CHAMBERS

DICTIONARY OF

Phrasal Verbs

CHAMBERS

DICTIONARY OF *Phrasal Verbs*

Compiled by
Kay Cullen
Howard Sargeant

CHAMBERS
English

Published by Chambers Harrap Publishers Ltd
43-45 Annandale Street, Edinburgh EH7 4AZ

A CIP catalogue record for this book is available from the British Library.

ISBN 0 550 10731 2

We have made every effort to mark as such all words which we believe to be trademarks. We should also like to make it clear that the presence of a word in the dictionary, whether marked or unmarked, in no way affects its legal status as a trademark.

The British National Corpus is a collaborative initiative carried out by Oxford University Press, Longman, Chambers Harrap, Oxford University Computing Services, Lancaster University's Unit for Computer Research in the English Language and the British Library.
The project received funding from the UK Department of Trade and Industry and the Science and Engineering Research Council and was supported by additional research grants from the British Academy and the British Library.

Typeset in Great Britain at Roger King Graphic Studio
Printed in China

CONTENTS

CONTRIBUTORS

Publishing Director
Robert Allen

Managing Editor
Elaine Higgleton

Senior Editor
Anne Seaton

Compilers
Penny Hands
Imogen Preston

Computer Officer
Ilona Morison

INTRODUCTION

One of the features of English that presents greatest difficulty for foreign learners is the use of idiomatic constructions, or phrases - frequent and almost instinctive for a native speaker - whose meaning is not deducible, or is not readily deducible, from their constituent parts. These constructions can be broadly categorized as **idioms** and **phrasal verbs.** Understanding and being able to use these constructions correctly in spoken and written English is essential if the learner is to develop a complete command of the language.

Idioms or 'fixed phrases', with their definitions and examples of their use in English, are dealt with in the companion volume to this dictionary, **Chambers Dictionary of Idioms**.

This dictionary concentrates on the second category, **phrasal verbs**.

What is a phrasal verb?

A phrasal verb is a short two-word (or sometimes three-word) phrase made up of a verb, such as **get, give, make, pull** and **see**, and an adverb (an adverbial particle) or a preposition, such as **in, off, on, out** and **up**. Learners find them difficult for two reasons: (1) meaning, and (2) verb and particle order.

1 Meaning

Strictly speaking, a phrasal verb is a form of idiom - that is, it has a meaning which 'is different from the sum of its parts'. In other words, knowing what the verb and adverb or preposition mean will not necessarily help you understand the combination when they are used together as a phrasal verb. For example, you may know the meaning of the verb **polish**, but may not know that the combination 'to **polish off**' means to finish something quickly and easily. In the sentence '*He polished off the last of the cakes*', clearly, **polish off** is a unit of meaning; omit the '*off*' and the sentence '*He polished the last of the cakes*' no longer makes much sense. Similarly, you may know the meaning of the verb **act**, but may not know that when someone **acts up** they behave badly, especially by being disruptive or uncooperative, as in '*The children were acting up again*'. The sentence '*The children were acting again*' has a wholly different meaning.

Learners will also encounter many *verb + adverb* and *verb + preposition* combinations that are not strictly 'idiomatic', that have either a literal meaning with a related idiomatic meaning, or a semi-idiomatic meaning, which may be quite easily deduced from the meaning of the verb alone. Although these are not strictly 'phrasal verbs', learners may nevertheless, quite understandably, expect to find them in a dictionary of phrasal verbs, so they have been included in this dictionary.

This dictionary therefore includes:

1. ***'idiomatic', or non-deducible phrasal verbs***. This category includes phrasal verbs or senses of the verb + particle in which the particle cannot be dropped without changing the meaning completely.

2. ***combinations that have a literal meaning***, and also idiomatic or semi-idiomatic senses. Examples include: **hold down, push around,** and **put up**.

3. ***combinations in which the particle functions as a intensifier***, suggesting the idea of completeness or thoroughness, without adding much to the basic meaning of the verb, as in **finish off, tidy up** and **eat up.** The use of a particle as an intensifier is one of the commonest ways of creating new phrasal verbs.

4. ***verbs which are always, or nearly always, accompanied by a particular adverb or preposition***, as in **rely on, abstain from, apprise of** and **consult with.**

2 Verb and particle order

Learners may find phrasal verbs difficult to use because they are not sure where to put the adverbial particle. Several different positions may be possible, or there may just be one fixed position. For example, in the phrasal verb **eat up**, in its transitive uses, **up** can come immediately after the verb, as in: *His mum told him to eat up his lunch*, or after the object, as in: *Amy ate her lunch up*. The object is regularly placed between the verb and particle when the object is a pronoun: *She ate it up*. When **eat up** is used intransitively, **up** always follows the verb: *Come on, Amy, eat up quickly!*

In this dictionary, there are no complicated codes to show the position of the particle, or whether a phrasal verb is transitive or intransitive. These are shown in this dictionary in two ways: (1) through the full-sentence definitions, and (2) in examples.

Full-sentence definitions show the phrasal verbs in context, and allow the learner to see immediately whether they are transitive or intransitive, and where the particle goes. Further usages - other common transitive or intransitive usages, and any alternative position for the particle - are shown in the examples. Showing syntactic behaviour in these ways allows the learner to see how the phrasal verb is used and to copy this usage in their own speech or writing.

Phrasal verbs in everyday speech and writing

The English language is constantly changing and evolving: new words and phrases enter the language all the time, and this new vocabulary includes phrasal verbs, such as *'grease out'* (= to pig out on greasy food). Native speakers of English intuitively create phrasal verbs, and intuitively understand those created by fellow native speakers, and this is naturally something that learners cannot do with anything like the same instinctive ease.

To help learners with this aspect of language use, this dictionary includes special entries on the adverbial particles and prepositions used to form phrasal verbs. These entries give the broad range of meanings that each particle has, and show which of the particles are used by native speakers to form new phrasal verbs. Examples of these phrasal verbs are taken from Chambers WordTrack, the Chambers new-words monitoring programme. New phrasal verbs from this source are usually informal in register, and are clearly labelled to show this.

While these entries may not make a learner use phrasal verbs intuitively like a native speaker, they will help learners who wish to develop their knowledge of how phrasal verbs are formed and how they function in English. By showing the range of meanings each particle has, and identifying those particles and meanings that are used in modern English to form phrasal verbs, we hope that learners will begin to understand phrasal verbs more easily, and feel more confident in their own use of them.

Chambers language databases

Chambers Dictionary of Phrasal Verbs has been compiled using computerized language resources consisting of: **Chambers WordTrack** and the **British National Corpus**.

Chambers WordTrack is a database of one of the most authoritative new-word monitoring programmes, and collects about 500 new words and meanings every month; approximately 40 000 citations are being monitored for inclusion in Chambers dictionaries and thesauruses at any one time. New words, usages and meanings are taken from a wide range of sources - newspapers, magazines, contemporary fiction, radio, television and film - from Britain, North America, Australia, New Zealand, Africa, India and the Far East, reflecting the use of English as an international language.

The **British National Corpus** is a database of modern English. It contains 100 million words of both written and spoken English, from a similarly wide range of recent sources, including books, magazines, newspapers, radio and television, formal meetings and everyday conversations.

Access to such a language corpus has revolutionized dictionary-making, helping us learn a lot of new things about what words mean and how they are used together.

How are the Chambers language databases used in this dictionary?

Learners can benefit directly from this new-found knowledge. Language databases help our task in the following ways:

- **new phrasal verbs**
  Chambers WordTrack monitors new phrasal verbs that are being invented all the time and used by native speakers of English.
- **new meanings**
  The language databases frequently reveal new meanings.
- **collocation**
  They show us which words are normally associated with a particular phrasal verb. For example, a search on *patter about* demonstrates that it is usually small or light people or animals that *patter about*.
- **context**
  They enable us to see what sort of situations phrasal verbs are used in.
- **register**
  They tell us which phrasal verbs are mainly used in informal situations and avoided in more formal situations. Most new phrasal verbs are either highly informal or slang.
- **gender, age, status**
  They allow us to see what kinds of people use certain phrasal verbs. They show us, for example, that many new and highly informal phrasal verbs are used by young people, such as the new phrasal verbs that are connected with drug-taking: *skin up* (= to roll a joint), *spliff up* (= to smoke a joint), *coke up* (= to get high on cocaine).

The language databases and examples

In addition, the language databases have been used extensively in this dictionary to provide material for examples. In particular, **Chambers WordTrack** has been used to provide examples of new phrasal verbs in the entries for the adverbial particles. These examples help show meaning, collocation and context and illustrate level of language. Where possible, material is authentic and has been taken directly from the language databases. In some cases, however, examples have been modified to keep them clear and useful, for instance where they contain obscure references or vocabulary.

PRONUNCIATION GUIDE

Key to the phonetic symbols used in the dictionary

Consonant

p	/piː/	**pea**
t	/tiː/	**tea**
k	kiː/	**key**
b	/biː/	**bee**
d	/daɪ/	**dye**
g	/gaɪ/	**guy**
m	/miː/	**me**
n	/njuː/	**new**
ŋ	/sɒŋ/	**song**
θ	/θɪn/	**thin**
ð	/ðɛn/	**then**
f	/fan/	**fan**
v	/van/	**van**
s	/siː/	**see**
z	/zuːm/	**zoom**
ʃ	/ʃiː/	**she**
ʒ	/beɪʒ/	**beige**
ʧ	/iːʧ/	**each**
dʒ	/ɛdʒ/	**edge**
h	/hat/	**hat**
l	/leɪ/	**lay**
r	/reɪ/	**ray**
j	/jɛs/	**yes**
w	/weɪ/	**way**

Vowels

Short vowels

ɪ	/bɪd/	**bid**
ɛ	/bɛd/	**bed**
a	/bad/	**bad**
ʌ	/bʌd/	**bud**
ɒ	/pɒt/	**pot**
ʊ	/pʊt/	**put**
ə	/ə'baʊt/	**about**

Long vowels

iː	/biːd/	**bead**
ɑː	/hɑːm/	**harm**
ɔː	/ɔːl/	**all**
uː	/buːt/	**boot**
ɜː	/bɜːd/	**bird**

Dipthongs

eɪ	/beɪ/	**bay**
aɪ	/baɪ/	**buy**
ɔɪ	/bɔɪ/	**boy**
ɑʊ	/hɑʊ/	**how**
oʊ	/goʊ/	**go**
ɪə	/bɪə(r)/	**beer**
ɛə	/bɛə(r)/	**bare**
ʊə	/pʊə(r)/	**poor**

Notes

1. The stress mark (') is placed before the stressed syllable (*eg* **fizzle** /'fɪzəl/)

2. The symbol '(r)' is used to represent *r* when it comes at the end of a word, to indicate that it is pronounced when followed by a vowel (as in the phrase *fritter away* /frɪtər ə'weɪ/).

ORGANIZATION OF ENTRIES

wake /weɪk/: **wakes, waking, woke** /woʊk/, **woken** /'woʊkən/

Pronunciation is given for the headword verb and irregular parts as necessary.

Verb parts – the third person singular, the present participle, past tense and past participle are shown for all verbs.

Note that in American English **waked** is often used as the past tense and past participle of **wake**.

Grammatical notes follow the headword verb.

tail /teɪl/: **tails, tailing, tailed**

tail away see **tail off**

Cross references: references are made to other phrasal verbs in the dictionary if information is given there, or if they are useful for comparison.

tail back

Traffic that **is tailing back** has formed a long queue that is moving slowly or waiting to move: *A huge queue of cars and lorries tailed back from the scene of the accident.* [compare **snarl up**]

• *noun* **tailback: tailbacks:** *a five-mile tailback on the M5.*

Derivatives: nouns and adjectives formed from phrasal verbs are given after the phrasal verb.

swivel /'swɪvəl/: **swivels, swivelling** (*AmE* **swiveling**), **swivelled** (*AmE* **swiveled**)

American spellings are shown in brackets.

swivel round

You **swivel round** when you quickly turn to face in the opposite direction: *She swivelled round to face me.* ❑ *She'd swivelled round in her chair.* [*same as* **swing round**]

Examples supported by the British National Corpus show the range of ways a phrasal verb can be used, and show where the adverbial particle can go.

Synonyms and antonyms are given at the end of the definitions, where appropriate.

wait up

1 You **wait up** when you don't go to bed at night at your usual time because you are waiting for someone's arrival or return, or some other event: *My mother always waits up for me, even when I come in after midnight.* ❑ *I'll be back late; don't wait up for me.* [*same as* **stay up**] **2** (*informal*) If you are about to leave or are ahead of someone and they say **'wait up'** they are asking or telling you to wait for them: *'Wait up, Ken, I'll just be a minute.'* [*same as* **hang on** (*informal*)]

Definitions are numbered and written as whole sentences, showing the phrasal verb being used in a natural and grammatically correct way. No abbreviations except *AmE*, *BrE* and *eg* (meaning 'for example') are used in the dictionary.

Register labels: phrasal verbs, synonyms and antonyms are labelled for register (for example, *informal* or *formal*) where necessary.

without /wɪ'ðaʊt/

Without is a preposition.
It is a fairly common word in English, but it only occurs in three phrasal verbs in this dictionary; **do without**, **go without** and **reckon without**; all of which have the idea of a lack or absence of something as part of their meaning.

Adverbial particles: entries for adverbial participles are in panels.

a

aback /ə'bak/

Aback is an adverb.
In the past, **aback** was a common adverb used in many of the ways that *back* is used now. In modern English, **aback** only appears in the phrasal verb **take aback**.

abide /ə'baɪd/: **abides**, **abiding**, **abided**

abide by
You **abide by** something such as a rule or a decision when you do what is ordered or what has been decided: *Israel knew that any failure to abide by the terms of the treaty would bring international condemnation.* [*same as* **keep to, stick to, observe**; *opposite* **flout, defy**]

abound /ə'baʊnd/: **abounds**, **abounding**, **abounded**

abound in *or* **abound with** (*formal*)
A place **abounds in** something, or **abounds with** it, when there is a large quantity or large numbers of it in that place: *The island abounds in lovely walks and beautiful scenery.* ❑ *This part of town abounds with bars, restaurants and nightclubs.* [*same as* **be full of**]

about see panel on next page

above see panel on next page

absorb /əb'zɔːb/: **absorbed**

absorb in
You **are absorbed in** something when it holds your attention completely, so that you're not aware of what is happening around you: *The men were so absorbed in their game that they didn't see us slip away.* [*same as* **be taken up with, be engrossed in**]

abstain /əb'steɪn/: **abstains**, **abstaining**, **abstained**

abstain from (*formal*)
You **abstain from** something that you enjoy, such as food or alcohol, when you choose not to have it; you **abstain from** doing something when you don't do it: *His doctor told him to abstain from cigarettes and alcohol.* ❑ *Several members of parliament abstained from voting.* [*same as* **leave off, refrain from** (*formal*)]

accede /ək'siːd/: **accedes**, **acceding**, **acceded**

accede to (*formal*)
1 You **accede to** a request when you agree to it: *The French government acceded to her request to be buried at Malmaison.* ❑ *The company has acceded to most of the strikers' demands.* [*same as* **grant**; *opposite* **turn down, refuse**] **2** You **accede to** a job, position or title when you gain it: *He had significant achievements behind him when he acceded to the job.*

about /ə'baut/

About is an adverb and a preposition. It is a very common word in English and is widely used in combination with verbs. It often has very little meaning at all, being used simply to link the verb with its object, as in **think about, talk about, know about** and **worry about. Around** or **round** can usually be substituted for **about** with no change of meaning.

1 MOVEMENT IN DIFFERENT DIRECTIONS
About refers to movement in several different directions, often movement without aim or purpose, as in **move about** and **look about,** and as in *drive about, toss about* and *tear about* in the following examples: *He continued to drive about his garden and woods.* ❑ *Any topic under the sun could be tossed about in the course of a morning's talk.* ❑ *They buy a jeep and think they can go tearing about the countryside.*

2 ACTION IN DIFFERENT PLACES
In a second sense, closely related to the first, and suggesting the same lack of plan or pattern, **about** refers to action taken in different places, as in **ask about,** or action that results in things being put in different places, as in **scatter about.** This action is often rough or violent, as in **throw about** and **hurl about.** In this sense, too, **about** frequently combines with verbs to form new combinations, such as *snuffle about, fling about* and *swap about,* in the examples: *There was the sound of something snuffling about in the soil.* ❑ *Paintings were pulled off the walls and flung about all over the room.* ❑ *There will inevitably be some changes; displays will get swapped about.*

above /ə'bʌv/

Above is a preposition and an adverb. Although it is a very common word in English, it is only found in a small number of phrasal verbs.

1 HIGHER POSITION OR LEVEL
The literal sense of **above** relates to a higher position or level, as in **get above** and **tower above** in the examples: *The noise has to get above a certain level before it can be classed a nuisance.* ❑ *The closer he got to the lamp, the bigger the shadow grew, until finally it spread across the ceiling and towered above him.*

2 BETTER OR MORE IMPORTANT POSITION
These literal combinations often have an extended meaning in which **above** refers to a better or more important position, so that when you **get above** yourself you behave as if you think you are better than others, and when one performer **towers above** all others they are considered by everyone to be the best by far.

accord /ə'kɔːd/: **accords, according, accorded**

accord with (*formal*)

One thing **accords with** another if it fits with, agrees with, or corresponds to, it: *The court has the ability to overturn legislation that does not accord with the constitution.* ❑ *This would accord with commonsense.* [*same as* **fit in with, correspond to, correspond with;** *opposite* **be at odds with**]

account /ə'kaunt/: **accounts, accounting, accounted**

account for

1 You **account for** something that has happened when you explain it: *He couldn't account for his behaviour.* ❑ *It was an odd feeling, and perhaps accounts for why I delayed my departure so long.* ❑ *What accounts for the Tories' success in winning again against the odds?* **2** Someone can **be accounted for** when you know where they are, and know that they have not been harmed or damaged: *The fire brigade said everyone in the building had been accounted for.* **3** Something **accounts for** a proportion of something if it amounts to or constitutes that proportion: *Fast food accounts for almost*

3 LACK OF ACTIVITY, PURPOSE OR PATTERN
In many informal phrasal verbs, **about** refers to lack of activity, as in **hang about**. Laziness is often suggested, as in **laze about, idle about** and **loaf about.** Lack of purpose or pattern is suggested in phrasal verbs such as **stand about** and **wander about**, combining with the idea of foolishness or irresponsibility in phrasal verbs such as **lark about, mess about, play about** and **muck about.** **About** in this sense sometimes combines with verbs to form new phrasal verbs, most of which are very informal or vulgar, as in *fanny about* in the following example: *He didn't see the point in fannying about* [= messing about] *with the guitars and drum kits.*

4 HAPPENING
In a small group of phrasal verbs, **about** refers to something happening or being caused, as in **bring about, come about** and **set about.**

5 TURNING
In a fairly formal use that is perhaps also a little old-fashioned, **about** can refer to the action of turning to face the opposite direction, as in **turn about** and **face about**, and is similar in this sense to **around** and **round.**

6 SURROUNDING OR ENCLOSING
In some phrasal verbs, with a slightly formal or literary use, **about** is used like **round** and **around** to refer to something being surrounded or enclosed, as in **throw about**. In this sense, it is occasionally used to form new phrasal verbs, such as *gather about* in the example: *Alice stepped gingerly over the stones with her skirts gathered about her.*

one meal in every ten served in the UK. ❑ *Forest burning currently accounts for 20% of the world's annual production of carbon dioxide.* [*same as* **make up, represent, constitute**] **4** A sum of money **is accounted for** when a record has been kept of how it has been, or will be, spent: *The finance director has discovered that £13.7m of funds could not be accounted for.* [compare **budget for**]

across see panel on next page

acquaint /ə'kweɪnt/: **acquaints, acquainting, acquainted**

acquaint with (*formal*)

1 You are **acquainted with** a person if you know them or have met them: *He tells me he is already acquainted with Mr Miller and Mr Rand.* **2** You are **acquainted with** something if you have some knowledge of it or are familiar with it: *You'll need to be acquainted with all the details.* ❑ *Experienced soldiers are fully acquainted with danger and know how to assess it.*

act /akt/: **acts, acting, acted**

act for

1 A lawyer or agent **acts for** you when he or she represents your interests in business dealings or discussions: *My husband and I have a solicitor who acts for both of us.* [*same as* **represent**] **2** You **act for** someone when you do their job because they are temporarily unable to: *In her absence, Jack Morris will act for her in negotiations with The Unico Corporation.* [*same as* **stand in** for, **fill in** for (*formal*)]

act on *or* act upon

1 You **act on** or **act upon** advice or suggestions when you do what is advised or suggested: *An experienced nurse can act on her own initiative.* ❑ *In a constitutional monarchy, the Queen acts on the advice of her Prime Minister.* [*same as* **follow**] **2** Something such as a drug, or an influence present in your surroundings, **acts on** you when it has an effect on you: *Caffeine is a stimulant which acts on the nervous system.* ❑ (*computers*) *The 'arrange icons' command acts upon the active window only.*

act out
1 You **act out** your feelings, emotions or fears when you express them in your behaviour, often unconsciously: *He is a man who acts out his principles.* ❑ *Teenagers sometimes act out their distress by running away.* **2** You **act out** an event or a story when you perform it as a play or a piece of theatre: *Children act out in miniature the dramas of adult life.* [*same as* **play out, enact**]

act up (*informal*)
1 Something such as a machine **is acting up** when it's not working properly: *The speakers seem alright, but the tape-deck's acting up again.* **2** Someone, especially a child, **is acting up** when they are behaving badly or uncooperatively, and causing trouble: *She couldn't trust him not to act up when something upset him.*
[*same as* **play up** (*informal*)]

add /ad/: adds, adding, added

add in
You **add** something **in** when you include it: *I'd add in a couple of paragraphs about her family background, just to give the character a little history.* ❑ *Stir the sauce until it thickens, and add in a little chopped parsley before you serve.*

add on
You **add** something **on** when you include it or attach it as an extra: *Add on £2.50 for postage and packing.* ❑ *You have space enough at the back of the house to add a conservatory on later, if you decide to.*
• *noun* **add-on**: **add-ons**
An **add-on** is any extra item or feature that you can get to add to something you already have: *This video-games machine comes with a cassette recorder and an add-on keyboard, which can be used for word-processing.* ❑ *You may also be able to get legal insurance as an add-on to a household policy for as little as £12.50.* ❑ *You can buy add-on*

across /ə'krɒs/

Across is a preposition and an adverb. It only occurs in a few phrasal verbs in this dictionary, with meanings that relate to movement from one side of something to the other, to discovering something, and to telling or communicating something.

1 MOVEMENT FROM ONE SIDE TO THE OTHER
Its literal meaning relates to movement from one side of something to the other, as in **run across** and **come across**. In this sense the appearance of new phrasal verbs is very common with **about** combining readily with many verbs of movement, such as *flood across*, *reach across* and *coil across* in the following examples: *The army came flooding across an unguarded frontier.* ❑ *He reached across and wiped a spot of ketchup from John's chin.* ❑ *She parked the car near where a stream coiled across the salt marsh.*
In an extension of this literal meaning, **across** is quite widely used to form new phrasal verbs, such as *gaze across*, *lean across* and *glance across*, as in the following examples: *He gazed across a sea of Union Flags.* ❑ *Fenn leaned across and flashed his card at the constable.* ❑ *She glanced scornfully across at Christina.*
Over can be substituted for **across** in most phrasal verbs with this sense, with little or no change of meaning.

2 DISCOVERING
Across combines with verbs to refer to the act of discovering something, usually unexpectedly or by chance, as in **come across, run across** and **stumble across.** Unlike senses senses 1 and 3, **over** cannot be substituted for **across** here.

3 TELLING OR COMMUNICATING
Across also relates to something being told or communicated, and particularly to the impression created or received, as in **put across, get across** and **come across.**
Over can be substituted for **across** in most phrasal verbs with this sense, with little or no change of meaning.

memory for your computer at $700 for 16 megabytes.

add to

One thing **adds to** another, or **adds** something **to** it, if it increases it: *The darkness of the night, the rain; it all adds to the atmosphere.* ❑ *The vast arched glass ceiling adds to the sense of space and grandeur.*

add together

1 You **add** numbers **together** when you combine them to make a greater number: *When you add together all the fees she receives from her various consultancies it makes a very healthy income indeed.* [*same as* **add up, count up, tot up** (*informal*)] **2** You **add** several things **together** when you combine them or mix them: *When added together, the gloss and matt paints give you a kind of eggshell finish.* [*same as* **blend**]

add up

1 You **add up** numbers or amounts when you calculate their total: *You haven't added the figures up correctly.* ❑ *You'll save 30p a week, and it all adds up.* [*same as* **count up, tot up** (*informal*)] **2** You say that figures or numbers don't **add up** if their total has been wrongly calculated. **3** (*informal*) Things **add up** if they make sense: *I can't think why she left so suddenly; it doesn't add up.* [*same as* **stand to reason**]

add up to

1 Numbers **add up to** an amount that is their total: *Errol gets £34.70, and Pam earns £75 a week. This adds up to £109.70.* [*same as* **come to, total**] **2** Circumstances **add up to** something if, taken together, they have a meaning or significance: *I can't see that this adds up to a motive for murder.* [*same as* **amount to, constitute**]

adhere /əd'hɪə(r)/: adheres, adhering, adhered

adhere to (*formal*)

1 You **adhere to** a plan, arrangement, agreement or rule when you do what it orders or requires: *Many Jews adhere scrupulously to Judaic law.* ❑ *It's important for staff to adhere strictly to the guidelines.* [*same as* **stick to, abide by, follow**; *opposite* **flout**] **2** You **adhere to** a belief, opinion or principles if you continue to support it: *He still adheres to the view that children need strict discipline.* [*same as* **hold to, stand by**]

after see panel below

after /'ɑːftə(r)/

After is a preposition.

As a preposition, its meaning relates to time, showing that one thing happens later than, or follows, another. This sense of following appears in our first group of phrasal verbs, the meanings of which relate to people and things being followed, chased or hunted. The other main meanings of **after** relate to wanting or desiring things, and to imitating or copying people or things.

1 FOLLOWING

After combines with verbs to refer to people or things being followed, chased or hunted, as in **come after, go after** and **run after**.

2 WANTING

After also combines with verbs to refer to the feeling of wanting something, or the action of trying to get it, as in **ask after**. In some combinations, this sense is developed from the idea of chasing or hunting, as in **go after** and **run after**. In others, the feeling suggested is a strong desire, as in **hunger after, hanker after** and **lust after**.

3 IMITATING OR COPYING

After also relates to the imitating or copying of people or things, in combinations such as **call after, name after** and **take after**.

against /ə'gɛnst/ *or* /ə'geɪnst/

Against is a preposition.
It is quite a common word in English, and its basic sense relates to relationships between two things, especially when these relationships involve difference, opposition or conflict. It has four main meanings when used in phrasal verbs, and frequently combines with verbs to form new combinations with all of these meanings.

1 OPPOSING
Against combines with verbs that refer to the actions of one person or thing that opposes another, as in **go against**, **plot against**, **set against** and **turn against**. It is very frequently used to form new phrasal verbs with this meaning, such as *protest against*, *lean against*, *appeal against*, *fight against* and *unite against*, as in the following examples: *The people are protesting against a hotel and golf development on their land.* ❑ *Courts will lean against allowing a tribunal to decide such matters.* ❑ *There are notorious difficulties in English law in appealing against an exercise of discretion.* ❑ *They would still be in the position of fighting against an independence movement.* ❑ *They invent a common enemy for the people to unite against.*

2 PROTECTING
In a second sense, **against** combines with verbs to refer to the idea of someone or something being protected, as in **protect against**. In some phrasal verbs, this protection is achieved by preventing what would cause harm, as in **guard against**, **insure against** and **provide against**. In this sense too, **against** frequently combines with verbs to form new phrasal verbs, such as *indemnify against*, *cover against* and *preserve against*, as in the following examples: *The company will indemnify us against all losses, claims and demands we may incur.* ❑ *Many people believe the E111 form covers you against any medical treatment you may need abroad.* ❑ *This will allow native tribes to preserve their territories against encroachment by developers.*

3 COMPARING
In a third sense, **against** forms phrasal verbs which refer to the comparing of two things, as in **balance against**, **match against** and **weigh against**. New phrasal verbs with **against** in this sense are also common: consider *check against* and *judge against* in the examples: *The most common search is that of checking a part against all others in its assembly.* ❑ *The Commission will not be judging its performance against local authority spending levels.*

4 BEING A DISADVANTAGE
The final sense of **against** relates to the fact of being a disadvantage. Things that **count against** you, **militate against** you, or **tell against** you make it less likely that you will succeed. **Against** combines freely with verbs in this sense, as can be seen in combinations such as *operate against*, *argue against* and *work against* in the following examples: *The scheme operates against every person who makes a claim in these circumstances.* ❑ *Our experience would argue against giving shareholders full status.* ❑ *In Vologsky's case, the very qualities which should have promoted him actually worked against him.*

In a few phrasal verbs, **against** occurs as the third element, as in **be up against** and **come up against**.

against see panel above

agree /ə'griː/: **agrees**, **agreeing**, **agreed**

agree with (*informal*)
Something, usually food, doesn't **agree with** you when it makes you feel ill: *These small, smoky rooms don't agree with his health.*

ahead see panel on next page

aim /eɪm/: **aims**, **aiming**, **aimed**

aim at
1 You **aim at** a person or thing when you point something in their direction:

I aimed at one of the trees, but the arrow hit the wall beyond. **2** Something **is aimed at** someone, or at doing something, when it is intended for them, or intended to do it: *Her articles are not aimed at a wide newspaper audience.* ❑ *This award is aimed at young and relatively unknown mountaineers.* **3** You **aim at** doing something when you are trying or intending to do it: *New government legislation is aimed at giving tenants greater protection.* ❑ *This is a project aimed at building a computer that can process huge amounts of data per second.* [*same as* **seek**]

aim for

1 You **aim for** something when you have it as a target, and you direct a weapon or other object towards it: *He was aiming for Swinton on the right wing, but the pass was intercepted.* **2** You also **aim for** something when you plan or intend to achieve it: *The Deutsche Bank is aiming for 30 branches in the former East Berlin by the end of the year.* [*same as* **aspire to** (*formal*), **work towards**]

> **ahead** /ə'hɛd/
>
> **Ahead** is an adverb.
> It is not a very common word in English, and it occurs in only a few phrasal verbs, with two main senses.
>
> 1 MAKING PROGRESS
> **Ahead** can refer to the idea of making progress, as in **go ahead**. In some phrasal verbs, the sense is of making faster progress than another person or thing, as in **get ahead** and **pull ahead**. In others, progress is made very rapidly or forcefully, as in **forge ahead**, **press ahead** and **push ahead**.
>
> 2 THE FUTURE
> In some phrasal verbs, **ahead** relates to the future. You **look ahead** and **think ahead** when you consider the future, and you **plan ahead** when you make decisions about how to deal with what will happen in the future. Something that **lies ahead** will happen in the future, and if it **looms ahead** it will happen very soon.

allow /ə'laʊ/: allows, allowing, allowed

allow for

You **allow for** something such as a possible delay or difficulty, or extra expense, when you take it into consideration in your planning: *This is not an income that allows for any luxuries.* ❑ *The trip will cost £10 per head, which allows £3.50 for coffee and sandwiches.* ❑ *You should allow for delays when planning your journey.* [*same as* **take into account, take account of**]

allude /ə'lu:d/: alludes, alluding, alluded

allude to (*formal*)

You **allude** to something when you refer to it in an indirect way, or mention it while talking of something else: *The Prime Minister only alluded to the problems of unemployment and health in his speech.* ❑ *The harsh realities of the bad old days were never alluded to.* [*same as* **touch on**; compare **refer to, hint at**]

along see panel on next page

among see panel on next page

amount /ə'maʊnt/: amounts, amounting, amounted

amount to

1 You use **amount to** to talk about total numbers or amounts: *The income from investments alone amounts to over £300,000.* ❑ *Such furniture as they had amounted to little more than would have furnished one room.* [*same as* **add up to, come to, total**] **2** People often use **amount to** to talk about what something seems to be, or what it really is: *I didn't think a bare explanation of the facts really amounted to a proper* *apology.* ❑ *Whether we go to Spain or Greece, it amounts to the same thing: a relaxing holiday in the sun.* [*same as* **add up to, constitute**] **3** You also use **amount to** to talk about how important or successful someone or something becomes: *A handful of residents wrote angry letters to councillors but their opposition never really amounted to much.* ❑ *All their children were good at school, but none of them amounted to anything.* [*same as* **come to**]

along /əˈlɒŋ/

Along is an adverb and a preposition. It is quite a common word in English. It occurs in phrasal verbs with four main meanings, and in the two most common meanings is often used to form new phrasal verbs.

1 MOVING
The literal meaning of **along** relates to movement. Used as a preposition, **along** suggests movement in the direction of the length of something such as a road or path, as in **go along, stroll along** and **move along**. In this sense, and as a preposition, **along** is frequently used to form new phrasal verbs, such as *jig along* and *roar along* in the following examples: *Spittals jigged along the corridor with the excited smile of a cat who'd got the cream.* ❑ *A motorcycle cop went roaring along the expressway.* Sometimes, an informal use modifies the idea of movement to suggest the idea of leaving or departing, as in **get along** and **push along**.

2 PROGRESSING
In an extension of the literal meaning of movement, **along** also combines with verbs to refer to the action of making progress, as in **come along, go along** and **help along**. In this sense, too, **along** is frequently used to form new phrasal verbs, such as *chug along* and *tear along* in the following examples: *A fast user is easily frustrated by a software package that chugs along a couple of paces behind them.* ❑ *Time was tearing along and there were the coals to fetch.*

3 GOING TOGETHER
Along occurs in a small number of phrasal verbs that express the idea of things going together or accompanying each other, as in **bring along, come along** and **tag along**.

4 AGREEING OR ACCEPTING
Along can also express the idea of agreeing to things or accepting them, as in **play along** and **go along with.**

among /əˈmʌŋ/

Among is a preposition.
In isolation, it is sometimes replaced by the slightly formal **amongst**, but this is rarely the case in phrasal verbs. It is not a very common word in English, and it occurs in only a small number of phrasal verbs in this dictionary, with two main meanings. In the first of these, it is used to form new phrasal verbs.

1 BEING SURROUNDED
In its literal sense, **among** refers to a position in which someone is surrounded by numerous people or things. It readily combines with verbs of movement to form new phrasal verbs, as in *wander among, kneel among, sit among* and *scatter among* in the following examples: *We would swim in one of the hotel pools or maybe wander among the old tombs in the Lodhi Gardens.* ❑ *He pushed clear and knelt among the waves.* ❑ *Debbie sat among them in her usual serene posture.* ❑ *Scattered among them were groups of tiny Mayan houses made of sticks.*
In **go among** and **walk among**, the idea of being surrounded is extended to suggest a close association with the surrounding people, perhaps becoming part of their group.

2 BEING PART OF A GROUP
The idea of a group is present in this second meaning of **among**, in the sense of *being* part of it rather than *becoming* part of it. The phrasal verbs **class among, number among** and **rank among** all have this meaning.

angle /'aŋgəl/: **angles**, **angling**, **angled**

angle for

You **angle for** something when you try to get it in an indirect way, without actually asking: *It was pretty obvious to everyone that she was angling for sympathy.* [*same as* **fish for**]

answer /'ɑːnsə(r)/: **answers**, **answering**, **answered**

answer back

Someone, especially a child, **answers** you **back**, or **answers back**, when they reply rudely: *She won't give him the job; he's answered back once too often.* [*same as* **talk back**]

answer for

1 You also use **answer for** as a way of stating who or what is responsible for something bad: *I can't answer for what happens to the horses; they're not my responsibility.* [*same as* **take the blame for**] **2** You use **answer for** as a way of stating that you're sure someone can be relied on or trusted: *There's no doubt about Tom's commitment to the company, but I couldn't answer for the others.* [*same as* **vouch for**]

answer to

1 You have to **answer to** someone for a mistake you make when you have to explain to them the reason for the mistake, perhaps also accepting whatever punishment they decide to give you: *Christians believe we will answer to God for our actions.* **2** Something or someone **answers to** a description if it matches or identifies them: *None of the boys answered to the description.*

apart see panel below

---

apart /ə'pɑːt/

Apart is an adverb.
It is a fairly common word in English. Its basic meaning is the opposite of **together**, and relates to the state of things that are not joined or touching but are at a distance from each other. In this dictionary, it occurs in phrasal verbs in two main meanings, and in each of these meanings it is used to form new phrasal verbs.

1 BREAKING OR DETACHING
Apart combines with verbs to refer to the action of breaking, as in **fall apart**, or detaching, as in **take apart**. Often, the meaning is more one of violence being used to break off a piece or part, as in **pull apart** and **tear apart**. In this particular sense, **apart** frequently occurs in new and often informal phrasal verbs such as *rip apart* and *yank apart*, as in the following examples: *Goodge watched the fight dispassionately for a few minutes, then waded into the crowd to rip the two men apart.* ❑ *With Donald's help, I managed to yank the clutch plates apart.*
Both **fall apart** and **tear apart** have meanings extended from this literal sense, which relate to emotional or psychological pain or collapse. An event that makes someone **fall apart** causes them to lose control of their emotions, and perhaps their ability to speak or think clearly; it **tears** them **apart** when it causes them a deep and lasting emotional pain.

2 SEPARATING
In a further extension of this literal sense of breaking or detaching, **apart** occurs in phrasal verbs whose meaning relates to the separating of people or things. Most commonly, the separation is of former partners or lovers, as in **drift apart** and **grow apart**. In this sense, we can find **apart** used to form new phrasal verbs, such as *float apart* and *stray apart* in the following examples: *It was as if, even after just a few days away from each other, we had begun to float apart spiritually.* ❑ *Going off to different colleges, and mixing with new people, boyfriends and girlfriends inevitably stray apart.*
In **tell apart**, you separate people or things by identifying the differences between them.

around /ə'raʊnd/

Around is an adverb and a preposition. It is a very common word in English and it occurs in a large number of phrasal verbs in this dictionary, in six main senses. In four of these senses, **around** combines freely with other verbs to form new phrasal verbs.
In many of the phrasal verbs in which **around** appears in this dictionary, **about** and **round** can often replace it with no change in meaning.

1 MOVING
The literal meaning of **around** relates broadly to movement in different directions, often without a definite aim or purpose, as in **run around**, **dance around**, **grope around** and **glance around**. In this broad sense, **around** can frequently be found forming new and often informal phrasal verbs such as *sweep around*, *phutter around* and *tool around* in the following examples: *Ginger Rogers swept around in yards of chiffon, spangles and ostrich feathers.* ❑ *He made coffee, phuttering around like a demented chemist with glass flasks and a meths burner.* ❑ *It's hard to imagine Nigel Mansell tooling around in a second-hand Metro.*

In a similar sense, **around** relates to movement or action in different places, as in **ask around**, **shop around** and **sleep around**, or to action that results in something being put in different places, as in **scatter around** and **spread around**.
Occasionally, new and often informal phrasal verbs are created with this sense, as in *kip around* in the following example: *At first, I kipped around* [= slept] *on friends' floors.*

2 LACK OF ACTIVITY OR PURPOSE
Another common use of **around** is in phrasal verbs that suggest a lack of activity or purpose, as in **hang around**, **lie around**, **stand around** and **wait around**. In this sense, too, **around** is frequently used to form new phrasal verbs such as *wander around*, *dabble around*, *grub around* and (*slang*) *ponce around* in the following examples: *We were wandering around on deck and we saw a man come out of the captain's cabin.* ❑ *It might suit you to dabble around here and there before settling on a career.* ❑ *He likes grubbing around in sandy holes.* ❑ *Why had Billy Tuckett been poncing around on the roof in the wee small hours?*

apprise /ə'praɪz/: **apprises**, **apprising**, **apprised**

apprise of (*formal*)
Someone **apprises** you **of** something when they tell you about it or inform you of it: *The judge hadn't been properly apprised of all her wishes.* [*same as* **let know**, **notify**]

approve /ə'pruːv/: **approves**, **approving**, **approved**

approve of
You **approve of** something if you think it is acceptable and are not offended by it: *Medical experts no longer approve of this method of dieting.* ❑ *He doesn't approve of that kind of language.*

around see panel above

arse /ɑːs/: **arses**, **arsing**, **arsed**

arse about *or* **arse around** (*vulgar slang*)
To **arse about** or **arse around** is to behave in a silly way that annoys or irritates others: *I wish they'd stop arsing around and get on with some work.* [*same as* **piss about** (*vulgar slang*), **bugger about** (*vulgar slang*), **muck about** (*informal*)]

as see panel on next page

aside see panel on page 12

ask /ɑːsk/: **asks**, **asking**, **asked**

ask after
You **ask after** someone when you ask for news about them: *I saw Phil in town yesterday; he was asking after you.* ❑ *He*

A number of phrasal verbs with **around** extend this meaning of lack of aim or purpose to suggest foolish or irresponsible behaviour, as in **fool around**, **mess around** and **muck around**; **mess around** and **muck around**, as well as **push around** and **jerk around**, also convey the idea of someone being badly or unfairly treated.
Again, new phrasal verbs are sometimes produced with this sense, as in (*vulgar*) *dick around* in the example: *Remember there's no-one will dick you around if you're sure what you want and know how much you want to pay.*

3 SURROUNDING
The third most common meaning of **around** in phrasal verbs relates to the surrounding of people and things, as in **gather around** and **cluster around**. Here again, **around** can be found frequently forming new phrasal verbs such as *fence around*, *mass around*, *press around* and *flock around* in the following examples: *Other areas were fenced around by fox-hunting landlords.* ❑ *General Bourbollon's troops are massing around the capital.* ❑ *They were far outnumbered by all the brief pants and yards of bare skin that pressed around them.* ❑ *They depict the forces of hell flocking around the Cross.*

4 FOCUSING
Around occurs in some phrasal verbs that refer to something that all other things relate to or are linked to, or something that everyone concentrates their attention on, as in **centre around** and **revolve around.** Phrasal verbs are freely formed with **around** in this sense also, such as *organize around*, *base around* and *build around* in the following examples: *There would still be a working class organized around production and trade unions.* ❑ *The course was based around questionnaires and structured interviews.* ❑ *The future of business is female; built around relationships.*

5 TURNING
Around occurs in a small number of phrasal verbs that relate to the action of turning, whether turning to face the opposite direction, as in **look around**, or turning repeatedly in a circular movement, as in **spin around** and **swivel around**.

6 AVOIDING
In a few phrasal verbs, the meaning of **around** relates to avoiding things, as in **skirt around** and **talk around**.

remembered to ask after my mother's health. [*same as* **inquire after**]

ask around

You **ask around** when you ask various people to give you information or advice about something: *When I asked around, I was told he hadn't been seen for weeks.*

as /az/ or /əz/

As is a preposition.
It is one of the most common words in English, but it occurs in only a small number of phrasal verbs in this dictionary. These combinations all refer to the function or nature of something, as in **know as** and **mark as**. Sometimes, this function or nature is false, as in **pass as** and **masquerade as**; sometimes, it is different from what was originally intended, as in **do as** and **serve as**.

ask for

1 You **ask for** something when you say you would like someone to give it to you: *You could ask for an increase on your overdraft limit.* ❑ *Don't be afraid to ask for help if there's anything you don't understand.* [*same as* **request** (*formal*)] **2** You **ask for** someone when you say you want to speak to them: *A Mr Davies phoned this morning asking for you personally.* **3** You say someone **is asking for** it, or **asking for** trouble, if the way they are behaving is certain to get them into trouble or difficulties: *It was asking for it to drive after drinking four whiskies.* ❑ *Walking through an area like that after dark is really asking for trouble.*

aside /ə'saɪd/

Aside is an adverb.
It is not a very common word in English, and only occurs in a few phrasal verbs in this dictionary. However, in three of its four main senses, it is used to form new phrasal verbs.

1 MOVEMENT TOWARDS THE SIDE
The basic sense of **aside** relates to movement towards the side, as in **stand aside** and **step aside**. It combines quite freely with verbs to form new phrasal verbs which convey this idea of movement towards the side, such as *toss aside*, *spring aside*, *look aside* and *smack aside* in the following examples: *He tossed aside his Guardian and smiled up at me.* ❑ *Mary, drunk as she was, managed to spring aside.* ❑ *He watched her from the corner of his eye, and saw her look aside and blush.* ❑ *Duvall smacked it dismissively aside.*

2 DISMISSING OR REJECTING
Aside occurs in phrasal verbs that relate to the dismissing or rejecting of people or things, as in **brush aside**, **sweep aside** and **wave aside**. It frequently forms new phrasal verbs with a similar meaning, such as *fight aside*, *shrug aside* and *shove aside* in the following examples: *She tried to fight the realisation aside.* ❑ *Criticisms have been made but he has shrugged them aside.* ❑ *Money worries will have to be shoved aside for the forseeable future.*

3 KEEPING SEPARATE AND SAVING FOR THE FUTURE
Aside also occurs in phrasal verbs that relate to things being separate or being kept separate, as in **lay aside** and **set aside**. **Aside** can be found forming new phrasal verbs with a similar sense, such as *lie aside* in the following example: *Avranches lies aside a little from the bypassing main road.*
Both **lay aside** and **set aside** have extended meanings that suggest that what is kept separate is saved for use in the future, and this is also the meaning of **leave aside**. New combinations with this meaning can also be found, such as *keep aside* in the following example: *The big banks have started to keep money aside as loan-loss protection.*

4 GIVING YOUR PLACE OR POSITION
Aside also occurs in the phrasal verbs **stand aside** and **step aside** which, in addition to their literal meaning relating to movement towards the side, can also refer to the act of giving your place or position to someone else.

ask in
You **ask** someone **in** when you invite them to come into your house or another place you are in, or to go in with you: *We stood on the doorstep chatting, and all the time I was waiting for her to ask me in for a drink.*

ask into
You **ask** someone **into** a place you are in when you invite them to come in: *They asked me into the boardroom, presumably to impress me with its splendour.* ❑ *She was met at the door by Arnold, and was immediately asked into his private office.* [compare **call in**]

ask out
You **ask** someone **out** when you invite them to go somewhere with you socially, *eg* to the cinema or to a restaurant: *I didn't know what to say: I'd never been asked out by a woman before.* ❑ *I think I might ask her out to dinner.*

ask over *or* ask round
You **ask** someone **over**, or **ask** them **round**, when you invite them to come to your house: *Isn't it about time you asked a few of your colleagues over for drinks?* ❑ *We've been asked round to my parents' house for the evening.*

aspire /ə'spaɪə(r)/: aspires, aspiring, aspired

aspire to (*formal*)
You **aspire to** something when it is your aim or ambition to achieve it: *Many of*

us who once aspired to fame and fortune are now stuck in fairly dead-end careers. ❑ *Some people aspire to greatness; others have greatness thrust upon them.* [*same as* **aim for**]

at see panel below

attend /ə'tɛnd/: **attends**, **attending**, **attended**

attend to

1 You **attend to** something such as a problem when you take what action is necessary: *There are one or two financial matters to attend to before we go in for dinner.* [*same as* **see to, deal with, take care of**] **2** You **attend to** someone when you give them the help or assistance they need: *Are there any customers not being attended to?* ❑ *The nurse will attend to your wounds as soon as she's free.* [*same as* **see to, take care of, look after**]

auction /'ɔːkʃən/: **auctions**, **auctioning**, **auctioned**

auction off

Something, especially something you want to get rid of, **is auctioned off** when it is sold at an auction: *I imagine they'll auction off most of the furniture from the old house.* ❑ *We could keep some and auction the rest off.*

average /'avərɪdʒ/: **averages**, **averaging**, **averaged**

average out

You **average out** several numbers when you calculate their average: *When we averaged it out, we found that we'd worked over thirteen hours a day.*

average out at

Several numbers **average out at** the number that is their average: *The total losses averaged out at over £30,000 per investor.*

away see panel on next page

at /at/ *or* /ət/

At is a preposition.
It is one of the commonest words in English and it occurs in numerous phrasal verbs in this dictionary. Its basic sense relates to identifying the position of something in space or time. There are two main meanings of phrasal verbs with **at** in this dictionary, and **at** can be found forming new phrasal verbs with both of these meanings.

1 AIMING OR DIRECTING
At links verbs of aiming or directing with their object, as in **aim at, look at** and **throw at**. New phrasal verbs with **at** performing this function are numerous, such as *grin at* and *target at* in the following examples: *How dared he grin at her like that?* ❑ *Targeted at species such as Norway pout and sand-eel, the operation undoubtedly destroys large numbers of immature fish.*

When the object is a person, there is sometimes the suggestion that they are suffering an attack of some kind, as in **laugh at**. Here too, **at** can be found forming new phrasal verbs, such as *fume at* in the following example: *There are no easy solutions when staff are fuming at each other.*

2 ATTACKING OR STRIKING
At also links to their object verbs that relate to physical attack, or to a physical striking of something, as in **fly at, grab at, jump at, pull at** and **strike at**. In this sense too, **at** can be found forming new phrasal verbs, such as *niggle at*, *swing at* and *stab at* in the following examples: *Doreen wanted to discuss matters that niggled at her mind.* ❑ *He lifted a pole and swung at Powers.* ❑ *Derain jumped back as the crazy woman stabbed at him with her passport.*

away /əˈweɪ/

Away is an adverb.

It is one of the commonest words in English and it occurs in many phrasal verbs in this dictionary, in seven main senses. In six of these senses, **away** frequently forms new phrasal verbs.

1 MOVING TO A FURTHER OR DISTANT PLACE

In its literal sense, **away** refers to movement to a further or distant place, as in **go away**, **move away** and **send away**. It occurs freely with other verbs to form new phrasal verbs, such as *trail away*, *slink away*, *drift away*, *step away* and *swirl away*: *He climbed the wall and trailed away across the fields.* ❑ *She slunk away and refused to answer the phone.* ❑ *The barrage balloons had drifted away and the morning sky was clear and cloudless.* ❑ *She stepped away as Eddie appeared with a cloth-wrapped bundle.* ❑ *His eyes were fixed on the silvery ribbon of water swirling away through the trees.*

2 NOT COMING AND NOT GETTING INVOLVED

Another common meaning of **away** in phrasal verbs refers to the fact of not coming or not getting involved, as in **stay away**, **keep away**, **shrink away** and **back away**. Phrasal verbs formed with this meaning too include *steer away*: *The policy should be to steer farmers away from high-yield farming.*

3 TAKING AND REMOVING

Another common meaning of **away** in phrasal verbs relates to the action of taking or removing something, or someone, as in **break away**, **pull away**, **snatch away** and **tear away**. This is perhaps the meaning in which **away** is most frequently used to form phrasal verbs, such as *hustle away*, *draw away*, *charm away* and *siphon away*: *He was hustled away by some of the extra police officers.* ❑ *The King's Cross development may draw money away from other projects.* ❑ *Could it charm a young London schoolteacher away from the crowded suburbs of the capital?* ❑ *£50 million was siphoned away from Lloyds' investors.*

4 DISAPPEARING AND DESTROYING

Away features in numerous phrasal verbs whose meanings relate to the fact of disappearing and to the act of destroying that causes something to disappear. In most cases, this happens slowly or gradually, as in **die away**, **drop away**, **eat away**, **fade away, melt away, waste away** and **wither away**. Phrasal verbs formed with this meaning include *drain away*, *chip away*, *gnaw away* and *dissolve away*: *The entire power supply seemed to drain away.* ❑ *It had begun to chip away at our commonsense approach.* ❑ *Emmie imagined the beetles in the roof, gnawing away at the rafters.* ❑ *It penetrates through armour easily and even dissolves part of it away.*

5 CONTINUING

Another common meaning of **away** in phrasal verbs relates to the idea of something continuing for some time, or being done repeatedly, as in **plug away** and **talk away**. Often, hard or fast work or other activity is suggested, as in **beaver away**, **hammer away**, **slog away** and **work away**. **Away** is commonly found forming phrasal verbs with these related meanings, such as *pine away*, *prod away*, *fret away*, *whizz away* and *tap away*: *It was clear to him that you were pining away for another man.* ❑ *Her conscience prodded away at her.* ❑ *Waking or sleeping, his mind fretted away at the case.* ❑ *It was a simple domestic scene: John whizzing away at the computer and me with my feet up.* ❑ *Alexis started tapping away at some fancy calculator.*

6 GETTING RID OF THINGS

A less common meaning of **away** in phrasal verbs relates to getting rid of things, or sometimes people, as in **drive away**, **frighten away**, **magic away**, **throw away** and **wipe away**. Phrasal verbs formed with this meaning include *trim away*, *polish away* and *flush away*: *Smooth over the dough and trim away any excess around the base.* ❑ *It had left wet stains on the varnish for the boy to polish away.* ❑ *Use it, rather than wastefully flushing it away.*

7 STORING AND HIDING

Lastly, **away** in the phrasal verbs in this dictionary relates to the storing or hiding of things. These are fairly fixed combinations, such as **file away**, **hoard away**, **put away**, **salt away** and **tidy away**.

b

back /bak/: **backs**, **backing**, **backed**

---

back away
You **back away** when you move slowly away or backwards, usually because you are nervous, afraid or disgusted: *He's the kind of creepy individual that children instinctively back away from.* [*same as* **back off**, **retreat** (*formal*), **withdraw** (*formal*)]

back away from
You **back away from** something such as an opinion or an idea when you show that you don't share it or support it: *The electricians' union appeared to back away from the view that industrial action was inevitable.* ❑ *Whilst the rebels backed away from criticizing the government outright, they made it clear they wouldn't be giving their support.*

back down
You **back down** when you stop demanding, insisting on, or fighting for something: *The unions refused to back down over pay and conditions.* ❑ *If we back down on a single issue, they'll sense weakness and walk all over us.* [*same as* **give in**, **yield** (*formal*); compare **climb down**]

back into
You **back into** something when you accidentally drive your vehicle backwards into it: *I became a little nervous when he backed into a petrol pump.*

back off
1 You **back off** when you show you don't want to become involved in an argument, fight or other confrontation: *Brewer pulled out his revolver and the two men backed off.* ❑ *Learn to back off a little, and that way you'll keep a cool head.* ❑ *This is nothing to do with you, so just back off!* [*same as* **retreat** (*formal*), **withdraw** (*formal*)] **2** You **back off** when you move slowly back, usually because you are nervous, afraid or disgusted: *She felt herself backing off when he stretched out his hand.* [*same as* **back away**, **retreat** (*formal*), **withdraw** (*formal*)]

back onto
A building or a piece of land **backs onto** something if its back is next to or facing it: *The vicarage backs onto a lane, from which anyone passing could have heard the shot.* [compare **give onto**, **open onto**]

back out
1 You **back out** when you decide not to do something you had previously agreed or promised to do: *If they back out of the contract at this stage, we'll be finished.* [*same as* **pull out**; compare **go back on**] **2** You **back out** when you drive your vehicle out backwards: *It's dangerous backing out onto such a busy road.* ❑ *She backed slowly out of the garage.*

back up
1 You **back** someone **up** when you support or help them: *They had, of course, sworn to back up the President no matter how shady or underhand his dealings with foreign powers were.* ❑ *Backed up by a network of loyal, if undisciplined, militiamen he had ruled*

the country with an iron fist. **2** You **back** someone **up** when you confirm that they are telling the truth; you **back up** a statement when you provide evidence to prove that it's true: *No-one would back up her story.* ❑ *Send photos*

back /bak/

Back is an adverb.
It is a very common word in English and it occurs in lots of phrasal verbs in this dictionary.

1 MOVING AND POSITIONING
The most common sense of **back** in phrasal verbs relates to the act of moving away from, or of positioning something away from, a front or central point, as in **drop back**, **fall back**, **hang back**, **stay back**, **step back**, **throw back** and **tie back**. **Back** is widely used to form phrasal verbs with this sense, such as *cast back*, *peel back*, *spring back* and *rock back* in the following examples: *She turned aside a little and cast her gaze back.* ❑ *To reveal these is to peel back a curtain.* ❑ *The position allows you to spring back or thrust forward without warning.* ❑ *Then you rock back into a cat stance.*
Sometimes, the movement relates to lack of progress, as in **hold back** and **set back**.

2 RETURNING
Back is widely used in phrasal verbs to refer to the notion of returning, in various related senses. In **double back** and **go back** the sense is literal, of returning to the place or position you were in before, and in this sense lots of phrasal verbs are formed with **back**, such as *drag back*, *inch back*, *trail back* and *head back* in the following examples: *The young boy screamed as he was dragged back to the plane that had brought him here.* ❑ *His reputation is gradually inching back to what it was.* ❑ *Patrick realizes life cannot change and trails back to his dull wife.* ❑ *I thought I would never find it here, so I headed back to the village.*
Give back, **hand back**, **pay back** and **send back** all refer to the action of returning to someone something you owed or had borrowed. In **answer back**, **fight back**, **hit back** and **strike back** someone responds to an attack by in turn attacking their attacker. In one sense of **call back**, **phone back** and **ring back**, you make a telephone call to the person who was trying to contact you earlier, or whom you have made an earlier telephone call to.

3 REGAINING POSSESSION
Back commonly occurs in phrasal verbs whose meaning relates to regaining possession of something, as in **claw back**, **get back**, **take back** and **win back**. It can be found forming phrasal verbs with this sense, such as *lure back* and *seize back* in the following examples: *They're preparing a campaign aimed at luring back some of the missing millions of tourists.* ❑ *When you lot seize the land back, make sure you know something about barn owls.*

4 REPEATING
In phrasal verbs such as **go back over**, **play back** and **read back** the sense is of an action being repeated.

5 PAST TIME
There are several phrasal verbs in this dictionary in which **back** relates to past time, such as **date back**, **flash back**, **hark back**, **look back** and **think back**. You can occasionally find it forming phrasal verbs in this sense, such as *plunge back* in the example: *The visitor has the feeling of being plunged back in time.*

6 CONTROLLING AND LIMITING
Back also occurs in phrasal verbs whose meanings relate to the act of controlling or limiting something. For example, the most common use of **cut back** relates to spending less money, and something **sets** you **back** when it limits your progress or causes delays. Often, it is emotions that are being controlled, as in **choke back**, **fight back**, **hold back** and **keep back**.
Sometimes phrasal verbs with this sense are used adjectivally, as in **scaled-back** in the following example: *In the Senate, his hastily assembled scaled-back bill failed to win a majority.*

of the damage and builders' estimates for repairs, to back up your claim. [*same as* **bear out, support**] **3** You **back up** when you drive your vehicle backwards: *You'll have to back up a little so I can open the gate.* ❑ *I asked him to back his car up a few feet, but he wouldn't.* [*same as* **reverse**] **4** You **back up** when you move back: *Could you get the spectators to back up a bit, to give me room for the shot.* [*same as* **retreat** (*formal*)] **5** To **back up** information stored on a computer is to make a copy of it, *eg* on a floppy disk.

• *noun* **back-up**: **back-ups**

1 Back-up is extra help or support, given now or ready to be given when it is needed: *We have over thirty officers available as back-up.* ❑ *Effects like these cannot be achieved without considerable technical back-up.* **2** A **back-up** is an extra thing you have ready to use if the first thing fails: *The system has a battery override as a back-up, in case of a power cut.*

backdate /bak'deɪt/ see **date back**

backdrop /'bakdrɒp/ see **drop back**

bail /beɪl/: **bails**, **bailing**, **bailed**

bail out

1 To **bail out** someone accused of a crime is to have them released from prison until their trial by paying the court a fixed sum of money: *Within an hour, a team of lawyers turned up to bail him out.* **2** You **bail** someone **out** when you help them out of a difficult situation, often by giving them money they urgently need: *The Bank soon grows tired of bailing out ailing businesses.* **3** (also **bale out**) To **bail out** a damaged boat is to remove the water that has flowed in through the hole, *eg* by scooping it out with buckets: *We spent a couple of exhausting hours bailing water out of the sleeping compartment.* ❑ *The water was gushing in so fast that bailing out seemed ridiculous.* **4** (also **bale out**) To **bail out** of an aircraft about to crash is to escape by jumping out with a parachute: *At the first sign of engine trouble, the pilot's instructions are to bail out.*

balance /'baləns/: **balances**, **balancing**, **balanced**

balance against

You **balance** one thing **against** another when you consider how important one is compared to the other: *Many directors find it difficult to balance their artistic values against the commercial pressures producers place upon them.* [*same as* **weigh against, set against**]

balance out *or* balance up

Two or more things **balance out** or **balance up** when they are equal; you **balance** them **out**, or **balance** them **up**, when you make them equal: *But income and expenses have to balance out if we're not to make a loss.* ❑ *It would take considerable skill and organization to balance up so many demands on your time.* [*same as* **even out, even up**]

bale see **bail**

balk *or* **baulk** /bɔːlk/: **balks**, **balking**, **balked**

balk at

You **balk at** something when you feel unwilling to do it, or when you refuse to do it: *I hadn't expected the builders to balk at providing an inflated estimate for the insurers; it was common practice.* [*same as* **demur** (*formal*)]

balls /bɔːlz/: **ballses**, **ballsing**, **ballsed**

balls up (*vulgar slang*)

To **balls** something **up** is to spoil it by making foolish mistakes: *Keep Taylor out of the way: we don't want him ballsing up another deal.* ❑ *If we let her* *anywhere near the filing system, she'll only balls things up again.* [*same as* **cock up** (*vulgar slang*), **mess up** (*informal*), **screw up** (*informal*), **bungle**]

• *noun (vulgar)* **balls-up**: **balls-ups**

A **balls-up** is a foolish mistake, or the disordered situation created by such a mistake: *Trust him to make a balls-up of the travel arrangements!*

band /band/: **bands**, **banding**, **banded**

band together

People **band together** when they form a group, and usually take action together to achieve a particular aim: *Disparate bunches of resistance fighters had banded together to form a united front.* ❑ *Dissenters were banding themselves together and the government was getting nervous.* [*same as* **team up**, **unite**; *opposite* **break up**, **split up**]

bandy /ˈbandɪ/: **bandies**, **bandying**, **bandied**

bandy about

People who **bandy about** words or ideas frequently use them or mention them, often too casually or without understanding their real meaning or importance: *Several names have been bandied about but no-one has been appointed to the job yet.* ❑ *'Ecosystem' is one of these trendy terms bandied about on university campuses by people who think they can save the world.* ❑ *People who read about such theories in second-rate journals shouldn't go bandying them about to reporters.*

bang /baŋ/: **bangs**, **banging**, **banged**

bang about *or* bang around

1 You **bang** something **about**, or **bang** it **around**, when you handle it very roughly: *When CDs first came out, we were told they couldn't be damaged no matter how much we banged them about.* ❑ *It's been banged around quite a bit but it still works fine.* [*same as* **knock about** (*informal*)] **2** You **bang about** or **bang around** when you go around doing things noisily: *I could hear him banging about in the bathroom; he'd clearly had a bad day.* [*same as* **crash about**] **3** Something **bangs about** or **bangs around** when it noisily and repeatedly hits things that surround it or are next to it: *You don't want the bottles banging about in the boot.* [*same as* **crash about**]

bang down

You **bang** something **down** when you put it down very roughly and noisily: *Ellen banged down her mug, spilling coffee all over the table.* [*same as* **slam down**]

bang into

You **bang into** something when you collide with it noisily or violently: *The handbrake cable snapped and the car banged into a van parked behind.* ❑ *Her kitchen was so small I kept banging into the fridge with my elbow.* [*same as* **bump into**]

bang on about (*informal*)

Someone **bangs on about** something when they talk about the same thing over and over again, so that it bores or irritates you: *I didn't think I could stand another evening of Barry banging on about how kids today have no respect.* [*same as* **go on about** (*informal*), **harp on**]

bang out (*informal*)

1 Someone **bangs out** a tune on a piano or similar instrument when they play it loudly and with energy, perhaps too loudly: *We all stood up and the organist banged out 'O Come All Ye Faithful'.* **2** You **bang out** work on a typewriter or computer keyboard when you type it fast and with energy: *He'd banged out the first chapter by lunchtime.* [compare **dash off**]

bang up

1 (*slang*) Someone **is banged up** when

they are put in prison: *She'll probably get a fine, but she might get banged up for a couple of months.* [*same as* **send down** (*informal*), **imprison**] 2 (*vulgar slang*) A woman **is banged up** when she becomes pregnant: *His parents kicked him out because he got his girlfriend banged up.* [*same as* **knock up** (*vulgar slang*)]

bank /baŋk/: banks, banking, banked

bank on

You **bank on** something happening when you expect it to happen, and perhaps make plans in advance: *We're all banking on good weather for the first meeting of the season.* ❑ *You can't bank on her train arriving on time.* ❑ *It's early days: I wouldn't bank on her support when it comes to the vote.* [*same as* **count on, bet on, rely on**]

bank up

1 To **bank up** something such as soil or snow is to form it into a heap or pile: *Through time, silt banks up and the course of the river is changed.* ❑ *We banked the compost up against a wall, where it would rot quicker.* [*same as* **pile up, heap up**] **2** To **bank up** a fire is to put a lot of coal on it so that it will burn slowly and for a long time: *In the winter, the coal fire was a real joy, and Dad banked it up every night before we went to bed.*

bargain /'bɑːgɪn/: bargains, bargaining, bargained

bargain for *or* bargain on

You **bargain for** something, or **bargain on** something happening, when you are expecting it or are relying on it happening: *Jenkins turned out to be a lazy, ignorant, womanizing scoundrel; not at all what the Dean had bargained for.* ❑ *We didn't bargain on them changing their mind at the last minute.* [*same as* **reckon on**]

barge /bɑːdʒ/: barges, barging, barged

barge in

Someone **barges in** when they rudely interrupt your conversation or what you are doing: *The children keep barging in on me when I'm talking on the phone.* [*same as* **burst in, butt in** (*informal*)]

barge into

1 Someone **barges into** a room when they enter it noisily and without waiting to be invited in: *I can't get used to the way people just barge into each other's offices.* **2** Someone **barges into** a conversation when they interrupt it rudely: *He can't stop himself barging into other people's conversations.* **3** Someone **barges into** you when they bump their body into yours roughly or clumsily: *If they can't get past, they just barge into you and knock you out of the way.*

barge through

Someone **barges through** a crowd of people when they walk into the crowd without waiting for people to move aside: *A doctor barged his way through to the front of the crowd.* [*same as* **push through**]

bark /bɑːk/: barks, barking, barked

bark out

Someone **barks out** an order when they shout it very loudly, and perhaps angrily: *The Sergeant-Major barked out an 'Eyes right!' and we turned to see the young princess passing in an open-top Daimler.*

base /beɪs/: bases, basing, based

base on *or* base upon

Something **is based on** or **upon** what it is broadly developed or created from: *Her arguments are based upon the findings of a team of Swiss scientists.* ❑ *Here is yet another television series* *based on a very successful Joanna Trollope book.* ❑ *I'm told you based the character of Reg on your own local supermarket manager.* [compare **derive from**]

bash /baʃ/: **bashes**, **bashing**, **bashed**

bash about (*informal*)
You **bash** something **about** when you treat it very roughly, and perhaps damage it: *I keep it locked so the kids don't go bashing it about.* ❑ *The table's been bashed about a bit but the chairs are in quite good condition.* [*same as* **knock about** (*informal*)]

bash on (*informal*)
You **bash on** with something when you continue doing it, perhaps with speed, energy or determination: *I'm a bit behind with my work, so I hope you don't mind if I just bash on while you wait.* [*same as* **press on, get on, push on** (*informal*); *opposite* **give up, abandon**]

bask /bɑːsk/: **basks**, **basking**, **basked**

bask in
1 You **bask in** sunshine when you enjoy the feeling of it on your body: *The beach was dotted with Atlantic seals basking in the afternoon sun.* **2** You **bask in** the praise or admiration other people give you when you greatly enjoy it, and perhaps show how delighted you are by it: *He seemed content to bask in the glory his wife's position bestowed on him and the family.* [*same as* **wallow in, revel in**]

batter /'batə(r)/: **batters**, **battering**, **battered**

batter down
Someone **batters down** something such as a door when they knock it down or destroy it by repeatedly hitting it hard: *In a frenzy of anger, he had battered the gate down with his feet.* [*same as* **break down**]

baulk see **balk**

bawl /bɔːl/: **bawls**, **bawling**, **bawled**

bawl out
1 You **bawl** something **out** when you shout or sing it loudly: *The three of them stood round the piano bawling out bar-room songs.* **2** (*informal*) Someone **bawls** you **out** when they speak angrily to you because you've done something wrong: *She seemed to get a thrill out of bawling out the trainees in front of the whole office.* [*same as* **tell off, dress down, rebuke** (*formal*)]

bear /bɛə(r)/: **bears**, **bearing**, **bore** /bɔː(r)/, **borne** /bɔːn/

bear down on
Someone or something **bears down on** you when they move towards you in a threatening way: *He saw her figure bearing down on him from the other end of the corridor.*

bear on *or* **bear upon** (*formal*)
Something **bears on** or **bears upon** what it affects or relates to: *The Secretary of State is perhaps forgetting that her rather casual remarks bear upon the medical care that is given to hundreds of thousands of patients.* [*same as* **have a bearing on**]

bear out
One thing **bears out** another when it supports it or proves that it's true: *Her allegations are not borne out by the facts.* ❑ *It was an attractive theory, but the results didn't bear it out.* [*same as* **confirm, substantiate**]

bear up
You **bear up** when you remain strong and brave in a difficult or upsetting situation: *She's bearing up wonderfully under the strain.*

bear with

You **bear with** someone when you are patient with them: *Please bear with me while I get everything ready.*

beat /biːt/: beats, beating, beat, beaten

beat down

1 The sun **beats down** when you feel it shining very strongly, perhaps so strongly that its heat makes you tired: *Scobie felt the noon sun beating down on his uncovered head.* **2** Rain **beats down** when it falls very hard: *The storm continued to beat down on their flimsy canvas shelter.* **3** You **beat** someone **down** when you force them to reduce the price of something they are selling you: *I managed to beat her down from £200 to £150.* ❑ *You can usually beat them down by around 50%.* [*same as* **knock down**]

beat off

You **beat off** something or someone who is challenging or attacking you when you stop them defeating you or overcoming you: *Liverpool's solid defending beat off yet another United attack.* ❑ *He came at me with a knife but I beat him off with my umbrella.* [compare **fend off, ward off**]

beat on (*AmE*)

Someone **beats on** you when they attack you with their hands and feet: *He was the kind of kid the others liked to beat on.* [*same as* **beat up**]

beat up

Someone **beats** you **up** when they punch, kick or hit you violently and repeatedly: *He claimed he'd been beaten up by the police.* ❑ *He'd want to beat up anyone who harmed his children in any way.* [*same as* **duff up** (*informal*), **work over** (*informal*), **assault**]

beat up on (*AmE*)

To **beat up on** someone is to beat them up: *Two guys cornered him in the locker room and beat up on him.*

beaver /ˈbiːvə(r)/: beavers, beavering, beavered

beaver away

Someone **is beavering away** at something when they are working hard at it, with all their energy and attention: *The children had been given homework and were already beavering away upstairs.* [*same as* **plug away** (*informal*); compare **slog away**]

become /bɪˈkʌm/: becomes, becoming, became /bɪˈkeɪm/, become

become of

People sometimes ask what **has become of** someone or something they haven't seen for a while or have had no recent news of, when they want to know what has happened to them: *She wondered what would become of the cottage if they sold it.*

bed /bɛd/: beds, bedding, bedded

bed down

You **bed down** somewhere when you make yourself a temporary bed and sleep there: *You could always bed down on the sofa.* [*same as* **doss down** (*informal*); compare **crash out**]

beef /biːf/: beefs, beefing, beefed

beef up (*informal*)

You **beef** something **up** when you add things to strengthen it or make it more important or impressive: *I felt the text needed beefing up a little.* [*same as* **enhance**]

before see panel on next page

beg /bɛg/: begs, begging, begged

beg off

You **beg off** when you say you will no longer do what you had promised or agreed to do: *Alex has had to beg off: his daughter's turned up for the weekend unexpectedly.* [*same as* **cry off, back out, cancel**]

before /bɪ'fɔː(r)/

Before is a preposition and an adverb. It is a very common word in English, but it only features in a handful of phrasal verbs in this dictionary, with two main senses.

1 TIME
Before is used in some phrasal verbs whose meanings relate to time. In one sense of **come before** and **go before,** a time earlier than the present is being referred to, whereas an experience that **lies before** you is one you will encounter in the future.

2 PRESENTING
In its other main sense, **before** occurs in phrasal verbs that refer to the action of presenting something to someone, so that they can consider it or make judgements on it. In a second sense of **come before** and **go before**, it is a person who presents themselves to someone in authority; you **lay** plans or ideas **before** someone, or **put** plans or ideas **before** them, when you ask for their opinion or judgement.

behind see panel in next column

believe /bɪ'liːv/: **believes, believing, believed**

believe in

1 You **believe in** something when you believe that it exists or is real: *There was the absurd case of the priest who didn't believe in God.* ❑ *The younger children still believed in Father Christmas.* **2** You also **believe in** something when you support or favour it because you think that it's right or has some value or worth: *I'm not sure how many members of the Party actually believed in Communism as a realistic model.* ❑ *Does the government still believe in giving free medical treatment to all who want it?* ❑ *They suspect that acupuncture is no longer believed in as an effective treatment for the more serious conditions.* **3** You can **believe in** something if it seems realistic or likely: *The film's two central characters are simply too outrageous to be believed in.* **4** You **believe in** someone when you are confident that they will be successful, or that they have made good decisions or judgements: *I'm lucky enough to have a husband who believes in me and in what I'm trying to achieve.* [*same as* **have faith in**]

belong /bɪ'lɒŋ/: **belongs, belonging, belonged**

belong to

1 Something **belongs to** you when you own or possess it: *He was, in effect, selling property that belonged to someone else.* ❑ *We looked at a house belonging to a retired couple.* **2** You **belong to** something such as a club when you are a member of it: *Less than 15% of our workforce belong to a trade union.* **3** People also use **belong to** to refer to connections or associations of various kinds: *She looked about 35, but her voice belonged to a much older woman.* ❑ *These attitudes really belong*

behind /bɪ'haɪnd/

Behind is an adverb and a preposition. It is a fairly common word in English, although it features in only a small number of phrasal verbs in this dictionary. Its basic meaning relates to position in space or time, and the senses featured here are related to this.

1 LEAVING AND STAYING
In its literal sense, **behind** occurs in a few phrasal verbs that refer to the action of leaving or the fact of staying. These are **leave behind, stay behind** and **stop behind**. You **put** an unpleasant experience **behind** you when you forget about it.

2 PROGRESS
In other phrasal verbs, **behind** refers to the notion of making poor progress compared to others or to the rest, as in **fall behind, get behind, lag behind.** If you **leave** someone **behind** you make much faster progress than them.

to a bygone age. ❑ *Plants belonging to a variety of species can be grown very successfully in containers.* ❑ *This challenges the notion of belonging to a particular culture or society.*

below see panel below

belt /bɛlt/: **belts**, **belting**, **belted**

belt out (*informal*)
Something **is belted out** when it is produced or expressed with great energy or power: *The furnace belted out a terrific heat.* ❑ *She was leaning against the upright piano belting out an old Sinatra number.*

belt up
1 (*informal*) Someone who tells you to **belt up** is rudely telling you to stop talking: *Just belt up for a second, will you!* [*same as* **shut up** (*informal*), **pipe down** (*informal*)] **2** You **belt up** when you fasten the seat belt in a car or other vehicle.

below /bɪ'lou/
Below is a preposition and an adverb.
It is not a very common word in English and it occurs in only one phrasal verb in this dictionary. Its basic meaning relates to a position lower than something; the phrasal verb **go below** means to move to a lower floor or level on a ship. You can occasionally find phrasal verbs formed with **below** in this sense, such as *dash below* in the following example: *One of the crew watched the bomb go off and dashed below to tell his shipmates.*

bend /bɛnd/: **bends**, **bending**, **bent**

bend down
You **bend down** when you lower your body, *eg* to place something on the floor, or to avoid a low ceiling: *He suffered from a bad back and couldn't bend down that far.* ❑ *She bent down and whispered in the child's ear.* [*same as* **stoop**]

bend over
You **bend over** when you move the top of your body forward and down, from the waist: *Ask them to bend over and touch their toes.*

beneath see panel below

beneath /bɪ'ni:θ/
Beneath is a preposition and an adverb.
Beneath is not a very common word in English, and is also slightly formal. It means the same as **under** and relates to the position of something. It only appears in this dictionary in the phrasal verb **marry beneath**, which means to marry someone from a lower class or position in society.

bet /bɛt/: **bets**, **betting**, **bet**

bet on
1 You **bet on** a race or other contest when you guess who the winner will be and risk money on your guess: *He always bets on the horse with the silliest name.* **2** People often use **bet on** when talking about what they expect or hope will happen: *They were all impressive candidates, but I'm betting on the fellow from Loughborough getting the job.* ❑ *I wouldn't bet on it being fine this weekend.* ❑ *This is a complex problem; don't bet on an early solution.* [*same as* **bank on, count on**]

between see panel below

between /bɪ'twi:n/
Between is a preposition.
It is a fairly common word in English. Its basic meaning relates to the middle position of something or someone. The phrasal verbs **come between** and **stand between** are both used to talk about what prevents someone from having or achieving something they want; something that **passes between** two people is communicated from one to the other.

beyond see panel below

bitch /bɪtʃ/: **bitches**, **bitching**, **bitched**

bitch up (*informal*; *especially AmE*)
Someone **bitches** something **up** when they spoil it, often deliberately: *There was always someone waiting to bitch up my special moments.* [*same as* **mess up** (*informal*), **wreck**, **ruin**]

bite /baɪt/: **bites**, **biting**, **bit** /bɪt/, **bitten** /ˈbɪtən/

bite back
You **bite back** a remark or sound when, as you're about to say it or express it, you manage to stop yourself: *Biting back his anger, Martin excused himself and left the room.* ❑ *She felt an apology forming itself in her mouth, but then bit it back.* [*same as* **choke back**, **suppress**]

> **beyond** /bɪˈjɒnd/
>
> **Beyond** is a preposition and an adverb. It is not a very common word in everyday English and it is used in only a few phrasal verbs in this dictionary. Its basic meaning relates to a position further than something or someone, and the phrasal verbs **get beyond** and **go beyond** both relate to making greater progress or further advances than someone or something else.

black /blak/: **blacks**, **blacking**, **blacked**

black out
1 A place or building **is blacked out** when all the lights are switched off and it is made completely dark, or windows and other openings are covered so that lights on inside the building cannot be seen from the outside: *Wardens patrolled the streets to make sure every house had been properly blacked out.* **2** Someone **blacks out** when they lose consciousness for a short time: *I must have blacked out: the next thing I remember is two men pulling me from the car.* [*same as* **pass out, faint**; compare **flake out, keel over**] **3** To **black out** a television or radio programme is to prevent it from being broadcast: *Orders from Beijing were to black out all scheduled news bulletins.*
• *noun* **blackout**: **blackouts**
1 Someone has a **blackout** when they lose consciousness for a short time: *Her blackouts were becoming more regular, and the doctors didn't seem able to do anything.* **2** A **blackout** is a period without lights or the state of having no lights, either because of a failure of the electricity supply, or because of orders to cover lighted windows, *eg* during a war: *There was a three-day blackout, during which we played cards by candlelight.* ❑ *In the blackout, on a clear night, you could see every star in the heavens.* **3** There is a radio or television **blackout** when programmes are prevented from being broadcast: *Two American journalists had defied the news blackout.*

blare /blɛə(r)/: **blares**, **blaring**, **blared**

blare out
Sound or music **blares out** when it is very loud, perhaps unpleasantly loud: *There were complaints about the disco music blaring out from one of the shops along the street.* ❑ *Radios all over town blared out the new national anthem.* [*same as* **blast out**; compare **boom out**]

blast /blɑːst/: **blasts**, **blasting**, **blasted**

blast off
A spacecraft **blasts off** when it leaves Earth to begin a journey into space: *The shuttle was due to blast off at two o'clock eastern time.*
• *noun* **blast-off**: **blast-offs**: *We were not notified of the problem until a couple of minutes before blast-off.* [*same as* **lift-off**]

blast out
Sound or music **blasts out** when it is very loud, perhaps unpleasantly loud: *The loudspeakers blasted out big band music, with interruptions for news from Saigon.* [*same as* **blare out**]

blaze /bleɪz/: **blazes, blazing, blazed**

blaze away
1 A fire **is blazing away** when it is burning with a bright and powerful heat: *It wasn't long before the logs were blazing away.* **2** (*informal*) To **blaze away** with an automatic gun is to fire it continuously: *And then you read about some psychopath walking into a shopping mall and blazing away with a submachine gun.*

blend /blɛnd/: **blends, blending, blended**

blend in *or* blend into
1 Someone or something **blends in** when they suit their surroundings, or other things, very well; they **blend into** surroundings that they suit very well: *The other students were much younger, and he wasn't sure if he would blend in.* ❑ *Ours is a modest little company which will perhaps struggle to blend into the high-powered international scene.* ❑ *It's difficult to see how such a conspicuously modern development could blend successfully into the largely medieval town centre.* ❑ *What they had planned blended in perfectly with our vision of a holiday away from it all.* [*same as* **fit in**] **2** Something that **blends in** is difficult to see because it is the same colour or shape as the things around it: *The tiger's stripes allow it to blend into its native jungle environment.* [compare **merge into**]

block /blɒk/: **blocks, blocking, blocked**

block in
1 Someone or something **blocks** you **in** when it is in a position that prevents you from moving or getting out: *Another car came and blocked me in.* ❑ *We'll have to move the long table, or the people at the back will be blocked in.* [compare **close in, shut in, hedge in**] **2** You **block in** something drawn in outline only when you add colour or shading inside the lines to make a solid figure. [compare **shade in, colour in**]

block off
To **block off** something such as a street or a door is to stop people entering or passing that way: *Because of roadworks, the back road will be blocked off for several days.* ❑ *If we blocked the front entrance off altogether, they'd have to go in by the side.* [*same as* **close off, seal off, cordon off**; *opposite* **open up**]

block out
1 Something **blocks out** light when it stops light from getting in: *If the tree grew any bigger it would block the sunlight out altogether.* [*same as* **shut out, exclude**; *opposite* **let in, admit** (*formal*)] **2** You **block** something **out** when you avoid thinking about it: *I couldn't block out of my mind the terrible things she had said.* [*same as* **shut out, blot out, suppress**]

block up
Something **is blocked up** when objects stuck inside it prevent water, air or some other substance from flowing through it in the normal way: *It dissolves the grease and grime that keeps blocking the sink up.* ❑ *Mucus blocks up the nose and forces the patient to breathe through their mouth.* [*same as* **bung up** (*informal*)]

blot /blɒt/: **blots, blotting, blotted**

blot out
1 One thing **blots out** another when it stops it from being seen or perceived: *What sunshine there was had now been blotted out by thick smoke from the fire.* ❑ *The smell was nauseating, and she poured on some bleach to blot it*

out. [*same as* **hide, mask, obscure**] **2** You **blot out** a painful or unpleasant memory when you avoid thinking about it or remembering it: *Most victims will try to blot the incident out completely.* [*same as* **block out, shut out, suppress**]

blow /blou/: **blows**, **blowing**, **blew** /blu:/, **blown**

blow away

1 Something **blows away**, or **is blown away**, when the wind takes it away: *Our map was blown away and we couldn't see anyone to ask for directions.* ❑ *We weighted it down with bricks, to stop it blowing away.* **2** Part of someone's body **is blown away** when it is destroyed or removed by the force of an explosion: *A terrorist bomb had blown one side of her face away.* **3** (*slang; especially AmE*) To **blow** someone **away** is to kill them by shooting them with a gun: *He threatened to blow them away if they came any closer.*

blow down

Something, especially something fixed firmly in position, **blows down** or **is blown down** when the wind causes it to fall to the ground: *One of the chimney pots blew down in the storm, and it damaged a neighbour's car.* ❑ *Last week's gales blew our apple tree down.*

blow out

1 You **blow out** a candle when you stop the flame burning by blowing air on it: *When we returned, the wind had blown the fire out.* [compare **put out**] **2** A storm **blows** itself **out** when it comes to an end; people often also say that things such as arguments **blow** themselves **out** when they come to an end: *These northerly gales should have blown themselves out by next week.* ❑ *Within a few days the whole furore had quite blown itself out.*

• *noun* **blowout**

1 A **blowout** occurs when a vehicle's tyre bursts, releasing all the air in the explosion: *A few miles outside Coventry, one of the vans had a blowout.* **2** (*informal*) A **blowout** is also a meal much larger than you normally have, often one eaten as part of a celebration: *He's still suffering from the customary Christmas blowout.*

blow over

1 Something such as an argument **blows over** when it ends and people forget about it: *It only took a few days for the scandal to blow over.* [*same as* **subside**; compare **die down**] **2** A storm **blows over** when it ends: *We huddled together in the cellar and waited for the hurricane to blow over.* [*same as* **subside**; compare **die down**] **3** The wind **blows** something **over**, especially something not firmly fixed to the ground, when it causes it to fall on to its side or fall upside down: *Gales of over 70mph blew over a number of vehicles in the Glasgow area.*

blow up

1 People **blow** something **up** when they destroy it with a bomb or other exploding weapon; something that **blows up** is destroyed in this way: *Once they'd blown up the main railway station, control of the city was theirs.* ❑ *It seems that the terrorist planting the device had accidentally triggered it, blowing himself up.* ❑ *If flames had reached the fuel store, the whole place would certainly have blown up.* [*same as* **explode**] **2** You **blow up** something such as a tyre or a balloon when you fill it with air or gas. [*same as* **inflate**] **3** To **blow up** a photograph is to make a bigger copy of it: *The detail will be much clearer if we blow it up.* [*same as* **enlarge**] **4** You **blow** something **up** when you make it seem more impressive, important or serious than it really is: *Once the newspapers got their hands on the story, it was blown up out of all proportion.* [*same as* **exaggerate**] **5** A storm **blows up** when it begins: *The horses get nervous when there's a storm blowing up.* **6** Something such as trouble or an argument **blows up** when it begins suddenly: *A heated row blew up between the director and the team manager.* **7** (*informal*) Someone **blows up** when they suddenly start shouting or behaving very angrily: *Peter blew up at one of the students for not handing her work in on time.* [*same as* **flare up**]

blurt /blɜːt/: **blurts**, **blurting**, **blurted**

blurt out
You **blurt** something **out** when you suddenly say it without thinking, or before you can stop yourself: *He was the defence minister who blurted out military secrets to a high-class prostitute.* ❑ *'Yes, we're leaving tomorrow,' he blurted out.*

board /bɔːd/: **boards**, **boarding**, **boarded**

board up
To **board up** a window or door is to cover it with wooden boards, *eg* because it is broken and has not yet been repaired: *There were rows of empty houses with their windows boarded up.* ❑ *Shopkeepers, terrified by rumours of street violence, had boarded their windows up.*

bog /bɒg/: **bogged**

bog down
You **are bogged down** by something when you give so much attention to it, or become so involved in it, that you fail to make proper progress or any progress at all: *We must be careful not to get bogged down in trifling detail.* ❑ *I thought we were becoming a little bogged down, so I tried to move the discussion on a bit.*

bog off (*informal*)
Someone who tells you to **bog off** is telling you rudely to go away: *I thought he would say 'Bog off,' but it seemed he really wanted to talk to someone.* [*same as* **piss off** (*vulgar slang*), **bugger off** (*vulgar slang*), **get lost** (*informal*)]

boil /bɔɪl/: **boils**, **boiling**, **boiled**

boil down to
People sometimes say that a complicated situation **boils down to** one particular thing when they are pointing out that that thing is its basic or most important aspect: *As with all committee decisions, it all boils down to money.* ❑ *What it boils down to is a fundamental difference in religious approach.* [*same as* **come down to**]

boil over
1 A liquid **boils over** when it is heated so fiercely that some of it spills over the edge of its container: *See that the milk doesn't boil over.* **2** A situation **boils over** when people lose their temper and start to behave very angrily or violently: *There were fears that the demonstration might boil over into a full-scale riot.*

boil up
You **boil up** a liquid when you heat it until it boils: *Use a large pan and boil up the water first, then plunge the pasta in.*

bomb /bɒm/: **bombs**, **bombing**, **bombed**

bomb out
1 A building **is bombed out** when it is destroyed by a bomb or bombs: *Friends in the city were bombed out in the first raids.* **2** (*informal*) Someone or something **is bombed out** when they are rejected or dismissed: *You spend weeks preparing a proposal, only to have it bombed out by councillors who wouldn't know a good idea if it slapped them in the face.* ❑ *She could get bombed out of her job if she carries on like this.* [*same as* **throw out**]

bone /boun/: **bones, boning, boned**

bone up on (*informal*)
You **bone up on** something you have been learning when you make sure you know it thoroughly, in preparation for an examination: *I'd better bone up on my irregular verbs.* [*same as* **swot up on** (*informal*), **revise**; compare **brush up on**]

book /buk/: **books, booking, booked**

book in *or* **book into**
You **book in** when you announce your arrival at a place, usually a hotel; you **book** someone **in** when you arrange for them to stay in a place such as a hotel: *When we booked in, we were asked to leave our passports.* ❑ *They decided to book into the first guesthouse they saw, to save time.* ❑ *Eddie had booked the group in to play four nights at the famous 'Lollipop Club'.* ❑ *She returned from her wanderings and booked herself straight into a London clinic for a couple of weeks.* [compare **check in**]

book up
1 You **book up** for something when you arrange to have it or take part in it at some time in the future: *Am I too late to book up for the Paris trip?* ❑ *Last year's holiday was a last-minute thing, but this year we decided to get booked up nice and early.* **2** Something you want to take part in or attend **is booked up** when there are no seats or tickets left: *I'm afraid the three o'clock flight is all booked up.* ❑ *The hotels along the front were all booked up solid the whole summer.*

boom /bu:m/: **booms, booming, boomed**

boom out
Someone **booms** something **out**, or their voice **booms out**, if they speak with a loud, deep, resounding voice: *The officer boomed out the commands.* ❑ *His voice booms out across the field.*

boot /bu:t/: **boots, booting, booted**

boot out (*informal*)
Someone **is booted out** when they are forced to leave: *People have been booted out of the Party for much less serious offences.* ❑ *They'll be trying their best to boot her out of her seat at the next election.* [*same as* **throw out, kick out** (*informal*)]

border /'bɔ:də(r)/: **borders, bordering, bordered**

border on
1 One country **borders on** another when it shares a border with it: *They stayed in Staffordshire and visited the counties that border on it.* [*same as* **neighbour**] **2** People often use **border on** when they are describing how extreme something is: *Her actions were at best unwise; at worst they bordered on stupidity.* ❑ *She had been in a miserable state bordering on depression.* [*same as* **verge on**]

boss /bɒs/: **bosses, bossing, bossed**

boss about *or* **boss around**
Someone **bosses** you **about**, or **bosses** you **around**, when they behave as if they had more authority than you and keep telling you what to do: *He was tired of being bossed around by his parents.* [*same as* **order about, push around, domineer**]

botch /bɒtʃ/: **botches, botching, botched**

botch up (*informal*)
You **botch** something **up** when you do it badly, without skill or carelessly: *Somebody botched up the order and we got a lot of stuff we didn't need.* [*same as* **mess up** (*informal*), **foul up** (*informal*), **cock up** (*vulgar slang*)]
• *noun* **botch-up**: **botch-ups**: *She was angry because Alan had made a*

botch-up of the seating plan.

bottle /ˈbɒtəl/: **bottles**, **bottling**, **bottled**

bottle out (*informal*)
You **bottle out** when you lose the courage to do something, and fail to do it: *I wouldn't be surprised if he bottles out at the last minute.* ❑ *I don't think her pride would let her bottle out of it now.* [*same as* **chicken out** (*informal*)]

bottle up
You **bottle up** a strong emotion you frequently feel when you don't allow yourself to express it: *You have to appreciate that she's been bottling this up for some time.* ❑ *She kept her anger bottled up inside her for years.* [*same as* **keep back, suppress**; *opposite* **let go, reveal**]

bottom /ˈbɒtəm/: **bottoms**, **bottoming**, **bottomed**

bottom out
Something that has been falling or getting worse **bottoms out** when it reaches its lowest level, beyond which it will not fall any further: *The good news is that the company's losses in the Far East appear to have bottomed out.* [*opposite* **peak**; compare **level out**]

bounce /baʊns/: **bounces**, **bouncing**, **bounced**

bounce back
You **bounce back** after a failure or disappointment when you soon become cheerful, hopeful or enthusiastic again: *I think you have to question how likely it is that British manufacturing can bounce back from such a sustained onslaught.* [compare **pick up, perk up**]

bow /baʊ/: **bows**, **bowing**, **bowed**

bow out
Someone **bows out** when they give up an important position or job, or when they stop taking part in something: *Navratilova may well play in one more Wimbledon before bowing out of the international circuit altogether.* [*same as* **retire, withdraw**; compare **pull out, back out**]

bow to
You **bow to** pressure from someone when you accept that you must do what they ask or demand: *The courts don't seem willing to bow to the arguments and entreaties of the animal rights lobby.* [*same as* **give in to, yield to**; *opposite* **stand up to, defy**]

bowl /boʊl/: **bowls**, **bowling**, **bowled**

bowl over
1 Someone **bowls** you **over** when they knock you to the ground with great force, perhaps such force that you roll over: *The poor lady was bowled over in the rush that followed.* [*same as* **knock over**] **2** You **are bowled over** by something or someone when you are immediately surprised or shocked by how impressive they are: *The friendliness of the Greeks just bowled me over.* [*same as* **take aback, overwhelm, stagger**]

box /bɒks/: **boxes**, **boxing**, **boxed**

box in
You **are boxed in** when the position of other people or things around you prevents you from moving or changing position: *An experienced jockey like Carson shouldn't allow himself to get boxed in on the rails.* [*same as* **hem in, confine, enclose**; compare **coop up**]

branch /brɑːntʃ/: **branches**, **branching**, **branched**

branch off
You **branch off** when you leave the main road or path and follow a smaller one connected to it: *About a hundred yards into the wood, take the narrow track that branches off the main path to the left.*

branch out
You **branch out** when you do something new or different, perhaps something rather exciting or a little uncertain or dangerous: *Several aeronautics companies branched out into the manufacture of weapons.* ❑ *I can't imagine Gerry branching out on his own.*

brave /breɪv/: **braves**, **braving**, **braved**

brave out
You **brave out** a difficult or unpleasant situation when, rather than trying to avoid it, you deal with it with courage and determination: *She's handled worse than this; I'm confident she'll brave this one out.*

brazen /ˈbreɪzən/: **brazens**, **brazening**, **brazened**

brazen out
Someone who **brazens** it **out** shows no feelings of shame, guilt or regret for the wrong they have done: *Most experienced politicians have the nerve to brazen it out.*

break /breɪk/: **breaks**, **breaking**, **broke** /brouk/, **broken** /ˈbroukən/

break away
1 You **break away** when you leave the group or association you have been part of: *They became so disillusioned, of course, that they broke away from the Labour Party altogether and formed the SDP.* ❑ *This has been the case with every self-proclaimed republic breaking away from the Soviet Union.* [compare **break with**] **2** You **break away** when you escape from someone who is holding you or keeping you prisoner: *Three of the prisoners managed to break away from their guard.*
• *adjective* **breakaway**: *He'll be meeting the leader of the breakaway republic in London next week.*

break down
1 A vehicle or machine **breaks down** when it stops working properly and needs to be repaired: *The policy covers you if you break down outside a five-mile radius of your home.* ❑ *We won't be able to afford the repair bill the next time the tumble-drier breaks down.* [*same as* **pack up** (*informal*), **conk out** (*informal*)] **2** Things such as relationships, partnerships and discussions **break down** when they come to an end, because of a disagreement: *When marriages break down, we have to put the interests of the children first.* [*same as* **fail**, **collapse**] **3** Someone **breaks down** when they completely lose control of their emotions and begin to cry, or perhaps laugh, uncontrollably: *We have often seen relatives of victims break down in front of the cameras.* [*same as* **collapse**] **4** Someone also **breaks down** when they suffer for a longer period from a serious illness of the nerves which makes them unable to deal with everyday life: *He simply broke down under the pressure.* [*same as* **crack up**] **5** To **break down** a door is to hit it so hard that parts of it break and it falls to the ground: *Two police officers with sledgehammers came to break the door down.* [*same as* **smash down**, **smash in**] **6** You **break** something **down** when you consider the separate parts that form it: *The national statistics can be broken down into four geographical sub-groups.* ❑ *Overall outgoings break down into household expenses, childcare, and the cost of running a car.* **7** A substance **breaks down** when chemical processes cause it to separate into the simpler substances that formed it: *Vegetable-based plastics readily break down when buried in soil.* ❑ *The body's own acids break down the food in your stomach.* ❑ *They've developed a drug that treats the poison by breaking it down.*

• *noun* **breakdown**: *Within an hour of the breakdown, we'll have your vehicle back on the road.* ❑ *The aggrieved partner finds it particularly difficult to cope with a mari-*

tal breakdown. ❑ *We all thought Colin was heading for a nervous breakdown.* ❑ *A breakdown of the figures reveals that people in the North do smoke more.*
• *adjective* **breakdown**: *We have a fleet of over thirty breakdown trucks.*

break in
1 Someone **breaks in** when they enter a building by force or dishonestly, usually intending to steal things inside: *They appear to have broken in through a rear window.* **2** You **break in** when you interrupt a conversation between other people: *I'm sorry to break in, but I think you're both wrong.* ❑ *'Isn't this all a bit irrelevant?' Sonia broke in.* [*same as* **cut in, butt in**] **3** You **break** someone **in** when you make them familiar with a new job or position: *It was Hanlon's responsibility to break in the new boys from the college.* **4** You **break in** new shoes when you make them lose their stiffness by wearing them a lot at first: *He wore the boots around the house to break them in.* **5** To **break in** a wild horse is to teach it to allow a rider on its back.
• *noun* **break-in**: **break-ins**
A **break-in** is an act of entering a building by force or dishonestly, usually intending to steal things inside: *They're concerned by the rising number of break-ins in rural areas.*

break in on
To **break in on** someone is to interrupt or disturb them, especially suddenly and noisily: *His peaceful reverie was broken in on by the sudden burst of a pneumatic drill in the street outside.* ❑ *I apologize for breaking in on you like this, but there's a man in reception who insists on seeing you immediately.*

break into
1 Someone **breaks into** a building or secure place when they enter it by force or dishonestly, usually intending to steal things inside: *The shop had already been broken into three times that year.* ❑ *Someone broke into the filing cabinet and removed all the financial documents.* **2** You also use **break into** to talk about things people suddenly begin to do with great energy: *We trotted for a few yards, then Myra's horse broke into a gallop.* ❑ *The men broke into raucous laughter.* [*same as* **burst into, launch into**] **3** To **break into** a new or different kind of business or activity is to become involved in it for the first time: *He's hoping to break into journalism when he leaves university.* [*same as* **launch into, move into**] **4** You **break into** a banknote or coin of high value when you use it to pay for something that costs much less, because you have no low-value notes or coins: *I don't want to have to break into a ten-pound note.* **5** You **break into** something, especially a supply of something you were keeping in reserve, when you use some of it: *Isn't it about time we broke into the next case of wine?* ❑ *The only way we could afford it now is by breaking into the holiday money.* [*same as* **dip into**]

break off
1 You **break** a piece of something **off** when you remove it from the main part by breaking it; something **breaks off** when it is removed from the main part by being broken: *They were shouted at for breaking a branch off the young tree.* ❑ *The aerial must have broken off in the car wash.* [*same as* **snap off, detach**] **2** You **break off** something such as a relationship when you end it: *No-one knows why she broke her engagement off.* [*same as* **terminate** (*formal*)] **3** You **break off** when you suddenly stop talking: *'Let me begin by ...' she broke off, seeing the minister leave the room.* **4** You **break off** when you temporarily stop what you're doing: *I thought we could break off for lunch around one.* ❑ *They didn't seem willing to break off their game to listen to his little speech.* [compare **knock off**]

break out

1 A prisoner **breaks out** of prison when they escape: *If three of us managed to break out, what would happen to the other two when the break-out was discovered?* **2** Violent, noisy and disturbing situations **break out** when they begin, often suddenly or unexpectedly: *Complete chaos broke out when the relief supplies arrived.* ❑ *They had had secret talks as late as the week before war broke out.* **3** You use **break out** to refer to the sudden spread of things such as sweat or spots on your skin: *Within seconds she was breaking out in a cold sweat.* ❑ *An angry red rash had broken out all over his body.* **4** You also use **break out** to talk about setting yourself free from something that prevents you from doing what you would like to do: *The only route to happiness seemed to lie in breaking out of this mind-numbing routine.* ❑ *Most kids want to leave the island and break out on their own.*

break through

1 You **break through** when you force a way through an obstacle or barrier to reach a place: *She managed to break through the police cordon to get to the house.* ❑ *No progress can be made unless we can break through the wall of indifference that surrounds the Ministry.* **2** Something hidden **breaks through** when it appears: *The sun never managed to break through the clouds.* ❑ *In spite of the scholarly trappings of much of his writing, an earthy, anti-intellectual tone occasionally breaks through.*

• *noun* **breakthrough**: **breakthroughs**
A **breakthrough** is an important discovery or other achievement, arrived at after a lot of hard work or struggling: *This is nothing less than a breakthrough in Anglo-Argentinian relations.* ❑ *a long list of scientific breakthroughs.*

break up

1 You **break** something **up** when you divide it into pieces or separate parts; something **breaks up** when it becomes separated into pieces: *He spent the first hour breaking up logs for firewood.* ❑ *If they got any closer, the boat would certainly break up on the rocks.* **2** To **break up** a gathering of people is to bring it to an end: *Neighbours called the police, who broke the party up.* ❑ *Then Mark, in a display of drink-inspired bravado, stepped in to break the fighting up.* ❑ *The meeting broke up at around eleven, and some of us went to the pub for a last drink.* **3** People **break up** when their relationship or partnership comes to an end: *How did you feel once you knew your parents were breaking up?* ❑ *If you go through with such an unwise marriage, you will only succeed in breaking up the family.* ❑ *We would be sad to see such a long-standing organization break up over such a trivial affair.* [*same as* **split up**; *opposite* **come together**] **4** To **break** something **up** is to add changes or variations to make it more interesting: *An expanse of plain wall needs a few pictures or posters to break it up.* ❑ *He took to strolling round the park at lunchtimes, to break up his day.* **5** (*informal*) A school **breaks up**, or the pupils in it **break up**, when the school term ends and the holidays begin: *My daughter doesn't break up until next week.*

break with

1 You **break with** partners or friends when you end your relationship or association with them, because of a disagreement: *Many Western intellectuals broke with the Communist Party in the Gorbachev era.* [compare **break away**] **2** You **break with** something such as a habit or tradition when you do something different from what is usual or expected: *Breaking with custom, the King leaves his residence in the middle of the night to welcome the Prince in person.*

breathe /briːð/: **breathes**, **breathing**, **breathed**

breathe in

You **breathe in** when you take air into your lungs through your nose or mouth: *Take the wine into your mouth and, holding it there, breathe in deeply through your nose.* ❑ *They wear masks to avoid breathing in the fumes.* ❑ *With gases of this kind, you must take care not to breathe them in.* [*same as* **inhale**]

breathe out

You **breathe out** when you send air out of your lungs through your nose or mouth: *Then breathe out slowly as you lower your arms.* [*same as* **exhale**]

breeze /briːz/: **breezes**, **breezing**, **breezed**

breeze in

You **breeze in** when you enter a place in a cheerful, confident or carefree way: *The door was flung open and in breezed Roger.* ❑ *He breezed in as if he didn't have a care in the world.* [*same as* **waltz in** (*informal*)]

breeze out

You **breeze out** when you leave a place in a cheerful, confident or carefree way: *The customer breezed out of the shop, calling over his shoulder for Menzies to follow him.* [*same as* **waltz out** (*informal*)]

brew /bruː/: **brews**, **brewing**, **brewed**

brew up (*BrE informal*)

You **brew up** when you make tea: *You're only working an hour before someone decides to brew up.*

brick /brɪk/: **bricks**, **bricking**, **bricked**

brick up

To **brick up** a doorway, window or other space is to build a wall of bricks in it to close it up: *The old fireplace was in an awkward place so we bricked it up.*

brighten /'braɪtən/: **brightens**, **brightening**, **brightened**

brighten up

1 To **brighten** a place **up** is to add colourful things to make it more attractive or pleasing: *A few posters would brighten up the walls.* **2** To **brighten up** an occasion is to make it more interesting or enjoyable: *They laid on a display of country dancing to brighten proceedings up a bit.* [*same as* **liven up**, **enliven** (*formal*)] **3** You **brighten up** when you become more cheerful: *She visibly brightened up at the mention of a holiday.* ❑ *We thought an afternoon in the country would brighten him up a little.* [*same as* **cheer up**, **perk up** (*informal*), **buck up** (*informal*)] **4** People often say it is **brightening up** when the weather is becoming sunnier: *Perhaps it'll brighten up later in the day.*

brim /brɪm/: **brims**, **brimming**, **brimmed**

brim over

1 A container **is brimming over** when it is so full that some of the liquid in it is spilling out over the edge: *Feet tapped, faces smiled and glasses brimmed over with champagne.* [*same as* **overflow**] **2** People often use **brim over** as a way of emphasizing how much there is of something: *He's brimming over with enthusiasm for this new job.* ❑ *The schoolkids were brimming over with great ideas for the show.* [*same as* **bubble over** (*informal*)]

bring /brɪŋ/: **brings**, **bringing**, **brought** /brɔːt/

bring about

You **bring** something **about** when you cause it to happen: *They're hoping this next round of talks will bring about a settlement of the pay dispute.* ❑ *This is a very strange attitude; I don't know what's brought it about.* [*same as* **produce**]

bring along

You **bring** someone or something **along** when you take them with you: *Numbers will be quite low, so please bring along a friend if you can.* ❑ *You're advised to bring a portfolio of your work along to the interview.*

bring back

1 You ask someone to **bring back** something they're taking away when you want them to return it to you later: *Please bring the book back on or before the date shown on the ticket.* **2** Something **brings back** memories when it makes you remember something or someone from the past: *I'd quite forgotten how pretty she had been, but the photo brought it all back.* **3** To **bring back** something that no longer exists is to establish it again: *Bringing democracy back to this chaotic country seems a near-impossible task.* ❑ *We find ourselves, at the close of the twentieth century, bringing back methods that were first used three hundred years ago.* [*same as* **restore, revive, reintroduce**]

bring down

1 To **bring down** a government or regime is to force it to give up power: *Even in '68, the students never looked like bringing the government down.* [*same as* **overthrow, topple**] **2** To **bring** something **down** is also to reduce it to a lower level or standard: *We have developed sound economic policies guaranteed to bring down inflation.* ❑ *Could unemployment be brought down to pre-1979 levels?* ❑ *They argue that mixed-ability classes bring down the brighter pupils.* **3** To **bring** someone **down**, *eg* in sports such as rugby, is to cause them to fall down on to the ground: *It looked to me as if Hoddle was brought down just inside the penalty box.* ❑ *He brought down the Milan striker with no intention of playing the ball.* **4** To **bring** something or someone **down** is also to cause them to fall to the ground by shooting them with a gun: *The bigger guns can bring down enemy planes within a range of three miles.* ❑ *Aim for his legs; we only want to bring him down.* **5** Something **brings** you **down** when it makes you feel unhappy or depressed: *It's a constant, nagging pain that brings down even the strongest of patients.* [*same as* **get down, weigh down**]

bring forth (*formal*)

Something **brings forth** what it produces or creates as a result or consequence: *The very suggestion would bring forth gasps of horror from committee members.* ❑ *It doesn't seem likely that this chitchat will bring forth any positive solution to the problem.* [*same as* **yield**]

bring forward

1 You **bring** something **forward** when you arrange for it to happen at an earlier date or time than you originally planned: *We'll have to bring the meeting forward to three o'clock.* ❑ *The trial has been brought forward to the beginning of February.* [*opposite* **put back, put off, postpone**] **2** You **bring forward** something such as a suggestion or proposal when you state it, especially in a formal way: *The marketing department has been invited to bring forward plans for the development of the business overseas.* [*same as* **put forward**]

bring in

1 An organization or authority **brings in** something such as a law, policy or system when they introduce it: *Why don't they bring in legislation to outlaw such cruelly low rates of pay?* [*same as* **establish**] **2** A person or industry **brings in** money when they make or earn it: *Workers at the assembly plant bring in little over $800 a month.* [*opposite* **pay out, lay out** (*informal*)] **3** You **bring** someone **in** when you ask or invite them to help or take part: *Air-accident experts have been brought in from North America to assist with the investigation.* ❑ *I could see them* *bringing in the local MP to lend weight to their campaign.* [*same as* **call in**] **4** You **bring** something **in** when you mention it or include it in discussion: *I feel they could bring in a little history of art to make the course more interesting.* [compare **bring up**] **5** A court or jury **brings** someone **in** either guilty or innocent when they decide if that person is guilty of a crime or not: *A verdict of 'not proven' was brought in.*

bring off (*informal*)
You **bring off** something difficult when you manage to do it: *It's a difficult dive but she should be able to bring it off.* [compare **pull off**]

bring on
1 Something that **brings on** a pain or illness causes you to suffer from it: *In midsummer, even opening a window can bring on his hay fever.* ❑ *She couldn't stray very far without bringing an anxiety attack on.* [compare **come on**] **2** To **bring** someone **on** is to help them to develop or improve in some way: *We need the coaching skills of experienced professionals to bring on our most talented youngsters.* ❑ *The hospital claims that a daily dose of soothing music brings the patients on no end.* **3** You **bring** something such as shame, embarrassment or trouble **on** or **upon** someone when you cause them to suffer it: *I don't feel in the least sorry for him; he brought it all on himself.* ❑ *Can you begin to understand the shame you have brought upon this family?*

bring out
1 A company that **brings out** a new product makes it available for people to buy; a publisher **brings out** a new book when they publish it: *The BBC decided to bring out a gardening book to accompany the television series.* ❑ *'You've brought a new album out, of songs collected on your journey round Ireland.'* **2** People often use **bring out** to refer to the way something is made more obvious or noticeable: *The reading of a talented and sensitive actor brings out the subtleties of Shakespeare's texts.* ❑ *The sight of a train brings out the little boy in most men.* ❑ *These tasks are designed to bring out the natural competitiveness in children.* ❑ *Football always brings out the worst in him.* [*same as* **reveal**] **3** To **bring** someone **out** is to help them to become less nervous about meeting or talking to other people: *I think membership of the uniformed organizations goes some way to bringing out the shy child.*

bring out in
Something **brings** you **out in** *eg* spots when it makes them appear on your skin: *Even being in the same room as cats brings him out in a rash.*

bring over
Someone **brings** something **over** when they bring it with them to the place where you are: *She's bringing the CD over, so we can all have a listen.* ❑ *This is just a sample from the collection of designs she brought over from Paris.*

bring round
1 You **bring** an unconscious person **round** when you make them become conscious again: *A sip of brandy usually brings them round.* [*same as* **bring to**; compare **come round, come to**] **2** You **bring** someone **round** when you persuade them to change their view and agree with you: *It won't be difficult to bring them round to our way of thinking.* ❑ *Within a matter of days, they'd been brought round to the view that a bridge would be a good idea.* [*same as* **win over, convert, sway**]

bring to
Someone who is unconscious **is brought to** when they are made conscious again: *It was a couple of minutes before we managed to bring him to.* [*same as* **bring round**]

bring together
1 You **bring** people **together** when you

cause them to gather in one place, *eg* by inviting them to attend an organized event: *The Festival brings together major musical talents from all parts of the world.* [*same as* **assemble**] **2** You also **bring** people **together** when you encourage them to begin a friendship or relationship, or restore one that had broken: *Our parties have been responsible for bringing together a number of couples.* ❑ *As is often the case, the children brought them back together.*

bring up
1 You **bring up** a child when you care for them and educate them: *She was brought up by her aunt.* ❑ *I'd like to think I brought my sons up to be kind and thoughtful.* ❑ *Their children were brought up rather strictly.* [*same as* **raise**, **rear**] **2** You **bring** a subject **up** when you mention it: *It does nobody any good to bring up painful episodes from the past.* [*same as* **raise**; compare **come up**] **3** You **bring up** food when your stomach throws it out through your mouth: *At least one of the babies will bring a feed up at some point in the day.* [*same as* **throw up** (*informal*), **spew up** (*informal*), **vomit**]

bring upon see **bring on**

bristle /ˈbrɪsəl/: **bristles**, **bristling**, **bristled**

---

bristle with
1 People sometimes use **bristle with** to emphasize how full of people or things a place is: *The hotel lobby bristled with famous names from stage and screen.* ❑ *The modern flight deck positively bristles with navigational equipment.* [compare **burst with**, **crawl with**] **2** Someone **bristles with** anger or other strong emotion when they display it in their behaviour: *She sat bristling with indignation, muttering on about the decline in standards of service.*

brood /bruːd/: **broods**, **brooding**, **brooded**

---

brood over *or* **brood on** *or* **brood upon**
You **brood over** something unpleasant, or **brood on** or **upon** it, when you spend time thinking about how unhappy it makes you or how much you regret it: *The secret is not to brood over your failures, but to accept them as inevitable.* [*same as* **dwell on**]

brown /braʊn/: **browns**, **browning**, **browned**

• *adjective (informal)* **browned off**
You are **browned off**, or **browned off** with something, when you are bored by it or annoyed about it: *I suppose we all get a bit browned off with our jobs from time to time.* [*same as* **cheesed off** (*informal*), **hacked off** (*informal*)]

brush /brʌʃ/: **brushes**, **brushing**, **brushed**

---

brush aside
You **brush** something **aside** when you refuse to consider it because you think it is unimportant: *She brushed aside the suggestion that the company's dealings might have been improper.* [*same as* **dismiss**; compare **sweep aside**]

brush past
You **brush past** someone when you walk quickly past them, so closely that you touch them lightly with your body or clothing: *I caught a whiff of expensive perfume as she brushed past me to the bar.*

brush up *or* **brush up on**
You **brush up** something, or **brush up on** it, when you refresh or improve your knowledge of it: *I'll need to brush up my Shakespeare before the course starts.* ❑ *You could do with brushing up on your French vocabulary.*

bubble /ˈbʌbəl/: **bubbles**, **bubbling**, **bubbled**

---

bubble over
1 Liquid **bubbles over** when it boils

violently and flows over the edge of its container: *It's possible for the water to bubble over and put the flame out.* [*same as* **boil over**] **2** People often use **bubble over** as a way of emphasizing how excited or enthusiastic someone is: *The boys bubbled over with delight at the prospect of a day at the farm.* ❑ *The cub scouts were fairly bubbling over with good ideas for the show.* [*same as* **brim over**]

buck /bʌk/: **bucks**, **bucking**, **bucked**

buck up
1 (*informal*) You **buck** someone **up** when you make them more cheerful; someone **bucks up** when they become more cheerful: *An evening out will buck you up a bit.* ❑ *I think a good holiday would buck up the whole family.* ❑ *I just wish they would buck up; all their moping around is making me tired.* [*same as* **cheer up**, **perk up** (*informal*)] **2** (*informal, old*) Someone who tells you to **buck up** wants you to hurry: *Buck up or we'll be late.* [*same as* **hurry up**, **get a move on** (*informal*)]

bucket /ˈbʌkɪt/: **buckets**, **bucketing**, **bucketed**

bucket down (*informal*)
People often say it **is bucketing down** when they mean it is raining very heavily: *Of course, the day we decide to go for a picnic is the day it buckets down.* [*same as* **pour down**, **pelt down** (*informal*), **sheet down**]

buckle /ˈbʌkəl/: **buckles**, **buckling**, **buckled**

buckle down
You **buckle down** when you begin to work seriously or hard: *It's time you buckled down to some work if you're going to pass that exam.* [*same as* **knuckle down** (*informal*); *opposite* **ease up**, **slacken off**]

budge /bʌdʒ/: **budges**, **budging**, **budged**

budge up (*informal*)
Someone who asks you to **budge up** wants you to move further along a seat, to make room for them to sit down next to you: *There might be room for one more if we all budged up a bit.* [*same as* **move up**]

budget /ˈbʌdʒɪt/: **budgets**, **budgeting**, **budgeted**

budget for
You **budget for** something when you include the cost of it in your calculations: *A lot of people forget to budget for road tax, insurance and petrol.* [compare **account for**]

bugger /ˈbʌgə(r)/: **buggers**, **buggering**, **buggered**

bugger about *or* **bugger around** (*vulgar slang*)
1 To **bugger about** or **bugger around** is to behave in a silly way that annoys or irritates others: *We'd have been finished by now if you hadn't buggered about so much this morning.* **2** To **bugger** someone **about**, or **bugger** them **around**, is to treat them very badly, *eg* by causing them a lot of inconvenience: *This is the second time I've been buggered about today.* [*same as* **piss about** (*vulgar slang*), **mess about** (*informal*)]

bugger off (*vulgar slang*)
Telling someone to **bugger off** is an offensive way of telling them to go away: *They collect the money and just bugger off.* [*same as* **piss off** (*vulgar slang*)]

bugger up (*vulgar slang*)
To **bugger** something **up** is to spoil it by making careless mistakes or bad judgements: *Sheila's buggered up the order again; we've got no sand and twice as much cement.* ❑ *Can he be relied on not to bugger things up?* [*same

as **cock up** (*vulgar slang*), **foul up** (*informal*), **mess up** (*informal*)]

build /bɪld/: **builds**, **building**, **built**

build in *or* **build into**

1 Furniture that is **built in** is fixed to a wall, or fixed firmly into a space bounded by walls, or built so that walls form its back and sides: *Of course, because the cupboards are built in, you can't take them with you when you move.* ❑ *The fish tank was built into an alcove at the side of the chimney breast.* **2** You **build** something **in** when you add it as a permanent part of something larger: *They've built a number of safety checks into the system.* ❑ *These are new contracts, with an escape clause built in.* [*same as* **incorporate**]

• *adjective* **built-in**: *With this range, you have the option of built-in or freestanding units.* ❑ *All tenancy agreements will have a built-in requirement to pay rent in advance.*

• *adjective* **inbuilt**

Inbuilt describes a part or feature of something that cannot be removed or separated because it forms part of its basic structure, or it already exists and does not need to be added: *Each system has its own inbuilt flaws.* ❑ *Children from such backgrounds seem to have inbuilt confidence.*

build on *or* **build upon**

1 You **build on** something, or **build upon** it, when you develop it further, or use it as an advantage: *We must build on previous experience and not make the same mistakes again.* ❑ *I would like to think that last year's successes can be built upon.* **2** Something **is built on**, or **built upon**, what it has as a base or foundation: *Her success as a lawyer was built on her ability to argue and discuss well.* ❑ *The strongest relationships are built upon mutual trust and understanding.* ❑ *We're building our hopes of an economic revival on the strength of the major European currencies.* [compare **base on**]

build up

1 Something **builds up** when it gradually increases in size, strength or amount; you **build** something **up** when you make it increase gradually in size, strength or amount: *Traffic is building up on the approach to the Newbridge roundabout.* ❑ *Money is urgently needed to help build up supplies of basic foodstuffs and medicines.* ❑ *We're looking for ways to build his confidence up a bit.* **2** You use **build up** to talk about how things such as organizations or systems have been created or formed: *From humble beginnings in Rochdale, they have built the company up into what is now a multinational concern.* ❑ *The industry was built up virtually from nothing, to become the backbone of the country's economy.* [*same as* **develop**] **3** You **build** someone or something **up** if you make them seem more impressive than they really are: *As a live performer, she was not all that she had been built up to be.* ❑ *By the end of the discussion, Frank had been built up into everyone's vision of the ideal man.* **4** To **build** someone **up** is to make them stronger and healthier, usually by giving them more to eat: *Doctors are insisting that he builds himself up a bit before they'll release him.* ❑ *Like mothers everywhere, Heather's seemed to think I needed building up.* [compare **feed up**] **5** An area that **is built up** has many buildings in it: *The farms are no longer there, and the woodland has been built up long since.*

• *noun* **build-up**: **build-ups**

1 A **build-up** is a gradual increase in the size, strength or amount of something: *Even in the rural parts, there's a build-up of traffic around five o'clock.* ❑ *Any dangerous build-up of gas will be shown on the gauge and released automatically via the safety valve.* **2** The **build-up** to an event is the time spent preparing for it, or the preparation itself: *These regional* *meetings are regarded as little more than the build-up to the national championships in May.* ❑ *With such a pathetic opponent, it's hard to see how Bruno can regard this as an adequate build-up for the title fight.*

• *adjective* **built-up**

A **built-up** area has a lot of buildings in it: *In built-up areas, the motorist has the additional hazard of people, particularly children, to think about.*

build upon see **build on**

bully /'bʊlɪ/: **bullies**, **bullying**, **bullied**

---

bully into

Someone **bullies** you **into** doing something when they force you to do it by making threats: *It appears that classmates had bullied him into stealing money from his parents.* [compare **force into**, **push into**]

bum /bʌm/: **bums**, **bumming**, **bummed**

---

bum about *or* **bum around** (*informal*)

1 You **bum about** or **bum around** when you spend your time lazily, doing nothing useful: *On a sunny day, we would walk the streets together, and just bum around.* ❑ *The prospect of simply bumming about for a few weeks was irresistible.* [*same as* **laze about**, **loaf about**] **2** You **bum around** or **round** when you spend time travelling for pleasure, usually with not much money: *The idea was to bum round France and Spain for a few months, until a real job came up.* [*same as* **wander about**]

bump /bʌmp/: **bumps**, **bumping**, **bumped**

---

bump into

1 You **bump into** a person or thing when you accidentally knock or hit them, sometimes damaging or hurting them as a result: *I can't see how bumping into a table could produce a bruise like that.* ❑ *Another car bumped into me from behind.* [*same as* **run into**, **bang into**] **2** (*informal*) You **bump into** someone if you meet them by chance: *You're bound to bump into him sooner or later.* [*same as* **run into**]

bump off (*slang*)

To **bump** someone **off** is to kill them: *Freddy'd bump off his old lady if he thought there was money in it.* ❑ *He opened his mouth once too often and got himself bumped off.* [*same as* **knock off** (*slang*), **do in** (*slang*), **murder**]

bump up (*informal*)

To **bump** something **up** is to raise the level of it, or increase it in number or amount: *Most places bump up the price if they know you're a tourist.*

bundle /'bʌndəl/: **bundles**, **bundling**, **bundled**

---

bundle off (*informal*)

You **bundle** someone **off** somewhere when you send them there in a hurry, or without care or consideration: *Children are simply bundled off to whatever school will take them.* ❑ *I had to bundle them off before my parents came back.* [*same as* **pack off** (*informal*), **send off**]

bundle up

You **bundle** things **up** when you gather them together in a bundle: *My papers were bundled up and stuffed into boxes.* [compare **parcel up**, **wrap up**]

bung /bʌŋ/: **bungs**, **bunging**, **bunged**

---

bung up

1 Something such as a pipe becomes **bunged up** when obstacles block it and prevent water, air or other substances passing through it: *Oil and grease will quickly bung up the sink.* ❑ *Instead of unblocking the pipes, the chemical sprays were bunging them up.* **2** (*informal*) You can say you **are bunged**

up if your nose is blocked with mucus, *eg* because you have a cold; you can also say you **are bunged up** if you are having difficulty passing solid waste out of your body: *She sounded a bit bunged up on the phone; perhaps her hay fever has already started.* ❑ *People who eat fried food all the time do tend to get a bit bunged up.*
[*same as* **block up**]

buoy /bɔɪ/: **buoys**, **buoying**, **buoyed**

buoy up
1 You **buoy** someone **up** when you keep them cheerful, or make them more cheerful, in a discouraging or depressing situation: *We have been buoyed up by reports of sightings of a couple making their way slowly across the mountainside.* ❑ *They needed news like this to buoy up their spirits.* [*same as* **cheer up, lift up, boost**] **2** To **buoy** something **up** is to prevent its level from falling, or prevent it from decreasing in number or amount: *The value of the dollar has been buoyed up by news that troops will be withdrawn from Somalia.* ❑ *It's only these tight controls on wage levels that have buoyed up the trade figures.* [*same as* **keep up**]

burn /bɜːn/: **burns**, **burning**, **burned** *or* **burnt**

Burned and **burnt** can both be used as the past tense and past participle of **burn**.

burn down
A building **burns down**, or **is burned down**, when it is destroyed by fire: *Most of the medieval abbeys were burned down in the sixteenth century.* ❑ *They were scared to leave the kids alone, in case they burned the place down.* ❑ *They would only get the money if the factory burned down completely.*

burn off
You **burn off** something such as paint when you remove it by heating or burning it: *Remove any old varnish completely, preferably by burning it off.*

burn out
1 A fire **burns out**, or **burns** itself **out**, when all the burning material is finally destroyed and the fire stops burning: *A few revellers stayed on until the bonfire had burnt out.* ❑ *The forest fire has been contained and will now be left to burn itself out.* **2** Electrical wires and pieces of electrical equipment **burn out** when they become damaged or destroyed by being used too much, or by having too much electric current passed through them: *The motor has burned out and will have to be replaced.* **3** (*informal*) You **burn** yourself **out** when you use up all your energy and become thoroughly exhausted: *Juantarina had nothing left for the last two laps: he'd burnt himself out in the first half of the race.*

• *adjective* **burnt-out** *or* **burned-out**
A **burnt-out** or **burned-out** vehicle or building has been completely destroyed by fire: *The roads were lined with burnt-out cars.*

burst /bɜːst/: **bursts**, **bursting**, **burst**

burst in *or* burst into
Someone **bursts in,** or **bursts into** a room, when they enter suddenly and noisily: *We were getting ready to leave when in burst Philip with news that the bridge had been destroyed.* ❑ *Alex burst into the room clutching a piece of paper, which he then crumpled up and threw at me.*

burst in on
You **burst in on** someone when you suddenly and noisily enter the room they are in, especially when you interrupt something they are doing: *I was sitting reading when the children burst in on me.*

burst into
1 You use **burst into** as a way of describing how suddenly and noisily someone begins to do something, such

as laugh or cry: *Then Henrietta burst into tears and refused to be consoled by anyone.* ❑ *We all burst into applause.* ❑ *Albert was drunk again: the chances of him bursting into song at any minute seemed pretty good.* [see also **burst in**] **2** Something **bursts into** flames when it suddenly catches fire and begins to burn.

burst out

You **burst out** crying or laughing when you suddenly begin to cry or laugh, usually noisily.

• *noun* **outburst**: **outbursts**

An **outburst** is a sudden expression of strong emotion, usually anger: *The children were used to witnessing such outbursts.*

burst with

You use **burst with** as a way of emphasizing how much of something there is, or how strong or intense it is: *Cream was always thick and yellow, and pies always bursting with fruit.* ❑ *The children are bursting with good ideas.* ❑ *Some of the childless couples are simply bursting with love to give to a little one.*

bury /'bɛrɪ/: **buries**, **burying**, **buried** •

bury in

You **bury** yourself **in** something you are reading when you give your complete attention to it: *I wanted to speak to Dennis before he had the chance to bury his head in the evening paper.* [compare **absorb in**]

bust /bʌst/: **busts**, **busting**, **busted** *or* **bust**

Busted and **bust** can both be used as the past tense and past participle.

bust up (*informal*)

1 To **bust up** an event at which people are gathered together is to force it to end by disturbing or interrupting it, often using violence: *The police called at around three in the morning to bust the party up.* **2** Partners in a relationship **bust up** when they end their relationship with each other: *The thing she's afraid of most is that her boyfriend will bust up with her.* [*same as* **break up**]

• *noun (informal)* **bust-up**: **bust-ups**

1 A **bust-up** is a quarrel, often one that ends a relationship: *Tom and Sally have had another bust-up.* **2** A **bust-up** is also a fight: *They still haven't repaired all the damage after the last bust-up.*

bustle /'bʌsəl/: **bustles**, **bustling**, **bustled**

bustle about *or* bustle around

You **bustle about** or **bustle around** when you walk about busily doing different things: *The worst kind of host bustles about ostentatiously shoving unwanted drinks and snacks into your hands.*

butt /bʌt/: **butts**, **butting**, **butted**

butt in

Someone **butts in** when they rudely interrupt you while you are speaking, or rudely interfere in what you are doing: *We can't hope to have a sensible discussion if Mr Portillo keeps butting in before I've finished my point.* ❑ *Companies want to run their own affairs, without the government butting in.*

butt out (*AmE informal*)

Someone who tells you to **butt out** is rudely telling you to stop interfering in their affairs: *I think her parents should just butt out and let her make her own mistakes.* [*opposite* **butt in**]

butter /'bʌtə(r)/: **butters**, **buttering**, **buttered**

butter up (*informal*)

Someone **butters** you **up** when they flatter or praise you as a way of persuading you to do something: *She thinks the money'll be no problem if* *she butters up her parents a bit.* ❑ *He tried to butter me up by telling me I was looking very nice tonight.* [compare **suck up to** (*informal*), **pander to**]

button /ˈbʌtən/: **buttons, buttoning, buttoned**

button up
You **button up** a piece of clothing when you fasten it using buttons: *Don't go out without buttoning your coat up.* [*same as* **do up**]

buy /baɪ/: **buys, buying, bought** /bɔːt/

buy in
You **buy in** something such as food when you buy large quantities of it, *eg* because you are expecting many guests: *At the first sign of winter, we all start buying in our flour, sugar and salt.* [*same as* **stock up, lay in**; compare **buy up**]

buy into
Someone **buys into** a business when they buy a share in the ownership of it: *The cousins were invited to buy into the farm.* [compare **come into**]

buy off (*informal*)
You **buy** someone **off** when you give them money to stop them opposing you or threatening you: *There was undoubtedly the impression that council members could be bought off.* ❑ *We usually advise them to buy off the blackmailer straight away.* [compare **pay off**]

buy out
You **buy** someone **out** when you buy their share in the ownership of a business, so that they no longer have any control: *The theory is that private*

by /baɪ/

By is an adverb and a preposition.
It is a very common word in English and it occurs in several phrasal verbs in this dictionary. Its meanings are numerous and very varied, but it has four main senses in phrasal verbs.

1 PASSING
The most common use of **by** is in phrasal verbs of passing. This can be a literal movement past something, as in **brush by** and **push by**. **By** is widely used to form new phrasal verbs with this meaning, such as *march by*, *pedal by*, *swan by*, *hurry by* and *saunter by* in the following examples: *A parade of people marched by with raised fists.* ❑ *Henry watched the flashy Japanese racers pedal by.* ❑ *As we swan by full of excitement, they show no emotion.* ❑ *It was the first time I had stopped to look: normally I hurried by.* ❑ *Conversation drifted over you as families sauntered by.*
There can also be a general reference to movement or progress of any kind. For example, time can **pass by, slip by** and **tick by**. In this sense, too, **by** often forms phrasal verbs such as *burn by* and *rocket by* in the examples: *The hours burned by.* ❑ *The summer had rocketed by.*
If you **sit by** or **stand by**, you fail to take the necessary action to prevent something bad from happening.

2 VISITING
In a group of fairly informal phrasal verbs, **by** refers to the idea of visiting someone; the visit is usually informal and brief. These phrasal verbs are **call by, come by, drop by** and **stop by**. You **go by** a place when you stop there briefly on your way somewhere else.

3 OBEYING AND REMAINING LOYAL
By is used in a few phrasal verbs that relate to the idea of obeying something or someone. For example, you **abide by** a law or a rule when you obey it, and you **live by** a certain principle when everything you do in your life follows that principle. In others, there is the idea of remaining loyal to someone or something, as in **stand by** and **stick by**.

4 STORING AND KEEPING
The phrasal verbs **lay by** and **put by** both refer to the action of someone who keeps something for later or future use.

investors will eventually buy out the government. [compare **pay out, sell out**]

buy up
You **buy up** something when you buy the whole stock of it, or buy as much as is available: *The council has been buying up land near the river.* ❑ *In reality, corporate investors buy up all the shares and the private investor doesn't get a chance.* [compare **buy in**]

buzz /bʌz/: **buzzes**, **buzzing**, **buzzed**

buzz off (*informal*)
When someone tells you to **buzz off** they are telling you rudely to go away: *We'll just buzz off when your guests show up.* [*same as* **clear off** (*informal*), **bugger off** (*vulgar slang*)]

by see panel on previous page

bypass /'baɪpɑːs/ see **pass by**

bystander /'baɪstandə(r)/ see **stand by**

C

call /kɔːl/: **calls**, **calling**, **called**

call after

Someone **is called after** another person, or a character in literature, when they are given the same name as that person or character: *She was called after Jane, her mother's oldest sister.* [*same as* **name after**, **name for**]

call away

When someone **is called away** from their home or normal place of work, they are summoned to deal with something, or attend to someone, elsewhere: *He's been called away on urgent business.*

call back

1 You **call back** when you visit someone again: *If you would rather your husband was here when we discuss it, I'll call back later when he's returned from work.* **2 a** If you have tried, unsuccessfully, to contact someone by telephone and you **call back**, you telephone them again: *Carol won't be home until seven. Can you call back later this evening?* **b** When someone has contacted you on the telephone and you tell them that you **will call** them **back**, you mean that you will telephone them later: *Your file isn't on my desk at the moment. Can I call you back in ten minutes when I've found it?* [*same as* **phone back**, **ring back**]

call by

You **call by** when you visit a place for a short time on your way to somewhere else: *I'll call by on my way to work and pick up the books from you.* [compare **call in**, **call round**]

call down (*formal*)

You **call down** the wrath or vengeance of some higher power or god on someone when you pray to that higher power to make something bad happen to that person: *He wanted to scream and shout, beat the wall, and call down the forces of destruction.*

call for

1 You **call for** a person or thing when you go or come to collect or fetch them: *He's calling for me at eight o'clock and we're going on to the theatre.* ❑ *Will you be able to call for the package on your way home from work?* [*same as* **pick up**] **2** A situation, problem or crisis **calls for** a particular thing if that is what is needed to solve it or deal with it, or if it is the appropriate thing to do in the circumstances: *It was an embarrassing situation that called for tact and diplomacy.* ❑ *What wonderful news! Come on everyone, this calls for a celebration!* ❑ *I don't think that remark was really called for.* [*same as* **require**] **3** You **call for** something when you ask or demand that it should happen: *The president made a radio broadcast calling for calm.*

call forth (*formal or literary*)

You **call** something **forth** when you make it appear or exist: *cruelty calls forth the sympathy of humane people* ❑ *Teachers whose daily lives are an eternal battle to contain the unease that noise calls forth in them.*

call in

1 a You **call in** to see someone *eg* at their home, at hospital, or at their place of work when you pay them a short visit there: *The district nurse will be calling in again tomorrow to see that you're all right.* **b** You **call in** at a place when you go there, usually when you are on your way to somewhere else: *Would you call in at the butcher's on your way home and pick up my order?* [compare **call by, call round**] **2** You **call** someone **in** when you ask them to come to give you help or advice: *If you don't stop that racket I'm going to call in the cops!* ❑ *Granny doesn't look too good; do you think we should call the doctor in?* ❑ *He had called in a firm of local builders to carry out the essential repairs.* [*same as* **call out, summon**] **3** A lender **calls in** a loan when they demand that it is paid immediately and in full, especially if the borrower has broken the terms of the loan agreement in some way: *When the bank heard of the firm's financial difficulties it called in its overdraft.*

call off

1 When an event that has already been scheduled or planned **is called off** it is cancelled: *Harry said he didn't see why the match should be called off just because there was snow forecast.* ❑ *Seven meetings have been called off in the last few days.* **2** A search or investigation **is called off** when it is stopped or halted: *The search for the missing climber had to be called off when it got too dark.* **3** You **call off** *eg* your dog when you order it to stop attacking someone: *I yelled to the man to call off his dog.*

call on

1 You **call on** someone when you pay them a visit: *One of our trained representatives will call on you some time in the next week.* **2 a** When you **call on** or **upon** someone to do something you ask or invite them to do it: *I'm now going to call on Professor Hutchins to give us the benefit of his expert opinion.* **b** When you **are called on** or **are called upon** to do something you are asked or required to do it: *All his colleagues will vouch for his honesty if called upon to do so.* **3** You **call on** or **upon** something that you would not normally use when you use it to help you through a difficult time: *He had to call on all his reserves of strength to get through the basic training course.* [*same as* **summon**]

call out

1 You **call out**, or **call** something **out**, when you speak in a loud voice, or say it loudly: *He called out to me to stop.* ❑ *Please say 'here' when I call out your name.* ❑ *He was calling out, 'I can't hold on any longer!'* [*same as* **shout**] **2** You **call** someone **out** when you ask them to come and help you or give you advice: *We had to call out an emergency plumber when the tank in the attic started leaking.* [*same as* **call in, summon**] **3 a** In an industrial dispute, members of a trade union **are called out** on strike when their union instructs them to stop working and leave their place of work: *ASLEF have called their members out on strike from 3 July.* **b** A military force **is called out** when they are ordered into action: *The president has had to call out the National Guard.*

• *noun* **call-out**: **call-outs**

A **call-out** is a request or summons made to someone to go and help someone in need: *Doctor Philips had to attend a 4 am call-out.*

call over

You **call** someone **over** when you ask them to come from some distance away to where you are, often so that you can speak to them or ask them something: *Call the waiter over and ask him to bring some more water.*

call round

You **call round** to a place, usually

somewhere that is not a very great distance away, when you go there to pay a short visit: *I'll call round at your flat sometime after work.* [compare **call by, call in**]

call up

1 You **call** someone **up** when you telephone them: *Barry called me up last night to ask me if I would like to go to the game with him.* [*same as* **phone up, ring up**] **2** When someone **is called up** they are officially ordered to join the armed forces of their country: *He was called up in 1941 and was wounded during the Normandy landings.* ❑ *a reservist called up in the course of the Gulf conflict.* [*same as* **draft**] **3** The person in charge of organizing an particular team or activity **calls** someone **up** when they select that person to be part of the team or take part in that activity: *The selectors have called up several younger and less experienced players for the Test against Australia.* **4** You **call up** information from a computer when you obtain it by instructing the computer to search for it in its memory: *Would you call up the latest sales figures and give me a printout before this morning's meeting.* **5** Something **calls up** something from the past, or an idea, when it causes you to think of it: *We were finding ways of starting to write in our own voice: through calling up early memories, waking up the senses, and developing an ear for the rhythms of speech.* ❑ *It really was what I'd dreamed about, a sort of crystal ball in which I could call up everything I had ever known.* [*same as* **bring back, evoke** (*formal*)]

• *noun* **call-up**

A **call-up** is an official order to members of the civilian population to join the armed forces of a country: *He got his call-up papers in this morning's post.*

call upon see **call on**

calm /kɑːm/: **calms**, **calming**, **calmed**

calm down

You **calm** someone **down** when you do something that helps them to stop feeling anxious, upset or angry; you **calm down** when you stop feeling anxious, upset or angry: *She'd become quite hysterical; the doctor had to give her a sedative to calm her down.* ❑ *For goodness sake, calm down! It's only a little spider.*

camp /kamp/: **camps**, **camping**, **camped**

camp out

1 You **camp out** when you sleep outdoors, with or without a tent: *They drove the cattle south, staying in the saddle all day and camping out at night under the stars.* **2** You can also say that you **are camping out** when you are sleeping somewhere indoors temporarily: *The refugees camped out at St Peter's School in Northampton.* ❑ *I'm afraid there's no spare beds, but if you don't mind camping out in the kitchen you're welcome to stay.*

camp up

Someone **is camping** it **up** when they are behaving in an unnaturally theatrical way, exaggerating their gestures, speech and movements as a bad actor may do: *There they all were at Cannes, the would-be stars of stage and screen, camping it up like mad hoping that some famous director would offer them a part in his latest movie.* [*same as* **ham it up** (*informal*)]

cancel /ˈkansəl/: **cancels**, **cancelling** (*AmE* **canceling**), **cancelled** (*AmE* **canceled**)

cancel out

When one thing **is cancelled out** by another, or when two things **cancel** each other **out**, each thing has the opposite effect of the other so that, when they occur together, no effect is produced: *Make sure the charges on your policy don't cancel out the tax savings.* ❑ *the increase in output in one market cancelling out the fall in output in the other.* [*same as* **neutralize** (*formal*), **nullify** (*formal*)]

care /kɛə(r)/: **cares, caring, cared**

care about

You **care about** someone or something when you are concerned about or interested in them: *I don't care about the money; I'm more concerned about you.* ❑ *She was an unpretentious designer but nevertheless she cared passionately about clothes.*

care for

1 You **care for** someone when you look after them: *lonely old people with no-one to care for them.* **2** You **care for** someone when you like or love them; you can say that you don't **care for** someone when you don't like them: *'Have you met her new boyfriend?' 'Yes, I have, and I have to say I don't much care for him.'*

carry /'karɪ/: **carries, carrying, carried**

carry away

1 A strong wind or current **carries** someone or something **away** when it takes or sweeps them away: *The flood waters carried away the flimsy wooden bridge.* **2** You get **carried away** by enthusiasm or excitement when you get so enthusiastic or excited about something that you are no longer able to behave in a rational or sensible way: *Just ignore her. She gets a bit carried away sometimes.*

carry back

An event or circumstance **carries** you **back** to some time in the past when it makes you remember past times or experiences: *Hearing his voice on tape carried me back to my childhood.*

carry forward (*rather formal*)

You **carry forward** a plan or scheme when you succeed in making progress with it: *We will carry forward a family support initiative, encouraging the voluntary sector in partnership with local authorities.*

carry off

1 Someone **carries** a person or thing **off** when they capture that person or thing and take them away: *The Highlanders raided the lowland farms and estates, carrying off their cattle and anything else of value.* **2** You **carry** something **off** when you manage to do it or deal with it successfully: *It's a difficult role, and it takes a very special type of actress to carry it off.* ❑ *She carried off a difficult and embarrassing situation with as much panache as she could muster.* **3** You **carry off** a prize when you win it: *For the second year running, Rangers have carried off all the footballing honours.* **4** An illness **carries** someone **off** when it causes their death: *He had become too frail to fight the pneumonia that finally carried him off.*

carry on

1 You **carry on** some activity or business when you do it or take part in it: *How do you expect us to carry on a conversation with all that noise going on?* ❑ *The business is now being carried on by the sons of the original proprietor.* ❑ *Conversation was carried on against a background of ear-splitting barking.* **2** You **carry on** doing something when you continue to do it without stopping: *I'd like to carry on working after I'm sixty.* ❑ *Don't let me interrupt you; just carry on with what you were doing before I came in.* ❑ *Take the first turn on the right and carry straight on until you reach the crossroads.* ❑ *Caspar took no notice of him, and carried on through the wood towards the field.* **3**

(*informal*) You can say that someone **is carrying on** when they are behaving in a silly, disruptive or annoying way: *A group of boys at the back of the bus spent the entire journey shouting and carrying on.*

• *noun (informal)* **carry-on**: **carry-ons**

1 When people are having a **carry-on** they are behaving in a silly, disruptive or annoying way: *If you don't stop that carry-on at once I'll send you both to the headmaster!* **2** A **carry-on** is also any annoying incident involving trouble, difficulty or an argument: *What a carry-on we had trying to get away on holiday! First, we thought we'd lost our tickets; then the taxi was late, and we nearly missed our flight!*

carry out

You **carry out** something such as a task, duty, procedure or order when you do it, complete it, or put it into operation or practice: *How to find the money necessary to carry out the charity's work has always been a worry.* ❑ *The union leaders had refused to carry out a ballot prior to calling a strike.* [*same as* **perform, undertake, execute, fulfil**]

carry over

Something **is carried over** from an earlier time when it is extended from that time so that it goes on happening or being done in a later period: *The habit of getting up early in the morning has been carried over from his childhood spent on a farm.*

carry through

1 You **carry** something **through** when you put it into practice or complete it: *It seems to me to be rather an ambitious plan. Do you think he's capable of carrying it through?* ❑ *A project is a project, he wrote, and once it is begun it should be carried through to the end.* [*same as* **accomplish**] **2** Something **carries** you **through** a difficult situation when it supports you and helps you to get through it: *It was my unshakeable faith in God that carried me through that desperate time.* ❑ *the work ethic that had carried her successfully through so many years of study and so many examinations.*

cart /kɑːt/: carts, carting, carted

cart off *or* cart away (*informal*)

Someone **is carted off** or **away** when they are taken away by force in an undignified way: *Several protestors were arrested and carted off to the police station.* ❑ *He glanced nervously at the police patrol and the slate-grey truck used to cart away vagrant minors.*

carve /kɑːv/: carves, carving, carved

carve out

You **carve out** something for yourself when you make or create it by your own efforts, often in difficult circumstances: *In carving out a distinctive niche for themselves, a number of options have been opened to them.* ❑ *Though he was forced to resign from the government, he gradually succeeded in carving out a new career for himself as an author and journalist.*

carve up

1 Something **is carved up** when it is divided into smaller parts and shared amongst two or more people or countries: *What guarantee have we that rural lines will survive when British Rail is carved up and privatised?* ❑ *It seemed as though the United States and the Soviet Union were carving up the world between them.* **2** (*slang*) If you **carve** someone **up** you wound them badly by cutting them repeatedly with a knife or razor: *A gang of young thugs had carved up his face with a broken bottle.* **3** (*informal*) If, when you are driving, another driver **carves** you **up** he or she drives dangerously by suddenly overtaking you and going into a space between you and the car in front so that you have to brake hard to avoid

a collision: *Did you see how that maniac in the Porsche carved me up?*
• *noun (informal)* **carve-up**: *the carve-up of Germany after the First World War.* ❑ *The Campaign for Real Ale attacks the carve-up of the brewing industry.*

cash /kaʃ/: **cashes**, **cashing**, **cashed**

---

cash in

1 You **cash in** an asset or investment when you convert it into money: *He raised the money he needed by cashing in his shares in British Telecom.* **2** In a casino, you **cash in** the chips you are left with when you have finished playing when you exchange them for money.

cash in on

You **cash in on** a situation when you take advantage of it so that you profit or benefit from it in some way, especially when you are able to do so by rather unfair or slightly dishonest means: *the continuing public outcry about senior management cashing in on the inflated profits of newly privatized companies* ❑ *local businessmen cashing in on the promotion of Goa as an affordable holiday destination for Europeans.* [*same as* **exploit**]

cash up

A shopkeeper **cashes up** when he or she adds up all the cash taken from customers in a certain period, especially at the end of each day: *After the bank closes, the staff stay on for another hour cashing up and updating the ledgers.*

cast /kɑːst/: **casts**, **casting**, **cast**

Note that **cast** is the present tense, the past tense and the past participle of the verb.

cast about *or* **cast around** (*formal*)

You **cast about, cast around,** or **cast round** for something when you try to find it or think of it: *Celia cast around in her mind for a less depressing topic.* ❑ *He hesitated for a moment while he cast about for appropriate words of comfort.*

cast aside (*formal*)

You **cast** someone or something **aside** when you get rid of them because you no longer want them or need them: *Many of his contemporaries had cast aside the old religion.* ❑ *Roger cast aside his rather sombre mood and listened with real interest.* [*same as* **abandon**]

cast away

When someone **is cast away** *eg* on a remote island they are left there, especially after being washed ashore from a shipwreck: *What would you miss most if you were cast away on a desert island?*
• *noun* **castaway**: **castaways**: *a lonely castaway walking barefoot on uncovered reefs in search of shellfish.*

cast back

You **cast** your mind or your thoughts **back** when you make yourself think of, or remember, an earlier time or event: *If you cast your mind back to our previous discussion, you'll remember that we agreed then to a pay rise for 1996 of no more that 5%.*

cast down

Someone **is cast down** when something has made them depressed and unhappy: *He seemed quite cast down by his friend's attitude, more than by all the other criticism that he had so far encountered.*
• *adjective* **downcast**: *He was sitting alone in a corner of the café looking downcast and somehow very vulnerable.*

cast off

1 (*formal*) You **cast** something **off** when you get rid of it because it is no longer useful: *Both sides have agreed to cast off the ideological narrowness of the past.* ❑ *No child should be expected to* *cast off the language and culture of the home as he and she crosses the school threshold.* [*same as* **throw off, reject, discard** (*formal*)] **2** You **cast off** when you untie a boat or ship from its mooring: *We cast off from the jetty and made our way, with the other small boats, out into the channel.* **3** You **cast off** in knitting when you form a finished edge by looping the yarn through two stitches at a time until none remain on the needle.

• *noun* **cast-offs**
You use or wear someone else's **cast-offs** when you use the things or wear the clothes that they no longer have any use for: *She said she wouldn't be seen dead in a charity shop trying on other people's cast-offs.*

• *adjective* **cast-off**: *I had to wear my sister's cast-off clothes.*

cast on
You **cast on** stitches in knitting when you create stitches by looping the yarn around the needle: *Begin the front of the sweater by casting on 106 stitches.* ❑ *Some knitters cast on by looping the yarn around their thumb.*

cast out (*formal*)
You **cast** someone **out** when you force them to leave and you abandon them, often because you think they have done something wrong: *The public's change of attitude to him after the trial made him feel as if he had been cast out into outer darkness.* [*same as* **expel, banish** (*formal*)]

cast round see **cast about**

cast up
1 Something **is cast up** on the beach or shore when it is left or thrown there by the sea or waves: *After several days at sea, their life-raft was cast up on an isolated island off the coast of Australia.* **2** (*informal*) If someone **casts** something **up** they remind you in an unkind way of a past failure in order to criticize you or make you feel guilty: *He's always casting up the fact that I wasn't clever enough to get into grammar school.*

catch /katʃ/: catches, catching, caught /kɔːt/

catch at
1 You **catch at** something when you try to grab it or take hold of it: *His arms flailed around as he tried to catch at something, anything, to prevent himself sinking in the mud.* **2** Something with a sharp point **catches at** your clothing when it pulls and tears it: *As he pushed his way through the thick hawthorn hedge, the thorns scratched his face and caught at his clothes.*

catch on (*informal*)
1 Something **catches on** when it becomes popular: *Baseball has never quite caught on in England; cricket is much more popular.* **2** You **catch on** when you begin to understand what is happening or being said; you **catch on** to something when you become aware that it is happening: *He's a smart kid; it doesn't take him long to catch on.* ❑ *It was some time before the police caught on to the fact that large quantities of drugs were being smuggled in through remote villages on the West Coast.*

catch out
1 You **catch** someone **out** when you trick them into making a mistake, especially one that shows that they have been lying or have done something wrong: *Be careful when you are giving evidence; the defence lawyer will do everything he can to catch you out.* **2** In cricket, a batsman **is caught out** when the ball he has just hit is caught by a member of the opposing team before it hits the ground.

catch up
1 You **catch up** with someone moving ahead of you when you manage to reach them by moving faster: *Slow down and let the others catch up.* ❑ *You'll have to run faster if you want to*

catch him up. **2** You **catch up** with someone when you reach the same standard or level as they are at: *She's fallen behind a little because she's been off school for so long, but if she works hard she'll soon catch up.* ❑ *We're so far behind the rest of Europe, I fear we'll never catch up.*

catch up in

You **are caught up in** some activity or situation when you are involved in it without really wanting to be, or you are so involved or interested in it that it takes all your attention: *The UN troops had become caught up in the fighting despite their efforts to limit their role to peacekeepers.* ❑ *He was so caught up in his private thoughts that he didn't hear the telephone ring.*

catch up on

1 You **catch up on** something that you had left undone until now when you spend time doing it: *Leave him in peace; he's got a lot of paperwork to catch up on.* [see also **catch up with**] **2** Something, usually something unpleasant, **catches up on** you when it begins to have an effect on your life: *My joints are getting stiff; I think old age is starting to catch up on me.* [*same as* **overtake**]

catch up with

1 You **catch up with** work that you should have done before when you spend time doing it and bringing it up to date: *Time to catch up with those jobs in the office that have been hanging over your head.* [see also **catch up on**] **2** The authorities, especially the police, **catch up with** someone who has broken the law when they find them after looking for them for some time, and are able to arrest them and bring them to justice: *He had defrauded dozens of old age pensioners of their life savings before the police eventually caught up with him.* **3** Something unpleasant, especially from your past, **catches up with** you when you can no longer hide it or avoid it and are forced to confront it or deal with it: *His involvement in many of the worst Nazi atrocities, which he had been so careful to keep secret, was bound to catch up with him eventually.*

cater /ˈkeɪtə(r)/: caters, catering, catered

cater for

A business or organization **caters for** a particular type of customer or group when they provide what that customer or group wants and needs: *financial consultants with specially trained advisors to cater for the needs of small businesses.*

cater to

Someone or something **caters to** a need or demand when they satisfy it: *A new service that caters to the needs of disabled people who want to go on living in their own homes.*

cave /keɪv/: caves, caving, caved

cave in

1 A structure such as a roof or ceiling **caves in** when it collapses: *The roof of the tunnel caved in bringing tons of rock and earth down on the men working beneath.* **2** (*informal*) If someone **caves in** they suddenly yield or surrender when they are under pressure to do so, usually after resisting for some time: *The unions kept up the pressure with a series of one-day strikes, hoping that the management would cave in and agree to all their demands.*

• *noun* **cave-in**: **cave-ins**: *They had to fit special steel props to prevent another cave-in.* ❑ *The home team was able to run away with the match after a complete cave-in by the opposition.*

centre (*AmE* center) /ˈsɛntə(r)/: centres, centring, centred

centre around *or* centre round

Something **centres around** or **round** a person or thing if that person or thing is its main focus: *There has been a clear shift of emphasis with the issue of new guidelines centred around what is best for the children in any given situation.* ❑ *language patterns centred around one cultural or language feature.*

centre on *or* **centre upon**
A particular thing **is centred on** or **upon** someone or something when it has that person or thing as its centre or main focus: *Their whole strategy was centred on their ambitions to break into the European market.* ❑ *He had always intended to produce a book on Greece, not centred on a single topic, but dealing with various aspects of Greek civilization.*

chain /tʃeɪn/: **chains**, **chaining**, **chained**

---

chain up
You **chain** something **up** when you tie it to something using a length of chain so that it cannot move about freely, escape, be opened or removed: *Their Alsatian has to be chained up to stop it attacking people who called at their house.* ❑ *You had better chain your bike up if you don't want to have it stolen.*

chalk /tʃɔːk/: **chains**, **chalking**, **chalked**

---

chalk up
You **chalk up** a success or victory when you achieve it: *Hendry has chalked up yet another win in a major championship.* [*same as* **notch up**]

chance /tʃɑːns/: **chances**, **chancing**, **chanced**

---

chance on *or* **chance upon**
(*formal*)
1 You **chance on** or **upon** someone when you meet or come across them by accident or chance: *Luckily for me, I chanced on a group of walkers who were able to give me directions.* **2** You **chance on** or **upon** something when you discover it by accident or chance: *While browsing in the library, I chanced upon an old volume of his poetry that had gone out of print long ago.*
[*same as* **come across**, **happen on**]

change /tʃeɪndʒ/: **changes**, **changing**, **changed**

---

change down
In a motor vehicle or on a bicycle with gears, you **change down** when you move the gear level into a lower gear; you **change up** when you move the gear lever into a higher gear: *He changed down to third as he approached the hill.* ❑ *As the car begins to pick up speed change up to second.*

change over
You **change over** from one thing to another when you replace one thing with another: *Many drivers are changing over from petrol to diesel vehicles because fuel is cheaper.*
• *noun* **changeover**: **changeovers**: *the changeover from coal-fired to gas-fired power stations.*

change round
1 The wind **changes round** when it begins to blow in a different direction. **2** You **change** something **round** when you alter the position of the things in it: *We changed our bedroom round so that the bed was under the window.* ❑ *Don't try to change the facts round so that I appear to be to blame.*

change up see **change down**

charge /tʃɑːdʒ/: **charges**, **charging**, **charged**

---

charge with
You **are charged with** a task or duty when you are given responsibility for making sure it is done: *a special envoy from the United Nations, charged with the task of bringing the two sides in the Bosnian civil war together for talks.*

chase /tʃeɪs/: **chases**, **chasing**, **chased**

---

chase after *or* **chase around after**

You **chase after** someone or something, or you **chase around after** them, when you rush around from place to place pursuing them or trying to keep up with them, or you put a lot of time and energy into finding them: *It's pretty embarrassing when your own mother starts chasing after all the young men in the village.* ❑ *I prefer to stay at home; I couldn't cope with chasing around after my husband when he's on tour.* ❑ *He spends most of his time chasing around after what little work is available.*

chase off

You **chase** a person or animal **off** when you force them to go away by threatening or frightening them: *He tried to enter the grounds but two huge guards dogs chased him off.*

chase up (*informal*)

1 You **chase** someone **up** when you get in touch with them to remind them of something they were supposed to do: *Chase up the caterers, will you, and ask them what has happened to the menus they promised me.* **2** You **chase** something **up** when you try to find it as quickly as possible because it is needed: *Could you chase up some balloons and paper hats for the children's party tomorrow?* [*same as* **hunt up, track down**]

chat /tʃat/: **chats**, **chatting**, **chatted**

chat up (*informal*)

1 When someone **chats** you **up** they talk to you in a friendly and amusing way in order to make themselves sexually attractive to you: *I came back to find some young lad chatting up my wife.* ❑ *If I didn't know you were already married, I'd think you were trying to chat me up!* **2** You also **chat** someone **up** when you use flattery or amusing conversation to persuade them to do something or give you something: *Go and chat up the hotel manager and see if he'll give us a room with a view of the sea.*

cheat /tʃiːt/: **cheats**, **cheating**, **cheated**

cheat on

1 You **cheat on** your sexual partner when you are unfaithful to him or her by secretly having a sexual relationship with someone else: *He's been cheating on his wife again.* **2** You **cheat on** something when you behave dishonestly or fraudulently: *He's been cheating on his expenses, claiming for trips he never made.*

check /tʃɛk/: **checks**, **checking**, **checked**

check in

1 You **check in** at an airport before you board a flight when you show your ticket so that the airline knows that you have arrived; the airline staff **check** you **in** when they examine your ticket before you get on a flight: *I'll just check in and then we can go and have a drink.* **2** You **check in** at a hotel, or you **check into** a hotel, when you arrive, sign your name in the register, and collect the key for your room: *We arrived at 2 am and were checked in by the night porter.* ❑ *The first thing we did when we arrived in New York was check into the Waldorf Astoria.* [*opposite* **check out**]
• *noun* **check-in**: **check-ins**
A **check-in**, or **check-in** desk, is a desk at an airport where passengers' tickets are checked before they board their flight, and their luggage is weighed and accepted for loading: *We joined the queue at the check-in.*

check off

You **check off** items on a list when you make marks on the list to show that each item is there or has been dealt with: *Pepita checked off another crate of bananas that would be shipped to lands she had never seen and never would see.*

check out

1 You **check out** of a hotel when you pay your bill and leave: *We'll have a room available after lunch when the couple in number 10 have checked out.* [*opposite* **check in**] **2** (*informal*) You **check** something **out** when you find out about it: *All I have to do now is check out the times of direct flights to Paris.* ❑ *We've had a report of a disturbance in Cambridge Street and I've sent two constables along to check it out.* [compare **check up on**] **3** (*informal*) You **check** someone **out** when you find out all that you can about them, usually without them knowing that you are doing so: *I don't know if he's who he says he is; we'll have to have him checked out.* [compare **check up on**] **4** You have the goods you want to buy in a shop or supermarket **checked out** when a cashier or till operator takes the price of each item and adds up the total you have to pay on the till.

• *noun* **checkout**: **checkouts**

A **checkout** in a shop or supermarket is a special desk where a cashier or till operator can add up the various prices of the goods you are buying: *There was a long queue at every checkout.*

check over

You **check** something **over** when you examine it to see whether it is working properly or has been done properly: *Peter's had a bad cough for weeks now. I'm going to have the doctor check him over.* ❑ *Just give me a moment to check over what you have written so far.*

check through

You **check through** a number of items when you look at each of them in turn in order to find a particular item or to see if everything is correct and in its proper order: *Can you just check through these lists to see if his name appears anywhere?*

check up

You **check up** to see if something is true or accurate when you make enquiries about it with a reliable source: *If you want to check up that their flight will be arriving on time, just phone the airport enquiry desk.* ❑ *I wasn't sure if I had taken his number down properly so I checked it up in the telephone directory.*

• *noun* **check-up**: **check-ups**

A doctor or dentist gives you a **check-up** when he or she gives you a general examination to see that you are in good health: *He seems to be clear of the cancer but he'll still have to go for regular check-ups every six months.*

check up on

You **check up on** someone or something when you find out if they are all right or are behaving or working as they should be: *Sometimes my parents drop in unexpectedly just to check up on me.*

cheer /tʃɪə(r)/: **cheers**, **cheering**, **cheered**

cheer on

You **cheer** someone **on** when you shout encouragement to them: *Standing stripped to the waist and cheered on by his mates, he won the body beautiful competition.* ❑ *All his friends came to the athletics meeting to cheer him on.*

cheer up

Someone or something **cheers** you **up** when they make you feel happier and more hopeful; you **cheer up** when you begin to feel happier and more hopeful: *I thought you were looking a bit down so I brought you a little present to cheer you up.* ❑ *Oh, do cheer up! You've nothing to be depressed about.*

cheese /tʃiːz/: **cheeses**, **cheesing**, **cheesed**

cheese off (*informal*)

Something **cheeses** you **off** when it makes you feel bored, irritated or unhappy: *His irresponsible attitude really cheeses me off.*

• *adjective* **cheesed off**: *You're*

looking a bit cheesed off. What's the matter? [*same as* **browned off** *(informal)*, **fed up** *(informal)*]

chew /tʃuː/: chews, chewing, chewed

chew on (*informal*)

You **chew on** a problem, proposal or idea when you think about it carefully for a long time before you decide what your opinion of it is or what you are going to do about it: *I'll have to go away and think about this; you've given me a lot to chew on.* [*same as* **ponder on** (*formal*), **consider**]

chew over (*informal*)

You **chew** something **over** when you spend time thinking carefully about it or discussing it in detail: *Now that we've told him what we want from him we better give him some time to chew it over.* ❑ *They have a meeting once a week to chew over any problems that have arisen in the meantime.*

chew up

1 You **chew** food **up** when you use your teeth to crush it or break it into smaller pieces before swallowing it. **2** (*informal*) Something **is chewed up** *eg* by a machine when it is crushed or damaged as if it has been chewed: *There's something wrong with the photocopier; it's chewing up the paper and jamming.*

chicken /ˈtʃɪkɪn/: chickens, chickening, chickened

chicken out (*informal*)

You **chicken out** when you don't do something risky or dangerous because you have lost the courage to do it: *Henry was going to do a parachute jump but he chickened out at the last minute.* ❑ *I prepared to bet that he'll chicken out of the fight when he finds out who his opponent is.* [*same as* **bottle out** (*informal*), **wimp out** (*informal*)]

chill /tʃɪl/: chills, chilling, chilled

chill out (*informal*)

People say they **are chilling out** when they are relaxing, either physically or mentally, after a period of very energetic activity or mental stress: *Sit down, have a beer, and chill out, man.*

chime /tʃaɪm/: chimes, chiming, chimed

chime in (*informal*)

Someone **chimes in** when they interrupt a conversation to add their own remarks or comments or express their own opinion: *We had almost reached agreement when Jim suddenly chimed in with an objection to the proposals.* ❑ *'Yes, that's quite true,' Peter chimed in, eagerly.* [*same as* **break in**]

chime in with (*informal*)

Something **chimes in with** something else when it fits in well with it: *I was delighted to discover that his attitude to this difficult question chimed in with my own.* [*same as* **accord with** (*formal*)]

chip /tʃɪp/: chips, chipping, chipped

chip in (*informal*)

1 A number of people **chip in** for something when they each give or contribute some of the money needed to pay for it: *We'll all have to chip in £50 if we decide to hire a car for the whole week.* **2** Someone **chips in** during a conversation when they interrupt it in order to say something: *Margaret chipped in with the suggestion that we should hold the meeting outdoors.*

chivvy *or* chivy /ˈtʃɪvɪ/: chivvies, chivvying, chivvied

chivvy along *or* chivvy up (*informal*)

You **chivvy** someone **along**, or you **chivvy** them **up**, when you continually do or say things to encourage them to hurry or do something they are very reluctant to do: *'He's going to be late! Go and chivvy him along, will you.'* [*same as* **annoy**]

choke /tʃouk/: chokes, choking, choked

choke back
You **choke back** an emotion or an expression of emotion when you try very hard to stop yourself showing it: *Biting hard on her knuckle to choke back her sobs, she fled from the room.* [*same as* **suppress**]

choke off (*informal*)
The availability or supply of something **is choked off** when forceful action is taken to stop it or bring it to an abrupt end: *Downing Street sources made little attempt to choke off speculation amongst MPs that a Cabinet reshuffle was on the cards.*

choke up
Something such as a pipe or drain **is choked up** when a number of things have blocked it so that nothing can flow through: *empty wine bottles with fur and fungus choking up their throats* ❑ *The drain is all choked up with leaves.* [*same as* **bung up**]

chop /tʃɒp/: chops, chopping, chopped

chop down
You **chop** a tree **down** when you cut through its trunk with an axe so that it falls to the ground: *They're going to chop down all these beautiful trees to build a motorway.*

chop off
You **chop** a part **off** something when you cut it off using an axe or sharp knife: *Mary, Queen of Scots, had her head chopped off.*

chop up
You **chop** something **up** when you cut it into small pieces using an axe or a sharp knife: *He chops up the old pallets for firewood.* ❑ *Coat the chopped-up chicken with seasoned flour.*

chuck /tʃʌk/: chucks, chucking, chucked

chuck away (*informal*)
You **chuck** something **away** when you get rid of it by throwing it away, often carelessly or casually: *Can you believe it? He's chucked away the chicken stock I was going to use for the sauce.* [*same as* **chuck out** (*informal*), **throw out**]

chuck in (*informal*)
You **chuck** your job **in** when you give it up, usually because you are dissatisfied or bored with it; you **chuck** something **in** when you stop doing it: *He's decided to chuck his job in and emigrate to Canada.* ❑ *I've told you twice to stop annoying your sister. If you don't chuck it in right now, you'll go straight to bed.* [*same as* **jack in** (*informal*), **pack in** (*informal*)]

chuck out (*informal*)
1 You **chuck** someone **out** when you force them to leave a place: *We were chucked out of the pub for singing football songs.* [*same as* **throw out**] **2** You **chuck** something **out** when you get rid of it by throwing it away: *As soon as I can afford a new one, I'm going to chuck this old sofa out.* [*same as* **chuck away** (*informal*), **throw out**]

chuck up (*informal*)
You **chuck up** your job when you give it up suddenly, without giving much notice: *He just chucked up his job and took off on a round-the-world trip.* [*same as* **throw up**]

chum /tʃʌm/: chums, chumming, chummed

chum up with (*informal*)
You **chum up with** someone when you form a friendship with them: *When in Venice, he chummed up with a couple of Italian students.*

churn /tʃɜːn/: **churns**, **churning**, **churned**

churn out

A person, organization, factory or machine **churns** things **out** when they produce them rapidly in large quantities: *The universities continue to churn out graduates with no vocational qualifications and many of them now find it very difficult to get jobs.* ❑ *Looking at the work he has been churning out lately, I wouldn't have recognised it as being the same author.*

churn up

Things such as heavy machines or vehicles **churn up** the earth when they break its surface up or make it soft and muddy; something **churns** water or mud **up** when it makes it splash about violently: *Buffalo and other animals had churned up the grass into a mass of muddy trails.* ❑ *It was as churned-up as a freshly harrowed field.*

claim /kleɪm/: **claims**, **claiming**, **claimed**

claim back

You **claim back** something that is yours or that you are entitled to when you ask for it to be returned to you: *He said he would pay for lunch and claim it back on his expenses.*

clam /klam/: **clams**, **clamming**, **clammed**

clam up

Someone **clams up** when they stop talking suddenly, especially refusing to answer any more questions: *Up to that point he had been chatting away quite happily but when I asked him where he had come from and who his parents were he just clammed up and looked sullen.*

clamp /klamp/: **clamps**, **clamping**, **clamped**

clamp down

People in authority **clamp down** on an activity when they bring it under very strict control or stop it altogether: *The company is going to clamp down on persistent absenteeism.*

• *noun* **clampdown**: **clampdowns**: *one of the police's periodic clampdowns on drinking and driving.*

clap /klap/: **claps**, **clapping**, **clapped**

clap in *or* clap into

Someone **is clapped in** or **into** prison when they are put there without delay and perhaps without being allowed a proper trial: *If you were even suspected of being involved with one of the terrorist organizations you were clapped in prison and left to rot.*

clap on *or* clap onto

You **clap** something **on** when you put it on quickly and roughly: *One policeman held him down while the other clapped the handcuffs on him.*

clap out

• *adjective* **clapped-out**

A **clapped-out** machine or vehicle is worn out because it is old and has been used a lot: *We travelled around in a clapped-out old van.*

class /klɑːs/: **classes**, **classing**, **classed**

class among

You **class** a person or thing **among** a particular group or category when you think of them as belonging to that group or category: *These could certainly be classed among the worst experiences of his life.*

claw /klɔː/: **claws**, **clawing**, **clawed**

claw at

A person or animal **claws at** something when they use their fingernails or claws to try to get a grip on it or scratch it: *The cat was clawing at the door, trying to get in.* ❑ *She screamed with rage and* *clawed at my face with her long painted fingernails.*

claw back

An organization or the government **claws back** the money that it has already paid to an individual, often in the form of a benefit or allowance, when it gets the money back through some form of deduction, especially through taxation.

• *noun* **clawback**: **clawbacks**: *The bidder might consider providing an open offer and clawback to its shareholders.*

clean /kliːn/: cleans, cleaning, cleaned

clean down

You **clean** a surface **down** when you clean it from top to bottom: *After sanding the door frames, clean the wood down before applying the varnish.*

clean out

1 You **clean out** something such as a cupboard or room when you empty it completely, get rid of the things you don't want, and clean it thoroughly: *Dad's cleaning out the garage and getting rid of all that old junk he's been hanging on to for years.* **2** (*informal*) If someone or something **cleans** you **out** they take all the money you have: *I can't afford to go out for a meal; today's trip to the garden centre cleaned me out completely.*

clean up

1 You **clean** something **up** when you make it clean again: *How did you manage to get chocolate all over your face? We'll have to clean you up before your mum comes to collect you.* **2** You **clean up** a mess when you get rid of it: *Get a damp cloth and clean up the blackcurrant juice you've spilt on the table.* **3** You **clean up** after someone when you clean a place that they have made dirty: *It's not fair to expect your mother to clean up after you all the time.* **4** (*informal*) Someone **cleans up** a place or organization when they take action to get rid of vice or crime there: *We would undoubtably require that the authorities be seen to have cleaned up their act.* ❑ *With all these accusations of 'sleaze' it's time someone did something to clean up the government's image.* **5** (*informal*) People say that an individual or business **cleans up** when that individual or business makes a particularly large profit from something: *He'd bought the houses cheaply and cleaned up when he sold them again.*

clear /klɪə(r)/: clears, clearing, cleared

clear away

You **clear away**, or **clear** things **away**, when you remove or put away the things you have been using, *eg* for a meal: *If everyone's finished I'll clear away now.* ❑ *Clear away all the dirty dishes and put them in the dishwasher.*

clear off

1 (*informal*) Someone **clears off** when they go or run away; if you say **'clear off!'** to someone you are telling them rudely to go away: *Here come the coppers; we'd better clear off quick!* ❑ *Clear off! This is private land.* **2** You **clear off** a debt when you pay it all back: *We've decided to use the money to clear off our mortgage.*

clear out

1 You **clear out** something such as a room or cupboard when you take everything out of it, throw away the things that you don't want to make more space, and tidy the things you want to keep: *Will you help me clear out this cupboard?* [*same as* **tidy out**] **2** You **clear out** when you leave a place quickly; you tell someone to **clear out** when you want them to leave immediately: *Her husband threatened to clear out that night if she didn't stop nagging him.* ❑ *The landlord has told* *us to clear out of the flat if we can't pay the rent we owe before the end of the week.*

clear up
1 You **clear up**, or **clear** a place **up**, when you make it tidy and put things away in their proper places: *I won't let you do any baking unless you promise to clear up afterwards.* ❑ *It's 4.30, and everyone is clearing up before going home.* **2** You **clear up** after someone when you tidy a place that they have made untidy: *You'd better put all these things away; I'm not going to clear up after you anymore.* **3** You **clear up** a mystery, misunderstanding or problem when you solve it or settle it satisfactorily; the police **clear up** a crime or crimes when they find out who the criminal or criminals are and arrest them: *I'd like to clear up a few minor points before I sign the contract.* ❑ *With the new powers the police have become more successful at clearing up crime.* **4** The weather **clears up** when it becomes fine again: *It's been raining all day even though the forecast said it would clear up in the afternoon.* **5** An illness or condition **clears up** when it gets better: *Has the rash cleared up yet?* ❑ *The joint and skin problems should be transient and will clear up in due course.*

climb /klaım/: **climbs**, **climbing**, **climbed**

climb down
In an argument or dispute, you **climb down** when you admit that you are wrong or have made a mistake: *He knows he's wrong but he's too stubborn and proud to climb down.*
• *noun* **climbdown**: **climbdowns**: *They're expecting a climbdown by management, but it's not going to happen.*

clock /klɒk/: **clocks**, **clocking**, **clocked**

clock in *or* **clock on**
Workers **clock in** or **on** when they push a special card into a machine so as to record the time that they arrive for work: *He always clocks in an hour before anyone else.* ❑ *Remember to clock on before you go to your work station.*

clock off *or* **clock out**
Workers **clock off** or **out** when they push a special card into a machine so as to record the time that they leave work: *The day-shift clocked off from the nearby factory at 4 pm.*

clock up (*informal*)
You **clock up** a particular speed, distance, score or total when you reach or achieve it: *Jerry's really been clocking up the miles* [= driving long distances] *in the last few weeks; he's had to drive from Manchester to London every day.* ❑ *He reached the final with apparent ease, clocking up some of the highest winning scores in the history of the tournament.* [*same as* **register**, **record**]

clog /klɒg/: **clogs**, **clogging**, **clogged**

clog up
Something **clogs up** a passage or opening when it blocks it so that nothing can get through or past: *convoys of heavy lorries clogging up the M1.*

close /klouz/: **closes**, **closing**, **closed**

close down
1 A factory or business **closes down,** or it **is closed down**, when it stops operating permanently: *The steel mill is closing down with the loss of 5000 jobs.* **2** A radio or television station **closes down** when it stops broadcasting for a time, especially during the night: *'We're closing down now until 6 o'clock tomorrow morning. I've just got time to wish all our listeners a peaceful night. Goodnight.'*
• *noun* **closedown**
1 (*uncount*) **Closedown** is the time

when a radio or television station stops broadcasting: *'What's on next?' 'It's 'Newsnight' followed by 'The Late Show', then closedown.* **2** A **closedown** is an instance of closing down a factory or industrial process: *If we can cut costs by closing a couple of departments we might be able to avoid a complete closedown.*

close in
1 When the days **close in** the hours of daylight become fewer and fewer as winter approaches; when night **closes in** it gets dark. [*same as* **draw in**] **2** Something **closes in** when it moves in from all sides to fill or envelop something: *We caught a brief glimpse of them before the fog closed in again and they were gone from view.* **3** People **close in** on someone or something when they all move towards that person or thing from different directions to surround and attack or capture them: *Police are closing in on the big Mafia bosses.*

close off
A area **is closed off** when a barrier is placed across it so that no-one can get into it or pass through it: *The northbound carriageway of the M8 has been closed off while police and firemen clear the wreckage from a collision between two articulated lorries.*

close on
You **close on** someone or something moving ahead of you when you gradually get closer and closer to them: *He saw that the police car was closing on him and looked around desperately for some way of escape.* ❑ *The horse on the inside was closing rapidly on the leaders.*

close out
You **close** something **out** when you put up some sort of barrier so that it cannot get in: *If you pull that blind down you'll close out most of the light.* ❑ *He tried to close the sound of their screams out by putting his fingers in his ears.*

close up
1 You **close up** a building or business premises when you close the doors and windows and lock them so that no-one can get in: *The librarian told us to choose our books quickly because she was just about to close up for the night.* ❑ *The house was closed up and everyone had gone.* **2** You **close** something **up**, or it **closes up**, when you close it, or it closes, completely: *the specially adapted leaf closes up trapping the unfortunate fly inside* ❑ *Father closed up the huge family Bible.* **3** People **close up**, or things **are closed up**, when they move, or are moved, closer together so that there are no spaces between them: *The sergeant-major gave the order to close up ranks.* ❑ *She looked for an escape gap, but the crowd had shifted again and closed up.*

cloud /klaud/: clouds, clouding, clouded

cloud over
1 It **clouds over** when the sky fills up with clouds that hide the sun: *By the time we got outside it had started to cloud over and there was the occasional spot of rain.* **2** Someone's face **clouds over** when their expression changes suddenly to one of worry or anger. **3** A clear or shiny surface **clouds over** when a thin layer of moisture covers it and makes it opaque or dull. [*same as* **mist over**]

club /klʌb/: clubs, clubbing, clubbed

club together
Several people **club together** to buy something when they each give some money towards the cost: *We're going to club together and buy a minibus so that we can all go off together at weekends.*

clue /kluː/: clues, cluing, clued

clue up
• *adjective (informal)* **clued up**

You are **clued up** about something when you are well informed about it: *He seems to be pretty clued up on the latest developments in information technology.* [compare **genned up**]

cluster /'klʌstə(r)/: **clusters, clustering, clustered**

cluster around *or* cluster round

People or things **cluster around** or **round** someone or something when they gather or come together round it in a tightly packed group or bunch: *They clustered round their pop idol clammering for his autograph.*

clutter /'klʌtə(r)/: **clutters, cluttering, cluttered**

clutter up

You **clutter up** a surface or area when you fill all the space available with things which ought not to be there and which are scattered about untidily: *Please stop cluttering up the hall with your skis and climbing equipment.*

coast /koust/: **coasts, coasting, coasted**

coast along

1 You **coast along** in a car or on a bicycle when you continue to move forwards after switching off the engine or stopping pedalling. **2** You **coast along** *eg* in your work when you do it without making much of an effort: *Henry doesn't try all that hard; he seems to prefer to coast along.*

cobble /'kɒbəl/: **cobbles, cobbling, cobbled**

cobble together

You **cobble** something **together** when you make or produce it in a hurry or in an emergency by putting together a number of conveniently-available things, instead of taking the time to obtain something new or specially designed for the purpose: *We had to cobble together a sort of stretcher from branches and an old blanket so that we could get the injured man to hospital.*

cock /kɒk/: **cocks, cocking, cocked**

cock up (*vulgar slang*)

You **cock** something **up** when you do it wrongly or very badly and so ruin it: *Don't, for goodness sake, leave the travel arrangements to Steven. He's sure to find some way of cocking them up.* ❑ *She cocked up the whole experiment by labelling the jars wrongly.*
• *noun (vulgar slang)* **cock-up**: **cock-ups**: *I haven't been able to process your application yet. There's been a bit of a cock-up at head office.* ❑ *This looks like yet another of their monumental cock-ups.*

coil /kɔɪl/: **coils, coiling, coiled**

coil around *or* coil round

Something long and flexible **is coiled around** or **round** something else when it is wound around it in a series of loops: *The python coiled itself around the goat crushing the life out of it.*

coil up

You **coil** something long and flexible **up** when you form it into a continuous series of loops or rings, one on top of the other: *She caught her foot in a coiled-up rope on the deck.*

collect /kə'lɛkt/: **collects, collecting, collected**

collect up

You **collect** things **up** when you pick them up and gather them all together: *Go round the tables and collect up all the dirty dishes.*

colour (*AmE* **color**) /'kʌlə(r)/: **colours, colouring, coloured**

colour in

You **colour in** a shape or outline drawn on paper, or you **colour** it **in**, when you

fill it with a colour or colours using paints, crayons or chalks: *That's a lovely house you've drawn. Are you going to colour it in now?*
• *noun* **colouring-in**: *Are you going to do the colouring-in now?*

colour up

When you **colour up** your face goes red because you suddenly feel embarrassed or guilty: *'Did you take Emily's pocket money?' 'No, I didn't, honestly,' he said, colouring up and avoiding his mother's eye.* [*same as* **blush**]

comb /koum/: combs, combing, combed

comb out

You **comb out** your hair, or you **comb** something **out** of it, when you draw a comb through it *eg* to loosen the tight curls made by hair curlers or remove tangles: *She was sitting on the edge of the pool combing the tangles out of her long brown hair.*

come /kʌm/: comes, coming, came /keim/

Come is both the present tense and the past participle.

come about

1 When you ask how something **came about** you are asking how it happened: *How did it come about that the patient was given the wrong dose of the drug?* ❑ *The situation came about through a misunderstanding.* [*same as* **happen, occur, come to pass** (*formal*)] **2** A boat, especially a sailing boat, **comes about** when it changes course so that it is facing or moving in the opposite direction: *When we reach the red marker we'll have to come about.* [see also **go about, put about**]

come across

1 You **come across** something when you discover or encounter it without looking for it or expecting it: *Digging in the garden, he came across a piece of broken pottery that looked as if it might be Roman.* ❑ *Did you happen to come across my old school tie when you were tidying out the wardrobe?* ❑ *Have you ever come across anything like this before?* ❑ *No matter how experienced you are you're bound to occasionally come across problems that you had never anticipated.* [*same as* **run across, run into**] **2 a** Someone or something **comes across** in a particular way if that is the impression they make on people: *His speech came across well.* ❑ *Some of the dancing was way below standard but the ballet still came across as one of Macmillan's most monumental pieces.* [*same as* **come over**] **b** Someone **comes across** as a particular type of person when that is how they appear to others: *She comes across as someone who is kind and caring.* **3** (*informal*) Someone **comes across** with *eg* money or information when they hand it over, especially reluctantly and after a delay: *He grumbled a bit but eventually he came across with the cash.* [*same as* **come up with** (*informal*), **produce**]

come after

1 One thing **comes after** another when it follows it, or when it happens or exists at a later time: *Who was the English king who came after Charles II?* ❑ *As far as I remember, the story of his affair with the actress came after his resignation, not before it.* ❑ *It's our responsibility to protect the environment for the generations who are to come after us.* [opposite **come before**] **2** Someone **comes after** you when they chase or pursue you: *We ran away, but he came after us, shouting and waving his hands in the air.* ❑ *'I'm warning you, if you don't stop now I'll come after you and see to it that you're sent down* [= sent to prison] *for a long, long time.'*

come along

1 Something such as an opportunity **comes along** when it occurs or arrives:

I don't think I'll take that job; I'll wait until something better comes along. [*same as* **crop up, turn up**] **2** When you ask how someone or something **is coming along** you want to know about their progress; someone or something **is coming along** when they are making good or satisfactory progress: *How's our young trainee coming along?* ❑ *'How's my father today, doctor?' 'He seems to be coming along fine; he might even be able to go home tomorrow.'* [*same as* **come on**] **3** You say **'come along'** to someone when you want them to hurry up, or do something that they do not want to do: *Come along now, ladies and gentlemen; it's closing time.* ❑ *Come along, eat up your vegetables like a good boy.*

come apart

Something **comes apart** when it breaks or splits, or can be separated, into two or more pieces: *He picked up what was left of the mummy but it came apart in his hands.* ❑ *The doll comes apart to reveal a series of smaller and smaller dolls each fitted inside the other.*

come around see **come round**

come at

1 Things **come at** you when they all reach you or are presented to you at the same time: *No wonder children get confused with so much information coming at them from advertising, television, and the like.* **2** Someone or something **comes at** you when they move towards you to attack you: *He came at me with a knife.* [see also **come for**]

come away

1 You **come away** when you leave the place where you are to go elsewhere, or when you move away from something: *He asked me to come away with him for the weekend.* ❑ *Come away from the water; you might fall in.* **2** Something **comes away** when it separates, often very easily, from the thing it has been attached to: *Plaster had come away from the walls from ceiling to floor.*

come away with (*informal*)

Someone **comes away with** a statement, remark or comment when they say it, often unexpectedly: *He comes away with some incredibly funny comments.* [*same as* **come out with** (*informal*)]

come back

1 You **come back** when you return to a place, often after being away for some time: *All these young men going off to war not knowing if they will ever come back.* **2** Something **comes back** to you when you remember it: *'Oh, what was his name?' 'Don't worry, it'll come back to you.'* ❑ *Yes, this was where it happened; it's all coming back to me now.* **3** Something **is coming back** when it is becoming fashionable again, after being out of fashion for a time: *I see those horrible platform shoes are coming back again.*

• *noun* **comeback**: **comebacks**

1 Someone makes a **comeback** when they return to the same level of fame or success that they had at some time in the past: *He's planning to make a comeback in the super-heavyweight division.* **2** When something you do has **comebacks**, it has bad or unpleasant consequences for you at some later date: *You better make sure this is all legal and above board. I don't want any comebacks.*

come back to

You **come back to** something when you return to it at a later time: *Let's come back to the question of grants when we have more information on what is available.*

come before

1 One thing **comes before** another when the one occurs or is placed in order before the other: *P comes before Q in the alphabet.* ❑ *It made a good* *symbol of harnessing of mighty powers for man's comfort, or perhaps of pride coming before a fall.* [*same as* **precede**; *opposite* **come after**] **2** Something to be decided, such as a legal case, **comes before** a court or tribunal when evidence is presented to the court or tribunal so that it can be examined or discussed and a judgement or decision made: *The bill is due to come before the House of Lords in September.* **3** One thing **comes before** another when the one is considered to be of greater importance than the other: *My family will always come before anything else.*

come between

Someone or something **comes between** two people who have a close relationship when it interferes with and spoils their relationship; something **comes between** somebody and the thing they want to do when it stops them doing it: *I won't let anyone come between me and my wife.* ❑ *He's determined to let nothing come between him and his ambition to reach the top of his profession.*

come by

1 Someone **comes by** when they move towards you and pass you: *She sat on the wall and watched as the parade came by.* [compare **go by**] **2** Someone **comes by** when they come to the place where you are to pay you a short visit: *Kirsty came by this morning to show me photographs of her latest work.* **3** You **come by** something when you get or obtain it, often by good luck or chance: *We were lucky to get it; these old farmhouses are hard to come by.* ❑ *Are you able to tell me how you came by all that money?* [*same as* **acquire**, **get hold of**]

come down

1 Something **comes down** when it moves, drops, falls or collapses downwards: *Some of the plaster on the ceiling has come down.* ❑ *They stood in a miserable huddle while the rain came down in buckets.* [= it was raining very heavily] ❑ *They have climbed out on to the prison roof and are refusing to come down.* **2** Levels or amounts **come down** when they decrease, are reduced, or get lower: *We are pleased to be able to announce that the unemployment rate has come down for the third month running.* [*opposite* **go up**] **3** In a dispute or argument, you **come down** on one side or the other when you decide finally which side you will support: *Unmistakably though, he has come down on the side of the demonstrators and against the East German leader.*

• *noun (informal)* **comedown**

1 A **comedown** is a loss or fall in rank, importance or social position: *He felt the job was a bit of a comedown from minister of state at the Foreign Office.* **2** A **comedown** is also an anticlimax: *We thought we had won thousands and it was an awful comedown to find it was only £50.*

come down on

You **come down on** someone hard when you criticize or punish them severely: *If any pupil is caught smoking in school, the headmaster will come down on them like a ton of bricks.* [*same as* **jump on**]

come down to

A complicated problem or situation **comes down to** a certain thing when that is the issue or factor on which everything else depends: *We would like to develop this side of the business more but it all comes down to money.* [= we may not be able to develop it if there is not enough money available] [*same as* **boil down to**]

come down with

You **come down with** an infectious illness when you catch it: *I suspect Will's coming down with flu.*

come for

1 Someone **comes for** you when they

come to where you are to fetch you and take you away: *Your dad said he would be coming for you around six o'clock.* **2** Someone or something **is coming for** you when they are moving towards you to attack you: *He appeared suddenly from behind a tree and came for me with what looked like a machete.* [*same as* **come at**; compare **go for**]

come forth (*formal or literary*)

1 Someone or something **comes forth** when it appears or is produced, and moves towards you: *Moses struck the rock with his rod twice; and water came forth abundantly.* [compare **go forth**] **2** Someone **comes forth** with a suggestion, idea or proposal when they present or offer it: *Our application was submitted prior to this information about the properties coming forth.* [*same as* **come forward with**]

• *adjective* **forthcoming**

1 A **forthcoming** event is one that will happen soon: *I'd like to congratulate Ron and Susan on their forthcoming marriage.* [*same as* **coming**] **2 a** Someone is **forthcoming** when they are willing or eager to tell you things: *I tried to talk to him but didn't find him very forthcoming.* [*same as* **communicative, talkative**] **b** Something such as information is **forthcoming** when it is made available: *We've sent them several reminders but to date no payment has been forthcoming.*

come forward

Someone **comes forward** when they offer to help or offer to give information: *We hope that anyone with any information about his whereabouts will come forward before another crime is committed.* [*same as* **step forward, volunteer**]

come forward with

Someone **comes forward with** an idea, suggestion or proposal when they make it: *Then Peter came forward with the suggestion that we should all meet again the following day.*

come from

1 a You **come from** a particular place or country when that is where you were born and brought up: *I know you've lived here for a long time but where did you come from originally?* ❑ *He's so weird I'm beginning to think he comes from another planet!* **b** You **come from** a particular family or class of people when you are descended from them; you **come from** a particular background when you were brought up in that way or you have experienced that type of life: *'I'm still as fit as I was twenty years ago. That's because I come from good peasant stock,' he said, with a smile.* ❑ *He doesn't come from a musical background.* [= his parents didn't sing or play a musical instrument] ❑ *Both men came from humble backgrounds.* **2** One thing **comes from** another when that other thing is its source or origin: *Where's this water coming from?* ❑ *I don't know where that story came from.* ❑ *He could hear the murmur of voices coming from the pigsties.* ❑ *Milk comes from cows and goats.* ❑ *The word used is 'chronos', from which comes our word 'chronology'.* **3** (*informal*) If you say you know where someone **is coming from**, you mean that you understand their intentions or motives: *Now I think I understand where he's coming from; he wants someone to look after him.*

come in

1 Someone **comes in** when they enter a place: *Hullo, it's nice to see you; do come in.* ❑ *'Come in,' called a lady's voice.* ❑ *Jack and Alison came in, followed by Marcus and Ludens.* ❑ *Caroline didn't even knock; she just came straight in.* **2** Something such as news **comes in** when you receive it: *The president's wife was in bed when news of the assassination attempt came in.* ❑ *Soon after the group was set up referrals were regularly coming in.* ❑ *There's a report coming in of a serious crash on the M5.* **3** Someone **comes in**

when they become involved or are included in a scheme, or have a role in it: *It's a family matter, so I don't quite see where someone who is complete stranger comes in.* **4** You have money **coming in** when you have an income: *With my husband out of work and me only working part-time we don't have much coming in.* **5 a** Something **comes in** when it becomes fashionable: *The so-called 'New Look' came in when rationing was ended after World War II.* [*opposite* **go out**] **b** Something new **comes in** when it comes into force, is introduced, or becomes available: *All new buses will have to be fitted with seat-belts when the law comes in in October.* ❑ *When telephone banking came in customers didn't have to visit their branch so often, so fewer staff were needed.* **c** A political party **comes in** when it wins an election and forms a government: *When the Tories came in, unemployment stood at over a million.* [*same as* **get in**] **6** You **come in** *eg* first, second or last when that is the position you finish in in a race or competition: *Sebastian Coe won the race, with the other British runners coming in third and sixth.* **7** The tide **comes in** when the level of the sea rises to a higher point on the shore. [*opposite* **go out**]

come in for

You **come in for** praise, blame or criticism when you are the subject of blame, praise or criticism: *The Labour leader came in for a bit of a battering in the Tory press.*

come in on

Someone **comes in on** a plan or scheme when they join it or make some contribution to it: *I know a couple of blokes who'll be willing to come in on the venture if they think they'll make a bit of money by it.*

come into

1 You **come into** money when you inherit it: *He's come into a fortune.* **2** You say that someone '**comes into** their own' when they have the opportunity, in particular circumstances, to display their talents, especially after a long period when their talents weren't recognized or known about: *Out on the hills, the four-wheel drive comes into its own.* **3** Something **comes into** a situation if it is one of the factors or issues involved in it: *Vanity doesn't come into it; I just want to look my best.*

come in with

Someone **comes in with** you when they join you in a business or scheme, especially when they invest money in it: *I'm not starting the business alone; I've asked a couple of friends to come in with me to spread the risk.*

come of

1 When something **comes of** something it has that result: *One of the big oil companies did show some interest in his invention but in the end nothing came of it.* ❑ *They've swindled her out of her savings. That's what comes of being too trusting.* **2** You **come of** the people you are descended from: *He comes of mixed parentage.*

come off

1 You **come off** a horse, a bicycle or a motorbike when you fall off it: *He hit a patch of oil on the road and came off his bike.* **2** A piece or part of something **comes off** when it becomes separated, or can be separated, from the main part: *The handle's come off the bathroom door.* ❑ *'The top of this jar won't come off.' 'Let me try. Look, it comes off quite easily.'* **3** A mark or stain **comes off** when it is removed or can be removed: *I hope to goodness this chocolate stain comes off.* **4** A scheme **comes off** if it is successful: *Our plans for early retirement didn't quite come off as we had hoped.* **5** (*informal*) An event **comes off** when it takes place: *There's a five-a-side football tourn-ament coming off next Saturday. Would* *you like to go along as a substitute?* **6** (*informal*) You **come off** well or badly when you end in a good or bad position after an event: *It was a hard fight for Bruno, but he came off the better of the two.* **7** You **come off** a drug when you stop using it: *He had a very bad time when he was coming off heroin.* ❑ *Carol's doctor told her she'd to come off the Pill because she has high blood pressure.* **8** (*informal*) When you say '**come off it!**' to someone you are telling them rather rudely that what they are saying is not true: *'His income was more than thirty thousand last year.' 'Oh, come off it, I've seen his accounts, and it wasn't even half that!'*

come on

1 When you ask how something **is coming on** you want to know about its progress; you say that something **is coming on** when it is progressing or growing well: *How's the science project coming on?* ❑ *'These carrots and beans are growing well.' 'Yes, they're coming on.'* [*same as* **come along**] **2** You say '**come on!**' to someone as a way of encouraging them to hurry up, or to do something, or to be more reasonable: *Come on, you two, we're going to be late!* ❑ *Oh, come on, Bill! Things aren't that bad.* **3** Something **comes on** when it begins: *We had just set up our picnic when the rain came on.* **4** A light **comes on** when it lights up or is switched on: *Someone must be in; I saw a light come on in one of the bedrooms.* **5** You have *eg* a cold **coming on** when it is starting: *Whenever I feel a migraine coming on I lie down in a darkened room.* **6** An actor **comes on** when he or she makes their entrance on stage; a player in a sporting team **comes on** when they join their team on the field while a match is being played: *You don't come on again until the last act.* ❑ *The fans roared their approval when Barnes came on in the second half.* **7** A film, play, television or radio programme **comes on** when it is shown, performed or broadcast: *When's the next series coming on?* ❑ *There's a new production of 'Fidelio' coming on at the Theatre Royal.*

come on to (*informal*)

Someone **comes on to** you when they flirt with you and behave in a sexually inviting way: *Maybe I got the signals wrong, but I could have swore she was coming on to me.*

come out

1 When the sun or moon **come out** they appear in the sky. **2** A fact or the truth **comes out** when it becomes known publicly: *What came out of the statistical analysis was how infrequently people actually use these idioms.* ❑ *The truth came out when she finally admitted that she was the one who had done it.* [*same as* **emerge**] **3** Marks or stains **come out** when they disappear or are removed as a result of washing or some other cleaning process: *I put my jacket into the dry cleaner's hoping that the wine stain would come out.* **4** Colour or dye **comes out** of a fabric if it fades, or is removed, *eg* as a result of washing: *This is a rinse, not a dye; it comes out of your hair in a couple of weeks.* **5** You **come out** in favour of something when you openly declare your support for it: *We were astonished when a life-long pacifist appeared to come out in favour of re-armament.* [*opposite* **come out against**] **6** You **come out** on top when you beat your opponent or opponents: *It looks as if it will be an American golfer who comes out on top.* **7** Workers **come out**, or **come out** on strike, when they stop working and leave their workplace because of an industrial dispute: *Do you really expect the miners to come out again after last time?* **8** The way something **comes out** is its final result or consequence: *It'll all come out okay in the end, you'll see.* **9** A photograph **comes out** when it is processed successfully and its subject can be clearly seen: *The photograph has come* *out a bit blurred.* **10** A new product **comes out** when it becomes available to the public; a book **comes out** when it is published: *The new model comes out in August.* ❑ *She's got another book of poetry coming out in the autumn.* **11** Flowers or buds **come out** when they appear on a plant: *It's guaranteed to rain as soon as the flowers on the cranesbill come out.*

• *noun* **outcome**

The **outcome** of a series of events or actions is their final result: *No-one can tell, at this stage, what the outcome of the surgery will be.*

come out against

You **come out against** something when you openly declare your opposition to it: *Many of the country's leading newspapers have come out against the government's plans for the health service.*

come out in

You **come out in** spots when they appear on your skin: *Quick, put on the heater! It's so cold in here I'm coming out in goosepimples.*

come out of

You **come out of** an event or process in a certain position when that is the position you are in at the end of it: *The minister came out of the affair with his reputation untarnished.*

come out with (*informal*)

Someone **comes out with** a remark, especially a funny one, when they make it: *He often comes out with these peculiar expressions that no-one else understands.* ❑ *What will that child come out with next?* [*same as* **come away with** (*informal*)]

come over

1 Something such as a violent emotion **comes over** you when it suddenly affects you: *I'm so sorry for losing my temper; I don't know what came over me.* **2** (*informal*) You **come over** faint or dizzy when you suddenly feel as if you are going to faint. **3** Someone or something **comes over** in a certain way if they make that impression on people: *She came over as very intelligent and enthusiastic at the interview.* [*same as* **come across**]

come round

1 Someone **comes round** to an idea when they change their mind and accept it: *I knew she would eventually come round to our way of thinking.* **2** A particular season or event **comes round** or **around** when it occurs at its regular time: *I can hardly believe it's nearly Christmas time again; it seems to come round more and more quickly as I get older.* ❑ *We'll do some decorating when spring comes around.* **3** Someone who is unconscious **comes round** when they regain consciousness: *I saw his eyelids flicker; I think he's coming round.* [*same as* **come to**]

come through

1 You **come through** a difficult or dangerous event or period of time when you survive it: *You can't expect to come through an awful experience like the death of a child without being affected by it in some way.* **2** A particular quality or meaning **comes through** to you when you notice or observe it in what is happening: *The conductor's sensitivity to the changes of mood came through in her handling of the orchestra.* **3** Something such as a document that you have been waiting for **comes through** when it arrives: *The date for your driving test has come through.* **4** Sounds **come through** a radio receiver when you can hear them: *Okay, Harry, you're coming through loud and clear.*

come to

1 Someone who is unconscious **comes to** when they regain consciousness: *When he came to he found himself in a hospital bed.* [*same as* **come round**] **2** A bill **comes to** a certain amount when that is the amount arrived at when all the items on it are added together:

Surely you've made a mistake; what we've eaten can't possibly come to £65! [*same as* **add up to, amount to**] **3** You **come to** something that you have to deal with when you reach it after dealing with a series of others before that thing: *'What about the new computer equipment?' 'I was just coming to that.'* **4** You can also use **come to** to talk about how successful someone or something becomes, or how they turn out in the end: *We'd great plans for expanding the business, but they didn't come to anything.* ❑ *Accepting charity! Surely we haven't come to this?*

come together

1 When two people or things **come together** they join up with each other or move so that they are touching each other: *They came together in a passionate embrace.* **2** Two people or groups that have been in opposition to, or in conflict with, each other **come together** when they settle their differences: *Workers and management have at last come together to work out a solution to the dispute.*

come under

1 Something **comes under** a heading if it is in the section or category that has that heading: *Mystery novels come under 'crime fiction'.* ❑ *Would you say dictionaries come under 'General Reference' or 'Language'?* **2** Something **comes under** a certain body or authority if that body or authority controls it or has responsibility for it: *Public transport comes under the regional rather than the district council.*

come up

1 Something **is coming up** when it is about to happen or appear: *Coming up after the break, Robert de Niro in his very first television interview.* **2** Something **comes up** when it happens suddenly and unexpectedly: *I'm afraid something's come up and I won't be able to go after all.* **3** A message **comes up** on a computer screen when it appears there: *An error message came up when I tried to load the file.* **4** Something **comes up** in a conversation or discussion when it is mentioned; a question on a particular topic **comes up** in an examination paper when it is included in the paper: *The question of the trade deficit is bound to come up in today's Cabinet meeting.* ❑ *I hope you've done some revision on the life cycles of the butterfly and the frog; one of them always comes up in the biology paper.*

come up against

You **come up against** opposition or a difficulty when you are faced with it: *There's likely to be a bit of a delay in getting the work finished on time. We've come up against a bit of a problem.*

come up for

1 Something **comes up for** sale when it comes on to the market and can be bought: *The manuscript, which was believed for many years to be lost, is coming up for auction next week.* **2** When someone **is coming up for** a certain age they will soon be that age: *He's coming up for eighteen and will be able to vote in the next election.* [*same as* **approach**] **3** When someone in office **is coming up for** re-election they are due to be considered as a candidate in a forthcoming election: *The President will try to push the legislation through Congress before he comes up for re-election in 1996.* **4** Someone or something **is coming up for** a particular process when they will soon begin that process or are due to be dealt with by it: *The car's coming up for its road test soon.* ❑ *He doesn't have time to go out in the evening these days; he's coming up for his exams.*

come upon

You **come upon** something when you find it by chance: *I came upon this bundle of letters when I was sorting* *through her desk.* [*same as* **chance upon** (*formal*), **encounter**]

come up to

1 Someone **comes up to** you when they approach you, *eg* to speak to you: *The horse came up to me and nuzzled my face.* ❑ *A strange man came up to her in the street and asked her where she lived.* **2** If someone or something **comes up to** a required standard they meet that standard: *The meal didn't come up to expectations.* [= it wasn't as good as we expected it to be] **3** To **come up to** a time is to approach it: *She must be coming up to retirement age.* ❑ *It was coming up to ten o'clock by the time I left the office last night.*

come up with

You **come up with** an idea when you think of it; you **come up** with a suggestion when you make it: *Who was it that came up with the bright idea to have a barbecue in March?*

come with

1 Something **comes with** something else when that other thing accompanies it or is included with it: *The steak comes with salad and french fries.* ❑ *The estate comes with its own stretch of salmon river.* **2** Something **comes with** something else when it follows naturally from that other thing: *Good judgement comes with experience.*

come within

Something **comes within** view or range when it comes near enough to be seen or reached: *He was perched on the edge of the precipice waiting for one of the birds to come within reach.*

conceive /kən'siːv/: conceives, conceiving, conceived

conceive of (*formal*)

You can **conceive of** something when you can imagine it or believe that it might happen: *We could not conceive of a situation where it would be necessary to leave the house that had been in our family for generations.* [*same as* **envisage**]

condemn /kən'dɛm/: condemns, condemning, condemned

condemn to

Someone **is condemned to** a particular punishment, or some other very unpleasant thing, when they are given it, or are forced to do or endure it: *He was condemned to death in the electric chair.* ❑ *It seemed as if we were condemned to spend the whole day in traffic jams.*

cone /koun/: cones, coning, coned

cone off

Workmen or the police **cone off** a road or area of ground when they put large, usually orange, plastic cones there to prevent traffic coming on to it: *The outside lane was coned off and workmen were busy digging up the tarmac.*

confer /kən'fɜː(r)/: confers, conferring, conferred

confer on *or* confer upon

You **confer** some quality or characteristic **on** or **upon** someone when you say, or suggest by what you say, that they have that quality or characteristic: *The great majority of people had never heard of her and it is an exaggeration to say that she ever achieved the degree of notoriety conferred on her in his biography.*

confess /kən'fɛs/: confesses, confessing, confessed

confess to

You **confess to** something when you acknowledge that it is true by telling someone about it: *He has confessed to the crime.* ❑ *Anne confessed to having been in love with Gerald for years.*

confide /kən'faɪd/: **confides, confiding, confided**

confide in
You **confide in** someone when you tell them things that you have been keeping secret: *I'm the only person he feels he can trust and confide in.*

confront /kən'frʌnt/: **confronts, confronting, confronted**

confront with
You **confront** someone **with** an accusation or criticism when you force them to respond to it; you **are confronted with** problems or difficulties when you have to deal with them: *When we confront him with such convincing evidence, he's bound to admit that we were right.* ❑ *His plan never had any hope of success, confronted, as he was, with such overwhelming opposition.* [*same as* **face with**]

conjure /'kʌndʒə(r)/: **conjures, conjuring, conjured**

conjure up
1 You **conjure** something **up** when you make it appear, as if by magic: *Do you really expect me to conjure up a meal for four people with these ingredients?*
2 You **conjure up** an image of something when you create an image of it in your mind or when your words create the image of it in other people's minds: *The sound of the pipes conjures up images of misty Highland glens and men in kilts.* [*same as* **call up, evoke** (*formal*)]

conk /kɒŋk/: **conks, conking, conked**

conk out (*informal*)
Something such as an engine or an organ in body **conks out** when it suddenly stops working: *The engine's making funny noises; I hope it doesn't conk out on us.* ❑ *His heart just conked out.* [*same as* **give out** (*informal*), **pack in** (*informal*)]

connect /kə'nɛkt/: **connects, connecting, connected**

connect up
You **connect** two things **up**, or they **are connected up**, when you join one to the other to form a connection: *We won't be able to use any of our electrical appliances until we're connected up to the mains.*

connect with
A bus or airplane **connects with** some other form of transport when its arrival time is organized so that its passengers can continue their journey with a minimum of delay: *Our flight from London to Boston connects with an internal flight to St Louis.*

connive /kə'naɪv/: **connives, conniving, connived**

connive at
Someone **connives at** some offence or wrongdoing when they know about it and help the people who are carrying out the offence by doing nothing to stop it happening: *The chauffeur connived at the kidnap of his employer's small daughter.*

consist /kən'sɪst/: **consists, consisting, consisted**

consist in (*formal*)
Something **consists in** the thing that is its essential or most important meaning: *True romantic love consists in being prepared to sacrifice everything for the person you love.*

consort /kən'sɔːt/: **consorts, consorting, consorted**

consort with (*formal*)
You **consort with** people, especially criminals or an enemy in war, when you spend time in their company or are in contact with them, taking part in their activities, or giving them information:

Those who consort with the enemy will be guilty of treason.

consult /kən'sʌlt/: **consults, consulting, consulted**

consult with

1 (*especially AmE*) You **consult with** someone, especially your lawyer or doctor, when you ask their advice: *They had taken powers to consult with the auditors and accountants of individual banks.* **2** People **consult with** their colleagues or others of equal status when they discuss some question that concerns them all: *The president will be consulting with other heads of state to see if some common approach to sanctions can be agreed amongst them.*

contend /kən'tɛnd/: **contends, contending, contended**

contend with

You have a problem to **contend with** when you are faced with it and must deal with it: *I've got enough problems to contend with without you creating more for me.* [*same as* **put up with**]

contract /'kɒntrakt/: **contracts, contracting, contracted**

contract in

You **contract in** to something when you agree, formally and in writing, to take part or participate in it: *People who contracted in to the state earnings-related pension scheme will continue to receive a higher level of pension.*

contract out

1 You **contract out** of something when you agree, formally and in writing, not to take part or participate in it: *Is it possible to contract out of their occupational pension scheme?* **2** A business or organization **contracts out** work when they make a contract with another business or individual to carry it out: *Usually they act as project managers contracting out the work to various specialist firms.*

converge /kən'vɜːdʒ/: **converges, converging, converged**

converge on

A number of people or things **converge on** a particular point when they all move towards it from different directions: *Thousands of New Age travellers converged on Stonehenge for the summer solstice.*

cook /kuk/: **cooks, cooking, cooked**

cook up (*informal*)

1 You **cook up** an excuse when you invent it: *When he was late for school, he cooked up this incredible story about the wheels falling off the bus.* **2** You **cook up** something such as a plan or scheme when you form or create it: *Most of the theories may seem outlandish curiosities, cooked up by teachers of literature who need to seem professional, or powerful.*

cool /kuːl/: **cools, cooling, cooled**

cool down

Someone **cools down** when they become calm after being angry: *Wait until he's cooled down a bit before you broach the subject again.*

cool off

You **cool off** when you become less warm, or less angry or excited: *The sun's too hot; I'm going for a swim to cool off.* ❑ *He lost his temper with one of the other kids so we put him in a room by himself to cool off.*

coop /kuːp/: **coops, cooping, cooped**

coop up (*usually in the passive*)

You **are cooped up** somewhere when you are shut in a small space: *He was cooped up all day in a tiny windowless* *office.* [*same as* **confine, imprison**]

cop /kɒp/: **cops**, **copping**, **copped**

cop out (*slang*)
You **cop out** when you avoid making a difficult decision or doing something risky: *Don't worry. This time I'm not going to cop out of telling her.*
• *noun* **cop-out**: **cop-outs**: *In the end the Bill was simply a cop-out which failed to address the problem in any constructive way.* ❑ *'I'm going to get someone else to do it for me.' 'Don't do that, it would be a cop-out.'*

copy /ˈkɒpɪ/: **copies**, **copying**, **copied**

copy down
You **copy down** what someone has said or written, or you **copy** it **down**, when you write it down exactly: *I copied down the figures from the blackboard in my maths jotter.*

copy out
You **copy out** something that has been written or printed, or you **copy** it **out**, when you write it out in full: *She copied out the whole letter for me in her impeccable handwriting.*

cordon /ˈkɔːdən/: **cordons**, **cordoning**, **cordoned**

cordon off
An area **is cordoned off** when some sort of official barrier is put around it, *eg* by the police, so that ordinary members of the public are prevented from entering it: *One end of the enclosure had been cordoned off and only owners and trainers were allowed into it.*

cork /kɔːk/: **corks**, **corking**, **corked**

cork up
To **cork up** a bottle is to close it by putting a cork into the opening in its neck: *This wine is bad; cork it up and take it back to the shop.*

correspond /kɒrɪˈspɒnd/: **corresponds**, **corresponding**, **corresponded**

correspond to *or* **correspond with**
One thing **corresponds to** another, or **corresponds with** it, when the one matches or is equivalent to the other: *This signature doesn't correspond to the one on your credit card.* ❑ *The forensic evidence didn't correspond with his theory about what had happened.*

cotton /ˈkɒtən/: **cottons**, **cottoning**, **cottoned**

cotton on (*informal*)
You **cotton on** to something when you realize what is happening or you understand it, especially after a time: *It took her ages to cotton on to the fact that we didn't want her to come with us.* ❑ *I kept hinting that Maria fancied him but he didn't cotton on.*

couch /kaʊtʃ/: **couches**, **couching**, **couched**

couch in
Something **is couched in** a stated type of language when it is expressed in that way: *explanations couched in the vocabulary of physics and neurochemistry.*

cough /kɒf/: **coughs**, **coughing**, **coughed**

cough up
1 You **cough up** mucus or blood when you bring it from your throat or lungs into your mouth by coughing. **2** (*informal*) **a** Someone **coughs up** when they give you the money that they owe you: *Where we got the money for it, I'm not sure. Perhaps Malcolm coughed up.* [compare **come across**] **b** Someone **coughs** something **up** when they tell it

to someone else: *'You're wondering something, boy; cough it up, spit it out, vomit it forth. In short, tell me.'* [*same as* **spit out**]

count /kaunt/: **counts, counting, counted**

---

count against
Something such as your age or lack of experience **counts against** you if you are rejected or penalized by others because of it: *You're certainly well enough qualified, but your lack of practical experience may count against you.*

count among
You **count** a particular person **among** your friends or the people who are like you when you consider that they are one of them: *When I have suffered as they have suffered, then I shall count myself among them.*

count down
You **count** something **down** when you prepare it by counting backwards from *eg* the number 10 so that it is ready to start when you reach zero: *A disembodied voice was counting down the seconds to launch.*

• *noun* **countdown**: **countdowns**

A **countdown** is the period of time that it takes to count backwards from a certain number to the number zero, or any fixed period of time just before an event is scheduled to happen: *the countdown to Christmas* ❑ *After a countdown from a minor celebrity, thousands of visitors rushed into the hall.*

count for
When you say that something **counts for** nothing or doesn't **count for** anything, you mean that it has no value or importance: *She said her parents liked him tremendously and surely that must count for something in this day and age!*

count in
You **count** someone **in** when you include them in an activity: *If you're looking for people to crew your yacht, count me in.* [*opposite* **count out**]

count on
1 You can **count on** or **upon** someone when you can rely on them: *I'm counting on Nancy being there to help.* ❑ *The Times could be counted upon for lengthy discussions of cricket and Rugby Union.* **2** You **count on** something when you are so sure that it will happen or be the case that you take account of it in your plans: *'I'm sure your father will lend us the money.' 'I wouldn't count on it if I were you.'* ❑ *We should count on taking at least three days to get there.*

count out
1 You **count out** an amount of money when you count the notes and coins one by one to find their total value: *He took a tin box out of the safe and counted out £5.50 in fifty pence pieces.* **2** When you ask people to **count** you **out** you are asking them not to include you in a scheme or activity: *'We're staging a sit-in at the university tomorrow.' 'Oh, are you indeed? Well, you can count me out.'* [*opposite* **count in**] **3** A boxer or wrestler **is counted out** when they are no longer allowed to continue with a fight because the referee has reached a count of ten while they are injured or knocked out.

count towards
In American English **count toward** is also used.

Something **counts towards** something when it makes a contribution to it: *the first event to count toward Ryder Cup qualification* ❑ *All such borrowings count towards the public sector borrowing requirement.*

count up
You **count up** all the things in a group or set when you add them all together to find the total: *Count up the number of days you've had off and I think you'll*

find you've used up your holiday entitlement for this year. [*same as* **add up, tot up** (*informal*)]

count upon see **count on**

couple /ˈkʌpəl/: **couples, coupling, coupled**

couple together
Two or more things **are coupled together** when they are joined or connected to each other: *The rigs slid rapidly into the dark water to be coupled together in twos and threes.*

couple with
One thing **is coupled with** another when the one is joined or connected with the other: *The prolonged delay, coupled with low spirits caused by cold, squalor, and hunger, had created a feeling of hopeless desperation.*

course /kɔːs/: **courses, coursing, coursed**

course down
If tears **are coursing down** someone's cheeks, they are flowing down their cheeks in a continuous stream.

course through
Your blood **courses through** your veins when it is pumped around your body quickly, especially after exercise.

cover /ˈkʌvə(r)/: **covers, covering, covered**

cover in
You **cover** an open area **in** when you put a covering over the top of it *eg* so that it is protected from the weather: *Pull the tarpaulin over so the hole is covered in.*

cover over
To **cover** something **over** is to cover it with something so that it cannot be seen or is no longer exposed: *If it rains the entire playing area can be covered over in seconds with an enormous electronically-operated roof.*

cover up
1 You **cover** something **up** when you put something over it to protect or hide it: *She lay down on the sofa and covered herself up with a rug.* ❑ *Make sure the delicate new growth is covered up at night to avoid frost damage.* ❑ *You're nearly naked! For goodness sake, cover yourself up.* **2** You **cover up** something dishonest or embarrassing when you try to hide it and prevent people from finding out about it: *She likes to cover up the truth like she covers up a naked light.* ❑ *Try as they might, they can't cover up the fact that he is a painter of no technical mastery, no intuitive feeling for pictorial space.* [*same as* **disguise**] **3** You **cover up** for someone else who has done something wrong when you try to prevent other people from finding them out: *Cameron covered up for Gillies without thinking it out.*
• *noun* **cover-up**: **cover-ups**
When there is a **cover-up** action is taken to prevent people finding out about something, especially something illegal, embarrassing, or dishonest: *The opposition is alleging that there has been a government cover-up.*

crack /krak/: **cracks, cracking, cracked**

crack down on
The authorities **crack down on** something when they take firm action to prevent or control it: *The Department of Social Security is cracking down on benefit fraud.*
• *noun* **crackdown**: **crackdowns**: *He was arrested during one of the government's periodic crackdowns on political dissidents.*

crack up
1 Someone **cracks up** when they have a nervous breakdown: *I don't seem to be able to handle stress anymore; I think I'm cracking up.* **2** (*informal*) Someone **cracks up** when they lose control of their emotions and become

extremely upset or angry: *Your father'll crack up when he sees the mess you've made!*

cram /kram/: **crams**, **cramming**, **crammed**

cram into
You **cram** something **into** a small space when you press it roughly into that space: *He crammed everything into a small battered suitcase and took off as quickly as he could.*

crane /kreɪn/: **cranes**, **craning**, **craned**

crane forward
You **crane forward** when you stretch your neck as far as it will go in order to look at something: *Like a helmsman in a storm, her head craned forward to peer past the flailing windscreen wipers at the road ahead.*

crank /kraŋk/: **cranks**, **cranking**, **cranked**

crank up
You **crank** a mechanism or engine **up** when you use an L-shaped bar called a crank to turn it and so make it operate: *The skunk then starts swaying its body back and forth as if cranking itself up for action.*

crash /kraʃ/: **crashes**, **crashing**, **crashed**

crash about *or* **crash around**
A person or animal **crashes about** or **around** when they move about clumsily and heavily, breaking or knocking things over as they go: *We couldn't see the elephants but we could hear them crashing about in the undergrowth.*

crash down
Something comes **crashing down** when it makes loud crashing sounds as it falls: *The shelves came crashing down scattering books and bric-a-brac all over the study floor.*

crash out (*informal*)
You **crash out** when you lie down and go to sleep, especially when you are extremely tired: *He staggered upstairs and crashed out without even getting undressed first.* ❑ *You can crash out on the sofa if you want.*

crawl /krɔːl/: **crawls**, **crawling**, **crawled**

crawl with
A place **is crawling with** live insects when it is full of them or covered with them: *We couldn't sunbathe because the whole place was crawling with ants and little biting flies.*

cream /kriːm/: **creams**, **creaming**, **creamed**

cream off
People or organizations **cream off** the best or most desirable parts from something when they select or take those and leave the rest: *The system is designed to cream off the most able pupils and concentrate resources on them, at the expense of the rest.*

crease /kriːs/: **creases**, **creasing**, **creased**

crease up
People **crease up**, or **crease up** with laughter, when something makes them laugh a lot: *When he made funny faces behind the teacher's back, we all creased up.*

credit /ˈkrɛdɪt/: **credits**, **crediting**, **credited**

credit with
1 You **credit** someone **with** a desirable quality such as commonsense when you think or assume that they have it: *I'm very disappointed in you; I had credited*

you with a little more imagination. **2** A person **is credited with** something such as an invention or improvement when they are publicly recognized as the person who has introduced it or developed it: *John Logie Baird, the Scotsman credited with the invention of television.*

creep /kriːp/: **creeps**, **creeping**, **crept** /krɛpt/

creep in
To **creep in** is to move in quietly and slowly, without attracting attention: *I turned the key in the door and crept in.* ❑ *Fog was creeping in off the sea.*

creep into
A particular feeling or tone **creeps into** something when it appears gradually: *A note of panic crept into her voice.*

creep up on
You **creep up on** someone when you move up behind them slowly and carefully without making a sound, so as to surprise or startle them: *He crept up on me and said 'boo!'.*

crisp /krɪsp/: **crisps**, **crisping**, **crisped**

crisp up
Something **crisps up**, or **is crisped up**, when it becomes, or is made crisp, or becomes or is made crisp again after becoming soft: *Turn the oven up to a high heat to crisp up the crackling on the roast pork.*

crop /krɒp/: **crops**, **cropping**, **cropped**

crop up
Something **crops up** when it occurs or appears, especially unexpectedly: *One or two problems have cropped up since our last meeting.* ❑ *We won't be able to come to your anniversary party; something's cropped up.* [*same as* **come up**]

cross /krɒs/: **crosses**, **crossing**, **crossed**

cross off
You **cross** a word or name **off** a list when you draw a line through it to indicate that it is no longer on the list: *If he doesn't apologise for what he did, I'll be crossing him off my Christmas card list.*

cross out
You **cross out** a word or letter in a text when you draw a line through it to get rid of it or replace it with another: *End the letter with 'Yours sincerely, William Grant'. No, on second thoughts, cross that out and put in 'Regards, Bill'.*

cross over
You **cross over** when you move to the other side of something: *They crossed over to the Italian side of the border.*

cross with
Farmers and animal breeders **cross** one breed of animal **with** another when they allow them to breed with each other so that they produce young that have a mixture of characteristics from both parents: *Traditional British breeds have been crossed with Continental breeds of cattle like the Charolais to increase their meat yield.*

crowd /kraud/: **crowds**, **crowding**, **crowded**

crowd around *or* crowd round
People **crowd around** or **round** someone or something when they gather together to form a large tightly-packed group around them: *Protestors were crowding round the Prime Minister shouting abuse.*

crowd in
People **crowd in** when a large number of them try to get in to a place at the same time: *The manager opened the doors at last and hundreds of eager bargain-hunters crowded in.*

crowd in on
People or things **crowd in on** you when they surround you in large numbers so that you feel overwhelmed by them: *With the problems that were crowding in on him, he felt trapped, crushed, defeated*

crowd into
People **crowd into** a place when large numbers of them try to get into it at once: *They were crowded into a small hall.*

crowd out
You **are crowded out** when people force you out of a place by taking up all the available space: *You must never allow yourself to be crowded out, neither must you retreat so far that you overstep the area boundary.* [*same as* **squeeze out**]

crumble /ˈkrʌmbəl/: crumbles, crumbling, crumbled

crumble away
Something, such as stone or wood, that is normally a solid mass **crumbles away** when it breaks down into small pieces: *The wood below the waterline was spongy and rotten: she could see it crumbling away in his hands.* ❑ *The few inches of rock beneath his feet threatened to crumble away.*

crumple /ˈkrʌmpəl/: crumples, crumpling, crumpled

crumple up
You **crumple** *eg* paper **up** when you crush or squeeze it in your hand to form a tight wrinkled ball; something **crumples up** when it collapses or is crushed into a series of wrinkles or folds: *I found the letter crumpled up in the wastepaper basket.* ❑ *Her face crumpled up, and she began to wail loudly.*

crush /krʌʃ/: crushes, crushing, crushed

crush in *or* crush into
People or things **are crushed in** when they are squashed up in a space that is too small; people or things **are crushed into** a space that is too small when they are squeezed or squashed into that space: *He was crushed in in a corner of the lift.* ❑ *Men, women, and children were crushed into cattle trucks.*

crush up
You **crush** something **up** when you reduce it to a powder by hitting it or pressing down on it with a heavy weight: *His mother crushed up the tablet and fed it to him in a spoonful of jam.*

cry /kraɪ/: cries, crying, cried

cry down
You **cry** something **down** when you talk about it in a way that makes it seem unimportant: *You have to battle against all those who would cry down your attempts to improve things.* [*same as* **denigrate** (*formal*)]

cry off
You **cry off** when you say you are not going to do something that you had previously arranged or agreed to do: *I know I said I would be there but I'm afraid I'm going to have to cry off.* ❑ *We were expecting Jane to come but she cried off at the last minute.*

cry out
You **cry out** when you shout or scream suddenly and loudly because you feel pain or want to get someone's attention: *Sometimes at night he'd cry out in his sleep.* ❑ *Someone cried out 'Where's the medic?'* ❑ *I draw in my breath and cry out for her: 'Mama! Mama!'*

• *noun* **outcry**: **outcries**

When there is an **outcry** about something many people object loudly and publicly about it.

cry out for
You can say that one thing **is crying**

out for another when it urgently needs or greatly deserves it: *human rights abuses crying out for justice* ❑ *What this party is crying out for is some decent music and a few extra bottles of wine.*

cuddle /ˈkʌdəl/: **cuddles, cuddling, cuddled**

cuddle up *or* **cuddle in**
You **cuddle up** to someone, or **cuddle in**, when you sit or lie close to them and hold them close: *She went in to check on the children and found them all cuddled up in bed.* ❑ *Come on, cuddle in and keep yourself warm.* [*same as* **snuggle up**]

cull /kʌl/: **culls, culling, culled**

cull from (*formal*)
You **cull** information **from** a number of sources when you take the bits of information you want from those sources: *All the secrets of his past life had been culled from police records in three continents, and from various victims of his frauds.*

culminate /ˈkʌlmɪneɪt/: **culminates, culminating, culminated**

culminate in (*formal*)
To **culminate in** something is to have that thing as the end or climax: *The whole sorry affair culminated in his being forced from office.* [*same as* **end in**]

curl /kɜːl/: **curls, curling, curled**

curl up
1 Something that is normally flat or straight **curls up** when its edges bend towards the centre: *The leaves had dried out and curled up in the heat of the sun.* **2** You **curl up** when you lie comfortably with your body bent round and your arms and legs drawn close to your body: *I just want to curl up in a chair and go to sleep.* **3** (*informal*) When someone says they **curled up** with embarrassment they mean that they were so embarrassed they instinctively made their body into as small a shape as possible so that they might not be seen: *When he said I was his sweet little pudding I just wanted to curl up and die.*

curtain /ˈkɜːtən/: **curtains, curtaining, curtained**

curtain off
You **curtain off** an area within a room when you put a curtain around it to separate it from the rest of the room: *We can curtain off this part of the room to give you a little more privacy.*

cut /kʌt/: **cuts, cutting, cut**

cut across
1 You **cut across** an area when you make your route shorter by crossing it: *We could get ahead of them if we cut across this field.* **2** Something **cuts across** the divisions between opposing groups when it affects all groups equally or forms a link between them: *There was potential here to cut across established Green-Orange divisions.*

cut away
You **cut** something **away** when you remove it by cutting: *The surgeon cut away all the diseased tissue.*

cut back
1 You **cut back**, or **cut back** spending, when you spend less money: *We've had to cut back a great deal since my husband lost his job. There are no expensive holidays now and we can't afford a new car.* **2** A plant, tree or shrub **is cut back** when most or all of its branches or stems are cut off: *You can cut it right back to the old wood without damaging it.*

cut back on
You **cut back on** something when you spend less money, or no money, on it;

you **cut back on** the total number of people or things when you reduce them: *The company is being forced to cut back on staff because of the recession.*

cut down

1 You **cut** a tree **down** when you cut or saw through its trunk so that it falls to the ground. [*same as* **fell**] **2** You **cut** something **down** when you reduce it in amount: *We'll have to find ways of cutting down our expenses.* ❑ *You'll have to cut down your beer-drinking if you want to lose weight.* ❑ *If we cut the text down we should be able to fit it into 400 pages.*

cut down on

You **cut down on** food or drink when you eat or drink less; you **cut down on** an activity when you do it less: *If you're really serious about lowering your blood pressure you'll have to cut down on smoking, or best of all, stop altogether.*

cut in

1 Someone **cuts in**, or **cuts in** on a conversation, when they interrupt: *'Wait a minute, I don't think you've got that right,' cut in Jack.* ❑ *If I could just cut in for a moment, I'll put you right on that last point.* ❑ *The operator cut in on our telephone conversation to tell me there was another call waiting.* [*same as* **interrupt**] **2** If someone else **cuts in** when you are dancing with someone, they take your partner and continue the dance leaving you without a partner: *I haven't had a chance to dance with Carrie all evening. Do you mind if I cut in?*

cut into

1 You **cut into** something when you make a cut in it by pushing the blade of a knife or other sharp implement into it: *You'll only be able to tell if the fruit is evenly distributed when you cut into the cake.* ❑ *The girth was so tight it was cutting into the horse's flesh.* **2** One thing **cuts into** another when it invades it or reduces the time available for it: *All these interruptions are cutting into the time left for checking and revising.*

cut off

1 You **cut** something **off** when you remove it by cutting: *Cut the fat off the meat before you cook it.* ❑ *You can see in this self-portrait the bandage where he cut his own ear off.* **2** One thing or person **is cut off** from others that they are normally linked to when they are separated or isolated from them: *Many of the smaller villages have been completely cut off by snow.* ❑ *She deliberately cut herself off from her family.* **3** A supply of something **is cut off** when it is stopped: *The electricity will be cut off during the repair work.* ❑ *If you don't pay your bill the gas company will cut you off.* **4** You **are cut off** while talking on the telephone to someone when you lose contact with them because the connection is broken: *We were cut off just when she was telling me some juicy gossip.* [*same as* **disconnect**]

• *noun* **offcut**: **offcuts**

Offcuts are small pieces that have been cut or trimmed off something larger, such as a carpet or piece of wood: *They'd ingeniously carpeted the little study with offcuts from all the other rooms.*

cut out

1 You **cut** something **out** when you cut around its edge to remove it from the object or material that it is part of: *I cut this article out of the newspaper for you.* ❑ *She was kneeling on the floor cutting out a dress.* ❑ *The peaches will taste perfectly okay if you cut out the mouldy bits.* **2** You **cut** something **out** of a text when you remove or delete it: *If you cut this last paragraph out, the essay will be much improved* ❑ *All references to her husband had been cut out of her autobiography.* **3** (*informal*) **a** You **cut** something **out** when you stop doing it: *I've felt a lot better since I cut out smoking.* **b** When someone says **'cut** it **out!'** or **'cut** that **out!'** to you, they are telling you angrily to stop doing whatever you are doing: *Come on now, cut that out! You're splashing water all over the floor.* [*same as* **give up**] **4** An engine **cuts out** when it suddenly stops working: *The engine keeps cutting out. What do you think's wrong with it?*

cut out for (*informal*)

You **are cut out for** a particular job or activity when you are suited to it: *She found after a couple of months that she wasn't really cut out for life in the country.*

cut through

1 You **cut through** something when you make a cut in it from one side to the other, or divide it by cutting: *You'll need a saw rather than secateurs if you want to cut through that thick branch.* ❑ *When he examined the brake pipe he found it had been completely cut through.* **2** Something **cuts through** something when it moves through it easily: *The old sailing ship made a magnificent sight as it cut through the waves.* **3** You **cut through** somewhere when you shorten your journey by going through it: *If you cut through the school playing-fields you'll get there five minutes earlier.* **4** You **cut through** something that is delaying your progress when you find a quick way to get round it: *He seems able to cut through all the government red tape and gets things done quickly.*

cut up

1 You **cut** something **up** when you divide it into pieces by cutting: *Thinking she was still at home with the children she absentmindedly cut her husband's meat up for him.* **2** (*informal*) You **are cut up about** something if you are upset about it: *She was very cut up about failing her driving test.*

d

dab /dab/: **dabs**, **dabbing**, **dabbed**

dab at

You **dab at** something when you touch it several times with light quick movements: *She dabbed at the cut with some cotton wool soaked in antiseptic.* ❑ *Gloria wrapped a corner of the hanky round her index finger and dabbed at Dot's cheeks until they were sore.*

dab off

You **dab** something **off** when you remove it by touching it with light gentle strokes *eg* using a soft cloth or cotton wool: *She was trying to dab the spilled wine off her blouse with her table napkin.*

dab on

You **dab** something **on** when you apply it to a surface with light quick movements of your fingers: *Anthea had her hair scraped back and was dabbing some sort of thick cream on her forehead and cheeks.*

dabble /ˈdabəl/: **dabbles**, **dabbling**, **dabbled**

dabble in

You **dabble in** an activity when you take part in it, take an interest in it, or work at it without getting too deeply or seriously involved in it: *She's interested in old pagan rituals and it's said that she has even dabbled in witchcraft.* [*same as* **dip into**]

dally /ˈdalɪ/: **dallies**, **dallying**, **dallied**

dally with

1 You **dally with** an idea when you consider it in a casual rather than a serious way: *I've often dallied with the idea of starting a market garden, but have never really done anything practical to make it happen.* [*same as* **toy with**] **2** (*old*) Someone **dallies with** a person of the opposite sex when they give that person the impression that they want a romantic relationship with them, but really have no serious intentions towards them. [*same as* **flirt with**]

dam /dam/: **dams**, **damming**, **dammed**

dam up

1 To **dam up** a river or stream is to build a dam across it, or to block it in some other way, so that the water is held up: *Only a trickle of dirty water ran in the bed of the stream below the point where it had been dammed up by rubbish.* **2** When someone **dams up** strong feelings they make a great effort not to show them, often doing so for a long time and putting themselves under a great deal of mental strain as a result: *She broke down at last, all the grief and frustration that had been dammed up for so long pouring out in helpless sobs.* [*same as* **bottle up**]

damp /damp/: **damps**, **damping**, **damped**

damp down

1 You **damp down** a fire when you put *eg* water or ash on it so that it stops burning so fiercely, or stops burning altogether: *The firefighters having been forced to draw back from the main building restricted their efforts to keeping the outbuildings damped down.* ❑ *The fire was nearly out but firemen continued to play their hoses on it to damp down the smouldering embers.* **2** You **damp down**, or **dampen down**, something that is dry or too dry when you put a small amount of water on it, often so that it can be more easily made smooth and flat: *Dampening down his hair with water and putting on aftershave was all he did to prepare for their date.* **3** If someone or something **damps down**, or **dampens down**, *eg* strong or violent feelings such as anger or enthusiasm, it has the effect of controlling or reducing their strength and intensity: *Brain dysfunction due to the effects of drugs or toxins damping down electrical activity will lead to disturbance or loss of consciousness.*

dampen /'dampən/: dampens, dampening, dampened

dampen down see damp down

dart /dɑːt/: darts, darting, darted

dart about *or* dart around

To **dart about** or **around** is to move quickly and lightly from place to place: *He sat on the river bank watching the swallows darting about as they gathered food for their chicks.* ❑ *His eyes darted around before he slipped a couple of bottles under his coat.*

dash /daʃ/: dashes, dashing, dashed

dash against

When something **is dashed against** a hard surface it is thrown there with such force that it breaks or is badly damaged: *The flimsy little boat was dashed to pieces against the rocks.* ❑ *The boy was flung forward dashing his head against the metal rail.*

dash off

1 You **dash off** when you go somewhere in a great hurry: *Where are you dashing off to?* [*same as* **rush off**] **2** You **dash off** something in writing when you write it very quickly without thinking too much about its presentation or content: *He dashed off a short reply thanking her for her invitation.*

date /deɪt/: dates, dating, dated

date back

Something **dates back** to a particular time in the past if that is when it began or was made: *His emotional problems date back to the day when his father walked out of the family home and never came back.* ❑ *These fossils are thought to date back as far as the Cambrian era.*

• *verb* **backdate: backdates, backdating, backdated**

When you **backdate** something such as a cheque you give it the date of a day before the actual date of writing; something **is backdated** when it begins or is put into effect from a date before the current date: *I was surprised to learn that my claim for invalidity benefit could not be backdated to the time of the accident.*

date from

Something **dates from** a specific time in the past if it began then, or was first made or used then: *Parts of the castle date from the 11th century.*

daub /dɔːb/: daubs, daubing, daubed

daub on

To **daub on** paint or some other soft or sticky substance is to put it on a surface roughly or carelessly in large uneven patches: *She was daubing on great blotches of red and orange, seemingly at random.* [*same as* **slap on**]

daub with

You **daub** something **with** *eg* paint or mud when you cover it with uneven patches or streaks of it: *The soldiers daubed their faces with mud so that they couldn't be seen so easily in the dark.*

dawn /dɔːn/: **dawns**, **dawning**, **dawned**

dawn on *or* dawn upon

A fact or the truth **dawns on** or **upon** someone when they suddenly or gradually realize or understand it: *Annabel was nowhere to be seen, and then it dawned on him that she had never intended to come.*

deal /diːl/: **deals**, **dealing**, **dealt** /dɛlt/

deal in

1 A person or company **deals in** a certain type of goods if they buy and sell them: *He made his fortune dealing in arms.* [*same as* **trade in**] **2 a** In card games, someone **is dealt in** when the dealer gives them the appropriate number of cards so that they can join in the game. **b** (*informal*) When a group of people plan to do something together and you want to join in on it, you can ask them to **deal** you **in**: *As long as you're going to go by car rather than on foot, you can deal me in.*

deal out

1 You **deal out** punishment or justice when you administer it or inflict it on people: *The courts have been dealing out stiff sentences to people found guilty of violent crimes.* [*same as* **hand out, mete out** (*formal*), **dispense**] **2** You **deal out** playing cards when you divide them among the players, or give each player the appropriate number of cards needed to play a particular game.

deal with

1 You **deal with** situations, problems, people, or other matters when you attend to them or take whatever action is necessary or appropriate in the circumstances: *Leave it to me; I'll deal with it.* ❑ *He's not very good at dealing with crises.* ❑ *What are the police doing to deal with the ever-increasing problem of drugs in Britain's inner cities?* ❑ *Have you dealt with those invoices yet, Miss Arnold?* ❑ *You'll be dealing with the public in this job so you should have a pleasant manner and a smart appearance.* ❑ *It's proved to be a particularly difficult problem to deal with.* **2** A book, article, speech or film **deals with** a particular subject or topic when that is what it is about: *The last two sections of the novel dealt with her attempt to rediscover herself.* ❑ *Her books deal mainly with feminist issues.* **3** You **deal with** a particular shop or business organization when you use their services or do business with them: *We've always dealt with Brodies' in the past.*

debar /dɪˈbɑː(r)/: **debars**, **debarring**, **debarred**

debar from (*formal*)

You **are debarred from** doing something when a rule or law prevents you from doing it: *His age debarred him from joining the army.* ❑ *She was effectively debarred from making any public statements.* [*same as* **shut out, exclude, prohibit**]

deceive /dɪˈsiːv/: **deceives**, **deceiving**, **deceived**

deceive into

You **are deceived into** doing or believing something when someone intentionally misleads you into doing or believing it: *She was deceived into signing the agreement by an unscrupulous salesman who told her it was a safe investment.* ❑ *The people were deceived into thinking that there was no alternative to war.*

decide /dɪˈsaɪd/: **decides**, **deciding**, **decided**

decide against

You **decide against** something when you make a choice not to do it or have it: *We thought about having double glazing, but when we saw what it would cost we decided against it.*

decide for

You **decide** something **for** someone when you make a decision about it on their behalf: *I can't make up my mind; you decide for me.* ❑ *He suggests that the scheme will give freedom of choice to people who are used to having most things decided for them.*

decide on *or* decide upon

You **decide on** or **upon** something when you choose that thing from amongst others: *Have you decided on a name for your baby yet?*

deck /dɛk/: decks, decking, decked

deck out *or* deck up

A place **is decked out** with colourful or attractive things for a special occasion when it is decorated with them; you **deck** yourself **out**, or **deck** yourself **up**, when you put on elaborate clothes: *The church was decked out with fruit and flowers for the harvest festival.* ❑ *They'd decked themselves out in beads and bangles.*

deck with

Something **is decked with** things when it is decorated all over with them: *a huge Christmas tree decked with gifts wrapped in brightly-coloured paper* ❑ *a barge decked with gaily-coloured streamers.*

declare /dɪ'klɛə(r)/: declares, declaring, declared

declare against

1 You **declare against** someone or something when you publicly announce your opposition to them: *More and more small landowners were declaring against the proposed reforms.* [*same as* **come out against**] **2** One country **declares** war **against** another when one announces publicly that they are officially at war with the other: *The United States immediately declared war against Japan.*

declare for

You **declare for** someone or something when you publicly announce your support for them: *The local branch has declared for the resumption of industrial action.* [*same as* **come out in favour of**]

dedicate /'dɛdɪkeit/: dedicates, dedicating, dedicated

dedicate to

1 You **dedicate** yourself **to** a particular cause or course of action when you give a lot of time and effort to it, because you believe it is worthwhile: *He dedicated himself to improving the lives of orphaned and abandoned children.* [*same as* **devote to**] **2** Something, especially a book, play or film **is dedicated to** a particular person or group of people when it is written, performed or produced in their honour, or to honour their memory: *The poem was dedicated to his mother.* ❑ *He dedicated it to his mother.*

defer /dɪ'fɜː(r)/: defers, deferring, deferred

defer to

You **defer to** someone, or **to** their experience, when you accept their opinion, or do as they want, out of respect for them or because you believe that they are right: *They were the sort of people who twenty-five years ago would have been deferred to because they were gents.*

delight /dɪ'laɪt/: delights, delighting, delighted

delight in

You **delight in** something, often something that causes hurt or embarrassment to others, if you enjoy it or get great pleasure from it: *She seems to delight in making him seems* *ridiculous in front of his friends.* ❑ *He delighted in his new-found freedom.*

deliver /dɪ'lɪvə(r)/: delivers, delivering, delivered

deliver of (*formal*)

1 A woman **is delivered of** a baby when she gives birth to it with the help of a doctor or midwife: *Mrs Fenchurch was safely delivered of twins at midnight on Wednesday.* **2** You **deliver** yourself **of** an opinion or speech when you state or make it in a self-important way: *Having delivered himself of these pearls of wisdom, he sat back with a smug smile.*

deliver up (*formal*)

You **deliver** something **up** to someone when you hand it over to them, especially when they have asked or ordered you to do so: *All the assets must be delivered up to the official receiver or trustee in bankruptcy.*

delve /dɛlv/: delves, delving, delved

delve in *or* delve into

You **delve in,** or **delve into** something, when you search through it thoroughly trying to find something: *He delved into his coat pocket and pulled out a ball of string.* ❑ *Campbell's been delving in some of the old parish records and has come up with some very interesting information about his family's history.* ❑ *If you just delve in any old way, it takes ages to find anything.*

depart /dɪ'pɑːt/: departs, departing, departed

depart from

You **depart from** an accepted or usual course of action or practise when you stop following it and do something different: *This year we have departed from our usual end-of-session programme and are having the prizegiving on the second last day of term.* ❑ *The minister departed from his prepared text to respond to journalists' questions.* [*same as* **deviate from** (*formal*)]

depend /dɪ'pɛnd/: depends, depending, depended

depend on *or* depend upon

1 You can **depend on** or **upon** someone when you can trust them to do what they have said they will do or when you can rely on them to behave in a certain way: *We can always depend on Ken to come up with a sensible solution.* ❑ *We did use that firm for a while but we found they just couldn't be depended on to turn up when they said they would.* ❑ *Are you certain that their support can be depended upon?* [*same as* **count on**] **2** You **depend on** someone or something when you rely on them to provide you with what you need to survive: *Many charities depend on the small donations they get from the general public.* **3** One thing **depends on** another when it is decided by or varies according to that other thing: *The amount you pay in council tax depends on the value of your house.*

deprive /dɪ'praɪv/: deprives, depriving, deprived

deprive of

You **are deprived of** something when it is taken away from you or you are prevented from having or using it: *He's been deprived of love and affection since early childhood.* ❑ *a whole section of society who have been deprived of their basic human rights.*

derive /dɪ'raɪv/: derives, deriving, derived

derive from (*formal*)

1 a You **derive** *eg* pleasure or satisfaction **from** something if you get pleasure or satisfaction from it: *I know she derives a lot of pleasure from the knowledge that her daughters are happily settled.* **b** You **derive** something **from** a particular source when you obtain it from that source: *Michael derived most of his income from rented* *property.* **2** One thing **is derived from** another when that is its source or origin or where it came from: *one of the many products derived from petroleum* ❑ *It's been given a local name 'fuglica' derived from Old Norse 'fugl' meaning bird.* ❑ *prejudices that derive from middle-class notions of respectability.*

descend /dɪ'sɛnd/: **descends, descending, descended**

descend from
You **are descended from** the people who are your ancestors: *He's descended from a long line of distinguished soldiers and politicians.*

descend on *or* **descend upon** (*informal*)
People **descend on** you when they arrive unexpectedly at your house to visit or stay: *I hope you don't mind us descending on you like this.*

descend to
You **descend to** some form of unpleasant or dishonourable behaviour when you lower your standards and behave in that way: *I was never really convinced that he was as wonderful as everyone else seemed to think he was, but I never thought he would descend to fraud and deception.*

despair /dɪ'spɛə(r)/: **despairs, despairing, despairs**

despair of
You **despair of** something when you lose hope that it will ever happen: *He was beginning to despair of ever finding a way out of his financial difficulties.*

deter /dɪ'tɜː(r)/: **deters, deterring, deterred**

deter from (*formal*)
You **are deterred from** doing something that you had previously wanted to do when something makes you feel that you no longer want to do it: *I don't think identity cards would deter poeple from travelling without tickets.* ❑ *Colonel Haldane made an example of him to deter others from doing the like.* [*same as* **put off**]

detract /dɪ'trakt/: **detracts, detracting, detracted**

detract from
Something **detracts from** the good or valuable qualities or effect that someone or something has when it makes them seem less attractive, admirable, useful or valuable: *Though the defects were very slight they detracted from the overall impression nevertheless.* [*opposite* **add to, enhance** (*formal*)]

deviate /'diːvɪeɪt/: **deviates, deviating, deviated**

deviate from (*formal*)
Something **deviates from** its normal route or path when it moves off it or away from it; someone **deviates from** a regular or normal routine or pattern of behaviour when they behave differently or do something unusual: *New Labour can't afford to deviate from the path it has set itself.* ❑ *The Smolensk, Kursk and Poltava gubernii deviated from central expectations and in many ways escaped rigid control from above.* [*same as* **depart from**]

devolve /dɪ'vɒlv/: **devolves, devolving, devolved**

devolve on *or* **devolve upon**
Work, power or responsibility **devolves on** or **upon** a person or group when it is passed down to them or transferred to them from a person or people at a higher level: *Responsibility for the day-to-day running of the department devolves on junior managers and section leaders.*

devolve to (*formal; legal*)
Property **devolves to** someone when its ownership is passed to them on the death of the previous owner: *Where no legitimate heir can be found, the estate*

devolves automatically to the crown.

devote /dɪ'vout/: **devotes**, **devoting**, **devoted**

devote to

1 You **devote** your life **to** something when you give all your time and effort to that thing; you **devote** time **to** something when you set aside time to do it: *He devoted his life to the theatre.* ❑ *Most of her spare time was devoted to helping others.* ❑ *Much as I would like to, we really can't devote any more time to discussion. We must get on now with implementing the plan.* **2** Something **is devoted to** a particular subject or area of interest when it deals exclusively with that subject: *There will be a whole pull-out section in next month's magazine devoted to music and the arts.* [*same as* **dedicate to**]

dictate /dɪk'teɪt/: **dictates**, **dictating**, **dictated**

dictate to

Someone **dictates to** you if they give you orders or tell you how you must do something, expecting that you will obey them: *He's fond of dictating to other members of the club, and he gets away with it because no-one will stand up to him.* ❑ *If he asks me nicely I may do it, but I certainly won't be dictated to.*

die /daɪ/: **dies**, **dying**, **died**

die away

1 A sound **dies away** when it becomes fainter and stops, or can no longer be heard; a light or a feeling **dies away** when it becomes weaker and disappears: *The sounds of their singing and laughter died away as they disappeared into the distance.* ❑ *The look of almost insane happiness in his eyes died away to be replaced by a blank stare.* [*same as* **fade away**] **2** The wind **dies away** when it blows with less and less strength and finally disappears: *As they approached the equator the light breeze that had carried them along died away and they were becalmed.*

die back

A plant **dies back** when some or all of its growth above the ground dies, with only its roots or bulb remaining alive: *herbaceous plants that die back in winter.*

die down

Something **dies down** when it decreases in level or intensity: *When the fever eventually dies down he is likely to feel very tired and weak for a while.* ❑ *By the time we get to Jerez hopefully most of the fuss will have died down.*

die for (*informal*)

1 You say you **are dying for** something when you want or need it very much: *Put the kettle on; I'm dying for a cup of tea.* [*same as* **long for, yearn for** (*formal*)] **2** People sometimes refer to something that they think is wonderful or very desirable as something to **die for:** *I must have it; it's a dress to die for.*

die off

People or other living things **die off** when they all die: *It's the time of year when wasps are beginning to die off.* ❑ *People who could have best helped him in his inquiries had died off one by one.*

die out

Something **dies out** when it gets rarer and rarer and finally disappears; families or races of people **die out** when there are none left alive: *The craft of thatching had died out locally.* ❑ *Families died out and were replaced with others over the course of the century.*

dig /dɪg/: **digs**, **digging**, **dug** /dʌg/

dig in

1 You **dig** things like fertilizer, compost or manure **in** when you mix it into garden soil by digging: *The plants can* *stay in the ground all winter and rot down, or be dug in, in the spring.* **2 a** Soldiers **dig** themselves and their equipment **in**, or they **dig in** somewhere, when they dig a hole or trench to protect themselves from enemy attack: *I could see guns that were dug in fairly close together. They looked like fifteen pounders.* **b** (*informal*) You **dig** yourself **in** somewhere when you establish a secure position for yourself there: *He's really dug himself in at Blenkinsop's. Nothing will shift him until he decides to retire.* **3** You **dig in**, or **dig** your heels **in**, when you stubbornly refuse to change your mind about something: *I could tell by his expression that he was going to dig in and refuse to grant our request.* ❑ *Sarah had dug her heels in, and refused the invitation.* **4** (*informal*) When someone tells you to **dig in** they are inviting you to help yourself to as much food as you want: *There's plenty of food, so dig in everyone!* [*same* **tuck in** (*informal*)]

dig into

1 You **dig** something hard or sharp **into** something when you push it firmly or roughly into that thing; something **is digging into** you when it is pressing into your flesh: *He dug his elbow into my ribs.* ❑ *The rough leather strap was digging into his shoulder making it red and sore.* **2** You **dig into** something when you search around in it or examine it thoroughly: *He's been digging into the company's foreign operations and has come up with what seem to be serious financial irregularities.* [*same as* **delve into**]

dig out

1 You **dig** something or someone **out** of somewhere when you get them out by digging: *The hunters used terriers to dig the fox out.* **2** (*informal*) You **dig out** something that has been stored away for some time when you search for it and find it: *You'll have to dig out all the old files relating to the case.* **3** (*informal*) You **dig** yourself **out** of a difficult situation when you manage to find a way to get out of it: *I'd like to see how you're going to dig yourself out of this mess.*

• *noun* **dug-out**: **dug-outs**

1 A **dug-out** is a hole that soldiers dig in the ground to protect themselves from enemy attack. **2** A **dug-out**, or a **dug-out** canoe, is a canoe made by carving out the inside of a tree trunk.

dig over

You **dig** *eg* a garden or flower bed **over** when you use a spade to break up the soil and turn over the upper layers: *The vegetable plot will have to be thoroughly dug over before planting.*

dig up

1 You **dig** ground **up** when you use a spade or similar implement to break up the top surface: *Why is it there always seems to be men digging up the roads on public holidays?* **2** You **dig** something that has been buried **up** when you remove it from the earth by digging: *Archaeologists have dug up a 3000-year-old skeleton.* [*same as* **unearth**] **3** (*informal*) You **dig up** information that very few people know about when you find it out through a careful search or investigation: *I've no idea where he dug up all these personal details about me.*

din /dɪn/: dins, dinning, dinned

din into

Facts or instructions about the correct way to do something **are dinned into** someone when they are told them over and over again so that they remember them: *As small children, road safety procedures were dinned into us by both our teachers and parents.* [*same as* **drum into**]

dine /daɪn/: dines, dining, dined

dine in (*formal*)

You **dine in** when you have your evening meal at home. [*opposite* **dine out**; compare **eat in**]

dine off *or* **dine on** (*old*)
You **dine off** or **on** a stated kind of food when you eat that food for dinner: *They dined on mince and slices of quince.*

dine out
You **dine out** when you have an evening meal away from home, *eg* at a restaurant or at someone else's house: *She told the maid to have the evening off because they were dining out.* [*opposite* **dine in**; compare **eat out**]

dine out on
When someone has had an experience that people are eager to hear about, and is regularly invited to dinner or other social occasions so that they can tell other people about it, you can say that that person **is dining out on** the story: *He'll be dining out for months to come on the fact that he met the Princess of Wales.*

dip /dɪp/: dips, dipping, dipped

dip into
1 You **dip into** a book when you open it occasionally and read a passage here and there, but don't read it from beginning to end; you **dip into** a subject when you study parts of it but not in any depth: *The lavish illustrations and photographs make it an interesting book to dip into.* **2** You **dip into** your savings, your pocket or your purse when you spend, or are obliged to spend, some of the money you have and wanted to keep: *We want to be able to pay for it without dipping into our savings.*

disabuse /dɪsə'bjuːz/: disabuses, disabusing, disabused

disabuse of (*formal*)
You **disabuse** someone **of** a wrong belief or idea that they have when you persuade or convince them that it is wrong or untrue: *'If you've some crazy notion that I've got designs on your person, allow me to disabuse you of it right now,' he told her bluntly.*

disagree /dɪsə'griː/: disagrees, disagreeing, disagreed

disagree with
1 You **disagree with** someone when you don't think that they are doing the right or proper thing or when you don't share their opinion: *Of course, the grandparents will routinely disagree with any new methods of child-rearing.* **2** Something **disagrees with** you when it makes you feel unwell: *I use soya milk now because I found that cow's milk disagreed with me.* ❑ *She found that the climate in Borneo disagreed with her so she came home two months early.*

discourse /dɪs'kɔːs/: discourses, discoursing, discoursed

discourse on *or* **discourse upon** (*formal*)
Someone **discourses on** or **upon** something when they talk or lecture about it at length: *He discoursed on aspects that were outside the usual limits of the corpus of collected material.*

dish /dɪʃ/: dishes, dishing, dished

dish out (*informal*)
1 You **dish out** something when you give some of it to each of a number of people, especially in generous amounts: *This government has been dishing out honours like so many sweets to all their supporters.* **2** You **dish** something unpleasant **out** to others when you give it to them: *He doesn't like being criticised but he's quite happy to dish it out.* [= to criticize others]

dish up
You **dish up** food when you put it on people's plates so that they can eat it: *The phone rang just when I was about to dish up the lasagne.* [*same as* **serve up**]

dispense /dɪ'spɛns/: dispenses, dispensing, dispensed

dispense with

You **dispense with** something you do not need or have stopped using when you get rid of it: *Now that we are doing all our own housework we can dispense with the services of a maid.*

dispose /dɪˈspouz/: disposes, disposing, disposed

dispose of

1 You **dispose of** something that you do not want or need when you get rid of it, *eg* by selling it or throwing it away: *companies disposing of assets* ❑ *They have to find a safe means for disposing of hazardous waste so that there is no risk to the environment.* ❑ *The police are trying to find out where the murderer disposed of the other bodies.* **2** You **dispose of** something difficult, inconvenient or tedious when you deal with it and get it out of the way: *The coalition would not exist for a period longer than was necessary to dispose of the emergency.* ❑ *Several people raised objections but he was able to dispose of them quite quickly.* **3** You **dispose of** a person or other living thing when you kill them: *Edmund had disposed of his father in a similar way to that in which St Mercurius had killed the emperor Julian.* [*same as* **dispatch**]

dispose to *or* dispose towards

Someone who is well **disposed to** or **disposed towards** you likes you or feels a friendly concern for you.

dissociate /dɪˈsouʃɪeɪt/ *or* /dɪˈsousɪeɪt/: dissociates, dissociating, dissociated

dissociate from

You **dissociate** yourself **from** someone or their ideas, when you make it known that you have no connection or involvement with them or do not share their views: *He was very careful to dissociate himself from the more extreme factions in the party.*

dissolve /dɪˈzɒlv/: dissolves, dissolving, dissolved

dissolve in *or* dissolve into

You **dissolve in** or **into** tears or laughter when you lose control of yourself and begin to weep or laugh helplessly: *He glared at her and was rather taken aback to see her dissolve into tears.*

distinguish /dɪˈstɪŋgwɪʃ/: distinguishes, distinguishing, distinguished

distinguish between *or* distinguish from

You can **distinguish between** two things when you are able to tell them apart or you can see that they are different; you can **distinguish** one thing **from** another, or others, when you can see that the one is different from the other, or others: *She doesn't seem capable of distinguishing between right and wrong.* ❑ *We need to distinguish between different elements of the media.* ❑ *it is referred to as academic illusionism, a style that can be distinguished from earlier forms of realism.*

dive /daɪv/: dives, diving, dived *or* dove /douv/

Note that the past tense **dove** is only used by American speakers of English.

dive in

You **dive in** when you start doing something with great enthusiasm but without preparing for it beforehand or knowing precisely how to do it: *When she was asked to organize the school concert she just dived in, though she had never done anything like it before.*

dive into

You **dive into** something such as a bag or cupboard when you suddenly start looking or searching inside it: *She dived into her handbag and brought out the letter.*

divest /daɪ'vɛst/: **divests, diverting, diverted**

---

divest of (*formal*)
1 a You **divest** yourself **of** clothing, especially a piece of heavy outer clothing or a ceremonial robe, when you take it off: *Having divested himself of his wet coat and hat, which he threw down carelessly in a corner, he proceeded to warm his hands at the fire.* ❑ *Divested of his robes, the Lord Mayor was indistinguishable from all the other pin-stripe-suited City businessmen.* **b** You **divest** yourself **of** something you are carrying, especially something heavy or awkward to carry, when you put it down: *He had divested himself of his heavy back-pack, and, as a result, was able to make much more rapid progress.* **c** You **divest** yourself **of** a particular attitude or way of thinking when you make a conscious effort to change it or get rid of it because you realize it is wrong. **2** You **divest** someone or something **of** property, power or rank, or they **are divested of** it, when you take it away from them, or they lose it: *I was stuck by what a pathetic sight the deposed king made divested, as he was, of his throne and the trappings of the court.* [*same as* **deprive of, strip of, relieve of**]

divide /dɪ'vaɪd/: **divides, dividing, divided**

---

divide among
Something **is divided among** a number of people when they are each given a part or a piece of it: *The residue of the estate to be divided among by children and grandchildren.*

divide between
1 Something **is divided between** a number of people when they are each given a part or a piece of it: *It had always been his intention to divide his property between his son and two daughters.* [*same as* **divide among**] **2** You **divide** your time **between** one activity and another when you spend some of your time doing one and some of your time doing the other: *Her time is divided between looking after her own young family and her elderly parents.*

divide by
You **divide** a larger number **by** a smaller one when you find out how many times the smaller number can go into the larger one: *100 divided by 10 is 10.* ❑ *Add these amounts together and divide the total by 7.* [compare **multiply by**]

divide from
Something **divides** one thing **from** another when it forms a barrier that separates them or keeps them apart; you **divide** one thing **from** another when you separate them: *Overgrown hedges with segments of barbed wire divided the hillside from the terraced gardens.* ❑ *Memories lingered of the strategy of trying to divide richer from poorer peasants.*

divide into
1 You **divide** a smaller number **into** a larger one when you find how many times the smaller number will go into the larger one: *If you divide 2.5 into 10 the answer is 4.* **2** You **divide** something **into** smaller parts when you cut it up or separate it into that number of smaller parts: *She divided the cake into four large pieces.* ❑ *grand Victorian houses divided into flats.*

divide off
Something **is divided off** from something else when there is a barrier or partition that separates them: *This showed how futile it was to try to divide off your private life from your public one.* ❑ *The dining area was divided off from the kitchen by a sliding door.*

divide up
1 You **divide up** something, or you **divide** it **up**, when you share it out between or among a number of people: *The land is to be divided up between*

his three sons. **2** You **divide** something **up** when you cut or separate it into a number of parts: *According to the terms of the will, the estate cannot be divided up and everything will go to the eldest son.*

divvy /'dɪvɪ/: **divvies**, **divvying**, **divvied**

divvy up (*slang*)
To **divvy up** is to share out or distribute the profits or winnings you have made from some enterprise, business deal or gamble between your shareholders or partners: *When eventually the syndicate chairman divvied up each member had won enough to go on an exotic holiday.*

do /duː/: **does** /dʌz/, **doing**, **did** /dɪd/, **done** /dʌn/

do about
You **do** something **about** some problem or difficulty when you deal with it, attend to it, or solve it: *Are you going to do something about this mess?* ❑ *Is something going to be done about the litter in the streets?* ❑ *It really is a terrible problem and I don't know what can be done about it.*

do as (*informal*)
You can say that something will **do as** or **do for** another thing when it can be used as a substitute for that other thing: *This flat rock will do as a table.* ❑ *Make the chicken's beak out of cardboard, and a big paper lampshade will do for the body.* [*same as* **serve as**]

do away with
1 You **do away with** something when you get rid of it or cause it to end: *There's a rumour going round that the government plans to do away with child benefit.* [*same as* **abolish, eliminate**] **2** (*informal*) You **do away with** someone when you murder them; if you **do away with** yourself when you commit suicide: *The police suspected him of having done away with his wife.* [*same as* **make away with** (*informal*)]

do down (*informal*)
You **do** someone or something **down** when you describe them in a critical or derogatory way to make them seem incompetent or stupid: *journalists who are only too eager to do the government down.*

do for (*informal*)
1 a Something **does for** you when it ruins or kills you: *It was the drink that did for him in the end.* **b** You **are done for** when you are ruined, destroyed or killed: *You'll be done for if you get caught.* **2** (*informal*) Someone **does for** you when you employ them, often on a part-time basis, to do your housework and cooking for you: *He has a young woman who comes in each morning to do for him.* ❑ *They're quite old enough to do for themselves now.*
[see also **do as**]

do in (*slang*)
To **do** someone **in** is to kill or murder them: *He threatened to do her in.* [*same as* **bump off** (*slang*)]
• *adjective (informal)* **done in**
People sometimes say they are **done in** when they are completely exhausted: *Come and sit down; you look done in.* [*same as* **tired out, worn out, fagged out** (*informal*)]

do out (*informal*)
You **do out** *eg* a room, drawer or cupboard when you tidy and clean it thoroughly: *When did you last do out these kitchen cupboards? They're absolutely filthy.*

do out in
You **do** a room **out in** a stated way when you decorate it in that way: *The kitchen was done out in green with hand-painted cupboards in solid wood.*

do out of (*informal*)
Someone **does** you **out of** something if they cause you to lose it *eg* by cheating you or treating you unfairly: *I'm sure that waiter's done me out of £5.* ❑ *I*

can't see the benefit of new technology if it does thousands of people out of a job. [*same as* **deprive of**]

do over

1 You **do** something such as a room **over** when you repaint it or put up new wallpaper, curtains, *etc*: *We're going to do the whole interior over in a more modern style.* **2** (*especially AmE*) You **do** something **over** when you do it again, usually because you have done it wrong the first time: *He'll have to do it over.* [*same as* **redo**] **3** (*slang*) Someone **is done over** when they are attacked and beaten severely; a house or business premises **is done over** when it is burgled or robbed: *We'd ring up the police, who'd take a bunch of these youths into the same exit and do them over.* ❑ *He returned home to find his flat had been done over for the third time in as many months.*

do up

1 You **do up** something such as a piece of clothing, or you **do** it **up**, when you fasten it: *He was seven before he learned how to do up his laces.* [*opposite* **undo**] **2** You **do up** something in a parcel or package when you wrap it and tie it with ribbon or string: *The present was done up in gold paper with a big pink bow.* **3** A girl or woman **does** her hair **up** in a particular style when she ties it up using such things as hairpins and ribbons: *She always does her little daughter's hair up in a ponytail.* **4** You **do up** a building when you repair or decorate it: *She buys old properties and does them up for letting.* ❑ *We'll need at least ten thousand pounds to do up the kitchen and bathroom.* [*same as* **renovate**]

do with

1 a You talk about one thing having something **to do with** another when you are discussing how or if they are related or connected to each other: *I don't see what it's got to do with him; it's our business, not his.* ❑ *How can I interfere? It doesn't have anything to do with me.* **b** Something is **to do with** something else when it concerns or involves that other thing: *I'm not quite sure what his exact job is but I know it's something to do with the security services.* **2** In questions and statements, you talk about what someone **did with** something when you are wondering where it is or where they've put it: *I don't know what I did with yesterday's newspaper. I may have thrown it away.* ❑ *What have you done with my black pen?* **3** You ask what is to be **done with** someone or something when you are wondering what action should be taken concerning them: *He just won't do what he is told. I don't know what's to be done with him.* ❑ *'What shall we do with these empty wine bottles?' 'Put them in a box and take them to the bottle bank for recycling.'* **4** When people say they could **do with** something they mean that they need or want it: *We could do with some new curtains in this room.* ❑ *I could do with a nice cold beer.* **5** You talk about what someone **does with** themselves when you are asking about or discussing what they spend their time doing: *He doesn't know what to do with himself now that he's retired.* ❑ *What did you do with yourselves when you were cut off from civilization for all those months?* **6** (*informal*) When people say they can't **be doing with** something they mean that they don't like it or can't tolerate it: *I can't be doing with people who make sarcastic comments all the time.*

do without

You **do without** something that you want or need, or that you would normally have, when you manage or survive though you don't or can't have it: *We can't afford to buy a car so we'll just have to do without until we've saved enough to buy one.* [*same as* **go without, forego** (*formal*)]

dole /doul/: doles, doling, doled

dole out (*informal*)
Someone **doles** something **out** when they share it out or hand it out, giving some to a number of people: *She's a bit too fond of doling out advice.* ❑ *The volume of work is very much dependent on local authority contracts doled out at yearly and half-yearly intervals.* [*same as* **deal out, dish out** (*informal*), **dispense** (*formal*)]

doll /dɒl/: dolls, dolling, dolled

doll up
A woman **dolls** herself **up**, or gets **dolled up**, when she dresses herself in smart or fancy clothes and does her hair in an elaborate style: *Can you wait for ten minutes; Jenny is still dolling herself up in the bedroom.* ❑ *What are you getting all dolled up for? We're only going down to the pub for half an hour.* [*same as* **titivate** (*formal*); compare **tart up**]

doom /duːm/: dooms, dooming, doomed

doom to (*usually passive*)
Someone or something **is doomed to** failure or some terrible fate when they must suffer it and cannot avoid it: *He knew that if he didn't escape he was doomed to die a horrible death.* [*same as* **condemn to**]

dope /doup/: dopes, doping, doped

dope up (*informal*)
Someone **is doped up** when they are given or take drugs, especially with the result that they become sleepy or do not know what is going on around them: *He'd been doped up with so many painkillers, he didn't know where he was.* ❑ *He'd doped himself up first with a mixture of drugs and alcohol.*

dose /dous/: doses, dosing, dosed

dose up
You **dose** yourself **up**, or you **are dosed up** with medicine, when you take, or are given, medicine, often in large quantities so as to make something such as a cold or sore throat better: *I thought I had a cold coming on so I dosed myself up with vitamin C tablets.* ❑ *Dosing the cattle up periodically with minerals ensures that they are getting sufficient amounts.*

doss /dɒs/: dosses, dossing, dossed

doss down (*informal*)
You **doss down** somewhere unusual or uncomfortable, especially somewhere that is not a proper bed, when you lie down there to sleep: *We couldn't find a hotel for the night so we dossed down in the back of the van.*

dote /dout/: dotes, doting, doted

dote on *or* **dote upon**
You **dote on** or **upon** someone when you love them very much, especially so much that you cannot see any faults that they may have: *She had no family except one nephew, whom she doted on.* [*same as* **adore, idolize**]

double /ˈdʌbəl/: doubles, doubling, doubled

double as
Something **doubles as** a particular thing when it has that function as well as its normal function: *The study doubles as a guest bedroom.*

double back
1 You **double back** when you turn and go back the way you came: *We came to a set of locked gates and had to double back and find another route.* **2** Something **is doubled back** on itself when it is bent so that it is formed into two connected lengths that are close to and parallel with each other: *The bottom sheet was doubled back on itself so that the unfortunate victim usually tore it when trying to force his feet towards the bottom of the bed.*

double over
1 You **double** something **over** when you fold it so that one half is on top of the other: *Doubling the card over she then proceeded to cut along the fold.* **2** You **double over** when you bend your body forwards at the waist: *He was doubled over in what looked like a very uncomfortable position.*

double up
1 You **double up** or **are doubled up** when you bend or are bent over from the waist: *We were doubled up with laughter.* ❑ *Her face was pure white and she was doubled up with pain.* **2** People **double up** when they get into pairs in order to share something or do something together: *Some of us may have to double up if there aren't enough bedrooms.*

dovetail /ˈdʌvteɪl/: dovetails, dovetailing, dovetailed

dovetail with *or* dovetail into
Things such as plans or events **dovetail with** each other, or **dovetail into** each other, when they fit neatly or perfectly together: *Arranging childcare so that it dovetails with our erratic work patterns isn't as easy as we would like it to be.*

down see panel on next page

downcast /ˈdaunkast/ see **cast down**

downplay /daunˈpleɪ/ see **play down**

downpour /ˈdaunpɔː(r)/ see **pour down**

downturn /ˈdauntɜːn/ see **turn down.**

doze /douz/: dozes, dozing, dozed

doze off
You **doze off** when you fall into a light sleep, often when you did not intend to: *I didn't hear you come in; I must have dozed off.* [*same as* **drift off, drop off**]

draft /drɑːft/: drafts, drafting, drafted

draft in *or* draft into
A person **is drafted into** one of the armed forces when they are ordered to serve in it; people **are drafted in**, or **are drafted into** an organization when they are taken into it, usually temporarily, to do some special job: *He was drafted into the navy in 1978.* ❑ *We drafted in a couple of extra computer programmers to help get the project off the ground.*

drag /drag/: drags, dragging, dragged

drag down
1 Something **drags** you **down** if it makes you feel weak, ill or depressed: *The pain was obviously dragging her down. She seemed quite unlike the person I used to know.* **2** Someone **drags** you **down** when they cause you, or your association with them causes you, to lose social status or reduce your standard of morals or behaviour: *He refused to be dragged down to their level.* ❑ *He'd no longer anything to lose, and someone like that is liable to drag down as many people as he can when he knows he has to go.*

drag in *or* drag into
You **drag** something **in**, or you **drag** it **into** a conversation or situation, when you mention it or introduce it unnecessarily: *There's no need to drag her name into this.*

drag on
Something **drags on** if it goes on for a long time, especially if it lasts longer than seems necessary or reasonable: *These claims for compensation tend to drag on for years.*

down /daun/

Down is an adverb and a preposition. It is a very common word in English and is frequently used to form phrasal verbs in its literal sense, referring to movement from above to a lower position, as in **fall down**, **jump down**, **pull down, ski down, sit down, throw down** and **walk down**. The movement may be of someone's body, or may refer to the action of someone who puts something down on a surface. The meaning of these combinations is often so clear that they may not be given an entry in this dictionary (unless they have other meanings). The following are examples of phrasal verbs with **down** used in its literal sense: *He plopped himself down on the nearest chair.* ❑ *He was unwilling to pull down a fine old specimen of a picturesque cottage.* ❑ *Mr Stych was canoeing down a tributary of the Mackenzie River.* ❑ *Bernice lowered the case gently down.* ❑ *The waiter glanced down at the tip of the silencer pointing at him.* ❑ *Jenna had to scramble down a bank.* ❑ *He carried the tray over to the cage and set it down just out of reach.*
Phrasal verbs with this sense of movement to a lower place or position include a group of combinations that specifically refer to rain, snow or sleet falling, as in **bucket down**, **lash down, pelt down** and **teem down**.
New and often informal phrasal verbs that refer to the action of rain or snow sometimes occur, as in *hose down* in the following example: *The next day it was hosing, absolutely hosing down.*
In its non-literal senses, **down** has the following meanings, some of which relate to its basic meaning of movement from a higher to a lower position.

1 MAKING OR BECOMING SMALLER OR LOWER
In combinations such as **come down**, **slow down, calm down** and **turn down**, **down** refers to reducing or lowering of the rate or level of something, as in the following examples: *The price of home computers has come down a lot making them more affordable for the ordinary man in the street.* ❑ *The driver slowed down as he approached the pedestrian crossing.* ❑ *She was relieved to see that he seemed to be calming down a little.* ❑ *German interest rates are edging down.* ❑ *The music is too loud. Would you turn it down, please.*
Many new and often informal phrasal verbs are formed using **down** in this sense, as in *dumb down* in the following example: *'He doesn't challenge you enough. Don't dumb down* [= make yourself seem less intelligent] *for security's sake.'*

2 FASTENING, SECURING AND FIXING
Down is also used in phrasal verbs such as **screw down**, **lash down, nail down, pin down, weigh down** and **batten down** to show that the fastening, fixing or securing action is made by pressing or pushing downwards from above, as in the following example of *strap down*: *He was sitting in a wooden chair strapped down to the deck, yelling instructions and waving his one arm.*

3 DESTROYING AND BREAKING
In another group of phrasal verbs **down** suggests that the action is one of ending something or its complete destruction, disintegration or failure, as in **burn down, break down**, and **bring down**. The following are some examples of its use in this sense: *Relations between the Soviet Union and the Western powers were rapidly breaking down.* ❑ *Our computer system has gone down.* ❑ *The government had no legal power to close down the newspaper.*
Many phrasal verbs are created with this meaning, as in *steam down* in the following example: *With large waves steaming you down, the body's store of oxygen is soon depleted.*

4 DEFEATING
Down occurs in a large number of phrasal verbs that have the notion of defeating someone or something as part of their meaning, such as **argue down**, **face down, fight down, grind down, knock down, stare down** and **vote down**.

5 RECORDING AND WRITING
Down is used in combinations such as **copy down**, **jot down, mark down, note down, set down, lay down** and **take down** to show that something is

continued on next page

recorded or written on paper, as in the following examples: *The policeman took down my name and address.* ❑ *You'll need to copy this down; it's something you'll do in the second year of your course.* ❑ *It might help you to know that I've been writing down my dreams on waking.* ❑ *The document which laid down precisely who got what in the case of divorce.*

6 EATING AND DRINKING
Down is also to form phrasal verbs that have to do with eating or swallowing actions, especially to emphasize that the action is quick or abrupt, as in **gobble down,** and **gulp down**. New phrasal verbs occasionally appear with this meaning as in *belt down, slip down* and *pack down* in the following examples: *He belted down a tumblerful of whisky, without pausing for air.* ❑ *Even if slimmers inadvertently slip down a couple of hundred more calories, the system can cope with it.* ❑ *You could well be packing down 400 calories before you even start your main course.*
You use **hold down, keep down** and **stay down** to talk about food and drink remaining in the stomach of a person who is ill, when you might have expected them to vomit.

7 FORCE, FIRMNESS AND AUTHORITY
Down can also suggest that the action of the verb is forceful or firm, or done with authority. The following are examples of the phrasal verbs **slam down, clamp down** and **crack down** which have this meaning: *He slammed the book down on the table.* ❑ *The authorities are clamping down on any form of political protest.* ❑ *The government seemed surprisingly unwilling to crack down on it.*

8 PASSING FROM ONE GENERATION TO THE NEXT
In combinations such as **pass down** and **hand down, down** refers to the transfer of something from the older generation to the younger generation.

9 CLEANING, POLISHING, SMOOTHING AND FLATTENING
Down refers to something being cleaned, polished or made flat or smooth in a group of phrasal verbs which include **sand down, wash down,** and **clean down**.
Again, new and often informal phrasal verbs with this sense are fairly common, as in *soap down* in the following example: *Her face and hair are washed before she's soaped down.*

Finally, some phrasal verbs with **down** have meanings that are entirely idiomatic, as in (*informal*) *go down* in the example: *He wanted to be able to tell his wife what had gone down.* [= what had happened]

drag out
1 You **drag** information **out** of someone who is unwilling to give it when you persuade them, with a great deal of difficulty, to tell you it: *Any information about his progress at school has to be dragged out of him.* **2** You **drag** something **out** when you make it go on for longer than is necessary or reasonable: *The government has a vested interest in dragging the inquiry out for as long as possible.* [*same as* **draw out, spin out, stretch out, prolong**]

drag up
1 When someone **drags up** some unpleasant event or story from the past that everyone had forgotten about they remind people unnecessarily about it: *Why do you go on dragging up the fact that he went bankrupt ten years ago?* [*same as* **bring up, dredge up**] **2** (*informal*) People say that a child **has been dragged up** when they think that its parents have not brought it up well, especially when they have not taught it good manners or have not been a good example: *What can you expect of kids who were dragged up by a mentally unstable mother and an alcoholic father?*

dragoon /drə'guːn/: **dragoons, dragooning, dragooned**

dragoon into

You **are dragooned into** something that you don't want to do when someone forces you to do it, especially when they use unreasonable pressure or threats to make you do it: *The boys had to be dragooned into helping with the haymaking.* [*same as* **bully, browbeat**]

draw /drɔː/: **draws**, **drawing**, **drew** /druː/, **drawn** /drɔːn/

---

draw back

1 You **draw back** from something unpleasant or frightening when you move back to get away from it: *When he moved towards her she drew back with a look of terror.* [*same as* **recoil** (*formal*)] **2** You **draw back** from something that involves you making a definite decision or commitment when you show that you are unwilling to proceed: *Faced with two such diametrically-opposed alternatives, in the end Klein drew back from agreeing to either one.*

• *noun* **drawback**: **drawbacks**

A **drawback** is a disadvantage or something that will create a difficulty: *One of the drawbacks of living in the country is having to travel long distances to go to the cinema or the theatre.* ❑ *Being tall has its drawbacks as well as its advantages.*

draw down

1 You **draw down** anger or criticism from others when you do something that makes them angry with you or direct criticism at you: *They hesitated to do anything that might draw down the wrath of the headmaster, knowing that his anger was a terrible thing.* **2** (*technical*) In banking and finance, money **is drawn down** when it is made available for the use of a person or organization by transferred it from a central fund to the customer's account: *Once the loan agreement is signed, the funds will normally be drawn down within 24 hours.*

draw for

People **draw for** things when they make a decision about which thing they are to do or have, or which order they will do something in, by each choosing something, such as a numbered or marked piece of paper, which indicates what they must do: *Will we draw for who's going to organize which stall at the jumble sale?*

draw in

1 The days **draw in** when there are fewer hours of daylight *eg* as autumn and winter approaches; evening **draws in** when it gradually gets dark: *As evening draws in, an apparent peace descends on the depot.* [*same as* **close in**; *opposite* **draw out**] **2** A train **draws in** at a station, or **draws into** a station, when it slows down as it approaches the station and stops when it reaches it. [*same as* **pull in**]

draw into

You **are drawn into** something when you become involved in it, though you did not intend to be; you **are drawn in** when you become involved in something, usually against your will: *I refused to be drawn into their argument.* ❑ *So central government gets drawn in willy-nilly; and when it is handing out money it will want to have some say over how it is spent.* [see also **draw in**]

draw off

You **draw off** some or all of the liquid in a container when you remove it gradually through a pipe or tube: *The sludge then settles to the bottom and can be drawn off with relative ease.*

draw on

1 You **draw on** or **upon** a supply or resource when you use it for what you need: *An huge organization like that has a wide variety of expertise to draw on.* ❑ *The research draws on fieldwork over a period of nearly 20 years.* ❑ *There's a gap between the historians' interpretations of the past and the more general remembrances drawn upon in public debate.* **2** Someone who is smoking **draws on** their pipe or cigarette when they suck air through it so that the smoke goes into their lungs: *Drawing contemplatively on his pipe and puffing out great billows of foul-smelling smoke, old Joe seemed not to be listening.*

draw out

1 You **draw** something **out** when you make it last longer than is necessary or reasonable: *Their side'll try to draw out the process for as long as possible.* ❑ *We don't want the case to turn out to be one of these long-drawn-out affairs where any settlement is eaten up by the legal costs.* ❑ *Moreover, the process of establishing credibility is long-drawn-out.* [*same as* **drag out**, **spin out**, **prolong**] **2** You **draw out** a sound when you make it longer than it would normally be: *a piercing shriek drawn out over what seemed like several minutes.* **3** A vehicle **draws out** when it moves out into the road from the side; a train **draws out** when it begins to move away from a station: *A lorry drew out into the outside lane and I had to swerve to avoid it.* ❑ *He drove up to the station just as his train was drawing out.* [*same as* **pull out**] **4** You **draw** money **out** of your bank or building society account when you take it out: *He went to the bank and drew out £1000 in five pound notes.* [*same as* **withdraw**] **5** Someone or something **draws** something hidden **out** when they do something that causes it to be clearly seen or expressed: *By a painstaking process, he succeeded in drawing out into the open what they had tried for so long to conceal.* [*same as* **bring out**, **elicit** (*formal*)] **6** You **draw** a shy person **out** when you encourage them to talk to you and express themselves freely: *Don't fall for this apparent reticence, but draw him out instead by providing openings.* [*same as* **bring out**] **7** The days **are drawing out** when there are more hours of daylight *eg* as spring or summer approaches. [*opposite* **draw in**, **close in**]

draw up

1 A vehicle **draws up** somewhere when it comes to a stop there: *A huge black limousine drew up outside the hotel, the doors flew open, and several secret service men jumped out.* [*same as* **pull up**] **2** You **draw up** a plan, schedule or document when you prepare it and produce it in a written form, often so that it can be shown to someone for their approval: *The enlightened bureaucrats responsible for drawing up the legislation may not have achieved everything they were striving for.* ❑ *I'm going to get my lawyer to draw me up a new will.* [*same as* **draft**] **3** You **draw up** a chair when you pull it nearer to someone or something so that you can sit close to them. **4** You **draw** yourself **up**, or you **draw** yourself **up** to your full height, when you stand upright, as tall and straight as you can.

draw upon see **draw on**

dream /driːm/: **dreams**, **dreaming**, **dreamt** /drɛmt/

---

dream away

You **dream** the hours **away** when you spend your time daydreaming and doing nothing else: *By the river in summer, you could dream your days away and relax completely.*

dream of

You can say you wouldn't **dream of** doing something to emphasize that you couldn't do it or would never consider it, because you think it is wrong: *I wouldn't dream of asking her how old she is.*

dream up

Someone **dreams up** something such as a scheme or plan when they invent it in their mind: *I'd like to meet the person who dreamed up this ridiculous scheme so that I could tell them what I thought of it.*

dredge /drɛdʒ/: **dredges**, **dredging**, **dredged**

---

dredge up (*informal*)
Something **dredges up** a memory from long ago when it makes you remember it; you **dredge up** something unpleasant that people have forgotten about when you mention it again: *A list of names that dredged up all these forgotten faces from the past.* ❑ *Of course, the tabloid press will dredge up every little bit of scandal they can find and make his life a misery.* [*same as* **drag up**]

dress /drɛs/: **dresses**, **dressing**, **dressed**

dress down
1 You **dress down** when you wear plain or simple clothes that will not draw people's attention to you: *He warned us we should dress down and carry little money.* ❑ *'Grunge' has been defined as a kind of downtown downdressing.* [*opposite* **dress up**] **2** You **dress** somebody **down** when you talk to them angrily to punish them for something they have done wrong: *Put a foot wrong and you'll be dressed down and utterly humiliated by one of the fearsome NCO's.* [*same as* **tell off**]
• *noun* **dressing-down**: *He was given a real dressing-down by his father.* [*same as* **telling-off**]

dress up
1 People **dress up** when they put on smart clothes: *Why are you getting all dressed up? It's only an informal lunch.* **2** People **dress up** when they put on fancy dress; you **dress up** as someone or something when you put on a special costume so that you look like that person or thing: *Every Christmas he dressed up as Santa Claus.* **3** You **dress** something **up** when you add things to it to make it more impressive or attractive; you **dress** something unpleasant **up** when you try to make it seem more acceptable: *This very basic dish can be dressed up with some homemade hollandaise sauce and seasonal vegetables.* ❑ *The plain fact is they are giving me the sack, however they try to dress it up.*

drift /drɪft/: **drifts**, **drifting**, **drifted**

drift along
Someone **drifts along** when they live their life without any real aim or purpose: *John just drifts along, seemingly without a care in the world, and certainly with no thought of his future.*

drift apart
Two people who have had a close friendship or relationship **drift apart** when they gradually become less and less close until they are no longer friendly or are no longer together: *The realisation that she and her husband were drifting apart filled Imogen with fear for the future.*

drift off
You **drift off** when you begin to fall asleep: *I was just drifting off when there was this terrific bang.* [*same as* **doze off**, **drop off**]

drill /drɪl/: **drills**, **drilling**, **drilled**

drill in
You **are drilled in** something when you are taught it by constant repetition: *Every employee in the nuclear industry is drilled in safety procedures.*

drill into
You **drill** something **into** someone when you make sure that they know or understand it by constantly repeating it: *You have to drill it into young people that drugs will ruin their lives.*

drink /drɪŋk/: **drinks**, **drinking**, **drank** /draŋk/, **drunk** /drʌŋk/

drink down
You **drink** a liquid **down** when you swallow it, usually quickly and often in one large mouthful: *The medicine tastes so vile you should drink it down as quickly as you can.*

drink in
You **drink in** sights, sounds or in-

formation when you concentrate on them eagerly so that you can experience them fully or take them all in: *We stood on the hill drinking in the almost hallucinatory detail of the visual field, before plunging downwards into our outdoor make-believe.* ❑ *Poppy sat with her mouth open, drinking in every word.*

drink to
People **drink to** someone or something when they raise their glasses and say their name before they drink, as a way of wishing them success and happiness: *They drank to the success of the campaign, then sent their glasses crashing into the fireplace.* [*same as* **toast**]

drink up
People tell you to **drink up** when they want you to finish your drink quickly: *Come on, gentlemen, drink up now. The bar closes in five minutes.*

drip /drɪp/: drips, dripping, dripped

drip with
1 You **are dripping with** sweat when you are so hot that sweat is running off your skin and falling to the ground in small drops: *The bare trees dripped with melting frost like chilling tears.* **2** People sometimes say that someone, usually a woman, **is dripping with** diamonds or gold jewellery when he or she is wearing a great many pieces of expensive jewellery.

drive /draɪv/: drives, driving, drove /droʊv/, driven /'drɪvən/

drive at
When you want to know what someone **is driving at** you want to understand what it is they are trying to say because they haven't made it very clear: *Do you know what he was driving at when he said he suspected some people were being disloyal?*

drive away
You **drive** someone or something **away** when you force them to go away *eg* by frightening them or by behaving badly: *Some of the new-style programmes are driving listeners away in droves.* ❑ *Her anger and bitterness has eaten her up and driven away all the people who once cared about her.*

drive back
1 You **drive back** somewhere when you return there by car: *Surely you're not going to drive back to Norwich to-night?* **2** Someone or something **is driven back** when they are forced to retreat: *The invaders were driven back to the sea.* ❑ *The beacons burned and burned, driving back the darkness.*

drive off
You **drive** people or animals **off** when you force or frighten them away from a place or you take them away by force: *They contented themselves with burning the village and driving off Dacre's and his people's cattle and horses.* ❑ *Thousands had been driven off their land.*

drive on
You **drive on** when you continue moving forwards in a vehicle or when you continue your journey after stopping for a time: *We waved at him to stop but he just drove on.* ❑ *We reached Fort William at four o'clock and drove on to Inverness the same day.*

drive out
You **drive** someone or something **out** when you force them to go away or disappear from a place: *The fire spread down through the timbers of the lighthouse lantern, driving the men out on to the rocks.* ❑ *But the Beaux-Arts was a short-lived fad, and not even its excesses could drive other styles out.* [*same as* **expel** (*formal*)]

drone /droʊn/: drones, droning, droned

drone on

Someone **drones on** when they go on speaking in the same monotonous tone of voice for a long time: *'Oh, I shall go mad,' Janine said, 'if I have to listen to Kitty droning on about the wedding.'* ❑ *I couldn't keep awake so I haven't a clue what he was droning on about.* [*same as* **go on, go on about**]

drool /druːl/: drools, drooling, drooled

drool over

You **drool over** someone or something when you look at them longingly, especially with your mouth hanging open, because you find them very desirable or attractive: *She's at that peculiar age when girls drool over their pop idols.*

drop /drɒp/: drops, dropping, dropped

drop away

Your friends or supporters **drop away** when they abandon you, often one by one or in small groups: *As national newspapers began to take up the story, his congregation dropped away to only about a dozen.*

drop back

You **drop back** when you begin to move more slowly than others so that they get ahead of you: *He seemed to pull a muscle and dropped back so that he was trailing the rest of the field.*

• *noun* **backdrop: backdrops**

1 A **backdrop** is a cloth with scenery painted on it hung at the back of a stage or film set. **2** A **backdrop** is also the circumstances or conditions that form the background for some event or series of events: *Negotiations were carried out against the backdrop of an increasingly shaky ceasefire.*

drop behind

You **drop behind** others when you begin to move or progress more slowly so that they are ahead of you: *He's dropped behind the rest of the class this term.*

drop by

Someone **drops by** when they visit you informally or unexpectedly: *Just drop by any time for a coffee.* [*same as* **call by**]

drop in

Someone **drops in**, or **drops in** on you, when they visit you without arranging to do so beforehand: *If you're going to drop in on me unexpectedly, don't be surprised if the place is in a mess.* ❑ *Adele dropped in unexpectedly this morning.* [*same as* **call in, pop in** (*informal*)]

• *adjective* **drop-in**

A **drop-in** centre is a building where people in need can go at any time to meet others or to get advice, without making an appointment.

drop off

1 You **drop off** when you fall asleep: *He had already dropped off to sleep when she began peeling the clothes from his back.* [*same as* **nod off** (*informal*)] **2** An amount or rate **drops off** when it decreases: *The latest statistics show that sales in the high street dropped off in January though they were forecast to rise.* ❑ *As you approach Bude the crowds increase, but one or two miles from the main centre the numbers quickly drop off.* **3** You **drop** a passenger in your vehicle **off** when you stop to let them get out somewhere, and then continue your journey; you **drop** something you have been carrying with you **off** when you leave it somewhere and continue on your journey: *My husband dropped me off at the station.*

• *noun* **dropping-off**

There is a **dropping-off** in the level of interest in or support for something when fewer people are interested in it or support it: *There seems to have been a dropping-off in the numbers of boys interested in joining the Scouts.* [*same as* **decline**]

• *adjective* **dropping-off**
A **dropping-off** point is a place where a bus or other vehicle stops to allow passengers to get out.

drop out
1 You **drop out** of a competition, or some planned activity, when you take no further part in it: *He had to drop out after the first round because he sprained his wrist.* **2** Students **drop out** of school or university when they leave it without finishing their course of study: *Some students are having to drop out because of lack of money.*
• *noun* **drop-out: drop-outs**
1 A **drop-out** is a student who leaves their school or university before they have completed their course of study: *For someone who was a high-school drop-out, he's made a great success of his life.* ❑ *The drop-out rate is reaching alarming proportions.* **2** A **drop-out** from society is a person who rejects normal social standards, *eg* by refusing to take a regular job, or dress or behave in an accepted way: *She's living in a squat with a group of hippies and drop-outs.*

drop round
You **drop round** at someone's house a short distance away when you visit them there without arranging to do so beforehand: *I'm just going to drop round to Mum's and see if she's okay.*

drown /draun/: drowns, drowning, drowned

drown out
A noise **drowns out** other sounds or people's voices when it is so loud that they cannot be heard because of it: *He turned up the music to drown out the sound of next-door's dog barking.*

drum /drʌm/: drums, drumming, drummed

drum into
You **drum** facts **into** someone when you keep repeating them until you are sure that they have learned them: *We had our multiplication tables drummed into us when we were at school.* [*same as* **din into**]

drum out
Someone **is drummed out** of an organization when they are forced to leave it, usually in disgrace: *The conviction for theft meant he was drummed out of the Guards.*

drum up
You **drum up** help or support when you go round persuading a number of people to give it: *'Is that why you're here? Still drumming up followers for your meetings?'*

dry /draɪ/: dries, drying, dried

dry off
Something **dries off** when the liquid that has been on its surface disappears; you **dry** yourself **off** *eg* after you have had a bath or have been swimming when you wipe the water off your skin with a towel.

dry out
1 Something **dries out** when all the moisture in it disappears: *The plants grow best in a reasonably fertile soil that doesn't dry out too readily.* **2** (*informal*) You can say that someone who is an alcoholic **is drying out** when they are trying to cure themselves of their addiction by drinking no alcohol at all.

dry up
1 a A river or lake **dries up** when the water in it becomes shallower and eventually disappears altogether. **b** Something **dries up** when it loses all its moisture, *eg* because it has been heated: *The peat in the plant pots has dried up completely because of the hot sun.* **2** A supply of something **dries up** when it decreases and comes to an end: *That cash is already drying up as Japan concentrates its resources at home.* ❑ *New construction projects have all but*

dried up during the recession. **3** (*informal*) If a speaker or actor **dries up** they stop speaking because they can't remember what they were going to say next: *He was so nervous he dried up in the middle of the soliloquy.* **4** (*informal*) If someone tells you to **dry up** they are telling you rudely or angrily that you are talking too much, or are taking nonsense and should be quiet: *'Oh, dry up, Frank. I'm fed up listening to you moaning!'* [*same as* **belt up** (*informal*), **shut up** (*informal*)] **5** You **dry up** when you use a cloth to wipe the water off dishes after they have been washed.

• *noun* **drying-up**

You do the **drying-up** when you dry dishes after they have been washed: *I'll wash if you'll do the drying-up.*

dub /dʌb/: **dubs**, **dubbing**, **dubbed**

dub into

A film or television programme in one language **is dubbed into** another language when a separate recording of the actors' voices is made in the second language and added to the soundtrack so that they seem to be talking in that language: *She spoke only French and Italian so her voice had to be dubbed into English.*

duck /dʌk/: **ducks**, **ducking**, **ducked**

duck out (*informal*)

You **duck out** of something you don't want to do when you avoid doing it: *I want you there to help me so don't try to duck out of it.*

duff /dʌf/: **duffs**, **duffing**, **duffed**

duff up (*informal*)

1 You **duff** something **up** when you spoil it or make a mess of it: *Look what you've done, you idiot! You've duffed up my painting!* [*same as* **cock up** (*vulgar slang*), **fuck up** (*vulgar slang*)] **2** You **duff** someone **up** when you hit them violently and repeatedly and injure them severely: *He ran away when the skinheads threatened to duff him up.*

dug-out /'dʌgaut/ see **dig out**

dump /dʌmp/: **dumps**, **dumping**, **dumped**

dump on (*informal*)

You **are dumped on** by people when they blame you unfairly for things that have gone wrong, or they criticize you continually: *He said he was going to leave home because he was sick of being dumped on by older brothers and sisters.* [*same as* **abuse**]

dust /dʌst/: **dusts**, **dusting**, **dusted**

dust down

You **dust** something **down** when you wipe or brush the dust from it: *He picked himself up, dusted himself down, and trying to look nonchalant, sauntered off as if nothing had happened.*

dust off

You **dust** something **off** when you remove the dust from it with a cloth or brush: *You'll have to dust off that work surface before you put anything down on it.* ❑ *The pitcher threw straight at his head so that he had to dive out of the way. He dusted off and glared.*

dwell /dwɛl/: **dwells**, **dwelling**, **dwelt** /dwɛlt/ *or* **dwelled**

dwell on *or* **dwell upon**

You **dwell on** or **upon** a subject if you keep thinking or talking about it: *I know it was a horrible experience, but you should try not to dwell on it.*

e

earmark /ˈɪəmɑːk/: earmarks, earmarking, earmarked

earmark for

You **earmark** something **for** a particular purpose when you decide that it will be used for that purpose, and perhaps mark it to show this: *Very little of it is spare cash; most of it is earmarked for household expenses of one kind or another.* ❑ *Coming out of the town centre there were a few fields, mostly full of thistles and earmarked for building.* [*same as* **set aside**]

ease /iːz/: eases, easing, eased

ease off

Something **eases off** when it becomes less intense or severe: *The rain was beginning to ease off so we packed up the car.* ❑ *The tension between them had not eased off a jot.* [compare **die down, let up**]

ease up

You **ease up** when you work less hard or use less effort or energy; a situation **eases up** when it becomes less busy or tiring: *When managers say ease up a little, it's time to listen.* ❑ *There's a crazy period for about four weeks, then things ease up again.* [*same as* **slow down, slacken off**]

eat /iːt/: eats, eating, ate /eɪt/, eaten

eat away

Something that **is being eaten away** is being gradually destroyed, *eg* by chemicals: *The side panel had been almost completely eaten away by rust.* ❑ *This kind of criticism can eat away at a child's confidence.* ❑ *It is as if the disease is steadily eating away his personality.* [*same as* **wear away, erode**; *opposite* **build up**; compare **waste away**]

eat in

You **eat in** when you have a meal at home, rather than going out to a restaurant: *With the kids, obviously most nights you're eating in.* [*opposite* **eat out**]

eat into

1 Chemicals and other substances **eat into** something when they begin to destroy it: *Moisture settles in the pipe and rust eats into it from the inside.* [*same as* **wear away**] **2** You **eat into** money or a supply of something when you use some of it, usually without wanting or expecting to: *Problems start when you have to eat into the winter fuel stocks.*

eat out

You **eat out** when you have a meal in a restaurant rather than at home: *We can still afford to eat out once in a while.* [*same as* **dine out**; *opposite* **eat in**]

eat up

1 You **eat up** your food when you finish all the food that has been given to you, or finish all the food available; you can tell someone to **eat up** as a way of encouraging them to eat all the food they've been given: *Only once they've eaten their vegetables up are the children offered sweets.* ❑ *Eat up and I'll cut you a piece of chocolate cake.*

2 You can say someone **is eaten up** by an undesirable emotion such as jealousy when it completely controls the way they feel or behave: *The surviving partner can be eaten up by guilt as much as by their sense of loss.* ❑ *You could see the curiosity eating them all up.* [*same as* **consume**] **3** Something **eats up** money or another resource when it uses it all, usually very quickly: *What with insurance and road tax, running a car can soon eat up all your spare cash.* [*same as* **use up**; compare **get through**]

ebb /ɛb/: ebbs, ebbing, ebbed

ebb away

Something **ebbs away** when it gradually loses its strength or intensity until it finally disappears: *Much of the old anger had ebbed away, and Lila had begun to smile again.* ❑ *For the first time, she saw her authority over the party ebbing slowly away.* [*same as* **fade away, die out, peter out**; *opposite* **build up**]

edit /ˈɛdɪt/: edits, editing, edited

edit out

To **edit out** parts of something such as a book or a broadcast is to remove them: *For television, much of the sex and violence has to be edited out.* ❑ *Don't worry about swearing off camera; we can edit that out later.* [*same as* **cut out, take out**; *opposite* **put in, add in**]

egg /ɛg/: eggs, egging, egged

egg on

Someone **eggs** you **on** when they encourage you to do something risky, foolish or wrong: *He was basically a good lad who'd been egged on by so-called friends.* [*opposite* **talk out of, hold back, put off**; compare **urge on, spur on**]

eke /iːk/: ekes, eking, eked

eke out

1 You **eke out** a supply of something when you make it last as long as possible by only using a little at a time: *Each family has to eke out their half-litre ration of paraffin.* ❑ *Food got harder to come by, and we got better at eking every bit out.* **2** You **eke out** a living when you manage to get only just as much food or money as you need to live: *Crofters eked out a meagre existence in harsh times and a hostile climate.* [*same as* **scrape, scratch**]

elaborate /ɪˈlabəreɪt/: elaborates, elaborating, elaborated

elaborate on (*formal*)

You **elaborate on** something when you explain it more fully or give further details about it: *The Defence Secretary was pressed to elaborate on UN policy in Bosnia.* [*same as* **expand on, enlarge on** (*formal*)]

emanate /ˈɛməneɪt/: emanates, emanating, emanated

emanate from

You can say that things such as information, feelings, or smells **emanate from** a place or source when they come from, or come out from, that place or source: *Rumours of an impending election have been emanating from Central Office since early last week.* ❑ *Worshippers seem genuinely uplifted by the collective goodwill that emanates from the congregation.* [*same as* **come from**]

embark /ɪmˈbɑːk/: embarks, embarking, embarked

embark on *or* embark upon (*formal*)

1 You **embark on** something new, exciting or risky, or you **embark upon** it, when you start it or start doing it: *We would never embark upon such an ambitious project without doing thorough research.* ❑ *Students will be embarking on a journey of self-dis-*

covery. **2** You can say that you **are embarked on** something, or **are embarked upon** it, when you have started it or started to do it: *Russia was embarked on a programme of rearmament that could not be reversed.*

empty /'ɛmptɪ/: **empties, emptying, emptied**

empty out

You **empty out** a container when you remove all its contents; you can also say that you **empty out** the contents: *Once you've emptied the compost out, you can use the bag as a liner for a hanging basket.* ❑ *You have to empty out the boot before you can get at the spare wheel.* [compare **clear out**]

encroach /ɪn'kroutʃ/: **encroaches, encroaching, encroached**

encroach on

Something **encroaches on** or **upon** *eg* your time or your freedom when it begins to take part of it away, or when it gradually takes more and more away: *The job began to encroach on her weekends, which had always been sacred.* ❑ *As the urban sprawl encroaches on our countryside, more native species of plants and animals are being lost.* [*same as* **infringe on, intrude on** (*formal*)]

encumber /ɪn'kʌmbə(r)/: **encumbers, encumbering, encumbered**

encumber with (*formal*)

You can say you **are encumbered with** something when it limits your freedom of action or is a very heavy burden that you are finding difficult to cope with: *You enter government not with a clean slate, but encumbered with systems created by your opponents.* ❑ *They had encumbered themselves with a lawsuit that even the richest of families would have struggled to finance.* [*same as* **lumber with** (*informal*), **saddle with, weigh down with**]

end /ɛnd/: **ends, ending, ended**

end in

1 Something **ends in** what is at its end or tip: *The cane ended in a sharp point, and was a formidable weapon.* ❑ *There was a long, narrow garden ending in a small wooded area that served as a retreat.* **2** Something **ends in** what happens as its result or conclusion: *Disputes of this kind frequently end in bitterness and recrimination.* [*same as* **culminate in** (*formal*)]

end up

You **end up** in a particular place or doing a particular thing when you find yourself in that place or doing that thing, especially when it was not your intention: *We took the first train that came in, and ended up in Florence.* ❑ *The car wouldn't start, so I ended up having to walk.* [*same as* **wind up** (*informal*), **finish up, land up** (*informal*)]

endear /ɪn'dɪə(r)/: **endears, endearing, endeared**

endear to

Your personality or your behaviour **endears** you **to** someone when it causes them to like you or feel affection for you: *His speech will not have endeared him to the voters.* ❑ *Her honesty and sincerity endeared itself to all who knew her.* [compare **win over**]

endow /ɪn'dau/: **endows, endowing, endowed**

endow with (*formal*)

Someone **is endowed with** a gift or talent, or a good or enviable quality, when they are lucky enough to have been given it or to have had it from birth: *A military background had endowed him with enviable self-discipline.* ❑ *one of those women endowed with a natural grace and poise.*

engage /ɪn'geɪdʒ/: **engages, engaging, engaged**

engage in (*formal*)
You **engage in** an activity when you take part in it or are involved in it: *It would hardly be seemly for a minister of the Crown to engage in such underhand dealings.* ❑ *We asked them to explain the scientific experiments they were currently engaged in.*

enlarge /ɪn'lɑːdʒ/: **enlarges**, **enlarging**, **enlarged**

enlarge on *or* **enlarge upon** (*formal*)
You **enlarge on** something, especially a brief statement, or you **enlarge upon** it, when you explain it more fully or give further details about it: *We're not clear about the actual sequence of events. Would you enlarge on your statement, giving dates and times?* ❑ *We could not give our approval until what sketchy details we have have been enlarged upon.* [*same as* **expand on**, **elaborate on** (*formal*)]

enquire see **inquire**

enter /'ɛntə(r)/: **enters**, **entering**, **entered**

enter for
You **enter for** something such as a competition when you state formally that you want to take part in it: *They had entered for three out of the five races.* ❑ *John's English teacher has entered him for a national poetry competition.* [*same as* **go in for**, **put in for**]

enter into
1 You **enter into** something when you begin it or start being involved in it: *We have no intention of entering into negotiations with management.* ❑ *The judges' decision will be final and no correspondence will be entered into.* ❑ *You should think seriously before entering into a relationship with a married man.* **2** Things that **enter into** a situation affect it, form a part of it, or are relevant to it: *This is a private affair: my professional abilities don't enter into it.* ❑ *There's no reason why potential changes in the weather should enter into our assessment of a particular site.* [*same as* **have a bearing on**]

enter upon *or* **enter on** (*formal*)
You **enter upon** a particular course of action, or **enter on** it, when you start to take it: *We knew that once we had entered upon these investigations, no area of public life would be immune from scrutiny.* [*same as* **embark on** (*formal*)]

entitle /ɪn'taɪtəl/: **entitles**, **entitling**, **entitled**

entitle to
You **are entitled to** something, or **are entitled to** do something, when you have the right to receive it or do it: *Junior members of staff are only entitled to 22 days holiday a year.* ❑ *Special membership entitles you to play without booking in advance.* [*same as* **allow**]

entrust /ɪn'trʌst/: **entrusts**, **entrusting**, **entrusted**

entrust to
You **entrust** something important or valuable **to** someone when you give them the responsibility of dealing with it or taking care of it: *I wouldn't entrust my child's education to such incompetent teachers.*

entrust with
You **entrust** someone **with** something important or valuable when you give them the responsibility of dealing with it or taking care of it: *Marjorie was entrusted with the task of finding partners for everyone.*

even /'iːvən/: **evens**, **evening**, **evened**

even out
Things **even out**, or **are evened out**,

when they become, or are made, more level or equal: *The path climbed steeply and then evened out towards the house.* ❑ *A rationing system was introduced to even the grain supply out over the whole year.*

even up

Things **even up** or **are evened up** when they become, or are made, more equal: *That's two points to Ian and Neil, which evens the scores up a bit.* [*same as* **balance up**]

expand /ɪk'spand/: expands, expanding, expanded

expand on *or* expand upon

You **expand on** something, or **expand upon** it, when you explain it more fully or give further details about it: *The essay would have been better if you had taken the time to expand on your opening argument.* [*same as* **enlarge on** (*formal*), **elaborate on** (*formal*), **flesh out**]

explain /ɪk'spleɪn/: explains, explaining, explained

explain away

You **explain away** a mistake or wrongdoing when you give good reasons why it is not your fault, or why people should not treat it as serious or important: *It was clearly a major cock-up; it would be fun listening to them trying to explain it away to management.*

eye /aɪ/: eyes, eyeing, eyed

eye up (*informal*)

1 Someone **eyes** you **up** when they look at you in a way that suggests they are sexually attracted to you: *He had the unfortunate habit of eyeing up other men's wives.* [*same as* **make eyes at, ogle**] **2** You can also say that someone **eyes** something **up** when they look at it, usually from a distance, and identify it as something they would like to have: *I had already eyed up a table in the conservatory, quite close to where he was seated.* [*same as* **pick out**]

f

face /feɪs/: **faces**, **facing**, **faced**

face about
Someone, *eg* a soldier on parade, **faces about** when they turn around so that they are facing in the opposite direction: *They marched to the end of the parade ground, faced about (*or *about-faced) and marched back again.*

face down
You **face down** an opponent when you confront them in such a bold and confident way that they are no longer able to challenge you effectively: *She was always able to face down any opposition spokesman who was foolish enough to challenge her in the House.* [compare **face out**]

face out
You **face** an unpleasant person or situation **out** when you oppose them or deal with it courageously and firmly: *It may seem like a disaster, but if we face it out together, we'll come through okay.* [compare **face down**]

face up to
You **face up to** something difficult or unpleasant when you are brave and honest enough to accept it and deal with it: *We've got to face up to reality.* ❑ *She had to face up to the fact that she was too old to be offered parts as the romantic lead.* [*same as* **come to terms with**]

face with
1 You **face** the outer surface of something **with** a different material when you cover it with a layer of that material: *a brick building faced with stone.* **2** You **are faced with** something unpleasant when you are confronted with it and cannot avoid looking at it or dealing with it: *He was faced with such overwhelming opposition that he was forced to back down.* [*same as* **come up against**, **confront with**]

fade /feɪd/: **fades**, **fading**, **faded**

fade away
Something **fades away** when it disappears or ends slowly and gradually: *The sounds of the orchestra faded away until only a single violin could be heard.* ❑ *There is a saying that old soldiers never die, they simply fade away.* [*same as* **die away**]

fade in *or* **fade up**
In radio, television or films, to **fade in** or **fade up** a sound or image is to introduce it gradually making it slowly louder or more distinct until it can be heard or seen clearly: *The poignant image of the hero's wife and family looking anxiously out to sea fades in as his ship sinks beneath the waves.*
• *noun* **fade-in** *or* **fade-up**: **fade-ins** *or* **fade-ups**: *one of the first directors to use innovative cinematic techniques like fade-ins.*

fade out
To **fade out** a sound or image is to make it gradually become fainter and fainter until it eventually disappears.
• *noun* • **fade-out**: **fade-outs**: *Then comes the inevitable fade-out of the music, and the DJ's voice is jangling in your ears.*

faff /faf/: **faffs**, **faffing**, **faffed**

faff about *or* **faff around** (*slang*)
People sometimes say that you **are faffing about** or **faffing around** when they think you are wasting time and effort on unimportant things or doing things in a disorganized way: *She had spent the whole morning faffing about and so wasn't ready when I called to collect her.* [*same as* **fart about** (*vulgar slang*), **mess about** (*informal*)]

fag /fag/: **fags**, **fagging**, **fagged**

fag out (*informal*)
Something **fags** you **out** when it makes you very tired: *All this running up and down stairs has fagged me out.* [*same as* **exhaust**]
• *adjective* **fagged out**
You are **fagged out** when you are extremely tired: *By the time I got home, I was fagged out and just wanted to crawl into bed.* [*same as* **done in** (*informal*), **exhausted**]

fall /fɔːl/: **falls**, **falling**, **fell** /fɛl/, **fallen** /'fɔːlən/

fall about (*informal*)
People **fall about** when they laugh uncontrollably or helplessly: *The audience fell about at his ludicrous antics.*

fall apart
1 Things **fall apart** when they break up into separate pieces because they are badly made or worn: *These shoes weren't the bargain I thought they were. They fell apart after just a couple of weeks.* [*same as* **come to pieces, fall to pieces**] **2 a** Something such as a system, organization or partnership **falls apart** when it collapses or fails: *No-one seems to be in control. The whole system is falling apart.* ❑ *Their marriage was showing signs of falling apart.* [*same as* **break up, disintegrate**] **b** Someone **falls apart** when they lose control of themselves and are unable to think clearly or behave in a sensible or rational way: *He spent weeks preparing for the trial but when he stood up in the witness box he just fell apart.* [*same as* **disintegrate**]

fall away
1 The land **falls away** where it slopes downwards, usually steeply: *At the bottom of the garden the land falls away to a sandy bay.* **2** Something **falls away** from the place where it was attached when it breaks off and falls down: *Part of the cliff face had fallen away leaving the fossils exposed.* **3** Your friends and supporters **fall away** when they begin to desert you and become fewer and fewer; the level of support for something **falls away** when it becomes less or smaller, especially gradually: *The Tories saw their support in rural constituencies falling away.* [*same as* **fall off**] **4** Something **falls away** when it disappears: *His old selfish attitudes fell away when he realized how much his friend had suffered by his thoughtless actions.* **5** You **fall away** from a position you have gained or achieved when you drop to a lower position: *Jose-Maria Olazabal made up some ground with a round of 72, but Feherty fell away with a 77.*

fall back
1 You **fall back** when you retreat or move back, usually because someone is attacking you or moving towards you in a threatening way: *Our troops had to fall back in the face of a determined assault by the enemy.* ❑ *The rioters fell back as the mounted policemen advanced.* [*same as* **draw back, retreat, retire** (*formal*)] **2** You **fall back** when you move backwards away from someone or something that you find frightening or horrifying: *Auguste fell back in horror when he saw what was in the box.* [*same as* **draw back, recoil**]

fall back on *or* **fall back upon**
You **fall back on** or **upon** a previously prepared plan or supply when you use it, *eg* when something else has failed or because there is no other alternative available: *If he loses his job, he has no*

savings to fall back on. [*same as* **resort to**]

fall behind

1 You **fall behind** when you progress more slowly than other people and they get ahead of you: *He's fallen behind the rest of the class and needs extra tuition to catch up.* ❑ *We mustn't let Britain fall behind in technology.* [*same as* **lag behind**] **2** You **fall behind** with payments that ought to be made at regular intervals when you fail to pay one or more of them when they become due; you **fall behind with** *eg* work that ought to be completed by a certain time when you do not complete it on time: *They've fallen behind with their mortgage payments and may have to sell their house.* ❑ *He's always falling behind with his paperwork.*

fall down

1 Something such as a plan or argument **falls down** when it fails because it is shown to be inadequate or false: *That is the point where his theory falls down.* **2** A building **is falling down** when it is in such a bad state of repair that parts of it are beginning to collapse or fall off: *They don't seem in the least concerned that the house is falling down around them.*

fall down on

Someone **falls down on** a job or task when they do not do it properly: *The police were accused of falling down on the job because the crime figures continued to rise.* [*same as* **fail**]

fall for

1 You **fall for** someone when you fall in love with them: *She always seems to fall for the most unsuitable men.* **2** You **fall for** something such as a lie when you are deceived by it or believe that it is true: *You didn't fall for that old story, did you?* ❑ *He told me he was an expert in antiques and, like a fool, I fell for it.*

fall in

1 A structure such as a ceiling or roof **falls in** when it collapses inwards: *The roof of the tunnel fell in, burying the unfortunate miners who were working at the coal face.* [*same as* **cave in**] **2** When soldiers **fall in** they take their places to form the lines or ranks of a military parade: *There was an undignified scramble as the sergeant major ordered the new recruits to fall in.* [compare **fall out**]

fall into

1 Someone or something **falls into** a particular state or condition when they reach or enter that state or condition, either suddenly or gradually: *She fell into a deep sleep.* ❑ *Many of the old dialects have fallen into disuse.* **2** You **fall into** a certain pattern of behaviour when you begin to behave in that way, often unintentionally: *He may come to feel that understanding is beyond him, and fall into that apathy which leaves everything to authority.* ❑ *He's fallen into some very bad habits recently.* [*same as* **get into**] **3** You **fall into** conversation with someone when you begin a conversation with that person, often by chance: *I fell into conversation with a very interesting old man on the plane journey home.*

fall in with

1 You **fall in with** an arrangement or suggestion made by someone else when you agree to it: *I trust him to do the right thing and will be quite happy to fall in with anything he might suggest.* **2** You **fall in with** a person or group of people when you meet them and follow what they do, or take the same direction as they do: *As a teenager, he fell in with a very bad crowd and was always in trouble with the police.* ❑ *The Captain informs us that we might expect to fall in with some homeward bound vessels.*

fall off

An amount, number, rate or standard **falls off** when it decreases or gets worse: *The number of competitors has fallen off in recent years.* [*same as* **fall**

away, lessen, deteriorate]

• *noun* **falling-off:** *Opinion polls show there has been a distinct falling-off in support for the Tories in the South East.*

fall on

1 (*formal or literary*) People **fall on** or **upon** an enemy when they attack them suddenly and fiercely: *Our troops fell on the enemy as they lay asleep.* ❑ *When a population gets out of balance with its environment disaster occurs, and it falls upon itself for a bit of frantic nibbling and other distressed rat-like behaviour.* **2** People **fall on** or **upon** food when they start eating it quickly and greedily: *The men fell upon the bread and cheese as if they hadn't eaten for days.* ❑ *You fall with relief upon your packed lunch.* **3** A duty, responsibility or cost **falls on** or **upon** you when you are the person who must bear it: *The responsibility for the expedition's failure fell squarely on his shoulders.* [*same as* **fall to**] **4** When one person **falls on** another they put their arms around that other person and hug them, usually because they are happy or excited: *She fell on his neck and kissed him over and over again in her joy and relief.* **5 a** If a date **falls on** a particular day, that is the day on which it occurs: *My birthday falls on a Sunday this year.* **b** Stress **falls on** a particular syllable when that is the syllable where the stress occurs. **6** Your eye or gaze **falls on** or **upon** someone or something when you catch sight of them: *His eyes fell on an interesting-looking book at the back of the top shelf.*

fall out

1 Hair, fur or teeth **fall out** when they become loose and come away from the body: *My hair fell out in handfuls.* **2** (*formal*) Events **fall out** in a particular way when that is the way that they happen: *And so it fell out that there was a new young king.* **3** One person **falls out** with another when they quarrel and are no longer friendly towards each other: *That was a silly thing for you and Andrew to have fallen out over.* ❑ *Even Mikhail Pogodin, the philosopher of Official Nationality, fell out with the authorities in the course of the war.* ❑ *I'm going to end up falling out with you if you keep criticizing my boyfriend.* **4** Soldiers **fall out** when they leave their positions in the lines or ranks of a military parade. [compare **fall in**]

• *noun* **fallout**

1 Radioactive **fallout** is the radioactive particles that settle on the earth after a nuclear explosion. **2** The **fallout** from an event is the bad or unpleasant consequences that result from it and which affect people who may not be directly involved in it: *one of the innocent victims of the fallout from the government's cost-cutting exercise.*

fall over

1 Someone or something that is upright **falls over** when they lose their balance or are knocked off balance, and finish lying on the ground: *Many of the gravestones were leaning over precariously, while others had fallen over and were lying smashed to pieces on the ground.* ❑ *She tripped and fell over.* **2** You **are falling over** yourself to do something when you are very eager to do it: *Banks and building societies are falling over themselves to lend you money and sell you new products like personal insurance.*

fall through

A plan **falls through** when it fails or cannot be achieved: *My plans for a winter break have fallen through.*

fall to

1 (*old or literary*) People **fall to** when they start something: *Dinner was served, and being extremely hungry, we all fell to immediately.* ❑ *Then goes he to the length of his arm, and, with his other hand thus o'er his brow, he falls to such perusal of my face, as he would draw it.* **2** (*formal*) It **falls to** you to do something if it is your responsibility or duty to do it: *It falls to me to propose the health of the bridesmaids.* [*same as* **fall on**]

fall under
If something **falls under** a particular heading or category, it is included under that heading or belongs to that category: *I don't think a trip to Singapore falls under the heading of incidental expenses.* ❑ *European mega-bids would fall under EC monopoly rules in current circumstances, anyway.* [*same as* **come under**]

fall upon see fall on

fan /fan/: fans, fanning, fanned

fan out
People or things **fan out** when they move forwards and outwards from the same starting point: *The six planes began the manoeuvre by flying in parallel formation, fanning out as they passed over the airfield.* ❑ *The villagers fanned out across the moor, looking in every nook and cranny for the missing child.*

farm /fɑːm/: farms, farming, farmed

farm out
1 A business **farms out** its work when it distributes what it cannot do itself to other businesses or individuals to complete: *now that so many new productions are farmed out to independent programme makers.* **2** Parents **farm out** their children when they give them to someone else to look after, usually because they want to spend time doing other things: *The boys were farmed out to relatives while their parents were abroad.*

fart /fɑːt/: farts, farting, farted

fart about *or* fart around (*vulgar slang*)
When someone says you **are farting about** or **around**, they mean you are wasting time doing silly or unnecessary things when you should be dealing with something that really needs to be done: *For God's sake, will you stop farting about and get on with cutting the grass!* [*same as* **faff about** (*slang*), **mess about** (*informal*)]

fasten /ˈfɑːsən/: fastens, fastening, fastened

fasten on *or* fasten upon
You **fasten on** or **upon** an idea, suggestion or proposal when you concentrate eagerly on it, and refuse to drop it: *But he was completely unsure how matter could affect mind, and, of course, Berkeley fastened on this.* [*same as* **seize on**]

fasten on to
Someone **fastens on to** you when they follow you about and won't let you get away from them: *Aubrey fastened on to me at the party and no matter what I did I couldn't get rid of him.* [*same as* **latch on to**]

fasten up
You **fasten** an opening in something **up** when you use buttons, hooks or straps to close it: *Put your hat on and fasten up the top button of your jacket so that you don't catch cold.*

father /ˈfɑːðə(r)/: fathers, fathering, fathered

father on *or* father upon (*formal*)
You **father** something **on** or **upon** someone when you say or suggest that they are the person who first thought of it or originated it: *Fathering the idea entirely on him was a convenient way of avoiding unpleasant confrontations with irate neighbours.* ❑ *How dare you try to father this shambles on me!*

fathom /ˈfaðəm/: fathoms, fathoming, fathomed

fathom out
You **fathom** a problem or mystery **out**

when you manage to solve it or find an explanation for it: *Most of the time he's perfectly sociable, then for no apparent reason he won't speak to anyone for days on end. I just can't fathom it out.* ❑ *It took me ages to fathom out what was going on.* [*same as* **work out**, **suss out** (*informal*)]

fatten /'fatən/: **fattens**, **fattening**, **fattened**

fatten up

An animal **is fattened up** when it is given plenty of food so that it gains enough weight, especially to be killed for food: *The bull calves were kept indoors and fattened up on a mixture of concentrates and silage.* ❑ *Connie is far too thin; she needs fattening up.*

favour (*AmE* **favor**) /'feɪvə(r)/: **favours**, **favouring**, **favoured**

favour with (*formal or humorous*)

You **favour** somebody **with** something when you do that thing for them or oblige them in that way: *Will you be favouring us with your presence this evening?*

fawn /fɔːn/: **fawns**, **fawning**, **fawned**

fawn on *or* fawn upon

Someone **fawns on** or **upon** you when they continually do or say things to flatter and please you and make you feel that you are very important: *He likes to surround himself with adoring acolytes who fawn on him and feed his vanity.*

fear /fɪə(r)/: **fears**, **fearing**, **feared**

fear for

You **fear for** someone when you are afraid that something bad might happen to them or that they might be in danger: *When we heard about the coup d'état, we feared for the safety of the British advisors who had been working with the deposed government.*

feature /'fiːtʃə(r)/: **features**, **featuring**, **featured**

feature in

Someone or something **features in** something, or they **are featured in** it, when they play a part, or are given a prominent role, in it: *Clint Eastwood featured in a series of popular 'spaghetti' westerns in the '60s and early '70s.* ❑ *He was featured in one of the tabloids as the man most likely to become prime minister.*

feed /fiːd/: **feeds**, **feeding**, **fed** /fɛd/

feed back

Reactions or ideas **are fed back** when they come back to the person or people in charge of monitoring or co-ordinating a process or method of working: *The kitchen staff expect the restaurant manager to feed back customer response.*

• *noun* **feedback:** *Have you had any feedback from customers on how they like the new software package?*

feed in *or* feed into

You **feed** things **in** or **into** a machine when you put them in, one after the other, for the machine to process: *Meat is fed into the machine at one end and comes out as sausages at the other end.* ❑ *Once the raw data has been fed into the computer, the draughtsman can play about with it to produce various effects.*

feed off

One thing **feeds off** or **feeds on** another when it uses that other thing as a supply for the things it needs to go on existing or growing: *Her resentment and anger grew day by day, feeding on her irrational jealousy and what she saw was his lack of attention to her needs.*

feed on

You **are fed on** a certain food or diet when that is what you are given as food: *The pigs were fed on scraps from the kitchen.* ❑ *a whole generation of young people fed on a diet of propaganda and misinformation.* [see also **feed off**]

feed to
Something **is fed to** a person or animal when it is given to them as food: *The fish heads can be fed to the cats.*

feed up
You **feed** a person or animal **up** by giving them plenty of good food to make them fatter: *You're much too thin; you look as if you need feeding up.*
• *adjective (informal)* **fed up**
You are **fed up** when you are bored, unhappy or dissatisfied; you are **fed up** with something when you are dissatisfied with it or it makes you bored and unhappy: *You look very fed up. What's wrong?* ❑ *I'm fed up with my job, my appearance, my marriage: everything, in fact.* [*same as* **cheesed off** (*informal*), **browned off** (*informal*)]

feel /fiːl/: feels, feeling, felt /fɛlt/

feel for
1 You **feel for** something that you cannot see when you use your hands to search for it: *The hallway was pitch dark and James had to feel for the light switch.* **2** You **feel for** someone in trouble or distress when you have feelings of sympathy for them because you understand what they are going through: *I can understand why you are so upset, and I feel for you, I really do.*

feel out
You **feel** someone **out** about something when you try to find out what they think about it, without asking them about it directly or being too specific: *Informal talks were held so that the UK representative could feel out what their likely response would be.* [*same as* **sound out**]

feel up (*informal*)
Someone **feels** another person **up** when they touch that person's body in an intimate way, either to arouse them sexually or for their own sexual satisfaction: *If he doesn't stop feeling up the girls in the office, one of these days he'll find himself accused of sexual harrassment.* [*same as* **touch up** (*informal*)]

feel up to
You **feel up to** something when you feel able to do it or cope with it: *'Let's go for a long walk.' 'No, I'm sorry, I just don't feel up to it at the moment.'* ❑ *'If you feel up to it,' Noreen said at breakfast, 'we'll take you down to the Arts Centre in the van.'*

fence /fɛns/: fences, fencing, fenced

fence in
You **fence in** something, or you **fence** it **in**, when you enclose or confine it within a fence: *The lions are safely fenced in and can't escape.*

fence off
You **fence off** a piece of land, or you **fence** it **off**, when you build a fence round it, or separate it from the land around it with a fence: *They've fenced off part of the park as a children's play area.*

fend /fɛnd/: fends, fending, fended

fend off
1 You **fend off** an attacker, or blows, when you stop them hurting you by turning or pushing them aside: *He put up his hands to fend off the birds.* **2** You **fend off** questions when you avoid answering them; you **fend off** criticism or a challenge when you prevent it from affecting or damaging you: *Exhibition organizers, in some instances, have to fend off proposals for inclusions with a political or particular cultural bias.* ❑ *His press agent successfully fended off inquiries from dozens of reporters.* [*same as* **ward off**]

ferret /ˈfɛrɪt/: ferrets, ferreting, ferreted

ferret out (*informal*)
You **ferret out** information when you

discover it after a determined search: *His unconventional methods of cross examination have proved to be very successful in ferreting out the truth.* [*same as* **unearth, bring to light**]

fetch /fɛtʃ/: **fetches**, **fetching**, **fetched**

---

fetch up (*informal*)
You **fetch up** somewhere when you arrive there, especially unexpectedly or unintentionally: *I broke my leg and fetched up in hospital.* [*same as* **land up** (*informal*)]

fiddle /ˈfɪdəl/: **fiddles**, **fiddling**, **fiddled**

---

fiddle about *or* **fiddle around**
1 You **fiddle about** or **around** when you waste time doing small unimportant things: *Stop fiddling about and get on with your work.* [*same as* **mess about** (*informal*)] **2** You **fiddle about** or **around** with something when you waste time making small unimportant changes or adjustments to it: *He spends all his time fiddling around with the engine of that motorbike but never goes anywhere on it.* [*same as* **tinker with, fool around with**]

fiddle with
1 You **fiddle with** something when you touch or move it repeatedly, *eg* because you are nervous: *He stood in the doorway, fiddling with his tie and looking embarrassed.* [*same as* **finger**] **2** You **fiddle with** something that does not belong to you when you touch or move it without permission: *Who's been fiddling with my tools; they aren't in their proper places.* [*same as* **interfere with, tamper with, monkey around with** (*informal*)]

fight /faɪt/: **fights**, **fighting**, **fought** /fɔːt/

---

fight back
1 You **fight back** against someone who has attacked you when you defend yourself and attack them in turn: *For a while we thought the cancer was going to kill him, but he seems to be fighting back now.* ❑ *If you don't fight back he'll just go on bullying you.* [*same as* **retaliate**; *opposite* **give way to, submit**] **2** You **fight back** the impulse or desire to do something when you make a great effort to control yourself and stop yourself doing it: *As the train drew out of the station, she stood on the platform fighting back her tears.* [*same as* **fight down**]
• *noun* **fight-back**: **fight-backs**
When someone who has been attacked stages or organizes a **fight-back** they begin to defend themselves by making an effort to fight their attacker.

fight down
You **fight down** strong emotions when you make a great effort not to show them: *She fought down an almost irresistible urge to scream.* [*same as* **repress, suppress**]

fight for
You **fight for** something when you struggle hard to obtain or achieve it: *He was lying on the floor fighting for breath and clutching his chest.*

fight off
1 You **fight off** an illness when you get rid of it and recover from it: *I thought I was going to get flu last week but I managed to fight it off.* [*same as* **ward off, stave off**] **2** You **fight off** people who are attacking you or bothering you, or you **fight** them **off**, when you manage to drive them away: *The enemy tried several times to storm the castle, but each time they were fought off.* ❑ *We had to fight off the reporters as we went into the house.* ❑ *He has so many women after him he literally has to fight them off.* [*same as* **beat off**]

fight out
People **fight** it **out** when they keep arguing or fighting about something until one person or group eventually

wins: *I don't know whose turn it is to wash the dishes; you'll have to fight it out between you.*

figure /'fɪgə(r)/ *or* /'fɪgjə(r)/: **figures**, **figuring**, **figured**

figure in

Something or someone **figures in** your plans or calculations when you have included it, or it forms part of your plans or calculations: *George hadn't figured in the cost of running the machine for twenty-four hours a day.*

figure on (*especially AmE; informal*)

1 You **figure on** doing something when that is what you intend to do: *I figure on finishing the book by the end of the year.* **2** You **figure on** something happening when you make plans that depend on it happening: *I hadn't figured on Luther turning up, so there wasn't enough room for us all in the van.* [*same as* **reckon on**]

figure out (*informal*)

1 You **figure** the cost of something **out** when you calculate it: *You'll have to figure out the compound interest to find the overall cost of the loan.* [*same as* **work out**] **2** You **figure out** something that you do not understand or do not know how to do, when you come to understand it or find out how to do it by thinking hard about it: *The engine came in so many bits it was impossible to figure out which went where.* ❑ *I can't figure out why she left home so suddenly.* [*same as* **work out**]

file /faɪl/: **files**, **filing**, **filed**

file away

You **file** a document or piece of information **away** when you put or store it away in a box or folder so that you can refer to it later if necessary: *I can't find my copy of the letter; my secretary must have filed it away.* ❑ *Be careful what you say to her. She files away every little scrap of gossip in her memory so that she can pass it on to her friends.*

file for (*legal*)

A person **files for** something in a court of law, especially divorce, when they ask the court to grant it by submitting an official request.

fill /fɪl/: **fills**, **filling**, **filled**

fill in

1 You **fill** a hole or gap **in** when you put in material to make it level with the surrounding surface, or you add something that will make it complete: *workmen filling in the holes in the road* ❑ *I had to fill in the gaps in the conversation by talking about the weather.* **2** You **fill in** a form, or you **fill** it **in**, when you write information in the spaces as required: *Take this form and fill in your name and age at the top.* ❑ *Fill this application form in and return it to the club secretary.* [*same as* **fill out, fill up**] **3** You **fill in** for someone when you do their job temporarily while they are ill or absent from work: *I'm going into hospital; could you fill in for me for a few days?* [*same as* **stand in, deputize**] **4** You **fill in** time when you do something to occupy or pass the time while waiting for something to happen: *We filled in the four hours between flights by taking a bus into town and exploring.*

• *noun (informal)* **fill-in**: **fill-ins**

A **fill-in** is someone or something that does someone else's job or takes something else's place temporarily: *We'll need to get an agency nurse as a fill-in while Karen's off on maternity leave.* [*same as* **stand-in**]

fill in on

You **fill** someone **in on** something when you inform them fully about it: *Could you fill me in on the latest developments?* ❑ *When you've been filled in on all the details we can have a meeting to discuss the project.*

fill out

1 You **fill out** a form when you write

information in the spaces as required: *He was getting tired of filling out application forms.* [*same as* **fill in, fill up**] **2** A thin person **fills out** when they gain weight: *After a few weeks of the healthy sea air and good food, her cheeks had filled out and acquired a healthy colour.* **3** You **fill** something such as a story **out** when you add whatever is needed to make it complete or more substantial: *Your essay is too short; you'll have to fill it out a bit if you want to get a good mark.* [*same as* **flesh out, expand**]

fill up

1 a You **fill up** a container when you put enough of something into it to make it full: *They filled up their water bottles at a little stream.* ❑ *He kept filling up our glasses and we got quite drunk.* **b** You **fill up** your motor vehicle when you fill its petrol tank with petrol: *I'm just going down to the garage to fill the car up.* **2** A place **fills up** with something when it becomes full of it: *The shop filled up with customers as soon as the doors opened.* ❑ *He peeped through the curtain and saw that the theatre was filling up nicely.* **3** You **fill up** a form when you write information in the spaces as required: *You have to fill up so many forms when you take your car abroad.* [*same as* **fill in, fill out**]

film /fɪlm/: films, filming, filmed

film over

A transparent surface **films over** when a dull or cloudy layer forms over it: *He had a lump in his throat and his eyes began to film over with tears.* [*same as* **cloud over, mist over**]

filter /fɪltə(r)/: filters, filtering, filtered

filter out

To **filter** something **out** is to remove it using a filter or filter-like process: *You can filter dirt out of the oil quite easily.* ❑ *Start by filtering out the applicants who have no computing experience.*

filter through

Information **filters through** when it reaches people gradually or by indirect means: *When reports of the victory began to filter through the citizens of Rome took to the streets to celebrate.*

find /faɪnd/: finds, finding, found /faʊnd/

find against (*legal*)

In a court case where there is a plaintiff and a defendant, the judge or jury **finds against** one of the two when they decide on the evidence they have heard that that person has not won the case: *If the judge finds against them they'll have to pay costs as well as any award for compensation.* [compare **find for**]

find for (*legal*)

In a court case where there is a plaintiff and a defendant, the judge or jury **finds for** one of the two when they decide on the evidence that that person has won the case: *After reviewing all the evidence, the court found for the plaintiff.* [compare **find against**]

find out

1 You **find out** something you did not know, or you **find** it **out**, when you discover it or learn about it, by chance or through investigation: *Could you find out when the bus leaves?* ❑ *I found out that she had left home three days earlier.* ❑ *Find something out about Columbus before tomorrow's lesson.* ❑ *Children enjoy finding out how things work.* **2** You **find** someone **out** when you discover that they have done something wrong or dishonest: *Though he had been very careful to cover his tracks, his wife found out that he was having an affair.* ❑ *Aren't you afraid of being found out?* ❑ *Be sure your sins will find you out.*

fine /faɪn/: fines, fining, fined

fine down
You **fine** something **down** when you make it more effective, efficient or economical by reducing it or cutting out whatever is unnecessary: *They have mastered the technical details and just need to fine down the manufacturing process to produce a marketable product.* [*same as* **refine**]

finish /ˈfɪnɪʃ/: **finishes**, **finishing**, **finished**

finish off
1 You **finish off** a task when you do everything that needs to be done to complete it: *I'm just finishing off this essay.* [*same as* **complete**] **2** You **finish off** food or drink when you eat or drink the last bit of it: *Finish off your pudding quickly.* **3** (*informal*) To **finish** someone **off** is to kill or destroy them, or defeat them completely: *A sudden thrust of the cavalry officer's sword finished him off.* ❑ *I had managed to wade through all six courses, but the chocolate pudding finished me off.* [= I couldn't eat anything else]

finish up
You **finish up** somewhere, or in some situation, if that is what happens to you in the end: *He'll finish up in jail.* ❑ *He started in the company as a tea boy and finished up as managing director.* [*same as* **end up**]

finish up with
You **finish up with** something when that is what you are left with at the end of a period of time: *If you don't stop smoking you're going to finish up with lung cancer or heart disease.*

finish with
1 You **finish with** a person when you end a relationship with them; you can also say you **are finished with** someone when you have no more to say to them, usually after scolding them or giving them instructions of some sort: *I finished with Jane last week.* ❑ *Wait; I haven't finished with you yet.* **2** You **finish with** something when you do not need it any more and stop using it: *You can have the newspaper when I've finished with it.* ❑ *I don't take drugs anymore; I've finished with all that.*

fire /faɪə(r)/: **fires**, **firing**, **fired**

fire ahead *or* **fire away** (*informal*)
Someone **fires ahead** or **fires away** when they start to say or ask whatever it is they want to: *Though I told him to wait until he could see Daddy alone, he just fired ahead and asked him for money in front of everyone.* ❑ *'May I ask you something?' 'Fire away!'* [*same as* **shoot** (*informal*)]

fire off
1 A bullet or other missile **is fired off** when it is shot from a gun: *The guard of honour fired off three rounds.* [*same as* **let off**] **2** (*informal*) You **fire off** questions when you ask them quickly one after the other; you **fire off** *eg* an angry protest when you send it out quickly, like a bullet from a gun: *The examiner was firing off questions so quickly I couldn't keep up.* ❑ *He fired off a letter to the newspaper threatening to sue them if they repeated the allegation.*

firm /fɜːm/: **firms**, **firming**, **firmed**

firm up
1 You **firm** your body **up** when you make your muscles firmer by doing exercise: *If you do the exercises every day you'll soon firm up those flabby tummy muscles.* [compare **tone up**] **2** You **firm up** *eg* an agreement or contract when you settle the details that have not yet been agreed or covered and include them in a fixed form: *Can we have a meeting to firm up the arrangements for next week's launch?* [*same as* **finalize**]

fish /fɪʃ/: **fishes**, **fishing**, **fished**

fish for

You can say that someone **is fishing for** information when they are trying to get it by subtle and indirect means; someone **is fishing for** compliments when they say something intended to prompt their listeners to pay them compliments: *The Sun reporter has talked to all his neighbours fishing for any whiff of scandal.* ❑ *When I said I wasn't happy with my appearance, I hope you didn't think I was fishing for compliments.* [*same as* **angle for**]

fish out (*informal*)

You **fish** something **out** when you pull it out of the place or container it is in: *He fell off the pier into the sea and we had to use a boathook to fish him out.* ❑ *He put his hand in his coat pocket and fished out a crumbled card with his name and address printed on it.* [*same as* **pull out**]

fish up

You **fish** something **up** from *eg* the bottom of a river or lake when you raise it out of the water: *The bundle of clothes Jonas had wanted so much to get rid of was fished up from the river.*

fit /fɪt/: **fits**, **fitting**, **fitted**

In American English, **fit** is sometimes used as the past tense and past participle.

fit in *or* fit into

1 You **fit** something **in** somewhere when you manage to find or make enough room or space for it; something **fits into** a space when the space is large enough for you to put it there: *I don't think we could fit all four chairs in the boot.* ❑ *There's a bit of room on the back seat; I'm sure a small person could fit in.* ❑ *Would the bookcase fit into that space under the window?* ❑ *Charlie could only just fit his swollen toes into the heavy leather boots.* [*same as* **get in, get into, go in, go into**] **2** Someone who doesn't **fit in** is different from others in a particular group or society, and doesn't really belong to it; you might also say that such a person doesn't **fit into** the group or society: *Thomas was a loner who never really tried to fit in.* ❑ *She knew her mother would never fit into the world of the idle rich.* [*same as* **blend in, belong, conform**; compare **stand out, stick out**] **3** You **fit** someone or something **in**, or **fit** them **into** your schedule, when you find time to deal with them: *I won't have the time to fit in everything I want to do.* ❑ *Could we fit a meeting in some time this afternoon?* ❑ *I'll see if the doctor can fit you in tomorrow morning.* [compare **squeeze in**] **4** You might use **fit in** or **fit into** when you're talking about someone's role, function or status, usually in relation to others: *I don't really see where the assistant manager fits in.* ❑ *Would this kind of letter fit into the category of 'customer complaints'?*

fit in with

1 To **fit in with** something such as a plan or system is to suit it or work as part of it: *Some convenience foods fit neatly in with ideas about healthy eating.* ❑ *These American methods don't really fit in with the way things have traditionally been done here.* [*same as* **match**; *opposite* **clash with, be at odds with**] **2** You **fit in with** someone else's plans when you adjust your own plans to suit theirs: *I'll fit in with whatever's convenient for you.*

fit out

To **fit** someone or something **out** is to supply them with the equipment they need: *On arrival, new recruits are fitted out with full combat kit.* ❑ *The cost of fitting out the older ships would be prohibitive.* [*same as* **kit out, rig out, equip**]

fit up (*informal*)

Someone **fits** you **up** if they invent false evidence that persuades the police, or another authority, that you've committed a crime or other offence: *Can't you see I've been fitted up?* [*same as* stitch up (*informal*), **frame**]

fix /fɪks/: **fixes**, **fixing**, **fixed**

fix on

1 You **fix on** something when you select it as a final or definite choice: *We haven't yet fixed on the kind of wedding we'd like.* **2** You **fix** your eyes or your attention **on** something when you look at, or concentrate on, that thing only: *Robert answered abstractedly, his gaze fixed on the woman in the red dress.* ❑ *Are they required to fix all their energies on the one project?* [*same as* **focus**, **concentrate**]

fix up

1 You **fix** something **up** when you make firm plans or arrangements for it to happen: *We've managed to fix up a two-week holiday at the end of September.* ❑ *I've fixed up for her to go and see Dr Graham.* ❑ *The secretary has the job of fixing up temporary accommodation for visitors.* ❑ *John's asked me to fix him up a three-o'clock meeting with the directors.* [*same as* **arrange**] **2** (*informal*) You **fix** someone **up** with something when you provide them with it: *I can easily fix you up with a bed for the night.* ❑ *She's offered to put me up in her flat, till I get myself fixed up.* ❑ *If you can fix yourself up with a pair of boots, there's a place for you in the team.* ❑ *It was Jed who got me fixed up with a new one.* **3** (*informal*) You **fix** something **up** when you make or build it quickly, using whatever materials are available: *They managed to fix up a rough shelter with sheets of plywood and some old tarpaulins.* ❑ *We've fixed her up a sandpit in the garden, from a couple of sawn-off teachests knocked together.* [*same as* **rig up** (*informal*), **knock up** (*informal*), **improvise**] **4** (*informal*) You **fix** something **up** when you carry out the repairs or improvements necessary to make it fit to use: *It wouldn't cost much to fix up the flat.* [*same as* **do up** (*informal*), **refurbish** (*formal*), **renovate** (*formal*)]

fix with (*formal*)

You **fix** someone **with** a stare when you stare at them intently: *The Doctor fixed Mortimer with a level gaze.* ❑ *Maggie had fixed him with her clear grey eyes.*

fizzle /ˈfɪzəl/: **fizzles**, **fizzling**, **fizzled**

fizzle out (*informal*)

Something such as anger or enthusiasm **fizzles out** when, soon after appearing or beginning to develop, it disappears or comes to nothing: *What initial outrage there was fizzled out as soon as the offer of money was made.* ❑ *The coup attempt fizzled out after widespread support failed to materialize.* [compare **peter out**]

flag /flag/: **flags**, **flagging**, **flagged**

flag down

You **flag down** a vehicle when you get the driver to stop by waving: *We flagged a taxi down in the Strand.* ❑ *Two men in police uniform flagged us down.*

flake /fleɪk/: **flakes**, **flaking**, **flaked**

flake off *or* flake away

Something that coats or covers a surface, such as paint, **flakes off** or **flakes away** when bits of it fall off the surface: *The rust flakes off if you rub it with wire wool.* ❑ *Some of the roughcast was flaking off the side walls.* ❑ *There were lighter patches where the old varnish had flaked away.* [compare **peel off**]

flake out (*informal*)

You **flake out** when you let yourself fall into a chair or on to a bed, and perhaps fall asleep, because you're exhausted: *We just dropped our rucksacks and flaked out on the grass.* [compare **flop down**, **pass out**, **black out**, **keel over**]

flare /flɛə(r)/: **flares**, **flaring**, **flared**

flare up

1 A fire **flares up** when it suddenly begins to burn brightly: *There was a gust of wind and the flames flared up.* **2** People often use **flare up** to talk about the moment when feelings, discussions or situations suddenly become angry or violent: *For an instant it looked as if long-awaited violence might flare up.* [*same as* **break out**, **boil over**] **3** Someone who **flares up** suddenly begins shouting angrily: *She would flare up at me for no apparent reason.* [*same as* **blow up** (*informal*), **fly off the handle** (*informal*), **blow one's top** (*informal*)]

• *noun* **flare-up**: **flare-ups**

A **flare-up** is a sudden outburst of anger or violence: *They feared that a failure to address prisoners' grievances swiftly would result in another flare-up of rioting.*

flash /flaʃ/: **flashes**, **flashing**, **flashed**

flash back to

Your mind **flashes back to** an event in your past when the memory of it suddenly comes into your mind, perhaps only briefly: *My thoughts kept flashing back to Grace, and what she had said.* [compare **drift back**]

• *noun* **flashback**: **flashbacks**

In a film or play, a **flashback** is a scene showing events from a character's past, as the character is remembering them: *Then there's a brief flashback to the row he had with his wife immediately before the accident.* ❑ *We're shown episodes from his childhood in flashback.*

flatten /ˈflatən/: **flattens**, **flattening**, **flattened**

flatten down

You **flatten** something **down** when you press or push it down to make it flat or smooth: *He rubbed the cream into his hair, combed it, then flattened it down with the palm of his hand.* ❑ *We need one of those hydraulic machines for flattening down soil.*

flatten out

An area of hilly or bumpy land **flattens out** when it becomes flat or flatter: *The garden flattens out towards the south side.* [*same as* **level out**; compare **even out**]

fleck /flɛk/: **flecked**

fleck with

A surface that **is flecked with** something such as light or colour has spots or small patches of light or colour on it: *The summer sky was brilliant blue, flecked with flimsy white clouds.*

flesh /flɛʃ/: **fleshes**, **fleshing**, **fleshed**

flesh out

You **flesh out** something such as a report or a story when you make it fuller or more complete by adding details to the brief summary or basic facts you've already given: *The first chapter would benefit from having a couple of the characters fleshed out a bit.* ❑ *Don't just give us the dates of battles; flesh the history out a bit for us.* [*same as* **expand on**, **enlarge on** (*formal*)]

flick /flɪk/: **flicks**, **flicking**, **flicked**

flick through

You **flick through** something such as a book or a magazine when you glance briefly at some of the pages: *I spent a nervous five minutes flicking through the in-flight magazine.* ❑ *She flicked through several pages then stood up and handed him the book.* [*same as* **flip through**, **browse through**, **leaf through**, **skim through**]

flinch /flɪntʃ/: **flinches**, **flinching**, **flinched**

flinch from

You don't **flinch from** difficult duties or tasks when you deal with them bravely, accepting that you mustn't avoid or ignore them: *It is a fact that elements of the service need improving, and this government will not flinch from the truth.* [*same as* **shy away, duck out** (*informal*); *opposite* **face up to, confront**]

fling /flɪŋ/: flings, flinging, flung /flʌŋ/

fling into

You **fling** yourself **into** an activity when you begin it with great enthusiasm and effort: *Bereaved partners tend to look for an escape, and many fling themselves into their work or a new hobby.* [*same as* **throw into**]

flip /flɪp/: flips, flipping, flipped

flip through

You **flip through** something such as a book or magazine when you glance briefly at some of the pages: *Some paced the floor and smoked; others sat flipping through the glossy presentations they would whip out in the middle of the interview.* [*same as* **flick through, browse through, leaf through, skim through**]

flirt /flɜːt/: flirts, flirting, flirted

flirt with

1 You **flirt with** someone when you have fun suggesting, usually not very seriously, that you're sexually attracted to them: *She can't resist flirting with older men.* ❑ *I used to annoy her by flirting outrageously with her husband.* [compare **chat up, get off with**] **2** You **flirt with** the idea of doing something when you think you might do it, but without making serious plans, and often dismissing the idea soon after: *She flirted for a time with the possibility of changing jobs.* [*same as* **toy with**]

float /fləʊt/: floats, floating, floated

float around

1 Something **is floating around** when people are talking about it or telling each other about it: *Various stories were floating around as to why she had resigned.* ❑ *There's this theory floating around the factory that the Canadian company has sold its share in order to protect British jobs.* [*same as* **go around, circulate**] **2** (*informal*) You can say that something **is floating around** when you think it is somewhere nearby, but you're not sure exactly where: *There are photos from last year's holiday floating around somewhere.* [*same as* **kick about** (*informal*), **knock about** (*informal*); compare **lie around**]

flock /flɒk/: flocks, flocking, flocked

flock in *or* flock into

People **are flocking in** when they're arriving in huge numbers; they **flock into** a place when crowds of them arrive there: *Once the new extension's finished, customers will come flocking in.* ❑ *Music-lovers of all ages have been flocking into the stadium all day.* [*same as* **flood in, pour in**]

flood /flʌd/: floods, flooding, flooded

flood in *or* flood into

People or things **flood in** when they arrive in huge numbers; they **flood into** a place when huge numbers of them arrive there: *Since last week's programme, letters have flooded in from people who supported our decision to broadcast.* ❑ *It's easy to imagine a situation in which refugees from all over the world would immediately start flooding into Europe's major cities.* [*same as* **pour in**; compare **flock in**]

flood out

People **are flooded out** when flood

water causes such severe damage to their home that they are forced to move out: *Nearly every house in this picturesque village has been flooded out.*

flop /flɒp/: **flops**, **flopping**, **flopped**

flop down (*informal*)
You **flop down** when you let yourself fall heavily down, *eg* into a chair or on to a bed, because you're exhausted: *I feel like just flopping down in front of the television for a few hours.* ❑ *Harry had flopped down on a rug with his arms extended and breathing rapidly in exhaustion.* [compare **flake out**]

flounder /'flaʊndə(r)/: **flounders**, **floundering**, **floundered**

flounder about *or* **flounder around**
1 A person or animal **flounders about** or **flounders around** when they move around in a clumsy, helpless way: *The injured deer floundered about for over an hour before dying.* ❑ *None of us was prepared to pay good money to watch two third-rate teams floundering around in the mud.* [compare **thrash about**] **2** Someone **is floundering about** or **floundering around** when they are struggling to think or speak clearly, *eg* because they are nervous or confused: *Paxman's brutally direct interviewing style has had many an eminent minister floundering about for credible answers.* ❑ *I sat back and listened to her floundering around, cobbling together feeble excuses.*

flow /floʊ/: **flows**, **flowing**, **flowed**

flow from
What **flows from** something is what naturally happens or appears as a result or consequence: *It's impossible to overestimate the social benefits that would flow from increased public awareness of environmental issues.* [compare **stem from, spring from**]

flow over
1 You let something **flow over** you when you don't allow yourself to be bothered or upset by it: *She manages to stay aloof: all the petty squabbles and tensions in the office just flow over her.* **2** A feeling **flows over** you when, suddenly and perhaps only briefly, you feel it very strongly: *Elliot felt a wave of jealousy flow over him.*
[*same as* **wash over**]

fluff /flʌf/: **fluffs**, **fluffing**, **fluffed**

fluff up
You **fluff up** a pillow or cushion that has been flattened down when you return it to its original rounded shape, *eg* by shaking it: *He quickly hoovered around the sofa and fluffed the cushions up.*

flunk /flʌŋk/: **flunks**, **flunking**, **flunked**

flunk out (*AmE informal*)
A student **flunks out** when they fail to make proper progress in their studies and are forced to leave without finishing their course: *The percentage of students who flunk out after the first year is surprisingly high.* [compare **drop out**]

flush /flʌʃ/: **flushes**, **flushing**, **flushed**

flush out
To **flush out** someone in hiding is to find them and force them to come out: *It is the civil defence force, not the police, that has taken upon itself the task of flushing the terrorists out.* ❑ *If they'd wanted to flush him out of hiding, they'd have done it already.* [compare **track down, sniff out**]

fly /flaɪ/: **flies**, **flying**, **flew** /fluː/, **flown** /floʊn/

fly at
Someone **flies at** you when they suddenly attack you, whether physically or with angry words or insults: *She*

suddenly flew at him, clawing with her nails. ❑ *She had a tendency to fly at journalists who questioned her motives.* [*same as* **lay into** (*informal*), **pitch into** (*informal*)]

fly in

Someone who **flies in** arrives by aeroplane; someone who **has been flown in** has been asked or ordered to come, and has come by air: *Jackson himself will be flying in from Mexico later today.* ❑ *Air-crash investigators from North America are being flown in to throw what light they can on the causes of the disaster.* ❑ *Further medical supplies will be flown in from Holland and Germany at the beginning of next week.*

fly into

Someone **flies into** a rage when they display extreme anger in a sudden outburst: *He had a tendency to fly into a temper for very little reason.*

fly out

Someone who **flies out** leaves by aeroplane; someone or something **is flown out** when they are sent by aeroplane: *Mr Major will meet her briefly before flying out to the Rio summit tomorrow.* ❑ *A further three hundred troops will be flown out next month.* [compare **jet off**]

fob /fɒb/: fobs, fobbing, fobbed

fob off

Someone **fobs** you **off** with something when they persuade you to accept something different from, and especially not as good as, what you asked for: *She tried to fob me off with a credit note, but I insisted on a full refund.* ❑ *Try to be firm with them; don't let yourself be fobbed off.* [compare **put off, palm off**]

focus /ˈfoukəs/: focuses, focusing, focused

focus on

To **focus on** something is to devote your attention or energy to dealing with, or considering, that thing only: *Government surveys have tended to focus on the effects of crime, without addressing its causes.* ❑ *The conference will seek to focus the minds of delegates on the very real issue of poverty in Western civilizations.* ❑ *This enables teachers to focus pupils' attention on a particular question.*

fog /fɒg/: fogs, fogging, fogged

fog up

A window **fogs up** when steam or warm air makes it cloudy and difficult to see through: *The heater wasn't clearing the windscreen; it was fogging it up.* [*same as* **steam up, mist up, mist over**; compare **cloud over**]

foist /fɔɪst/: foists, foisting, foisted

foist on

You **foist** something **on** someone when you force them to accept or deal with something they don't want or don't welcome: *Our aim is to get them to think for themselves, not to foist our own views on them.* ❑ *The neighbour's kids were foisted on us for the afternoon.* [*same as* **force on, impose on**]

fold /fould/: folds, folding, folded

fold up

1 You **fold** something **up** when you get it into a small neat shape by folding it, often so that it's ready to put away or store somewhere: *She watched him fold up the newspaper carefully and tuck it into his bag.* ❑ *The rug'll be easier to carry if you fold it up.* ❑ *These lightweight, easy-to-clean garden chairs fold up for easy storage.* **2** An unsuccessful business **folds up** when it collapses or closes down: *You never imagine that a high-street chain like Rumbelows will fold up.* [*same as* **go under**]

follow /ˈfɒləu/: **follows**, **following**, **followed**

follow through

You **follow** something **through** when you continue to do or consider it until you reach the end or reach a conclusion: *We had a number of business plans but we didn't follow any of them through.* ❑ *In the first couple of chapters, she develops an interesting theory, but unfortunately she doesn't follow it through.* [compare **see through**]

follow up

1 You **follow up** what little information you have when you try to find out more: *Information from members of the public has given us some fresh leads, and we're following them up at the moment.* ❑ *Before I assign my best journalist to the story, I have to be sure it's worth following up.* [*same as* **pursue**; compare **look into, check out**] **2** You **follow up** something you have done when you do something else that develops it further or adds to it: *The success of the original dictionary was followed up by a series of workbooks and other spin-offs.* ❑ *We're proud of our achievements in the league and we're hoping to follow them up with good performances in the cup competitions.*

• *noun* **follow-up**: **follow-ups**

A **follow-up** is something that is designed to develop, or add to, something done earlier: *As a follow-up to the May conference, in June we'll be running a number of workshops in key areas around the country.* ❑ *Chief Inspector Harris will lead the follow-up investigation.*

fool /fuːl/: **fools**, **fooling**, **fooled**

fool about *or* fool around

You **fool about** or **fool around** when you behave in a deliberately silly way, sometimes to amuse people: *The boys went down to the river to swim and fool about.* ❑ *There were one or two serious students, but most of them fooled around all day until it was time to go to the pub.* [*same as* **muck about** (*informal*), **lark about** (*informal*)]

fool about with *or* fool around with

1 Someone who **fools about** or **around with** something treats it too casually, and foolishly disregards the harm they might cause or the danger they are exposed to: *Tim and I got nervous when she started fooling about with her dad's gun.* ❑ *When you're fooling around with people's feelings, someone's bound to get hurt.* [*same as* **mess about with** (*informal*), **muck about** (*informal*)] **2** One person **fools about with**, or **fools around with**, another when they have a casual sexual relationship with them, especially when one or both people are married to someone else: *He's released from jail only to find that his wife has been fooling around with his best friend.*

for see panel on next page

force /fɔːs/: **forces**, **forcing**, **forced**

force back

You **force back** emotions or desires when you make a great effort to prevent yourself from expressing them: *I could see he was having to force back the tears.* ❑ *I had a sudden urge to slap him, but I forced it back.* [*same as* **fight back, hold back, keep back, suppress**; *opposite* **let go**]

force into

You **force** someone **into** doing something when you make them do something they don't want to: *In a free market economy, you see, a government can't force a company into putting up wages.* ❑ *It seems he was forced into stealing from his parents by older, so-called 'friends'.*

force on *or* force upon

You **force** something **on** someone when you make them accept something they don't want; you might also say that such a person **has** something **forced upon** them: *Because of this government's casual attitude, other countries are forcing more and more of their nuclear waste on us.* ❑ *I don't imagine they want any additional responsibilities forced upon them.* [*same as* **foist on, impose on**]

forge /fɔːdʒ/: **forges**, **forging**, **forged**

forge ahead
You **forge ahead** when you make fast progress, often so fast that you are in a leading position, ahead of all your competitors: *Repairs to the castle are forging ahead.* ❑ *With the sale of Rover to BMW, it is the Germans who are forging ahead at the luxury end of the car market.* [*opposite* **lag behind, drop behind, trail**]

fork /fɔːk/: **forks**, **forking**, **forked**

fork out (*informal*)
You **fork out** on something when you spend money on it, especially a large sum of money that you spend unwillingly: *Don't expect me to fork out more money to tax and insure it.* ❑ *Ratepayers have already forked out a fortune on repairs to council buildings.* [*same as* **shell out** (*informal*), **lay out** (*informal*), **cough up** (*informal*)]

forth see panel on next page

forthcoming /fɔːθˈkʌmɪŋ/ see **come forth**

forward see panel on page 131

for /fɔː(r)/

For is a preposition.
It is one of the most common words in English, and is widely used in combination with verbs. It often has very little meaning at all, but is used simply as a way of linking the verb with its object. For example, you **ask for** something when you ask someone to give it to you, and you can **account for** something if you are able to explain where it is or why it has happened. **For** can occur as the third element in a phrasal verb, as in **come in for, go in for, hold out for** and **stand up for**.
Perhaps because its meaning can be so slight or so vague, **for** is rarely used to form new phrasal verbs with special meanings.
The two commonest meanings of **for** refer to aims or purposes, as in **make for** and **look for**, and to actions or states relating to other people, as in **vouch for** and **fear for**.

1 AIMS AND PURPOSES
For can refer to an aim or a purpose, as in **apply for** and **head for**. It sometimes suggests that the aim or purpose is the result of a decision or choice, so that you **press for** something, or **push for** something, when you urge others to support it, often in opposition to some other thing; and you **plump for** something, or **opt for** it, when you choose it from a number of alternatives.

2 ACTIONS AND STATES RELATING TO OTHER PEOPLE
For can also refer to actions or states that relate to other people, and in this sense it can often be replaced by the phrase *on behalf of*. For example, you **plead for** someone when you ask a person in authority, such as a judge, not to punish them too harshly; you **root for** someone when you support them enthusiastically; and you **feel for** someone who is sad or in trouble when you feel sympathy for them.
For is also used in a number of phrasal verbs with very idiomatic meanings. For example, you **are spoiling for** a fight when you are eager to fight someone or have an argument with them; you **fall for** someone when you fall deeply in love with them; and you **live for** something when it is the only thing in your life that you care about or think is important.

foul /faʊl/: **fouls, fouling, fouled**

foul up (*informal*)
Someone **fouls** something **up** when they spoil it by making careless mistakes or bad judgements: *I don't know how he managed to foul up the travel arrangements.* ❑ *If it doesn't arrive on time, you can bet it's because the Glasgow office has fouled up again.* [*same as* **mess up** (*informal*), **muck up** (*informal*), **cock up** (*vulgar slang*)]
• *noun (informal)* **foul-up**: **foul-ups**: *This is the kind of annoying foul-up we'd hoped to avoid at this stage.*

freak /friːk/: **freaks, freaking, freaked**

freak out
1 (*informal*) Someone **freaks out** when they react to something with extreme behaviour, usually either becoming very angry or very worried and frightened: *Her parents will freak out when they get the bill.* ❑ *I nearly freaked out when I read the first question.* ❑ *The weird way she rolled her eyes really freaked me out.* **2** (*slang*) People who take drugs for pleasure **freak out** when, as a reaction to the drugs, they behave in a wild, uncontrolled way: *We'd never seen anyone on acid freak out like that before.*

free /friː/: **frees, freeing, freed**

free up
You **free up** something such as time or a resource when you make some available so that it can be used for a

forth /fɔːθ/

Forth is an adverb.
As an adverb, **forth** is a rather literary or formal word, and it is now most commonly found as part of a phrasal verb. It is often used to form phrasal verbs.
In its basic sense, **forth** refers to going out or coming out. Its principal meanings relate to movement forward, as in **go forth**; to things appearing or being produced, as in **call forth**; and to the presenting of things, as in **put forth**.

1 MOVEMENT FORWARD
Forth refers to energetic movement forward, away from a place. The person or thing that is moving usually has some firm purpose or intention, as in **sally forth** and **venture forth**.
Forth can be combined with verbs of movement to create phrasal verbs which mean, or imply, energetic or strong movement forward, such as **charge forth, hurtle forth**, and **sail forth**; and *march forth* and *troop forth*, as in the following examples: *The Romans marched forth to devour the world.* ❑ *Bullied into submission, former opponents now trooped forth to support the idea.*

2 APPEARING OR BEING PRODUCED
In a second sense, **forth** refers to something appearing or being produced. It sometimes suggests that what appears has a powerful effect, or comes or goes forcefully, like a rushing flow of water, as in **pour forth, cascade forth** and **send forth**.
Forth is frequently used to form phrasal verbs with this meaning, such as *belch forth, spew forth* and *vomit forth*, as in the following examples: *Smoke and gas bubbles belch forth from the underground chimney.* ❑ *The machine was spewing forth yet more urgent reports from all over the world.* ❑ *We drank in the sleek images and snappy messages vomited forth by the advertising industry.*

3 PRESENTING
Forth is also used to refer to the idea of presenting, declaring or describing something such as an opinion or plan, usually energetically or forcefully, as in **hold forth** and **set forth**.
It is often used to create new phrasal verbs, such as: *He sat in the office, spouting forth.* There is also the noun **bodying-forth**, from the old phrasal verb **body forth** [= to represent or to stand for], as in: *People see the river's muddy turmoil as a bodying-forth of their own turbulent inner selves.*

particular purpose: *He said he would try to free up a couple of hours the following week.* [*opposite* **tie up**]

freeze /friːz/: freezes, freezing, froze /frouz/, frozen /'frouzən/

> **forward** /'fɔːwəd/
>
> **Forward** is an adverb.
> It is one of the most common adverbs in English, and is frequently used to form phrasal verbs in its literal sense, referring to movement in a direction ahead or in front. Combinations such as **creep forward**, **draw forward, ease forward, lean forward, leap forward, press forward, sit forward** and **surge forward** are so numerous, and their meaning so clear, that they may not be listed in this dictionary.
> In its non-literal senses, **forward** refers to movement in time, as in **look forward to**; to the presenting and offering of things, as in **put forward**; and to things developing or making progress, as in **move forward**.
>
> 1 MOVEMENT IN TIME
> **Forward** refers to movement in time, whether to an earlier or later time, as in **bring forward, take forward, carry forward** and **put forward**.
> The adjectival form **fast-forward**, as in *the fast-forward button*, is quite common, and there is also a related phrasal verb, as in: *He fast-forwarded the tape until he came to the bit he wanted to watch.* ❑ *I will fast-forward 15 years.* ❑ *He wished he could fast-forward time and know what was to be discovered.*
>
> 2 PRESENTING AND OFFERING
> **Forward** also refers to the presenting or offering of something, often of yourself, as in **come forward** and **step forward**.
>
> 3 DEVELOPING OR MAKING PROGRESS
> In a third sense, **forward** refers to something developing or making progress. It sometimes suggests the idea of concentrating on the future, and forgetting the past, as in **go forward**.

freeze out (*informal*)
You **freeze** someone **out** when you prevent them from taking part in something, often by ignoring them or being unfriendly to them: *It was clear that a Western alliance had been formed, with the purpose of freezing out Eastern bloc countries.* ❑ *If you answer more than three questions incorrectly, you'll be frozen out of the next round.* [compare **squeeze out**]

freeze over
A lake **freezes over** when it becomes covered with ice: *Where do the ducks go in the winter when the pond freezes over?* ❑ *There's no way they'll give us the money — there's more chance of Hell freezing over.* [*same as* **ice over**]

freeze up
Mechanical devices with moving parts **freeze up** when ice prevents the parts from moving: *All the locks had frozen up and we couldn't get into the car.* [*same as* **ice up**; compare **seize up**]

freshen /'frɛʃən/: freshens, freshening, freshened

freshen up
You **freshen up** when you get washed and make yourself neat, perhaps by changing your clothes: *They'll probably want to freshen up before dinner.* ❑ *I'll take some time to freshen myself up a bit.*

frighten /'fraɪtən/: frightens, frightening, frightened

frighten away *or* frighten off
1 You **frighten away** or **frighten off** someone who is threatening you when you make them so afraid that they go away or stay away: *They kept the camp fire burning to frighten the bears away.* ❑ *It's clear the thief had only just entered the building when the sound of police sirens frightened him off.* [*same as* **scare off**] **2** You also **frighten** someone **away**, or **frighten** them **off**, when what you do makes them

unwilling to approach you or join you: *He's desperate for marriage and children, and this has frightened away every woman he's met so far.* ❑ *Blair's task is to remain loyal to the party's socialist roots whilst being careful not to frighten off the middle-class voter.* [*same as* **scare off**; compare **ward off**]

frighten into

Someone **frightens** you **into** doing something when they use threats to persuade you, so that you are afraid of not doing it: *Some witnesses had been frightened into giving false evidence.*

fritter /ˈfrɪtə(r)/: fritters, frittering, frittered

fritter away

You **fritter away** your time or money when, little by little, you waste it by spending it on unimportant or unnecessary things: *It was all too easy to fritter the whole holiday away sunbathing and splashing in the sea.* [*same as* **squander**]

from see panel on next page

frost /frɒst/: frosts, frosting, frosted

frost over *or* frost up

A surface **frosts over** or **frosts up** when it becomes covered with frost: *The pavements had frosted over and it was treacherous underfoot.* ❑ *The windscreen has frosted up during the night and I can't find my scraper.*

frown /fraʊn/: frowns, frowning, frowned

frown on *or* frown upon

Something **is frowned on** or **frowned upon** if people disapprove of it: *Increasingly, smoking is frowned on in public buildings.* ❑ *The company makes a great show of frowning upon any hint of sexist behaviour.*

fuck /fʌk/: fucks, fucking, fucked

fuck about *or* fuck around (*vulgar slang*)

1 To **fuck about** or **fuck around** is to behave in a silly way that annoys or irritates others: *Tell them to stop fucking about and get some work done.* **2** To **fuck** someone **about**, or **fuck** them **around**, is to treat them very badly, *eg* by causing them a lot of inconvenience: *I came here to do business, not to be fucked around by a bunch of snotty-nosed accountants.* [*same as* **piss about** (*vulgar slang*), **bugger about** (*vulgar slang*), **mess about** (*informal*)]

fuck off (*vulgar slang*)

Telling someone to **fuck off** is an extremely offensive way of telling them to go away: *Why don't you fuck off back to America where you belong!* [*same as* **piss off** (*vulgar slang*), **bugger off** (*vulgar slang*), **get lost** (*informal*)]

fuck up (*vulgar slang*)

To **fuck** something **up** is to spoil it by making careless mistakes or bad judgements: *He's managed to fuck up the last chance we had of making any serious money.* ❑ *Don't get Norris involved; he'll only fuck up again.* [*same as* **cock up** (*vulgar*), **foul up** (*informal*), **mess up** (*informal*)]

• *noun (vulgar slang)* **fuck-up**: **fuck-ups**: *He's been sent to sort out another fuck-up in the Shrewsbury office.*

fuss /fʌs/: fusses, fussing, fussed

fuss over

Someone who **fusses over** you is constantly looking for ways to make you happy, or worrying that you might not be happy or well, perhaps so much that they annoy or irritate you: *She doesn't realize that fussing over the children will only make them soft.* ❑ *I think that, to varying degrees, we all like to be fussed over a bit.*

from /frɒm/

From is a preposition.
It is a very common word in English, but occurs in a fairly small number of phrasal verbs in this dictionary. These phrasal verbs can be identified as having two distinct meanings.

1 SOURCE OR ORIGIN
From is used to form phrasal verbs that indicate the source or origin of something, as in **make from**, or who or what the provider of something is, as in **spring from**.
The first group within this broad meaning show where or from what period of history someone or something comes from and include **hail from** and **date from**, as in the following examples: *The plant hails from the Caucasus Mountains and is quite hardy.* ❑ *an important collection of leather goods dating from Egyptian times.*
The second group of phrasal verbs are more specific to the gathering of information and indicate how and from where this information is obtained, as in **derive from** and **cull from** in the following examples: *Golspie, whose name is derived from the old Gaelic word meaning 'the place of strangers'.* ❑ *a series of case studies culled from members of the network.*
The last loose group of phrasal verbs with this sense include combinations like **emanate from** which have the same idea of source or origin as part of their meaning, but in the sense that something is sent out or provided, as in the example: *A literature such as that which emanated from Rousseau between 1749 and 1762.*

2 HIDING, EXCLUDING, SEPARATING
The second broad sense of **from** used in phrasal verbs suggests that something is hidden or someone prevents it from being seen or becoming known. Phrasal verbs with this sense include **keep from** and **conceal from**.
The slight extension of this sense which contains the idea of stopping or resisting is present in combinations such as **shield from** and **withhold from**.

From is also used as the second element of phrasal verbs as in **get away from**, **break away from** and **set apart from**.

g

gabble /ˈgabəl/: **gabbles, gabbling, gabbled**

gabble away *or* **gabble on**
(*informal*)
You can say that someone **is gabbling away**, or **is gabbling on** about something, when he or she is talking so quickly that it is difficult for others to follow or understand what he or she is saying: *Old Mrs Bates gabbles away quite happily when we visit her, though she doesn't remember who we are.* ❑ *What were you gabbling on about? It didn't make any sense.*

gad /gad/: **gads, gadding, gadded**

gad about *or* **gad around**
(*informal, often derogatory*)
You **gad about** or **gad around** when you go from one place to another looking for entertainment and amusement, especially when other people think you ought to be doing something more serious or important: *She's always gadding about and never seems to spend any time with her children.* ❑ *Don't you think it's time you stopped gadding around and got a job?* [*same as* **gallivant about**; compare **run around**]
• *noun* **gadabout**: **gadabouts**: *She's always been a bit of a gadabout.*

gain /geɪn/: **gains, gaining, gained**

gain in
1 You **gain in** something such as weight or height when you get heavier or grow taller: *The sledge gained in speed as it went down the slope.* **2** You **gain in** some quality when you get more of it: *He felt he had gained in wisdom and experience, but at a high personal cost.*

gain on *or* **gain upon**
1 You **gain on** someone or something ahead of you when you reduce the distance that separates you from them and come closer and closer to them: *I look back and see that Stewpid is gaining on me. I keep running.* ❑ *Recent opinion polls show the Social Democrats gaining on the Christian Democrats.* [*same as* **catch up with, catch up on**] **2** You **gain on** someone or something behind you when you move further ahead of them: *The gap between the runners began to widen as the leading group began to gain another few yards on the rest of the field.*

gallivant /ˈgalɪvant/: **gallivants, gallivanting, gallivanted**

gallivant about *or* **gallivant around** (*informal*)
You **gallivant about** or **around** when you spend your time wandering from one place to another in a carefree way: *He's spent the last six months gallivanting about Europe.* [*same as* **gad about** (*informal*); compare **run around**]

gallop /ˈgaləp/: **gallops, galloping, galloped**

gallop through (*informal*)
You **gallop through** something that you have to do or say when you do or say it very quickly: *There's nothing very complicated about this test. You should*

be able to gallop through it in no time. ❏ *They galloped through the various items on the agenda so that they could get finished by 5pm.*

gamble /'gambəl/: **gambles**, **gambling**, **gambled**

gamble away

You **gamble away** money, or you **gamble** it **away**, when you lose it by gambling unsuccessfully: *He gambled away his entire fortune in three short months.* ❏ *By putting his faith in quacks, he was gambling away his only real chance of a cure.*

gamble on

1 You **gamble on** a race, game or competition when you bet money on the result hoping that you will win: *He demanded a windfall tax and said that those that gambled on currencies should be treated the same as racehorse punters.* ❏ *Each week millions of people gamble on the National Lottery hoping to win a fortune.* **2** When you **gamble on** something happening or being the case, you act or make a decision hoping that it will turn out the way you want it to, even though there is a risk it will not: *We gambled on the weather remaining fine and left our raincoats at home.* ❏ *The government is gambling on the support of several minor parties to push the legislation through parliament.*

gang /gaŋ/: **gangs**, **ganging**, **ganged**

gang together *or* gang up

Two or more groups of people **gang together**, or they **gang up** with each other, when they come together to form a larger group, usually in order to do something: *We will be ganging up with English, Welsh and Irish Scouts for the national jamboree.*

gang up on

When two or more people **gang up on** another person, they act together as a group against that person, especially in a fight or argument: *He was ganged up on by several bigger boys.* ❏ *Several of his former political allies ganged up on him.*

gasp /gɑːsp/ *or* /gasp/: **gasps**, **gasping**, **gasped**

gasp out

You **gasp out** a statement, message or warning when you say it in short bursts because you are finding it difficult to breathe properly, *eg* because you have been running: *He gasped out, 'Help me, I think I'm dying,' as he sank to his knees.*

gather /'gaðə(r)/: **gathers**, **gathering**, **gathered**

gather around see **gather round**.

gather in

Crops **are gathered in** when they are harvested: *They are working round the clock to gather in the wheat and barley.*

gather round

1 A group of people **gather round** or **around** a person or place when they all move towards it and stand near it: *Come on, children, gather round, and I'll show you how to make a cake.* ❏ *Knots of people had gathered around each visitor, eager for news of England.* **2** People **gather round** or **around** a person in trouble when they give that person their support: *The bereaved woman's friends had all gathered round to help.*

gather together

You **gather together** a number of things from various places, or you **gather** them **together**, when you collect them together so that they are all in the same place: *He has gathered together all the experts in the field so that they can exchange ideas.* ❏ *The geese gather together in a dense fleet a thousand or so strong.* ❏ *It was* *essential, Dexter knew, to gather together as powerful a case as possible.*

gather up

You **gather** things **up** when you pick them up so that they are in one heap or pile: *Without a word Andreyev gathered up the papers in front of him and strode after his former colleague.* ❑ *They were gathering great armfuls of hay up and tossing them on the cart.*

gear /gɪə(r)/: gears, gearing, geared

gear down

1 You **gear down** when you shift the gear lever of a motor vehicle to a lower gear: *McRae geared down as he approached the bend.* **2** An operation or activity **is geared down** when its scope or intensity is reduced to suit new circumstances: *We'll be forced to gear down our production now that demand is falling.* [*opposite* **gear up**]

gear to *or* gear towards

A system or way of operating **is geared to** or **geared towards** a particular purpose or group of people when it is organized so that it suits their requirements: *This was in the context of a world trading system geared to the industrial needs of Europe.* ❑ *Obviously the service has to provide value for money, but it must be geared first and foremost towards the needs of patients.*

gear up

Someone or something **gears up** to do something, or they **are geared up** to do it, when they get ready, or are made ready, to do it: *The newly industrialized nations of the Far East are gearing themselves up for entry into international markets.* ❑ *He spent a few days at base camp getting himself geared up for the assault on the summit.*

gee /dʒiː/: gees, geeing, geed

gee up (*informal*)

You **gee** yourself **up** to do something when you summon the energy or enthusiasm to do it; someone or something **gees** you **up** when you are feeling tired or lazy if they make you feel more energetic: *He was feeling the effects of the long flight and had to gee himself up to go out and do some sightseeing.*

gen /dʒɛn/: gens, genning, genned

gen up (*informal*)

When someone **gens** you **up** they give you all the information that you need to know about a particular subject: *Go and see Arthur and he will gen you up on the latest developments.* [*same as* **brief, put in the picture** (*informal*)]
• *adjective (informal)* **genned up**
You are **genned up** when you have all the information you need: *You won't be able to make an informed choice if you're not genned up on all the options available.* [*same as* **clued up**]

get /gɛt/: gets, getting, got /gɒt/

In British English the past tense and past participle of **get** is **got**. In American English **gotten** is often used as the past participle.

get about *or* get around

(*informal*)

1 You **get about** or **get around** if you move around or travel to different places: *'She was in Cardiff on Monday, Birmingham on Tuesday and Edinburgh on Wednesday.' 'Yes, she gets about, doesn't she.'* ❑ *He's lost the use of his legs and doesn't get about much any more.* **2** If you can **get about** or **get around** you are able to walk or move about: *He's broken his ankle but he can still get about on crutches.* **3** News or information **gets about** or **gets around** as more and more people are told about it: *Keep this information to yourself; I wouldn't want it to get about.*

get across

1 You **get across** an obstacle when you manage to cross it: *How are we going to get across the river when there's no bridge and we don't have a boat?* [*same* *as* **get over**] **2** You **get** an idea, feeling or message **across** when you succeed in making other people understand it: *It's up to us to get across the message that, once again, the government has got it wrong.* [*same as* **get over, communicate**]

get after

You **get after** someone when you follow them and try to catch them: *'John's just left. Get after him and tell him the flight's been cancelled.'*

get ahead

1 You **get ahead** of someone when you move or progress so that you pass them: *Schumaker accelerated approaching the bend and got ahead of Hill as they came into the straight.* **2** You **get ahead** with *eg* work when you complete more of it than you need to, or are required to, by a given time: *I want to get ahead with this project so that I'll have more free time later on.* [*opposite* **get behind**] **3** You **get ahead** when you are successful in your career and you reach a senior position: *How do you expect to get ahead if you're not willing to work?*

get along (*informal*)

One person **gets along** with another, or two people **get along**, when they have a friendly relationship, or they live or work well together: *I'm so glad you brought Mary; we've been getting along like a house on fire.* [= very well] ❑ *Somehow I never seemed to be able to get along with my parents-in-law.* [see also **get on**]

get around

1 You **get around** or **get round** to doing something when you finally do it, especially after a difficulty or delay: *Steven eventually got round to painting the garden gate.* **2** News or information **gets around** or **gets round** when more and more people hear about it: *It's a mystery to me how these rumours get around.* [see also **get about**] **3 a** You **get around** or **get round** a problem or difficulty when you find a way of avoiding it rather than dealing with it directly: *We'll just have to face it; I can't see any way of getting around it.* **b** You **get around** or **get round** someone when you manage to persuade them to do something, or to allow you to do something: *Don't worry about Mum; I can easily get around her.*

get at (*informal*)

1 When you ask or wonder what someone **is getting at** you want them to explain more clearly what they are suggesting or what they mean: *Do you know what he was getting at when he said there was trouble on the horizon?* **2** You **get at** someone when you criticize or find fault with them: *Do you think he was getting at me when he said he thought the system could be improved?* ❑ *I'm fed up with that teacher; she's always getting at me.* [*same as* **pick on**]

get away

1 You **get away** when you escape: *The police managed to catch three of the robbers but the leader of the gang got away.* ❑ *fishermen standing in the pub talking about the one that got away.* [= the big fish that they say they caught but which managed to escape] **2** You **get away** when you are able to leave, especially having been prevented from doing so earlier: *I'll have to get away by 11 o'clock if I'm to catch the last train.* **3** You **get away** when you are able to go away from your home or work on a holiday: *We're hoping to get away for a couple of weeks in the summer.*

• *noun* **getaway**: **getaways**

A person, especially a criminal, makes their **getaway** when they manage to escape from the police or people who are trying to catch them: *The robbers made their getaway in a stolen car.*

get away from

1 When you tell someone to **get away from** something you are ordering them to move away from it: *Get away from the window; someone might see you!* **2**

You **get away from** someone or something when you escape from them: *I go to a night class to get away from the children for a few hours.*

get away with

1 You **get away with** something when you escape taking that thing with you: *The robbers had got away with nearly £100,000 worth of diamonds.* **2 a** Someone who **gets away with** something illegal or dishonest manages to avoid being caught or punished for it: *He's apparently been getting away with tax fraud for years.* **b** You **get away with** something that others would normally find unacceptable when you manage to do it without being criticized or found out: *I sang the first verse twice, but no-one seems to have noticed so I think I got away with it.*

get back

1 You **get back** when you return to your home or the place where you started out from: *Our train was late and we didn't get back until after midnight.* ❑ *This has been rather a long lunch; we'd better be getting back to the office.* ❑ *He got back just in time to dress for dinner.* **2** You **get** someone or something **back** when you return them to the place that they came from, or you get them to come back to a place: *I don't think we'll be able to get his dislocated shoulder back into its socket without giving him an anaesthetic.* ❑ *Do you think we should get him back for a second interview?* **3** You tell someone to **get back** when you order them to move to a position further back or away from you: *'Get back! I've got a gun, and I'll use it if you come any closer!'* **4** You **get back** something that belongs to you when it is returned to you; you **get** something that you have lost **back** when it returns or is returned: *I lent him my Bon Jovi tapes months ago and I don't think I'm ever going to get them back.* ❑ *After looking so pale and ill for so long, she's now got her normal healthy glow back.* [*same as* **recover**, **regain**]

get back at (*informal*)

You **get back at** someone when you get your revenge on them: *She racked her brains trying to think of a way to get back at Elizabeth.* [*same as* **get even with**]

get back into (*informal*)

You **get back into** some activity when you begin to do it again after a period when you did not, or were not able to, do it: *After years spent at home, it took her a while to get back into the routine of going out to work every day.*

get back to

1 You **get back to** work or some other activity when you return to it after an absence or a period when you had been doing something else: *The best thing for him would be to get back to his everyday routine.* **2** You **get back to** someone when you contact them again, especially by telephone, so that you can give them information that you weren't able to give them when you spoke to them earlier: *I don't have the price list handy. Can I get back to you on it?*

get behind

1 You **get behind** someone or something when you move so that you are in a position behind them: *If you get behind that curtain no-one will see you.* **2 a** You **get behind** with *eg* work when you do not keep up to date with it: *This delay was due to one or other of the works departments getting behind with the manufacture.* **b** You **get behind** *eg* with your rent or with loan repayments when you do not pay them at the times they are due: *Because the sums involved were so much larger, getting behind with mortgage payments became a much more serious debt trap than bills at retailers.* [*same as* **fall behind**] **3** You **get behind** someone when you give them your support and encouragement: *The supporters should get behind their team instead of continually criticizing them.*

get beyond
Something **gets beyond** a certain point or stage when it progresses so that it passes that point or stage: *I laid a bet that he couldn't get beyond level two of Super Mario Brothers.* ❑ *This has got beyond a joke.* [= it is now serious and no longer amusing]

get by
1 People or things **get by** an obstacle when there is enough space for them to get through or past it: *There was a lorry blocking the road and the police car couldn't get by.* **2** You **get by** when you manage to live or survive without much money, help or other resources: *Money has always been a worry but we've always managed to get by somehow.* [*same as* **exist**, **subsist** (*formal*)]

get by on
You **get by on** a certain sum of money or a certain level of income when you manage to live on that amount of money or income: *Few young couples nowadays are able to get by on only one income.*

get by with
You **get by with** something when you use it as a reasonably acceptable substitute for the thing that is considered to be the most desirable or appropriate to the circumstances: *I don't have a decent suit. Do you think I could get by with a blazer and grey trousers for the interview?* [*same as* **get away with**]

get down
1 You **get down** from a high position, or from a position above the ground, when you move down to a lower position, or on to the ground; you **get down** on your knees when you kneel: *The cat's climbed to the top of the tree and can't get down again.* [*same as* **descend**] **2** You **get** something **down** when you record it by writing it on paper, especially quickly: *The professor talks so quickly those of us who can't do shorthand find it difficult to get everything down.* ❑ *As soon as things quietened down he'd get as much down on paper as possible.* **3** (*informal*) Something **gets** you **down** when it makes you sad or depressed: *His constant criticisms are beginning to get me down.* ❑ *It was the fourth time in two weeks she had slept late, and it was beginning to get her down.*

get down to (*informal*)
1 You **get down to** something when you begin working hard or seriously at it: *After the Easter break you'll have to get down to some serious study for your exams.* **2** You **get down to** the essential or most basic aspects of something when you concentrate on them or begin to deal with them: *They're more likely to attack opponents than get down to the specifics of their own party programmes.*

get in
1 A politician or political party **gets in** when they are elected to power: *Do you think the Tories will get in again at the next election?* **2** You **get** something **in** when you find the time or opportunity for it: *I'd like to get another hour's work in before dinner.* ❑ *It was difficult to get a comment in, everyone was talking so furiously.* **3** You **get** someone **in** to do work of some kind for you when you get them to come to your home or place of work to do it: *'Will you be putting the new bathroom in yourselves?' 'No, we're getting a local firm of plumbers in.'* **4** A train or bus **gets in** when it arrives at its destination: *The last train gets in at midnight.*

get in on (*informal*)
You **get in on** an activity when you succeed in taking part in it: *He's always trying to get in on our discussions, even though we make it obvious he isn't welcome.*

get into
1 You **get into** a car or some other vehicle when you move inside it: *It took*

four ambulance workers and Jack to finally get him into the ambulance. **2 a** You **get into** a particular situation when you become involved in it; someone or something **gets** you **into** a particular situation if they get you involved in it: *It was very foolish of them to get themselves into so much debt.* ❑ *His habit of saying the first thing that comes into his head will get him into trouble one of these days.* **b** You **get into** a rage, panic or some other emotional state when you enter that state: *She got into a real panic when she discovered the baby was missing.* **3** (*informal*) You **get into** something when you develop a liking or enthusiasm for it: *Since he's been working in Edinburgh, he's really got into Scottish history and culture.* **4** (*informal*) You ask what **has got into** someone if they are behaving in an unusual way, especially when this is unwelcome or disturbing: *I wonder what's got into Peter? He was quite rude to me!* **5 a** You **get into** a school, college or university when you are given a place to study there: *Do you think he'll get good enough grades in his A-levels to get into Oxford?* **b** A politician **gets into** parliament when they are elected to represent a constituency in parliament: *He got into parliament with the slimmest of majorities.* [*see also* **get in**] **6** A train, bus or ferry **gets into** a place when it arrives there: *When does the ferry leaving Ullapool at 11am get into Stornaway?* **7** You **get into** clothes or shoes when you put them on or they are large enough to fit you: *The astronauts couldn't get into their heavy space suits without help.* ❑ *I've got so fat I can't get into any of my clothes.*

get in with

You **get in with** a particular group of people when you become involved with them or form a relationship with them, especially when you think that by doing so you will gain some advantage for yourself: *I've been trying to get in with some of the more experienced players hoping to learn something.*

get off

1 If someone tells you to **get off** something they are telling you to move off or away from it: *Get off my land immediately or I'll have you prosecuted.* ❑ *'Ouch! Get off! You're standing on my toe.* ❑ *Get your dirty feet off my clean floor!* **2** You **get** something **off** when you remove it: *I'll never get this stain off the carpet.* ❑ *Isn't there some sort of special solution that gets graffiti off?* **3 a** You **get off** a bus, train, or plane when you get out of it: *Stop the bus! I want to get off!* ❑ *Have my seat. I'm getting off at the next station.* [*same as* **alight**] **b** You **get off** a bicycle, motorbike or horse when you dismount from it: *He had to get off his bike and push it up the hill.* **4 a** You **get off** when you leave *eg* to go on a journey: *We've packed all our camping equipment and are hoping to get off as soon as it's light.* ❑ *Get yourself off to school now; it's nearly half past eight.* **b** You **get** a letter or message **off** when you send it by post, facsimile or radio: *Can you make sure this letter gets off before the last post tonight?* **5** You **get off**, or someone **gets you off**, when you are given little or no punishment for something wrong, illegal or dishonest that you have done: *I'd say you got off rather lightly.* ❑ *The lawyers got him off with a small fine.* **6** You **get** clothes **off** when you take them off or undress: *It's so hot! I must get this thick jersey off.* [*same as* **take off**]

get off on (*slang*)

You **get off on** something when it makes you very excited or gives you great satisfaction: *He seems to get off on having all that power.*

get off with (*informal*)

You **get off with** someone when you attract them into beginning a romantic or sexual relationship with you: *She thought I was trying to get off with her boyfriend.*

get on

1 People **get on**, or one person **gets on** with another, when they have a friendly relationship and live or work together harmoniously: *I don't think my son and his wife have been getting on very well recently.* ❑ *She doesn't really get on with her parents.* [*same as* **get along**] **2** You **get on** when you make progress in your career: *It seems that, in order to get on, you have to socialize with the bosses.* [*same as* **get ahead**] **3** (*informal*) When you say that someone **is getting on**, you mean they are becoming old: *I don't think Dad will be able to come on a walking holiday with us; he's getting on a bit, you know.* **4** (*informal*) When you ask or wonder how someone **is getting on**, you want to know generally what they are doing, or what progress they are making; someone **is getting on** well when they are making good progress: *'How's David getting on in his new job?' 'He seems to be getting on fine.'* **5** You **get on** a bus or train when you board it at the start of a journey: *Several people got on at the next stop.* ❑ *Hurry up and get on the bus.* [*same as* **board**; *opposite* **get off**, **alight**] **6** You **get** clothes **on** when you put them on or dress: *She was trying to get her new jeans on.*

get on at (*informal*)

When someone **gets on at** you, they criticize you repeatedly, especially for not having done something they think you should have done: *My wife's been getting on at me to get a job.* [*same as* **nag**; compare **keep on at**]

get on for

Something **is getting on for** a stated amount or time when it is approaching that amount or time; someone **is getting on for** a stated age when they are nearly that age: *We must have had getting on for three hundred applications so far.* ❑ *It was getting on for 3am by the time they found their way back to the road.* ❑ *Jim's father still goes riding even though he must be getting on for ninety.*

get on to

You **get on to** someone when you contact them, especially by telephone: *Get on to the suppliers and find out why our order hasn't arrived.*

get on with

1 You **get on with** someone when you have a good or friendly relationship with them: *She wants to leave home because she doesn't get on with her stepmother.* **2** You **get on with** something when you begin to do it, or you carry on doing it: *I had better get on with this work if I want to finish it today.* ❑ *Have you got enough work to be getting on with?*

get out

1 When you tell someone to **get out** you are telling them to leave: *Go on, get out; I don't want you here.* ❑ *Get out of my sight, you disgusting child!* **2** A secret **gets out** when it becomes known publicly: *If this gets out, we'll be in real trouble.* **3** Someone or something **gets out** of the place where they have been kept prisoner, or contained, when they escape or can leave and go outside: *When he eventually gets out, he'll find it pretty difficult to adjust to life outside prison.* ❑ *Someone left the gate open and the dog got out.* **4** You **get out** when you spend time outside your home: *She's a bit frail now and doesn't get out much any more.*

get out of

You **get out of** something, or **get out of** doing it, when you manage to avoid doing it: *I don't want to go to their stupid dinner party but how on earth am I going to get out of it?* [*same as* **avoid**, **duck out** (*informal*)]

get over

1 You **get over** an obstacle when you manage to move over it to the other side: *I don't think that little pony will get over that big jump.* **2** You **get over**

something such as an illness, shock or disappointment when you recover from it: *She's never really got over the death of her husband.* **3** You **get over** a problem or a difficulty when you deal with it successfully: *We'll be able to relax a little once we've got over the busy period in the summer.* **4** You **get** a message **over** when you make other people understand it: *a concerted effort by the Labour Party to get the message over to the electorate that they aren't the 'tax and spend' party any longer.* [*same as* **get across, communicate**]

get over with
You **get** something unpleasant **over with** when you do it as quickly as possible so that you don't have to go on thinking or worrying about it: *She said she just wanted to get the funeral over with so that she could get on with her life.*

get round see get about

get through
1 You **get through** work or a task when you finish or complete it: *It'll take me hours to get through all these letters.* **2** You **get through** an amount or supply of something when you use all of it: *We seem to be getting through an awful lot of coffee.* **3 a** You **get through** to someone when you succeed in contacting them by telephone: *I tried ringing him at the cottage but I couldn't get through.* **b** You **get through** to someone, or **get** something **through** to them, when you make them understand or realize something: *I can't seem to get through to them how important this is.* ❑ *This is vitally important. Am I getting through to you?*

get to
1 You **get to** a place or stage when you reach it or arrive at it: *What's the best way to get to the British Museum from here?* ❑ *'Where did you get to before Mr Campbell went off sick?' 'We got to the part where Hamlet saw the ghost of his father in his mother's bedroom.'* ❑ *He felt he was getting to the point where he couldn't cope anymore.* **2** You wonder where someone **has got to** when they haven't arrived at the time or place they were expected: *He should have been here ages ago. Have you any idea where he might have got to?* **3** (*informal*) Someone or something **gets to** you when they upset or annoy you: *You shouldn't let him get to you. He's like that to everyone.* [compare **get at**]

get together
People **get together** when they meet, especially informally: *We must get together soon and discuss the project.*

get up
1 You **get up** when you stand from a sitting or lying position, or when you leave your bed after waking: *Everyone got up when she came in the room.* ❑ *Raymond found it hard to get up on winter mornings.* [*same as* **rise**] **2** You **get** someone **up** when you make them get out of bed, usually earlier than they had intended: *She got me up at six o'clock just to watch the sun rise.*

get up to
You talk about what someone **is getting up to** when you are referring to what they are doing, especially if you think it is likely to be something you will disapprove of: *I hate to think what he and his mates are getting up to in Greece.*

get with (*informal*)
When someone tells you to '**get with** it' they are telling you that your ideas or attitudes are old-fashioned or out-of-date and that you should get to know about what is happening now: *Nobody wears their hair like that any more. You should try to get with it, Mum.*

gibe or jibe /dʒaɪb/: gibes, gibing, gibed

gibe at
You **gibe at** someone or something when you make unkind remarks to find

fault with them or make them look foolish: *He battled through his statement to the House, continually gibed and laughed at by the opposition.* [*same as* **mock**]

ginger /ˈdʒɪndʒə(r)/: **gingers**, **gingering**, **gingered**

ginger up

You **ginger up** something that is dull or slow-moving, or you **ginger** it **up**, when you do something or add something to it to make it more interesting, exciting or active: *Unless the government does something soon to ginger up the housing market it looks as if it will, at best, continue to stagnate, and, at worst, house prices will continue to decline.* ❑ *They brought on Dejon Saunders to ginger the team up a bit.*

give /gɪv/: **gives**, **giving**, **gave** /geɪv/, **given** /ˈgɪvən/

give away

1 a You **give** something **away** when you give it to someone else, usually because you no longer want it: *Her mother gave most of her old baby clothes away.* **b** You **give** something **away** when you lose it carelessly: *The centre forward gave that ball away.* [= allowed a member of the opposing team to get the ball through his carelessness] **2** Someone **gives away** the prizes at a prize-giving ceremony when they present them to the people who have won them: *We've asked Mrs Andrews of the PTA to give away the prizes.* [*same as* **give out, present**] **3 a** You **give** information **away** when you allow it to become known to other people, especially when you should have kept it secret: *It seems he had been giving away all sorts of valuable trade secrets.* **b** You **give** someone **away** when you betray them: *I don't want him to find me; you won't give me away, will you?* **4** You **give away** personal thoughts or feelings without intending to when your appearance or behaviour makes it clear what they are: *I wondered what she was thinking; her expression gave very little away.* **5** At the beginning of a wedding ceremony, the bride's father **gives** her **away** when he takes her to the altar of the church and officially hands her to her future husband so that they can be married: *Her father's dead so her uncle will be giving her away.*

• *noun* (*informal*) **giveaway**

You can refer to something someone does as a **giveaway** if it shows clearly how they really feel about something, when they have been trying to hide their true feelings: *I could tell that she didn't mean what she said; her expression was a dead giveaway.*

give back

You **give** something **back** when you return it to its owner; something **is given back** to someone when it is returned to them: *Give me back my ball.* ❑ *The unexpected win gave the team its confidence back.*

give in

1 You **give in** when you admit that you have been defeated, allow yourself to be defeated, or agree to stop opposing or resisting something and allow it: *Others give in, decide they are past the stage where beauty has any relevance, and concentrate on looking tidy and presentable.* ❑ *They just keep battling on and refuse to give in.* ❑ *'They say that unless they have the money we'll fall behind the Russians. So I give in.'* [*same as* **surrender**] **2** You **give** something that has to be returned **in** when you hand it back to the person responsible for dealing with it: *Has everyone given their homework in to the teacher?* [*same as* **hand in**]

give in to

You **give in to** someone or something when you stop arguing or resisting, and agree to what they demand, or allow it to happen: *She cradled Ari's head on her lap as the girl gave in to the overwhelming sensations crashing through her nervous system.* ❑ *He's* *trying his best not to give in to temptation.* [*same as* **give way to**]

give of (*formal*)

Someone **gives of** their time or energy when they give it to others or do something for others, usually without expecting anything in return: *But talent can be developed and trained and provide a sound basis for you to give of the best that is inside you.*

give off

Something **gives off** heat, light or a smell when it produces it or sends it out: *Most light bulbs give off more heat than light.* ❑ *The chemical gave off acrid fumes, stinging their eyes.* ❑ *... contracting and giving off gravitational energy as heat and light.*

give onto

The door or window in a room **gives onto** somewhere when it leads straight to that place, or has a view of it: *The french doors give onto a little courtyard.*

give out

1 You **give** things **out** when you give one to each of a number of people: *We stood in the High Street giving out leaflets.* ❑ *Most neighbourhood police place the emphasis upon community service and informal contact, giving out few parking tickets.* [*same as* **hand out**, **distribute**] **2** News or information **is given out** when it is announced or made known to the public: *I shall let it be given out that she fell from her horse.* ❑ *It's been given out by the Prime Minister's office that he and the Irish Taoiseach are close to agreement.* **3** A person or thing **gives out** a noise or sound when they send it out or make it: *The old engine was giving out a strange rattling noise.* ❑ *He jumped up and gave out the most tremendous shout of triumph.* **4** A supply of something **gives out** when it has been completely used up and there is none of it left: *Jane tried to climb Kilimanjaro, but her strength gave out about 2000 feet from the summit.* [*same as* **run out**] **5** (*informal*) Something **gives out** when it stops working, especially suddenly: *The strain was too much and his heart just gave out.* **6** In cricket, a batsman **is given out** when the umpire decides and indicates that he is out: *When England batted, Gooch was given out caught behind and it seemed to dispirit his team-mates.*

give over

1 You **give** something **over** to someone when you pass or hand it over an object or space to them: *That's my book. Give it over.* ❑ *I cannot give over any of the powers that I, as a Member of Parliament, was given when I came to this Parliament.* **2** (*informal*) If you tell someone to **give over**, or to **give over** doing something, you are telling them to stop what they are doing: *Oh, give over, will you! I'm fed up listening to your excuses.* ❑ *I wish he would give over droning on about his holiday.*

give over to

1 A time or place **is given over to** something when it is used for that thing only: *Every available piece of land was given over to cereal production.* ❑ *The last years of his life seem to have been largely given over to this task.* **2** You **give** yourself **over to** something when you devote yourself entirely to it: *She wanted the world to go away so that she could give herself over to her lover's embrace.*

give up

1 You **give up** something, or **give up** doing something, when you decide not to do it any longer: *Giving up smoking together is much more likely to be successful than doing it alone.* ❑ *Why are you giving up your job?* ❑ *Yet it's easy to cut down on fat without giving up all your favourite foods.* **2** You **give up**, or **give up** something you have been trying to do, when you stop trying to do it or stop trying to hold on to it, and admit defeat: *When I saw it, I felt like giving up, curling up into a tiny* *ball to be forgotten by everyone.* ❑ *I've given up trying to talk sense to him.* ❑ *'Come on, have another guess.' 'No, I give up, I haven't a clue what it is.'* **3** You **give** someone **up** when you stop having a relationship with them: *But I have given her up, and in any case she has meant nothing to me for years.* ❑ *If you don't give that boy up your father and I will stop your allowance.* **4** You **give** someone **up** for dead when you believe that they are dead; you **give** someone or something **up** as lost when you believe that they will never be found or recovered: *We had all given her up* [= believed she would die] *when she made this miraculous recovery.* **5** You **give** yourself **up** when you surrender yourself to someone in authority and become their prisoner: *The thieves were cornered by police and forced to give themselves up.* **6** You **give** something you have **up** to someone else when you allow them to have or take it: *They weren't prepared to entertain anything that entailed France giving up military sovereignty.* ❑ *They went round the town calling on the people to give up their dead.* [*same as* **deliver up** (*formal*), **hand over, surrender**]

give up on (*informal*)

You **give up on** someone when you stop trying to get them to behave in a reasonable way, or you lose hope that they will ever begin to behave reasonably or do what you hoped they would do: *Here you are at last! We'd almost given up on you.* ❑ *It would be immoral of me to give up on my son.* ❑ *To do that almost seemed to entail giving up on the course altogether.*

give up to

You **give** yourself **up to** some feeling or state of mind when you allow yourself to be taken over by it: *Fabia felt even more light-headed and gave herself up to the pleasure of her walk with Ven.* [*same as* **give over to**]

glance /glɑːns/: **glances**, **glancing**, **glanced**

glance off

A moving object **glances off** a surface when it strikes it lightly and moves on: *The left corner of the rear bumper crumpled in a flash of sparks as it glanced off the wall.*

glaze /gleɪz/: **glazes**, **glazing**, **glazed**

glaze over

You can say that someone's eyes **glaze over** when their expression shows that they are no longer interested in what they are watching or listening to: *She went on and on. I could see that Ken's eyes had glazed over, and the kids were wriggling in their chairs, desperate to escape.*

glory /'glɔːrɪ/: **glories**, **glorying**, **gloried**

glory in

You **glory in** something when you feel or show great delight or pride in it: *She didn't just enjoy her position at the apex of the town's social scene; she positively gloried in it.*

gloss /glɒs/: **glosses**, **glossing**, **glossed**

gloss over

You **gloss over** an awkward problem or question when you ignore it or deal with it quickly, hoping to take the attention of other people away from it: *It's no use the Minister trying to gloss over his department's mistakes.* ❑ *The company has also neatly glossed over the fact that with the gas come added nasties, including benzene.*

go /goʊ/: **goes**, **going**, **went** /wɛnt/, **gone** /gɒn/

The usual past participle of **go** is **gone**, but **been** is also sometimes used.

go about

1 To **go about** is to move from place to

place, often, but not necessarily, with a particular purpose: *William Kunster went about the world protesting against the trial on the grounds that it was political.* ❑ *We don't go about in cars, not in London.* **2** You **go about** something in a particular way when you deal with it or handle it in that way: *I couldn't think how to go about breaking the news to her.* ❑ *This seems an odd way to go about things.* **3** You **go about** doing something, often something other people disapprove of, when you do it often: *They both go about with permanent scowls.* ❑ *She'd gone about in awe of these adults.* ❑ *There's no need for him to go about insulting people like that.* [*same as* **go around**, **go round**] **4** You say that something **is going about** when more and more people are talking about it, know about it, or are being affected by it: *There's a rumour going about that his wife's left him.* ❑ *Isn't there a bad cold going about?* [*same as* **go around**, **go round**]

go about with

You **go about with** someone when you are friendly with them and you do things together: *He used to go about with one of the lads from the village, but I haven't seen them together for a while.*

go after

1 You **go after** someone or something when you follow them, trying to catch up with them: *Don't let her leave like that; go after her and tell her you're sorry for what you said.* [compare **get after**] **2** You **go after** a job when you try to get it: *He went after several jobs but didn't succeed in getting any of them.*

go against

1 You **go against** someone else's wishes when you do something that they do not want you to do; something **goes against** your principles when it is the opposite of what you believe is right: *She went against her father's express wishes and married before she was twenty one.* ❑ *It goes against everything I have been brought up to believe.* ❑ *It goes against all commonsense to sell it off for profit.* **2** Opinion **goes against** you when it is unfavourable to you; a judgement or verdict in a court case **goes against** you when you lose: *'Can you tell us how you felt when the vote went against you?'*

go ahead

1 You **go ahead** of someone when you move forward so that they are in a position behind you or following you: *He went ahead of us to see if he could find a way across the river.* ❑ *Sheffield went ahead after 30 minutes when Gage knocked the ball past Allen.* **2** Something **goes ahead** when it takes place as planned: *Do you think their marriage will go ahead now that she's found out about his criminal record?* ❑ *Both events will go ahead amid tightened security.* ❑ *I assume that this can go ahead immediately.* **3** You **go ahead** with something when you do it as intended; if someone tells you to **go ahead** they mean that you should begin something, or they give you permission to do what you have said you want to do: *'Paul is going to tell us about his hobbies. Go ahead, Paul.'* ❑ *'Can I look through your record collection?' 'Yes, go ahead.'* ❑ *It was against the advice of most of his staff that he went ahead with it.* ❑ *The referendum, approved by Cabinet last night, will go ahead with all speed.*

• *noun* **go-ahead**

Something is given the **go-ahead** when permission is given for it to be put into action, or begin.

• *adjective* **go-ahead**

A **go-ahead** person or organization is prepared to use new methods or develop new ideas.

go along

1 You **go along**, or you **go along** somewhere, when you travel or go there: *I fixed things up with Donald and went along to explain the plan.* ❑ *Just go* *along the corridor and it's the first on your left.* ❑ *'Are you going to the party?' 'I think I'll go along for half an hour or so.'* **2** You do something as you **go along** if you do it while you are continuing with some more general activity: *I couldn't speak any French when I came to France. I just learnt it as I was going along.* ❑ *Selected applicants begin to serve as trainees on the boats, literally learning the ropes as they go along.*

go along with

You **go along with** a plan or decision when you agree with it and support it: *I'll go along with anything you might suggest.* ❑ *I think you're simply going along with what he wants, and frankly that's out of character.*

go around

1 Something such as a rumour or an illness **is going around** or **round** when it is being passed from one person to the other: *Have you heard the rumour that's going round that the Prime Minister is thinking of resigning.* ❑ *There's a tummy bug going around the office.* ❑ *One idea going around is that French troops might be mixed in with brigades from Britain and other NATO countries.* [*same as* **go about**] **2** If there is enough to **go around** or **round** there is enough for everyone: *Would you mind having white wine? There isn't enough champagne to go around.* ❑ *With less capital to go around, banks must make fewer loans.*

go around with

You **go around with** someone, or **go round with** them, when you are often in their company in public: *'Perhaps there isn't all that much fun in going around with a married bloke, after all?'* ❑ *He goes around with a very strange crowd.* [*same as* **go about with**]

go at

1 Two people **go at** each other when they attack each other, physically or with words: *We could hear them in the other room, going at each other hammer and tongs.* **2** (*informal*) You **go at** something when you start to do it with a great deal of effort or energy: *When he was asked to knock down the wall he went at it like a man possessed.* [*same as* **tackle**]

go away

1 You **go away** when you leave a place: *They've gone away on holiday.* ❑ *I hated the idea of her going away to school.* ❑ *Now he must go away and I daresay I shall never see him again.* ❑ *Unable to go away for weekends or holidays, she never goes out at night to dinner parties, discos or evening classes.* **2** When you tell someone to **go away** you are telling them to leave, especially to leave your presence: *He came round to see me but I told him to go away.* ❑ *'Fenna, it's over, go away.'* ❑ *The men motioned me to go away.* ❑ *So they asked him to go away and come back in a week.* **3** Something **goes away** when it disappears: *The issue would not go away.* ❑ *The recession they have caused and which so nearly ditched them will not go away automatically.* ❑ *The rash seems to be going away now.*

go back

1 You **go back** when you return to a place or position that you have been in before, or a method that you have used before: *She should go back home. She's old.* ❑ *I'll go back tonight and see what's to be done.* ❑ *They have gone through too much to go back now.* ❑ *The doctors told me to go back to Cambridge and continue the research.* ❑ *I go back into her room and have a look around.* ❑ *Go back down the road for half a mile.* ❑ *When I retire I want to go back to the Highlands.* ❑ *The teacher told him he hadn't done any of the work properly so he had to go back to the beginning.* **2** Something **goes back** to an earlier time when it has its origins in that earlier time: *Go back a few hundred years and look around.* ❑ *Their quarrel goes back to the time when they fought* *over the same girl at school.* ❑ *His family tree goes back to just after the Norman Conquest.* **3** The clocks **go back** when they are set to an earlier time so as to give an extra hour of daylight. [*opposite* **go forward**]

go back on

You **go back on** a promise or agreement when you decide not to do what you promised or agreed to do: *He could not honestly have gone back on that undertaking.*

go back over

You **go back over** something that you have finished when you redo it or look at it for a second time: *We'll have to go back over this chapter so that the people who weren't in class last week know what it is about.* ❑ *Going back over previous months' editions, I found three letters all in praise of Steffi.*

go back to

1 You **go back to** something that you stopped doing earlier when you return to it and start doing it again: *She went back to work two weeks after her baby was born.* ❑ *Angela said she would find it hard to go back to using an old-fashioned typewriter after using a word-processor.* [*same as* **go back**] **2** When things **go back to** normal they become normal again.

go before

1 The people who **have gone before** you are the people who have lived before you were born; something that **has gone before** is something that has happened in the past: *The floors and walls of the church were incised with the records of those that had gone before.* ❑ *Greenaway said he hated the thought of a shot in a film being like a preposition, linking what went before and after.* ❑ *This is a completely new issue and has nothing to do with anything that has gone before.* **2** A matter **goes before** a court or committee when it is presented to that court or committee so that an official judgement, decision or recommendation can be made about it: *So he went before the court and pleaded 'Not Guilty'.* ❑ *His claim for unfair dismissal will go before an industrial tribunal.*

go below

On a boat or ship, you **go below** when you leave the deck and go down the stairs to the inner part of the hull: *It started to rain so we all went below and shut the hatch.*

go beyond

Something **goes beyond** a particular level or the normal scope of something when it passes it or extends further than it: *His behaviour goes beyond mere enthusiasm; it's obsessive.* ❑ *These powers go well beyond those of the Scottish transport users' consultative committee in relation to rail and ferry services in Scotland.* [*same as* **exceed**, **surpass**]

go by

1 Someone or something **goes by** when they pass along in front of you: *I saw a number 88 bus go by with a bright yellow ad proclaiming 'Britain needs its universities'.* ❑ *He sat on the verge and watched the traffic go by.* **2** You **go by** a place when you pass it: *If you're going by the chemist's would you drop in and collect my prescription?* ❑ *Melanie felt a shudder of dread as she went by every door.* **3** Time **goes by** when it passes: *As time went by they became closer and closer.* ❑ *Twenty years went by before he saw his homeland again.* ❑ *The Broomielaw Quay was enlarged as years went by.* [*same as* **elapse**] **4** You **go by** something, *eg* someone's advice, when it influences your actions or decisions: *You shouldn't go by what you read in the paper; sometimes journalists get their facts wrong.* ❑ *Local music appears to be on the wane, if recent developments are anything to go by.* ❑ *Isn't my word enough to go by, after all these years?* **5** You **go by** a particular name when that is the name you are generally known by: *A singer who goes by the name of Rocking Ronnie.*

go down

1 Someone or something **goes down** when they move or travel from a higher level or position to a lower one: *He's always wanted to go down the Cresta Run.* ❑ *His office is the first on the right as you go down the stairs.* ❑ *Go down to reception and ask if there have been any messages for me.* ❑ *Men went down the main shaft and tried to clear it.* **2** The sun **goes down** when it sinks below the horizon and it begins to get dark: *I watched the sun go down in the trees behind Thornfield.* **3** Something **goes down** when it falls, reduces or gets lower: *The water level in the lake has gone down during the drought.* ❑ *The value of the company's shares has been going down for the last few days.* ❑ *Our supply of food is going down rather quickly.* ❑ *The quality of life will go down.* **4** A ship **goes down** when it sinks; its crew **goes down** with the ship when they are drowned: *The suction of the ship going down could pull the lifeboat under.* ❑ *The trawler went down in heavy seas.* ❑ *Only two crew members were rescued; the rest are believed to have gone down with the ship.* **5** Someone **goes down** when they fall to the ground, usually after receiving a stunning blow: *The bottle hit him on the forehead and he went down like a stone.* ❑ *Limeking went down as if shot, and his rider desperately tried to get him to his feet.* [*same as* **fall down, collapse**] **6** A sportsman or sporting team **goes down** when they are defeated in a match or competition: *Lendl went down by five sets to three in a thrilling final.* ❑ *He produced one of the best performances by an Irish horse when going down narrowly to Garrison Savannah at Cheltenham.* **7** Something like a remark or piece of humour **goes down** well when people like it or enjoy it: *His jokes didn't go down very well with the older folks.* **8** (*informal*) When someone talks about food or drink **going down** well, they mean that it is eaten or drunk with enjoyment: *A glass of dry white wine would go down well with this fish.* **9** (*informal*) A person found guilty of a crime **goes down** when they go to prison: *'I'm expecting to go down for this one. I can't face five years in prison.'* [compare **send down**]

go down in

Something **goes down in** writing when it is recorded by writing it down; an event **goes down in** history when it will be remembered for a long time: *Everything he said went down in the copper's notebook.* ❑ *He'll go down in history as the best Prime Minister that never was.*

go down with

You **go down with** an illness when you begin to suffer from it: *At the start of the holiday they all went down with measles.*

go for

1 You **go for** someone when you attack them, physically or with words: *You should keep that brute of a dog under control. It went for me when I opened the gate.* **2** You **go for** someone or something when you like or are attracted by them: *She goes for him in a big way.* ❑ *We don't go much for classical music, I'm afraid.* **3** You **go for** something when you choose it: *There were lots of unusual desserts but in the end I went for the chocolate mousse.* ❑ *Parke thought the old version was 'a bit Seventies' and went for something 'more authoritative'.* **4** (*informal*) You also **go for** something when you decide to try to achieve it: *There's definitely a market for this type of service. I think we should go for it.* ❑ *'I'm thinking of becoming a professional jockey.' 'That's a good idea, go for it.'*

go forth (*old or literary*)

1 Someone **goes forth** when they go out of the place, usually in a purposeful manner: *Follow the suggestions to break out of old patterns and go forth courageously into new and uncertain territory.* **2** Something such as a message or call **goes forth** when it is issued or sent out: *The clear message that went forth was that they would never compromise on the issue of disarmament.*

go forward

1 Something **goes forward** when it progresses or begins to be put into effect: *Listen to the genuine concerns, sort out the issues from the power politics, and then hopefully go forward in the manner of conciliation.* ❑ *The scheme can't go forward unless we get planning permission.* **2** Someone involved in a competition **goes forward** to the next round when they win enough votes or points to take part in, or be included in, the next stage of the competition. **3** The clocks **go forward** when everyone sets their clocks to a later time, usually so as to allow an extra hour of daylight. [*opposite* **go back**]

go in

1 You **go in** when you enter a building or room; you **go into** a building or room when you enter it: *Please do go in.* ❑ *It's got cold; I'm going in.* ❑ *They all went into the dining room for lunch.* ❑ *If you go into the cupboard under the stairs, you'll find a stepladder.* **2** Something that **goes in**, or **goes into** a space, fits, or fits into that space: *He tried to put his new car into his garage but it was too wide to go in.* ❑ *Where does this piece of the jigsaw go in?* ❑ *The old key went into the lock surprisingly easily.* **3** (*informal*) A piece of information or news **goes in** when you understand it: *I told him that his mother was dead but I don't think it went in.* [compare **take in**] **4** The sun, moon or stars **go in** when they disappear behind a cloud or clouds: *The moon went in and we were left stumbling along in the dark.*

go in for

1 You **go in for** a contest when you enter it: *Are you going in for the sculpture competition?* **2** You **go in for** an activity or occupation when you enjoy it and do it regularly: *Schools went in for a lot of physical education, which involved jumping about in a draughty hall with your shirt tucked into your knickers.* ❑ *He doesn't go in for outdoor sports much.*

go into

1 a You **go into** a job or profession when you choose it as a career: *I'd never thought of going into the police force.* **b** Someone **goes into** business when they offer their services or products to customers in the hope of making a profit: *He's thinking of going into business for himself.* **2 a** You **go into** hospital when you are admitted as a patient. **b** Someone **goes into** lodgings when they go and live in someone else's house and pay them rent. **3** You **go into** something when you discuss or explain it in detail: *There isn't time to go into the precise reasons for the decision.* **4** You **go into** something when you examine it thoroughly to find out all you can about it: *Have you gone into all the risks associated with taking this drug for long periods?* [*see also* **go in**]

go in with

You **go in with** someone when you form a business partnership with them: *Dave said he was surprised that Tom was going in with his brother. They were so different he doubted if it would work.*

go off

1 A bomb or gun **goes off** when it explodes or is fired: *The gun went off accidently.* **2** Food **goes off** when it becomes rotten and unfit to eat: *The fridge broke down, and all the milk went off.* **3** An electrical device such as a light, or a system controlled by an electrical switch, **goes off** when it stops functioning: *He set the timer so that the TV would go off after 30 minutes.* ❑ *At midnight all the lights and heating went off.* **4** You **go off** someone or something when you stop liking them: *It sounds like she's beginning to go off Simon.* ❑ *I've gone off the idea completely.* **5** An event **goes off** well when it is successful: *The party went off really well.*

go off with

You **go off with** someone when you leave in their company, especially when you leave your partner and go away with someone else: *I took Jenny to the dance, but as soon as we got there she went off with some bloke who was there with the band.*

go on

1 You **go on** doing something, or **go on** with something, when you continue to do it: *Mark went on working while the others were out.* ❑ *I'll just go on with my guitar practice.* ❑ *He went on talking after most of the audience had left.* ❑ *If you had gone on with your studies you might have been able to get a better job now.* **2** You **go on** in a particular direction when you continue travelling or moving in that direction: *Go on until you reach the church and then turn left.* **3** You **go on** when you continue to talk or tell a story, often after an interruption or pause: *'I'm sorry for interrupting you; please go on,' he said.* ❑ *She went on to tell them how it was she had become a painter.* **4** You say '**Go on!**' to someone when you want to encourage them to do something: *'This cake is delicious. Go on, try a piece.'* **5** People sometimes say '**Go on!**' to someone to show that they don't believe them: *'Go on! That surely can't be true!'* **6** Something **goes on** when it continues to happen: *Do you think this will go on much longer?* ❑ *He didn't want it to stop. He wanted it to go on and on for ever.* ❑ *Do you think this hot weather will go on for much longer?* ❑ *The strike went on for another two months.* **7** Time **goes on** when it passes: *As time went on she got more used to his funny little habits.* **8** An actor or other performer **goes on** when they make their entrance on stage: *She didn't go on till the second act.* **9** You **go on** somewhere when you go there after being somewhere else: *Do you think he'll go on to university when he leaves school?* ❑ *We've all decided to go on to Archie's after the play.* **10** You **go on** to do something when you do it after doing something else: *He started his acting career in rep, and went on to star in several successful West End productions.* **11** When you ask what **is going on** you want to know what is happening, or what the people you are talking to are doing, especially if you suspect they are doing something wrong: *Someone's moved my desk. Would someone please tell me what's going on?* ❑ *Right, what's going on in here?* **12** When you have something to **go on**, you have some piece of evidence or information to support your theory or opinion: *From what I've been able to gather, the police don't have much to go on.* **13** An electrical device such as a light, or a system controlled by an electrical switch, **goes on** when it starts to function: *I heard a click and the security lights went on.* [compare **come on**] **14** You **go on** a course of drugs when you start taking them: *She said she might go on the Pill.* **15** A supply of something **goes on** something else when it is used for that thing: *Most of his money goes on feeding his heroin habit.* ❑ *All his wages go on paying back his debts.*

go on about (*informal*)

You **go on about** something when you talk about it constantly and tediously: *He went on and on about how wonderful she was, until we were all fed up listening to him.* ❑ *They've been going on about having to find poor old Jenny a new man.* ❑ *'What are you going on about?' he said, his mind on the bees.*

go on at (*informal*)
Someone **goes on at** you when they continually find fault with you or urge you to do something: *She's always going on at me about my schoolwork.*

go out
1 You **go out** when you leave the room, building or other place you have been in: *Will you be going out today?* ❑ *We went out into the garden.* ❑ *No-one dared go out at night.* ❑ *Beyond, go out of the square by the left exit, Via Baracchini.* ❑ *I went out and slammed the door behind me.* **2 a** A light **goes out** when it is switched off or no longer shines: *The lights suddenly went out.* ❑ *The stars lost their sheen and went out as the first strain of light eased away the darkness.* **b** A fire or something that is burning **goes out** when it stops burning: *There was a sudden draught and the candle went out.* **3** The tide **goes out** when the level of the sea falls back and the water reaches a lower point on the shore: *The tide in the estuary went out as fast as it came in and it wasn't unusual for large fish to be stranded.* [*opposite* **come in**] **4** You **go out** when you do something socially, such as visit the cinema or the theatre or go to a restaurant: *Before the children were born we went out two or three times a week.* ❑ *We don't seem to have the money to go out any more.* ❑ *They dress up then go out to dinner in some restaurant.* **5** Something **goes out** when it is no longer fashionable or popular: *That hairstyle went out in the Seventies.* **6** A message or news **goes out** when it is announced; a letter **goes out** when it is sent: *The call went out for volunteers to help clear up the flood damage.* ❑ *From the leadership, the word went out quickly: no triumphalism.* **7** A radio or television programme **goes out** when it is broadcast: *The programme will be going out all over Britain.* **8** The money that you have **going out** is the money that you spend on bills and other expenditure: *We'll have to cut down on our spending; we've got more going out than we have coming in.* [= we are spending more than we are earning]
• *adjective* **outgoing**
An **outgoing** person is someone who enjoys talking to and being with others. [*same as* **sociable**, **extrovert**]

go out with
You **go out with** someone when you have a romantic or sexual relationship with them, but are not living with them: *So I promised I wouldn't go out with him again.* ❑ *They've been going out together for years.* [*same as* **go together**]

go over
1 You **go over** something when you cross it, or move from one side of it to the other: *You go over a stile from one field into another.* ❑ *It was flattened as if a steamroller had gone over it.* ❑ *He went over the Tay to Aberfeldy.* **2** You **go over** something when you examine or check it carefully, or discuss it in detail: *It's worth going over her story again to prevent others from falling into the same trap.* ❑ *We need to go over these accounts again.* ❑ *They went over the main points of his scheme to decide whether it was practical.*
• *noun* **going-over**
1 You give something a good **going-over** when you examine it thoroughly to find out if all its parts are working properly, or you clean every part of it: *The first task is to give this work surface a good going-over.* **2** (*informal*) Someone gives you a **going-over** when they beat you severely: *They held him down and gave him a proper going-over with a brush-handle.*

go overboard
You can say that someone **goes overboard** about or for someone or something when they are wildly enthusiastic about them: *On the other hand, talk to*

him about a book, like the one Gordon lent him, and he'd go overboard about it.

go over to

1 You **go over to** someone or something when you move across the space that separates them from you so that you are close or closer to them: *He went over to her and put his arm around her shoulder.* ❑ *Ali went over to the mantelpiece and picked up one of the china figurines.* **2** You **go over to** someone's house when you pay them a visit at their home: *He went over to Andrew's to watch a video.* **3** You **go over to** somewhere overseas when you travel there: *He said he had to go over to Brussels that weekend.* **4** Someone **goes over to** the enemy or the opposition when they change sides: *The king of Bohemia, the archbishop of Cologne and the duke of Brabant all went over to Philip, mainly inspired by their own self-interests.*

go round see go around

go through

1 To **go through** an object or place is to travel or pass in at one side and out at the other: *His head went through the windscreen.* ❑ *Will you be going through Edinburgh on your way to the Borders?* ❑ *The path goes through fields.* ❑ *The 5th Brigade had gone clean through enemy lines.* **2** You **go through** an amount or supply of something when you use it all up: *He can go through ten pairs of shoes in a year.* ❑ *We went through a week's supply of food in three days.* [*same as* **get through**] **3** You **go through** something such as a room or container when you check the contents carefully: *She'd gone through her briefcase twice, and the letter wasn't there.* **4** You **go through** a number of things when you examine or consider each one carefully: *Would you go through these old clothes and see if there are any you want to keep.* **5** You **go through** an unpleasant experience when you suffer or endure it: *Looking back, it was a serious situation that I wouldn't wish to go through again.* ❑ *You must have gone through hell when your husband's affair was made public.*

go through with

You **go through with** something when you decide to do it even though it may be difficult or unpleasant: *She threatened to sue, but I doubt if she'll go through with it.* ❑ *He asked Madge if she wanted to go through with it, which of course she didn't.*

go to

1 You **go to** a school, college or university when you attend classes there: *She wasn't yet home from the local girls' school she goes to.* [*same as* **attend**] **2** (*informal*) Someone **goes to** a task when they do it with a lot of energy and determination: *Look! He's going to score! Go to it, Andy!* **3** Someone **goes to** *eg* a lot of trouble when they make extraordinary efforts to do or achieve something: *They went to a lot of trouble to discover who had been making the nuisance calls.* ❑ *Nigel was disgusted but intrigued by the lengths Eleanor had gone to.*

go together

1 Two or more things **go together** when they match or fit together well, or are closely associated: *I don't think red lipstick and green eyeshadow go together.* ❑ *It is often observed that misogyny and homophobia go together.* [*same as* **go with**] **2** Two people **are going together** when they are having a romantic or sexual relationship, but are not living together: *They've been going together for six months now.* [*same as* **go with**]

go towards *or* go toward

1 You **go towards** someone or something when you move in their direction: *He neither went towards her nor withdrew.* **2** An amount of money **goes towards** something when it is used to pay part of the cost: *My bonus can go towards the cost of a holiday.* ❑ *The* *money given will go towards nutritional programmes in one of the poorest areas of Cairo.*

go under

1 You **go under** something when you pass beneath it or move so that you are under it: *Smoke was blown into the carriages when the train went under a bridge.* ❑ *The mouse has gone under that cupboard.* **2** Something that has been floating on the surface of water **goes under** when it sinks below the surface: *The ship struck a rock and went under.* **3** A business **goes under** when it fails: *They'll lose everything if the company goes under.*

go up

1 Something **goes up** when it moves to a higher position: *He went up the stairs.* ❑ *The lift attendant asked me if I was going up.* ❑ *The rocket went straight up.* ❑ *I'm going to go up into the attic and look for my old school photographs.* [*opposite* **go down**] **2** To **go up** is also to increase or rise: *The temperature went up into the nineties.* ❑ *The price of fresh vegetables goes up when they are in short supply.* ❑ *Interest rates are going up again.* [*opposite* **go down**; compare **come down**] **3** (*informal*) People talk about something **going up** when it explodes or is destroyed by fire: *If you lit a match in our kitchen, it'd go up with a roar.* **4** Something **goes up** to a certain point when it extends as far as that point: *Her legs were so long they seemed to go up to her armpits.* ❑ *There's a damp patch on the wall that goes up to the ceiling.*

go with

1 One thing **goes with** another when they match or compliment each other: *That tie doesn't go with that shirt.* ❑ *This claret will go nicely with the beef.* **2** (*informal*) You **are going with** someone when you are having a romantic or sexual relationship with them: *She's been going with him for a couple of months as far as I know.* **3** (*informal*) You **go with** something when you allow it to happen, or decide to use it or put it into action: *We didn't think much of the name at first, but somehow came round to it and decided to go with it.*

go without

You **go without** something, especially something needed or expected, when you have to manage without it: *Our parents didn't have the money for Christmas presents, so we went without.* [*same as* **do without**]

goad /goud/: goads, goading, goaded

goad into

You **goad** someone **into** doing something, especially something foolish, violent or illegal, when you continually annoy them until they do it: *He said he was goaded into hitting his wife by her constant nagging.* ❑ *She was goaded by this into a direct and emphatic reply.*

goad on

You **are goaded on** to do something when others continually encourage or challenge you to do it or go on with it: *His friends stood around the bottom of the tree goading him on to climb higher and higher.*

goof /guːf/: goofs, goofing, goofed

goof about *or* goof around

(*informal*)

You **goof about** or **around** when you behave in a foolish or amusing way: *Stop goofing about and give me back my jacket.*

goof off (*AmE informal*)

You **goof off** when you deliberately avoid work or school, and waste time: *Sometimes, we'd goof off and go down to the river.*

goof up (*AmE informal*)

You **goof up** when you make a silly mistake: *You gentlemen have the wrong* *documents; I'm afraid my secretary's goofed up.*

gouge /gaudʒ/: **gouges**, **gouging**, **gouged**

gouge out
You **gouge** part of a solid object or mass **out** when you use your fingernails or some other sharp implement to remove it: *Someone's gouged a big piece out of the cheese.*

grab /grab/: **grabs**, **grabbing**, **grabbed**

grab at
You **grab at** someone or something when you try to catch hold of them with a quick grasping movement of your hand: *The chimpanzee tried to grab at me through the bars of its cage.*

grapple /'grapəl/: **grapples**, **grappling**, **grappled**

grapple with
1 You **grapple with** someone when you take hold of them and struggle with them in an attempt to overpower them: *The security guard was on the floor grappling with one of the bank robbers.*
2 You **grapple with** a problem or difficulty when you struggle hard to solve it or deal with it: *Leave him in peace to do his homework; he's grappling with quadratic equations.*

grasp /grɑːsp/ *or* /grasp/: **grasps**, **grasping**, **grasped**

grasp at
You **grasp at** something when you reach for it and try to take it or hold on to it: *He was grasping at some smallest, most irrelevant piece of evidence in the hope that he could prove his theory.*

grass /grɑːs/ *or* /gras/: **grasses**, **grassing**, **grassed**

grass on *or* **grass up** (*slang*)
One criminal **grasses on** others, or they **grass** others **up**, when they tell the police or other people in authority about the crimes they have committed or are planning to commit: *You know what'll happen to you if you grass on us.* ❑ *You wouldn't grass us up, would you Johnny?*

grass over
You **grass** an area of bare earth **over**, or it **grasses over**, when you sow grass seed or lay turf on it, or grass grows over it naturally: *We've decided to grass over the area at the bottom of the garden so that the boys have somewhere to play football.*

green /griːn/: **greens**, **greening**, **greened**

green up
You **green up** grass on a lawn when you add fertilizer to it so that it becomes greener: *The mixture has the dual effect of killing moss and greening up your lawn in one easy operation.*

grind /graɪnd/: **grinds**, **grinding**, **ground** /graund/

grind down
Something **grinds** you **down** when it makes you lose hope and become depressed: *He's been quite ground down by all the problems he has had to face.* ❑ *The relentless pressure of work was grinding her down.*

gross /grous/: **grosses**, **grossing**, **grossed**

gross out (*especially AmE informal*)
Someone **grosses out** when they behave in a disgusting or excessive way: *They were lying slumped in front of the television grossing out on beer and ice cream.* [*same as* **pig out** (*informal*)]

ground /graund/: **grounds**, **grounding**, **grounded**

ground in
You **are grounded in** a particular subject when you are taught or learn

its basic or most important points or rules so that you are able to apply them more generally: *We try to make sure that every pupil is well grounded in the subjects that make up the core curriculum.*

ground on

An argument, theory or belief **is grounded on** a particular thing when that thing forms its basis or foundation: *It's an interesting point he makes, but is it or isn't it grounded on fact?*

grow /grou/: grows, growing, grew /gru:/: grown /groun/

grow apart

People who were once close to each other **grow apart** when they become less close: *She's developed her own interests outside the home with the result that she and her husband have grown apart.* [*same as* **drift apart**]

grow into

Children **grow into** clothes that were once too big when they grow enough for the clothes to fit properly: *It's a little big across the shoulders, but he'll soon grow into it.*

grow on

1 You can say that something **grows on** you when you gradually begin to like it more: *I didn't like the music at first, but the more you listen to it, the more it grows on you.* **2** Seedlings **are grown on** when they are put in larger containers or in the earth so that they have enough room to grow: *Grow them on in a cold frame.*

grow out of

1 Children **grow out of** clothes when their body grows so much that the clothes no longer fit properly: *Niall seems to grow out of new shoes in less than a month!* [*same as* **outgrow**] **2** You **grow out of** something such as a hobby or interest when you gradually stop liking it or wanting to do it, especially when you come to think that it is too childish: *I've rather grown out of late-night parties.*

grow up

1 A person **grows up** when they gradually change from a child into an adult, or they reach the stage of being an adult: *Young Peter is really growing up fast.* ❑ *She's grown up so much since I last saw her.* [*same as* **mature**] **2 a** You can also say that someone **grows up** or **is growing up** when they start to behave in an adult way, no matter how old they are: *He's grown up a lot since he went away to school.* **b** You can tell someone to **grow up** when you want them to behave in a more mature or less childish way: *Oh, grow up, Martin!*

grow up on

You say that you **have grown up on** something when you have been used to having it since childhood: *We grew up on stories of odd happenings at the old grange.*

grub /grʌb/: grubs, grubbing, grubbed

grub about *or* grub around

A person or animal **grubs about** or **around** when they scrape or scratch in the earth or dirt looking for something: *I found him grubbing about in the dustbins.*

grub out *or* grub up

You **grub out** weeds or other plants, or you **grub** them **up**, when you pull them out of the ground removing the whole plant including the roots: *Howls of protest followed the announcement that the old hedge was to be grubbed up.*

guard /gɑ:d/: guards, guarding, guarded

guard against

You **guard against** something when you try to avoid it or prevent it happening by taking sensible precautions: *All* *the equipment should be properly sterilized to guard against infection.*

guess /gɛs/: **guesses**, **guessing**, **guessed**

guess at
You **guess at** something when you try to find the answer by guessing: *He could hardly have guessed at the difficulties.* ❑ *How these amazing animals took off and landed can only be guessed at.*

gull /gʌl/: **gulls**, **gulling**, **gulled**

gull into *or* **gull out of** (*old or formal*)
When someone **is gulled into** doing something, they are tricked into doing it by someone else; if someone **is gulled out of** something they have they are deceived into giving it to someone else: *He was gulled into guaranteeing the loan.* ❑ *Appleby was effectively gulled out of the property that was rightfully his.*

gulp /gʌlp/: **gulps**, **gulping**, **gulped**

gulp back
You **gulp back** a sound when you make swallowing movements to prevent it being heard: *She gulped back her sobs.*

gulp down
You **gulp down** food or drink when you swallow it quickly, often in large mouthfuls: *He crammed the papers in his briefcase, gulped down a cup of tea, and rushed out to the car.*

gum /gʌm/: **gums**, **gumming**, **gummed**

gum up
1 Something **is gummed up** when it is blocked with a sticky or glue-like substance: *Her eyelids were all gummed up.* **2** You **gum** something **up** when you do something to prevent it working properly: *You've gummed up the whole works by sending those parts to the wrong depot.*

gun /gʌn/: **guns**, **gunning**, **gunned**

gun down
To **gun** someone **down** is to shoot them, often when they are unable to defend themselves, killing them or wounding them severely: *Two masked men gunned him down outside his front door.*

gun for
Someone who **is gunning for** you is trying to find any opportunity to find fault with you or attack you: *The boss's gunning for you; you'd better keep out of his way!*

gunge /gʌndʒ/: **gunges**, **gunging**, **gunged**

gunge up (*informal*)
Something **is gunged up** when it is filled or blocked with a thick sticky mass: *This drain is all gunged up with dead leaves and kitchen waste.*

h

hack /hak/: **hacks**, **hacking**, **hacked**

hack about

1 You **hack** something **about** when you seriously damage it by cutting it roughly or violently with a knife or other sharp instrument: *None of the Shropshire victims have been hacked about like this.* **2** To **hack** a piece of writing **about** is to make so many changes to it, especially by cutting out large parts, that it looks completely different from what was originally written: *You would spend days on a speech only to have it hacked about in a matter of minutes.*

hack at

You **hack at** something when you attack it with rough or violent cutting strokes with a knife or other sharp instrument: *He entered the room with a long-handled axe and hacked at the man's naked backside.*

hack down

To **hack down** something such as a tree is to cause it to fall to the ground with rough or violent cutting strokes with an axe or other tool: *A thoughtless builder had hacked our lilac bush down.* [*same as* **chop down**]

hack off

1 You **hack** something **off** when you detach it with rough or violent cutting strokes with an axe or other tool: *Would a panicky murderer take the time to hack off his victim's hands?* [*same as* **cut off**, **chop off**; compare **lop off**] **2** (*informal*) Someone who **hacks** you **off** annoys or irritates you: *'It's petty officials who hack me off,' she said.*

• *adjective (informal)* **hacked off**
Someone who **is hacked off** is annoyed or irritated: *Both instructor and pupil had finished the lesson wet through and hacked off.* [*same as* **fed up**, **cheesed off** (*informal*), **browned off** (*informal*)]

hack through

You **hack through** an area of thickly growing trees or bushes when you move through it making a path for yourself by roughly chopping off branches: *Endill tried to hack his way through but there were too many plants blocking his way.* [*same as* **cut through**]

haggle /'hagəl/: **haggles**, **haggling**, **haggled**

haggle over

You **haggle over** something, such as the price of goods for sale, or the details of an agreement, when you argue that it should be changed to suit you better: *It takes nerve to haggle over the small print if you are told that your new colleagues have worked under similar terms for years.* [compare **beat down**]

hail /heɪl/: **hails**, **hailing**, **hailed**

hail as

You use **hail as** to talk about the way someone or something is praised or admired in public: *Although hailed by Randolph Churchill as being 'Tory democracy in action', the 1963 process was no more open.*

hail from (*informal*)
You **hail from** the place where you were born, or where you come from: *The plant has spectacular yellow flowers, hails from the Caucasus mountains, and is well suited to all but dry or exposed conditions.* ❑ *Isn't he the chap that hails from Erracht near Fort William?*

ham /ham/: **hams**, **hamming**, **hammed**

---

ham up (*informal*)
You can say that an actor **hams** it **up** when they act in a very exaggerated and unnatural way, especially when this is done deliberately in order to amuse the audience: *It is a delight to see Mason ham the drunken scene up.*

hammer /ˈhamə(r)/: **hammers**, **hammering**, **hammered**

---

hammer away at (*informal*)
You **hammer away at** something when you say it repeatedly, so that people realize how important it is and remember it: *I keep hammering away at this point, but it applies to so many areas and it's so rarely done.* [*same as* **bang on about** (*informal*)]

hammer out
1 People **hammer out** an agreement when they work long and hard to achieve it: *We were determined to hammer some sort of solution out, if it took all night.* [*same as* **work out, thrash out**] **2** To **hammer out** a tune is to play it loudly and with force: *A man with a '70s haircut hammered out some old rock clichés.*

hand /hand/: **hands**, **handing**, **handed**

---

hand back
You **hand** something **back** when you return it to the person you took or borrowed it from: *Following Portugal's revolution in 1974, Lisbon tried to hand back Macao to China; Peking wasn't interested.* [*same as* **give back**]

hand down
Things that **are handed down** are given or left to people who are younger, or to people who come after: *Traditional storytelling skills were handed down through the generations.* ❑ *Each government hands its failures down to the next lot.* [*same as* **pass on, pass down, hand on**]

hand in
1 You **hand** something **in** when you give it to someone, especially someone in authority: *I stopped off at the library to hand in some books.* ❑ *We're giving all young people at risk of offending the chance to hand their weapons in to their local police station.* [*same as* **give in**] **2** You **hand in** a piece of work when you give it to the person who has the responsibility of judging it: *You must have a good reason for handing essays in late.* [*same as* **submit**] **3** You **hand in** your notice or your resignation when you give your employer a letter stating that you are giving up your job.

hand on
You **hand** something **on** when you give or leave it to younger people or people who come after you: *There was a fear that any outstanding debts would be handed on to the children.* [*same as* **pass on, pass down, hand down**]

hand out
You **hand** things **out** when you give one to each of several people: *The class prefect would hand out books and pens to the others.* [*same as* **give out, dish out** (*informal*); compare **dole out**]
● *noun* **handout**: **handouts**
1 A **handout** is a gift of something such as money or clothing to a poor person, *eg* by a charitable organization: *Many families were too proud to accept handouts.* **2** A **handout** is also a piece of printed information given to people, *eg* to students attending a lecture: *It was just one of those advertising handouts you get thrust on you in the street.*

hand over
1 You **hand** something **over** to someone when you give it to them to own or keep: *The BBC have refused to hand over film of the event without a court order.* [*same as* **turn over, surrender** (*formal*)] **2** You also **hand** something **over** to someone when you give them the responsibility of dealing with it or looking after it: *Who are you going to hand the presentation over to after you've given the introduction?* [*same as* **turn over**]

hand round
You **hand** something **round** when you pass it to each of several people: *I'll serve the food while you hand round drinks.* [*same as* **pass round**]

hang /haŋ/: **hangs, hanging, hung** /hʌŋ/

---

hang about (*informal*)
1 You **hang about, hang around** or **hang round** somewhere when you spend a long time there doing nothing, or waiting for someone or something: *I don't know why he had come hanging about here instead of hearing his own minister preach.* ❑ *Many young prostitutes are preyed upon by men who hang around railway stations waiting for runaways to arrive.* ❑ *French students had been hanging round the fringes of the course all week, trying to pick up girls at the college doors.* ❑ *Anthony had just left university and was hanging round, not trying very hard for a job.* **2** The people you **hang about, hang around** or **hang round** with are your friends, the people you spend a lot of your time with: *Charlie spends time with his family while the rest of the band hang about together.* **3** You can tell someone to **hang about** when you want them to wait: *The wolf says to the rabbit, 'Hang about 'til 8pm and I'll eat you for supper'.* [*same as* **hang on** (*informal*), **hold on** (*informal*)]

hang back
Someone who **hangs back** says or does nothing, because they are nervous, cautious or afraid: *She mentally urged him not to hang back, but she didn't want to make the first move.* ❑ *We must all join in; there is no room for anyone to hang back.* [compare **hold back, shrink back**]

hang on
1 (*informal*) You can tell someone to **hang on** if you want them to wait or stop: *Hang on a minute; that's not fair!* [*same as* **hold on** (*informal*)] **2** You **hang on** when you grip something tightly to prevent yourself from being thrown or bumped around: *We all hung on for dear life as the boat plunged into the rapids.*

hang on to
You **hang on to** something when you keep it: *I'd hang on to the old shoes; you could use them in the garden.* ❑ *It's frustrating for them to see the old leaders hanging on to power.* [*same as* **hold on to**]

hang out
1 You **hang out** washing when you hang it on a line outside, to dry: *Some residents fled with such haste that their washing is still hanging out.* **2** (*informal*) You **hang out** somewhere when you spend a lot of time there; you **hang out** with the people you spend a lot of time with: *In LA, you hung out with your contemporaries.* ❑ *Over here, I hang out with traditional musicians from the folk scene.*

hang over
1 You can use **hang over** to describe the position of something such as fog or smoke above an area: *Looking down, I could see a thick mist over the water and patches of mist hanging over the corn.* **2** You can also use **hang over** to refer to the presence of something bad or undesirable, such as a problem or a hostile atmosphere: *There are problems worldwide, but the biggest question*

mark hangs over the United States operation.

• *noun* **hangover**: **hangovers**

You have a **hangover** if you feel weak, tired or ill after drinking too much alcohol.

• *adjective* **hung over**

You are **hung over** when you have a hangover: *Adrian just sat with his hands on his stomach looking very hung over.*

hang round see **hang about**

hang together

1 Two or more people or groups **hang together** when they remain partners with each other: *The autonomous regions that make up the Russian Federation have an incentive to hang together.* [*same as* **stick together**] **2** You can say that something such as a story **hangs together** if its different parts combine well to form a proper or satisfactory whole: *Out of the nine poems he set to music, Cale eventually chose the four 'that seemed to hang together best'.* [compare **go together**]

hang up

1 You **hang up** things such as clothes when you store them by hanging them on a hook, rail or other fitting: *She kicked off her shoes and hung her suit up.* **2** You **hang up** when you end a telephone conversation by replacing the receiver: *I tried to reason with her but she hung up on me.* ❑ *If they call back, just hang up the phone.* **3** You can say that you **hang up** the equipment you use for a job or activity when you stop using it because you are giving up the job or activity: *I think it's probably time he hung his boots up.*

• *noun* **hang-up**: **hang-ups**

You have a **hang-up** about something if dealing with it or thinking about it makes you feel nervous, embarrassed, frightened or uncomfortable in some other way: *I don't think it can be dismissed as just another teenage hang-up.*

hanker /ˈhaŋkə(r)/: **hankers**, **hankering**, **hankered**

hanker after *or* **hanker for**

You **hanker after** something, or **hanker for** it, when you want it very much, especially when you have wanted it for a long time: *There are still athletes who hanker after a British shoe that is strong and reliable.* ❑ *Some sort of automatic payment scheme is what we've been hankering for.* [*same as* **long for, crave for, yearn for** (*formal*)]

happen /ˈhapən/: **happens**, **happening**, **happened**

happen along

Someone or something that **happens along** arrives unexpectedly: *Accidents like this don't just happen along; something pretty sinister has to cause them.*

hark /hɑːk/: **harks**, **harking**, **harked**

hark at (*informal*)

Some people use **hark at** as a way of drawing attention to what someone has just said, before commenting on how surprising, annoying or ridiculous it is: *Hark at her! Anyone would think she was the Queen of Sheba!*

hark back to

1 You **hark back to** a past time or event when you remember it or talk about it: *It's the kind of gathering where everyone in the room is harking back to their schooldays.* **2** When something **harks back to** an earlier time or period, it reminds you of that time or period, or seems to belong to it: *They wore elaborate dresses that harked back to the days of the Paris salons.*

harp /hɑːp/: **harps**, **harping**, **harped**

harp on

Someone who **harps on** a subject keeps talking about it so much that they bore or annoy others: *They're the kind of parents who harp on the terrible* *expense of everything.* [*same as* **go on about** (*informal*)]

haul /hɔːl/: **hauls, hauling, hauled**

haul up

Someone who **is hauled up** in front of a person or group of people in authority is forced to explain their wrong or criminal behaviour to them, and perhaps receive punishment: *We could have him hauled up before the magistrates in a matter of hours.* ❏ *Hauling him up in front of the headmaster isn't going to do any good. The thing is that he doesn't belong here.*

have /hav/: **has** /haz/, **having, had** /had/

have against

You **have** something **against** someone when you have a particular reason for disliking them or disapproving of them: *I have nothing against thorns or prickles so long as you can admire them from a safe distance.*

have back

You can use **have back** to tell someone when you want them to return what they are borrowing from you: *I must have it back by Friday at the latest.* ❏ *Don't worry; I'll have it back to you for the weekend.* [compare **get back, give back**]

have in

You can use **have in** to refer to a visit to your home or workplace by someone who carries out work there: *The plan was to have the builders in before Christmas, so the whole thing would be finished before the baby was born.* [compare **call in**]

have on

1 What you **have on** is what you are wearing: *I don't think you can have seen this dress; it's the first time I've had it on.* **2** You **have on** something such as a radio or television when it is switched on and you are listening to or watching it: *They had their music on so loud that the glasses in our cupboards were shaking.* **3** Someone who asks if you **have** anything **on** at a particular time wants to know if you will be busy at that time: *You could come over for Sunday lunch if you've got nothing on.* **4** (*informal*) Someone **is having** you **on** when they are teasing you by pretending that something is true when it is not: *Was he having me on about his brother being in the Foreign Legion?*

have out

1 You use **have out** to refer to the surgical removal of a part of someone's body: *Her little girl had to have another tooth out.* ❏ *Do you know if you've had your appendix out?* **2** You **have** something **out** with someone when you discuss openly something that has been causing bad feeling between you: *Sheila decided to go straight over there and have the whole thing out with him there and then.*

head /hɛd/: **heads, heading, headed**

head back

You **head back** when you travel towards the place you started your journey from: *We left the remote mountains of the north and west and headed back towards the central highlands.* ❏ *They negotiated the turn and were heading back along the other side of the village green.* [*same as* **return**]

head for

1 You **head for** a place when you travel or move towards it: *We decided to abandon fishing and head for home before I froze to death.* **2** You can also say that you **are heading for** something, or **are headed for** it, when it is going to happen to you: *He warns that the Arab world is headed 'for a period of turbulence like never before'.* [*same as* **head towards**]

head off

1 You **head off** when you leave, often in a particular direction: *I'm afraid we'll have to head off soon; we both have an early start tomorrow.* ❑ *I watched her head off towards the Tube.* ❑ *The canoeists headed off downstream towards Grandtully.* [compare **clear off, set off**] **2** You **head** someone **off** when you prevent them from reaching a place by blocking their path towards it: *They sent two riders around the rocks to the north, to head the cattle off.* **3** You **head off** something unpleasant when you prevent it from happening: *Another rise in VAT was rumoured, but recent economic surveys suggest the Treasury may have headed it off.*

head towards

1 You **head towards** a place when you move or travel in that direction: *The grey saloon car had pulled on to the hard shoulder and was heading towards her.* [*same as* **head for**] **2** You can also say that you **are heading towards** something, or **are headed towards** it, when it is going to happen to you: *UK mortgage interest rates are heading towards 14.75%.* [*same as* **head for**]

head up

You can say that someone **heads** something **up** when they lead it or are in charge of it: *The man Bleasdale picked to head up its new Charter Train Unit was David Ward.* [*same as* **head**]

heap /hiːp/: heaps, heaping, heaped

heap up

You **heap** things **up** when you make a large, untidy pile by putting one on top of the other: *It was difficult to see how a plate heaped up with so many potatoes could possibly stay on the tray.* [*same as* **pile up**]

heap upon

When someone is praised or insulted a lot, you can say that praises or insults **are heaped upon** them: *They don't have to earn or even deserve the praise or the cascade of 'goodies' heaped upon them.*

hear /hɪə(r)/: hears, hearing, heard /hɜːd/

hear about

You **hear about** something when someone tells you about it: *I hear about these artists who work all day and all night.* ❑ *A few days after he died, they came to the house and said they were sorry to hear about my husband.*

hear from

1 You **hear from** someone when they send you a letter or telephone you: *If you haven't heard from the firm within 28 days, write to their head office.* **2** You can also say that you **hear from** someone when they speak or say something: *Let's hear more from Mr Bridges before returning to the audience for their opinions.*

hear of

1 You **hear of** something when someone tells you about it: *When the king heard of the revolt he was seized by an epileptic fit.* ❑ *You hear of actresses being temperamental; this girl isn't.* **2** You can say that you **have heard of** something or someone when you recognize their name, or when you know that they exist: *Charsky mentioned Ivan Sakulin; we've heard of him before.* ❑ *Le Bugue is a place you've probably never heard of before.* ❑ *Whoever heard of apprentices as old as that?* **3** (*formal*) People sometimes say they won't **hear of** something to mean that they refuse to allow it: *She is advised to rest but won't hear of it, saying the summer will restore her strength.*

hear out

You **hear** someone **out** when you allow them to say all they want to say, without interrupting: *Eliza was determined that, they would hear her out.*

heat /hiːt/: **heats**, **heating**, **heated**

heat up

1 You **heat** something **up** when you cause it to become hot or hotter; something **heats up** when it becomes hot or hotter: *It'll only take a few seconds to heat up the milk.* ❑ *The car was beginning to heat up and I was worried about possible damage to the animal's health.* [compare **warm up**] **2** You can also say that a situation **heats up** when it becomes more angry or violent: *That will make the East Germans feel even more imprisoned and could heat up resentment against the government.* [*same as* **hot up**]

heave /hiːv/: **heaves**, **heaving**, **heaved**

heave up (*informal*)

Someone **heaves up** when food or drink comes back up from their stomach and is forced out through their mouth: *I spent the morning lying on their bathroom floor heaving up.* [*same as* **throw up** (*informal*), **chuck up** (*informal*), **sick up**, **vomit**]

hedge /hɛdʒ/: **hedges**, **hedging**, **hedged**

hedge around *or* hedge round

You use **hedge around** or **hedge round** to talk about situations in which problems limit freedom or prevent progress or success: *The whole scheme was hedged around with difficulties.* ❑ *This was just one of the pitfalls her life seemed hedged round with.*

hedge in

You feel **hedged in** when things prevent you from doing what you want or need to do: *The company's petty restrictions had us hedged in on all sides.* [*same as* **hem in**, **fence in**]

help /hɛlp/: **helps**, **helping**, **helped**

help along

You **help** something **along** when you make its progress faster or easier, or make its success more complete: *Today, helped along by Fitch Benoy's radical interventions, the new building is much more than the sum of its parts.*

help off with

You **help** someone **off with** a piece of clothing when you help them to take it off: *Leonard hovers round the older ladies, ready to help them off with their coats.*

help on with

You **help** someone **on with** a piece of clothing when you help them to put it on: *Now she's a bit older, she doesn't need to be helped on with her clothes.*

help out

You **help out** when you give someone help that they need; you can also say that you **help** them **out**: *Marie could help out with the baby and I could help out by going to the shops.* ❑ *If we're ever stuck for money I'm sure my parents would help us out if they could.*

help up

You **help** someone **up** when you help them to stand up from where they are sitting or where they have fallen down: *She's embarrassed at having to ask the younger ones to help her up out of the chair.*

hem /hɛm/: **hems**, **hemming**, **hemmed**

hem in

You **are hemmed in** when things prevent you from doing what you want or need to do, or prevent you from moving around freely: *It's quite natural for Western women to feel that Muslim traditions hem them in.* ❑ *It was an oblong barrack building with a narrow paved yard, hemmed in by high walls spiked on top.* [*same as* **fence in**, **hedge in**]

herd /hɜːd/: **herds**, **herding**, **herded**

herd together
People **are herded together** when they are gathered together in a group or crowd, especially roughly or without politeness: *We had been herded together to discuss this and other issues by Dr Derek Booth.* [compare **get together**]

hide /haɪd/: **hides**, **hiding**, **hid** /hɪd/, **hidden** /ˈhɪdən/

hide away
1 You **hide** something **away** when you put it in a place where nobody will see it or find it: *The passport forms had been hidden away at the back of a pile of stuff about film processing.* **2** Someone who **hides away** stays in a place where others won't see them or find them: *All this hassle would make anyone else want to hide away. But not Steffi.* [compare **hide out**] **3** You can say that something such as a house **is hidden away** when it is in an area that few people go to, or a place that is difficult to see or find: *The Sheldrake place was hidden away in a cove at the north end of the bay.*

• *noun* **hideaway**: **hideaways**
A **hideaway** is a secret place you go to in order to be alone: *There was a field here, with high hedges that we'd built a hideaway in.*

hide behind
People who **hide behind** a certain way of behaving adopt that behaviour so as not to show their real feelings or personality: *There's also the ruthless realist routine he hides behind at work.* ❑ *Geoff managed to hide what was basically misanthropy behind a haughty disregard for personal relationships.*

hide from
1 You **hide from** someone when you go to a place where they cannot see or find you: *He decided to hide from the others until it was dark.* **2** You **hide** something **from** someone when you put it in a place where they can't see or find it: *I need to find somewhere good to hide these presents from the kids.* **3** You also **hide** something **from** someone when you try to prevent them from finding out about it: *There was never any need to explain things to him; equally, it was impossible to hide anything from him.* **4** You **hide from** something when you try to pretend that you don't know about it: *They're right when they say that you can't hide from the truth.*

hide out
You **hide out** somewhere when you stay there so that people don't find you, especially people you are escaping from: *Is there anywhere you know of where he might go to hide out until the fuss dies down?* [compare **hide away**]

hike /haɪk/: **hikes**, **hiking**, **hiked**

hike up
1 You **hike up** a piece of clothing when you pull it up so that its lower edge is in a higher position: *The women hiked their skirts up, so they wouldn't get caught on the wire.* [*same as* **hitch up**] **2** (*informal*) To **hike up** a price or other sum of money is to increase it suddenly and by a large amount: *As soon as you mention Oxford or Cambridge the salary gets hiked up a couple of thousand.* ❑ *They hike their rates up during the tourist season.* [*same as* **push up**]

hinge /hɪndʒ/: **hinges**, **hinging**, **hinged**

hinge on *or* hinge upon
One thing **hinges on** another, or **hinges upon** it, when the first depends on the second: *It was a nail-biting season, with the championship hinging on the very last match.* ❑ *Success abroad seems to hinge on American-Japanese trade relations.* [*same as* **rest on**]

hint /hɪnt/: hints, hinting, hinted

hint at

You **hint at** something when you suggest in an indirect way that it is true or that it exists, or that it could be true or could exist in the future: *He told her how cold his wife had always been: Eleanor started hinting at an affair.* ❑ *The introductory document hints at formal examinations at the end of key stages.*

hire /haɪə(r)/: hires, hiring, hired

hire out

To **hire** something **out** is to allow others to use it in return for money: *The leisure centre hires out bikes for £5 a day.* [*same as* **rent out**]

hit /hɪt/: hits, hitting, hit

hit back

You **hit back** when you attack in return someone who has attacked you; you can also say that you **hit back** at them: *If one of the other boys hits you, make sure you hit them back just as hard.* ❑ *The minister in question hit back with an attack on the paper's 'lack of editorial independence'.*

hit on *or* hit upon

You **hit on** something, or **hit upon** it, when you discover it or realize it: *Looking for trousers, he hit on a pair of corduroy breeches.* ❑ *They exhibited all the satisfaction of someone who has just hit upon a method of causing water to flow uphill.*

hit out

You **hit out** when you attack someone, especially with criticisms or insults: *They in turn hit out at the festival organizers, claiming not enough has been done to promote the city.*

hitch /hɪtʃ/: hitches, hitching, hitched

hitch up

You **hitch up** a piece of clothing you are wearing when you pull it up so that its lower edge is in a higher position: *Gerald had a habit of hitching his trousers legs up before he sat down, exposing an expanse of faded sock.* [*same as* **hike up, pull up**]

hive /haɪv/: hives, hiving, hived

hive off

Part of a business company or other concern **is hived off** when it is sold to someone else, especially making a large profit: *Legal services was the first section to be hived off to the private sector.* [*same as* **sell off**]

hold /hould/: holds, holding, held /hɛld/

hold against

You **hold** something **against** someone when you deal with them harshly or unfairly because you disapprove of or dislike something about them: *Her father says, 'So, you married an Englishman. We won't hold it against you.'* ❑ *Perhaps their lack of computer competence will be held against them.* [compare **count against**]

hold back

1 You **hold** something or someone **back** when you prevent them from moving or leaving: *I would like to have seen the guard holding back the tourists with an old sword.* [*same as* **keep back**] **2** To **hold** something **back** is to prevent or delay its progress; to **hold** someone **back** is to prevent them from making good or proper progress, usually in their career: *Smoking can affect the developing baby by holding back its growth.* ❑ *Transplant programmes have been held back because of a shortage of donor organs.* ❑ *I'm sure your parents never meant to hold you back in any way.* [compare **cut back**] **3** You **hold back** information when you don't tell everything you know: *The Inspector feels Evans is holding something back.* [*same as* **withhold**] **4** You **hold back**

something such as tears or laughter when you prevent yourself from crying or laughing when you feel you want to: *I could see Moira working hard to hold her anger back.* [*same as* **choke back, stifle, suppress**] **5** You **hold back**, or **hold back** from doing something, when you don't do what you intended or wanted to do: *It is necessary to be patient, to hold back and do nothing.* ❑ *This was something Poindexter could hardly hold back from revealing.*

hold down

1 To **hold** something **down** is to keep it at a low level and prevent it from rising or increasing: *There are too many market-makers in these areas, which holds down everyone's earnings.* [*same as* **keep down**] **2** You can say that someone **holds down** a job when they manage to keep it, when you might have expected them to lose it: *Peter had never held any job down for longer than a couple of months.* **3** You **hold** feelings or emotions **down** when you prevent yourself from expressing them: *It isn't easy for people like Janey to hold down the waves of panic that surge up inside them every time they have to deal with confrontation.* [*same as* **hold back, keep back, stifle**] **4** Someone who can't **hold down** food vomits after they've eaten: *At least she's managed to hold her breakfast down.* [*same as* **keep down**] **5** To **hold** people **down** is to use force to control their behaviour, giving them no rights or freedoms: *It was to be expected that the African peoples, after being held down for so long, would rise up against their oppressors.*

hold forth

Someone who **is holding forth** is talking about something in a boring or self-important way: *The army officer holds forth about the unscrupulousness of the moneylender, saying he would kill her without conscience.* [*same as* **spout forth**]

hold in

You **hold** your feelings or emotions **in** when you prevent yourself from expressing them: *As a man, you're expected to hold in your fear and accept your fate bravely.* [*same as* **hold back, keep in**]

hold off

1 You **hold off**, or **hold off** doing something, when you delay doing it; something **holds off** when it doesn't happen, when you expected it would: *The pilot knows he will eject, but holds off until the aircraft is clear of habitation.* ❑ *Could you hold off announcing it to the press until the family has been informed?* ❑ *We just need the rains to hold off for another few days, until we can get the wheat in.* **2** You **hold off** someone who is attacking you, or **hold off** their attack, when you prevent them from defeating you: *If they can hold the Madrid side off until half time, they'll consider that an achievement in itself.*

hold on

1 (*informal*) People often say '**Hold on!**' when they want you to wait: *Tell them to hold on a few seconds until we get the rest of the cartons unpacked.* [*same as* **hang on**] **2** You **hold on** when you support yourself by holding something; you **hold on** to something when you hold it in order to support yourself: *You tight-rope walk on the single strand below and hold on to the other two lines for balance.* ❑ *Two tired men were holding on to each other for support.* ❑ *The ride can be a bit bumpy, so you're advised to hold on tight.* **3** You **hold on** to something when you keep it; you can also say that you **are holding on** when you manage to continue doing something: *Mr Quiles is probably more concerned to hold on to his job.* ❑ *There will be more battles like this in the coming years, whether or not the Conservatives hold on to power.* ❑ *I felt a twinge in my leg and eased down, just holding on for the silver medal.* [*same as* **hang on**]

hold out

1 You **hold** something **out** when you hold it at some distance in front of your body, often in a gesture of offering: *You lie flat on the bench with the weights held out above your chest.* ❑ *I approached and held a piece of chicken out to him.* ❑ *The Syrian soldier nearest the door held out his arms in friendship.* ❑ *They held out the possibility of talks with the government as an incentive to call off the demonstration.* **2** You **hold out** when you manage to resist attacks made against you over a period of time: *I'm not sure how long the Arsenal defence can hold out against such sustained pressure.* ❑ *The Hussites took the territory and managed to hold out successfully until 1436.* [*same as* **last out**; *opposite* **give up, give in**] **3** A supply of something **holds out** when it lasts: *We weren't even sure that our stock of firewood would hold out.* [*same as* **last out**] **4** You **hold out** hope of something when you still hope that it will happen: *Few of us at that stage held out much hope for eventual rescue.*

hold out for

You **hold out for** something you are asking for when you refuse to accept anything less than it: *With the unions holding out for a full five per cent, a strike of some sort seems inevitable.*

hold out on (*informal*)

You **hold out on** someone when you don't tell them everything you know: *You know I wouldn't risk holding out on you, Benny.*

hold over

1 Something that **is held over** is not done or dealt with when expected, but delayed until later: *There is talk that the whole tournament could be held over until next month, when the Americans will be available.* [*same as* **put off, put back, postpone**] **2** Someone **holds** something **over** you when they threaten you with it or use the threat of it to influence you: *They are holding the threat of a national strike over the people of this country.*

hold to

1 You **hold** one thing **to** another when you hold it against it, so that the two are touching each other: *Jack was still kneeling beside Bunty and holding her hand to his cheek.* **2** You **hold** someone **to** a decision or promise they have made when you force them not to abandon it: *Leaders only just managed to hold the Party to a multilateralist line on disarmament.* ❑ *'We must have you over to dinner some time.' 'I'll hold you to that.'* **3** You can use **hold to** to talk about opinions and beliefs that people have: *The Provisionals hold to similar understandings of the necessity of violence under certain circumstances.* [*same as* **adhere to** (*formal*)]

hold together

1 Something that **holds together** stays in good order, and does not collapse or break: *I'm just hoping my old moped will hold together for another winter.* **2** People or groups who **hold together** stay in agreement or in partnership with each other; you **hold** them **together** when you persuade them not to disagree or end their partnership: *It's difficult to see how the party can hold together in light of such public declarations of discontent.* ❑ *The King encouraged MacDonald to hold the government together and to fight the election as a government.* [compare **stay together, stick together**]

hold up

1 You **hold** something **up** when you lift it into a position in front of you, and perhaps slightly above you, often in a gesture of showing: *Agnes was now holding up the coat before her.* **2** Something **is held up** by what supports it or prevents it from collapsing: *The rocks below seemed to be wobbling under the strain of holding the building up.* [*same as* **prop up**] **3** To **hold** something **up** is also to prevent it from failing: *The company's financial fortunes had been shaky and we needed* *a prop to hold us up.* **4** You **hold** something **up** when you stop or delay its progress: *The object was not to provide refreshment but to hold up the party for a few minutes.* ❑ *Spot checks cannot be carried out without holding other traffic up.* **5** You can use **hold up** to talk about how effective something remains after it has been used or tested: *The Goretex jackets tended to hold up better in winter conditions.* ❑ *None of their theories would hold up under close examination.* [*same as* **stand up**] **6** You can use **hold up** to talk about the way someone or something is referred to or described by others: *Singers like LL Cool J are held up as authentic voices of teenage youth.* ❑ *She was embarrassed by the teachers' habit of holding her up to be some sort of model pupil.* **7** To **hold up** people, or places such as banks, is to steal money from them using threats of violence, *eg* with guns: *Trains carrying tourists are regularly held up north of the mountains.*

• *noun* **hold-up**: **hold-ups**

1 A **hold-up** is a delay: *We had one or two hold-ups on the way and arrived over an hour late.* ❑ *Hold-ups are expected throughout the morning on the M6 and A74.* **2** A **hold-up** is also an act of stealing money using threats of violence: *He's suspected of being responsible for the hold-up in the High Street last month.*

hold up to

A person or thing **is held up to** ridicule or scorn when someone ridicules or scorns them in front of others or in public: *We had to sit there while Lewis held modern poetry up to contempt.*

hold with

You can say that you don't **hold with** something if you don't approve of it: *Newman and the other traditionalists didn't hold with the communicative approach to language learning.* [*same as* **agree with, subscribe to** (*formal*)]

hole /houl/: holes, holing, holed

hole up (*informal*)

Someone who **holes up** somewhere stays in a place where others, usually the police, won't find them: *We suspected all along that they were holed up somewhere along the Cornish coast.* [*same as* **hide out**]

home /houm/: homes, homing, homed

home in on

1 Something such as a missile **homes in on** a target when its electronic aiming device fixes it on a direct course that it travels along towards the target: *Enemy vehicles can home in on our signals if we don't use a scrambler.* ❑ *From distances of up to half a mile, the young hyenas home in on the scent of blood.* **2** You **home in on** something when you concentrate all your attention or efforts on it: *Ministers always seem to home in on fraud at the lower or poorer end of the scale.* [*same as* **focus on**]

hook /huk/: hooks, hooking, hooked

hook up

1 You **hook** one thing **up** to another when you attach it using hooks or other fittings: *It'll be a good half hour before they can get a new engine hooked up.* [*same as* **couple up**] **2** A piece of electrical or electronic equipment **is hooked up** when it is connected to a power supply; two such pieces of equipment **are hooked up** when they are connected to each other: *The first job is to get the telephone system hooked up.* ❑ *You just hook your PC up to a modem and you can speak to other computers virtually anywhere in the world.* [*same as* **link up**]

hop /hɒp/: hops, hopping, hopped

hop off (*informal*)

Someone who tells you to **hop off** is rudely telling you to go away: *You kids had better hop off, before I take a* *broom to you!* [*same as* **buzz off** (*informal*), **clear off**]

hope /hoʊp/: **hopes**, **hoping**, **hoped**

hope for
You **hope for** something when you want or expect it to happen, or you want or expect to have it: *The best that the government can hope for is to ride out the crisis until the next election.* ❑ *He asked me what the realities of the medical situation were and what could be hoped for in the best of circumstances.*

horse /hɔːs/: **horses**, **horsing**, **horsed**

horse about *or* horse around
(*informal*)
People **horse about** or **horse around** when they play in a lively, rough and noisy way: *We don't want the children horsing around anywhere near the pool.* [*same as* **mess about** (*informal*), **fool about**, **lark about** (*informal*)]

hose /hoʊz/: **hoses**, **hosing**, **hosed**

hose down
You **hose** something **down** when you clean it thoroughly using water squirted from a hose: *Our quarters were hosed down regularly to minimize the risk of infection.* [compare **wash down**]

hot /hɒt/: **hots**, **hotting**, **hotted**

hot up
A situation **hots up** when it becomes busier or more exciting, or when people's feelings become more intense: *Things were hotting up but he just couldn't think what to do next, without getting into trouble.* ❑ *Undoubtedly, international industrial competition was hotting up.* [*same as* **heat up**]

hound /haʊnd/: **hounds**, **hounding**, **hounded**

hound out
Someone who **is hounded out** of a place is forced to leave it, often by others who have grouped together against them: *He found himself hounded out of the post within six months.*

howl /haʊl/: **howls**, **howling**, **howled**

howl down
Someone speaking in public **is howled down** when others force them to stop speaking by shouting insults: *They did send one representative, but the locals mercilessly howled him down.* [*same as* **shout down**]

huddle /ˈhʌdəl/: **huddles**, **huddling**, **huddled**

huddle round
People **huddle round** something when they gather in a close group around it: *James and the other men huddled round the dying fire.* [*same as* **gather round**]

huddle together
People **huddle together** when each has their body pressed closely against the others, *eg* for warmth or safety: *The crew said they had survived by sleeping huddled together.* ❑ *The ducks were all huddling together trying to keep warm.*

hum /hʌm/: **hums**, **humming**, **hummed**

hum with
People often use **hum with** to describe how busy a place is: *Hotels' public areas are humming with personalities and film and TV crews.* [*same as* **bustle with**]

hunger /ˈhʌŋgə(r)/: **hungers**, **hungering**, **hungered**

hunger for
You **hunger for** something when you want it very much, especially when you have wanted it for a very long time: *By the end of the winter you're hungering*

for a bit of sunshine. [*same as* **die for, hanker after**]

hunker /ˈhʌŋkə(r)/: **hunkers, hunkering, hunkered**

hunker down (*AmE*)

You **hunker down** when you lower your body into a position with knees fully bent so that your buttocks approach your heels: *She watched the two men hunker down behind a bush.* [*same as* **crouch down**]

hunt /hʌnt/: **hunts, hunting, hunted**

hunt down

You **hunt** someone **down** when you finally find them after a long search: *The image is of drunken, crazed locals hunting down interlopers and murdering them in the night.* ❑ *Green will hunt you down, both of you, wherever you go.* [*same as* **track down**]

hunt out

You **hunt out** something that was stored away somewhere a long time ago when you find it after a long search: *We spent all of last evening hunting out the photos from the first InterRail holiday.* [*same as* **look out, dig out**]

hunt up

You **hunt** something **up** when you manage to find it: *Most of her time is spent hunting up references in the British Library.* [*same as* **chase up**]

hurl /hɜːl/: **hurls, hurling, hurled**

hurl about *or* hurl around

You **hurl** something **about**, or **hurl** it **around**, when you throw it roughly or violently in many directions or from place to place: *Furniture had been overturned and books and records hurled about the place.* ❑ *The yellow ball had been hurled around by the kids and was much softer.* [*same as* **throw about**]

hurry /ˈhʌrɪ/: **hurries, hurrying, hurried**

hurry on

You **hurry on** when, rather than stopping, you continue to walk quickly, perhaps a little quicker than before: *A woman with a clipboard approached him but he dropped his shoulders and hurried on.*

hurry up

1 You tell someone to **hurry up** when you want them to move or act more quickly: *Hurry up, Bill; people will be standing in line for the loo.* ❑ *If the kids don't hurry up we'll still be here at teatime.* **2** You **hurry** someone **up** when you make them move or act more quickly: *Miss Jones stood in the corridor hurrying up the stragglers.* **3** You **hurry** something **up** when you make it progress faster or happen sooner: *I wrote them a letter begging them to hurry up the settlement of our claim.* [*same as* **speed up, accelerate** (*formal*)]

hush /hʌʃ/: **hushes, hushing, hushed**

hush up

1 To **hush** something **up** is to keep it secret, so that nobody finds out about it: *It was Ingrams' job to hush up affairs like this.* [*same as* **cover up, suppress** (*formal*)] **2** You can tell someone to **hush up** when you want them to stop talking; you **hush** someone **up** when you make them stop talking: *Get the ones at the back to hush up.* ❑ *Anyone daring to whisper was unceremoniously hushed up.* [*same as* **shut up**] **3** You can also say that someone **is hushed up** when they are forced not to tell what they know: *It wouldn't be the first time that Adamson had managed to hush a witness up.* [*same as* **shut up**]

hype /haɪp/: **hypes, hyping, hyped**

hype up

1 You **hype** something **up** when you make it seem more impressive, important or exciting than it really is: *The Minister is continuing his practice of hyping up every issue.* [compare **talk up**] **2** To **hype** someone **up** is to make them eager to do something: *Men inside the vans were hyped up by one or two officers running their batons along the grilling over the windows.* [compare **psych up**]

i

ice /aɪs/: **ices**, **icing**, **iced**

ice over

A surface **ices over** when it becomes covered with ice: *That was the year the lake iced over in November.* [*same as* **freeze over**]

ice up

Something **ices up** when ice develops inside or around it and prevents it from moving or working properly: *All the locks had iced up during the night.* [*same as* **freeze up**; compare **seize up**]

identify /aɪ'dɛntɪfaɪ/: **identifies**, **identifying**, **identified**

identify with

1 You **identify with** someone when you feel sympathy and understanding for them because they are like you or their situation is similar to your own: *You can't expect readers to identify with a hero whose only problem in life is what to spend his money on.* [*same as* **relate to**] **2** You can use **identify with** to talk about links or connections made between people and things: *None of these poets set out to be identified with a movement of any kind.* ❑ *In the public's mind, the name Jaguar is still identified with quality and excellence in motor cars.* [*same as* **associate with**]

idle /'aɪdəl/: **idles**, **idling**, **idled**

idle about *or* idle around

Someone who **idles about** or **idles around** spends time lazily, doing nothing: *Seeing him idling about was making me angrier by the day.* ❑ *We spent the first couple of weeks idling around the beach and the nearby campsites.* [*same as* **laze about**, **loaf about**; compare **lounge about**, **hang about**]

idle away

You **idle** time **away** when you spend it lazily, doing nothing: *Mitsy and the others went down to the river to idle away the afternoon.* [*same as* **while away**]

impinge /ɪm'pɪndʒ/: **impinges**, **impinging**, **impinged**

impinge on *or* impinge upon

(*formal*)

One thing **impinges on** another when it affects it, especially when it disturbs it or interferes with it: *At times of crisis, my work schedule inevitably impinges on my private life.* [*same as* **encroach on**, **intrude on**]

impose /ɪm'poʊz/: **imposes**, **imposing**, **imposed**

impose on *or* impose upon

1 Someone **imposes** something **on** you when they force you to accept or suffer it: *I wouldn't want to impose my religious beliefs on anyone.* ❑ *The new tax will not be imposed on people's savings.* ❑ *They didn't stop to think it might not be right to impose themselves upon her so soon after she'd had the baby.* **2** Someone **imposes on** you when they cause you bother or inconvenience: *I hate to impose on you, but my car won't start and I wondered if you would give me a lift.* ❑ *He's the kind of* *person who will always be imposed upon.*

impress /ɪm'prɛs/: **impresses**, **impressing**, **impressed**

impress on *or* **impress upon**
You **impress** something **on** or **upon** someone when you stress or emphasize it: *We're hoping to impress on the Health Secretary the need for a nationally negotiated settlement.* ❑ *They have impressed it upon us that we are the groundbreakers in this field of study.*

improve /ɪm'pruːv/: **improves**, **improving**, **improved**

improve on *or* **improve upon**
You **improve on** something you have done, or **improve upon** it, when you do it better a second time; you **improve on** something someone else has done, or **improve upon** it, when you make it better by changing it or by doing it differently: *She'll find it difficult to improve on her first-round score.* ❑ *Last year's performance must be improved upon.* [*same as* **better**]

in see panel on next page

inbuilt /'ɪnbɪlt/ see **build in**

indulge /ɪn'dʌldʒ/: **indulges**, **indulging**, **indulged**

indulge in
You **indulge in** something when you allow yourself the pleasure of doing or having it: *Would you care to indulge in a sherry before dinner?* ❑ *Anyone indulging in casual sex should be aware of the risks.*

inflict /ɪn'flɪkt/: **inflicts**, **inflicting**, **inflicted**

inflict on *or* **inflict upon**
You **inflict** something unpleasant **on** someone, or **inflict** it **upon** them, when you force them to suffer it: *Frank never hesitated to inflict his troubles on others.* ❑ *Our parents will have their grandchildren inflicted upon them for the weekend.*

inform /ɪn'fɔːm/: **informs**, **informing**, **informed**

inform on
To **inform on** someone is to give information about their crimes or wrongdoings to the police or other authority: *Few of us would inform on a close friend or relative, I think.* [*same as* **betray**; compare **tell on**]

infringe /ɪn'frɪndʒ/: **infringes**, **infringing**, **infringed**

infringe on *or* **infringe upon**
Something **infringes on** things such as rights or freedoms when it takes some or a part of them away: *People see the introduction of identity cards as infringing on their civil liberties.* ❑ *The manager's traditional privileges were being infringed upon.* [compare **encroach on, impinge on, intrude on**]

ink /ɪŋk/: **inks**, **inking**, **inked**

ink in
You **ink** something **in** when you write in ink what you had previously only written in pencil, to show that a firm or final decision has now been made about it; you can also say that you **ink** something or someone **in** when you make a firm or final decision about them: *I'll get my diary and ink in the date.* ❑ *The date is definitely the 25th, but the venue hasn't been inked in yet.* [compare **pencil in**]

input /'ɪnput/ see **put in**

inquire *or* **enquire** /ɪŋ'kwaɪə(r)/: **inquires**, **inquiring**, **inquired**

inquire after
You **inquire after** someone when you ask for news of them: *She always inquires after the children.* ❑ *I said*

in /ɪn/

In is an adverb and a preposition.
It is one of the most common words in English. Its basic sense relates to movement from the outside of something to the inside, and this sense is present in many of its principal meanings.

1 ENTERING AND ARRIVING
There are many combinations in which **in** has this literal sense, and their meanings are very clear. These include **come in**, **go in** and **invite in**. More numerous are combinations which mean the same but whose meanings are less clear, often because the verb is not used in its literal sense. For example, you can say that a bus or train **pulls in** when it arrives. You **check in**, **book in** or **sign in** when you formally register your arrival. People **crowd in**, **flood in**, **pile in** and **pour in** when they arrive in large numbers.
The sense of entering is present in a group of combinations that suggest movement through something, such as **soak in**, where the movement is often into the body, or part of it, as in **breathe in**, **drink in**, **sink in** and **take in**.

2 GATHERING AND COLLECTING
In can refer to the gathering and collecting of things. Combinations with the verb in its literal sense include **bring in**, **get in**, **fetch in** and **take in**. The phrasal verbs **cash in** and **trade in** combine the sense of collecting with the sense of exchanging.

3 ADDING AND INCLUDING
There are many combinations in which **in** relates to the adding or including of things. You can **add in**, **build in**, **include in**, **fit in** and **put in** things that will form a new part of something. Several combinations suggest the idea of things being mixed together, such as **dig in**, **merge in**, **mix in** and **stir in**. This sense of mixing is extended in some combinations to suggest that the things that are combined or mixed match each other very well, as in **blend in** and **tone in**.

4 INTERRUPTING AND INVOLVING
In some combinations, **in** relates to interrupting and involving, as in **barge in**, **break in**, **cut in** and **want in**. Often it relates to the actions of people who interrupt by involving themselves in situations where they are not wanted, such as in **butt in** and **muscle in**.
In this sense, **in** as an adverb is sometimes followed by *on* as a preposition, as in **burst in on**.

5 PREVENTING AND LIMITING
In a number of combinations, **in** refers to the actions of people and things that prevent or limit something, as in **lock in** and **block in**. Combinations in this group sometimes refer not to physical states, but to the way people feel, as in **hem in** and **pen in**.

6 BREAKING
In some combinations, **in** refers to breaking, suggesting that the broken parts fall or are forced towards the inside of something, as in **break in**, **cave in**, **kick in** and **smash in**.

7 REMAINING
In is used in several combinations that relate to remaining somewhere, often at home, instead of going away or going out. For example, you **stay in** and **stop in** when you stay at home; you **wait in** when you wait at home for an expected visitor; and you **eat in** when you dine at home, rather than going out to a restaurant.
[see also **into**]

'Good morning' and inquired after her husband's health. [*same as* **ask after**]

inquire into
To **inquire into** something is to investigate it formally, often in order to find out why or how it happened: *It seems astounding that the precise cause of death was not inquired into.* ❑ *The committee was set up primarily to inquire into standards in public life.* [*same as* **look into**]

insist /ɪn'sɪst/: **insists**, **insisting**, **insisted**

insist on *or* insist upon
You **insist on** something, or you **insist**

upon it, when you state firmly that you want it and will not be satisfied until it is given or done: *Life can be difficult for schoolkids whose parents insist on taking them to school.* ❑ *My client will have to insist on an hourly rate that reflects her experience and expertise.* ❑ *The smallest details can be insisted upon in a formal contract.*

intake /ˈɪnteɪk/ see **take in**

interfere /ɪntəˈfɪə(r)/: **interferes**, **interfering**, **interfered**

interfere in

Someone **interferes in** something if they involve themselves in it when their involvement is not wanted: *It must be difficult for parents not to interfere in the children's lives.* [*same as* **pry into**]

interfere with

1 To **interfere with** something is to disturb the way it is arranged or ordered, or the way it progresses: *She found the job was interfering too much with her family life.* ❑ *The story has the familiar theme of the scientist who interferes with nature and gets his fingers burnt.* **2** Someone **interferes with** something when they touch or disturb it without the permission of the person it belongs to: *Someone had clearly interfered with the papers on my desk while I had been out of the room.* [*same as* **meddle with**, **monkey with** (*informal*), **tamper with**] **3** Someone who **interferes with** someone, usually a child, touches them in a sexual way or tries to have sex with them: *We were shocked and saddened by yet another report of a priest who had interfered with children in his care.* [*same as* **molest**, **abuse**]

into see panel on next page

intrude /ɪnˈtruːd/: **intrudes**, **intruding**, **intruded**

intrude on *or* intrude upon

(*formal*)

To **intrude on** something is to disturb it by entering or being present when not wanted or not welcome: *A horrible realisation intruded itself upon his relaxation.* ❑ *It wouldn't be right for us to intrude on them in their time of grief.*

invite /ɪnˈvaɪt/: **invites**, **inviting**, **invited**

invite in

You **invite** someone **in** when you ask them to come into your home, or your room: *Well, aren't you going to invite me in?* [*same as* **ask in**]

invite out

You **invite** someone **out** when you ask them to go to a restaurant, theatre or other place with you, in order to spend time together socially: *Go round and invite her out, even if it's only for a walk.* [*same as* **ask out**; compare **go out with**]

invite over *or* invite round

You **invite** someone **over**, or **invite** them **round**, when you ask them to come to your home: *We've invited over some of our neighbours.* ❑ *Perhaps we'll be invited round to their house some time.* [*same as* **ask over**, **ask round**]

iron /ˈaɪən/: **irons**, **ironing**, **ironed**

iron out

You **iron out** difficulties or problems when you solve them or get rid of them: *We were determined to iron it out before the end of the day.* [*same as* **sort out**, **clear up**]

itch /ɪtʃ/: **itches**, **itching**, **itched**

itch for (*informal*)

You can say that you **are itching for** something when you are very eager to have it: *She was itching for a chance to prove what she could do.* [*same as* **long for**]

into /ˈɪntuː/

Into is a preposition.

It is one of the most common prepositions in English, and its basic sense relates to movement from the outside of something to the inside of it. This sense is present in some of its principal meanings.

1 ENTERING AND ARRIVING

There are many combinations in which **into** has this literal sense, and their meanings are very clear. These include **come into**, **go into** and **invite into**. More numerous are combinations which mean the same but whose meanings are less clear, often because the verb is not used in its literal sense. For example, you can say that a bus or train **pulls into** a place when it arrives there. You **check into**, **book into** or **sign into** a place when you formally register your arrival there. People **flood into** and **pour into** a place when they arrive there in large numbers.

The sense of entering is present in a group of combinations that refer to the action of one thing that hits or strikes another violently, such as **bump into** and **plough into**.

2 PUTTING AND PLACING

There are many combinations in which **into** relates to the putting or placing of things somewhere, such as **fit into, set into** and **slot into**. A number of phrasal verbs combine this sense of putting with the sense of entering, as in **drum into, sink into** and **tap into**.

3 CHANGING IN SUBSTANCE OR NATURE

In a large number of combinations, **into** relates to the process by which the nature or substance of something changes, as in **fall into, grow into, lapse into** and **make into**. With some phrasal verbs, this change in substance or nature is the result of different things being combined or mixed, as in **blend into, melt into, merge into** and **shade into.**

4 FORCING AND PERSUADING

In a number of combinations, **into** refers to something that someone is forced or persuaded to do, as in **press into, push into** and **talk into**.

[see also **in**]

j

jabber /'dʒabə(r)/: **jabbers, jabbering, jabbered**

jabber away (*informal*)
Someone **is jabbering away** when they are talking very quickly, perhaps so quickly that you cannot understand them: *A group of foreign students sat jabbering away in the corner.* [*same as* **gabble away** (*informal*), **babble, prattle**]

jack /dʒak/: **jacks, jacking, jacked**

jack in (*informal*)
You **jack** something **in** when you stop doing it: *I'm getting tired; let's jack this in.* ❑ *There are days when I feel like jacking in my job and starting a whole new life for myself.* [*same as* **pack in, give up, abandon**; *opposite* **carry on, keep on**]

jack off (*vulgar slang; especially AmE*)
To **jack off** is to stroke your own sexual organs in order to achieve sexual climax or orgasm. [*same as* **jerk off, masturbate**]

jack up
1 You **jack up** something heavy, especially a car or other vehicle, when you lift it, or lift one end of it, off the ground using a mechanical device called a jack, placed underneath: *We'd better jack it up and check the underside.* **2** (*informal*) To **jack up** something such as a price is to raise or increase it, especially suddenly and greatly: *They take any opportunity to jack up their charges.* [*same as* **put up, hike up**; *opposite* **put down, drop**] **3** (*slang*) People who **jack up** inject illegal drugs into their body. [*same as* **shoot up** (*informal*)]

jam /dʒam/: **jams, jamming, jammed**

jam on (*informal*)
A driver **jams on** the brakes when they put them on suddenly and with force: *Then Andy jammed the brake on and the van went into a spin.* [*same as* **slam on, put on**]

jazz /dʒaz/: **jazzes, jazzing, jazzed**

jazz up (*informal*)
You **jazz** something **up** when you do something to make it look or seem brighter or livelier: *I suppose we could jazz up the walls with a few posters.* ❑ *She thinks the costumes should be jazzed up a bit.* [*same as* **brighten up, liven up**]

jerk /dʒɜːk/: **jerks, jerking, jerked**

jerk around *or* **jerk about** (*slang; especially AmE*)
Someone **jerks** you **around**, or **jerks** you **about**, when they treat you badly, *eg* by causing you a lot of inconvenience: *I won't stand for them jerking me around like that.* ❑ *The bigger the company, the more they feel they can jerk you about.* [*same as* **mess around, muck about, abuse**; *opposite* **do right by**]

jerk off (*vulgar slang; especially AmE*)

To **jerk off** is to stroke your own sexual organs in order to achieve sexual climax or orgasm. [*same as* **jack off** (*slang*), **masturbate**]

jet /dʒɛt/: jets, jetting, jetted

jet off (*informal*)
You can say that someone **jets off** somewhere, especially to a distant and exciting place, when they go there by plane: *Harold and Ida will be jetting off to the Canaries for the winter.* [*same as* **fly off**]

jibe see gibe

jog /dʒɒg/: jogs, jogging, jogged

jog along (*informal*)
You might say that something **is jogging along** when it is making steady progress, or its usual progress, perhaps when you wish it would change or become more interesting: *Life at the office continued to jog along at its usual pace.*

join /dʒɔɪn/: joins, joining, joined

join in
You **join in** when you become involved in something that other people are doing: *She used to watch the other children playing but wouldn't join in.* ❑ *Soon everyone was joining in the discussion.* [*same as* **muck in** (*informal*), **pitch in** (*informal*), **participate**; *opposite* **stand apart, shy away**]

join up
1 You **join** things **up** when you connect or attach them to each other: *If you join up these three photos you get a panorama effect.* ❑ *Shorter lengths had been joined up to make one long pipe.* [*same as* **link up**; *opposite* **take apart, break up**] **2** Someone **joins up** when they become a member of one of the armed forces: *She joined up in 1940 and was immediately posted abroad.* [*same as* **enlist**; compare **call up**]

join with
You might ask someone to **join with** you in doing something when you want them to do it with you: *Please rise and join with me now in drinking a toast to the bride and groom.*

jolly /ˈdʒɒlɪ/: jollies, jollying, jollied

jolly along (*informal*)
You **jolly** someone **along** when you try to keep them contented or satisfied, usually so that they will continue to help you: *The cook was always threatening to leave, but Mr Banks jollied her along with constant compliments and the occasional small gift.* [*same as* **humour, keep sweet** (*informal*); *opposite* **chase away, antagonize**]

jot /dʒɒt/: jots, jotting, jotted

jot down
You **jot** something **down** when you write it down quickly and informally: *I jotted down the number on the back of an envelope.* [*same as* **take down, make a note of**]

juggle /ˈdʒʌgəl/: juggles, juggling, juggled

juggle with
You **juggle with** several things when you have to try hard to deal successfully with all of them at the same time: *modern parents juggling with the pressures of a full-time job and the responsibilities of bringing up a young family.* [*same as* **balance**; compare **cope with**]

juice /dʒuːs/: juices, juicing, juiced

juice up (*informal*; *especially AmE*)
You **juice** something **up** when you make it livelier, more energetic or more interesting: *The first part of the song*

needed juicing up a little, so we added some electric guitar. ❑ *They could juice up the presentation by hiring a celebrity to do it.* [*same as* **pep up, enhance**; *opposite* **detract from, spoil, impoverish**]

jumble /ˈdʒʌmbəl/: **jumbles, jumbling, jumbled**

jumble up

You **jumble** things **up** when you put them into a confused order or state: *Names and pictures had been jumbled up so we didn't know who was who.* [*same as* **mix up, muddle up**; *opposite* **sort out, order**]

jump /dʒʌmp/: **jumps, jumping, jumped**

jump at

You **jump at** a suggestion or offer when you accept it eagerly: *He'll jump at the chance to spend a bit of time in the country.* [*same as* **seize upon**]

jump on

Someone **jumps on** you when they suddenly attack you with insults or words of criticism: *Any mention of workers' rights was jumped on by the manager.* [compare **tell off, bawl out**]

jump out

Someone **jumps out** when they suddenly appear from a hiding place: *I opened the door and a gang of children in Hallowe'en masks jumped out.* [*same as* **leap out**]

jump out at

Something, such as a word on a page of writing, **jumps out at** you when you notice it immediately because it is very striking or obvious: *A name from the past jumped out at me from the page.* [*same as* **leap out at**]

jut /dʒʌt/: **juts, jutting, jutted**

jut out

Something that **juts out** projects or sticks out from a surface: *He glanced up to see a rock ledge jutting out above him.* [*same as* **poke out**; *opposite* **recede**]

k

keel /kiːl/: **keels**, **keeling**, **keeled**

keel over (*informal*)
Someone **keels over** when they fall to the ground, usually sideways, because they suddenly lose consciousness or feel very ill: *Several soldiers keeled over in the heat.* [*same as* **fall down**, **collapse**; compare **black out**, **pass out**]

keep /kiːp/: **keeps**, **keeping**, **kept** /kɛpt/

keep away
1 You **keep away** from somewhere when you don't go there: *In the afternoons, when the shops were busiest, I tended to keep away.* [*same as* **stay away**, **avoid**] **2** You might tell someone to **keep away** when you don't want them to come near: *She threatened to turn the dogs on him if he didn't keep away.* ❑ *Keep those children away from the fire.*

keep back
1 You **keep** something **back** when you don't tell others everything: *He seemed frank and sincere, but I got the impression he was keeping something back.* ❑ *She had kept back important evidence, which obstructed police investigations.* [*same as* **hold back**, **withhold**; *opposite* **give away**, **blurt out**, **confess**] **2** You **keep back** emotions when you control them and don't show others how you feel: *I was finding it hard to keep back the tears.* ❑ *He's been used to keeping his feelings back.* [*same as* **hold back**, **stifle**, **suppress**; *opposite* **let go**, **reveal**, **disclose**] **3** You **keep back** when you stand some distance away: *Keep back and let the ambulance through.* ❑ *Marshals are employed to keep spectators back.* [*same as* **stand back**, **stay back**; *opposite* **crowd round**, **gather round**] **4** You **keep** part of something **back** when you don't give or use all of it now, but save some for later: *Remember to keep back a little of the meat juices to make a gravy with.* ❑ *They insisted on keeping back £4000 of our mortgage until we had carried out some repairs.* [*same as* **reserve**, **retain**; *opposite* **use up**, **give up**, **surrender**]

keep down
1 You **keep** things such as costs or prices **down** when you prevent them from rising or increasing: *We have introduced sensible economic policies to keep down inflation.* [*same as* **hold down**, **control**, **contain**, **curb**] **2** You can't **keep down** what you eat or drink when you vomit it back up because you are ill: *She's kept her breakfast down, so far at least.* [*opposite* **throw up** (*informal*), **spew up** (*informal*)]

keep from
1 You **keep** someone **from** doing something when you stop them doing it; you **keep from** doing something you want to do when you don't do it: *It's a way of keeping her from telling everyone in the college about it.* ❑ *She clung on to the rail to keep herself from falling.* ❑ *We'll talk more later; I mustn't keep you from your celebrations any longer.* ❑ *It was all I could do to keep from slapping his face.* [*same as* **prevent**; *opposite* **allow**] **2** You **keep** something

from someone when you don't tell them about it: *She was never very good at keeping anything from her parents.* [*same as* **hold back, keep back, withhold**; *opposite* **reveal, disclose**]

keep in

1 You **keep** someone **in** when you don't allow them to go out or leave, *eg* as a punishment: *When the weather's this cold, younger children should be kept in.* ❑ *The headmaster kept in a number of boys, for over an hour.* [*opposite* **let out, allow out**] **2** You **keep** someone **in** something when you provide them with a regular supply of it: *My husband's wages were barely enough to keep us in food.*

keep in with

You **keep in with** someone when you do things that make them continue to like you, usually for selfish reasons: *Your uncle is the kind of powerful man every young boy should keep in with.* [*opposite* **alienate, antagonize**]

keep off

1 You **keep** someone or something **off** an area when you don't let them enter it; you **keep off** when you don't enter it yourself: *If you don't keep your dog off my land, next time I'll shoot it!* ❑ *I just think bikes should be kept off the roads in busy cities.* ❑ *People using the park are requested to keep off the grass.* ❑ *A large sign read: Private Estate. Keep Off.* [*same as* **keep away from, stay off**; *opposite* **allow on, give access to**] **2** You **keep** something unwanted **off** something else when you stop it from touching, harming or spoiling it: *There didn't seem to be any way we could keep the insects off our baby.* ❑ *We'll light a fire, to keep off the cold.* [*same as* **keep away, ward off, deter, repel**; *opposite* **attract, invite**] **3** You **keep off** something when you no longer eat or drink it, *eg* because you know it would make you ill: *The doctor has told me to keep off alcohol of any kind.* ❑ *His wife was instructed to keep him off the cigars.* [*same as* **stay off, lay off** (*informal*), **go without**; compare **give up**] **4** You **keep off** something when you avoid talking about it: *Thank God we managed to keep off the subject of politics.* [*same as* **steer clear of**] **5** Rain or snow that **keeps off** doesn't come, when you expected it would. [*same as* **hold off**; *opposite* **come on**]

keep on

1 You **keep on** doing something when you continue to do it or do it repeatedly: *They kept on walking in spite of their hunger and tiredness.* ❑ *She keeps on talking about her childhood, as if she wants to return to the past.* ❑ *As I keep on telling you, your parents know best.* [*same as* **carry on, persist in**; *opposite* **stop, give up, leave off**] **2** Someone **keeps** you **on** when they continue to employ you: *If you're a good worker, they might keep you on for another few weeks.* ❑ *Most of them will go when the office closes; the best will be kept on in other jobs.* [*same as* **hold on to, retain**; *opposite* **get rid of, sack, give the sack**]

keep on about

Someone **keeps on** about something when they continue to talk about it, or talk about it often, especially so often that you have become bored or annoyed by them: *I wish he wouldn't keep on about how cold it is.* [*same as* **go on about, harp on about**; *opposite* **shut up about**]

keep on at

Someone **keeps on at** you when they bother you with repeated questions, complaints or demands: *My mother keeps on at me to settle down and have kids.* ❑ *They replied to none of our letters, so we just kept on and on at them.* [*same as* **go on at** (*informal*), **nag, badger**]

keep out

You tell someone to **keep out** when you don't want them to enter a place or an area: *A handwritten sign on the door said 'DANGER. KEEP OUT!'.* ❑ *We tried all sorts of ways of keeping the neighbour's dogs out of our garden.* [*same as* **keep away, stay out**; *opposite* **bring in, go in, come in**]

keep out of

You **keep** someone **out of** danger or other unpleasantness when you prevent them from being harmed or becoming involved: *Good friends will do their best to keep you out of trouble.* ❑ *You would do best to keep out of other people's affairs altogether.* [*same as* **stay out of**]

keep to

1 You **keep to** something when you follow its line or course and don't go away from it: *Keep to the path and you won't get lost.* ❑ *Our discussion time is limited, so we must keep to the subject.* ❑ *When you work shifts, it's difficult to keep to a regular routine.* ❑ *There'd be no problems if they'd kept to the original plan.* [*same as* **stick to, stay with**; *opposite* **go off, wander from, stray from**] **2** You **keep** something **to** a certain amount when you limit it to that amount: *Pocket money should be kept to about £5 per child per week.* ❑ *We try to keep waste to an absolute minimum.* [*same as* **restrict**; compare **keep down**] **3** You **keep** someone **to** a decision or promise when you make them do what they have decided or promised: *He had said he was willing to marry the girl and they were determined to keep him to it.* ❑ *Patrick was kept to his word by pressure from close friends and family.* [*same as* **hold to**] **4** You **keep** something **to** yourself when you don't tell others about it: *I'd like you to keep our little discussion to yourself.* ❑ *She'd always kept her feelings to herself.*

keep up

1 One person or thing **keeps up** with another that is moving or progressing when they move or progress at the same speed as the other: *She walked so fast that I had to trot to keep up with her.* ❑ *Salaries are increased regularly to keep up with inflation.* ❑ *One or two of the pupils are finding it difficult to keep up with the rest of the class.* ❑ *You'll have to work a little faster if you want to keep up.* [*same as* **keep pace**; *opposite* **fall behind, get left behind, drop back**] **2** You **keep up** with things that are happening if you make sure you know about them: *I do try to keep up with the latest developments in world politics.* ❑ *So many changes are being made all the time that it's impossible to keep up.* [*same as* **stay abreast, keep in touch**; *opposite* **lose touch, lose track of**] **3** You **keep** something **up** when you continue to do or achieve it, not letting it decline or stop: *I knew he couldn't keep that pace up for long.* ❑ *Her work has improved greatly in recent weeks; let's hope she can keep it up.* ❑ *They kept up the attack for most of the game, but without creating a single real scoring chance.* ❑ *It's important that academic standards should be kept up.* ❑ *Marching soldiers would sing to keep their spirits up.* ❑ *The doctor says you must eat to keep your strength up.* ❑ *If this hot weather keeps up, there could be a drought.* [*same as* **maintain, sustain, persist**; *opposite* **let fall, let drop, drop off, let up**] **4** You **keep** someone **up** when you cause them not to go to bed until later than usual or later than they would like: *A phone call from Floyd kept her up past her normal bedtime.* ❑ *I must apologise for keeping you up so late.*

• *noun (uncount)* **upkeep**
The **upkeep** of something such as a building is the cost of keeping it running or in good repair: *You may want a larger house but can you really afford the upkeep?*

keep up with

You **keep up with** someone when you remain in contact with them, for example by regularly writing to them or telephoning them: *They've kept up with many of their old university friends.* [*same as* **keep in touch, stay in touch**; *opposite* **lose contact, lose touch**]

key /kiː/: keys, keying, keyed

key in

In computing, you **key in** information when you enter it into a computer by pressing the keys on a keyboard: *You need to key in the password to open up the program.* [*same as* **type in, punch in, input**]

• *adjective* **keyed up**

You are **keyed up** when you are very nervous or excited about something, especially something that is about to happen: *I feel at my most keyed up around half an hour before I go on stage.* ❑ *What is everyone so keyed up about?* [*same as* **worked up, tensed up, on edge**; *opposite* **laid back** (*informal*)]

kick /kɪk/: kicks, kicking, kicked

kick about *or* kick around

(*informal*)

1 You can use **kick about** or **kick around** to talk about where something is, or to say that it exists: *His old schoolbooks were kicking about in the attic.* ❑ *The notion that women were being unfairly treated was kicking around even then.* [*same as* **knock about, knock around**] **2** You can say that people **kick** something such as an idea or a suggestion **about** or **around** when they discuss or consider it, especially in an informal way: *We kicked around a few alternatives, but came up with nothing we liked as much.* [*same as* **toss about, toss around**]

kick against

You **kick against** something fixed or established, such as a law or a tradition, when you oppose it or react against it, usually strongly or angrily: *Any small company that kicked against the system would be crushed by the banks.* [*same as* **defy, rebel**; opposite **go along with, comply, conform**]

kick back (*informal*)

A person or company **kicks back** money when, as an illegal way of encouraging someone to buy their goods or services, they return part of the money that the buyer pays them: *The building company had apparently agreed to kick back 10% to one of the councillors on the planning committee.*

• *noun* **kickback**: **kickbacks**: *There's no question that they have been getting kickbacks from every contract they award.*

kick down

Someone **kicks down** a door when they kick it hard so that it falls down: *Neighbours said they saw two police officers kick the door down.* ❑ *We had to kick down the gate to get in.* [*same as* **break down, smash down**]

kick in

Someone **kicks** something **in** when they damage or destroy it by kicking it violently: *Vandals had slashed the furniture and kicked the TV in.* ❑ *He'd had his face kicked in by a gang of thugs.* [*same as* **smash in**]

kick off

1 A football match **kicks off** when play begins: *One of their players arrived late, so we didn't kick off until quarter past.* **2** (*informal*) To **kick off** is also to start or begin anything: *The course kicked off with coffee and an introductory chat.* ❑ *I suppose we should kick off by learning one another's names.* ❑ *They kicked off the concert with a couple of their best-known songs.* [*same as* **open, commence**] **3** You **kick off** your shoes when you casually push each shoe off with the opposite foot: *She flopped into a chair and kicked her boots off.*

• *noun* **kick-off**: **kick-offs**

A **kick-off** is the start of a football game, or the time when it starts: *a twelve-o'clock kick-off* ❑ *We got there* *just before the kick-off.*

kick out (*informal*)
To **kick** someone **out** of somewhere is to force them to leave: *A group on a table in the corner got a bit rowdy and the manager kicked them out.* ❑ *He's been kicked out of his job.* ❑ *She was expelled from two schools, and later managed to get herself kicked out of college.* [*same as* **throw out, boot out** (*informal*), **turn out**]

kick over
Someone **kicks** something **over** when they kick it so that it overturns or falls over: *One of the men kicked over a table and a fight started.* [compare **knock over**]

kick up (*informal*)
Someone **kicks up** a fuss or a row when they start arguing or protesting loudly and angrily, often unnecessarily: *If any of us were late, the manager kicked up a terrible stink.*

kid /kɪd/: kids, kidding, kidded

kid on (*informal*)
Someone **kids** you **on** when, for fun, they try to make you believe something that isn't true: *Of course they weren't really offended; they were just kidding us on.* [*same as* **have on** (*informal*), **pull someone's leg, joke**]

kill /kɪl/: kills, killing, killed

kill off
You **kill** something **off** when you destroy it completely: *Early frosts killed off most of the fruit.* ❑ *Any opposition to the scheme would have to be killed off in the early stages.* [*same as* **wipe out, do for** (*informal*)]

kip /kɪp/: kips, kipping, kipped

kip down (*informal*)
You **kip down** somewhere when you make yourself a temporary bed and sleep there: *We could give them each a sleeping-bag and they could kip down on the floor.* [*same as* **doss down** (*informal*), **crash** (*informal*)]

kiss /kɪs/: kisses, kissing, kissed

kiss away
When you comfort someone by kissing them, you can say that you **kiss away** their worries, fears or other unpleasant feelings: *a mother kissing away her baby's tears.*

kiss off (*AmE informal*)
You **kiss** something **off** when you dismiss it as unimportant, uninteresting or of very poor quality: *Writers like Archer were kissed off as 'cheap' or, even worse, 'popular'.* [*same as* **look down on, sniff at, reject**; *opposite* **cry up, acclaim, applaud**]

kit /kɪt/: kits, kitting, kitted

kit out
You **kit** someone **out** when you provide them with the clothes and equipment they need for a particular activity or job: *You could kit yourself out with the basics for around £200.* ❑ *Now you're fully kitted out and ready to play your first game.* [*same as* **fit out, rig out, equip**]

kneel /niːl/: kneels, kneeling, knelt /nɛlt/ *or* kneeled

kneel down
You **kneel down** when you lower your body into the position of resting your weight on your knees, instead of on your feet: *The priest gave a sign, and ten thousand people knelt down to pray.*

knit /nɪt/: knits, knitting, knitted

knit together
Two or more things **knit together** when they become very closely or firmly joined, forming a solid unit or whole: *The broken bones should knit together in around six to eight weeks.* ❑ *It's the editor's job to knit together the various*

bits of film as seamlessly as possible. [*same as* **fuse, bind, link**; *opposite* **break apart, split up**]

knock /nɒk/: knocks, knocking, knocked

knock about *or* knock around

(*informal*)

1 A person **is knocked about** or **knocked around** when someone hits them repeatedly: *He seems like the kind of man who would knock his wife about.* [*same as* **beat up, batter, mistreat**] **2** You can use **knock about** or **knock around** to talk about where something is: *I'm sure there's another copy knocking about somewhere in the office.* ❑ *The usual crowd of autograph hunters was knocking around the stage door.* [*same as* **kick about, kick around**] **3** You **knock about** or **knock around** when you travel from place to place, or pass time, in a casual way, without any very serious purpose; someone who **has knocked about** or **knocked around** has had experience of a large variety of places and circumstances: *She spent a year knocking about France.* ❑ *Uncle Ted always played down his youthful exploits, but if pushed would admit that he'd 'knocked around a bit'.* [*same as* **have been about**] **4** You **knock about** or **knock around** with someone when you spend a lot of your time with them: *At weekends I mostly knock around with my friends from college.* ❑ *How long have they been knocking about together?* [*same as* **go about, go around**]

knock back (*informal*)

1 You **knock** a drink **back** when you drink it quickly or drink a lot of it: *He knocked back three whiskies in the space of a couple of minutes.* ❑ *I think she's been knocking back the gin lately.* [*same as* **gulp down, quaff**; compare **put away** (*informal*), **pack away**] **2** Something such as a suggestion, or an application for a job, **is knocked back** when it is rejected: *I was knocked back by four universities before I finally got a place at Exeter.* ❑ *She applied for a more junior post, but they knocked her back again.* ❑ *We applied for a loan, but the bank knocked us back.* [*same as* **turn down**]

knock down

1 A vehicle or its driver **knocks** someone **down** when they crash into them and injure or kill them: *If they don't build a crossing there, it's only a matter of time before a child is knocked down.* ❑ *She was knocked down by a lorry.* [*same as* **knock over, run over**] **2** To **knock down** a building is to destroy it deliberately: *A row of houses had to be knocked down to make way for the new road.* ❑ *We could knock the dividing wall down and make one big room.* [*same as* **pull down, demolish**; *opposite* **put up, build**] **3** (*informal*) You **knock** someone **down** when you persuade them to lower the price of what they are selling you; you **knock down** a price when you lower it: *He would never buy anything without trying to knock the salesman down a few quid.* ❑ *We've knocked the offer price down three times, but there are still no takers.* [*same as* **beat down, bring down**] **4** You **knock** someone **down** when you push or hit them so that they fall to the ground: *One of the older boys had knocked him down in the playground.* [*same as* **knock over**]

knock off

1 You **knock** something **off** a table, shelf or other surface when you hit it and cause it to fall to the ground: *He caught the clock with his coat and knocked it off the mantelpiece.* **2** (*informal*) You **knock** an amount **off** something when you reduce it by that amount: *He knocked £75 off the car because it had a dent in one door.* ❑ *They've already knocked ten minutes off our lunch break.* [*same as* **take off, deduct**; *opposite* **add on, slap on** (*informal*)] **3** (*informal*) You **knock off,**

or **knock off** work, when you stop work for a break or at the end of the day: *Some people used to knock off early on Fridays.* [*same as* **clock off, pack up**] **4** (*informal*) You **knock** something **off** when you do it quickly and with little or no effort or care: *If he's stuck for money, all he has to do is knock off another best-selling novel.* [*same as* **knock out** (*informal*), **churn out, rattle off**] **5** (*slang*) Someone **knocks** something **off** when they steal it: *We spotted a customer trying to knock off a handful of CDs.* [*same as* **nick** (*informal*), **pinch, lift**] **6** (*slang*) Someone **knocks off** a bank, shop or other premises when they carry out a robbery there: *They were amateurs who'd never knocked off anything really big.* [*same as* **hold up, do over** (*informal*), **rob**] **7** (*slang*) To **knock** someone **off** is to murder them: *He'd knock off his granny if he thought there was money in it.* ❑ *His brother was knocked off by one of the Chicago gangs.* [*same as* **bump off** (*slang*), **do in** (*slang*), **kill**]

knock out

1 Someone **is knocked out** when they are made unconscious by being hit on the head, or made sleepy or unconscious by drugs or alcohol: *The blow seemed to have knocked him out.* ❑ *A whisky before bedtime usually knocks me out.* [*opposite* **bring round, perk up, pep up**] **2** A competitor or team **is knocked out** of a competition when they are defeated at one of its stages and do not take any further part in it: *We were knocked out in the third round.* [*same as* **beat, eliminate**; *opposite* **go through**] **3** You **knock** something **out** when you force it out by a sharp blow: *She walked into a door and knocked one of her teeth out.* **4** (*informal*) You **knock** something **out** when you produce it quickly and with little or no effort or care: *You can spot the students who just knock out their essays in a couple of hours.* [*same as* **knock off, churn out, rattle off**] **5** (*informal*) You might say that something **knocks** you **out** when you are very impressed by it: *The poems just knocked me out; I'd never read anything like them before.* [*same as* **bowl over**]

• *noun* **knockout**

1 If a boxing match ends in a **knockout**, one boxer hits the other so hard that he knocks him unconscious; a **knockout** blow is one that makes your opponent unconscious or unable to continue with the contest. **2** A **knockout** is also a competition in which only the winning teams or competitors go forward to the next round.

knock out of

Things such as opinions, feelings or ways of behaving **are knocked out of** you when you are taught, harshly and perhaps with frequent punishment, to change or get rid of them: *He's always been arrogant, but a spell in the army will soon knock that out of him.* ❑ *The war had knocked every last ounce of humanity out of them.*

knock over

1 You **knock** something **over** when you cause it to overturn or fall to the ground by hitting or pushing it, often accidentally: *One of the kids had knocked over a vase of flowers.* ❑ *They saw an old lady knocked over by a man on a bike.* [*same as* **tip over, upset**; compare **knock down**] **2** (*informal*) To **knock** something **over** is to steal it: *Guerrillas had knocked over a truck-load of government supplies.* [*same as* **knock off**] **3** (*informal*) To **knock over** something such as a bank or a shop is to steal things from it: *They could make a living simply by knocking over the occasional warehouse.* [*same as* **knock off** (*slang*), **rob**]

knock up

1 (*informal*) You **knock** something **up** when you make it quickly: *She was one of those people who could knock up a dress in an evening.* **2** You **knock** someone **up** when you wake them by knocking on their door: *We asked John and Betty, who were early risers, to* *knock us up around 7.30.* [*same as* **get up, rouse**] **3** Players of games like tennis **knock up** when they spend a few minutes practising their shots before a match begins. **4** (*vulgar slang*) A man **knocks** a woman **up** when he makes her pregnant: *I told her if she got knocked up I'd throw her out of the house.*

know /nou/: **knows**, **knowing**, **knew** /nju:/, **known**

know about

You **know about** something when you have discovered it, learned it or been told about it: *There wasn't much he didn't know about British history.* ❑ *Did you know about Lewis's decision to leave?* ❑ *Not much is known about what happened after that.*

know as

Someone or something **is known as** a name when that is the name people usually call them, even though other names for them may exist: *William was known to everyone in the family as 'Wee Billy'.* ❑ *The bison is now most common in North America, where it is known as the buffalo.*

know of

You **know of** something or someone when you know they exist, or you have heard others talk about them, but you don't know much about them yourself: *I wouldn't say I exactly know her, but I do know of her.* ❑ *She knows of a man who drank so much beer he killed himself.* [*same as* **hear of, hear tell of**]

knuckle /ˈnʌkəl/: **knuckles**, **knuckling**, **knuckled**

knuckle down (*informal*)

You **knuckle down**, or **knuckle down** to work, when you begin to work hard or seriously, often after a period of doing very little: *With only four weeks to the exams, most students are knuckling down to some serious revision.* [*same as* **buckle down, get down to**; *opposite* **ease up, slacken off**]

knuckle under (*informal*)

You **knuckle under** when you agree or submit to what someone is trying to force you to do: *Wayward pupils were punished systematically until they knuckled under.* ❑ *It seems they've knuckled under to pressure from the European Parliament.* [*same as* **cave in, give in, give way**; *opposite* **hold out against, stand up to**]

l

labour (*AmE* **labor**) /'leɪbə(r)/: **labours** (*AmE* **labors**), **labouring** (*AmE* **laboring**), **laboured** (*AmE* **labored**)

labour under (*formal*)
1 You **labour under** something when it is a disadvantage or handicap that slows down your progress or makes your situation difficult: *The ship had laboured all day under a severe head-wind.* ❑ *The local physician labours under the name of Dr Death.* [*same as* **struggle against**] **2** When someone believes something that is not true, you can say that they **labour under** a false belief or false notion, often when this causes them to waste their time or effort: *The Government is labouring under the mistaken idea that the country supports its pay policies.* ❑ *I told her she was labouring under a misapprehension.*

lace /leɪs/: **laces**, **lacing**, **laced**

lace up
You **lace up** shoes with laces when you fasten them by tying the laces: *You'll have to wait while I lace my boots up.* [*same as* **tie up**, **do up**; *opposite* **untie**]
• *noun (plural)* **lace-ups**
Lace-ups are shoes that are fastened with laces. [compare **slip-ons**]

lace with
1 You **lace** a drink such as coffee or tea **with** alcohol when you add alcohol to it: *He passed round a mug of hot coffee laced with rum.* [*same as* **flavour**; compare **spike with**] **2** You can also use **lace with** to talk about anything that has something added to it, especially something that makes it richer or more interesting: *His lectures were always liberally laced with jokes and funny stories.* [*same as* **spice with**, **colour**]

ladle /'leɪdəl/: **ladles**, **ladling**, **ladled**

ladle out
1 You **ladle out** soup when you serve it with a large deep spoon called a ladle: *She put the vegetables in a bowl while her father ladled out the casserole.* **2** (*informal*) People often say that something such as information or advice **is ladled out** when it is given in large quantities, especially if you disapprove of this: *This kind of propaganda is ladled out to schoolchildren every day.* [*same as* **dish out** (*informal*), **dole out** (*informal*)]

lag /lag/: **lags**, **lagging**, **lagged**

lag behind
A person or thing **lags behind** another or others when they move or progress more slowly and become left behind: *Mum strode out purposefully, with Dad and the kids lagging behind.* ❑ *Salaries in Britain lag behind those in many other European countries.* [*same as* **fall behind**]

lam /lam/: **lams**, **lamming**, **lammed**

lam into (*informal*)
You **lam into** someone when you attack them fiercely, either with punches and kicks, or with insults or criticisms: *the frightening spectacle of a world-class*

boxer lamming into an unprepared amateur ❑ *We were made to stand and watch as the editor lammed into him for missing the deadline.* [*same as* **tear into** (*informal*), **lay into** (*informal*)]

land /land/: **lands**, **landing**, **landed**

land in
Someone or something **lands** you **in** a difficult situation when they cause or create it for you: *Comments like that could land the whole government in trouble.* ❑ *You're going to land yourself in an intolerable mess if you don't assert yourself now.* [*same as* **get into**]

land up (*informal*)
You **land up** in a particular place or situation when you arrive there, especially without particularly intending to, after a journey or a series of events: *After months of travelling she landed up in Istanbul.* ❑ *I didn't want to land up teaching English in some remote place.* ❑ *Over half of them will land up in prison by the time they're twenty.* [*same as* **end up**, **wind up** (*informal*)]

land with (*informal*)
Someone **lands** you **with** a problem or something unwanted when they leave you to deal with it: *I found myself landed with the bill for the whole meal.* ❑ *She always seemed to get landed with the clumsiest dancers.* [*same as* **lumber with** (*informal*), **saddle with** (*informal*)]

lap /lap/: **laps**, **lapping**, **lapped**

lap up
1 An animal **laps up** a drink when it drinks it quickly, and often eagerly or greedily: *Henry's dog sat lapping up the beer that had been spilt on the floor.* **2** (*informal*) You **lap up** something you are offered or given when you accept it eagerly or with pleasure: *No matter what they say about not seeking praise, you can see that they really lap it up.* ❑ *First-year students lap up whatever information you can give them.* [*same as* **soak up**, **devour**]

lapse /laps/: **lapses**, **lapsing**, **lapsed**

lapse into
You can say that someone or something **lapses into** a particular state, condition or manner of behaviour when you think that it is a worse one than that person or thing was in before: *After a promising first ten minutes, the film soon lapsed into the familiar exploitation of sex and violence.* ❑ *Fearing he might lapse into tearfulness again, he turned away.* [*same as* **sink into**, **degenerate**]

lark /lɑːk/: **larks**, **larking**, **larked**

lark about *or* **lark around** (*informal*)
You **lark about** or **lark around** when you do silly things for fun: *I want less larking about and more doing your homework.* [*same as* **mess about** (*informal*), **muck about** (*informal*)]

lash /laʃ/: **lashes**, **lashing**, **lashed**

lash down
1 To **lash** something **down** is to tie it firmly in position with ropes: *Clearly all ferries would be safer if passenger vehicles were lashed down.* [*same as* **tie down**, **fasten down**, **secure**] **2** Rain **lashes down** when it falls very heavily. [*same as* **pour down**, **beat down**]

lash out
You **lash out** when you make a sudden violent attack on someone, either physically or with angry words: *When I stepped forward he lashed out at me with a knife.* ❑ *They're fierce animals that will lash out if cornered.* ❑ *She took the opportunity to lash out against the unfairness of the system.* [*same as* **hit out**, **tear into** (*informal*), **pitch into** (*informal*)]

lash out on (*informal*)

You **lash out on** something when you spend a lot of money on it: *They lashed out over £5000 on resurfacing their driveway.* [*same as* **splash out on** (*informal*); compare **fork out, cough up**]

last /lɑːst/: **lasts**, **lasting**, **lasted**

---

last out
1 A supply of something **lasts out** when it is not used up too soon: *A pile of firewood that size should last out the winter.* ❑ *I wasn't sure how long our oil reserves would last out.* [*same as* **hold out, subsist** (*formal*); *opposite* **run out, dry up**] **2** To **last out** is to survive, especially to remain strong or in good working order for a certain period or as long as is necessary: *He wasn't sure he could last out the whole evening without a whisky.* ❑ *Mexico was only another twenty miles or so, and I was sure my horse would last out.* [*same as* **hold out, hang on, come through**; *opposite* **break down, crack up** (*informal*)]

latch /latʃ/: **latches**, **latching**, **latched**

---

latch onto
1 Someone who **has latched onto** you seems eager always to be with you, because they like you or find you interesting: *The boy soon latched onto Charlie, mesmerised by his magic tricks and his funny stories.* [*same as* **take up with, hang around** (*informal*)] **2** You **latch onto** something when, finally, you realize or understand it: *It took her a moment to latch onto what they were arguing about.* [*same as* **catch on, cotton on** (*informal*), **figure out, grasp**]

laugh /lɑːf/: **laughs**, **laughing**, **laughed**

---

laugh at
You **laugh at** someone or something when you show that you think they are foolish or ridiculous: *He was afraid that the other children would laugh at him for not knowing the answer.* ❑ *Any suggestion she made was laughed at by the rest of the committee.* [*same as* **scoff at, make fun of, ridicule**]

laugh off
You **laugh off** a problem or difficulty when you treat it as unimportant or as a joke: *Actors learn to laugh off criticisms in the press.* ❑ *If anyone said anything nasty about her, she would laugh it off.* [*same as* **shrug off, make light of**; *opposite* **take seriously, take to heart**]

launch /lɔːntʃ/: **launches**, **launching**, **launched**

---

launch into
You **launch into** something, such as a speech or a story, when you begin it with energy or enthusiasm: *Then she launched into a detailed account of her academic career.* ❑ *He imagined Sheila launching into one of her gripes about interfering parents.* [*same as* **burst into**]

lavish /ˈlavɪʃ/: **lavishes**, **lavishing**, **lavished**

---

lavish on *or* **lavish upon**
You **lavish** something such as money, affection or praise **on** or **upon** someone when you give them a large or generous amount of it: *So much time and energy has already been lavished on this project.* ❑ *She has the love of four doting grandparents lavished upon her.* [*same as* **shower on, pour on, heap on**]

lay /leɪ/: **lays**, **laying**, **laid**

---

lay about
Someone **lays about** you when they attack you violently: *Three youths laid about him with sticks.* [*same as* **lay into** (*informal*), **set about** (*informal*)]

lay aside
1 You **lay** something **aside** when you keep or save it to use later: *We always*

have some spare cash laid aside for emergencies. ❏ *Could you lay it aside for me if I promise to collect it next week?* [*same as* **lay by**, **set aside**, **put aside**] **2** You **lay aside** something you are using or doing when you put it down and take a break or rest: *It must have been three o'clock before I finally laid my books aside.* [*same as* **set aside**, **put aside**] **3** You **lay aside** your feelings or opinions when you take a decision to abandon them and adopt new ones: *It was hard to see how they could lay aside years of mutual dislike.* ❏ *She will have to lay her old fears aside and get on with the future.* [*same as* **cast aside**, **set aside**, **dismiss**]

lay away
To **lay** something **away** is to keep or save it for later: *Goods may be laid away in our warehouse for up to six months, until full payment is made.*

lay before
You **lay** something such as a proposal or problem **before** someone when you present it to them for their advice, opinion or judgement: *New plans are to be laid before the committee.* [*same as* **put before**]

lay by
You **lay** something **by** when you save or keep it to use in the future: *That way you could lay by a small sum for your retirement.* [*same as* **lay aside**, **put by**]
• *noun* **lay-by**: **lay-bys**
A **lay-by** is a small area at the side of a road where drivers may stop out of the way of the traffic: *Henry pulled in to a lay-by and had a short nap.*

lay down
1 You **lay** something **down** when you put it down, *eg* on a table or on the floor: *The gunmen were then ordered to lay down their weapons.* [*same as* **set down**; *opposite* **pick up**, **take up**] **2** A rule, or a person in authority, **lays down** what should be done when they state officially what must be done: *The government have issued a new booklet laying down guidelines for safety at work.* ❏ *Conditions for membership are laid down in the club rules.* [*same as* **set out**, **stipulate**] **3** Someone **lays down** their life when they die fighting for a cause or to save someone else. [*same as* **sacrifice**] **4** Wine **is laid down** when it is stored, to be drunk in the future: *All too often, people who have laid down a cellarful of expensive wine feel obliged to prepare a feast to go with it.* **5** When something is being built on an area of land, people sometimes say that it **is being laid down**: *Where before there was only wasteland, beautiful gardens have been laid down.*

lay in
You **lay** something **in** when you buy a supply of it and store it somewhere: *The snows had cut us off again, but luckily Irma had laid in enough food for the whole winter.* [*same as* **lay up**, **stock up with**]

lay into (*informal*)
Someone **lays into** you when they attack you fiercely, either physically or with angry words: *He was badly injured; the boys had really laid into him this time.* ❏ *When I arrived, she was laying into June about her untidy appearance and casual attitude.* [*same as* **tear into** (*informal*), **rip into** (*informal*), **pitch into** (*informal*)]

lay off
1 A company **lays** people **off** when it stops employing them, permanently or often only temporarily: *They'll be laying off another fifty employees in the new year.* ❏ *We've been laid off indefinitely until business picks up.* [*opposite* **take on**, **hire**; compare **sack**, **pay off**] **2** (*informal*) People sometimes tell someone who is annoying them or attacking them to **lay off** when they want them to stop: *He'd been warned to lay off, but was too drunk to take notice.* ❏ *Lay off him, Tom; he's just a kid.* [*same as* **leave off**, **give over** (*informal*), **quit**] **3** (*informal*) You **lay**

off something when you stop doing, using or consuming it: *The doctor's told him to cut out the big lunches and lay off the beer and whisky.* ❑ *It's a good idea to lay off the chemical fertilizers and make your own organic compost.* [*same as* **stay off, give up**]

• *noun* **layoff: layoffs**

There are **layoffs** in a company or organization when it stops employing people because there is no work for them.

lay on

1 You **lay** something **on** when you provide or supply it: *Up till now the management has always laid on a Christmas party for the staff.* ❑ *They even laid a car on, to take him to the airport.* **2** People often use **lay on**, or **lay upon**, where 'put on' would be used in a general sense: *They tried to lay the blame on us.* ❑ *Emphasis was always laid upon the importance of classical training.*

lay out

1 You **lay** things **out** when you arrange them in a neat, ordered way: *She laid all her photographs out on the floor.* ❑ *He would methodically lay out all his clothes for the morning.* [*same as* **set out, spread out**] **2** Things such as gardens, towns and streets **are laid out** when they are designed and arranged according to a certain plan: *splendidly laid-out gardens.* **3** Things such as ideas or plans **are laid out** when they are described or presented in detail: *The inspector's recommendations are laid out in a paper entitled 'Options for Improvement'.* [*same as* **set out**] **4** (*informal*) You **lay out** money on something when you spend a lot of money on it: *The company simply wouldn't be prepared to lay out sums of that kind.* [*same as* **fork out** (*informal*), **shell out** (*informal*)] **5** (*informal*) A person **is laid out** when someone hits them, knocks them to the ground, usually making them unconscious: *The blow laid him out flat on the floor.* [*same as* **knock out**]

• *noun* **layout: layouts**

A **layout** is an arrangement or plan showing how *eg* land, buildings or printed material is to be organized: *The newspaper now has a different layout with more colour pictures.*

lay up

1 (*informal*) An illness **lays** you **up** when it makes you so ill that you have to lie down or stay in bed: *Frank has been laid up with the flu for over a week.* [*same as* **debilitate**] **2** Something such as a vehicle **is laid up** when it is not being used, *eg* because it is broken and is being repaired: *It was not unusual for the boats to be laid up for the whole winter.* **3** You **lay up** a store or supply of something when you collect it gradually and keep it to use in the future: *It's normal practice in these parts to lay up stocks of flour and salt for the winter.* [*same as* **lay in, stock up with**] **4** (*informal*) You **lay up** somewhere when you hide there for a while: *We're covering all ports and the airport, but my guess is they'll lay up somewhere on the island.* [*same as* **hole up** (*informal*), **hide out, lie low**]

lay upon see lay on

layabout /'leɪəbaʊt/ see **lie about**

---

laze /leɪz/: **lazes**, **lazing**, **lazed**

---

laze about *or* laze around

You **laze about** or **laze around** when you spend your time doing nothing or just relaxing: *We spent the afternoon lazing about on the beach.* ❑ *It's no use just lazing around; you have to get out and do something.* [*same as* **lounge about, hang about** (*informal*), **lie around**]

lead /liːd/: **leads**, **leading**, **led** /lɛd/

---

lead astray

Someone **leads** you **astray** when they persuade you to do something that is bad or wrong: *Many young criminals are first led astray by an older person, often a member of their family.* ❑ *You don't expect the teachers to be leading them astray.* [*same as* **corrupt**; compare **go astray**]

lead in

You **lead in** when you give an introduction to something such as a speech or a performance: *You could lead in with a brief history of the town, before beginning the lecture proper.* [*same as* **open**]

• *noun* **lead-in**

The **lead-in** to something, such as a speech, event or performance is the short introduction that precedes it, or the period just before it.

lead off

1 You **lead off** when you are the person who begins something such as a discussion: *We'll introduce ourselves first. Roger, would you like to lead off?* [*same as* **kick off** (*informal*), **start the ball rolling** (*informal*)] **2** A road or passage **leads off** from the place where it starts; one room **leads off** another when it is entered from the other: *The road leading off to the right will take you to the beach.* ❑ *The normal pattern of student accommodation is a large sitting room with two bedrooms leading off it.*

lead on

Someone **leads** you **on** when they make you believe something that is not true, *eg* by telling you a series of lies or giving you false impressions: *The boy, it seems, was really in love, but Eleanor was just leading him on.* ❑ *Are we just being led on by the advertisers?* [*same as* **string along** (*informal*), **deceive**, **lead up the garden path** (*informal*)]

lead up to

1 A series of events **lead up to** a particular situation if one develops from another so as to cause or create that situation: *Let's examine the events leading up to World War I.* **2** You **lead up to** a particular subject in a conversation when you carefully direct the conversation towards it: *I wondered what you were leading up to.* [*same as* **work up to**]

leaf /liːf/: leafs, leafing, leafed

leaf through

You **leaf through** a book, or the pages of a book, when you turn the pages quickly and look briefly at what is written or printed on them: *She sat at a table in the corner, leafing through a magazine.* [*same as* **flick through**, **thumb through**, **skim through**]

leak /liːk/: leaks, leaking, leaked

leak out

Secret news or information **leaks out** when it becomes known to the public: *Palace officials were distressed to discover that news of the royal divorce had leaked out.* [*same as* **get out**, **come out**]

lean /liːn/ leans, leaning, leaned *or* leant /lɛnt/

Leaned and **leant** are both used as the past tense and past participle of the verb.

lean on (*informal*)

1 Someone **leans on** you when they use threats or other forms of pressure to try to make you do what they want: *If he won't pay up, we'll have to lean on him a bit.* [*same as* **coerce**, **pressurize**] **2** You **lean on** someone when you need their help or support, and you expect them to give it whenever you ask for it: *The youngest boy has always leant a lot on his parents.* ❑ *For too long the company has been leaning on its reputation and its past glories, forgetting that in the modern world you have to earn your business.* [*same as* **rely on**, **depend on**]

lean out

You **lean out** of a window when you have your head and shoulders projecting out through it: *It's madness to lean* *out when another train is coming.*

lean over

You **lean over** when you bend down to bring your head closer to someone or something, *eg* so that you can see or hear them better: *She leaned over and kissed him on the cheek.* ❑ *It really irritates her the way her mother leans over her when she's cooking.*

lean towards *or* lean toward

American speakers of English usually use **toward** instead of **towards**.

People often say that they **lean towards** something that they support or prefer, or something that they are in favour of: *It is clear that NATO is leaning increasingly towards a military solution.* ❑ *If anything, I lean towards the Liberals on this issue.* [*same as* **tend towards, incline towards** (*formal*); *opposite* **be against, oppose**]

leap /liːp/: leaps, leaping, leaped /liːpt/ *or* /lɛpt/, leapt /lɛpt/

Leaped and **leapt** are both used as the past tense and past participle of the verb.

leap at

You **leap at** something when you accept it eagerly: *I imagine she would leap at the chance to spend her summer working in Australia.* [*same as* **jump at, grab**]

leap on

1 Someone **leaps on** you when they make a sudden violent attack on you: *The dog broke free and leapt on her before she could shut the gate.* [*same as* **jump on, pounce on**] **2** You **leap on** something when you immediately show great interest in it or enthusiasm for it: *Candidates who said they were from Oxford were automatically leapt on.* [*same as* **pounce on**]

leap out

Someone **leaps out** when they suddenly appear from a hiding place: *At the moment the camera stopped, the dog was to leap out and start barking.* [*same as* **jump out, emerge**]

leap out at

Something **leaps out at** you when you notice it immediately because it is very striking or obvious: *Bad grammar and punctuation leapt out at him from every page.* [*same as* **jump out at, shout at**]

leave /liːv/: leaves, leaving, left /lɛft/

Left is used as both the past tense and past participle of the verb.

leave aside

You **leave** something **aside** when you don't mention, discuss or consider it, although perhaps you will later: *Leaving aside the issue of pay, do you think the deal is fair?* [*same as* **put aside, disregard, ignore**; compare **set aside**]

leave behind

1 You **leave** someone or something **behind** when you don't take them with you, whether by accident or on purpose: *The passenger jets off happily to the sun while their luggage is left behind in London.* ❑ *They frequently go off by themselves and leave the children behind with Granny.* [*opposite* **take, bring**] **2** You use **leave behind** to talk about things, often unpleasant or unwanted things, that remain in a place as a result of someone or something having been there: *Gigantic tankers ply coastal waters and leave a trail of oil and debris behind them that eventually washes up on our beaches.* ❑ *She has taken care not to make herself responsible for any business debts that may be left behind after his death.* ❑ *The Romans departed, leaving behind them a network of roads that was to form the backbone of our transport system for centuries.* **3** Someone who **is left behind** fails to progress or advance as well as others: *The child who can already read doesn't leave his classmates behind; rather he is held back while they struggle to bring themselves up to his level.* [*same as* **outstrip**; compare **fall behind**]

leave off

1 You **leave** something **off** your list when you do not include it: *Mark recounted his experience of Spanish trains, with the result that Spain was promptly left off our itinerary.* [*opposite* **put on, add to**] **2** You **leave off** a piece of clothing when you don't put it on or wear it: *If you think it's too hot, leave your jacket off.* [compare **take off**] **3** You **leave off** doing something when you stop doing it: *Let's start from where we left off last week.* ❑ *When was it that he left off drinking beer?* [*same as* **break off**] 4 (*informal*) You tell someone to **leave off** doing something annoying when you want them to stop doing it: *I wish Frank would leave off filling the kids' heads with that nonsense.* ❑ *Tell her to leave off; we've got enough to worry about already.* [*same as* **give over** (*informal*), **quit**; *opposite* **keep on**]

leave out

1 You **leave** something or someone **out** when you don't include them: *After such a poor performance, he risks being left out of the squad for the winter tour.* ❑ *I told her what you'd said, leaving out the bit about her husband.* [*same as* **omit**; *opposite* **put in, add**] **2** (*informal*) People sometimes say **leave it out** as a way of telling someone to stop doing something, especially to stop telling lies or pretending: *'This has been one of the greatest days of my life!' 'Oh, leave it out; it's not been that exciting.'* [*same as* **turn in**]

leave over

Something **is left over** when it remains after the rest or the others have been used up or taken away: *There's still some drink left over from the party.*

• *adjective* **leftover**

Leftover describes things that remain when the rest or the others have been used up or taken away: *We gathered leftover bits of charcoal from the beach, to make our own barbecue.*

• *noun* **leftovers**

Leftovers are food that remains uneaten at the end of a meal: *Lunch invariably consists of the previous evening's leftovers reheated.*

let /lɛt/: lets, letting, let

Let is used as the past tense and past participle of the verb.

let down

1 Someone **lets** you **down** when they fail to do what they agreed or promised they would do, or what you expected they would do: *That would be letting down my whole family; could never do that.* ❑ *It's understandable that people feel let down by a government that said it would bring taxes down.* **2** You **let down** something that is filled with air, such as a tyre, when you allow the air inside it to escape: *They'd let one of the teachers' tyres down.* [*same as* **deflate**; *opposite* **blow up, pump up, inflate**] **3** To **let down** garments such as skirts and dresses is to make them longer by unfolding material that forms their bottom edge: *For my sister, who was taller, we had to let the coat down by a good couple of inches.* [*opposite* **take up**; see also **let out**]

• *noun* **letdown**: **letdowns**

A **letdown** is something that is much less exciting or impressive than you expected it would be: *We loved Paris, but all agreed that London was a bit of a letdown.*

let in

1 You **let** someone **in** when you allow them to enter, *eg* by opening a door: *The dwarves warn her not to let anyone in the house.* ❑ *Although he'd booked a table, they wouldn't let him in without a tie on.* ❑ *You had a key; why didn't you just let yourself in?* [*same as* **admit** (*formal*); see also **let into**] **2** To **let in** things such as air, water and light is to allow them to enter, through a hole, gap or crack: *Open the windows and let some fresh air in.* ❑ *It wasn't until we were half way up that I realized my boots were letting in water.*

let in for (*informal*)
You wonder what you have **let** yourself **in for** when you realize you may have involved yourself in something difficult or unpleasant: *She was very vague about today's programme, so I've no idea what we've been let in for.*

let in on (*informal*)
You **let** someone **in on** something that is secret, or is reserved for a few people only, when you tell them about it, or allow them to take part in it: *I'll let you in on a little secret; I'm going to go for that job at the Sorbonne.* ❑ *If they'd let anyone else in on the scam it would have meant smaller shares for everyone.*

let into
1 You **let** someone **into** a place when you allow them to enter it, *eg* by opening a door: *One of the servants could have let him into the house via the kitchen.* ❑ *Non-members are not to be let into the casino under any circumstances.* [see also **let in**] **2** You **let** someone **into** a secret when you tell them something that others don't know. [*same as* **let in on**]

let off
1 Someone who **is let off** is given a punishment less severe than they deserve, or no punishment at all: *I'll let you off this time; next time it'll be no football for a week.* ❑ *The papers reported it as a rapist being let off with a fine.* [compare **get off**] **2** Someone who **is let off** a duty or task is allowed not to do it: *The beauty of a holiday is being let off cooking and housework.* ❑ *Some teachers would let you off homework if you played in the orchestra.* **3** To **let off** a gun is to fire it; to **let off** a bomb or other exploding device is to make it explode: *They dress up in bright costumes and let off fireworks.* ❑ *He wouldn't have dared let the gun off inside the house, for fear someone would hear it.* [compare **go off, set off**] **4** Smoke, gases or fumes **are let off** when they are released: *The steam that the boiler lets off could be harnessed to produce electricity.* [*same as* **give off, emit**] **5** The driver of a vehicle you are travelling in **lets** you **off** when they stop to allow you to get out: *We made an unscheduled stop at Igoumenitsa, to let off a couple of sick passengers.* ❑ *She said she had errands to run; I let her off at the post office.* [*same as* **drop off, put off, set down**] **6** (*slang*) Someone who **lets off** releases gases from their stomach through their anus: *If any of the boys let off, the whole class descended into hysterics.* [*same as* **fart** (*informal*), **break wind**]

let on (*informal*)
You don't **let on** about something when you don't tell others about it, or don't reveal it to them in any way: *If you see Alec, don't let on that I've mentioned the party.* ❑ *If I tell you, you mustn't let on to my parents.*

let out
1 You **let** someone **out** when you allow them to leave, usually by opening or unlocking a door: *There was opposition to the policy of letting prisoners out for Christmas.* ❑ *Food and drink are brought in to her; she's never let out of the room for anything.* ❑ *Don't interrupt your meal; I can let myself out.* [compare **see out**] **2** To **let out** something such as air or water is to allow it to escape or flow out: *Lift the baby out before you let the water out of the bath.* ❑ *Try to let the breath out slowly and evenly.* [*same as* **release**] **3** You **let out** sounds or noises when you make them: *Tristan squeezed the damaged paw and the dog let out a yelp.* [*same as* **emit, utter**] **4** You **let** something **out** when you say something that should be kept secret: *It seemed clear that a member of the team had let out the details of our meeting.* [*same as* **let slip**; compare **come out, get out**] **5** (*informal*) Something **lets** you **out** when it allows you to avoid doing something or to escape something,

usually something unpleasant: *The meeting has been fixed for next Wednesday, which lets me out as I'll be in Amsterdam.* ❑ *'They're looking for talented young musicians.' 'That lets you out, then!'* **6** You **let out** a house or other property that you own when you rent it to other people: *They could easily let a couple of rooms out to students, to make a bit of extra money.* [*same as* **rent out**; compare **hire out**] **7** To **let out** a garment is to make it wider by repositioning the joins at its sides, bringing out material that was inside the original joins: *I let it out a couple of inches when I was pregnant.* [*opposite* **take in**; see also **let down**]
• *noun* **outlet**: **outlets**
1 An **outlet** is a hole, pipe or passage through which *eg* water or steam can flow out or escape. **2** An **outlet** is also a shop in which a particular manufacturer's goods are sold: *The company has opened several new outlets throughout the UK and France.* **3** An **outlet** for things such as energy or strong feelings is something that allows you to use them up or get rid of them: *The teenagers need to have some outlet for their frustrations.*

let through
To **let** someone **through** is to allow them to pass: *Officers were under orders not to let anyone through without searching their vehicle.* ❑ *Only cars bearing a Ministry of Defence sticker were let through the road block.* [compare **wave through**]

let up
Something **lets up** when it becomes less strong or intense, or when it stops altogether: *There'll be serious flooding if the rain doesn't let up soon.* ❑ *The good interviewer puts the pressure on with the first couple of questions and never lets up for the whole interview.*
• *noun* • **let-up**: **let-ups**: *There's been no let-up in fighting in the two days since the agreement was signed.*

level /ˈlɛvəl/: levels, levelling (*AmE* leveling), levelled (*AmE* leveled)

level at *or* level against
You **level** something such as criticism or blame **at** someone, or **level** it **against** them, when you criticize or blame them: *My client refutes all charges of professional misconduct levelled at him in the press.* ❑ *They levelled accusations of disloyalty at almost every member of the Cabinet.*

level off *or* level out
1 You **level off** a surface when you make it smooth or level: *Once the concrete begins to set you can level it off with a square edge, or a plasterer's float, for a really smooth finish.* **2** Something that is rising or falling in number, amount, degree or extent **levels off** or **levels out** when it stops rising or falling and remains steady or level: *Student intake had reached over 25,000 before it began to level off.* ❑ *The road climbed steeply and then levelled out.* **3** An aircraft **levels off** or **levels out** when it begins to fly horizontally after flying up or down: *We levelled out at 35,000 feet.*

level with (*informal*)
You **level with** someone when you're honest with them and tell them the whole truth: *I don't think they're levelling with me about their plans for the land.* [*same as* **be straight with** (*informal*)]

lie /laɪ/: lies, lying, lay /leɪ/, lain /leɪn/

lie about *or* lie around
1 Someone who **is lying about** or **lying around** is lying, or perhaps sitting, in a very casual, relaxed or lazy way, and doing nothing: *We just lay around on the beach all afternoon.* [*same as* **lounge about**; compare **hang about**] **2** Things that **are lying about** or **lying around** have been left somewhere carelessly or in an untidy state: *She left her books lying about on the floor.* ❑ *If you leave your tools lying around*

they're bound to get lost. [compare **kick about**]

• *noun* **layabout**: **layabouts**

A **layabout** is someone who is lazy and does no work.

lie ahead

You can use **lie ahead** to talk about what will happen, or what you will experience, in the future: *None of us could have imagined the difficulties that lay ahead.* ❑ *Ahead of them lay months of hardship and near-starvation.* [compare **lie before**]

lie around see **lie about**

lie back

You **lie back** when you lower your body backwards from a sitting position into a position that is, or is closer to being, horizontal, resting on your back: *She lay back against the cushions.* ❑ *Try to breathe out as you lie back.* [compare **lie down**]

lie before (*formal*)

You can use **lie before** to talk about what will happen to someone, usually in the near-future, or what they will experience or have to deal with: *Some difficult decisions lay before them.* [compare **lie ahead**]

lie behind

What **lies behind** something is what causes it or what the reason is for it: *It was perhaps a vague sense of guilt that lay behind his reluctance to visit Thomas.* ❑ *What lies behind such crimes is rarely more than pure and simple greed.* [*same as* **underlie**]

lie down

1 You **lie down** when you get into a flat or horizontal position, especially to sleep or have a rest: *I lay down on the grass and went to sleep.* ❑ *We were ordered to lie down and place our hands behind our heads.* [compare **lie back**]
2 Someone who refuses to **lie down** is determined not to stop fighting or struggling: *Local protesters say they will not lie down over the issue of the proposed bridge.* [*same as* **give in, give up, yield**; *opposite* **fight on**]

• *noun* **lie-down**

You have a **lie-down** when you rest your body in a horizontal position, *eg* on a bed: *I'll take the kids for a few hours while you have a lie-down.*

lie in

You **lie in** when you intentionally stay in bed until after the time you usually get up in the mornings: *The twins slept on until after nine, which gave us a rare opportunity to lie in.* [compare **sleep in**]

• *noun* **lie-in**: *We always had a lie-in on Sunday mornings.*

lie up

Someone **lies up** somewhere when they hide there, *eg* to escape from someone who is chasing them: *There are any number of derelict farmhouses where fugitives might lie up.* [*same as* **hole up** (*informal*), **lie low**]

lie with

People often use **lie with** when saying who is responsible for something, or whom things such as powers, duties and choices belong to: *The real blame lies with the parents.* ❑ *I disagree that the decision should lie with committee members.*

lift /lɪft/: lifts, lifting, lifted

lift off

A spacecraft **lifts off** when it rises up from the ground at the beginning of a flight.

• *noun* **lift-off**: **lift-offs**: *It was only a few minutes before lift-off that we identified the problem.*

light /laɪt/: lights, lighting, lit /lɪt/, lighted

Lighted and **lit** can both be used as the past tense and past participle of the verb, though **lit** is more usual.

light on see **light upon**

light out (*AmE informal*)

You **light out** when you leave a place in a hurry, often to escape from someone or something: *Then we heard voices and decided to light out.* ❑ *When they hear her coming, the dogs light out of the whole damn place.* [*same as* **get out, pull out** (*informal*), **clear out** (*informal*)]

light up

1 To **light** something **up** is to shine lights on it or make it bright with light; something **lights up** when a light inside it is switched on: *Fires all along the hillside lit up the night sky.* ❑ *It makes a difference having public buildings lit up at night.* ❑ *The control panel lights up automatically when you go through a tunnel.* [*same as* **illuminate**] **2** People's faces or eyes **light up** when an expression of happiness or excitement comes into them: *Young eyes light up at the mention of Christmas.* **3** (*informal*) Someone **lights up** when they light a cigarette or pipe and begin to smoke it: *You see the smokers lighting up as soon as they get off the coach.* ❑ *He lit up a favourite pipe and sank into the armchair.*

• *adjective* **lighting-up**

Lighting-up time is the time when drivers are required by law to switch their vehicle's lights on.

light upon *or* light on (*formal*)

You **light upon** something, or **light on** it, when you discover it by chance: *They had, almost in spite of their research, lighted upon the perfect explanation.* [*same as* **hit upon, come across, chance upon, happen upon**]

lighten /ˈlaɪtən/: lightens, lightening, lightened

lighten up (*informal; especially AmE*)

You can tell someone to **lighten up** if you think they are too serious or tense and should relax more: *The whole damn deal might be blown if Rizzo doesn't lighten up a little.*

liken /ˈlaɪkən/: likens, likening, likened

liken to

You **liken** one thing **to** another when you describe it as being similar to the other: *The computer is often likened to the human brain, but the comparison is rather flawed.* [*same as* **compare**]

limber /ˈlɪmbə(r)/: limbers, limbering, limbered

limber up

You **limber up** when you do stretching exercises to warm your muscles before taking part in sport or other physical activity. [*same as* **loosen up, warm up**]

line /laɪn/: lines, lining, lined

line up

1 People **line up** when they form a straight line or queue; you **line** them **up** when you put them into a straight line or queue. **2** You **line** one thing **up** with another when you make it straight, or in the right position, in relation to the other: *Skoda, now a member of the Volkswagen group, is lining up right alongside companies such as BMW and Mercedes in the pursuit of motoring excellence.* ❑ *Don't rush the shot; take time to line up the camera.* ❑ *The casual effect of a dry-stone wall is ruined if you try to line stones up with each other perfectly.* 3 (*informal*) You **line** something **up** when you organize or arrange it: *She's got a job lined up for the summer.* ❑ *A singer has been lined up for the party.* [*same as* **fix up, lay on**] **4** People often use **line up** to say whom, in a dispute or conflict, they give their support to and whom they oppose: *A number of prominent backbenchers were lining up against the Cabinet.*

• *noun* **line-up: line-ups**

1 A **line-up** is a group of people or things gathered together for a particular purpose: *There are a few new faces in the Scotland line-up for the game against France.* ❑ *There's entertainment from an impressive line-up of* *showbiz personalities.* **2** A **line-up** is also a row of people that includes someone suspected of committing a crime, whom a witness of the crime tries to identify: *Do you think you could pick her out of a line-up?* [*same as* **identification parade**]

linger /ˈlɪŋgə(r)/: lingers, lingering, lingered

linger on

Someone or something **lingers on** when they stay or remain for a long time, often longer than was expected or longer than you would like: *The taste lingers on the tongue long after you've swallowed it.* ❑ *Pete and June lingered on till around four, and would have stayed all night I'm sure, if we'd let them.*

linger over

You **linger over** something when you do it slowly, or take a lot of time to do it, usually so that you can enjoy it better: *When we do linger over breakfast, there's always the feeling that half the day's gone and you've done nothing with it.*

link /lɪŋk/: links, linking, linked

link up

You **link up** two people, places or things when you connect or join them in some way: *The Edinburgh office is linked up with the London office by computer.*
• *noun* **link-up**: **link-ups**: *We'll do a satellite link-up with Hollywood for a live broadcast of the main awards.*

listen /ˈlɪsən/: listens, listening, listened

listen in

1 You **listen in** to a private conversation, *eg* on the telephone, when you listen to it secretly: *Her parents sit outside the door to listen in on her conversations with friends.* ❑ *We can't talk about anything without your father listening in.* [*same as* **eavesdrop**] **2** You **listen in** to a radio programme when you listen to it: *If you were listening in last week, you'll remember that Eric Clapton was in the studio.* [compare **tune in**]

listen out for

You **listen out for** something when you prepare to hear and identify the sound of it when it comes: *I lie awake, listening out for the sound of her key in the door.* [compare **look out for, watch out for**]

live /lɪv/: lives, living, lived

live apart

Two people who are married to each other **live apart** when each lives in a different house, separate from the other: *He's been living apart from his wife for the last six months.* [compare **break up, split up**]

live by

You **live by** certain principles or beliefs when they guide the way you behave in everyday life: *But how many people who call themselves Christians actually live by the teachings of Christ?* [*same as* **keep to, stick to, abide by, follow**]

live down

You'll never **live down** something you've done when it is so very foolish, embarrassing or wrong that people will never forget it or forgive you for it: *I'll never live it down if I fail my driving test again.*

live for

You **live for** something when it is the most important thing in your life: *You have to consume poetry; live for it, in fact.*

live in

To **live in** is to have as your home the place where you also work or study: *Over 50% of the students in his college live in.* ❑ *We expected at least three of the servants to live in.*
• *adjective* **live-in**
1 Live-in describes people who also

live in the place where they work or study: *We couldn't afford a live-in housekeeper.* **2** A person's **live-in** boyfriend or girlfriend is one who lives in the same house as them.

• *adjective* **lived-in**

A room that is **lived-in** is used a lot, and is not so neat and tidy that you feel unable to relax in it; some people also use **lived-in** to mean untidy: *The first place had a warm, lived-in atmosphere.* ❑ *I suppose it has a kind of lived-in charm.*

live off

1 You **live off** a certain kind of food when it is the only kind you eat, often because no other kinds are available: *We slept on the ground and lived off whatever was growing on the trees and in the fields.* [*same as* **live on**] **2** People use **live off** to say where they get the money they need to live: *The interest from his UK investments alone is enough for them to live off.* ❑ *We were made to feel that we'd lived off our parents long enough.* [compare **sponge off, scrounge off**]

live on

1 People use **live on** to say how much money they have to buy food, clothes and other things they need: *I wasn't sure the family could live on one wage only.* **2** You **live on** a certain kind of food when that is the only kind of food you eat, perhaps because there are no other kinds available: *Health problems of one sort or another are inevitable in children who live predominantly on fried food and sweets.* [*same as* **live off**] **3** You can use **live on** to talk about what still exists, or what people in general still remember: *His widow lived on into her nineties.* **4** Something **lives on** if people go on remembering it: *The disaster lives on in people's memories, kept alive perhaps by its frequent treatment in film.*

live out

1 People **live out** when their home is not the place where they work or study. **2** You can use **live out** to talk about how or where someone spends their life, especially the last part of their life: *He wanted to live out his remaining days in the sun.*

live through

To **live through** an unpleasant event or period is to experience it: *What is the feeling among the younger generation, who didn't live through the war?* [*same as* **go through**]

live together

People who are having a sexual relationship **live together** when they live in the same house as if they were married. [compare **live with**]

live under

You can use **live under** to talk about the kind of government, political system or ruler that is in authority over people: *What are the perceptions of those who lived in the East under communism?*

live up (*informal*)

Someone who **is living** it **up** is having a wild, exciting time full of pleasures, especially the kind of pleasures that cost a lot of money: *He said he had worked long and hard for more than twenty years and now he was going to live it up a bit.*

live up to

Something that **lives up to** expectations is as good, or sometimes as bad, as you expected it to be: *Barry spent the evening living up to his reputation as a ladies' man.* ❑ *Very few of the products lived up to the claims of their manufacturers.* [*same as* **match up to, measure up to**]

live with

1 You **live with** someone when you share the same house as them: *She's twenty-six and still living with her mum and dad.* **2** You **live with** someone you are having a sexual relationship with when you share a house with them. **3** You **live with** something unpleasant when you continue to suffer from it or remember it; you learn to **live with** something when you accept it as part of your life: *He will have to live with the mistake for the rest of his life.* ❑ *In these situations, parents often find themselves unable to live with the guilt.* [compare **put up with**]

liven /'laɪvən/: **livens, livening, livened**

liven up

1 To **liven** something **up** is to make it livelier or more interesting or exciting: *Some pictures on the walls should liven up the room a bit.* ❑ *A dull party momentarily livened up when a fist-fight broke out between two of her colleagues.* [*same as* **pep up, enliven** (*formal*); compare **jazz up**] **2** You **liven up**, or something **livens** you **up**, when you become, or it makes you, livelier or happier and more energetic: *The guests livened up a bit when food was served.* ❑ *The holiday has livened him up a lot.* [*same as* **buck up** (*informal*), **perk up** (*informal*), **cheer up**]

load /loud/: **loads, loading, loaded**

load down

1 Someone **is loaded down** when they have a lot of heavy things to hold or carry: *The assistant was loaded down with packages and instructed to bring them to the car.* [*same as* **weigh down**] **2** You can also say you **are loaded down** when you have a lot of things to do or deal with: *The production department will be loaded down with work for the next couple of months.* [*same as* **snow under**]

load up

You **load** a vehicle **up** when you put in it everything that is to be taken; you **load** things **up** when you put them into a vehicle: *It took us a couple hours to load up the trailer.* ❑ *Once the furniture was loaded up, there was no room for the carpets.* [compare **pack up, pile up, stack up**]

loaf /louf/: **loafs, loafing, loafed**

loaf about *or* loaf around

Someone who **loafs about** or **loafs around** spends time being lazy: *The students we saw did very little except loaf about the campus.* ❑ *I'll try loafing around for a while and see how it suits me.* [*same as* **laze about, lounge about**]

lock /lɒk/: **locks, locking, locked**

lock away

1 You **lock** something **away,** or you **lock** it **up**, when you put it in a safe, locked place: *It makes me angry to think that most of her paintings are locked away in a bank vault.* ❑ *The old lady locks up her diamonds in a drawer by her bed.* [compare **shut away, close up**] **2** Someone **is locked away**, or **is locked up**, when they are put either in prison or in a psychiatric hospital: *Victims' families want the law to lock these people away for a very long time.* ❑ *People like you should be locked up.* **3** You **lock** yourself **away** when you go to a private room or other place where you won't be disturbed by other people: *She's one of those writers who stays locked away for days on end.*

lock in

Someone **locks** you **in** a room when they lock the door to prevent you from leaving; you **lock** yourself **in** when you accidentally close a door that you can't then open again from the inside to let yourself out: *No prisoners are locked in, not even at night.* ❑ *Hall had pulled the fire door to and locked himself in by mistake.*

lock out

1 You **lock** someone **out** when you prevent them from entering by locking a door: *Staff were locked out the room until the meeting was over.* **2** You **lock** yourself **out** of a place when you accidentally close a door that you can't then open again from the outside to let yourself in: *The driver's door can't be locked from the inside, so you can never lock yourself out.* **3** The management in a factory or other workplace **lock** the workers **out** when they prevent them from entering to do their work, because the workers have refused to accept the pay or working conditions offered.

• *noun* **lockout: lockouts**

In an industrial dispute, there is a **lockout** when the management of a factory or other workplace prevent the workers from entering to do their work.

lock up

You **lock up**, or **lock** a house or other building **up**, when you lock all the doors and windows securely, so that burglars can't get in: *The understanding always was that the last person to leave locked up.* ❑ *I wanted to lock up the garage before coming to bed.* [see also **lock away**]

• *noun* **lockup: lockups**

1 A **lockup** is a place where prisoners, such as criminals arrested by the police, are kept, especially temporarily. **2** A **lockup**, or a **lockup** garage, is a garage that may be locked securely, especially one that is some distance away from the user's home or base.

log /lɒg/: logs, logging, logged

log in *or* log on

To **log in** or **log on** is to enter a computer system by typing the required word or sequence of words.

log into

To **log into** a computer system is to enter it by typing the required word or sequence of words.

log out *or* log off

To **log out** or **log off** is to leave a computer system by typing the required word or sequence of words.

loll /lɒl/: lolls, lolling, lolled

loll about *or* loll around

Someone who **lolls about** or **lolls around** sits or lies lazily somewhere, doing nothing: *The campus teemed with students lolling about on the grass.* [*same as* **lounge about**; compare **hang about**]

long /lɒŋ/: longs, longing, longed

You **long for** something when you have a very strong desire to have it: *The cold wet winters depressed her; she longed for balmy Mediterranean evenings.* [*same as* **be dying for, yearn for** (*formal*), **hunger for, hanker for**]

• *adjective* **longed-for**: *It can be pretty upsetting when a much longed-for holiday goes disastrously wrong.*

look /luk/: looks, looking, looked

look after

1 You **look after** someone, usually a child or someone ill, when you do and give what they need and keep them safe and well: *Women, as much as men, are surprised to learn that fathers are capable of looking after their babies.* [*same as* **care for, take care of**] **2** You **look after** something when you keep it in good condition: *A reliable car, well looked after, should last you at least six years.* [*same as* **take care of**] **3** Someone who **looks after** something is responsible for doing it, dealing with it or making decisions about it: *This company books the venue and the band, and even looks after the catering.* ❑ *You often find that cleaning is looked after by an outside contractor.* [*same as* **see to, attend to, take care of**] **4** You **look after** something for someone when you make sure that it is not damaged, lost or stolen, perhaps while they are away: *Would you look after my cases while I go to the toilet?* ❑ *We're looking after the house next door while the neighbours are on holiday.* [*same as* **watch, mind, keep an eye on**] **5** You say you can **look after** yourself to tell someone you are able to protect yourself from people who try to harm or deceive you: *He said I wasn't to worry about John, that he was a big boy now and could look after himself.*

look ahead

You **look ahead** when you consider the future, and perhaps prepare for what you expect will happen: *Looking ahead ten years, we can see the South East Asian countries dominating the market.*

look around see look round

look at

1 You **look at** something when you turn your eyes towards it so that you are able to see it: *Whenever I look at him, I see his father at his age.* **2** You **look at** something when you consider, study or examine it: *The first chapter looks at the history of the period.* ❑ *Get an expert to look at it and give you a valuation.* ❑ *I've changed the oil but there's still the brakes to be looked at.* **3** The way you **look at** a fact or situation reveals your attitude towards it or opinion about it: *The film is the director's baby but, looking at it as a producer, I have to decide if it'll make money.* ❑ *Let's look at the problem from a different angle.* **4** You **look at** something written or printed when you read it, usually only briefly: *I haven't had the chance to look at the report.* **5** Someone who won't **look at** something won't consider it; someone who would not **look** twice **at** something is not interested in it at all: *I don't think they'd look at any candidate who didn't have a First from Oxford or Cambridge.* ❑ *She won't look twice at a job in industry.* ❑ *He's an ordinary looking man, who normally you wouldn't have looked twice at.*

look back *or* look back on

1 You **look back**, or **look back on** something, when you think about the past: *She looks back on her childhood with fond memories.* **2** You say someone has **never looked back** if they have been very successful: *She opened her first shop at the age of twenty and never looked back.*

look down on

Someone who **looks down on** you thinks you are not very important, or less important than they are: *It's amazing to think how goods from Japan were once looked down on.* [*same as* **sneer at, look down one's nose at, turn one's nose up at**]

look for

You **look for** someone or something when you try to find them: *I looked everywhere for the photographs.* ❑ *We're looking for a solution to the problem and hoping it lies in the former Soviet Union.* [*same as* **seek** (*formal*)]

look forward to

You **look forward to** something that is going to happen when you feel happy because you know you are going to enjoy it: *She's looking forward to the birth of her baby.* ❑ *Are they looking forward to going to Australia?* ❑ *I think we can look forward to a period of sustained economic growth.*

look in

You **look in** somewhere when you pay a brief visit there: *Would you look in at the library on your way home and collect my books?* ❑ *Would there be time to look in on Jan and Mike while we were passing?* [*same as* **drop in, call in**]

look into

You **look into** something when you investigate it: *I've offered to look into the problem for him.*

look on

1 You **look on** when you watch something without taking part: *The boys were presented with their medals as proud parents and friends looked on.* **2** You can use **look on** or **look upon** to talk about the way you regard or consider something: *Some men do look upon marriage as an unnecessary restriction on personal freedom.* ❑ *They* *made it clear that they would not look kindly on applications from Blacks.*

• *noun* **onlooker: onlookers**

Onlookers are people who watch something without taking part or being involved in it: *She was jeered by a crowd of onlookers.*

look out

1 You say '**look out!**' to warn someone of danger: *Look out! There's a car coming!* [*same as* **watch out**] **2** You use **look out** to talk about looking for something when you're not sure where it is because you haven't used or seen it for a long time: *Chris and Dave came down, and we looked out some old photos from our schooldays.* ❑ *There's a hand drill in the garage; I'll look it out for you.* [*same as* **dig out** (*informal*)]

• *noun* **lookout: lookouts**

1 A **lookout** is a place high up, from where you can see all around an area: *Alan sat up in the homemade lookout and watched for foxes.* **2** A **lookout** is also a person who watches for danger: *There were three of us in all: two working on the safe, and the driver acting as lookout.* **3** (*informal*) You can say that someone's foolish behaviour is their **lookout** to emphasize that they, and nobody else, will be responsible for what happens as a result: *Some climbers think if people want to go into the mountains with no equipment or training then it should be their lookout.*

look out for

1 You **look out for** something when you are ready to notice and identify it when it comes or when it becomes available: *I've got Tom looking out for one in the Edinburgh secondhand shops.* ❑ *Look out for a sign on the right.* [*same as* **watch out for**] **2** You **look out for** someone when you are ready to give protection when they need it: *With a close-knit extended family, they all look out for each other.*

look over

You **look over** something, or **look** it **over**, when you examine it: *We've looked over several flats in this part of town.* ❑ *Could you briefly look over this report for me?* ❑ *Why don't you let the doctor look you over to make sure you haven't broken anything?*

look round

1 You **look round** or **look around** when you turn your head to look at something behind you, or when you look in all directions around you: *I shouted a name but none of them looked round.* ❑ *She was looking round for somewhere to put the box.* ❑ *Looking around the room, I noticed there were no pictures on the walls.* **2** You **look round** a place or building when you visit it: *Let's look round the castle this afternoon.* [*same as* **go round**] **3** You **look round** for something when you try to find it by looking in different places: *Did I tell you Helen's started looking round for another job?*

look through

1 You **look through** things when you examine them one by one: *I looked through my clothes but found nothing suitable for the funeral.* ❑ *Neil asked me to look through all the cupboards again, but I knew we wouldn't find anything.* [*same as* **go through**] **2** You **look through** something written or printed when you read it briefly: *I only get about ten minutes at breakfast to look through the morning's headlines.* [compare **flick through, browse through**]

look to

1 You **look to** someone for something when you rely on or expect them to do or provide it: *She has always looked to her parents for support.* ❑ *It would seem fanciful to look to poetry to inspire a revolution of any kind.* [*same as* **turn to**] **2** You **look to** the future when you consider it: *He said they had put all the bad times behind them and were now looking to the future with confidence.*

look up

1 You **look up** when you direct your eyes towards what is above you: *I heard the noise and looked up to see a woman falling to the ground.* ❑ *She passed me the towel slowly, without even looking up from her book.* **2** You **look** information **up** when you look for it in books or other printed material where it may be found: *I had to look up the spelling in a dictionary.* ❑ *They gave me the street-name and I looked it up on the map.* **3** (*informal*) You **look** someone **up** whom you haven't seen for a while when you visit them: *Look us up if you're ever in Edinburgh.* **4** (*informal*) You can say that a situation **is looking up** when it is improving: *The weather is beginning to look up.* ❑ *With cuts in interest rates, things are beginning to look up for small businesses.*

look upon see look on

look up to

You **look up to** someone that you admire and respect: *Because students automatically look up to you, you have a responsibility not to talk rubbish.*

loom /luːm/: **looms**, **looming**, **loomed**

loom ahead

When you know you will soon experience or have to deal with something unpleasant, you can say that it **looms ahead**: *The written exam was over, but already the oral in Paris loomed ahead.*

loom up

Something you are approaching **looms up** when you are suddenly able to see it, and are perhaps a rather frightened or unnerved by it: *The figure of an unnaturally large dog loomed up out of the darkness.*

loose /luːs/: **looses**, **loosing**, **loosed**

loose off

To **loose off** a gun or other exploding weapon is to fire or explode it: *They loosed a few rounds off over the heads of the rioters.*

loosen /ˈluːsən/: **loosens**, **loosening**, **loosened**

loosen up

1 You **loosen up**, or **loosen** part of your body **up**, when you do exercises to make your muscles less stiff: *The 'dog down' posture is the best way to loosen up the area around the backs of the knees.* ❑ *Never run a race without first loosening up.* [compare **warm up**] **2** (*informal*) You can tell someone to **loosen up** if you think they look nervous or tense and should relax more: *Hey, loosen up a little; here, have a drink.* [*same as* **lighten up**]

lop /lɒp/: **lops**, **lopping**, **lopped**

lop off

1 To **lop** something **off**, *eg* a branch of a tree, is to cut it off, usually with a single heavy blow: *There was the sailor who got his leg lopped off when the cord snapped and came whipping back.* [*same as* **chop off**, **sever**] **2** You can use **lop off** to talk about large amounts or proportions that are removed or deducted: *Don't forget the agent lops about 15% off for arranging the investment.* [*same as* **cut off**, **take off**, **knock off**]

lord /lɔːd/: **lords**, **lording**, **lorded**

lord over

Someone who **lords** it **over** you behaves as if they are superior to you, *eg* by giving you orders: *They obviously don't think there's anything wrong with a young boy lording it over his aunts and uncles.* [compare **boss about**, **push around**, **queen over**]

lose /luːz/: **loses**, **losing**, **lost** /lɒst/

lose out

You **lose out** as a result of something

if it causes you to suffer a loss or other disadvantage: *A spread of investments safeguards you if you lose out on any single investment.* ❑ *With indirect taxes like VAT, it's always the people at the bottom of the scale who lose out.* [compare **miss out**]

lose out to
You **lose out to** something or someone who competes with you when you lose or suffer because they gain or win: *The BBC's music stations have lost out considerably to Atlantic 252 and the other new commercial stations.*

lounge /laundʒ/: **lounges, lounging, lounged**

lounge about *or* **lounge around**
You **lounge about** or **lounge around** when you spend your time lazily, doing nothing: *Isn't it time you stopped lounging about and actually started to take an interest in something?* ❑ *He's the typical apathetic teenager who spends most of his time lounging around the house.* [*same as* **laze about, loaf about, bum about** (*informal*); compare **hang about, loll about**]

louse /laus/: **louses, lousing, loused**

louse up (*informal*)
Someone **louses** something **up** when they spoil it, often by making careless mistakes: *He thinks it's fun to go around lousing up people's lives.* [*same as* **mess up** (*informal*), **foul up**]

luck /lʌk/: **lucks, lucking, lucked**

luck out *or* **luck up** (*AmE informal*)
You **luck out** or **luck up** when you have good luck or good fortune: *We lucked out and found a cheap place near the beach that had just come empty.* ❑ *Was he destined for great things or had he simply lucked out?* ❑ *Just so happens, I lucked up and got all his attention.* [compare **strike out**]

lumber /ˈlʌmbə(r)/: **lumbers, lumbering, lumbered**

lumber with (*informal*)
You can say that you **are lumbered with** a job or responsibility that you don't want when you have been given it: *I was about to get lumbered with my young cousins for the whole weekend.* [*same as* **saddle with, land with**]

lump /lʌmp/: **lumps, lumping, lumped**

lump together (*informal*)
Separate things **are lumped together** when they are treated as a single unit or whole: *Inevitably, in these arguments, single parents and unemployed people are lumped together with new-age travellers, drug addicts and every other group perceived as undesirable.*

lure /ljuə(r)/: **lures, luring, lured**

lure away
You **lure** someone **away** when you persuade them to leave and come with you: *One of the big city companies had lured him away from banking with the promise of a fantastic salary package.*

lust /lʌst/: **lusts, lusting, lusted**

lust after
To **lust after** someone is to feel a strong sexual desire for them: *Of course, I'd been lusting after his brother for months.*

m

magic /ˈmadʒɪk/: **magics, magicking, magicked**

magic away
To **magic** something **away** is to make it disappear immediately: *The problem of debt is an international one and can't be magicked away with some secret formula.* [compare **spirit away**]

major /ˈmeɪdʒə(r)/: **majors, majoring, majored**

major in
A student **majors in** a particular subject when it is their main subject of study: *You don't decide what to major in until the end of third semester.*

make /meɪk/: **makes, making, made** /meɪd/

make after
You **make after** something or someone when you chase them: *A black car swerved out of a side street and made after the van at top speed.* [*same as* **go after**]

make away with (*informal*)
1 Someone **makes away with** something when they steal it and run away with it: *You wouldn't leave the pram outside in case someone made away with your baby.* [*same as* **make off with**] **2** People sometimes use **make away with** to mean kill or murder: *They watched him day and night so he didn't try to make away with himself.* [*same as* **do away with** (*informal*), **bump off** (*informal*), **do in** (*informal*)]

make for
1 You **make for** a place when you move towards it: *We didn't tell them we were really making for Athens.* ❑ *He jumped up and made hastily for the door.* [*same as* **head for**] **2** Something **makes for** a certain situation if that situation is likely to occur as a result: *Fine weather made for an enjoyable holiday.*

make into
1 You **make** one thing **into** another when you cause it to change and become the other: *There were plans to dig over the lawns and make them into vegetable beds.* **2** To **make** someone **into** a particular kind of person is to influence the way they think or behave so that they become that kind of person: *It's doubtful whether such programmes can make bad parents into good parents.* [*same as* **turn into**]

make of
What you **make of** something is the opinion you form of it, or the impression you get of it, or what you understand it to mean: *So, what did you make of the new manager?* ❑ *I didn't know what to make of her strange response.*

make off (*informal*)
You **make off** when you leave, especially hurriedly: *The thieves made off in a yellow Transit van.* [*same as* **take off**]

make off with (*informal*)
Someone **makes off with** something when they steal it: *Anyone might walk in and make off with the family silver.* [*same as* **make away with**]

make out

1 You can **make** something **out** when you are able to see or hear it, usually with difficulty: *I could make out the faint outline of a car in the fog.* ❑ *I couldn't make out all the words of the song.* [compare **pick out**] **2** You can **make** something **out** when you can understand it, usually with difficulty: *I couldn't make out whether he was pleased or not.* ❑ *From his account of events, it was difficult to make out how it had happened.* [*same as* **work out, figure out**] **3** You can't **make** someone **out** if you can't decide what kind of person they are, or you can't understand why they behave the way they do: *None of us could really make Phil out; he had every reason to be happy.* [*same as* **figure out**] **4** You **make out** that something is so when you try to convince people that it is: *She's been making out that checking windows was not her responsibility.* ❑ *The programme made her out to be concerned only with holding on to power.* ❑ *It's not as difficult as some people make out.* **5** You can use **make out** to talk about the way you describe someone or something, or the impression you give of them, particularly when it is a false or wrong impression: *The press had made him out to be a shameless philanderer who trifled with unsuspecting women's hearts.* ❑ *The situation is not as black as it is made out to be.* ❑ *She makes herself out to be something of an expert in the field.* **6** You **make out** things such as cheques and receipts when you write the necessary details on them: *Could you make the cheque out to Breakages Ltd?* [*same as* **write out**; compare **fill in**] **7** (*informal*) You can ask how someone **is making out** when you want to know how they are, or what progress they are making; someone who says they **are making out** means they are dealing successfully with the situation they are in: *I don't know how they'll make out in the big city.* ❑ *You shouldn't worry about Clancy; he'll make out all right on his own.* [*same as* **get on, get along, cope, manage**] **8** (*slang*) To **make out** is to have sexual intercourse: *I could see a couple of kids making out in the back of my truck.* ❑ *None of the guys had ever made out with Lucy; she was our ambition.* [*same as* **score** (*slang*), **get it on** (*slang*), **have it off** (*slang*)]

make over

You **make over** something you own to someone else when you legally make them the owner of it: *Our personal wealth was at risk and accountants advised us to make it all over to our children.* [*same as* **sign over, turn over**]

make up

1 The things that **make up** something are its parts, or the things that form it: *The potting compost is made up of moss peat, sharp sand, garden soil and fertiliser.* ❑ *Blacks still make up only 2% of our representation nationwide.* [*same as* **comprise, constitute**] **2** You **make up** something that is not true when you invent it, perhaps to deceive others: *She made up some feeble excuse to do with washing her hair.* ❑ *They had accused him of making the whole thing up.* [*same as* **cook up** (*informal*), **trump up** (*informal*), **concoct**] **3** You **make** something **up** when you prepare it by putting various things together: *The kitchen staff will be happy to make up packed lunches for guests that require them.* **4** You **make up** something when you add the number or amount of things that are missing, to make it complete: *We need another player to make up the team.* **5** You **make up** your mind when you make a firm and final decision or choice: *I couldn't make up my mind whether he was lying or not.* ❑ *She made her mind up to get on the first train that came in.* **6** Someone **makes** themselves **up** when they put cosmetics on their face. **7** People who have quarrelled **make up**, or **make** it **up**, when they settle their differences and become friends again: *Have you* *made it up with Janice yet?* **8** You **make up** a bed when you prepare a bed that is not currently being used, *eg* for an unexpected guest: *Don't go to the bother of making the camp bed up; I'm just as happy on the sofa.*

• *adjective* **made-up**

A **made-up** story or excuse is one that someone has invented, that is false or untrue.

• *noun* **make-up**

1 Make-up consists of things such as lipstick, face powder and other cosmetics put on the face. **2** The **make-up** of something or someone is their character or nature: *She argued that the average jury's make-up was overwhelmingly middle class.* ❑ *Such petty emotions are simply not part of her make-up.*

make up for

1 Something **makes up for** something else that is lacking or lost if it replaces it and restores the balance: *We'll have to work hard to make up for lost time.* **2** You **make up for** something bad or wrong that you have done when you do something good or right as an apology or to restore a good relationship with someone: *I hoped this would make up for my earlier rudeness.* ❑ *She wanted to do something to make up for coming home late the previous evening.* [*same as* **compensate for, atone for**]

make up to

You **make up to** someone when you are deliberately very pleasant to them, either because you are sexually attracted to them or because you want them to do something for you: *He was the kind of bloke who couldn't resist making up to every woman in his company.* ❑ *Why don't you try making up to the Principal?* [*same as* **chat up, butter up**]

make with (*informal; especially AmE*)

Someone who tells you to **make with** something wants you to bring or produce it: *Hey, waitress! Let's make with the coffee over here!* ❑ *So he sits me down and starts making with the soft words and the loving eyes.*

map /map/: maps, mapping, mapped

map out

You **map out** future plans, intentions or schemes when you decide or explain how they will happen: *Her parents appear to have her career all mapped out for her.* ❑ *We took a number of options and mapped them out for the students to consider.* [*same as* **set out, lay out**]

march /mɑːtʃ/: marches, marching, marched

march on

Soldiers **march on** a place when they walk towards it in order to attack it: *An entire battalion would march on Zaragoza and would be prepared to accept the consequences.* ❑ *Protesters from a range of organizations will march on Shell headquarters and demand a conference with managers.*

mark /mɑːk/: marks, marking, marked

mark as

You can use **mark as** to talk about the bad impression you have of someone that makes you decide what kind of person they are: *Failure in this would mark me as someone who can't cope in a crisis.* [*same as* **label as**; compare **mark down as**]

mark down

1 You can say that you **mark** something **down** when you write it down: *I had marked down his address on the back of my cheque book.* [*same as* **jot down, note down**] **2** Goods for sale **are marked down** when their price is reduced or lowered: *We had to mark them down by 50% to get rid of them.* ❑ *The trousers had been marked down from £45 to £15.* [*same as* **put down,**

take down, cut] **3** A student **is marked down** for mistakes they make in their work when marks are taken off because of the mistakes: *They mark you down for poor spelling, no matter how good your ideas are.* [opposite **mark up**] **4** To **mark down** a student's work is later to award it a lower mark or grade than the one originally given: *The external examiner marked you down a couple of percent.* [opposite **mark up**]

• *noun* **markdown**: **markdowns**

A **markdown** is a reduction in the price of goods for sale: *There are incredible markdowns of up to 60%.*

mark down as

You can use **mark down as** to talk about the impressions you have of someone that make you decide what kind of person they are: *From his appearance, you wouldn't mark him down as an aid worker.* [*same as* **have down as, put down as**; compare **mark as**]

mark off

1 You **mark off** items on a list when you mark them with a symbol to show that they have been selected or dealt with: *On the telephone list he had marked well-used numbers off in red.* [*same as* **tick off**; compare **cross off**] **2** You **mark** something **off** when you mark its boundary or limit in order to separate or isolate it: *Damaged areas had been marked off with wire fences.* [compare **cordon off**] **3** The features of something that **mark** it **off** from something else show that it is different or distinct: *There was about him a gentle quality that marked him off from the other men.* [*same as* **mark out, distinguish**]

mark out

1 You **mark** something **out** on a surface when you show where it will be built or created on that surface by drawing lines, or when you draw the lines that form it: *We've marked out windows here and here.* ❑ *When you need an athletics track you just mark one out around the football pitch.* **2** The features of something that **mark** it **out** from something else show that it is different or distinct: *What marked out the successful candidates was a willingness to challenge traditional methods.* [*same as* **mark off, distinguish**] **3** You can say that someone **is marked out** to achieve something when circumstances or other people seem to have decided that they will achieve it: *Even at that early stage, Party bosses had marked him out as a high-flier.*

mark up

1 To **mark up** a price is to raise or increase it: *They mark the imported lagers up by anything up to 200%.* [*same as* **put up, hike up**; opposite **mark down**] **2** A student **is marked up** when they are given extra marks for particularly good elements in their work: *Any reference to the films of Godard gets you marked up a couple of percent.* [opposite **mark down**] **3** To **mark up** a student's work is later to award it a higher mark than was originally given: *Professor Gerrard marked up first-year essays as a matter of course.* [opposite **mark down**] **4** You **mark up** items on a list when you show you have selected them by writing a mark or symbol next to them: *From your list of eight favourite records choose the one you like best and mark it up.* [*same as* **highlight**]

• *noun* **markup**

The **markup** on goods is the percentage added to the cost or wholesale price by the seller or retailer: *There's a markup of as much as 100% on gold jewellery.*

marry /'marɪ/: marries, marrying, married

marry above

Someone who **marries above** themselves marries someone of higher social rank: *They never gave me the feeling that I had married above myself.*

marry beneath

Someone who **marries beneath** themselves marries someone of lower social rank: *Technically, the Prince had married beneath himself.*

marry into
You **marry into** a family, social class, religion or other group when you become part of it by marrying someone from it: *Their mothers dream of their marrying into the aristocracy.* ❑ *It makes you wonder what you've married into.*

marry off
To **marry off** a child, usually a daughter, is to find a partner for them to marry, and so to get rid of the responsibility of looking after them: *By the time she was eighteen, they couldn't wait to get her married off.* ❑ *Arrangements had been made to marry her off to the Bedsloe boy.*

marry out
Someone who **marries out** marries someone of a different religion to their own: *Marrying out is no longer the taboo it once was.*

marry up
You **marry** one thing **up** with another, or **marry** the two **up**, when you join or combine them; you can also say that the two things **marry up**: *The second platform is hoisted up to marry up with the first.* ❑ *If infantry units fail to marry up at Gaza, the whole operation will be jeopardised.* [*same as* **join up**, **link up**]

marvel /ˈmɑːvəl/: **marvels**, **marvelling** (*AmE* **marveling**), **marvelled** (*AmE* **marveled**)

---

marvel at
You **marvel at** something when you are very surprised, or perhaps shocked, by how impressive it is: *The younger visitors usually marvel at the size of some of the aeroplanes.* [*same as* **wonder at**]

mash /maʃ/: **mashes**, **mashing**, **mashed**

---

mash up
You **mash up** solid pieces of food when you press or crush them to make a soft mass: *We don't serve vegetables to these patients without mashing them up first.*

mask /mɑːsk/: **masks**, **masking**, **masked**

---

mask out
In photography, you **mask out** part of a negative print when you cover it so that it does not appear in the final photograph.

masquerade /maskəˈreɪd/: **masquerades**, **masquerading**, **masqueraded**

---

masquerade as
You can use **masquerade as** to talk about people or things that pretend to be something they are not: *The thieves gain entry to people's houses by masquerading as telephone engineers.* ❑ *You often get a batch of statistics masquerading as research.* [*same as* **pose as**]

match /matʃ/: **matches**, **matching**, **matched**

---

match against
1 You **match** one person or thing **against** another when you make them compete with each other to find out who or which is better: *The string of third-rate fighters matched against him is in no way fit preparation for a title fight.* [*same as* **pit against**, **set against**]
2 You **match** one thing **against** another when you compare the two: *The list of candidates is then matched against the scripts, to check that everyone on the course has taken the exam.*

match up
Things **match up** when they are the same or similar, when they are suited to each other, or when they fit together correctly: *If you can match up the names with the faces, you win a prize.*

❑ *Genetic fingerprinting techniques confirmed that crime and suspect matched up.*

match up to

You can use **match up to** when talking about whether people or things achieve certain standards or satisfy certain requirements: *It was widely thought that Jean didn't match up to the demands of a senior post.* [*same as* **measure up to, be up to**]

maul /mɔːl/: mauls, mauling, mauled

maul around

You **maul** something **around** when you roughly or violently pull it from position to position: *It makes you cringe to see the removal men mauling around your prized items of furniture.*

measure /ˈmɛʒə(r)/: measures, measuring, measured

measure against

You **measure** people or things **against** each other when you compare them: *Measured against competitor profits, our performance last year was a modest achievement at best.* ❑ *It's not so fantastical when you measure it against the technological developments of the last 20 years.* [*same as* **set against**]

measure off

You **measure off** a certain length of something when that measured length is to be cut off: *Measure me off a four-foot length for the plinth.* ❑ *I've measured three metres off; will that be enough?* [compare **measure out, mark off**]

measure out

You **measure out** a certain amount of something when that amount is to be taken or served: *Measure out 5ml of powder and mix it with half a litre of water.* ❑ *A blocked plan is drawn and we measure the required carpet out according to that.* [compare **measure off, mark out**]

measure up

1 Someone or something that **measures up** reaches a required or desired standard: *She's a competent manager, but I'm not sure she'd measure up to the new position.* ❑ *Compared with last year's results, how do this year's students measure up?* **2** To **measure up** is to take measurements related to something you are going to make, build or fit: *The shop will send a carpet fitter round to measure up.*

meddle /ˈmɛdəl/: meddles, meddling, meddled

meddle in

Someone **meddles in** something when they involve themselves in it though their involvement is not wanted: *I didn't want to be accused of meddling in Stimpson's affairs.* [*same as* **pry in, intrude in, interfere in**]

meddle with

Someone **meddles with** something when they touch or disturb it without the permission of the person it belongs to: *I put a lock on the door to stop the kids meddling with my computer.* [*same as* **tamper with, interfere with**]

mediate /ˈmiːdɪeɪt/: mediates, mediating, mediated

mediate between

To **mediate between** people or groups who disagree is to try to make them reach an agreement with each other: *Mediating between the warring factions proved to be much more difficult than had been anticipated.*

meet /miːt/: meets, meeting, met /mɛt/

meet up

1 You **meet up** with someone when you each go to the same place at the same time by arrangement, to do something together: *We parted in Cologne, arranging to meet up in Venice a week later.* **2** Things **meet up** at the point where they connect with or join each other: *An extra signal box was positioned where the old track meets up with the new.* [*same as* **link up, join up, come together**]

meet with

1 You **meet with** people when you come together for a discussion: *She is meeting with her solicitors this morning.* [*same as* **meet**] **2** Something **meets with**, or **is met with**, a certain response or reaction if that is the way people respond or react to it: *My suggestion met with contempt.* ❑ *Reports of atrocities had initially been met with disbelief.* ❑ *Her first novel met with considerable success.* **3** You can use **meet with** to talk about what happens to you, or what you experience: *If patients meet with an accident whilst in your care, you want to be sure your insurance will cover it.* [*same as* **encounter**]

melt /mɛlt/: melts, melting, melted

melt away

1 Heat **melts** something **away** when it causes it to melt and eventually disappear: *The old layers of paint were quickly melted away.* ❑ *The addition of oil will help the residue to melt away.* **2** You can say that anything **melts away** when it slowly or gradually disappears: *Any support he once had amongst his colleagues had melted away.* [*same as* **fade away, die away, peter out, dwindle**] **3** (*literary*) You can say that people **melt away** when they move away quietly or secretly: *When Derek launched into his salesman routine, most of the guests melted away.* [*same as* **disperse**]

melt down

To **melt down** an object, especially one made of metal, is to heat it until it melts and can be reshaped or re-used: *Environmental groups opposed plans to melt the structures down.*

• *noun* **meltdown**

There is a **meltdown** in a nuclear reactor when parts of it accidentally melt, releasing radioactivity into the atmosphere: *The older reactors were more at risk of meltdown.*

melt into

1 You can use **melt into** to describe the way strong feelings such as anger change into gentler feelings: *Her initial severity melted instantly into a sort of apologetic camaraderie.* [*same as* **dissolve into, evaporate into**] **2** A person you are chasing **melts into** a crowd when they hide from you by becoming part of the crowd: *Hannay melts into a Salvation Army street march.*

merge /mɜːdʒ/: merges, merging, merged

merge in

Something **merges in** with its surroundings when it is so similar to them in its colour, shape or patterning that it is difficult to see or distinguish: *Being in the same typeface, there is a danger that the headwords will merge in and the user won't be able to pick them out from the rest of the text.* [*opposite* **stick out, stand out**; compare **blend in**]

merge into

One thing **merges into** another when it becomes difficult to see or distinguish each one because the two are so similar in colour, shape or patterning: *bands of colour that were so similar they seemed to merge into each other* ❑ *The zebra's stripes help it to merge into its natural grassland landscape.*

merge with

Business companies **merge with** each other when they combine to form a single company: *We are merging with a Canadian publishing company.*

mess /mɛs/: messes, messing, messed

mess about *or* mess around

(*informal*)

1 You **mess about** or **mess around**

when you spend time doing silly or foolish things: *The teacher told them off for messing about in the toilets.* **2** Someone **messes** you **about** or **messes** you **around** when they treat you badly or unfairly: *I wish they'd stop messing me around and tell me what job they want me to do.*
[*same as* **fool about** (*informal*), **muck about** (*informal*), **piss about** (*vulgar slang*), **bugger about** (*vulgar slang*)]

mess about with *or* **mess around with** (*informal*)
Someone **messes about with** something, or **messes around with** it, when they touch or disturb it when they shouldn't, especially without the permission of the person it belongs to: *I don't mess around with the engine; that way, I know I can't damage anything.* [*same as* **meddle with, interfere with, tamper with**]

mess up (*informal*)
1 You **mess** something **up** when you make it dirty or untidy: *Don't mess up my dress; I've just ironed it.* [*same as* **muck up** (*informal*)] **2** You **mess** something **up** when you spoil or damage it: *This strike has really messed up our plans.* [*same as* **muck up** (*informal*), **foul up** (*informal*), **screw up** (*vulgar slang*)] **3** (*AmE*) Someone **messes up** when they make a mistake or do something badly: *This is your last chance; don't mess up.* [*same as* **foul up** (*informal*), **screw up** (*vulgar slang*)]
• *noun (informal)* **mess-up**
There is a **mess-up** when a mistake has been made or something has been done badly: *There was some mess-up over the billing of business calls.*

mess with (*informal*)
You **mess with** someone when you involve yourself in an argument or conflict with them: *the kind of violent man you wouldn't want to mess with.*

mete /miːt/: metes, meting, meted

mete out (*formal*)
To **mete out** punishment is to give it out: *Stricter sentences have been meted out to relatively minor offenders.* [compare **deal out, dole out, hand out**]

militate /ˈmɪlɪteɪt/: militates, militating, militated

militate against (*formal*)
A fact, event or situation **militates against** something happening or being successful when it is a disadvantage or drawback that is very likely to prevent it happening or being successful: *There's no reason why her age should militate against her finding another job.* [*same as* **go against, tell against**]

mill /mɪl/: mills, milling, milled

mill about *or* **mill around** (*informal*)
A crowd of people **are milling about** or **milling around** when they are moving idly about, especially when they are waiting for something to happen: *As early as six o'clock, bunches of devoted fans start milling around outside the gates.* [*same as* **hang about**]

mind /maɪnd/: minds, minding, minded

mind out (*informal*)
You say **mind out!** to someone to warn them to be careful: *Mind out! There's a car coming.* ❑ *You'll fall down that hole if you don't mind out.* [*same as* **watch out, look out**]

minister /ˈmɪnɪstə(r)/: ministers, ministering, ministered

minister to (*formal*)
You **minister to** people, or **minister to** their needs, when you provide the things they need or want: *Their mothers will continue to minister to their every need.* [*same as* **attend to, look after**]

miss /mɪs/: misses, missing, missed

miss out

You **miss** something **out** when you fail to include it or decide not to include it: *When I read through the form, I noticed that he'd missed out his date of birth.* ❑ *Have I missed anyone out?* [*same as* **leave out, omit**]

miss out on

You **miss out on** something that others enjoy when you don't receive it or don't take part in it: *You mustn't miss out on all the free food.* ❑ *I don't want my children to feel that they're missing out, not having the toys the others have.* [compare **lose out on**]

mist /mɪst/: mists, misting, misted

mist over *or* mist up

1 A glass surface **mists over** or **mists up** when it becomes covered with tiny drops of water, making it difficult for people to see through it: *It wasn't long before his glasses started misting over.* ❑ *The windscreen was misting up at such a rate that the blower couldn't clear it.* ❑ *The heat misted my spectacles up.* [*same as* **steam up, fog up**] **2** Your eyes **mist over** when they fill with tears, making it difficult for you to see clearly: *You see him mist over every time someone mentions it.* [compare **fill up, well up, cloud over**] **3** You can say that your mind or your brain **mists over** when you feel unable to think clearly: *Geoffrey's mind has a tendency to mist over when there is more than one thing to think about.* [*same as* **fog up**]

mistake /mɪ'steɪk/: mistakes, mistaking, mistaken

mistake for

You **mistake** one person or thing **for** another when you falsely believe that the one is the other: *She mistook my silence for disapproval.* ❑ *I'm sorry; I mistook you for a colleague of my wife's.* [*same as* **take for, take to be**; compare **mix up, muddle up**]

mix /mɪks/: mixes, mixing, mixed

mix in

1 You **mix** a substance **in** when you add it to another and combine the two to form a new substance: *When you've thoroughly mixed in the salt, mix the yeast and water in.* [*same as* **add in**; compare **blend in**] **2** You can say that someone **is mixing in** when they are involving themselves in the activities or discussions of others: *Why don't you mix in a bit and enjoy yourself?* [*same as* **join in, muck in** (*informal*), **pitch in** (*informal*), **participate**; *opposite* **stand apart, shy away**]

mix into

You **mix** one substance **into** another when you add it to the other and combine the two to form a new substance: *Mix the salt into the flour with your hands.*

mix up

1 You **mix up** two people or things when you identify them wrongly and think one is the other: *I always mix him up with his brother.* ❑ *Even now, after knowing them for years, I still sometimes get them mixed up.* [*same as* **muddle up**; compare **mistake for**] **2** You **mix** things **up** when you upset their usual or correct order, whether deliberately or by accident: *Your papers fell on the floor, and I may have mixed them up in retrieving them.* [*same as* **muddle up, jumble up**] **3** You **mix** something **up** when you prepare it by combining different ingredients: *Mix up another barrowload of concrete.* ❑ *Sheila mixed up a salt and lemon solution and soaked the area with it.* [*same as* **prepare**]

• *noun (informal)* **mix-up**: **mix-ups**
A **mix-up** is a mistake caused by confusion or misunderstanding: *There was a mix-up with the bags and our luggage was put on a different plane.*

• *adjective (informal)* **mixed up**
You can say that someone is **mixed up** if they are confused about what kind of person they are or how they should behave with others, usually because of

social or emotional problems in the past: *Sitting in a classroom with a bunch of mixed-up teenagers isn't my idea of fun.* [*same as* **screwed up**]

mix up in
You can use **mix up in** to describe someone's involvement in something, often a crime or other dishonest activity: *This is the kind of scandal that no government minister wants to get mixed up in.*

mix up with
You can use **mix up with** to describe someone's involvement with a group of people you disapprove of, *eg* criminals: *She'd got herself mixed up with a gang of thugs at school who were taking money off the younger pupils.* ❑ *Before you know it, you're getting mixed up with someone else's wife.*

mix with (*slang*)
You **mix** it **with** someone when you involve yourself in an argument or conflict with them: *They all know better than to mix it with Ray.* [compare **mess with**]

model /ˈmɒdəl/: **models, modelling** (*AmE* **modeling**), **modelled** (*AmE* **modeled**)

model on
1 You **model** one thing **on** another when you create it to be similar to the other, or develop it from the other: *The structure of degree courses here is modelled on the American universities.* [*same as* **base on, found on**] **2** You **model** yourself **on** someone you admire when you try to be like them: *I've tried to be an original singer, not modelling myself on anyone in particular.*

molder see **moulder**

monkey /ˈmʌŋkɪ/: **monkeys, monkeying, monkeyed**

monkey about *or* **monkey around** (*informal*)
Someone **monkeys about** or **monkeys around** when they enjoy behaving in a lively, silly way: *They should spend more time working and less time monkeying around on that bike.* [*same as* **fool about** (*informal*), **lark about** (*informal*)]

monkey about with *or* **monkey around with** (*informal*)
Someone who **monkeys about with** something, or **monkeys around with** it, treats it too casually, and foolishly disregards the harm they might cause or the danger they are exposed to: *That way there would be little temptation for the boys to go monkeying around with my chisels.* [*same as* **fool about with** (*informal*), **mess about with** (*informal*), **play about with**]

mooch /muːtʃ/: **mooches, mooching, mooched**

mooch about *or* **mooch around**
Someone who **mooches about** or **mooches around** somewhere moves around there feeling bored or lazy, without a definite aim or purpose: *She spends her days off mooching about the house in her nightie.* ❑ *Most of them just mooched around outside the pub, waiting for something to happen.* [*same as* **hang about, idle about**]

moon /muːn/: **moons, mooning, mooned**

moon about *or* **moon around**
Someone who **moons about** or **moons around** spends their time feeling rather sad or depressed and doing nothing: *I don't think I could face another weekend of Tom mooning about the house.* [*same as* **mope about**]

moon over
You **moon over** someone you are in love with when you spend your time doing nothing but think about them: *She's up in her room mooning over some boy at school.* [compare **swoon over**]

mop /mɒp/: **mops**, **mopping**, **mopped**

mop up

1 You **mop up** a liquid that has been spilt when you remove it using a cloth that it soaks into: *I'd mop it up before it stains the table.* [*same as* **wipe up**] **2** (*informal*) To **mop** someone **up** is to finally get rid of them by destroying or killing them, or defeating them in a battle or other contest: *You have visions of your children being mopped up by a forty-foot juggernaut.* ❑ *The Russians rolled into Berlin and mopped up what resistance they met within a matter of hours.*

mope /moʊp/: **mopes**, **moping**, **moped**

mope about *or* **mope around**

Someone who **mopes about** or **mopes around** spends their time feeling sad or depressed and doing nothing: *Moping around in the garden all morning isn't going to solve the problem.* [*same as* **moon about**]

moulder (*AmE* **molder**) /ˈmoʊldə(r)/: **moulders**, **mouldering**, **mouldered**

moulder away

Something that **is mouldering away** is rotting or decaying slowly: *A few bits of salad were mouldering away at the back of her fridge.* ❑ *She had a vision of herself mouldering away in some dark corner of local government.* [*same as* **rot away**]

mount /maʊnt/: **mounts**, **mounting**, **mounted**

mount up

Something **mounts up** when it increases in amount until there is a lot of it: *Our savings will soon mount up if we don't touch them.* [*same as* **build up, grow**]

mourn /mɔːn/: **mourns**, **mourning**, **mourned**

mourn for

1 You **mourn for** someone when you feel deep sorrow because they have died: *It's not until after the inquest that you feel you can really mourn for your lost loved one.* [*same as* **grieve for, weep for**] **2** You **mourn for** something when you feel very sad because you don't have or experience it any longer: *It does no good to mourn for the success of bygone years.* [compare **long for**]

mouth /maʊθ/: **mouths**, **mouthing**, **mouthed**

mouth off (*informal*)

Someone who **mouths off** gives their opinions in a loud or forceful way that irritates others: *I wasn't staying to listen to her mouthing off about the need for greater parental supervision.*

move /muːv/: **moves**, **moving**, **moved**

move about *or* **move around**

1 You **move about** or **move around** when you keep moving or changing your place or position: *I could hear someone moving about upstairs.* ❑ *He's another of these players who move around the court at lightning speed.* **2** You also **move about** or **move around** when you frequently move house or change your job: *She said she was fed up moving about and wanted to buy a house somewhere and settle down.* **3** You **move** something **about**, or **move** it **around**, when you move it from one place to another, usually several times: *If she couldn't sleep, my mum would move the furniture around a bit, to see what it looked like.* **4** A worker **is moved about** or **moved around** when their employer moves them to a different job, especially more than once: *They move us around at will, creating vacancies that the high-flyers can fill.*

move along

1 A police officer or other person in authority tells someone to **move along** as an order to leave the place they are standing or sitting in: *The gathering crowds were moved along by police.* [*same as* **move on**] **2** You **move along** when you move to a position further along something such as a road or a row of theatre seats: *If we all move along a bit there would be room for another one on the end.* [compare **move up**] **3** You can say that something **is moving along** when it is making good progress: *They're fairly moving along with the new library extension; it'll be finished for Easter.* [compare **come along**]

move around see move about and move round

move away

1 To **move away** is to leave, or to go away; you **move** something **away** when you put it in a place away from where it was before: *I tried to move quietly away before the discussion turned to religion.* ❑ *Move away from the desk and keep your hands in the air.* ❑ *She went to grab me but I moved my arm away.* [compare **slip away**] **2** You **move away** when you go and live in a different place, away from where you lived before: *There's the usual grief when your kids' best pals move away to a different town.*

move away from

You **move away from** things such as opinions or beliefs when you no longer have or support them: *The younger members sought to move away from traditional forms.* [*opposite* **move towards**]

move down

1 To **move down** is to go from a higher place to a lower one; to **move** something **down** is to change its place or position to a lower one: *These books could be moved down a couple of shelves to make room for the CDs.* **2** To **move down** is also to move to a position that is lower on a scale: *Everton have moved down to fourth place, behind Manchester United.* ❑ *She had very poor exam results in second year and was moved down a class.* **3** You can say that you **move down** when you go to a place that is further south, especially to live or settle there: *Her sister is moving down to London with the Bank.* **4** A level, value or standard **moves down** when it becomes lower: *Oil prices have moved steadily down since the May crisis.* [*same as* **come down**, **go down**, **fall**]

move in

1 You **move in** when you start to live in a new or different house: *We get the keys on Friday and will begin moving in at the weekend.* [*opposite* **move out**; compare **settle in**] **2** Someone **moves in** with you when they come to live in your home: *Then she told us her boyfriend wanted to move in.* **3** People who **move in** arrive in order to take action or take control: *The order was given and officers with riot shields moved in.* ❑ *Rival ice-cream sellers moved in on each other's territory.* **4** To **move in** on someone is to approach them in order to attack them: *The boys moved in on him from all sides.* ❑ *Interviewers like Humphries soften you up a bit before they move in for the kill.* [*same as* **close in**]

move into

1 You **move into** a new or different house or area when you start to live there: *A few younger couples with kids had moved into the street.* [*opposite* **move out**] **2** You **move** someone or something **into** a place when you put them in that place: *We could always move the bookcase from the dining room into the hall.* ❑ *They had moved troops into the demilitarized zone and broken the terms of the Easter agreement.* **3** To **move into** a particular activity is to start to be involved in it: *From a low-key acting career they can move right into the pop business and be millionaires within months.* ❑ *They move from trading gas and telecom shares into risky stuff like futures.* **4**

To **move into** a place is to arrive there in order to take action or take control: *Mounted police moved into the park to disperse the crowds.*

move off

A vehicle **moves off** when it starts moving after being stationary: *Don't move off until I've got the children safely strapped in.* [compare **set off**]

move on

1 You **move on** when, after stopping or staying for a while, you leave, often to continue a journey: *No job could keep her for longer than a year; she would get itchy feet and feel it was time to move on.* ❑ *We packed up the trailer and moved on down the coast to Montpelier.* [compare **carry on, go on**] **2** You **move on** from one thing to the next when you stop doing one thing, or finish doing it, and begin dealing with the next: *Moving on to the question of the concert, we still need volunteers to sell tickets.* [*same as* **go on**] **3** A police officer or other person in authority **moves** you **on** when they order you to leave the place you are standing or sitting in: *A bloke in a uniform said we had to move on.* [*same as* **move along**] **4** You **move on** when you change to something, *eg* a job or a house, that is better than the one you had before: *If he does well, they might move him on to a sales position.* ❑ *He moved on from a late-night slot on Radio Stoke to a high-profile show on national radio.* [*same as* **progress**] **5** Things such as ideas and methods **move on** when they become more modern or more advanced: *Surgical techniques have moved on astonishingly fast in the last five years.* **6** You can say that time **moves on** when it passes, often suggesting that it seems to pass quickly: *We'd better order the dress soon; time is moving on.*

move on to *or* move onto

You **move on to** something, or **move onto** it, when you begin dealing with or discussing it as the next subject: *Moving on to the issue of funding, I think we all realise that much work needs to be done in tightening up budgets.*

move out

1 You **move out** when you leave your house to go and live elsewhere: *We're moving out of the flat in April.* ❑ *They've moved out of this area altogether.* **2** People **are moved out** of a place when they are taken from it or ordered to leave: *We will not be satisfied until the British government moves its troops out of Northern Ireland.* **3** To **move out** of a particular activity or business is to stop being involved in it: *It seemed prudent at the time to move out of sheet metal products altogether.* ❑ *We were certainly taking risks picking up our share of the market at a time when all the big companies were moving out.* [*opposite* **move in, move into**]

move over

1 Something **moves over** a surface when it goes across it: *We watched the shadows moving slowly over the hills.* **2** You ask someone to **move over** when you want them to change their position to make space for you to sit or lie next to them: *Move over a bit; I'm falling off the edge of the bed.* [compare **move along, move up**] **3** Someone who tells you to **move over** wants to take your place and do what you've been doing: *It's time for the old boys like me to move over and make way for younger players.* [*same as* **step aside, step down**]

move over to

You can use **move over to** to describe changes to something new or different: *We are considering moving over to the metric system favoured by our European partners.*

move round *or* move around

You **move round** something, or **move around** it, when you move or travel past it along a circular course, or when you keep circling it: *He sprang up and moved round the table towards me, his fists clenched.* ❑ *Who was it who discovered that the Earth moves round the Sun?* [see also **move about**]

move towards

1 You **move towards** something when you approach it: *It was only when he moved towards me that I noticed his eyes were different colours.* **2** You can also say that you **move towards** something when you come closer to achieving it, supporting it or agreeing to it: *They're moving towards the French position on nuclear testing.* ❑ *We seem to be moving towards a solution of the oil crisis.* [opposite **move away from**]

move up

1 People in a row or line **move up** when they move so that they are standing or sitting more closely together, usually so as to make room for others: *If we all moved up a little Phil could get on the end.* [*same as* **move along**; compare **move over**] **2** You **move up** or **are moved up** when you progress to a higher grade, rank, level or position: *He moves up to the senior school next term.* ❑ *If he's moved up a class now, he'll only be sixteen in his final year.* **3** A level, standard or value **moves up** when it rises or increases: *The pound has moved up half a cent against the dollar.* **4** Something **moves up** when it moves to a higher position: *She watched an ant move slowly up a tree, carrying a twig three times its size.* ❑ *Move the middle picture up a bit, in the line with the other two.* **5** You **move up** when you move to a position from which you are ready to take action or make an attack: *Two further divisions have been moved up to reinforce the eastern front.*

mow /mou/: mows, mowing, mowed, mown *or* mowed

Large numbers of people **are mowed down** or **mown down** when they are killed violently in a single incident: *Then some lunatic with a machine gun mows down a trainload of commuters.* [*same as* **cut down, slaughter, massacre**]

muck /mʌk/: mucks, mucking, mucked

muck about *or* muck around

(*informal*)

1 Someone **mucks about** or **mucks around** when they behave in a silly way: *He got told off by the teacher for mucking about in class.* [*same as* **mess about** (*informal*), **fool about** (*informal*)] **2** (*informal*) When you **muck** someone **about**, or **muck** them **around**, you treat them badly or unfairly: *He feels he's been mucked about enough already.* [*same as* **mess about**]

muck in (*informal*)

Several people **muck in** when they all work together to achieve something: *We might as well muck in with the rest of them.* [compare **chip in, pitch in**]

muck out

You **muck out** a place where animals are kept when you clean it; you can also say that you **muck** the animals **out**: *It was Sally's job to muck out the pigs.* ❑ *One of the lads from the village comes in at weekends to muck the stables out.*

muck up (*informal*)

1 You **muck** something **up** when you do it very badly and fail at it: *She thinks she's mucked up her exams.* [*same as* **mess up** (*informal*), **foul up** (*informal*), **cock up** (*vulgar slang*)] **2** You can also say you **muck** something **up** when you get it dirty: *Watch what you're doing; you'll muck up my dress.*

muddle /ˈmʌdəl/: muddles, muddling, muddled

muddle along

You **muddle along** when your life or work follows a confused and unplanned course from one event to the next: *We* *can't go on like this, muddling along from one crisis to the next.*

muddle through
You **muddle through** when you succeed in spite of foolish mistakes or lack of organization: *Things will certainly not go as smoothly in practice, but we'll muddle through to the end.*

muddle up
1 You **muddle up** two people or things when you identify them wrongly and think one is the other: *They're so similar in so many ways, it's understandable that people keep muddling them up.* [*same as* **mix up**; compare **mistake for**] **2** You **muddle** things **up** when you upset their usual or correct order, whether deliberately or by accident: *We muddle names and faces up and panel members have to match them up again.* [*same as* **jumble up**]

muffle /'mʌfəl/: muffles, muffling, muffled

You **muffle** yourself **up** when you wrap a thick, heavy scarf or other covering round your neck to keep warm: *Even on hot days, she keeps the kids muffled up in cardigans and hats.* [*same as* **wrap up**; compare **cover up**]

mug /mʌg/: mugs, mugging, mugged

mug up (*informal*)
You **mug up** a subject of study, or you **mug up** on it, when you try to learn as much about it as you can in the short time available, usually in preparation for an exam: *I'll spend the week before the test mugging up my Highway Code.* [*same as* **swot up**]

mull /mʌl/: mulls, mulling, mulled

mull over
You **mull** something **over** when you spend time thinking about it carefully: *I sat down to mull over what she had said.*

multiply /'mʌltɪplaɪ/: multiplies, multiplying, multiplied

multiply out
People sometimes say they **multiply out** two numbers when they multiply them: *Take the first and the last figures and multiply them out.*

muscle /'mʌsəl/: muscles, muscling, muscled

muscle in
You **muscle in** when you forcefully involve yourself in something that does not concern you, or take a share of something that you have no right to: *We didn't want the parents muscling in on our plans.* [*same as* **interfere in**, **butt in**]

muscle out
Someone who **is muscled out** of a position or job is forced to leave by someone who uses unkind or unfair methods: *Colleagues she had trusted muscled her out of the chairmanship when they heard the news.*

muse /mjuːz/: muses, musing, mused

muse on *or* muse over
You **muse on** something, especially something that is pleasant and not very serious, or you **muse over** it, when you spend time thinking about it: *Students sit on the terrace musing on the fate of their respective essays.*

muss /mʌs/: musses, mussing, mussed

muss up (*informal*)
Your hair or clothing **is mussed up** when it is disarranged and looks untidy: *She didn't go out into the garden in case the wind mussed her new hairdo up.*

muster /'mʌstə(r)/: musters, mustering, mustered

muster up
You **muster up** qualities such as

strength or patience when you try to find within yourself as much of it as you can, in order to deal with a situation: *I was hoping I would be able to muster up enough courage to tell her what I really thought.* [*same as* **summon up**]

n

naff /naf/: **naffs**, **naffing**, **naffed**

naff off (*informal*)

If someone tells you to **naff off** they are telling you very rudely to go away and stop bothering them: *He hid his face behind a newspaper and told the paparazzi to naff off.* ❑ *No-one seemed to want me there so I just naffed off.* [compare **sod off, piss off**]

nag /nag/: **nags**, **nagging**, **nagged**

nag at

1 Someone who **nags at** you repeatedly finds fault with you or criticizes you for doing, or not doing, something that they think you shouldn't, or should, have done: *She's been nagging at me for months to fix the hinge on the garden gate.* [*same as* **go on at** (*informal*), **keep on at, harp on**] **2** A thought or suspicion **nags at** you when you keep thinking or worrying about it; a pain **nags at** you when it is there all the time: *The thought went on nagging at me until I just had to talk to someone about it.* ❑ *There it was, that thought again, nagging at the back of his mind. Had she gone to meet her lover?* ❑ *A dull toothachy pain nagged at him and made him especially irritable.*

nail /neɪl/: **nails**, **nailing**, **nailed**

nail down

1 You **nail** something **down** when you fasten it with nails so that it cannot be moved or opened: *You'll need a hammer, of course, for all those jobs like driving in picture pins and nailing down loose floorboards.* ❑ *They'll steal anything that isn't nailed down, you know.* **2** If you have been unable to find someone, or they have been unwilling to give you clear and accurate information about something, and you **nail** them **down,** you succeed in finding them, or you get them to give you the information you want: *Eventually, after chasing around for three days we managed to nail him down in the Newcastle office.* ❑ *Don't let the minister off the hook; nail him down and make him answer the question directly.* [*same as* **pin down**] **3** (*informal*) You can **nail** something **down** if you are able to say exactly what it is or describe it precisely: *There's something distinctly odd about Joe, but it's difficult to nail down precisely what it is.* [*same as* **pin down**]

nail up

1 You **nail** something **up** when you fix it to an upright surface with nails: *On 21 October 1517, Martin Luther nailed up his Ninety Five Articles of Religion on the door of Wittenberg Cathedral.* **2** Something such as a door **is nailed up** when it is secured with nails to prevent it being opened easily: *The shutters had been nailed up long ago and the room was dark and airless.*

name /neɪm/: **names**, **naming**, **named**

name after

A child **is named after** another person when they are given the same first or Christian name as that other person, often as a way of showing respect or affection for them; something **is named after** someone or something when it is given the same name as that person or thing: *They named the baby after her mother's father.* ❑ *Peter is named after his maternal grandfather.* ❑ *Behind the apse of the Duomo the visitor passes the Palazzo dell'Orologio, named after the clock at the top.* ❑ *Thrushcross Grange, named after the mansion in Wuthering Heights.* [*same as* **call after**]

name for

Name for is mainly used in American English and means the same as **name after**: *He was named for John Edward Grant, his maternal grandfather.* ❑ *the Hoover Dam, named for Herbert Hoover.*

narrow /'narou/: narrows, narrowing, narrowed

narrow down

When you **narrow down** a number of choices or possibilities, you reduce their number so that you are left with only those that are most likely or most appropriate: *The police have narrowed down the number of possible suspects to two.* ❑ *This one is too expensive, and this one is shoddy-looking. That narrows the choice down a bit.* [*same as* **restrict**]

nestle /'nɛsəl/: nestles, nestling, nestled

nestle up

You **nestle up** to someone when you move close to them and press your body against theirs, especially for warmth or comfort: *The puppies nestled up to their mother's warm body.* ❑ *She put her head on his shoulder and nestled up close to him.* [*same as* **cuddle up, snuggle up**]

nibble /'nɪbəl/: nibbles, nibbling, nibbled

nibble at

1 An animal **nibbles at** something when it takes small bites off it: *a mouse nibbling at a piece of cheese.* **2** You **nibble at** your food when you eat only a little of it, or eat only small mouthfuls, usually because you have no appetite: *She nibbled unenthusiastically at a dry biscuit.* [*same as* **peck at, pick at**]

nip /nɪp/: nips, nipping, nipped

nip off (*informal*)

You **nip off**, or **nip off** somewhere, when you leave in a hurry: *They're nipping off to a health farm for the weekend, leaving the children with the nanny.* ❑ *The little devil nipped off as soon as my back was turned.*

nip out (*informal*)

People often say that they **are nipping out**, or **are nipping out** somewhere, when they are going out for a short time: *Fred isn't here; he's just nipped out for a moment.* ❑ *I'm just nipping out to the chemist for a bottle of shampoo.* [*same as* **pop out**]

nod /nɒd/: nods, nodding, nodded

nod off (*informal*)

You **nod off** when you go to sleep, especially without intending to and when you are somewhere other than in bed: *'Would you like to lie down, lass? You were just about to nod off there.'* ❑ *I settled down in a pew at the back and nodded off.* [*same as* **doze off, drop off** (*informal*)]

nose /nouz/: nose, nosing, nosed

nose about *or* nose around (*informal*)

You **nose about** in a place, or you **nose around** or **round**, especially somewhere where you shouldn't be or haven't been invited to, when you look for something there or simply look around because you are curious: *There's someone I don't know nosing about in the lane.* ❑ *The landlady came in to tell him there was a private detective nosing around yesterday.* [*same as* **poke**

about, **snoop**]

nose out
When someone **noses** hidden or secret information **out** they discover it after a careful or determined search in places where no-one else has looked or thought of looking: *It's guaranteed that some Fleet Street hack will nose out what we've been up to and splash it all over the newspapers.* [*same as* **root out**, **smell out**, **sniff out**, **uncover**]

nose round see **nose about**

notch /nɒtʃ/: notches, notching, notched

notch up (*informal*)
You **notch up** a particular score when you gain that number of points; people also talk about someone **notching up** a win or victory when that person has gained or achieved it, especially if they have had several wins or victories in succession: *Jim proceeded to notch up his 500th League appearance against Birmingham on 18th October.* ❑ *A number of pilots in the squadron had notched up 70 or more sorties.* [*same as* **chalk up** (*informal*), **rack up** (*informal*), **attain** (*formal*)]

note /nout/: notes, noting, noted

note down
You **note down** something, or you **note** it **down**, when you write it quickly on paper, often in an abbreviated form, so that you can refer to it later: *A couple of pressmen were following him, noting down everything he said.* ❑ *I'm just noting down the registration number of that car.* ❑ *Are you noting this down?* [*same as* **jot down**, **take down**, **write down**]

number /ˈnʌmbə(r)/: numbers, numbering, numbered

number among
Someone or something **is numbered among** a particular group or category of people or things when they are included or considered as one of that group or category: *I number Joseph among my most intimate friends.* ❑ *He's numbered among a small group of international statesmen who might be expected to bring the negotations to a successful conclusion.* [*same as* **count among**]

nurse /nɜːs/: nurses, nursing, nursed

nurse through
Someone **nurses** you **through** an illness when they look after you until you recover, *eg* by giving you the medicine or treatment you need, keeping you warm and watching over you at night: *She stayed with him and nursed him through a particularly rough bout of malaria.*

O

object /əb'dʒɛkt/: **objects**, **objecting**, **objected**

object to
Someone **objects to** something when they say that they do not like it or do not approve of it: *I honestly didn't think they would object to my marrying Madeleine on the grounds of my birth.* ❑ *What they objected to was the cut in the standard rate of benefit.* ❑ *The staff strongly objected to this arrangement, yet it went ahead.* [*same as* **raise objections to**]

oblige /ə'blaɪdʒ/: **obliges**, **obliging**, **obliged**

oblige with (*rather old*)
When someone asks you if you could or would **oblige** them **with** something they are asking you politely if you will give it to them: *Please be good enough to oblige me with an immediate response to this letter.*

occur /ə'kɜː(r)/: **occurs**, **occurring**, **occurred**

occur to
A thought or idea **occurs to** you when you think of it or it comes into your mind: *That I might be too old simply didn't occur to me. I feel the same as I did when I was 30.* ❑ *It was so simple she wondered why the idea hadn't occurred to her before.* ❑ *The first thing that occurs to me, frankly, is that you must be a saint to put up with it.* [*same as* **enter your head, cross your mind**]

of see panel on next page

off see panel on next page

offcut /'ɒfkʌt/ see **cut off**

offend /ə'fɛnd/: **offends**, **offending**, **offended**

offend against
A particular action or type of behaviour **offends against** an established code, rule or principle when it breaks or goes against that code, rule or principle: *The obvious answer is to fuse national insurance with income tax, but that would offend against the notion that national insurance is 'contributory'.*

offer /'ɒfə(r)/: **offers**, **offering**, **offered**

offer up
1 To **offer up** a prayer or sacrifice is to pray to God or make a sacrifice to Him: *Lord, we offer up this prayer to Thee.*
2 When you **offer up** something to someone you present it to them: *He even attempted to reduce the troublesome rat population on the island by having them killed, dressed and offered up to his tenants and workmen to eat.*

off-putting /ɒf'pʊtɪŋ/ see **put off**

onlooker /'ɒnlʊkə(r)/ see **look on**

of /ɒv/ *or* /əv/

Of is a preposition.

It is a very common word in English and is used to show various relationships between things. When combined with verbs it often has very little meaning except to show the connection between the verb + preposition and the noun or noun phrase that follows. It is sometimes used to show what something is made from or made up of. For example, you can say that a committee **is composed of** politicians from various parties when its members are drawn from various political parties. In formal English, the usual meaning of certain verbs is changed when they are followed by **of.** For example, **admit of, allow of**, and **permit of** all have similar meanings relating to the possibilities of the situation being referred to, as in the following examples: *His reluctance to defend himself against the accusation admits of no other interpretation but that he is guilty.* ❑ *Michael's strict moral code would allow of no compromise with those whose actions he deemed to be wrong.* ❑ *Our present difficulties permit of no freedom to act as we might otherwise have chosen to do.*

1 CAUSE OR ORIGIN

Of is used to show that the thing referred to is the cause or origin of a particular situation. For example, someone **dies of** hunger when lack of food is the cause of their death; and, a situation **born of** a particular event or set of circumstances comes about because of it, as in the following example: *The alliance of America, Russia and Britain was born of dire necessity.*

2 COMMUNICATION AND INTERPRETATION

Of is used with another group of verbs that have to do with communication and interpretation of information and knowledge. For example, what someone **says of** you is what they say about you; you **apprise** someone **of** something when you inform them about it; you **assure** someone **of** something when you make them feel certain about it; and, when someone asks you what you **make of** something they want to know what interpretation you have put on it.

3 QUALITY OR CHARACTERISTIC

Other verbs with **of** indicate that someone or something has a stated quality or characteristic. For example, if someone **reeks of** perfume, the smell of perfume coming from them is very strong and overpowering; and, when you say that someone's behaviour or attitude **smacks of** complacency or some other unacceptable quality, you mean that their behaviour or attitude has that quality.

4 REMOVAL

Of is also used in some phrasal verbs to show that something is removed, taken away or kept from the person concerned. For example, someone **is stripped of** their rank when it is removed, often because they have abused it; someone **is starved of** affection when they are not given the affection they need or want; and, someone **robs** you **of** something when they steal it from you.

off /ɒf/

Off is an adverb and a preposition.

Off has several meanings when used in phrasal verbs. Its basic meaning, of which the other meanings are extensions, is of movement away or departure.

1 MOVING AWAY OR LEAVING

Off is used in its literal sense to suggest leaving or departure: for example, you **set off** when you begin a journey; a vehicle **moves off** when it begins to move away from the place where it has been stationary for a time; and, a plane **takes off** when it leaves the ground. It also has this meaning in many non-literal combinations. For example, to **waltz off** means to move away in a carefree and casual way; and, if a vehicle **roars off** it leaves with its engine making a loud noise. **Away** is sometimes used instead of **off** in phrasal verbs with this sense;

continued on next page

for example, **run off** and **run away** have more or less the same meaning. The following are some more examples of literal and non-literal combinations with this meaning: *The kids ran off* (or *away*), embarrassed. ❑ *He walked away, thrusting the swing door out of his way, and striding off down the corridor.* ❑ *He stormed off to his dressing room.* ❑ *She leapt off her chair as though a firecracker had gone off underneath her.*

2 MOVEMENT FROM A HIGHER TO A LOWER POSITION

Off is also used in combinations that have the same basic meaning of movement away, but in the more specific sense of movement from a higher position to reach a lower position. For example, you **get off** a bus when you alight from it; you **get off** a horse when you dismount; and, you **jump off** a wall when you get down from it by jumping. Other combinations with this sense include **fall off**, **slide off**, **slip off**, and **step off**, as in the following example: *As he stepped off the pavement to cross the side street, he felt he was stepping off a cliff.*

3 DECREASING, LESSENING OR DECLINING

Off is also combined with verbs to indicate that the intensity or volume of something goes down or declines. For example, you **cool off** when you become less warm or less angry, and the wind **slackens off** when it gradually blows less and less strongly. It is also used in a non-literal sense to show that something's quality has declined. For example, food **goes off** when it becomes unfit to eat; you **go off** someone or something when you stop feeling enthusiastic about, or friendly towards them; and, the effect of a drug or alcohol **wears off** when it gradually becomes less and less and finally disappears. **Away** can be substituted for **off** in certain combinations with this sense; for example, you can say that the level of attendance at, or support for, something **falls off** or **falls away** when fewer and fewer people attend or support it.

4 SEPARATING OR BLOCKING

Off can also refer to actions or states in which things are separated from others by putting up a barrier or creating a blockage or division of some kind. Thus, you **partition off** part of a room when you separate it from the rest of the room by putting up a partition. Phrasal verbs with this meaning are often formed by combining a verb that is more usually used as a noun with **off**, as in *cordon off*, *cone off*, *bollard off* and *hive off*. The following are some examples of phrasal verbs with this sense: *The vegetable plot was divided off from the rest of the garden by a trellis covered with climbing roses.* ❑ *Oxford Street and nearby Maddox Street were cordoned off following warnings of bombs.* ❑ *It is quite common to see mile upon mile of pristine tarmac bollarded off for no apparent reason at all.* ❑ *Responsibility for various specific public services is hived off to a range of special agencies.*

5 STOPPING OR PREVENTING

In another sense, **off** indicates that the action is one of preventing an attack of some sort, or protecting yourself or others from something unpleasant by doing something to stop it or get rid of it. For example, you **fight** an attacker **off** when you fight back so that they are forced to stop attacking you; and, you **stave off** hunger pangs when you eat something to stop yourself feeling hungry. Other phrasal verbs with this sense include **head off** and **hold off**, and more are shown in the following examples: *Later, loaves were marked with a cross to ward off evil spirits that might prevent the bread from rising.* ❑ *Once the body's system has beaten off the disease, it builds some resistance against it.*

6 REMOVING, ELIMINATING OR DISPOSING

Off is used in another group of phrasal verbs to emphasize that someone or something is completely removed, often using some degree of force. For example, you **break** something **off** when you remove it from the place where it was attached, and, you **scrape** paint **off** when you remove it from a surface by scraping at it with a sharp-edged tool. Someone **is pensioned off** when they are removed from their job or post, but are paid a pension by their employer; and, someone **makes off** with something that does not belong to them when they secretly take it away with them. There are many literal combinations with this sense, such as **chop off**, **scrub off**, **shear off**, **wash off**; and, **cross off** and **suck off**, as in the following examples: *I cross off each day on the calendar when I go to bed, and lie there and think of you.* ❑ *I think it's best to suck it off with one of these tiny battery-powered vacuum cleaners.*

This general meaning of removing or getting rid of something is extended in a small group of more idiomatic phrasal verbs. For example, to **bump** someone **off** is to murder them; and, someone **is carted off** when they are taken away by force or against their will.

7 BEGINNING OR STARTING

Combinations with this meaning show that something is beginning, or something causes it to start happening. Thus, you **lead off** when you do something first and others follow; and, a golfer **tees off** when they begin the round by hitting the first ball. Other combinations with this sense include **trigger off**, **spark off** and **kick off**, as in the following examples: *It triggered off a savings and loan crisis in Maryland in 1985.* ❑ *The case sparked off an intense national debate about the safety of children in private nurseries.* ❑ *He kicked off the discussion by asking everyone what they thought of the council's policy.*

8 ENDING, STOPPING, DISCONNECTING AND CANCELLING

Other combinations with **off** indicate or imply that something is ended or cancelled, or, it is disconnected from something. Phrasal verbs with this sense are often formed, especially in informal speech or writing. For example, someone or something **turns** you **off** when their behaviour makes you feel less enthusiastic or excited; and, you tell someone to **leave off** when you want them to stop doing something. You **call** an event **off** when you cancel it, and you **switch** an electrical appliance **off** when you operate a switch so that the power is disconnected and it stops working. Many combinations with this sense have an opposite meaning when **on** is substituted for **off**. The following are some more examples of phrasal verbs with this sense: *He broke off* [= stopped speaking], *apparently only to finish his drink.* ❑ *Georgia had broken off all official relations with the USSR.* ❑ *The explosion may have destroyed the controls in which case, I imagine, the engines shut off automatically.* ❑ *From the time of his marriage, he cut himself off entirely from his brother.* ❑ *The England game was rained off.* [= cancelled because it was raining]

9 FINALITY OR COMPLETENESS

Off is also used as an intensifier in combinations such as **kill off**, **finish off**, and **sell off** suggesting that actions have finality or completeness. For example, you **pay off** a loan when you repay all the money that you owe to the lender, usually by paying the final instalment. The following are more examples of phrasal verbs using **off** in this way: *A cream tea was the perfect way to round off a fabulous week's walking on the South West Coast Path.* ❑ (*informal*) *He's on course for his best scoring season yet with his goal that killed off Watford.*

10 REJECTING, DISMISSING, OR IGNORING

Off can also imply that the action is one of rejecting, dismissing or ignoring. It is sometimes used to form phrasal verbs with this meaning. For example, you **yawn** something **off** when you dismiss it or disregard it because you find it boring or unoriginal, as in: *This continuous assault on the senses could easily be yawned off as nothing new.*

More commonly used combinations with this sense include **brush off**, **shrug off**, **write off** and **laugh off**, as in the following examples: *Aunt Lucy would not take her back, Polly knew; she had shrugged Polly off.* ❑ *Commonsense would tell her it's unlikely to be written off as another accident.*

11 PUBLIC DISPLAY OR ATTENTION-SEEKING

Off is also used in some, often derogatory, phrasal verbs to suggest that the main aim of the action is getting other people's attention. For example, someone **shows off** when they deliberately

continued on next page

make a public display of themselves or what they see as their talents; and, someone **mouths off** or **sounds off** when they express their opinion too loudly and forcefully, in a way that other people find objectionable.

12 ABSENT FROM WORK OR SCHOOL
Off is used in another sense to show that someone is absent from work, because they are ill or on holiday, or, they are deliberately avoiding work or school. Most phrasal verbs with this sense are informal; for example, someone **skives off** when they avoid doing the work that they ought to be doing; and, a pupil **dogs off** or **bunks off** school or classes when they are absent without permission or are playing truant.

13 AVOIDING HEAVY PUNISHMENT
You **get off**, or someone **gets** you **off**, with a light sentence or punishment, when you avoid, or they help you avoid, a heavier sentence or punishment for a crime that you have committed, as in these examples: *You'll get off with a caution or three months community work.* ❑ *We're hoping he gets off with a very light sentence.* **Let off** has a similar meaning: *He was let off with a fine.*

14 USING OR CONSUMING
Phrasal verbs such as **dine off** and **live off** indicate that someone or something is used as a source of food, energy or power, or as a means of existence or survival. For example, people **live off** the land when they get their food and other things they need to survive from the things that grow or can be found in the countryside; and, you **sponge off** someone else when you get them to provide you with what you need without doing, or giving them, anything in return. Phrasal verbs with this sense can also refer to the fuel that is used to provide power for a machine or vehicle, so that a machine or system that **runs off** the mains gets its power from the mains electricity. **On** may be substituted for **off** in most combinations with this sense.

15 GETTING RID OF OR TAKING, USING DECEPTION OR DISHONESTY
Off is used in a number of non-literal combinations that suggest that deception or dishonesty is used to get rid of a person or thing, or to take something from someone. For example, you **fob** someone **off** when you give them something other than the thing they asked for or expected, in order to get rid of them; someone **rips** you **off** when they cheat you out of something that is rightfully yours; and, someone is **palmed off** with something inferior when they are given it instead of what they might reasonably have expected to be given, as in: *Usually he got palmed off with the Mile End Road, stabbings in Chinatown, opium dens; you name it, Stich was put on the case.*

16 FALLING ASLEEP
Off is used in several phrasal verbs whose meaning has to do with the transition from a waking to a sleeping state. For example, you **get off**, or **get off** to sleep, when you manage to fall asleep, often after a spell when you were finding it difficult to sleep. Other phrasal verbs with this sense are shown in the following examples: *She finally drifted off to sleep about 2 am.* ❑ *'Tell me how the film ended. I dozed off half way through.'*

17 EXPLODING OR FIRING
Off is also used when referring to actions concerning firearms or other explosive devices, so that when you **set off** a firework you light the touchpaper so that it explodes; and, a rocket **blasts off** when the explosive force of its fuel igniting forces it up and away from its launching site. A bomb **goes off** when it explodes, and a gun **goes off** when it fires a bullet or cartridge, as in the following example: *The case for the defence was that the revolver went off accidentally.*

on see panel on next pages

onto see panel on pages 235 and 236

on /ɒn/

On is an adverb and a preposition.
It is used in a great many phrasal verbs, both in its literal sense and in non-literal senses. Its basic meaning has to do with place or position. It is also combined with many rather formal verbs to indicate that the noun or noun phrase that follows is the thing that is connected to or affected by the action of the verb, as in **confer on**, **devolve on**, **enlarge on**, **ponder on**, **impinge on**, **reflect on**, and **touch on**. **Upon** can be substituted for **on** in many combinations of this kind, some of which are shown in the following examples: *Hopefully, it'll give some severely disabled people a means of getting out of the bath without having to rely on another person.* ❑ *powers which impinge on the citizen's ordinary rights* ❑ *It conferred on certain military commanders administrative and judicial powers.* ❑ *The discussion was of a general nature and we only touched on the subject of prisons.*

1 PLACE OR POSITION
On is combined with many verbs that refer to place or position or movement to a particular place or position. It often indicates that direct contact is made with something, usually from above. For example, you **rest** your head **on** someone's shoulder when you bring your head into contact with that person's shoulder; something **is placed on** a table when it is put there; you **lie on** a bed when you stretch your body in a horizontal position on top of it; something that has been travelling or falling through the air **lands on** something if that is where it comes to rest; a bird **perches on** a branch when it sits or comes to rest there; and, you **step on** something when you bring your foot down on top of it. **On** is also used in combinations that indicate that the action referred to is directed towards a particular thing or place. For example, you **focus on** a particular thing when that is what you look at or pay particular attention to; soldiers or the police **fire on** someone or something when they fire their guns in their direction; you **look on** when you watch something happening but don't get involved in the action; and, someone **fixates on** someone or something when they become unhealthily obsessed with or emotionally attached to that person or thing. Some phrasal verbs with this meaning have both literal and non-literal senses. For example, you **sit on** something when you rest your bottom on top of it; but, if you say that someone **is sitting on** something they ought to be dealing with, you mean that they are deliberately delaying dealing with it.

2 IN OR INTO A VEHICLE, SHIP OR AIRCRAFT
Some phrasal verbs with **on** refer specifically to movement to a position inside or on top of a vehicle. Thus, you **get on** a bus or plane when you move inside it so that it can carry you to the place you want to go to; and, a plane or ship **takes on** fuel or supplies when fuel or supplies are transferred on board. Other combinations with this meaning include **hop on**, **jump on**, **pile on** and **climb on**, as in the following examples: *She hopped on a Tube train.* ❑ *One of the men tried to jump on board, but the Jeep was travelling too fast.* ❑ *Jumping on her bike, Brenda pedalled away furiously.* ❑ *He put on the helmet and climbed on the pillion.*

3 CONTINUING
On is used with many verbs to indicate that the action continues beyond a certain point or for an extended period of time. New phrasal verbs with this sense are often created in both British and American English. Examples of commonly used phrasal verbs with this sense include **work on**, **follow on**, and **get on**: so that, you **work on** when you continue to work, especially after the time when you would normally have finished for the day; one thing **follows on** from another when the second thing comes after the first, especially as a natural progression from the first; and, if someone says they must **get on** they mean that they must continue with their journey or with the work they have to do and cannot be delayed any longer. Some combinations with this sense are more idiomatic in meaning. For example, you **carry on** when you con-

continued on next page

tinue with something that you have been doing before; and, people sometimes say that someone **is wittering on** when that person has been talking for a long time about things that are unimportant, irrelevant, or of no interest to their listeners. Some combinations suggest that the action of continuing or progressing is very slow or difficult, as in **plod on**, **struggle on**, **battle on**, and **soldier on**. For example, if something **drags on** it continues for too long; and, if someone who is dying **lingers on** they take a longer than expected time to die.

4 ENCOURAGING TO CONTINUE OR GO FORWARD

On is combined with certain verbs to show the action referred to is one of encouraging someone to go forward or continue with some course of action. You say **'come on!'** to someone to encourage them to do something they are slow or reluctant to do; you **are spurred on** by something when it gives you the incentive to make a greater effort to reach your goal or achieve what you are aiming for; people **cheer** someone **on** when they shout loudly to encourage them; and, someone **leads** you **on** when their actions are intended to encourage you to continue with something, even though you know that it might be wrong to do so.

5 DRESSING

On is used in several phrasal verbs that have to do with the action of dressing, such as **put on** and **pull on**. For example, if you can't **get** some item of clothing **on** you aren't able to fit part of your body into it *eg* because your movements are restricted by disability or your body is too large to fit it; and, you **throw** clothes **on** when you put them on carelessly, usually because you are in a hurry.

6 ATTACHING, FASTENING OR ADDING

On is also used to form phrasal verbs that indicate or suggest that something is attached or fastened securely to something else. For example, something **is pegged on** when it is attached to something by small wooden or plastic pegs; and, you **pin** something **on** your clothing when you attach it with a pin or pins. The basic meaning of attaching, fastening or adding something is also extended to non-literal combinations. For example, someone **piles on** the pressure when their actions add to the amount of pressure you are under; someone **latches on** to you when they follow you everywhere and you can't get rid of them; you **pin** your hopes **on** something if that is the thing that must happen if things are to turn out as you want them to; and, you **seize on** some useful fact or circumstance when you suddenly focus all your interest or attention on it. In more formal or literary English **upon** is sometimes used instead of **on** in combinations with this sense.

7 BEGINNING, CONNECTING OR CAUSING TO WORK

Another meaning of **on** in phrasal verbs shows that something is begun, or is connected to the thing that provides it with the power to start operating. For example, you **switch on** or **turn on** a machine when you press, pull or turn the switch that makes it start working; and, workers **clock on** when they operate a machine that records the time they have started work. **Off** is used in phrasal verbs with the opposite meaning. This sense of beginning or starting some process or course of action is also used in combinations such as **embark on** where the more formal or literary **upon** may be used instead of **on.**

8 USING AS A BASIS OR SOURCE

On is used in another group of phrasal verbs to show that the person or thing referred to after the verb + preposition is what is used as the source or basis for the action, or, is the cause of the condition of the subject. For example, if someone **thrives on** hard work they seem to be full of energy and good spirits as a result of it, rather than being tired by it as you might expect them to be; if you **act on** information you take action based on what you have been told; and, you **draw on** your resources or reserves when you use them in order to do or accomplish something.

9 CONSUMING

On in this sense is used in combinations that refer to eating, or using something as a fuel. For example, you **breakfast on** orange juice and croissants when that is what you have for breakfast; and, a machine **runs on** a particular type of fuel when it uses that fuel in order to work. **Off** can be substituted for **on** in combinations with this meaning; and, in combinations that refer to eating, **upon** is sometimes used in more formal English. Thus, **dine on** and **dine upon** have the same meaning as **dine off**.

10 ATTACKING
On is used in another group of phrasal verbs to suggest a sudden attack or violent action directed against a particular person or target. For example, if someone **turns on** you they suddenly and unexpectedly begin to attack you physically or with words; and, someone **rounds on** people who have been criticizing or attacking them when they respond by attacking them in turn.

11 ARRANGING TO HAPPEN
A small number of verbs combined with **on** suggest that something is arranged or made available at a particular place or time. For example, if a group of people **put on** a theatrical show of some sort, they bring together the actors, supply the costumes and props, and make all the necessary arrangements for its performance. Similarly, when food or transport **is laid on** someone provides it for others, free of charge.

12 DISCOVERING
On is also used with verbs to show that something is discovered or comes into view suddenly or unexpectedly. For example, you **stumble on** something when you come across it suddenly; and, you **chance on** something when you come across it by chance. **Upon** is sometimes used instead of **on** in combinations with this sense, especially in formal or literary English.

13 TRANSFERRING
Hand on and **pass on** are examples of another group of phrasal verbs whose meanings have to do with the transfer of something from one person to another, or from one generation to the next.

Some phrasal verbs with **on** are purely idiomatic. For example, you **have** someone **on**, or you **kid** them **on**, when you playfully make them think that something is true when it isn't; and, if you say 'Don't **take on**' to someone you mean that they shouldn't get so upset.

On also forms the third element of many phrasal verbs, as in **cash in on, crack down on, grow up on, home in on** and **take out on.**

onto /ɒntə/

Onto is a preposition.

Many people consider that **onto** should be written as two words, **on to**. However, it is often used as one word in phrasal verbs that refer specifically to movements ending in or on a stated position or place.

1 MOVEMENT ENDING IN A STATED POSITION OR PLACE
For example, you **jump onto** a bus when you jump so that you land on or inside it, and you **throw** logs **onto** a fire when you throw them so that they land on it. There are many combinations with this meaning of movement ending in a specific place or position, including **fall onto, dash onto, lower onto, scramble onto, load onto, topple onto, focus onto, project onto,** and **shine onto**. The following are some examples using combinations with this sense: *She sank onto a kitchen chair.* ❑ *We were herded onto a train which didn't move for 40 minutes.* ❑ *An older model of history based on the rise and fall of empires could be projected onto the fossil record.*

2 ATTACHED OR FASTENED
Another group of phrasal verbs use **onto** to indicate that something is attached, fastened, applied or transferred to something else, as in **build onto, cling onto, fix onto, glue onto, graft onto, bolt onto, splice onto, spray onto** and **stretch onto**. For example, you **stitch** something **onto** something else when you attach the one to the other with stitches made using a needle and thread; and, you **hang onto** something when

continued on next page

you keep it or hold it in a tight grip and do not let go. The following are some more examples of combinations with this sense: *You can copy a file onto a floppy disk without having to unload everything.* ❑ *The office was built onto the end of what had been an external wall.* ❑ *Programs and data were, at one time, punched onto cards.* ❑ *Cotton or fine linen stretched onto a wooden frame or glued onto hardboard can be used as a support for oil or acrylic paints.* ❑ *The language known as Middle English developed after the Norman Conquest with French grafted onto the old Anglo-Saxon.*

3 DIRECTION
Onto is also used in some combinations to indicate the direction in which a window, room or building faces, or the place or area that a window or door leads to. Phrasal verbs with this meaning include **open onto, lead onto, look onto, give onto, run onto, back onto** and **emerge onto.** The following are some examples showing the use of phrasal verbs with this meaning: *a window looking onto a majestic cedar tree* ❑ *An unmarked door opened onto a plush modern office.* ❑ *a kilometre-long cutting emerging onto a longer embankment* ❑ *19th century cottages which back onto the river.*

ooze /uːz/: **oozes, oozing, oozed**

ooze out
A thick liquid, or dense gas or smoke, **oozes out**, or **oozes out** of something, when it comes out very slowly: *As the medics were carrying him away, I could see blood oozing out of his boots and dripping on the ground.* ❑ *foul-smelling gas oozed out of the metal containers.*

open /ˈoupən/: **opens, opening, opened**

open into
A door or window **opens into** another room, or **into** a space such as a courtyard, when it allows you to pass or see directly into it: *The dining room and sitting room open into each other.* ❑ *Adjoining was a funeral parlour with a window opening into the studio.*

open off
A room or area **opens off** a corridor, path or street if you can pass directly into it from the corridor, path or street: *a long, dark corridor with tiny cell-like rooms opening off it.*

open onto
A door or window **opens onto** a place, such as a garden or patio, when you can reach or see that place through it: *A central corridor opened onto bedrooms on one side, and a sitting room and dining room on the other.* ❑ *The windows of the little room opened onto the garden.* [*same as* **give onto**]

open out
1 You **open out** something that is folded when you unfold it or spread it out: *He took out a folded sheet of paper, opened it out, and smoothed it flat on the table.* ❑ *Opening out the map, he began to look for a route that led to the nearest village.* **2** A flower or flower bud **opens out** when the petals unfold and spread out: *The buds had formed but for some unknown reason they didn't open out.* **3** Something narrow such as a corridor, road, valley or river **opens out** when it gradually widens: *A deep groove in the rock opened out into a chimney in which he could brace his feet against the sides.* ❑ *He saw that the vaulted passageway opened out into a large courtyard.* **4** A view or prospect **opens out** when you are able to see more of it because there is nothing in the way: *It's worth taking the funicular railway just to experience the journey and marvel at the views opening out below.* ❑ *The whole panorama of life was opening out in front of him.* **5** Someone **opens out** when they begin to express their feelings or thoughts more freely: *After*

some hesitation, she opened out and told us a bit more about her life in the secret service. [*same as* **open up**]

open up

1 You **open up** a building or room when you unlock the door or doors so that people can come in: *Father had gone on ahead to open up the house.* ❑ *He hammered on the door and shouted that he'd wake the whole hotel if I didn't open up.* **2** A new shop or business **opens up** when it begins trading; the shops **open up** when they open their doors so that customers can come in and buy things: *She's opening up a boutique in the high street.* ❑ *They often came past the shop to see when it was going to open up again.* ❑ *He knew that by the time he'd walked into town they'd have opened up the covered market.* **3** You **open up** a package, or a locked container, when you unwrap it or unlock it so that you can see inside or take something out: *Using a huge old key, he opened up the trunk and took out what looked like a jewelled mask.* ❑ *The dogs bounded across the drive to their master who was opening up the car boot to remove his luggage.* **4** A gap or passageway through something **is opened up** when the things that have been blocking it are removed allowing people or things to pass through: *I've been campaigning to open up the unofficial footpath bordering the golf course.* **5** A region or territory **is opened up** when it is made easier to get to, or easier to have trading links with: *opening up new territories like China* ❑ *Thomas Cook opened up the world to men and women who had never dreamed of travelling before.* **6** Opportunities **open up**, or a circumstance **opens up** opportunities to you, when it creates opportunities for you to make progress or experience new things: *They all thought that the value of the course was in the career opportunities it opened up.* ❑ *Far from ruining his life, he found it had opened up all sorts of undreamt-of opportunities.* **7** You **open** yourself **up** to criticism or abuse from others when you make yourself vulnerable to it: *When stepping forth with an idea, an individual may open himself up to personal rejection.* ❑ *'Be careful! You may be opening yourself up to ridicule, or even worse.'* **8** (*informal*) Someone previously unwilling to talk about themselves or their feelings **opens up** when they begin to talk more freely: *We had a couple of glasses of wine, and she opened up a little after that.* ❑ *He played the role of my psychoanalyst by helping me to open up.* **9** (*informal*) A surgeon **opens** you **up** when he or she cuts into your body so that a diseased or damaged organ or part can be repaired or removed: *What worries me is that when the surgeon opens me up he might find something nasty, like a tumour.* [*same as* **cut open**] **10** (*informal*) Someone with a gun **opens up** when they begin firing: *He burst through the doors and just opened up on innocent by-standers.* ❑ *The German guns then opened up and bombarded our positions.* [*same as* **open fire**] **11** (*informal*) You **open** the vehicle you are driving **up** when you make it go much faster, or as fast as it will go: *Once you get out on the autobahn you can open her up and really see how she performs.* [*same as* **accelerate**] **12** A game such as football **opens up**, or the players **open** it **up**, when it begins to be played in a more exciting way with the players moving around a lot and playing less defensively. **13** A competitor in a race **opens up** a lead when they get well ahead of their opponents: *Arkle swept past Mill House and opened up an unassailable lead.*

operate /'ɒpəreɪt/: **operates**, **operating**, **operated**

operate on

A surgeon **operates on** a patient when

he or she performs surgery on that patient: *It's much easier to operate on people if you give them a general anaethestic.* ❑ *Whether the foot is operated on or not, it will never be normal again.*

oppose /ə'pouz/: **opposes**, **opposing**, **opposed**

• *adjective* **opposed to**

1 When someone is **opposed to** something, they are against it or disagree with it: *He said he was opposed to corporal and capital punishment.* ❑ *Laing is opposed to the appointment of so-called worker directors.* **2** When two things are **opposed to** each other they are opposite each other or completely different from each other: *He had an image of a different kind of economic order, opposed to Islamic socialism.*

opt /ɒpt/: **opts**, **opting**, **opted**

opt for

You **opt for** something when you choose or select it, rather than any of the other possibilities that are available: *They both opted for the guinea fowl casseroled in red wine.* ❑ *The American people opted for a return to isolationism.* ❑ *You can do a full-time course, or you can opt for one that is part-time, or evening classes.* [*same as* **decide on**, **plump for**, **pick**]

opt in

You **opt in** when you choose or decide to do or take part in something: *The new organ-donor scheme will be more satisfactory because, by allowing people to opt in, we can be sure of their wishes in advance.*

opt out

You **opt out** when you choose or decide not to do or take part in something: *Nigel, by opting out of the computer course, had already made his compromise with ambitious dreams.*

order /'ɔːdə(r)/: **orders**, **ordering**, **ordered**

order about *or* order around

When someone **orders** you **about**, or **orders** you **around**, they tell you to do things in a rude and unpleasant way and don't allow you to make your own decisions or choices: *She ordered her daughters about and made their lives impossible with hundreds of petty rules.* ❑ *'Stop ordering me about!'* [*same as* **boss about**, **push around**]

order off

Players in a game such as football **are ordered off** when the referee or some other official tells them to leave the playing area, *eg* because they have behaved badly or have committed a serious foul. [*same as* **send off**]

out see panel on next page

outbreak /'autbreɪk/ see **break out**

outburst /'autbɜːst/ see **burst out**

outcast /'autkɑːst/ see **cast out**

outcome /'autkʌm/ see **come out**

outcry /'autkraɪ/ see **cry out**

outgoing /aut'gouɪŋ/ see **go out**

outlay /'autləɪ/ see **lay out**

outlet /'autlɛt/ see **let out**

out /aut/

Out is an adverb.

Out is a very common word in English and is widely used in combination with verbs. Its basic meaning is of movement from the inside to the outside. For example, when someone **gets out** of hospital they are discharged and allowed to go home; and, a prisoner **breaks out** of prison when he or she escapes to the outside.

1 LEAVING

Out is used in its literal meaning in phrasal verbs that refer to someone or something leaving a place or moving outside or away from it. For example, a train **pulls out** when it moves away from a station, and you **fly out** when you leave somewhere by aeroplane.

2 REMOVING AND DELETING

In combinations with this sense, **out** indicates that something is removed, pulled or taken from the inside. For example, a dentist **takes** a tooth **out** when he or she removes it from a patient's mouth; you **squeeze** something **out** when you remove it by squeezing the container it is in; and, you **gouge** something **out** when you remove it by making rough scooping movements with a sharp tool. **Out** is also used in combinations that refer to something being deleted, so that when you **cross out** something you have written you remove it by making a line or series of lines through it.

New and often informal phrasal verbs with this meaning are quite common, as in *scissor out* and *zap out* in the following examples: *Newspaper reviews had been scissored out.* ❑ *I would write rubbish on my computer and have to zap it all out the next day.*

3 EXCLUDING, OMITTING

Another sense of **out** used in phrasal verbs indicates that someone or something is excluded, omitted, rejected or forced out of a place or group. Thus, you **rule** something **out** when you decide not to do it or consider it; and, you **leave** or **miss** something **out** when you do not include it, either by mistake or intentionally. You **blot out** an unpleasant memory when you don't allow yourself to remember it; and, someone **is cast out** when they are forced by others to leave a place.

4 SEARCHING, OBTAINING, DISCOVERING, SOLVING

In phrasal verbs such as **find out** and **dig out**, **out** is used to show that the action is one of discovering information, especially information that is not previously known or is difficult to obtain. Thus, when you **ferret out** or **root out** information you find it after a careful and thorough search; and, you **seek** someone **out** when you go and look for that particular person, usually so that you can consult them about something. You **work** a problem **out** when you find the answer or solution; and, you **check** information **out** when you confirm if it is true or not by checking with various reliable sources.

5 EMERGING, APPEARING OR BEGINNING

Out is used in some phrasal verbs that refer to something appearing or emerging, often from a place where it has been hidden. For example, people say that the sun **has come out** when it has appeared from behind the clouds; a baby bird or reptile **hatches out** when it emerges from its egg; when you **break out** in a rash many small spots appear on your skin; and, fighting **breaks out** somewhere when opposing groups begin to attack and fight each other.

6 PROJECTING

Out is also used in some phrasal verbs to indicate that something projects outwards or away from a surface or object. **Jut out**, **poke out** and **stick out** are phrasal verbs with this sense.

7 OUTSIDE, OUTDOORS OR AWAY FROM HOME

Some verbs combined with **out** mean that an event or activity goes on outside or away from your home or place of work. For example, you **camp out** when you sleep outdoors, and a business **farms out** work when they give it to someone outside the company to do or complete. You **ask** someone of the opposite sex **out** when you ask them to go with you on a

continued on next page

date to somewhere like a restaurant or the cinema. You **send** something **out** in the mail when you use the postal service to carry it away from your home or office to the person or company you want it to go to; and, you **send out** for something such as a meal when you ask an outside supplier to deliver it to your home or office. Other combinations with this meaning include **dine out** and **eat out**, **lease out** and **invite out**.

Some phrasal verbs with this sense are more idiomatic. For example, someone who has been involved in a relatively narrow field or sphere **branches out** when they begin to become involved in a wider variety of things, or they spread their activities beyond their normal sphere.

8 CHOOSING OR SELECTING

A few phrasal verbs with **out** have the meaning of choosing or selecting, so that when someone **is singled out** they are only person chosen from a group; and, you **pick** something **out** when you choose it from a number of possible alternatives.

9 MAKING A SUDDEN OR LOUD NOISE

Out is used in many phrasal verbs to suggest that a noise is made suddenly or loudly, often causing the listener to be startled by its suddenness and volume, as in **bark out**, **bawl out**, **blare out**, **blurt out**, **cry out**, **rap out,** and **shout out**.

10 PRODUCING

Out can also indicate that things of the same kind are produced rapidly or in large quantities. For example, you **trot out** the same excuse when you use the same excuse again and again; and, someone **churns** or **rattles** things **out** when they produce them in a continuous stream.

Again, in this sense, new phrasal verbs regularly appear, such as *crank out* in the following example: *I wouldn't be cranking all these books out if I was spending all my time in night-clubs!*

11 FINISHING, EXTINGUISHING OR DISAPPEARING COMPLETELY

This sense of **out** suggests that something is finished, extinguished, or disappears completely. A fire or light **goes out** when it stops burning; a custom or species of animal **dies out** when it disappears completely; a supply **runs out** when it comes to an end and there is none left; something **peters out** when it gradually comes to an end; and, an engine **conks out** when it stops working suddenly.

This sense is extended to combinations that refer to actions or states that result in a person becoming unconscious. For example, you **are knocked out** when you are struck on the head so hard that you lose consciousness; and, you **black out** or **pass out** when you faint. New phrasal verbs with this sense are continually been created; examples include the informal phrasal verbs **punch out**, **crash out**, and **zonk out**.

12 DISTRIBUTING

Out is used in another group of phrasal verbs, including **give out**, **hand out**, **dole out**, **divide out** and **pay out**, to show that something is distributed or shared amongst a number of people.

13 EXTENDING AND STRETCHING

Another sense of **out** in phrasal verbs shows that the action is one of extending or stretching, so that you **hold out** your hand when you stretch it out in front of you, and you **reach out** for something when you try to get hold of it by stretching out one or both of your arms. You **eke** a limited supply of something **out** when you make it last as long as possible by using only a small amount at a time.

14 EXPANDING AND INCREASING

Out is also used in literal and non-literal combinations which refer to expanding or increasing. For example, you **let** a piece of clothing **out** when you add more material to it so that it is large enough to fit; you **flesh out** a report or piece of writing when you add more detail to it; and, a sail **bellies out** when the wind fills it and forms it into a large rounded shape.

15 COMPLETENESS

Out is used in many phrasal verbs as an

intensifier to show that an action or state has an element of thoroughness or completeness. For example, you **work out** when you do a series of physical exercises in order to achieve or maintain a high level of fitness; you **clear out** a room or cupboard when you take everything out of it and clean it thoroughly; and, people **iron out** problems when they find satisfactory solutions to them. A great many new phrasal verbs, especially informal ones, are being created with this meaning, very often by making a verb from a noun and adding **out**: for example, **luck out** meaning to have an extraordinary amount of good luck; **chill out** meaning to relax your mind or body after a period of stress or physical activity; **grease out** meaning to eat large quantities of greasy, and therefore unhealthy, food; **bliss out** meaning to reach a state of blissful happiness; and, **cool out**, a verbal use of the adjective **cool**, meaning restrained and relaxed, as in the example: *He's cooling out the brash Eighties look in this new incarnation for the Nineties.*

16 CONTINUING, OFTEN WITH DIFFICULTY, UNTIL SOMETHING IS COMPLETE

Phrasal verbs with **out** used in this sense imply that the action is continued for some time until the situation referred to is over or can be brought to an end. For example, you **stick** a difficult or unpleasant situation **out** when you endure it until it ends or is over. Other phrasal verbs with this sense include **face out**, **see out**, **hold out** and **last out**. New and often informal phrasal verbs with this sense are quite common. For example, you **tough** it **out** when you get through a difficult situation by being resolute, perhaps rather aggressively so, as in the example: *We decided to tough it out when the cops questioned us.*

17 RECORDING, DEMONSTRATING OR PUTTING DOWN ON PAPER

Out is combined with many verbs indicating that a particular method of demonstrating, planning or recording its details or measurements is used. For example, you **map out** how you will approach some task or problem when you show how you will deal with its various stages in general terms. **Sketch out** and **rough out** are further examples of phrasal verbs with this sense.

18 ATTACKING

Some phrasal verbs with **out** refer to attacking movements or actions. You **hit out** or **lash out** when you aim a blow at someone or something, often not very accurately, or, you attack them by criticizing them or saying cruel or hurtful things to them.

Out is also used in some phrasal verbs that have very idiomatic meanings. For example, you **make** something **out** when you can see it, recognize it, or understand it, and some people talk about **making out** with someone they have had sexual intercourse with; you **fall out** with someone when you argue with them and stop being friendly with them as a result; and, you **carry** something **out** when you put it into practice.

outpouring /ˈaʊtpɔːrɪŋ/ see **pour out**

output /ˈaʊtpʊt/ see **put out**

outstanding /aʊtˈstandɪŋ/ see **stand out**

over see panel on following pages

overboard see panel on page 244

overpass /ˈoʊvəpɑːs/ see **pass over**

overrun /oʊvəˈrʌn/ see **run over**

overspill /ˈoʊvəspɪl/ see **spill over**

over /ˈouvə(r)/

Over is a preposition and an adverb. It is very common in English and is frequently used in phrasal verbs. Its basic meaning is similar to **above**. As a preposition it often follows verbs to show that the following noun or noun phrase is the object of the action, or the person or thing that the action is directed towards. For example, two people **argue over** something when that is the thing their argument is about; and, someone **fusses over** you when they show a lot of concern for you or give you a lot of attention in a way that you find irritating.

1 ABOVE OR DIRECTLY ABOVE
Over is used in its literal sense to indicate that something happens in a place or position above something else. For example, a plane **flies over** when it travels through the sky above you; someone **towers over** you when they are so tall that they make you feel small; and, the owner of a business **lives over** the shop when their home is in the same building, directly above the shop. **Over** is also used in combinations that refer to movement from a higher to a lower position. For example, you **bend over** when you bend your body at the waist bringing the top half of your body closer to the ground. A small group of phrasal verbs with this sense indicate that someone has the role of supervising others or being in charge of something. For example, someone **presides over** a meeting when they are the person in overall charge who makes sure that it is conducted properly; people **are ruled over** by a king or dictator when a king or dictator governs them and makes the laws; and, you **watch over** someone when you supervise what they are doing and make sure they don't come to any harm.

2 MOVEMENT ACROSS FROM ONE SIDE TO THE OTHER
Over is used in many phrasal verbs in the literal sense to indicate that something moves across something from one side to the other. Combinations with this sense include **clamber over**, **climb over**, **crawl over**, **cross over**, **hop over**, **leap over**, **stride over**, **vault over** and **walk over**, and they show that the movement is made across an obstacle or from one side to the other of a space or surface. Some combinations have a slightly extended meaning and indicate that something is placed so that it goes over the top of something and down on either side, such as **drape over** and **sling over**.

3 COVERING OR HIDING
Over is combined with some verbs to show that the action is one of covering or hiding. For example, you **paint over** or **concrete over** something, when you cover it with paint, or concrete; the sky **clouds over** when it becomes covered with clouds, and a lake **freezes over** when a layer of ice covers its surface completely; you **cover** something **over** when you put something on top of it so that it is hidden or protected; and, something **is spread over** a wide area when it covers all of that area. There are some phrasal verbs with this sense of covering or hiding that are metaphorical. For example, you can say that some unpleasant fact or circumstance **has been glossed over** when it has been dealt with in a way that hides or disguises its worst or most unpleasant aspects.

4 MOVEMENT TO THE SIDE
Some phrasal verbs with **over** indicate that the movement referred to is to one side or sideways. For example, a vehicle **pulls over** when it moves to the side of the road and stops; and, if someone tells you to **move over** or **slide over** they are telling you to move your body sideways.

5 OVERFLOWING
Another sense of **over** indicates that a liquid flows out of or escapes from a container because the level has reached the point where the container cannot hold any more. Combinations with this sense include **boil over**, **brim over** and **spill over**. The literal sense of some of these combinations can be extended to refer to things other than liquids that grow so much in volume or extent that they cannot be contained. For example, if violence **spills over** from a place where it was previously concentrated it begins to happen in other places nearby;

and, you can say that someone **is bubbling over** with enthusiasm when they are so full of enthusiasm that they can't stop themselves from showing it.

6 COMMUNICATING A FEELING OR IMPRESSION
Over is used in a small number of phrasal verbs to show that something is communicated to others. For example, you **get** a message **over** to people when you succeed in making them understand it; you **put** something **over** well or badly when that is the way you communicate it to others; and, you **come over** in a certain way when that is the impression you make on other people. **Across** is often used instead of **over** in phrasal verbs with this meaning.

7 ENDING, FINISHING OR COMPLETING
Another use of **over** in phrasal verbs shows that a temporary situation is ended or finished and things have returned to normal. For example, a quarrel or disagreement **blows over** when it comes to an end and the people involved re-establish normal friendly relations with each other; and someone **gets over** an illness or disappointment when they recover from it. **Over** is also used in this sense as the second element of the phrasal verb **get over with**; so that when you **get** something unpleasant **over with**, you get it done as quickly as possible.

8 DOING SOMETHING AGAIN
Over is also used in a small number of phrasal verbs, especially in American English, to show that something is done again. For example, you **start over** when you go back and start something again from the beginning; and, you have to **do** something **over** when you have to do it again because you did it incorrectly the first time.

9 LOOKING AT, EXAMINING, OR CONSIDERING
Another sense of **over** occurs in phrasal verbs that have to do with looking at, examining, or considering something from the beginning to the end, often in a careful methodical way. Combinations with this sense include **check over**, **go over**, **read over**, **talk over** and **think over**. Thus, when you **talk** something **over** with someone else you discuss it with them so that they can give you their opinion of it and help you to come to a sensible decision about it.

10 FALLING
Over is also combined with many verbs to indicate that something falls or is pushed from an upright position to a horizontal one, on the ground. Combinations with this meaning include **blow over**, **fall over**, **knock over**, **tip over**, **trip over**, and **topple over**. Some phrasal verbs with this meaning are more idiomatic. For example, if you say that you **were bowled over** by something, you mean that you were so impressed by it, or it affected you so strongly, that you were overwhelmed and made helpless.
A small number of very idiomatic phrasal verbs use **over** to emphasize that something is done thoroughly, especially in combinations that have to do with attacking or robbing a person or place. You can say that people **have worked** someone **over** when they have beaten that person severely; and, that a house or business premises **has been done over** when it has been robbed.

11 TRANSFERRING OR CHANGING POSITION
Over is also combined with verbs to show that something is transferred from one person to another or changed from one position to another. For example, you **switch** things **over** when you put each one in the other's place; and you **hand over** something when you give it to someone else, especially reluctantly. It is also combined with verbs to indicate that something moves or is moved so that its opposite side is the one that is facing upwards. For example, you **turn over** the pages of a book when you move them so that you can look at the other side.

12 REMAINING
Over is used in some combinations to suggest that something stays in the same place or the same state for a certain period of time. For example, you **sleep over** at someone else's house when you visit them and spend the night there; and, if something **is held over** until a later time it is not done until then.

overboard /ˈouvəbɔːd/

Overboard is an adverb.

Overboard is used in its literal sense with verbs of movement to show that movement is made from a position on a ship or boat into the water, as in **dive overboard, fall overboard, jump overboard, leap overboard, toss overboard, tip overboard, chuck overboard** and **sweep overboard**. The meaning of these combinations is so clear that they may not be given a separate entry in this dictionary.

Overboard is used in a small number of phrasal verbs that have both literal and non-literal senses. For example, you can talk about someone **going overboard** when you think they are behaving in an extreme way or are doing something to excess; and, if you **go overboard** for someone or something, you are very enthusiastic about them or are extremely impressed by them, as in the following example: *'I'm beginning to understand why Gary went overboard for you,' he said huskily.*

Throw overboard also has an additional sense beyond its literal meaning, so that when people talk about **throwing** something **overboard** they mean that they are abandoning it or getting rid of it completely, as in this example: *The old system of division of labour is thrown overboard.*

own /oun/: **owns, owning, owned**

own to (*formal*)

You **own to** something when you admit to it: *He admits he can't even own to despair.* ❑ *Any man that owned to being afraid was treated with utter contempt.*

own up

Someone who has done something wrong **owns up** when they admit that they did it; someone **owns up** to something wrong or illegal when they admit that they did it: *'Come on, own up. I know you did it.'* ❑ *He said he wasn't going to own up to something that would get him expelled.* [*same as* **confess, come clean** (*informal*)]

p

pace /peɪs/: paces, pacing, paced

pace off *or* pace out

You **pace off** part or parts of a total length or distance, or you **pace** a length or area **out**, when you measure it by counting the number of equally spaced steps you take to cover it: *Pacing off about twenty yards, he made a mark in the sand with the heel of his boot.* ❑ *Peter paced out the length and breadth of the room.*

pack /pak/: packs, packing, packed

pack away

You **pack** things **away** when you put them in a bag, box, cupboard or other container and store them for future use: *Any spare eggs are frozen and packed away in special containers.* [*same as* **put away**]

pack in

1 You **pack** things **in** when you put them in a container or space so that they fit tightly and neatly; people or things **are packed into** a space or container when they are fitted into it tightly with little or no space between them: *Dolly had opened the case and was packing in the neatly-ironed shirts.* ❑ *The investigators said the explosive could have been illegally packed into the hold as part of the cargo.* ❑ *Simmer the pears in the syrup and pack into sterilised jars.* **2** You **pack** a lot **in**, or you **pack** a lot **into** a relatively short period of time, when you succeed in doing a great many things in that time: *If you are well organized, you can pack a lot into a single weekend.* **3** (*informal*) People sometimes say that an event or performance, especially one in a theatre, **is packing** them **in** when it is attracting very large crowds or audiences: *The tiny island theatre has been packing them in every week since it opened.* **4** (*informal*) **a** You **pack** something **in** when you stop doing it, especially suddenly or abruptly: *After a couple of weeks working in those terrible conditions, I felt like packing it in and going home.* [*same as* **jack in** (*informal*), **chuck in** (*informal*)] **b** When someone tells you to **pack** something **in** they are telling you rudely or angrily to stop doing it: *You had better pack that nonsense in if you don't want to end up being sent out of the room!* **5** (*informal*) You **pack** your boyfriend or girlfriend **in** when you decide to end the relationship: *'Are you still going out with Tracy?' 'No, I packed her in last week.'* [*same as* **finish with, chuck in** (*informal*)] **6** (*informal*) People say that a machine **has packed in** when it has stopped working altogether; they also sometimes say that an organ or organs in someone's body, such as the liver or the kidneys, **has** or **have packed in** when they have stopped functioning altogether: *Don't tell me the generator's packed in again!* ❑ *It's not surprising that his liver packed in after thirty years of heavy drinking.* [*same as* **pack up** (*informal*)]

pack into see **pack in**.

pack off (*informal*)

You **pack** someone **off** somewhere when you send them there without wasting any time, even though they may not want to go: *After Mario had been packed off to be charged with attempted murder, the police started to search the apartment.* ❑ *part of a scheme to brush the whole racial problem under the carpet by packing the black majority off to rural 'homelands' dotted around the country.* [*same as* **bundle off** (*informal*), **send off, dispatch** (*formal*)]

pack out

You can say a place **is packed out** if it is as full of people as it is possible to be; people **pack** a place **out** when they crowd into it and fill it completely: *They gave a series of special concerts and the village hall was packed out every evening.* ❑ *Jostling and shoving, they packed the assembly rooms out, and still more people tried to get in.* [*same as* **mob**]

pack up

1 You **pack up** your belongings when you put them in a suitcase, bag or other container so that you can take them with you when you are leaving: *I gave her a hand packing up her clothes.* ❑ *She packed up her car as if about to go away for the weekend.* **2** You **pack up** at the end of the working or school day when you tidy your desk or work area and put everything away before you leave: *By the time the bell rang, the kids had cleared their desks, packed up, and put on their outdoor clothes.* **3** (*informal*) You **pack up** some activity, or you **pack** it **up**, when you stop doing it: *If I had a cough like that I'd pack up smoking right away!* [*same as* **pack in** (*informal*)] **4** (*informal*) People say that a machine or an organ in the body **has packed up** if it has broken down or stopped working altogether: *'Do you have a torch? This one's packed up.'* ❑ *We're hoping he gets a transplant before his kidneys pack up completely.* [*same as* **pack in** (*informal*)]

pad /pad/: pads, padding, padded

pad out

1 To **pad** something **out** is to fill it out with soft material so that it is the right size: *polyester wadding covered with white cotton can be used to pad out the shoulders* (or *pad the shoulders out*). **2** You **pad out** a speech or something you have written such as a letter or an essay, when you add things to it that are not strictly necessary to make it longer: *He's padded his speech out with a lot of meaningless waffle.* [*opposite* **cut down, condense, shorten**]

paint /peɪnt/: paints, painting, painted

paint in

You **paint in** the details of a picture when you add them using paint: *I then paint in the bulk of the solid colour, screwing up my eyes and obliterating any detail, but getting the tones hopefully right.*

paint on

Something **is painted on** when it is created on, or applied to, a surface using paint: *They were looking for the wooden markers with thistles painted on.*

paint out

To **paint out** something that has been painted or drawn on a surface is to cover it with paint so that it can no longer be seen: *It seems one of the figures in the original version was painted out; perhaps because the artist wasn't satisfied with the composition.*

paint over

To **paint over** something is to apply a layer or layers of paint on top of it: *The Eastons restored the ornamental brickwork, most of it imitation brickwork painted over the original brick.*

pair /pɛə(r)/: **pairs**, **pairing**, **paired**

pair off

When people **pair off**, or **are paired off**, they come together, or are put together, in twos, pairs or couples: *Within a couple of days all my friends had paired off with English boys they met in the Spanish bars.* ❑ *My aunts were always trying to pair me off with 'suitable' girls.*

pair up

A person or animal **pairs up** with another when they come together to form a pair or couple, usually in order to do something together: *Then the birds pair up and build a nest.* ❑ *Ronnie paired up with Joe for the three-legged race.*

pal /pal/: **pals**, **palling**, **palled**

pal around (*informal*)

People, especially children or young adults, **pal around** together when they are friends with each other and spend a lot of their time in each other's company: *Wasn't she one of the girls you palled around with at school?* ❑ *Who does your son pal around with?*

pal up with (*informal*)

You **pal up with** someone when you become friends with them: *When he first went into the army, he'd palled up with a couple of Welsh lads.* [*same as* **chum up with** (*informal*)]

pall /pɔːl/: **palls**, **palling**, **palled**

pall on (*formal*)

Something that you previously found interesting or exciting **palls on** you when you begin to find it boring or less interesting, usually because it has gone on for too long or never changes: *After a couple of months, even the stunning scenery was beginning to pall on Gerard and he longed for the bustle of the city.*

palm /pɑːm/: **palms**, **palming**, **palmed**

palm off (*informal, derogatory*)

1 Someone **palms** something useless or worthless **off** on you when they get rid of it by persuading you to take it or buy it: *He tried to palm some cheap imitation off on me, but I insisted on the real thing.* [*same as* **fob off**] **2** If you are trying to get a straightforward answer to a question and the person you expect to give it to you **palms** you **off** with an excuse or a lie, they try to get rid of you that way instead of giving you the proper or true answer to your question: *Henry tried to palm me off by telling me that he hadn't had time to look at the script.* [*same as* **fob off**]

pan /pan/: **pans**, **panning**, **panned**

pan out (*informal*)

Something **pans out** when it develops or happens in the way that you hoped or expected; how a situation **pans out** is the way it happens or develops: *What will we do if this doesn't pan out?* ❑ *He wasn't too pleased about how things had panned out.* [*same as* **turn out**, **work out**]

pander /ˈpandə(r)/: **panders**, **pandering**, **pandered**

pander to (*derogatory*)

You **pander to** someone when you give or tell them what they want or like, even when it may be wrong to do so: *The problem had been exaggerated by the popular press in order to boost their circulation and pander to the prejudices of their readers.* ❑ *A Jesuit declared that by approving the rightness of contraception the Anglican Communion was pandering to paganism.* [*same as* **cater to**, **gratify** (*formal*), **indulge**]

pant /pant/: **pants**, **panting**, **panted**

pant for

If you say that you **are panting for** something you mean that you want to have it or do it very much: *I'm panting for a cold drink!* ❑ *He was one of those Scotsmen who pant for London, but who was nevertheless in his own way an ardent patriot.* [*same as* **long for, yearn for** (*formal*)]

pant out

You **pant out** words when you say them while taking short quick breaths between the words because you have been running or are finding it difficult to breathe for some other reason: *Bent double with the effort of running so quickly upstairs, Joss panted out, 'Come quick, Dad's ill.'*

paper /'peɪpə(r)/: papers, papering, papered

paper over

You **paper over** a disagreement, fault or difficulty when you hide or disguise it so that you can give the impression that there is agreement or that things are going well: *We should try to discuss this honestly and without trying to paper over the difficulties which we all know exist.* ❑ *As far as they were concerned it was just an attempt to paper over the racial tensions that existed.* [*same as* **cover up, gloss over, camouflage**]

parcel /'pɑːsəl/: parcels, parcelling (*AmE* parceling), parcelled (*AmE* parceled)

parcel out

Something, usually land, **is parcelled out** when it is divided into smaller parts or sections so that it can be distributed amongst a number of people: *They had parcelled the land out into small plots.* ❑ *Land was parcelled out to the powerful military class to enrich themselves.* [*same as* **divide out, portion out**]

parcel up

You **parcel** something **up** when you wrap it in a parcel using paper, cardboard, string, sticky tape, *etc*: *She parcelled up the books and wrote 'please handle with care' on the address label.*

pare /pɛə(r)/: pares, paring, pared

pare away

You **pare away** the outer layers of something when you cut them off it in thin strips so reducing its size; you **pare away** at something when you reduce its size or extent bit by bit: *If you pare away all the glitz and glamour, all you're left with is a rather inferior production.* ❑ *Niche shops have been paring away at the department stores share of the high street market.*

pare down

You **pare down** something, or you **pare** it **down**, when you make it smaller or reduce it bit by bit: *Pare down your weight until you are carrying as little excess as possible.* ❑ *The company has announced that it will be paring down the workforce as part of a package of cutbacks.*

pare off

To **pare** something **off** something else is to remove it from that thing in thin strips using *eg* a small sharp knife: *Pare off the outer layers until you reach the young green wood.* ❑ *He sat on the edge of the bath paring the hard skin off his feet.*

part /pɑːt/: parts, parting, parted

part from

1 You **are parted from** someone or something when you are separated from them: *Shaposhnikov refused to be parted from his headgear.* ❑ *A process that has, since the sixteenth century, relentlessly parted the commoner from his freehold, and reduced him to a landless labourer.* **2** You **part from** someone with whom you have had some sort of close relationship when you leave them, so ending the relationship: *... all the hopes and frustrations that make up a life, meeting people and parting from them, listening* *to them and speaking to them* ... ❑ *How could he bear to part from his wife and children?*

part with

You **part with** something when you give or sell it to someone else, especially when you do so reluctantly: *Thomas just couldn't bear to part with his toy rabbit.* ❑ *Bingham appeared happy to part with the money.* ❑ *Few farmers can now afford to part with such valuable by-products as manure without charging for them.* [*same as* **give up, let go of, relinquish** (*formal*)]

partake /pɑːˈteɪk/: partakes, partaking, partook /pɑːˈtʊk/

partake in (*old or formal*)

You **partake in** a particular activity when you take some part in it or are involved in it: *He was insistent that he had never partaken in any of their illegal activities.* [*same as* **participate**]

partake of (*old or formal*)

1 (*often humorous*) You **partake of** food or drink when you eat or drink it: *Shall we move into the shade and partake of a little wine?* **2** Something **partakes of** a particular quality or characteristic when it has or suggests that quality or characteristic in some degree: *Their relationship partook somewhat of the nature of a tropical storm.* [*same as* **smack of, suggest**]

partition /pɑːˈtɪʃən/: partitions, partitioning, partitioned

partition off

Part of a room or other enclosed space **is partitioned off** when a thin internal wall or partition is put up to separate or divide it from the rest of the room or space: *The foreman's office was partitioned off from the shop floor.* ❑ *They're partitioning part of the main hall off to create a small office and cloakroom.*

pass /pɑːs/: passes, passing, passed

pass along

1 You **pass** something you have been given **along** when you give it to someone else next to you: *Take a chocolate and pass the box along.* **2** You **pass along** a route when you travel or move from one end of it to the other: *Frankie could never pass along that section of corridor without feeling that there was someone hiding in the shadows.*

pass around see pass round

pass as see pass for

pass away

1 Something **passes away** when it gradually disappears; something that **has passed away** is no longer there or no longer exists: *When at last the pain passed away, Norma was able to open her eyes again.* ❑ *a powerful nostalgia for the world that has passed away.* **2** (*euphemistic*) People often say that a person **has passed away** when that person has died: *A police spokesman said: 'It seems Mrs Soper died and then her husband passed away a short time later.'* [*same as* **pass on, pass over**]

pass between

1 Things such as information, letters, or looks **pass between** people when they are exchanged by those people: *Few words had passed between them over the last month.* **2** Something **passes between** two people or things when it moves so that those people or things are in a position on either side of it: *The driveway passes between two rows of stately copper-beech trees.*

pass by

1 People or things **pass by** when they go past; you **pass by** a place when you go past it on your way to somewhere else: *He backed into a doorway to allow the boisterous crowd to pass by.* ❑ *Through the café window I watched*

London nightlife pass by. ❑ *I would, of course, have to write to Miss Kenton to tell her I might be passing by.* **2** Time **passes by** when it elapses: *A day, a week, then a month passed by, and still there was no news.* **3** You **pass** things or people **by** if you go past them without stopping; someone or something **passes** you **by** when they ignore you or avoid you, or go on their way without involving or coming into contact with you: *I simply can't pass the island by without a further look at its highlight, the Black Cuillin.* ❑ *Women in her position can have that desperate feeling that life has passed them by.* ❑ *He said firmly that he wouldn't let such an opportunity pass him by again.*

• *noun* **bypass: bypasses**

1 A **bypass** is a road carrying traffic around the outskirts of a busy city or town built to avoid congestion in the city or town centre. **2** A **bypass** is also a surgical operation in which a tube replacing a length of vein or artery that has become blocked is inserted in the body so that the blood can flow properly.

• *noun* **passer-by: passers-by**

A **passer-by** is someone who happens to be walking past, *eg* when something is happening: *Several passers-by had witnessed the accident.*

pass down

Things such as stories, customs, physical characteristics or skills **are passed down** when they are taught to, or reappear in, the next and subsequent generations: *The craft of metal-working was passed down from father to son.* [*same as* **hand down, pass on**]

pass for

Someone or something **passes for** or **passes as** something else when they appear to be that thing, or are a reasonable substitute for it: *With a new outfit and hairstyle, she felt she could almost pass for human.* ❑ *Is this then what passes as witty conversation amongst the younger generation?* [*same as* **be taken for**]

pass into

1 You **pass into** a place when you move inside it from the outside: *He descended a series of flagged steps and passed into a green tunnel.* ❑ *He passed into the kitchen without a word.* **2** Something **passes into** history or legend when it becomes part of it: *'British Business', for 103 years the official organ of the Department of Trade and Industry, has not passed into history without comment.* ❑ *And so it was ensured that his escapades would pass into legend.*

pass off

1 A temporary feeling or effect **passes off** when it disappears: *He sat down until the feeling of nausea passed off.* [*same as* **wear off**] **2** An event **passes off** when it takes place or ends; it **passes off** well or badly when it goes well or badly: *Despite our misgivings, the whole thing passed off without a hitch.* **3** You **pass** an unpleasant event or incident **off** lightly, *eg* with a shrug or a joke, when you try to suggest by your attitude that it is not really important, or has not affected you in any serious way: *I could tell that Barbara was hurt, though she passed the comment off with a wry smile.*

pass off as

People **pass** one thing **off as** another when they make other people believe that it is that other thing; a person **passes** himself or herself **off** as someone different from their true self when they pretend they are that person: *No attempt was made to pass the cheeses off as the great traditional products of an unmechanized age.* ❑ *He had tried to pass the painting off as a genuine Picasso.* ❑ *She gained access to the castle by passing herself off as a kitchenmaid.*

pass on

1 You **pass on** something, or you **pass**

it **on**, when you give or tell it to another person or other people: *She wants to pass on the message that the world is still a great place despite everything.* ❑ *You can pass on the infection without knowing.* ❑ *Those fugitives who congregated on the Omsk railway passed on spotted typhus to 60% of the regional railway workers.* ❑ *Radiation is absorbed by the living material, and thus passes on its energy to it.* **2 a** You **pass on** things such as skills, customs or wealth when you teach them or give them to the next generation: *The farm will be passed on to the eldest son when he dies.* ❑ *He sees it as part of his responsibility to the game to pass his skills on to the next generation of players.* [*same as* **hand on, hand down, pass down**] **b** You **pass on** your genes, or a specific gene, when you have children and they have some of your genes, or when that particular gene appears in one or all of your children, and in subsequent generations of your family: *Haemophilia doesn't appear in the carrier mother, but is, instead, passed on to her male children.* [*same as* **transmit**] **3** You **pass on** from one place, activity, subject or stage to another when you progress or move from one to the next: *With so little space available in newspapers, the critic only has time to mention a painter or sculptor, make a brief observation, and pass on.* [*same as* **go on, proceed** (*formal*)] **4** You **pass** someone **on** to someone else when you refer them to or put them in touch with that other person so that they can deal with them or give them the help they want: *'I'm going to pass you on to my colleague, Mr Adams, who knows all about your case.'* **5** (*euphemistic*) Sometimes people say that a person **has passed on** when that person has died: *She passed on two weeks ago.* [*same as* **pass away**] **6** Increased costs or financial savings **are passed on** to a business company's customers when the company adjusts the price they charge for their goods, either upwards or downwards, to take account of any rise or fall in their production costs: *A threefold increase in the price of our raw material will have to be passed on to our customers somehow.*

pass out

1 People or things **pass out** of an opening when they move through it to the outside: *Cars passed out of the iron gates, one by one, and sped after the hearse.* **2** People you have known **pass out** of your life when you no longer have any contact with them: *At New Year, I think about the year that's gone past, and perhaps, people who've passed out of my life.* **3** You **pass** things **out** when you give or distribute them to a number of people: *The exam papers were passed out and we had a few moments to look at them before we had to begin.* [*same as* **give out, hand out**] **4** Someone **passes out** when they become unconscious for a short time: *If your attacker tries to strangle you, you can pass out in a matter of seconds.* ❑ *It was so hot I was near passing out at times.* [*same as* **black out, faint**] **5** Students or cadets being trained at a military or police college **pass out** when they finish their course successfully.

• *adjective* **passing-out**

A **passing-out** parade or ceremony is one in which those students or cadets at a military or police college who have completed their course successfully take part.

pass over

1 Something **passes over** something else when it moves above or across it, or follows a route from one side of it to the other: *Two beautiful night herons passed over our heads.* ❑ *The train passed over huge bridges that looked as if they were made of matchsticks.* ❑ *a coast path that passes over National Trust property.* **2** Someone **is passed over** for a job or promotion if they are not selected for it, especially when a younger or less experienced person is chosen instead: *Why were the first and second prize-winners in the competition passed over and Scott appointed instead?* ❑ *She has been passed over for promotion yet again.* [*same as* **overlook**] **3 a** You **pass over** something when you fail to mention it or notice it: *This is the sort of CD that the ordinary music-lover is likely to pass over in favour of something better known.* [*same as* **ignore**, **disregard** (*formal*)] **b** You **pass over** some unpleasant fact when you deliberately avoid mentioning it or dealing with it: *He passed quickly over the section of the report that criticized his department.* [*same as* **gloss over**, **skirt around**, **skate around**; *opposite* **confront**] **4** Some people say that someone who has died **has passed over** meaning that their spirit has left their body and entered the spirit world or 'gone over to the other side'.

• *noun (especially AmE)* **overpass**: **overpasses**

An **overpass** is a road that carries traffic over another road. [*same as* **flyover**]

pass round

1 People **pass** something **round** when they give or hand it to one another in turn; something **is passed around** when one person gives or hands it to another person, who gives or hands it to the next person, and so on: *Traditionally, African beer is drunk from a large cup, passed round the group of drinkers.* ❑ *We passed books around, swapped the names of authors, and discussed the latest writing in literary magazines.* ❑ *Copies of their first report were being passed around, and avidly perused.* [*same as* **hand round**, **circulate**] **2** You **pass** something such as a length of rope or yarn **round** something else when you form it into a loop or circle around that other thing: *Pass the elastic round your fingertip, then slip the end through the loop.*

pass through

1 You **pass through** a place when you travel through it on your way to somewhere else; when you say you **are passing through** you mean you are only stopping briefly where you are before you continue on your journey to somewhere else: *Some refugees jumped on the trains as they passed through East Germany.* ❑ *He didn't want to get too deeply involved, because, as he told himself, after all he was just passing through.* **2** Something **passes through** or **is passed through** something else when it moves or is moved through it going in at one side and out at the other: *The wafer-thin ears of many bats act as sound frequency filters allowing all but the most ultrasonic frequencies to pass through.* ❑ *Some molluscs live as filter feeders passing water through or over their bodies.* ❑ *He then passed quickly through the crowd.* **3** You **pass through** a school or other teaching establishment when you spend a number of years being educated there: *They had passed through Kingsmarkham Primary School together.* **4** Something **passes through** a number of stages or phases when it goes through them, changing or being changed as it progresses from one stage or phase to the next: *Comte maintained that all societies necessarily passed through the same three stages of development.* ❑ *These are phases of 'normal development' that we pass through as we progress to being mature, integrated people.*

pass to

A duty, responsibility or property **passes to** someone when it becomes theirs: *presidential powers passed to the Chair of the Supreme Soviet.*

pass under

A road or vehicle **passes under** something when it goes underneath it from one side to the other: *Drive east from the ferry, and after passing under the motorway, follow the winding road*

up and onto where Emmetten stands.
• *noun* **underpass: underpasses**
An **underpass** is a tunnel under a busy road or motorway that walkers or cyclists use to cross from one side of the road to the other safely.

pass up (*informal*)
You **pass up** an opportunity or chance, or you **pass** it **up**, when you don't use it or take advantage of it: *Surely you wouldn't pass up a chance to study in France?*

past see panel in next column

paste /peɪst/: **pastes**, **pasting**, **pasted**

paste up
1 You **paste up** a poster or notice when you attach it to a wall using paste or a similar sticky substance. **2** In book, newspaper and magazine production, text and illustrations **are pasted up** when they are arranged and stuck down on page-sized pieces of paper for photographing and printing, or as a guide to how they should appear in the final printed version.
• *noun* **paste-up: paste-ups**
A **paste-up** is a sheet of paper on which the text and illustrations for a page of a book, magazine or newspaper have been arranged and stuck down.

pat /pat/: **pats**, **patting**, **patted**

pat down
You **pat down** something that is sticking up, such as your hair, when you flatten it by striking it gently with your hand several times: *She filled in the hole and patted the earth down so that it didn't look as if there had been anyone digging.*

patch /patʃ/: **patches**, **patching**, **patched**

patch together
You **patch** something **together** when you create it in a hurry using various parts or elements which don't necessarily fit together well but are all available at the time: *For several weeks,*

---

past /pɑːst/
Past is a preposition and an adverb.

1 MOVEMENT PAST
Past is used in phrasal verbs to show that the movement referred to involves coming up to or alongside someone or something, and then continuing beyond them. For example, when someone or something **goes past**, it moves towards you and then continues by; when you **brush past** someone you pass them quickly, with your body or clothing coming into contact with them as you go by; something **hurtles past** when it goes by very quickly; you **squeeze past** someone or something when you get by them with difficulty by forcing your way through a narrow space. There are many literal combinations using **past**, such as **drive past, float past, flow past, sweep past, race past, hurry past** and **sidle past.** It is also used to create new and often informal phrasal verbs, as is shown in the following two examples: *She ghosted* [= seemed to float through the air like a ghost] *past me, and curled up in an armchair.* ❑ *Lorries bullied past* [= forced smaller vehicles out of their way] *on a road that had once been a towpath.*

2 MOVEMENT IN TIME
Past is also used in phrasal verbs that refer to movement in time. For example, the days, weeks or years **fly past** when time seems to go by very quickly; and they **drag past** when time seems to pass very slowly.
The only phrasal verb with **past** that has a non-literal meaning is **put past,** and it is normally used with a negative in the form of a fixed phrase; so that, when you say you wouldn't **put** something **past** someone you mean that you wouldn't be surprised if they did it or had done it, as in the following example: *'Surely he wouldn't have taken his father's car without permission!' 'I wouldn't put it past him!'*

he scurried back and forth trying to patch together an arrangement for co-operation with the Tory dissidents. [*same as* **cobble together**]

patch up

1 You **patch up** a quarrel or disagreement that you've been having with someone, or you **patch** things **up**, when you both agree not to quarrel or disagree any more: *I'm glad to hear they've patched things up and are friends again.* **2 a** You **patch up** something that has been broken or damaged, or you **patch** it **up**, when you do a quick temporary repair on it so that it can be used again: *The garage patched up the bodywork but it really isn't a very satisfactory job.* **b** (*informal*) A doctor or surgeon **patches up** a wounded or injured patient when they give them temporary treatment *eg* by cleaning, stitching and bandaging their wounds or performing an emergency operation at the scene of an accident to repair as much damage as possible.

patter /'patə(r)/: patters, pattering, pattered

patter about *or* patter around

A small, light person or animal **patters about** or **around** when they move about or run from place to place with light, tapping footsteps: *He could hear the puppy pattering about on the tiled floor.*

pattern /'patən/: patterns, patterning, patterned

pattern on

Someone **patterns** themselves **on** another person when they copy what that person has done or follow the example they have set; something **is patterned on** something else that already exists when its design or construction has been based on, and is therefore similar to, that other thing: *The complex was patterned on an American-style shopping mall, with everything under one roof.* ❑ *As a military strategist, he patterned himself on Napoleon.* [*same as* **model on**]

pave /peɪv/: paves, paving, paved

pave over

An area of ground **is paved over** when it is covered with paving stones or bricks to form a hard level surface: *The plan is to take up the lawn and pave over the entire area.*

paw /pɔː/: paws, pawing, pawed

paw at

1 An animal **paws at** something when it touches it repeatedly with its paw or hoof: *The reindeer pawed at the ice and snow to reach the lichens beneath.* **2** (*informal*) Someone **paws at** you when they touch you repeatedly in a way that you find annoying or offensive: *She said he was a very nice man, but she couldn't bear it when he pawed at her.*

pay /peɪ/: pays, paying, paid

pay back

1 You **pay back** money that someone has lent you when you return it to them; you **pay** someone **back** when you return the money that you owe them: *Grants intended to help meet the cost of extra fuel in very cold weather do not have to be paid back.* ❑ *Budgeting loans are paid back by weekly deductions from benefit.* ❑ *I can lend you something as long as you pay me back this week.* [*same as* **repay**] **2** You **pay** someone **back** for something bad they have done to you when you get your revenge on them or punish them for it: *'It was awful what he did to you!' 'Don't fret, I'll pay him back; make his life a misery.'* [*same as* **pay out**]

• *noun (AmE informal)* **payback**
You give someone **payback** when you do something bad to them to get revenge for something bad they have done to you.

pay for

1 You **pay for** something when you give money in exchange for it: *By far the safest way to pay for mail order goods is by credit card.* ❑ *The inclusive tour, in which every item of travel arrangement was paid for in advance, was Thomas Cook's invention.* **2** Someone **pays for** something they have done wrong when they are punished for it or are made to suffer because of it: *He paid for his mistake with his life.* **3** Something you have bought, especially something that may have cost you a lot of money at the time, **pays for** itself when its use saves you more money than it cost because it enables you to do things more cheaply or efficiently: *The machine is so cheap to run it'll have paid for itself in a couple of years.*

pay in

You **pay** money **in** when you put it in your bank or building society account: *Have you paid that cheque in yet?* [*opposite* **draw out, withdraw**]

• *adjective* **pay-in**

A **pay-in** slip or form is a printed form from a bank that you use to pay money into your account.

pay into

You **pay** money **into** a bank or building society account when you put or transfer it into the account: *You can vary the amount you pay into the savings plan, more when you can afford it, less when you have less money available.*

pay off

1 You **pay off** a debt when you return to the lender all the money you owe them: *The crunch came when my bank asked me for my credit card back and demanded I pay off the overdraft at once.* ❑ *Never borrow more money to pay off existing debts.* [*same as* **repay, settle, discharge**] **2** A business or organization **pays off** workers when it makes them redundant, paying them the wages or salary that they are entitled to up to the time of redundancy; a worker **is paid off** when their employer makes them redundant: *Another slump in the construction industry meant that most companies were paying off men.* ❑ *It came as a very nasty shock when he heard he was being paid off.* [*opposite* **take on**] **3** Something you do **pays off** if it has profitable results: *It was at this stage that the intensive training in navigation paid off.* ❑ *My persistence paid off when the RCA allowed me to take up my place on a joint MA course in the departments of Environmental Media and Design Education.* **4** You **pay** someone **off** when you bribe them with money in order to get rid of them, usually because they have been threatening you or blackmailing you: *If you pay him off this time, he'll just come back for more.*

• *noun (informal)* **payoff: payoffs**

1 A **payoff** is a successful or profitable result from a course of action or policy which involved a certain amount of risk or uncertainty. [*same as* **reward**] **2** A **payoff** is also money paid to someone as a bribe.

pay out

1 You **pay out** money for something when you spend it, especially reluctantly, on that thing: *You won't be paying out any more money than you did before.* ❑ *The Western Australian government paid out $13 million to cover land purchases in 1975.* [*same as* **lay out** (*informal*), **shell out** (*informal*), **spend**] **2** You **pay out** money when you give someone what they are due or entitled to receive *eg* as wages or winnings from a bet: *He announced that the full prize money would be paid out.* **3** (*informal*) You **pay** someone **out** for some wrong they have done you when you get your revenge or punish them for it. [*same as* **pay back**] **4** To **pay out** a length of rope is to release it bit by bit: *The tow rope was made fast, and paid out enough to keep the crippled yacht two waves astern of the lifeboat.*

• *noun* **pay-out**: **pay-outs**
A **pay-out** is money paid to people entitled to receive it, *eg* the total amount paid to winners in various forms of gambling: *The total payout on this week's lottery was 14 million pounds.*

pay up (*informal*)
1 You **pay up** when you give someone the money you owe them, especially when you do so unwillingly: *It became obvious that Mrs Schofield wasn't going to pay up without a struggle.* **2** (*informal*) You **pay** something **up** when you pay for it in instalments: *You can put down 20% now and pay the rest up over six months.*
• *adjective* **paid-up**
Paid-up members of a society, club, or political party are members who have paid in full the money or subscription required to be a member.

peal /piːl/: peals, pealing, pealed

peal out
Someone's voice or laughter **peals out** when it makes a loud sound that reverberates like bells ringing: *Heads turned in surprise as her raucous laughter pealed out in the hushed reading-room.* [*same as* **ring out, resound**]

peck /pɛk/: pecks, pecking, pecked

peck at
You **peck at** your food when you eat only small mouthfuls of it because you have no appetite or because you don't want to appear greedy: *And there was Aunt Mabel, ever so genteel, pecking at her food and piercing us with her disapproving gaze.* [*same as* **pick at**]

peel /piːl/: peels, peeling, peeled

peel off
1 You **peel** something **off** a surface when you pull it off carefully, usually in one piece; the outer covering of something **peels off** when it becomes detached from the surface in small pieces or strips: *I bought a sandwich and carefully peeled off the cellophane.* ❑ *Use a soft cloth to ease the strip into place, peeling off more backing paper as you progress.* ❑ *For sliced veneers, the timber is clamped and slices peeled off by a machine like a very large plane.* ❑ *She went through six weeks of agony after her skin literally peeled off.* **2 a** (*informal*) You **peel off** when you undress: *Blanche peeled off, throwing her clothes over the back of a chair.* [*same as* **strip off**] **b** You **peel off** a piece of tight or wet clothing when you take it off slowly and gradually using pulling movements: *She peeled the wet trousers off.* **3** A vehicle or aeroplane that has been travelling along as part of a tightly-packed group **peels off** when it suddenly leaves the group by turning away to one side and moving off in a different direction: *One of the accompanying destroyers peeled off from the convoy and began the search for the submarine.*

peg /pɛg/: pegs, pegging, pegged

peg away *or* **peg away at** (*informal*)
You **peg away**, or you **peg away at** something, when you go on working steadily and determinedly in order to achieve your aim or objective or to complete a task successfully: *They had been pegging away for years trying to get the council to make the road one-way.* ❑ *The team pegged away at the opposition all through the first half and when Ashurst was careless with his feet, Pilgrim kicked the penalty goal.* [**plug away (at)** (*informal*), **work away (at)**]

peg out
1 You **peg** wet washing **out** when you hang it on a washing line to dry, fixing it with clothes pegs. [*same as* **hang out**] **2** You **peg out** something on the ground when you stretch it out and fix it in place with wooden or metal pegs driven

into the ground: *The animal skins were pegged out and left to dry in the sun.* **3** (*informal*) When you say that someone **has pegged out** you mean that they have died: *He must have been at least 95 when he eventually pegged out.* [*same as* **die**]

pelt /pɛlt/: pelts, pelting, pelted

pelt down (*informal*)
Rain **pelts down** when it falls very quickly and heavily: *The dust was washed away as the rain continued to pelt down.* [*same as* **bucket down** (*informal*), **pour down**]

pen /pɛn/: pens, penning, penned

pen in
You **pen** people or animals **in** when you confine them or shut them up in a small space or pen; you **are penned in** by something when it restricts your freedom to move or act in the way you want to: *Jay penned her in, one hand on each armrest of the chair she was sitting in.* ❑ *François felt penned in and suffocated by his overly-protective parents.*

pen up
Animals or people **are penned up** when they are kept in a small confined space or pen: *The calves were penned up in a long low shed.*

pencil /ˈpɛnsəl/: pencils, pencilling (*AmE* penciling), pencilled (*AmE* penciled)

pencil in
You **pencil in** something such as an appointment in your diary, or you **pencil** it **in**, when you write it in pencil rather than in ink, or include it only provisionally, so that it can be altered later if necessary: *My secretary will pencil our meeting in for 2.30 pm tomorrow.* ❑ *Next year they see profits increasing to £113 million with £143 million pencilled in for the following year.* [compare **ink in**]

pension /ˈpɛnʃən/: pensions, pensioning, pensioned

pension off
1 Someone **is pensioned off** when they are forced to retire from their job or work, but are given a pension by their employer: *Most clearing banks are pensioning off the local branch manager who had personal knowledge of his customers.* **2** (*informal*) You **pension off** a machine or piece of equipment that you've used for a long time when you stop using it and begin to use something more modern or efficient instead: *Don't you think it's time you pensioned off that old horse and got a tractor?*

people /ˈpiːpəl/: peoples, peopling, peopled

people by *or* people with
A place, especially a place that is created in someone's imagination, is **peopled by** or **is peopled with** a particular group or type of people or animals, when those are the people or animals that exist there, or are created in the person's imagination to populate that place: *a great stairway linking heaven and earth, peopled by angels ascending and descending* ❑ *She peopled her fantasy island with plumed parrots, preening dodos, and psychedelic land crabs.*

pep /pɛp/: peps, pepping, pepped

pep up (*informal*)
1 You **pep** something **up** when you make it more interesting or lively: *A shop-bought jar of cranberry sauce will benefit from a tablespoon or two of rum or brandy to pep the flavour up.* ❑ *It would be good if he pepped up his lectures with a few jokes.* [*same as* **liven up, enliven** (*formal*)] **2** Something **peps** you **up** when it makes you feel more energetic or lively, especially if you have been feeling tired or depressed: *A holiday in the sun is just the sort of*

tonic you need to pep you up. [*same as* **perk up** (*informal*)]

pepper /'pɛpə(r)/: **peppers, peppering, peppered**

pepper with
1 To **pepper** someone or something **with** a number of small missiles is to throw or fire a shower of them in their direction hitting them in various places at the same time: *He fired at the intruder peppering him with lead shot.* **2** Something **is peppered with** things when there are many of those things scattered around in various places on or in it: *a wide rolling plain, peppered with tiny villages.* **3** If someone **peppers** their speech or a piece of writing **with** a certain kind of language, or references to a particular thing, they use that kind of language, or refer to that thing many times when they are speaking or writing: *His speech was peppered with some of the most colourful oaths I have ever heard.*

perk /pɜːk/: **perks, perking, perked**

perk up (*informal*)
1 Someone who has been ill, depressed or unhappy **perks up** when they become more lively or cheerful; something **perks** them **up** when it makes them feel more lively or cheerful: *As he thought about the evening ahead he perked up slightly.* ❑ *Meals seemed to be the only thing that would perk them up.* [*same as* **buck up** (*informal*), **cheer up**] **2** You **perk** something **up** when you make it more interesting or exciting: *You can perk up the basic stew by adding some chilli powder.* [*same as* **liven up, spice up, pep up** (*informal*)]

permit /pə'mɪt/: **permits, permitting, permitted**

permit of (*formal*)
If a situation **permits of** a particular thing it allows it or makes it possible: *The rigidity of their rules and procedures permits of no freedom of thought or action.*

persist /pə'sɪst/: **persists, persisting, persisted**

persist in
Someone **persists in** a particular course of action or type of behaviour when they continue with it even when other people oppose them or say that they are wrong to do so: *I must warn you that if you persist in this reckless behaviour you risk losing everything.* ❑ *Why do you think he persists in going home early every Friday when he knows it is our busiest day?* [*same as* **go on, keep up**]

pertain /pə'teɪn/: **pertains, pertaining, pertained**

pertain to (*formal*)
If something **pertains to** another thing it concerns or is relevant to that other thing, or is connected or associated with it: *Sort out any booklets or manuals pertaining to the heating system or any other fixture you are leaving.*

peter /'piːtə(r)/: **peters, petering, petered**

peter out
Something **peters out** when it reduces, fades or gets less intense and comes gradually to an end: *Within a short distance from the airport, roads peter out to cattle tracks.* ❑ *The orchestra faded and finally Lachlan's fine solo baritone petered out.* ❑ *The artillery petered out between 3am and 4am, and then started again.*

phase /feɪz/: **phases, phasing, phased**

phase down
Something **is phased down** when it is gradually reduced to a lower or less

intense level of activity over a period of time: *Production will peak next month and then'll be phased down over the next six months.*

phase in

Something new **is phased in** when it is introduced slowly and gradually, or in stages, over a period of time: *The new tax allowances will be phased in over three years.* ❑ *Radical changes like this should be phased in gradually so that people have time to get used to them.* [*opposite* **phase out**]

phase into

Something new **is phased into** an existing system when it is introduced slowly and gradually into that system over a period of time: *Robots were phased into car-assembly plants across Europe.*

phase out

Something **is phased out** when it is taken away or removed slowly and gradually, or in stages, over a period of time: *Child tax allowances were phased out following the introduction of child benefit in 1977.* [*opposite* **phase in**]

phone /foun/: phones, phoning, phoned

phone around see phone round

phone back

Someone **phones back** or **phones** you **back** when they contact you by telephone some time after you have telephoned them, or they telephone you for a second time: *I waited to hear from him again, but he didn't phone back.* ❑ *Sorry, I can't speak to you just now; I'll phone you back later.* [*same as* **call back, ring back**]

phone for

You **phone for** someone when you telephone them to ask them to come and help you or do something for you; you **phone for** something when you telephone someone to ask them to bring or deliver it to you: *Quick! Phone for the doctor.* ❑ *Customers phoning for a pizza are guaranteed delivery within 20 minutes.*

phone in

1 Someone **phones in** when they contact a radio or television station by telephone either to make a comment on something that the station has broadcast or to take part in a programme in which the public's comments or questions are broadcast: *Listeners are invited to phone in with their comments.* ❑ *He's always phoning in to the BBC complaining about something or other.* **2** You **phone in** when you telephone your workplace, usually to inform them you can't come in because you are ill: *Quite a number of the staff phoned in sick after the Christmas break.* ❑ *Jill isn't at work today and she hasn't phoned in yet.*

• *noun* **phone-in**: **phone-ins**

A **phone-in** is a radio or television programme in which members of the public are invited to telephone the station to make comments or ask questions.

phone round

You **phone round** or **around** when you contact a number of people or companies by telephone to get or give them information about something: *Would you phone round the local florists and find out which can deliver a bouquet this afternoon?*

phone through

You **phone** information **through** to someone when you give it to them by telephone: *One of the CIA men had to phone a message through to Reagan.*

phone up

You **phone** someone **up** when you dial their telephone number and talk to them on the telephone: *The man from the council told me I could phone up any time and ask for rubbish to be collected.* ❑ *Sometimes he would phone* *her up and threaten her.* [*same as* **call up**, **ring up**]

pick /pɪk/: **picks**, **picking**, **picked**

pick at

1 You **pick at** your food when you eat very little of it: *Families sit around self-consciously picking at their dinners.* ❑ *He describes this way of eating as 'grazing'; picking at this and that all day long.* [*same as* **nibble at**, **peck at**] **2** You **pick at** something when you scrape pieces off it with your fingernails: *She was picking at the flaking paint.* ❑ *He seated himself on the cold tiles and picked at their dark dusty colours with one finger.*

pick off

1 You **pick off** something, or you **pick** it **off**, when you remove it from the place where it is attached using your fingers or fingernails: *A hair was stuck to the helmet. Philip picked it off carefully.* ❑ *If you pick off the scab the wound might get infected.* **2** Individuals in a group of *eg* soldiers **are picked off** by a gunman or gunmen when they are shot down one by one: *It was known as 'sniper alley' where both civilians and soldiers were regularly picked off.* ❑ *The men inside would then be fired on through the roof, picked off like pigeons in a cote.*

pick on

1 You **pick on** someone when you select them from a group: *The teacher always seems to pick on one of the girls to read aloud.* ❑ *I was picked on to lead the singing.* [*same as* **pick out**, **choose**] **2** Someone **picks on** you when they choose you, often unfairly and repeatedly, as a target for criticism or bullying: *Because he was different, he was picked on by the other boys.*

pick out

1 You **pick** something **out** when you select it from a group: *She picked out the most expensive engagement ring in the display.* [*same as* **choose**] **2** You **pick** someone or something **out** from a crowd or mass when you recognize or identify them: *It was hard to pick out faces he knew from the swaying mass of heads.* ❑ *My eyes became accustomed to the semi-darkness, so that I could pick out shapes about seventy-five yards away.* [*same as* **make out**, **distinguish**] **3** You **pick out** certain things from a mass or group when you remove them: *Wash the lentils and pick out any that look discoloured.* **4** A detail **is picked out** in a separate colour when it is painted or given a different colour from the background to emphasize it or make it more noticeable: *The room had a chimney-piece picked out in false stone-effect.* **5** You **pick out** a tune on a musical instrument when you play it slowly note by note: *By the age of two, she could pick out a tune on the piano.*

pick over

When you **pick over** a collection or mass of things you look or sort through them, taking or keeping any parts that are useful or usable: *He makes his living picking rubbish over and selling bits and pieces for cash.* ❑ *She found Rodney and Veronica in the kitchen picking over a pile of fungi.*

pick through

1 You **pick** your way **through** something when you find a way through it taking care to avoid obstacles: *We picked our way through the lush undergrowth.* ❑ *Picking her way through the rubble, she eventually came to the place where her house had stood.* **2** You **pick through** something when you select the parts or things you want and leave the rest: *Crows are perfectly adapted for a life among craggy rocks, devouring a few mice, picking through a nice gamey carcass occasionally, but mostly just hovering gracefully on thermals below cliffs.*

pick up

1 You **pick** something **up** when you

take hold of it and lift it, usually with your hands or fingers; something **is picked up** when someone or something lifts it off the ground: *Stanley picked up a newspaper and started to read.* ❑ *He saw an envelope on the floor, and bending down, picked it up.* ❑ *Women in brown shawls picked up their babies and shouted to their children to come inside.* ❑ *a machine with great gaping jaws that could pick up cars and move them around the junk-yard.* **2 a** You **pick** yourself **up** when you stand up again after falling: *Astonishingly, after tumbling headlong down the steps, she picked herself up and walked away as if nothing had happened.* **b** You **pick up** your feet when you lift each foot off the ground as you walk, instead of dragging or scuffing your feet along the ground: *Major Vine snapped at the men to pick up their feet and straighten their shoulders.* **3** You **pick** someone or something **up** when you go and fetch them from the place where they are waiting to be collected: *You can pick me up about half past two.* ❑ *Next night he remembered to pick up the video on the way home from work.* **4** You **are picked up** by a passing car, helicopter or boat when it stops to give you a lift or take you on board: *The crew of the stricken tanker were picked up by the Peterhead lifeboat.* **5** You **pick up** something such as a skill or language when you learn it casually through observation and practice, rather than through formal teaching or training: *You may know only a few German phrases now, but you'll soon pick it up.* **6** You **pick up** a habit, especially a bad one, when you copy other people who do it: *He'd picked up a few nasty little habits since I last came across him.* **7** You **pick up** an infectious disease when you get it by coming into contact with the thing that infects you: *Paul's picked up a throat infection that's proving very difficult to get rid of.* [*same as* **catch, contract** (*formal*)] **8** You **pick up** things like news or ideas when you gather them from various sources or hear about them through casual contact with other people: *Along the way you pick up little techniques that help you control your behaviour, or get your own way.* ❑ *I wonder where he picks up ideas for new recipes?* **9** You **pick** things **up** when you get them or buy them cheaply: *You can pick up all sorts of bargains at car-boot sales.* **10** You **pick up** points or penalties when you gain them during a match or competition: *Hull picked up their first win of the season against Leeds on Sunday.* ❑ *The Republicans also picked up an estimated 14,000 votes from the Social Democrats.* ❑ *You will pick up penalties for stepping out of the area.* **11** You **pick up** a radio or television transmission when you receive it on your equipment: *The only programme our radio would pick up was Soviet propaganda, in English.* ❑ *TV programmes picked up by the satellite on Bykov's roof.* **12** Someone **is picked up** by the police when they are arrested and taken to the police station: *Never before have so many young men been picked up for questioning in one day.* **13** An individual or organization **picks up** the bill for something when they pay for it: *It doesn't seem fair that the taxpayer should have to pick up the bill for their incompetence.* **14** You **pick up** when you recover from an illness, or your health improves; something that has been in a bad or poor state **picks up** when it improves: *Iain wasn't at all well, but thankfully he's beginning to pick up now.* ❑ *Trade picked up slowly towards the end of the year.* ❑ *He reckons the economy will soon pick up again.* [*same as* **get better**] **15** You can say that something **picks** you **up** when it makes you feel better or more cheerful: *It was the only hangover remedy that really did pick him up the morning after.* **16** A vehicle or vessel **picks up** speed when it starts going faster; the wind **picks up** when its force increases: *As they picked up speed* *along the main tarmac road, it was already 3 am.* ❑ *We steered clear of the crashing waves off Rubha Dubh Tighary as a Force 5 gale picked up from behind.* ❑ *The wind has picked up a bit.* **17** You **pick up** a story that someone else has left unfinished, or cannot finish because they do not know what happened next, when you continue with it: *Anton picked up the story from the point when I had left the group to do some shopping.* **18** (*informal*) Someone who tries to **pick** you **up** tries to get to know you in the hope of having a sexual relationship with you: *Maybe he's taken a course in French film as a way of learning to pick up girls.* ❑ *A couple of American sailors tried, unsuccessfully, of course, to pick us up.*

• *noun* **pick-up**: **pick-ups**

A **pick-up**, or a **pick-up** truck, is a type of small open-backed lorry that can be easily loaded and unloaded.

pick up on

1 You **pick up on** something when you return to it after doing or discussing something else for a time: *He has a habit of picking up on topics discussed in previous conversations.* **2** You **pick up on** something when you notice it and draw others' attention to it by beginning to discuss it or challenge it: *Neither of these points were picked up on in the debate.* **3** (*informal*) Someone **picks** you **up on** something that you have said when they point out that it is wrong: *The interviewer failed to pick him up on the obvious contradictions in his argument.*

pick up with

You **pick up with** a person or a group of people, often one that others disapprove of, when you begin to spend time regularly in their company: *Since he came home he's picked up with those young thugs again.*

piece /piːs/: pieces, piecing, pieced

piece out

You **piece out** a story or picture of something when you manage to complete it by discovering or fitting together its several parts or details: *Archaeologists are painstakingly piecing out the mystery of what happened to the once-thriving Iron Age community.*

piece together

1 You **piece together** something such as a story or the truth when you gradually collect all the relevant facts and understand how they fit together: *Police piecing together the events of Tuesday night have discovered that the killer robbed another couple a few minutes earlier.* ❑ *It's difficult to know what of the last few days I remember, or have pieced together, or have been told by Nathan.* **2** To **piece together** something broken or torn into fragments is to mend it, or reform it, by fitting all the pieces together again: *Piecing together and gluing the broken shards is a job for an expert.* ❑ *Eliot's poem seems at times to be attempting to piece together some new religion out of the fragments of the old.*

pig /pɪg/: pigs, pigging, pigged

pig out (*informal*)

To **pig out** is to eat a lot of food in a very short time, especially fattening food such as ice cream or cakes: *I drove back, pigged out on a high-calorie breakfast, and read the Sunday papers.* [*same as* **gross out** (*informal*), **overeat, overindulge**]

pile /paɪl/: piles, piling, piled

pile in

People **pile in** when they all move in quickly to a place or vehicle in a disorderly crowd: *Then the lads all piled in and the bus moved off.*

pile into

People **pile into** a place or vehicle when they move inside it quickly in a disorderly crowd: *We all had to pile into a speedboat and literally flee for our lives.*

pile on
1 (*informal*) You can say that someone **is piling on** something such as work or pressure when they are giving you more and more of it: *Labour is beginning to pile the pressure on in this pre-election period.* ❑ *Duncan Ferguson smashed a shot into the crossbar as the home side piled on the pressure.* **2** You can say that people **pile on** when they get on a vehicle or raised platform in a disorderly crowd: *The minibus arrived and we piled on with all our gear.*

pile out
People **pile out** of a place or vehicle when they leave it quickly, in a disorderly crowd: *Around twenty Scotland supporters piled out of the carriage, shouting and singing.*

pile up
1 You **pile** things **up** when you put them one on top of the other in a pile: *Clean plates were piled up on the draining board.* ❑ *an old lady with silvery hair piled up high and a pale, invalid's face.* [*same as* **stack up**] **2** Things **pile up** when they accumulate so that there is a great amount or number of them in one place; work **piles up** when it accumulates so that there is a large amount to deal with: *There was a long halt as the traffic jam piled up ahead.* ❑ *Rotting rubbish was piling up in the streets.*

• *noun* **pile-up**: **pile-ups**
A **pile-up** is a road accident in which several vehicles crash into each other: *a four-car pile-up on the first lap of the British Formula Three Championships as Silverstone.*

pilot /'paılət/: **pilots**, **piloting**, **piloted**

---

pilot through
You **pilot** someone or something **through** when you guide them safely through something that is full of dangers or obstacles: *It was a real achievement to have piloted the legislation through a largely hostile Commons.*

pin /pın/: **pins**, **pinning**, **pinned**

---

pin down
1 Someone **is pinned down** when they are trapped because someone or something is preventing them from moving, progressing or escaping: *They found themselves pinned down by snipers in a narrow gully.* ❑ *Firemen battled to free the man from the steel beam that was pinning him down.* **2** You can **pin** something **down** if you are able to describe or identify exactly what it is: *She had an eerie sense that she was acting out something she had done before, but she couldn't pin it down.* [*same as* **put one's finger on**] **3** You **pin** somebody **down** to something, or to a specific time, when you force them to decide to do it, or do it at that time: *He wasn't too keen to commit himself to an exact time, but I managed to pin him down to the next afternoon at 3pm.*

pin on *or* **pin upon**
1 You **pin** something **on** or **upon** something else when you fasten it to that other thing with a pin or pins: *A distinctive gold badge was pinned on her chest.* **2** You **pin** the blame for something **on** someone when you say that they are responsible for it: *We were trying to pin the blame on each other for messing up the day.*

pin up
You **pin** something **up** when you attach it to a vertical surface such as a wall or noticeboard with a pin or pins: *The notices were pinned up high to avoid any graffiti.* ❑ *Draw the line out in pencil first, using your spirit level, and then pin up the battens and check the level again.*

• *noun* **pin-up**: **pin-ups**
A **pin-up** is an attractive woman or

man whose photograph is often used to decorate people's walls: *Overnight it seemed, he'd become a teenage pin-up.* ❑ *Betty Grable, the American forces' favourite pin-up girl.*

pine /paɪn/: **pines**, **pining**, **pined**

pine for

You **pine for** someone or something that you have lost or can't be with when you long for them so much that it makes you unhappy: *The 31-year-old actor plays Nestor Castillo, a melancholic trumpet player who pines for Maria, the love he left behind in Cuba.*

pine away

Someone **pines away** when they are so unhappy that they gradually become weaker and weaker, and eventually die: *The dog refused to eat and simply pined away.*

pipe /paɪp/: **pipes**, **piping**, **piped**

pipe down (*informal*)

When someone tells you to **pipe down**, they are telling you firmly to be quiet or to stop talking: *'Pipe down, you lot, and listen to what Miss Hudson has to say.'* [*same as* **shut up** (*informal*), **belt up** (*informal*)]

pipe up

Someone **pipes up** when they speak unexpectedly or break the silence by saying something: *And then, out of the blue, Cooper piped up, 'I know, miss.'*

piss /pɪs/: **pisses**, **pissing**, **pissed**

piss about *or* piss around (*vulgar slang*)

1 People sometimes say that you **are pissing about** or **pissing around** when they are very annoyed with you because they think you are wasting time: *As per usual, Tom spent half an hour pissing about in the garage before we could leave.* [*same as* **arse about** (*vulgar slang*), **faff about** (*informal*), **fart about** (*vulgar slang*), **mess about** (*informal*)] **2** To **piss** someone **about** is to treat them badly or unfairly: *Nicola had gone out about 9am saying she was going on an executive management course on How to Piss People About.* [*same as* **mess about** (*informal*)]

piss down (*vulgar slang*)

People sometimes say it **is pissing down** when it is raining heavily: *'Is it still pissing down at Achnacarry?' he asked.*

piss off (*vulgar slang*)

1 When someone tells you to **piss off** they are telling you very rudely to go away: *'Piss off, will you,' one of them hissed at me.* **2** When people say that someone or something **pisses** them **off** they mean that person or thing annoys or bores them very much: *Quite honestly I'm getting pretty pissed off with Wilko.*

pit /pɪt/: **pits**, **pitting**, **pitted**

pit against

You can say that someone **is pitted against** another person or thing when they are set against each other in a fight or contest: *Pilots pitting their skills against the forces of nature.*

pitch /pɪtʃ/: **pitches**, **pitching**, **pitched**

pitch in *or* pitch into (*informal*)

1 You **pitch in** when you start something or join in something with a great deal of energy and enthusiasm; you **pitch into** something such as work or food when you start doing it or eating it with a great deal of energy or appetite: *There was a great deal to do, so we all had to pitch in.* ❑ *Like ravenous dogs, they pitched into the cakes and chocolates.* [*same as* **wade in, weigh in**] **2** You **pitch into** someone when you start to attack them or criticize them vigorously: *The Shadow Chancellor pitched into his opposite number and accused him of misleading* *the House.* [*same as* **lay into** (*informal*), **wade into** (*informal*), **weigh into** (*informal*)]

plague /pleɪg/: plagues, plaguing, plagued

plague with

1 Someone who **is plagued with** irritating or unpleasant things suffers from, or is bothered by, them continually and can't get rid of them: *Britain, as a society, continued to be plagued with social division after 1945.* **2** You **plague** someone **with** questions or demands when you bother them with a constant stream of them: *He said he didn't want to be plagued with embarrassing questions by the press, so was getting away until the fuss died down.*

plan /plan/: plans, planning, planned

plan ahead

You **plan ahead** when you make plans for the future: *When you reach retirement age, you are planning ahead for the time when you may not be as capable as you were.* ❏ *They were able to plan ahead with confidence.*

plan for

You **plan for** something when you make plans that include it or take it into account: *We now need to plan for increasing numbers of elderly people.*

plan on

When you **plan on** doing something you decide in advance to do it: *When organizing a jumble sale, don't plan on selling too much at more than 10 pence an item.*

plan out

You **plan** something **out** when you make a detailed plan so that you know exactly how or when you will do it: *You should plan out your time so that you can get through the work reasonably comfortably.*

plane /pleɪn/: planes, planing, planed

plane away *or* plane off

You **plane away** or **plane off** uneven or excess parts from wood when you remove them with a sharp-bladed tool called a plane: *Strip the paint off the windows, then plane off a little wood before repainting.*

plane down

You **plane** wood **down** when you make its surface smooth using a plane.

plant /plɑːnt/: plants, planting, planted

plant out

To **plant out** seedlings or small plants that have been grown in a tray or pot is to put them in the ground outside with enough space to grow: *Over winter keep cuttings in pots indoors and plant them out in the spring.*

play /pleɪ/: plays, playing, played

play about *or* play around

1 You can say that someone **is playing about** or **playing around** if they are doing something in a not very serious way: *You had better stop playing about and take school a bit more seriously.* **2** (*informal*) **a** Someone who **plays around** has one or more casual sexual relationships with other people while they are married or have a permanent partner: *The judge told the court that even if the accused's wife was playing around, that was no excuse for murder.* **b** You **play around** with someone when you have a casual sexual relationship with them while you are married or in a permanent relationship: *He'd been playing around with one of the young researchers in his office.* **3** You **play about** or **play around** with things such as ideas when you think about them or experiment with them to find out how they might work or what sort of result they might produce: *Murray's been playing around with a few ideas for the* *new model; making it more environmentally-friendly.*

play along

1 You **play along**, or **play along** with someone, when you keep them happy by co-operating or agreeing with them, or pretending to do so: *He was the one who masterminded it. I just played along because I was scared of him.* ❑ *Perhaps if we play along with them they might let us go.* **2** You **play** someone **along** when you make them believe that that you will eventually do what you have no intention of doing: *She's been playing him along for years, but doesn't have the least intention of marrying him.*

play at

1 a Someone who **is playing at** some activity is not doing it in a serious or responsible way: *You can't just play at being a parent; it takes total commitment all the way.* **b** Someone who **is playing at** a job or role is pretending that they have that job or role: *They spend their weekends playing at being soldiers.* **2** You ask what someone **is playing at** when you are annoyed at them for doing something foolish or wrong: *You nearly got yourself killed back there: what on earth did you think you were playing at?*

play back

You **play back** a film or sound recording when you watch it or listen to it immediately after the filming or recording: *Camcorders can play back their recordings immediately after they have put them onto tape.* ❑ *She played back the messages on her answerphone.*
• *noun* **playback:** *playback on low band equipment* ❑ *a playback deck.*

play down

You **play** something **down**, or you **play down** its importance or significance, when you try to make it seem unimportant or of no significance: *The government had tried to play down the dangers of pollution.* ❑ *She talks about her beauty as a fact which she will neither boast about nor play down.*
• *verb* **downplay: downplays, downplaying, downplayed**
You **downplay** something when you try to make it seem less important or significant than it really is: *Many graduates, in such a world, learn to downplay their qualifications.* ❑ *While they downplay the importance of routine in their daily lives, they can usually be found in the local pub by 7pm.*

play off

Two sporting teams **play off** when they play against each other to decide which will be the winner.
• *noun* **play-off**: **play-offs**: *a sudden-death play-off between O'Connor and Kite* ❑ *The National Football League play-offs are about to begin.*

play off against

When someone **plays** one person **off against** another they deliberately try to make them quarrel or be suspicious of each other, usually in order to gain some advantage for themselves: *The tension between the Soviet Union and the West allowed national liberation movements to play one side off against the other.* ❑ *The playwright plays one neighbour off against the other.*

play on

1 Sportsmen or musicians **play on** when they continue to play after an interruption or through something that might have been expected to have caused them to stop: *The ref ignored their pleas for a penalty and ordered them to play on.* **2** Light **plays on** an object or surface when it falls on or is directed towards it, often moving back and forth across it: *The sergeant's torch played on a single figure ten yards away.* **3** Someone or something **plays on** or **upon** your feelings when they have a strong effect or influence on them; someone **plays on** or **upon your** good nature or weaknesses when they take advantage of them for their own benefit: *The condition of his sister still played on his mind.* ❑ *music that plays on the emotions* ❑ *The Tories played on the electorate's fears that Labour was the 'tax and spend' party.*

play out

1 An event **is played out** when it is acted or happens as if it were a play or a scene in a play: *Though every second customer is probably just like me, this charade is going to be played out on the basis that I'm being difficult.* ❑ *This initially provincial dispute was played out on the national stage.* **2** (*informal*) Someone or something **is played out** when they are exhausted or finished, or have no further usefulness or relevance: *The notion that women can't function without a man is played out.*

play through

1 You **play** a piece of music **through** when you play it from beginning to end: *Play the adagio through and then I'll make comments or suggestions.* **2** In golf, you **play through** when you take your next shot without waiting for your partner or other players on the course to take their turn or play their shots first.

play up (*informal*)

1 A machine **is playing up** when it is not working properly: *Suspecting that the compass was playing up again, Wood altered course by 5 degrees.* [*same as* **act up** (*informal*)] **2** A part of your body, especially a diseased or injured part, **is playing up**, or **is playing** you **up**, when it is giving you a lot of pain: *I see the Major's limping again. His old wound must be playing him up.* **3** Children who **are playing up** are behaving badly and refusing to cooperate: *Some of the older boys were playing up and wouldn't sing.* [*same as* **act up** (*informal*)]

play upon see play on

play up to (*informal*)

1 You **play up to** someone when you flatter them or make them feel important: *It's quite sickening the way she plays up to the party bosses.* **2** You **play up to** some quality or characteristic that people believe you have when you behave in a way that makes them go on believing that you have it: *They think she's only about seven or eight, and she plays up to this for all she's worth.*

play with

1 Children **play with** things when they spend time amusing themselves with them and using them as toys: *The baby had crawled behind the sofa and lay there playing with his toes.* **2** You **play with** a sporting team when you are a member of that team: *the New Zealand prop forward who plays with the Canberra Raiders in Australia.* **3** You have a certain amount of something to **play with** when you have more of it than you are likely to need: *There were four of us, climbing the route in two parties of two, with four 50 metre ropes to play with.*

plead /pliːd/: pleads, pleading, pleaded *or* pled /plɛd/

Note that the usual past tense and past participle is **pleaded**. However, American and Scottish speakers of English also use **pled**, as in the phrase '*He pled guilty*'.

plead for

1 You **plead for** something when you ask or beg for it in an urgent or emotional way: *Signs pleading for slower driving seemed to have no effect.* **2** Someone **pleads for** someone else when they argue or speak in defence or support of that person; a lawyer **pleads for** his or her client when they represent them and speak for them in a court of law: *No master pleaded for his future.* ❑ *Mullach and Lionan departed leaving Marsco to plead for them.*

plead with

You **plead with** someone to do something when you beg them to do it in an urgent and emotional way: *Wilson heard Mr Browning plead with his wife to say something to him.* ❑ *Jakali's husband's ploughing bull had died and he'd pleaded with Kalchu to lend him one of his.*

plod /plɒd/: plods, plodding, plodded

plod away
You **plod away** when you work very slowly but steadily at something: *He'll never be a high-flier, but he plods away and gets through the work I set him.*

plod on
You **plod on** when you continue walking or making progress at a very slow but steady pace: *The rest of the walkers plodded on through the rain.*

plonk /plɒŋk/: plonks, plonking, plonked

plonk down (*informal*)
You **plonk** something **down** when you put it down heavily without taking very much care where you put it; you **plonk** yourself **down** when you sit down heavily, or you sit down in a place where you have not been invited to sit: *Carrie came in and plonked her bucket down on the newly polished table.* ❑ *He roamed around the room before plonking himself down in a chair by the fire.* [*same as* **plump down**]

plot /plɒt/: plots, plotting, plotted

plot against
Someone **plots against** you when they make secret plans to damage your reputation, disrupt your plans or undermine your position: *He started to imagine that some of his closest advisors were plotting against him.*

plot out
You **plot out** *eg* a route, or you **plot** it **out**, when you work it out by marking it on a map: *They used a large-scale ordnance survey map to plot out their route.*

plough (*AmE* plow) /plaʊ/: ploughs, ploughing, ploughed

plough back
Profits **are ploughed back** into a business when they are reinvested in the business that made them.

plough in
When farmers **plough** a crop **in** they cover it with soil turned over by a plough to make the ground more fertile or because the crop is not worth harvesting: *Prices fell so catastrophically it made more financial sense to plough the crop in.*

plough into
1 When a vehicle **ploughs into** another vehicle or some other obstacle it crashes into it violently: *The two girls died when the car ploughed into them from behind.* **2** You **plough** money **into** something when you invest large amounts of money in it: *The message from the north is that the Rugby Football Union needs to plough more resources into its missionary work in the area.* **3** Manure or a crop **is ploughed into** the earth when it is mixed with the soil using a plough.

plough on
You **plough on** when you continue doing something despite its difficulty: *The temptation is to plough on regardless instead of cutting your losses.*

plough through
1 When something **ploughs through** something else, it forces a way through it: *I ploughed through the trough in the snow.* **2** When you say that you **are ploughing through** something you mean that you are working your way through it slowly and with some difficulty: *Five hundred and thirty-one pages is a lot to plough through.* ❑ *Not wanting to appear rude we ploughed through a bucket of beer between us.*

plough up
A crop or land **is ploughed up** when the soil is broken up and turned over with a plough: *In those days we ploughed the sugar beet up, then chopped the tops off and put them in heaps.*

pluck /plʌk/: plucks, plucking, plucked

pluck at
To **pluck at** something is to take hold of it and pull it with a quick movement before letting go again: *A small boy was plucking at his sleeve.* ❑ *One fan sang along and plucked at an imaginary guitar.*

pluck out
To **pluck out** something, or to **pluck** it **out**, is to take it out by taking hold of it and making a quick pulling movement: *He plucked out the thorn from her finger.* ❑ *If thine eye offend thee, pluck it out.*

plug /plʌg/: plugs, plugging, plugged

plug away *or* plug away at
(*informal*)
To **plug away**, or **plug away at** something, is to work slowly and steadily at it in order to finish it successfully or achieve your aims: *The company needs to keep plugging away to get the City to really sit up and take notice.* ❑ *British auction houses continue to plug away at the Japanese market.* [*same as* **peg away (at)** (*informal*), **work away (at)**]

plug in
You **plug in** an electrical appliance, or you **plug** it **in**, when you connect it to the power supply by means of an electrical plug: *They had the headsets on and plugged in at the console.* ❑ *'This lamp isn't working.' 'Have you tried plugging it in?' she asked in a sarcastic tone.*

plug into
1 You **plug** an electrical appliance **into** the mains when you connect it to the mains by pushing its plug into an electrical socket: *Plug the computer into the mains and switch on.* **2** (*informal*) You **plug into** a particular activity or movement when you find out things about it such as what makes it work or what motivates the people involved, so that you can understand it: *After all, one of the reasons I'm doing this job is that I'm plugged into what's going on in the musical world.*

plug up
To **plug up** a gap or hole, or **plug** it **up**, is to fill it or block it by pushing something into it: *A sticky mixture of tar and horsehair was used to plug up any gaps.*

plumb /plʌm/: plumbs, plumbing, plumbed

plumb in
You **plumb in** a washing machine or dishwasher when you connect it to the water supply and waste pipe so that it will fill and drain when it is switched on.

plumb into
A washing machine or dishwasher **is plumbed into** the main water supply when it is connected to it.

plump /plʌmp/: plumps, plumping, plumped

plump down
You **plump** something **down** somewhere you put it down suddenly or let it drop or fall heavily or carelessly; you **plump** yourself **down** when you sit down suddenly and heavily: *Pamela plumped her rounded behind down on the chair next to Norman's.* ❑ *He'd plumped the carcasses down in the middle of the kitchen floor.* [*same as* **plonk down** (*informal*)]

plump for
You **plump for** something when you suddenly make a decision to select it

from a number of things that you might choose, especially after a period of hesitation or careful thought: *Her heart sank when she thought of her husband's stupidity at plumping for the easy money rather than a more secure job.* ❑ *We're not certain which it is, but we're going to plump for the first definition.*

plump out *or* plump up

You **plump out** or **plump up** cushions or pillows when you shake and squeeze them so that they form fat rounded shapes: *The hen settled in the nest, plumping out her feathers to cover the chicks.*

plunge /plʌndʒ/: plunges, plunging, plunged

plunge in

1 You **plunge in** when you dive suddenly into deep water so that you are immersed in it: *Sometimes a kingfisher will perch on an overhanging twig, cock its eye at the water and plunge in for fish.* **2** You **plunge in** when you say something or become involved in something suddenly without thinking too much about it beforehand: *Tony plunged in with a spirited but rather ill-thought-out defence of their actions.* [*same as* **leap in**]

plunge into

1 To **plunge** one thing **into** another is to push the first into the second with so much force that it sinks into it: *Richard plunged his sword into William's horse.* **2** To **plunge into** water is to dive or be pushed into it quickly and become immersed: *He slithered down the slope and plunged into the stinking waters of Muddy Beck.* **3** A place **is plunged into** darkness when it is suddenly made dark: *They were plunged into shadow between the woods of Birnam.* **4** You **plunge into** something when you begin doing it suddenly or become deeply involved in it very quickly without thinking too much about it beforehand: *I literally had to plunge into the abyss and find out what I could about what they wanted me to do.* ❑ *He has plunged into the knowledge of the East and extended the borders of occidental knowledge.*

ply /plaɪ/: plies, plying, plied

ply between

A ship, plane or bus **plies between** two places when it travels from one to the other and back again regularly: *a local Indonesian vessel plying between Anjer in Java and Telok Betong in Sumatra.*

ply with

You **ply** someone **with** food, drink or questions when you keep offering or giving them food or drink, or asking them questions: *The landlord of the Ostrich would ply wealthy travellers with drink.* ❑ *She plied him with questions about his visit to Tamar's home. 'What was it like?' she asked.*

point /pɔɪnt/: points, pointing, pointed

point out

1 a You **point** something **out**, or you **point** it **out** to someone when you indicate it to them in some way: *The islands of Capri, Procida and Ischia had been pointed out to her.* ❑ *He can take you to the loch and point out precisely where you will be sure to catch fish.* **b** You **point** a particular person **out** when you identify them from amongst a group, especially by pointing your index finger in their direction: *I don't know who the director is. Can you point him out to me?* **2** You **point out** something when you mention it to people for consideration, or draw it to their attention: *I examined my contract and pointed out a minor discrepancy in it to Personnel.* ❑ *Sceptics point out that the Conservatives' share of the vote is less than it was in the 1960s.*

point to

1 You **point to** something when you indicate it or identify it by holding out your index finger in its direction; the hand of a watch or the needle of a compass **points to** a particular figure or letter on the dial when that is the time or direction it is indicating: *Aggie pointed to the seat at the front of the cart.* ❑ *It is one o'clock when the big hand is pointing to 12 and the little hand is pointing to 1.* **2** Something **points to** something else when it draws people's attention to it: *Good presentation points to and highlights the message that you want to get across.*

point towards
1 Something **is pointed towards** something else when it is in a position or is placed so that it facing in the direction of that thing: *With your knees flexed comfortably and your racquet pointing towards your opponent, move your weight on to the balls of your feet.* **2** Something **points towards** something else when it indicates, or seems to indicate, that other thing: *a recent batch of opinion polls pointing towards a hung parliament.*

point up
You **point up** something, or you **point** it **up**, when you draw particular attention to it or highlight it: *She compares the two activities, drawing parallels and pointing up interesting distinctions.*

poke /pouk/: pokes, poking, poked

poke about *or* poke around
1 Someone **pokes about**, or they **poke around** or **round** somewhere when they look or search through it, either looking for something in particular or looking to see if there is anything interesting there: *He saw the light again, flashing in and out of the crumbling walls. Someone was in there, poking about.* ❑ *We can take the lid off the box and poke around inside.* **2** You can say that someone **is poking about**, or they **are poking around** or **round**, when they are making enquiries or trying to find information out about something that you think is none of their business: *He was poking around in his sly way.*

poke at
You **poke at** something when you push something sharp into it with jabbing movements: *Anna poked at her soggy cereal until the milk spilled on to the table.* [*same as* **prod at**]

poke out
1 Something **pokes out** when it protrudes or sticks out from some-where: *There was his big toe, poking out of a hole in his sock.* **2** You **poke** part of your body **out**, especially your head, when you push it out of a hole or opening: *He poked his head out of the bedcovers to listen.* ❑ *Wardens in tin helmets poked their noses out of sandbagged alarm posts as we walked by.* **3** You **poke** something **out** when you remove it from somewhere using a sharp implement: *You have to poke them out of their shells with a pin.*

poke round see poke about

poke through
Something **pokes through** when part of it appears through or is pushed through a narrow gap or hole in something: *Look closely and you'll see the tips of new shoots poking through the leaf litter.*

poke up
1 Something **pokes up** when it appears out of, or above the level of, something, having pushed through it or through a narrow gap from beneath: *Some sort of home-made aerial poked up from the top of the bunker.* **2** You **poke up** a fire when you jab at the wood or coals with a poker to make them burn more brightly and give off more heat: *Grandad rose, poked up the fire, and then settled himself again cosily in a big leather chair.*

polish /ˈpɒlɪʃ/: polishes, polishing, polished

polish off (*informal*)
You can say that you **polished** some-

thing **off** when you finished it quickly and easily: *He watched her polishing off the final remains of her large meal.* ❑ *He'd polished off his first two matches in three sets.*

polish up

1 You **polish up** an object or piece of furniture when you rub it with polish so that it shines: *Will you be polishing up your medals for the big parade?* **2** You **polish up** a skill or technique when you improve it by practising: *If you're going to camp out on the mountain, you'd better polish up your survival skills.* ❑ *The cast were polishing up their lines.*

ponce /pɒns/: **ponces**, **poncing**, **ponced**

ponce about *or* **ponce around** (*offensive, slang*)

Sometimes people say that someone **is poncing about** or **around** when they think that person is behaving in a silly way or isn't doing what they should be doing: *All he does is ponce about the office trying to look important.*

ponder /'pɒndə(r)/: **ponders**, **pondering**, **pondered**

ponder on *or* **ponder upon** (*formal or literary*)

You **ponder on** or **upon** something when you think about it carefully, especially when you are trying to work out how best to deal with it: *He pondered on the afternoon ahead and was so involved in his thoughts that he didn't hear the boy speak.* ❑ *He has certainly given us something to ponder on.*

pop /pɒp/: **pops**, **popping**, **popped**

pop in *or* **pop into** (*informal*)

1 You **pop in** somewhere, or you **pop into** a place, when you go in for a short while, usually without arranging to do so beforehand: *We'll pop in somewhere for a drink and a snack on the way to the theatre.* ❑ *'I'm just popping into the butcher's,' she said brightly.* **2** You **pop** something **into** your mouth or a container when you put it there with a quick movement of your hand; something **pops into** your mind or your head when you suddenly think of it: *Will you pop this card into his pigeonhole, please?* ❑ *The idea just popped into my head.*

pop off (*informal*)

1 You **pop off** when you go away, usually in a hurry; you **pop off** somewhere when you go there quickly: *'I'm just popping off now. Cheerio, everyone.'* ❑ *She said she had to pop off home.* **2** People sometimes say that a person **has popped off** when that person has died: *When I eventually pop off I want all my friends to have a big party.*

pop out

Something **pops out** when it comes out of somewhere quickly; something **pops out** when it is forced out, sometimes making a popping sound as it comes out: *A figure popped out of a doorway to Alexei's left.* ❑ *His eyes seemed to be popping out of his head with uncontrollable anger.*

pop up

Something **pops up** when it appears or occurs suddenly and unexpectedly: *With so much spare cash floating around, it was inevitable that entrepreneurs would pop up and try to claim it for themselves.*

pore /pɔː(r)/: **pores**, **poring**, **pored**

pore over

You **pore over** something such as a book when you study it carefully and with great concentration: *Alicia found him poring over the documents, his brow furrowed with concentration.*

portion /'pɔːʃən/: **portions**, **portioning**, **portioned**

portion out

You **portion** something **out** when you

share it out by first dividing it into parts or portions: *We want to be able to portion the work out fairly.* [*same as* **share out**]

post /poust/: **posts**, **posting**, **posted**

post up

Information **is posted up** when it is displayed on something such as a wall or noticeboard so that people can read it: *The exam results will be posted up in the main hall tomorrow morning.*

potter /'pɒtə(r)/: **potters**, **pottering**, **pottered**

potter about *or* potter around

When you **potter about** or **around** you move from place to place in a slow or relaxed way, sometimes doing small unimportant jobs: *When I was feeling a little better, I pottered about the house in pyjamas.* ❑ *A cruising dinghy is an ideal boat for the whole family to use and generally potter around in.*

pounce /pɑuns/: **pounces**, **pouncing**, **pounced**

pounce on *or* pounce upon

A person or animal **pounces on** you when they suddenly jump towards you and grab you: *He thought there were bears that pounced on you if you stepped in the lines in the pavement.* ❑ *Edward, hoping to slink past unnoticed, was pounced upon and told to hurry to his classroom.*

pour /pɔː(r)/: **pours**, **pouring**, **poured**

pour away

You **pour** a liquid **away** when you get rid of it by pouring it out of a container into a drain: *The farmers were each losing £1000 a week pouring away milk supplies.*

pour down

Rain **pours down** when it falls very heavily: *The rain poured down in Carmarthen and the streets were like rivers.*

• *noun* **downpour**: **downpours**
A **downpour** is a very heavy shower of rain: *They looked as if they had been caught in a sudden downpour.*

pour forth

Something **pours forth** when it comes out in a continuous stream or dense mass: *She wasted no time, the words pouring forth before he could draw breath.* ❑ *a scene of devastation with buildings pouring forth black smoke as they burned.*

pour in *or* pour into

People or things **pour in** when large numbers of them come into a place in a continuous stream; you can also say that they **pour into** the place: *Huge quantities of mail are beginning to pour in.* ❑ *More cavalry poured in from the woods and fields.* ❑ *Its vast volume of water pours into a huge cleft in the earth.*

pour off

You **pour off** liquid when you tip the container it is in so that some or all of it pours out: *Pour off the fat before it solidifies.*

pour on

You **pour** scorn or ridicule **on** or **upon** someone or something for something they have said or done, when you make scornful remarks about them to show your contempt: *His article poured scorn on their thesis.*

pour onto

People **pour onto** a place or area when large numbers of them move onto it in a steady stream: *People poured onto the streets waving flags.*

pour out

1 You **pour out** liquid from a container when you make it flow out of that container into another: *He poured out a large measure of whisky.* **2** Something such as liquid or smoke **pours out** of a place when it comes out in a rapid flow: *Petrol was pouring out of the tanker*

and spreading over the road. **3** Someone **pours out** their feelings or worries when they tell them to another person in a continuous flow with no hesitations: *There was the Contessa pouring her heart out to Rudolpho, who looked as if he would rather she didn't.*
• *noun* **outpouring**
When there is an **outpouring** of strong feeling many people express that feeling publicly: *This outpouring of compassion was greater than they had ever anticipated.*

pour over
You **pour** liquid **over** something when you pour it on top so that it covers it: *Arrange the tagliatelle on a serving dish and pour over the sauce.* ❑ *Pour the sauce over the fish.*

pour upon see **pour on**

pour with (*informal*)
People often say it **is pouring with** rain when it is raining heavily; you can also say you **are pouring with** sweat when you are sweating so heavily that it is running off your body: *It poured with rain all day.*

prance /prɑːns/: **prances**, **prancing**, **pranced**

---

prance about
People **prance about** or **around** when they move about in a light-hearted or foolish way, often with exaggerated or comical movements: *In the film, two well-known actors prance about in women's clothes.*

preclude /prɪˈkluːd/: **precludes**, **precluding**, **precluded**

---

preclude from (*formal*)
Something **precludes** you **from** doing something when it prevents you from doing it or makes it impossible for you to do it: *The school authorities took the view that J's learning difficulties did not preclude him from following the normal curriculum.*

predispose /priːdɪsˈpouz/: **predisposes**, **predisposing**, **predisposed**

---

predispose to *or* **predispose towards** (*formal*)
Something **predisposes** you **to** an illness or unpleasant medical condition when it makes you very likely to suffer from that illness at some time in the future; something **predisposes** you **to** or **towards** a particular course of action or set of beliefs when it makes you very likely to take that course of action or adopt those beliefs at some time in the future: *A diet too high in refined sugar and fat will predispose people to either obesity or a shortage of nutrients, including essential minerals.* ❑ *His upbringing predisposed him towards scepticism.*

preface /ˈprɛfɪs/: **prefaces**, **prefacing**, **prefaced**

---

preface with *or* **preface by**
To **preface** something **with** something else is to introduce or precede the second thing with the first; something **is prefaced by** something else when that other thing comes before it and acts as an introduction to it: *Their embrace had been prefaced with romantic dialogue and declarations of love.* ❑ *a catalogue of painting by Noël Coward prefaced by a memoir of the playwright, describing his interest in painting.*

present /prɪˈzɛnt/: **presents**, **presenting**, **presented**

---

present to
1 An award or gift **is presented to** someone when they are given it, often as part of a ceremony and by somebody important: *Gold medals were again being presented to tennis players at the Seoul Olympics in 1988.* **2** You **are presented to** some important person when you are formally introduced to them: *He was presented to the governor, Lord Plunkett.*

present with
1 You **are presented with** something when you are given it in a formal ceremony: *The prizewinner was presented with a cup which had been awarded for the first time in 1987.* **2** You **are presented with** a problem or difficulty when you are given it to deal with: *In this case, the neighbourhood police were presented with a dilemma.* [*same as* **face with**]

preside /prɪˈzaɪd/: **presides, presiding, presided**

preside over
Someone **presides over** a group of people or a state when they act as the president of that group or state: *Agostinho Neta, politician and poet, was to preside over the new state.*

press /prɛs/: **presses, pressing, pressed**

press ahead
You **press ahead** with something you intend to do when you carry it out with determination as quickly as possible: *The other 10 EC nations were determined to press ahead with the Maastricht Treaty.*

press for
You **press for** something when you ask for it urgently and repeatedly: *MPs had been pressing for an enquiry following publication of a damning report on school discipline.*

press into
You **press** someone **into** a course of action or activity when you force them to do it: *Haddow was pressed into service as his assistant.*

press on
You **press on** with something you are doing when you continue with it in a determined way; you **press on** somewhere when you continue your journey there without delay: *He is keen to press on with modernizing the party's policy-making machinery.* ❑ *She pressed on, her legs aching, until she could walk no further.*

press upon
You **press** something **upon** someone when you force them to take it even when they don't want it: *Dotty made alarming potions from herbs and pressed them upon her unwilling neighbours and friends.*

presume /prɪˈzjuːm/: **presumes, presuming, presumed**

presume on *or* **presume upon** (*formal*)
Someone **presumes on** or **upon** your good nature or generosity when they take it for granted or take advantage of it: *We wouldn't presume upon your hospitality unless it was a dire emergency.*

pretend /prɪˈtɛnd/: **pretends, pretending, pretended**

pretend to (*formal*)
Someone **pretends to** an important title or property when they claim they have a right to it: *'Should any other prince pretend to any right to these lands, I am ready to defy him and defend them in the name of the Kings of Castile.'*

pretty /ˈprɪtɪ/: **pretties, prettying, prettied**

pretty up
Something that people regard as ugly or unpleasant **is prettied up** when it is given a more attractive or acceptable appearance or image: *The publics relations people are trying to pretty it up and make it seem less shocking and shameful.*

prevail /prɪˈveɪl/: **prevails, prevailing, prevailed**

prevail on *or* **prevail upon**
You **prevail on** someone to do something, or you **prevail upon** them to do it, when you persuade them to do it: *Our mothers would be prevailed upon*

to lend us metal meat skewers which we used to bore holes in the conkers. ❏ *Can he be prevailed on to give us a little more time to pay?*

prey /preɪ/: **preys**, **preying**, **preyed**

prey on *or* **prey upon**
1 A bird or animal **preys on** or **upon** another when it hunts and kills it for food: *The young fish prey on plankton, and, as they grow, larger species.* ❏ *Many smaller species of lizard are heavily preyed upon.* **2** Something **preys on** your mind when you can't stop worrying or thinking about it: *She was allowing Amy's predicament to prey on her nerves, sapping her confidence.* ❏ *His unannounced departure preyed on her thoughts. Had she done something wrong?*

prick /prɪk/: **pricks**, **pricking**, **pricked**

prick out
You **prick out** seedlings when you plant them in soil in small holes made with your finger or a thin stick.

prick up (*informal*)
1 An animal **pricks up** its ears, or its ears **prick up**, when its ears stand up straight in response to a sound: *The horse's ears pricked up at the unfamiliar noise.* **2** You **prick up** your ears, or your ears **prick up**, when you begin to listen more carefully because you have heard something interesting: *She thought she heard voices coming from the next room. She moved closer to the door and pricked up her ears.*

print /prɪnt/: **prints**, **printing**, **printed**

print off
You **print off** a certain number of copies of something such as a book or photograph when you print that number: *They'll print off ten thousand leaflets to begin with, more if we need them.*

print out
You **print out** data from a computer when you produce a printed copy of it: *You can print out what's on the screen at any time.* ❏ *Parish records are available in printed-out form from a microcomputer.*
• *noun* **printout**: **printouts**: *He was tearing off sections of printout as it came tumbling out of the machine.* ❏ *We've received the material on disks, but we haven't done printouts yet.*

prise *or* **prize** /praɪz/: **prises**, **prising**, **prised**

prise off
You **prise off** something that is fixed tightly to something else when you remove it by placing something under it to act as a lever: *The workmen prised the lid off the coffin.* ❏ *We thankfully prised off our crampons; the end of 17 hours climbing.*

prise out
To **prise out** something that is fitted tightly into something else is to remove it gradually and with some difficulty using some sort of lever or levering movement: *He tried to prise himself out of the chair, as the figure moved towards him.*

proceed /prə'siːd/: **proceeds**, **proceeding**, **proceeded**

proceed against (*formal; legal*)
To **proceed against** somebody is to take legal action against them: *Her barrister has advised that she proceed against both companies.*

proceed from (*formal*)
One thing **proceeds from** another when the first happens or exists as a result of the second, or comes from it: *Michelangelo's works have a strong and marked character and seem to proceed from his own mind entirely.*

prod /prɒd/: **prods**, **prodding**, **prodded**

prod at
You **prod at** something when you push your fingertip or some other long implement towards it or against it: *Smith was prodding unenthusiastically at the goat stew.* ❑ *Lee prodded at the dead animal with a stick.* [*same as* **poke at**]

profit /'prɒfɪt/: **profits**, **profiting**, **profited**

---

profit by *or* **profit from**
You **profit from** something when you gain something from it; you **profit by** something when you make a gain as a result of doing it: *The more one plays a piece of music through, the better it goes, and even the poorest conductors profit from this.*

prohibit /prə'hɪbɪt/: **prohibits**, **prohibiting**, **prohibited**

---

prohibit from (*formal*)
You **are prohibited from** doing something when you are not allowed to do it: *His wife and son are prohibited from participating in any kind of public political activity.*

pronounce /prə'nɑuns/: **pronounces**, **pronouncing**, **pronounced**

---

pronounce on *or* **pronounce upon** (*formal*)
When someone **pronounces on** or **upon** something they give an authoritative judgement or opinion on it: *Once the European Court of Human Rights had pronounced upon the matter they had no choice but to comply with their ruling.*

prop /prɒp/: **props**, **propping**, **propped**

---

prop up
1 You **prop** something or someone **up** when you support them or keep them upright by leaning them on or against something: *She propped herself up on one elbow.* ❑ *The roof had to be propped up before the damage could be assessed fully.* **2** One person or group **props up** another when they support or help the other financially: *a benefit system that will prop up the rich in temporary difficulty but is reluctant to help people who are literally out on the streets* ❑ *The industry had to be propped up with government money.*

protect /prə'tɛkt/: **protects**, **protecting**, **protected**

---

protect against
1 Something that **protects against** harm or a harmful effect prevents it from happening or affecting you: *Use a sunscreen that protects against both UVA and UVB rays.* ❑ *Breast feeding helps protect babies against allergy and infection.* **2** An insurance policy or guarantee **protects against** some kind of loss, illness or injury when it guarantees to pay a sum of money in the event of that loss, illness or injury happening: *The policy protects against redundancy and critical illness.*

protect from
You **are protected from** something unpleasant when something prevents it happening to you or affecting you: *I pulled on the wool socks and thick trousers I wore to protect me from the cold.* ❑ *Younger women are protected from heart disease, but in later life are just as vulnerable as men.*

protest /prə'tɛst/: **protests**, **protesting**, **protested**

---

protest against
You **protest against** something when you hold a protest or use some other means of expressing your opposition to it: *violent clashes between police and students protesting against the arrest of two of their leaders* ❑ *He protested vehemently against what he regarded as a demotion.*

provide /prə'vaɪd/: **provides**, **providing**, **provided**

---

provide against
You **provide against** something which

might happen in the future, especially the risk of financial loss, when you make arrangements to ensure that it doesn't happen, *eg* by insuring against it: *With increased job insecurity, it makes sense to provide against loss of income, even if it is only temporary.*

provide for

1 You **provide for** someone when you supply money and other things they need to live: *He wasn't able to provide adequately for his family on his meagre pay.* **2** You **provide for** an event or situation when you include it in an arrangement or make it part of a plan, agreement or contract: *The plan provided for the withdrawal of Soviet troops in exchange for the guaranteed neutrality of Afghanistan.* ❑ *Finland's constitution provides for a parliamentary system of government as well as a presidency with considerable powers.*

provide with

Someone or something **provides** you **with** something when they give it to you; you **are provided with** something when it is given to you or made available for you to use: *We will provide you with a free uniform.* ❑ *This should provide you with the incentive to train harder and achieve even more.* ❑ *He was provided with a map and a compass, and nothing else.*

provoke /prə'vouk/: provokes, provoking, provoked

provoke into

Someone **provokes** you **into** doing something unreasonable or violent when they make you so angry that you react in that way: *He was provoked into giving the youth a quick slap on the ear, which he later regretted.* ❑ *Major was provoked by the Euro-sceptics into resigning as party leader.*

prowl /praul/: prowls, prowling, prowled

prowl about *or* prowl around

Someone **prowls about** or **around** when they move about in a stealthy way, especially when they are looking for something to steal: *He hasn't believed in Santa since he caught his parents prowling about with Christmas stockings in the dead of night.* ❑ *This was the third time she'd come across unauthorized people prowling around the ward.*

pry /praɪ/: pries, prying, pried

pry into

Someone **pries into** your affairs when they try to find out things about you when they have no right to do so: *The press has no right to pry into their private lives the way they did.*

psych *or* psyche /saɪk/: psychs, psyching, psyched

psych out (*informal*)

You **psych** someone **out** when you say or do things that make them lose confidence in their ability to compete against you successfully: *Of course, it's all a pantomime, intending to psych the opposition out.*

psych up (*informal*)

You **psych** yourself **up** to do something when you prepare yourself mentally for it by getting yourself into a confident mood: *You can see him talking to himself, trying to psych himself up.* [compare **hype up**]

puff /pʌf/: puffs, puffing, puffed

puff away

Someone who **is puffing away** is repeatedly drawing smoke into their lungs from a cigarette or pipe and blowing it out again in small clouds: *One of the boys produced a packet of cigarettes and soon all four of them were puffing away merrily.*

puff out

1 You **puff** something **out**, or it **puffs**

out when you make it, or it becomes, larger or fuller, *eg* by filling it with air or causing it to swell: *He was portrayed as a sort of elderly cherub, with puffed out cheeks.* **2** (*informal*) Something, especially vigorous exercise, **puffs** you **out** when it makes you exhausted or makes your breathing difficult: *She had felt full of energy till the long climb up the hill puffed her out.* ❑ *'What've you been doing? You look puffed out.'*

puff up
Something **puffs up** when it fills with air and becomes larger; if part of your body **puffs up** the soft tissues swell after a blow or injury: *It puffs up its body so that predators are deterred.* ❑ *From this photograph you can see that he has the typical puffed-up moon face of someone who has been taking steroids for a long time.*

pull /pʊl/: pulls, pulling, pulled

pull about *or* pull around
You **pull** someone or something **about** or **around** when you handle them roughly or violently: *The younger ones are often pulled about by their older siblings, but never seem to come to much harm.* ❑ *He was pulled around in the scrum, his shirt was torn, and his hair was standing up on end.*

pull ahead
Someone or something **pulls ahead** when they gradually get in front of others or go into the lead: *Labour was level with the Tories in the opinion polls in July 1978, and was threatening to pull ahead.*

pull apart
1 You **pull** a thing or things **apart** when you tear it into one or more pieces or separate them by pulling at either side: *The puppy had pulled the soft toy apart and was playing with the stuffing.* ❑ *Jack moved to the window and pulled apart the curtains.* **2** Someone **pulls** an idea or piece of work **apart** when they point out the faults in it or criticize it in a humiliating way: *His latest offering was pulled apart by the art critic on the 'Guardian'.* ❑ *She'd read my stuff, pull it apart, and then suggest I start all over again.* [*same as* **take apart**]

pull around see pull round

pull aside
1 You **pull** something **aside** when you move it to one side so that you can pass or see what is behind it: *Pulling aside the screen of overgrown plants, she found a door in the wall.* **2** You **pull** someone **aside** when you take them away from a group of people so that you can have a private conversation with them: *Francis pulled me aside and warned me to take care what I said to him.*

pull at
1 You **pull at** something when you grasp it, pull it towards you, and then let it go: *Someone was pulling urgently at my coat. I turned to find Jess standing just behind me.* ❑ *Four men pulled at the rope, but the boat was firmly stuck in the sand.* [*same as* **tug at**] **2** Someone **pulls at** a cigarette or pipe when they take long deep breaths to draw the smoke into their mouth and lungs: *'Hmm, let me see,' he said, pulling meditatively at a foul-smelling clay pipe.*

pull away
1 A vehicle or its driver **pulls away** when it starts moving after being stationary, *eg* at the side of the road or at traffic lights: *James Hunt pulled away from the start line.* ❑ *The two policemen gave chase but the white car pulled away before they could reach it.* **2** Something, especially a vehicle, that is moving ahead of you **pulls away** when it moves more quickly than you are moving so increasing the distance between you and it: *The boat was pulling swiftly away towards a distant ship.* **3** A person **pulls away** from someone who is holding them or touching them when they move back

and away from that person suddenly in alarm or surprise: *'Leave me alone, it wasn't me!' I cried, trying to pull away.* **4** You **pull** yourself **away** from something when you force yourself to leave, though you are very reluctant to do so: *It was all she could do to pull herself away from such a fascinating spectacle.*

pull back

1 Troops **are pulled back** when they are moved away from the front line: *The German forces had pulled back towards the Seine taking all their equipment with them.* **2** You **pull back** from something that you had been thinking of doing when you decide not to do it or be involved in it: *They've pulled back from all-out confrontation with the unions.* **3** You **pull** something **back** from a difficult situation you have got yourself into when you succeed in doing something that makes the situation better than it was: *They were a goal down when the captain scored, pulling them back from almost certain relegation.*

pull down

1 You **pull** something **down** when you lower it by pulling: *He watched me pull down the Jolly Roger and throw it overboard.* ❑ *Agnes bolted the door and pulled down the blind.* **2** A building or other structure **is pulled down** when it is deliberately taken down, *eg* to clear land or because it is unsafe: *A beautiful old Georgian terrace was pulled down to make way for the motorway extension.* ❑ *They had no choice but to pull it down before it fell down.* [*same as* **demolish**] **3** Worry, stress or an illness **pulls** you **down** when it makes you depressed or weakens you physically: *If you're already undernourished, the virus will pull you down very rapidly.* **4** (*informal*) If someone **pulls** you **down** they say or do something that lowers your standing or personal esteem, or your association with them causes you to fall to a lower social position: *She should leave him before he pulls her down any further.* **5** A mark or test **pulls** you **down** when it causes you to fail or move to a lower position in a class: *His overall mark was pulled down by the last assessment, which was very poor.* **6** (*especially AmE; informal*) When people talk about someone **pulling down** a certain amount of money each week or month they are referring to the amount of salary or profit that that person earns in that period: *Some of those city whizz-kids are pulling down a hundred grand a year.*

pull for (*informal*)

If someone is going through a difficult or testing time, you **are pulling for** them when you are giving them support or help, hoping that they will get through it successfully: *He felt utterly alone, as if there was no-one pulling for him, no-one on his side.* [*same as* **root for** (*informal*)]

pull in *or* pull into

1 A vehicle or its driver **pulls in**, or **pulls into** a place, when the vehicle leaves the road it has been travelling on and turns off and stops, *eg* at the side of the road or at a filling station: *We stopped and the police car pulled in behind.* ❑ *I pulled into the driveway of the third house on the right.* **2** A train **pulls in**, or **pulls into** a station, when it arrives there: *We tried to get a clear view of the platform and the hundreds of people watching the troop train pull in.* ❑ *At 6.30 am the next morning the train pulled into Central Station, Glasgow.* [opposite **pull out, leave**] **3** (*informal*) People sometimes say that someone **is pulling in** a large amount of money or large profits when they are earning it, often from various sources: *After a couple of successful shows in the Big Apple, you'll soon be pulling in the cash.* [*same as* **rake in** (*informal*)] **4** An event **pulls in** the crowds when a lot of people go to it: *He said he was getting out of the business; circuses* *weren't pulling in the crowds like they used to.* [*same as* **attract**]

pull off

1 You **pull** clothes **off** when you take them off in a hurry: *Georgina pulled off her coat and flung it on a chair.* ❑ *She could hear Ben pulling covers off chairs and tables, searching, restlessly searching for something.* **2** You **pull** something difficult **off** when you succeed in it or manage to achieve it: *He is backing his old club to pull off the first Premier League title.* [compare **bring off**] **3** A vehicle **pulls off** when it starts moving forward after being stationary: *The guard blew his whistle and we pulled off in clouds of steam.* [*same as* **pull away**] **4** A vehicle or its driver **pulls off** the road when the vehicle leaves the road and parks, or joins another road: *Ellwood saw them pull off the road into the driveway of a hotel.*

pull on

1 You **pull on** clothes when you put them on with a certain amount of difficulty, or in a hurry: *He pulled on his coat in silence.* **2** Someone **pulls on** a cigarette or pipe when they suck air through it with long steady breaths so that smoke goes into their mouth and lungs: *He pulled on a hand-rolled Havana cigar and smiled complacently.*

pull out

1 You **pull** something **out** when you take hold of it and remove it with a rapid movement of your hand from a container or the place where it is kept; you **pull out** something that has been embedded in something else when you remove it with a quick forceful movement: *He opened one of his desk drawers and pulled out a little tin box.* ❑ *He pulled a wad of hundred-dollar bills out of his pocket.* ❑ *a claw hammer, which can pull nails out as well as drive them in.* **2** A vehicle or its driver **pulls out** when it moves out from the side of the road, or moves to the centre of the road in order to overtake another vehicle going in the same direction: *He was struck by a van pulling out of a side street.* **3** A train **pulls out** when it leaves a station: *Several minutes before the express was due to pull out, there was no-one on the platform.* [*same as* **leave;** *opposite* **pull in**] **4** A person or organization **pulls out** of an agreement, undertaking or previously-arranged event when they withdraw from it: *He pulled out of the tournament with a sprained wrist.* ❑ *His chance for gold was gone when the US pulled out of the Moscow Olympics.* **5** An army **pulls out** or **is pulled out** when it leaves the place that it has been occupying or fighting in: *some of the British forces being pulled out of Northern Ireland.*

pull over

1 A vehicle or its driver **pulls over** when the vehicle moves closer to the side of the road, usually to park or to let other vehicles overtake: *We pulled over at a roadside café to have a cup of coffee.* **2** When the police **pull** you **over** they signal to you to move your car to the side of the road and stop: *The police can pull you over and check that your vehicle is roadworthy.*

• *noun* **pullover: pullovers**

A **pullover** is a piece of clothing you wear on the top half of your body, that you pull over your head to put on. [*same as* **jumper, sweater**]

pull round

1 To **pull** someone or something **round** is to turn them so that they face in the opposite direction: *Wilson grabbed me then and pulled me round to face him.* **2** You **pull** a bad situation **round** or **around** when you succeed in preventing it from ending in disaster: *The banks have given them six months to pull the business round.* **3** You **pull round** or **around** after an illness or an anaesthetic when you begin to recover or regain consciousness: *The doctors say that if he doesn't pull round in twenty-four hours, there isn't much hope.*

pull through

Someone **pulls through** when they recover from a serious illness or injury so that their life is no longer in danger; someone **pulls through** when they survive or overcome their personal troubles and difficulties; you **pull** someone **through** when you give them the help or support they need in order to recover or survive: *He's a fighter, and hopefully he will pull through.* ❑ *It was the love and support of our family that pulled us through.*

pull to

You **pull** a door or window **to** when you pull it so that it closes: *Bob pushed her onto the landing and pulled the bedroom door to behind him.*

pull together

1 People **pull together** when they work together to achieve a common aim or purpose: *'France and England never really pulled together, for all they might find themselves on the same side.'* **2** You **pull** the various elements of some scheme or plan **together** when you succeed in making it work: *I hope we can pull it together, but sometimes I have my doubts.* **3** You **pull** yourself **together** after being shocked or upset by something when you get your feelings under control so that you are able to act more rationally: *I saw him go pale and then visibly pull himself together before proceeding.* ❑ *Slowly the tears subsided and gradually I began to pull myself together.*

pull under

If you are swimming or paddling in water and something **pulls** you **under**, it drags you downwards so that you are under the surface: *The currents off the coast can pull even the strongest swimmer under.*

pull up

1 You **pull** yourself **up** when you are sitting or lying down when you bring your body into a more upright position using your arms: *The baby can pull himself up using the sides of the cot.* **2** You **pull up** a chair when you move it closer to someone or something: *Maggie pulled up a chair to be close to the fire.* **3** You **pull up** plants when you remove them from the ground by their roots: *Vandals had pulled up all the tulips and strewn them over the grass.* **4** A moving vehicle or its driver **pulls up** at a certain place when the vehicle comes to a stop there: *By the time he pulled up she was beginning to feel much better.* **5** You **pull** yourself **up** when you suddenly stop yourself doing or saying something: *He was just about to dive, saw the pool was empty, and pulled himself up just in time.* **6** (*informal*) You **pull** someone **up** when you scold or reprimand them: *He pulled me up about my work, saying it wasn't up to the required standard.*

pump /pʌmp/: pumps, pumping, pumped

pump in *or* pump into

1 You **pump** liquid or air **in** when you use a pump to force it in; you **pump** it **into** a place or container when you transfer it there using a pump: *The water was pumped in from a nearby tanker.* ❑ *Water from the Chattahoochee river is pumped into the peanut fields.* **2** Money **is pumped into** a business when large amounts of it are invested in that business over a period of time: *In the period between the wars, even more money was pumped into enlarging and rebuilding old pubs.*

pump out

1 Liquid or air **is pumped out** when it is forced out using a pump or as if it is being pumped: *The ocean pumping out waves that trip up against the jutting kerbs of the land.* **2** You **pump out** a container when you remove the liquid from it using a pump: *The tin mines nearer the coast had to be pumped out continuously.*

pump up

1 Liquid or gas **is pumped up** when it

is forced upwards using a pump: *Oil is pumped up from deep below the ground.* **2** You **pump up** a tyre or a football when you force air into it using a pump so that it reaches it correct size or pressure: *He'd checked the oil and pumped up the tyres.* [*same as* **blow up**]

punch /pʌntʃ/: punches, punching, punched

punch in
To **punch in** a series of letters or numbers is to enter them by hitting the appropriate keys on a keyboard: *Vic went to the console by the door and punched in a numerical code.*

punch out
1 A hole or shape **is punched out** when it is made by using a special machine with a part that cuts through wood, metal, plastic or paper when it is pressed down: *The star shapes were punched out using a steam press.* **2** (*slang*) You **punch** someone **out** when you hit them with a powerful punch that knocks them unconscious or makes them incapable of fighting back: *Come on, go for the knock-out! Punch him out!*

punch up
An amount **is punched up** on a cash register when the operator presses the appropriate keys with sharp tapping movements of their fingers: *He'd already punched it up on the till.*
• *noun* **punch-up**: **punch-ups**
A **punch-up** is a violent fight in which people hit each other with their fists: *Many of their recent matches have been marred by punch-ups on the pitch.*

push /pʊʃ/: pushes, pushing, pushed

push about *or* push around
1 You **push** something **about** or **around** when you move it across a surface from one place to the other: *Her walking-frame squeaked on the lino as she pushed it about.* ❑ *He was taken to L'Escargot to eat but just pushed his gourmet food around on his plate.* **2** Someone **pushes** you **around**, or they **push** you **about**, when they bully you or treat you roughly: *'You'd never have stayed around so long if I'd pushed you about.'* ❑ *I told him he couldn't push me around any more like a football from one job to another.* ❑ *a public body that felt pushed around by the Tories.*

push ahead
You **push ahead** when you continue to make progress in a determined and energetic way; you **push ahead** with a plan or scheme when you continue with it in a determined way despite difficulties or opposition: *Several of us felt we should push ahead as quickly as possible.* ❑ *The group is pushing ahead with an ambitious expansion strategy.* ❑ *Unfortunately, they weren't able to push ahead as fast with their plans as they had wanted.* [*same as* **push forward, push on** (*informal*)]

push along (*informal*)
When someone who has been spending time in your company or having a conversation with you says they must **push along** they mean that they must leave because they have somewhere else to go: *We'll have to be pushing along soon, George.* [*same as* **push off**]

push aside
1 You **push** someone or something **aside** when you push them out of your way: *He pushed her aside roughly, and opened the door.* **2** You **push** something **aside** when you dismiss it or treat it as unimportant: *Her request for clarification had been pushed aside and ignored.* [*same as* **brush aside, disregard**]

push back
1 You **push** something **back** when you move it backwards or back to the position it was in before: *Jonathan pushed back his chair and got up.* ❑ *She pushed back the lock of hair that had flopped over her eyes.* ❑ *Bob pushed*

her back onto the landing. **2** An army or a crowd **is pushed back** when they are forced to move back or retreat: *There was a possibility that the German Army might push the Commando Brigade back to the sea.*

push by
You **push by** someone who is blocking your path when you press your body against them roughly or rudely as you go past them: *Her eyes stared unseeingly at the people pushing by her into the Metro.* ❑ *The woman suddenly crossed the room, pushed by him, and ran down the stairs.* [*same as* **push past**]

push for
If you **push for** something to be done or to happen, you strongly recommend it to others or constantly ask people to support you and so help you achieve it: *The Irish government has been pushing for more rapid progress since September.* [*same as* **press for**]

push forward
1 Something **is pushed forward** when it is moved from the back towards the front: *This muscle makes it possible to pull the legs back, push the hips forward and straighten the legs.* **2** You **push forward** when you continue to make progress or advance in a determined way; you **push forward** with something you want to do or achieve when you continue with it in a determined way: *The crowd pushed forward eagerly.* ❑ *They announced that they would be pushing forward with plans for a single currency.* [*same as* **push ahead**, **push on**] **3** If someone **pushes** themselves **forward** they deliberately try to be noticed: *You have to push yourself forward in this business, or else you'll get nowhere.*

push in (*informal*)
When someone **pushes in** they force their way into a queue and take a place ahead of the people who were there before them; when someone **pushes in** they force their way into a place or group where they are not welcome: *I was here first. He pushed in ahead of me.* ❑ *Some of the demonstrators had pushed in to interrupt the meeting.*

push into
1 Something **is pushed into** place when it is put there with a pushing movement: *A dust bag is supplied and it very simply pushes into the side of the machine.* **2** You **are pushed into** doing something when someone else forces you to do it: *He said he wouldn't be pushed into resigning.*

push off
1 When you are in a boat or on a bicycle, you **push off** when you push against the shore or the ground so that you can begin to move away: *She put one foot on the pedal, pushed off with the other, and began to cycle away.* **2** (*informal*) If you say you are going to **push off** you mean that you are about to leave; when you tell someone to **push off** you are telling them rudely to go away: *'We'll push off now and see you in a couple of hours.'*

push on
1 Someone or something **pushes on** when they continue in a certain direction: *We stopped at the inn for a mid-day meal and then pushed on to Aubeterre.* ❑ *There were times when even the thought of the money wasn't enough to push him on to success.* **2** (*informal*) You **push on** with something that you want to complete when you continue to work steadily at it: *Raymond's working at the weekend so that he can push on with the job.*

push out
If someone **is pushed out** they are forced to leave their job or position by someone else: *Grieves didn't leave of his own accord; he was pushed out by the powers that be.* ❑ *He'd decided to get out before he was pushed out.*

push over

You **push** someone or something **over** when you knock them down or cause them to fall to the ground: *Some of the standing stones had fallen down or been pushed over.* ❑ *It was an obvious foul. He pushed the striker over deliberately.*

• *noun* (*informal*) **pushover**: **pushovers**

1 A **pushover** is a task that is easily accomplished or done: *He's clever and has worked hard all year, so he'll probably find the exam a pushover.* **2** A person can be referred to as a **pushover** if they can be very easily persuaded or influenced: *He's certainly not the pushover some people expected him to be.*

push past

Someone **pushes past** you when they press their body against yours rudely to force you out of their way: *The man started to push past, but Alexei caught his arm.* ❑ *He said something rude under his breath and tried to push past.* ❑ *She pushed past him roughly on her way to the kitchen.*

push through

1 You **push through** a solid mass of people or things when you force your way through them to the other side: *Bragg pushed through the crowd and bent over the body.* ❑ *She twisted out of his grasp and pushed through the swing doors.* ❑ *In a week or two the catkins will be out and spring flowers will begin to push through.* **2** You **push through** a proposal or plan, or you **push** it **through**, when you make a determined effort to get it accepted or put into effect: *Bandiera even admitted to doubts about some of the deals he had pushed through.* ❑ *Important bills were pushed through using the swift but effective parliamentary guillotine.* ❑ *Gorbachev used his powers to rule by decree to push the reform through.*

push to

You **push** a door or window **to** when you close it by pushing against it: *Bodo put out a large hand and pushed the door to.*

push towards

Someone **pushes towards** something when they make a determined effort to reach it: *To push him towards a record, Scott will be challenged by the six-times winner of the Nice Triathlon.*

push up

1 You **push** yourself **up** when you move upwards or move to a more upright position by pressing part of your body against a firm surface: *He used his heels to push himself up the slates on his backside.* **2** The level of something **is pushed up** when it is forced upwards: *Higher mortgage rates will push up inflation towards 8%.* ❑ *The markets have already pushed up rates by half a point.*

• *noun* **push-up**: **push-ups**

Push-ups are exercises done while lying face down in which you use your arms to lift the weight of your body off the ground: *I did a few push-ups and other exercises.*

put /put/: puts, putting, put

put about

1 Something such as a lie or rumour **is put about** when someone deliberately tells it to a lot of people in order to influence them: *They even suggest that these are lies put about by foreigners who don't understand the country's history and culture.* [*same as* **put round**] **2** A ship or boat **puts about** when it turns and begins to sail in the opposite direction. **3** (*informal*) You can say that someone **is putting** themselves **about** when they are making contact with a great many people, often to impress them or to achieve some aim: *You have to put yourself about a bit if you want the right people to notice you.*

put above

You **put** one thing **above** another or

others when you consider it is more important or valuable: *He puts creativity and originality above musicianship.*

put across

You **put** ideas **across** well, or you **put** them **over** well, if you express them so that they are clearly understood by your listeners or readers: *Keep it simple. Put it across as something they can't do without.* ❑ *They're increasingly dependent on 'spin-doctors' to put over the party message.*

put around see put round

put aside

1 You **put** something **aside** when you separate it from other things, often so that you can keep it for use later: *Their gardener put aside some of the best plants to take cuttings for next season.* **2** You **put** money **aside** when you save it, especially for a particular purpose: *Surely you have some money. Have you really got nothing put aside?* [*same as* **save**] **3** (*formal*) You **put** someone or something **aside** when you abandon them: *He'd put his first wife aside to marry a princess whose dowry included large areas of the adjoining province.* [*same as* **discard**]

put at

If the value or cost of something **is put at** a certain figure that is what it is estimated to be; if someone's age **is put at** a certain number of years that is the age that they are thought to be: *I would put it at nearer a thousand.* ❑ *The skeleton's age was put at about eighteen or nineteen years.*

put away

1 You **put** something **away** when you put it into the place where it is to be kept or stored: *'I have put away my paints and brushes for ever,' he said.* ❑ *The girls had washed and put away the cups and plates.* ❑ *The dishes had been washed and put away.* ❑ *It started to rain heavily before he could roll up and put away his prayer mat.* ❑ *It was time to put away childish things.* **2** (*informal*) You **put** money **away** when you save it: *You don't have to invest large sums; you can put away as little as £10 per month.* [*same as* **put by**] **3** In games such as football and snooker, a player **puts away** the ball when they kick it into the back of the goal net or hit it into the pocket: *Shortly afterwards Chandler put away the second.* **4** (*informal*) When people say that you can **put away** food or drink they mean that you can eat or drink a lot: *He was putting away cakes and sandwiches as if he hadn't seen food for a month.* **5** (*informal*) People **are put away** when they are sent to prison or to a secure hospital for people with severe mental illness: *She's a danger to herself and to others. She ought to be put away.* ❑ *The evidence we have should be enough to put him away for at least ten years.*

put back

1 You **put** something **back** when you return it to its proper place, or to the place it came from: *Iona picked up one of the figures, saw what it cost, and put it back hurriedly.* ❑ *The stones were collected in a trailer and taken away, instead of being put back on the field.* ❑ *You will begin to realize what action you need to take to put everything back on course.* **2** To **put** a planned event or procedure **back** is to delay it until a later time: *It meant that dinner had to be put back an hour.* [*same as* **postpone**] **3** You **put** a clock **back** when you adjust it so that it shows an earlier time, often one hour earlier. **4** People talk about **putting** the clock **back** when they would like to change something that has happened, or do it in a different way: *It's too late now; nothing can be done to put the clock back.* [*same as* **turn back**]

put before

You **put** a proposal or plan **before** someone when you offer it for their consideration: *proposals on electoral* *reform which could be put before the electorate either in a referendum or at the next general election.*

put behind

You **put** an unpleasant experience **behind** you when you decide that it will no longer affect you or influence you: *I can put all that fear behind me now.*

put by

You **put** something **by** when you keep or save it so that you have a supply for future use or emergencies: *Mrs Vane told him she might be able to help since she had a little money put by.* [*same as* **put away**]

put down

1 You **put** something you have been holding or carrying **down** when you place it somewhere *eg* on the floor or on a table: *Chief Inspector Kuhlman put down the phone and looked at Kurt Meyer.* ❑ *The small boy put down the basket he was weaving.* ❑ *I lifted the receiver, listened to the dialling tone, and put it down again.* **2** The police or army **put down** a revolt or rebellion when they use force to stop it: *The Americans dispatched marines to put down an uprising in Grenada.* [*same as* **crush**] **3** (*informal*) You **put** someone **down** when you criticize them and make them feel stupid: *Some women put her down for working with a man.* **4** An animal **is put down** when it is killed painlessly, *eg* because it is ill, old, or considered dangerous: *Poor old thing shouldn't be allowed to suffer any longer. I want him to be put down humanely.* [*same as* **put to sleep**, **destroy**] **5** You **put down** *eg* suggestions or ideas when you write them on paper: *I've put down four different headings.* ❑ *He put down whatever came into his head.* [*same as* **set down**, **note down**, **jot down**, **put in writing**] **6** Delegates to a conference or members of parliament **put down** a motion when they submit it in writing so that it can be debated: *This year 1073 motions have been put down, but only 18 will be debated.* **7** An aircraft **puts down** somewhere when it lands there: *The aircraft was put down very quickly on a small lake.*

• *noun (informal)* **put-down**: **put-downs**

A **put-down** is something that you say that makes someone appear foolish or stupid, or that criticizes them: *Miss Parker was an expert in the witty put-down.*

put down as

1 You **put** something **down as** something it is not when you write down or record it as being that thing, often in order to deceive: *He'd put it down as incidental expenses.* **2** You **put** someone **down as** a particular type of person when you decide that this what or who they are: *I hadn't put him down as the romantic type.*

put down for

1 You **put** your name **down for** something when you put your name on a list so that you can be considered or included: *They'd put his name down for Winchester when he was less than a year old.* **2** If someone is organizing a collection of money for something and you tell them to **put** you **down for** a certain amount you mean that you will pay them that amount later: *Put me down for 50 pence a mile.*

put down to

You **put** one thing **down to** another if you think the first is caused by the second: *I'd been having these terrible headaches, but I put them down to stress. It never occurred to me that I might need glasses.* ❑ *The accident could be put down to failure to maintain a safe airspeed at low altitudes.* ❑ *The evening's success should be put down to music that never ceases to delight.* ❑ *The decline of the forest was put down to a condition known as progressive spruce death.*

put forth

1 Someone **puts forth** an idea or opinion when they make it known to others or to the public in general: *A similar idea to Linde's was put forth independently some months earlier.* ❑ *The book accepts many of the arguments put forth by scholars of the judicial system.* [*same as* **put forward**] **2** (*rather formal*) To **put forth** something is to send it outwards: *The sun put forth all its power; it blazed and scorched.* ❑ *The plant grows quickly and puts forth floating leaves.* ❑ *Then the plants will bush out, putting forth fresh shoots at frequent intervals.*

put forward

1 a You **put forward** an idea when you suggest it for other people's consideration: *The arguments he put forward were very persuasive indeed.* ❑ *In his book Herbert Read took up the categories of types put forward by Jung.* ❑ *The case put forward by the pensions industry was less than persuasive.* **b** You **put** your name **forward** for something when you offer yourself as a possible candidate for a post or role; someone else **puts** your name **forward** when they suggest that you be considered as a candidate for a post or role: *It was then that Gordon Brown decided not to put his name forward for party leader.* **2** You **put** a clock **forward** when you adjust it so that it shows a later time. **3** You **put** a planned event **forward** when you arrange that it should happen earlier than originally scheduled: *Mother put lunch forward an hour so that we could leave to catch the 2.30 train.*

put in

1 You **put** something **in** a container or other enclosed space when you place it inside it: *She put her thumb in her mouth again as soon as her mother's back was turned.* ❑ *The children were wrapped in blankets and put in the car.* **2** You **put in** time or effort when you spend it on some activity: *He puts in the hours but the standard of his work is still not as good as it should be.* ❑ *Crisp was putting in an astonishing performance.* **3** You **put in** a claim when you make it officially or submit it to someone in authority: *Postal workers have put in a claim for a 10% pay rise.* **4** Someone **puts in** a remark when they make it: *'But it's not the same one,' Meg put in.*

• *noun* **input**

1 The **input** to a computer is the information or data that is put into it; **input** is also anything that is put in so as to produce some result. **2** Your **input** to *eg* a discussion is the contribution you make to it: *His input was pretty minimal.*

• *verb* **input: inputs, inputing, input**: *Open the file, then input the data you want to include.*

put in for

You **put in for** something when you formally apply for it: *He's put in for a transfer to another part of the company.*

put into

1 Someone or something **is put into** something when they are placed inside it or made to go inside it: *They were separated from the other passengers, put into a van and driven around for several hours.* **2** Someone sick or elderly **is put into** a retirement or nursing home when they are sent to live there, often by their own relatives. **3** You **put** money **into** something when you invest it or save it there: *The trust fund was set up to put capital into small businesses.* ❑ *She had her own flat bought with money that had been put into trust until her eighteenth birthday.* **4** You **put** a lot of thought, time or effort **into** something when you think about it for a long time or work at it for a long time: *What sickens me about it being destroyed is not the object itself but the time and thought I had put into it.* ❑ *A course for real enthusiasts who know that you only get out of a course what you put into it.* **5** You **put** a theory or plan **into** practice when you do it to see how it really works: *It gave them an opportunity to put into practice what they had learned.* **6** You **put** your thoughts or feelings **into** words when you express them using words: *They were too frightened to put into words what they had felt.*

put off

1 You **put** something **off** when you delay doing it: *The Mozarts set out for Salzburg to visit Leopold, a visit promised since their marriage but constantly put off.* [*same as* **postpone**] **2** Something **puts** you **off** doing something when it makes you unwilling to do what you wanted or intended to do: *The weather conditions weren't severe enough to put us off going for a sail.* ❑ *The house still had the gaunt, haunted look that had so put Meg off before.* [*same as* **deter**, **discourage**]

• *adjective* **off-putting**

Something is **off-putting** when it causes you to be less willing to do or continue with something: *Sudden and abrupt changes of direction will be off-putting for your opponent.* ❑ *The thought of cycling uphill for eight miles was a bit off-putting.*

put on

1 You **put** something **on** something else when you place it on top of that other thing: *Philip took the vase and put it on the table.* **2** You **put** clothes **on** when you put them on your body: *I sprinted back to the changing room to put on my gym shoes.* ❑ *She had put the hat on and taken it off again three times.* **3** You **put on** something such as a light when you press or turn the switch so that it begins to operate: *She led the way into a miniature kitchen and put on the kettle.* **4** You **put on** a record or tape when you place it on or in the record player or tape recorder so that it will play: *She put on another record.* **5** You **put on** a play or other entertainment when you organize it and perform it in public: *The drama society put on a short comic sketch.* ❑ *We put on three new plays by Will in the next year, and some plays by other writers.* **6** You **put on** weight when you gain weight: *He's put on a lot of weight since last year.* **7** You **put on** a certain type of behaviour when you deliberately behave in an unnatural way: *Then she puts on her little-girl-lost face.* ❑ *Can you really believe he's that concerned? I think he puts it on.* **8** Stress or strain **is put on** you when something causes you to feel it or suffer from it: *He was aware of the strain it had put on his relationship with George.*

put on to (*informal*)

When someone or something **puts** you **on to** something you hear about or discover it from them: *Fred put me on to this much cheaper place.*

put out

1 You **put** something **out** when you take it from inside a place and put it outside: *He put the cat out, locking the back door before he came to bed.* **2** You **put out** a light when you switch it off; you **put out** a fire when you extinguish it: *'Would you put out the light, please, dear?'* ❑ *Firemen who were called to put out the fire discovered the child's body.* **3** Someone or something **puts** you **out** when they inconvenience you: *Don't do it unless you have time. I don't want to put you out.* **4** You **are put out** by something when it causes you to feel anxious and upset: *He had to admit he was a little put out by her reaction.* ❑ *The Commandos in the trench with me didn't seem to be put out by the noise of the explosions.* [*same as* **disturb**] **5** You **put out** a message, request or warning on the radio when you broadcast it: *We couldn't put a message out on the radio because there was something wrong with the equipment.* ❑ *Jamieson worried about the non-appearance of MacFadyen and wondered if they should put out on all stations for him.*

• *noun* **output**

The **output** from a factory is the things it produces; the **output** from a computer is the data it produces.

put out of
You **are put of** a place when you are forced to leave it; you **are put out of** an event when someone else defeats you or something else happens to prevent you from continuing: *Jobs had been lost, mortgages forfeited and folk put out of their homes.* ❑ *20 horses were put out of the race at the smallest fence on the course.*

put over see **put across**

put past
If you say you wouldn't **put** something **past** someone you mean that you wouldn't be surprised if they did it: *'You know what he's like; I wouldn't put it past him to say yes just to spite me.'* ❑ *He said he wouldn't put it past his Mum to leave work early.*

put round
1 You **put** something **round** or **around** something else when you place it so that it encircles that other thing: *She put her arms round his neck but he pushed her away.* ❑ *The senator put his arm lightly around his son's shoulder.* **2** Information **is put round** or **around** when it is deliberately told to a number of people, often in order to influence them: *A view was put around that individual companies in the group were worth more separately than as a group.* [*same as* **put about**]

put through
1 You **put** a caller **through** on the telephone when you connect them with the person they want to speak to: *'I'm putting you through now, caller.'* ❑ *She put a call through to Riorbak.* ❑ *The staff were refusing to put calls through to Scotland Yard.* **2** Someone **puts** you **through** an unpleasant experience when they make you suffer it: *This is typical of the pain Dustin would put himself through in order to get 'inside' a character.* ❑ *She acted in a very calm manner considering the trauma she had been put through.* ❑ *How could I put the people I love through so much pain?*
• *noun* **through-put**
The **through-put** in a factory or system is the volume of things that pass through it: *The device will ensure there is an adequate through-put of water in the system.*

put to
1 You **put** something **to** something else when you place it against that other thing: *She put the damp cloth to his forehead.* **2** You **put** a proposal or idea **to** someone when you ask them to consider it: *The new offer was put to the men.* ❑ *'I put it to you that millions of people will rely on occupational rather than state pensions when they retire.'*

put together
1 You **put** people or things **together** when you put them with each other in the same place: *When horses are put together in the same paddock they need to be carefully chosen for their compatibility.* **2** You **put** something **together** when you join a number of separate parts to make a whole or complete thing, or you gather a number of separate things together and make them part of something larger or more complete: *The way sleeping bags are put together is one of the main factors affecting their efficiency.* ❑ *Now that he'd put the facts together the story sounded absolutely ridiculous.* ❑ *Our buying power with the major hotel chains means we can put together an excellent package, complete with rail and coach fares.* ❑ *Hopefully, he'll be interested in being in this band that we're trying to put together.* **3** You **put together** a piece of work when you create it, bringing together all the necessary elements: *She knows how to put a business letter together all right.* ❑ *The company was fully prepared to give her the freedom necessary to put*

together the type of programme she truly wanted to make. **4** You **put together** an event when you organize all the different elements into a workable whole: *They're putting together an exhibition of post-war British painting.* **5** You can say that one thing excels or is worth several other things **put together** if even in combination they cannot beat it: *He seemed to have more money than all the rest of us put together.*

put towards
You **put** money **towards** something when you use it to meet part of the total required: *The money I was going to save on rent could be put towards a deposit on a house.* ❑ *He wanted to earn a higher salary so that he would have something to put towards his eventual retirement.*

put under (*informal*)
When you are having a surgical operation, a doctor or nurse **puts** you **under** when they give you an anaesthetic to make you unconscious: *The nurse gave me an injection to put me under.* [*same as* **knock out**]

put up
1 To **put up** a building or other structure is to build or erect it: *Her parents had put up a marquee in the garden.* **2** You **put up** something such as an umbrella when you unfold it and raise it ready for use: *Lucia took her umbrella with her but didn't put it up despite the light drizzle.* **3** You **put up** something such as a poster or notice when you attach it to a wall or noticeboard: *He took a hand in the redecorating, splashing on paint and putting up wallpaper.* **4** Prices **are put up** when they are increased: *Most high-street banks have put up their charges to customers who go into overdraft.* **5** You **put up** money for some cause when you provide money for it: *No-one is willing to put up the funds for a proper training course.* **6** You **put** property **up** for sale when you make it available to be bought: *On the way they stopped at a farmhouse that was about to be put up for sale.* **7** You **put up** a struggle or fight when you resist an attack or fight in a determined way: *He decided it wasn't worth putting up a fight and risking a beating.* ❑ *The Nissan of Bailey and Blundell put up a strong challenge and took second.* **8** You **put** someone **up** when you give them accommodation in your house, especially by providing them with a bed for the night: *Would your brother be willing to put us up for a few nights?* **9** A political party **puts up** a candidate in an election when they choose that candidate to contest the election: *The Republicans put up candidates in about half the constituencies.*

put upon
If you feel **put upon** you feel that someone is taking advantage of you or forcing you do things you do not want to do: *It is easy to get the impression that he was the only one to suffer, constantly put upon by Mrs Moore and bored by her daughter.* ❑ *This sympathy and attention hardened my resolve not to be put upon.*

put up to
One person **puts** another **up to** something wrong, silly or dishonest when they tell them or encourage them to do it: *It wasn't something he'd have thought of by himself. Someone must have put him up to it.* [compare **egg on, goad into, incite**]

put up with
You **put up with** something unpleasant or unsatisfactory when you accept or tolerate it: *Over the years, Anne had put up with an awful lot from me.* ❑ *Violence in the home is as much a crime as violence from a stranger, so don't put up with it.*

puzzle /ˈpʌzəl/: **puzzles, puzzling, puzzled**

---

puzzle out
You **puzzle** something **out** when you

come to understand it or find an answer to it after thinking hard: *She seemed to be trying to puzzle out who the midnight caller might be.*

puzzle over

You **puzzle over** a problem or question when you wonder about it or try to solve it: *Just as they were puzzling over the next move the man rang back to say they were on a wild goose chase.* ❑ *The question I'm puzzling over, is why do you or don't you go to clubs? What is their appeal?*

q

quail /kweɪl/: **quails**, **quailing**, **quailed**

quail at (*formal* or *literary*)
You **quail at** something when it makes you tremble or draw back with fear: *Irene quailed at the thought of making the presentation in front of so many people.*

quarrel /'kwɒrəl/: **quarrels**, **quarrelling** (*AmE* **quarreling**), **quarrelled** (*AmE* **quarreled**)

quarrel with
1 You **quarrel with** someone when you have an angry disagreement or argument with them: *They're the sort of people who are always quarrelling with their neighbours.* **2** When you say that you would or would not **quarrel with** someone else's statement, opinion or conclusion you mean that you would, or would not, disagree with them: *'It's one of the best paintings in the exhibition.' 'I don't think many people would quarrel with that.'*

queen /kwiːn/: **queens**, **queening**, **queened**

queen over
People sometimes say that a girl or woman **is queening** it **over** other people, when she is ordering them about and behaves in a haughty way towards them because she thinks she is better than they are: *No more Bet Lynch queening it over the customers of the Rovers' Return.* [compare **lord over**]

queue /kjuː/: **queues**, **queuing**, **queued**

queue up
People **queue up** when they stand one behind the other in a queue, *eg* because they are waiting to get into a place or are waiting for service in a shop or post office: *At noon things get busy as customers queue up for sandwiches and take-away meals.* ❑ *I wouldn't mind betting people will be queuing up for these products as soon as they come on the market.*

quibble /'kwɪbəl/: **quibbles**, **quibbling**, **quibbled**

quibble about or **quibble over**
You **quibble about** something unimportant when you ask unnecessary questions or raise petty objections; you **quibble over** something small or unimportant when you question it unnecessarily: *The only thing they might quibble about is the cost.* ❑ *They quibbled over some of the minor details but agreed finally that they should go ahead.*

quicken /'kwɪkən/: **quickens**, **quickening**, **quickened**

quicken up
You **quicken** something **up** when you do it faster or increase its speed; something's speed or the rate at which it is done **quickens up** when it becomes faster: *You'll have to quicken up your typing speed if you want to get a job as a secretary.* ❑ *The pace quickened up*

and Don had to pedal like mad to keep up with the leaders.

quiet /'kwaɪət/: **quiets**, **quieting**, **quieted**

quiet down

Quiet down is mostly used in American English and has the same meaning as **quieten down**: *When things had quieted down a little, we went into the garden to look at the stars.*

quieten /'kwaɪətən/: **quietens**, **quietening**, **quietened**

quieten down

You **quieten** someone or something **down** when you calm them or do something to make them less noisy; someone or something **quietens down** when they becomes quiet or calm: *Four months in France had quietened her down and given her a veneer of sophistication quite lacking before.*

r

rabbit /ˈrabɪt/: **rabbits**, **rabbiting**, **rabbited**

rabbit on (*informal, derogatory*)
Someone who **rabbits on** talks for a long time about uninteresting, irrelevant or unimportant things; if you ask what someone **is rabbiting on** about you want to know what they are talking about: *I still don't know what he was rabbiting on about, do you?* ❑ *She can spend a full hour on the phone rabbiting on about nothing in particular.* [*same as* **gabble on** (*informal*), **rattle on** (*informal*)]

rack /rak/: **racks**, **racking**, **racked**

rack up (*informal*)
Someone **racks up** points or victories when they add another point or victory to the total they have already gained: *The Red Baron was airborne again, racking up his score of kills.* ❑ *Kasparov had racked up another easy victory.*

rage /reɪdʒ/: **rages**, **raging**, **raged**

rage against
You **rage against** something you think is wrong or unjust when you express or display violent anger or protest about it: *She found herself raging against all those people who had never had to face poverty and deprivation.* ❑ *Jay raged against her former husband and all the lovers Lucy was sure to have had in between.*

rail /reɪl/: **rails**, **railing**, **railed**

rail against
You **rail against** injustice or something that you are being forced to do when you express your strong disapproval of it or complain bitterly and loudly about it: *He railed against what he saw as falling standards of conduct and dress.* ❑ *Jill was protesting loudly, railing against the imposition of wholly unrealistic targets.*

railroad /ˈreɪlroud/: **railroads**, **railroading**, **railroaded**

railroad into
Someone **is railroaded into** doing something when they are hurried into doing it without being given enough time to consider whether it might be good or bad: *He felt he was being railroaded into it despite having serious doubts about the plan.*

railroad through
Legislation or a plan **is railroaded through** when it is put into practice or made law using great force or pressure to overcome any opposition: *The legislation was railroaded through Congress without any proper consultation with groups that would be directly affected by it.*

rain /reɪn/: **rains**, **raining**, **rained**

rain down
Things **rain down** when a great many of them fall from above at the same time, like raindrops: *As soon as they announced they were to have a baby loads of letters of congratulation, bibs*

and baby boots rained down on them. ❑ *Bombs were raining down on the city day and night.*

rain off

1 An event, especially a sporting event, **is rained off** when rain prevents it from taking place or continuing: *Cricket fans were given a ticket refund when the England game was rained off.* **2** Workers, especially building workers, **are rained off** when they are prevented from continuing with their work because of heavy rain: *The work isn't progressing as planned, principally because the men were rained off all last week.*

rake /reɪk/: rakes, raking, raked

rake in (*informal*)

A person or organization **is raking in** money or cash, or **is raking** it **in**, when they are earning lots of money, especially without much apparent effort: *The top football clubs are raking in millions from sales of merchandise, bringing out a new strip each season which their fans feel obliged to buy.* ❑ *Some of the vendors at the car-boot sale are really raking it in.* [*same as* **pull in** (*informal*)]

rake over

Someone **rakes over** something from the past, especially something that people would prefer to forget because it is upsetting or unpleasant, when they talk about it again in detail: *The press will insist on raking over all the details of his past indiscretions.*

rake up (*informal*)

1 You **rake up** the past when you talk about unpleasant things that happened some time ago, that people would prefer to forget: *It may be regarded as of historical interest by some, but as far as I'm concerned it's just raking up a past that is best forgotten.* **2** You **rake up** the people or things needed for a particular purpose when you look in various places for them, find them and bring them all together: *I think I might be able to rake up enough people to make two 5-a-side football teams.* [*same as* **dredge up**]

rally /ˈralɪ/: rallies, rallying, rallied

rally round

People **rally round** someone when they come together to support and help that person through a time of difficulty: *Everyone in the village rallied round, and they were soon fixed up with a bed for the night and dry clothes.*

ram /ram/: rams, ramming, rammed

ram down

1 To **ram** something **down** is to force it downwards with heavy pressure from above: *A mixture of large stone chips called hardcore is rammed down into the hole, and the concrete replaced.* **2** If someone tries to **ram** opinions or facts **down** your throat they force them on you in a very determined way ignoring the fact that you may not agree with them or are not interested in what they are saying.

ram in *or* ram into

1 To **ram** something **in,** or to **ram** it **into** something, is to use force to push it in, or push it into that thing: *He won't pay any attention unless we find some way to ram it into his head that drugs can kill.* ❑ *I jumped into the driver's seat and rammed the key into the ignition.* **2** A moving vehicle **rams into** another vehicle or stationary object when it crashes into it violently: *The lorry rammed into the crash-barrier, shedding its load on the carriageway.* ❑ *a massive pile-up as vehicle after vehicle rammed into the back of each other.*

ramble /ˈrambəl/: rambles, rambling, rambled

ramble on

Someone **rambles on** when they talk

or write in a long-winded, disorganized or confusing way so that what they are trying to say isn't very clear to their listeners or readers: *He has a tendency to ramble on, and risks losing readers' interest as a result.* ❑ *Grandma sat in her favourite chair, rambling on as usual about life when she was a girl.* [*same as* **run on**]

range /reɪndʒ/: **ranges**, **ranging**, **ranged**

range against

A number of people or things **are ranged against** a person or group when they have all taken up a position ready to oppose or fight that person or group: *The dictator threatened that it was in his power to sponsor terrorist attacks on the countries ranged against him.* ❑ *Incredibly, he seemed quite undaunted by the powerful forces ranged against him.*

rank /raŋk/: **ranks**, **ranking**, **ranked**

rank among

A person or thing **ranks among** a stated group, grade or category when they are included in or are considered to belong to it because they have the necessary qualities or skill: *Young Balinese who rank among the world's top competitive surfers.* ❑ *Britain's researchers still rank among the world's best in the science that underpins biotechnology.*

rap /rap/: **raps**, **rapping**, **rapped**

rap out

Someone **raps out** an order, question or statement when they say it suddenly using a abrupt and forceful tone of voice: *The sergeant-major was rapping out orders.* ❑ *'What the hell do you think you're doing?' he rapped out.*

rat /rat/: **rats**, **ratting**, **ratted**

rat on (*informal*)

Someone **rats on** their friends or associates when they betray them, usually by telling someone in authority about something wrong or illegal that they have done: *Lloydie said, 'I bet it was that little sneak McQuade who ratted on us.'* [*same as* **squeal on** (*informal*)]

ration /ˈraʃən/: **rations**, **rationing**, **rationed**

ration out

Something that is in short supply **is rationed out** when the amount each individual is allowed to have is restricted so that the supply can be divided amongst the greatest number of people or can be made to last longer: *Emergency aid was being rationed out, but still many people went without.* ❑ *Flour and rice had to be rationed out at two sacks per family per month.*

rattle /ˈratəl/: **rattles**, **rattling**, **rattled**

rattle off (*informal*)

You **rattle off** something, or you **rattle it off**, if you say or do it very quickly because you find it so easy that you don't have to think about it: *Williams Junior can rattle off the dates of all the British kings and queens since Henry VIII.* ❑ *Clearly, the album had not, like some, been rattled off in a weekend.* [*same as* **reel off**]

rattle on (*informal*)

Someone **rattles on**, or **rattles on** about something, when they speak quickly and go on talking for a long time, unaware of or ignoring the fact that their listeners may not be interested in what they are saying: *You won't be able to stop him once he gets started. He rattles on non-stop.* ❑ *Try as he might he couldn't get away and had to listen to old Mrs Murray rattling on about the faulty plumbing.* [*same as* **rabbit on** (*informal*)]

rattle out (*informal*)

You **rattle** things **out** when you make

them very quickly: *With up-to-date machinery the firm could rattle out twice as many parts as they can now.* ❑ *He rattles out novels like a factory making nuts and bolts.*

rattle through (*informal*)
You **rattle through** something that you have to do when you finish it very quickly and easily: *They rattled through all the business on the agenda and were finished before lunchtime.*

rattle up (*informal*)
Someone **rattles** something **up** when they make it easily in a very short time, especially because they are skilled or are using special equipment to make the work easier: *Give John a couple of planks of wood and a handful of nails and he'll rattle you up a set of bookshelves in no time.* [*same as* **knock up** (*informal*)]

rave /reɪv/: **raves**, **raving**, **raved**

rave about (*informal*)
People **rave about** something when they talk about it in a very enthusiastic, passionate or admiring way: *He was raving about the young actress, saying that she was the discovery of the decade.* ❑ *The picturesque Lune Valley that Mrs Radcliffe raved about and Turner painted.*

rave on (*informal*)
Someone **raves on** when they talk in a wild, uncontrolled way without making much sense, usually because they feel very passionate or enthusiastic about the thing they are talking about: *'Just think,' she raved on, 'six months in New Zealand; hot springs, kiwis, spectacular scenery...'* ❑ *Do you have any idea what he was raving on about?*

rave up (*informal*)
People **rave** it **up** when they enjoy themselves or celebrate, *eg* by drinking, dancing to pop music or having noisy and lively parties: *Just occasionally they like to rave it up a bit at a disco.*

• *noun* **rave-up**: **rave-ups**: *Judging by the racket, the students next door are having a bit of a rave-up.*

reach /riːtʃ/: **reaches**, **reaching**, **reached**

reach down
You **reach down** when you bend or lie flat and stretch out your arm or arms so that you can touch or get hold of something beneath you: *Suddenly a metal door opened and arms reached down to pull us up.*

reach down to
Something **reaches down to** a particular point or level when it extends downwards as far as that point or level: *Gerald was wearing an extraordinary coat that reached down almost to his ankles.*

reach for
You **reach for** something when you stretch out your hand and arm as far as you can so that you can grasp it: *Reaching for a cup, her hand accidently brushed his arm.*

reach out
You **reach out** when you stretch your arm out in a particular direction so that you can touch or grasp something that is some distance away from you: *He reached out and switched on the lamp.*

reach out for
You **reach out for** something when you stretch your arm out to get it: *Instinctively hands reached out for support that might brace them and help guard against the blow.*

reach out to
1 You **reach out to** people in need when you try to give them help or comfort: *Charities and support groups reaching out to the needy and victims of injustice of all kinds.* **2** An organization **reaches out to** people when they try to involve, inform or make contact with as many of them as possible: *Particularly at election time, television reaches out to*

people who are less well informed about politics.

reach up
You **reach up** when you stretch your arm or arms above your head to touch or get hold of something above you: *She reached up and put her hand over his mouth.* ❑ *She reached up to the hook for her dressing-gown.*

reach up to
Something **reaches up to** a particular point or level when it extends upwards as far as that point or level: *The water rose steadily until it reached up to his chin.*

read /riːd/: reads, reading, read /rɛd/

read back
When you have written something down and you **read** it **back** you read it from beginning to end, often aloud, as a way of checking that it is accurate: *He asked his secretary to read back what he had just dictated.*

read for
1 You **read for** a particular university degree when you study and do the work necessary to obtain it: *My younger son is reading for a BA in medieval history.* ❑ *At that time he was reading for the bar.* [= studying to become a barrister] **2** An actor **reads for** a part in a play when they learn the lines for that role: *He was reading for a part in an Agatha Christie film.* ❑ *The director has asked Findlay to read for the part of Prince Hal.*

read into
You **read** something **into** what someone says or does when you find some extra meaning in it, often one which they did not intend: *No matter what he does now, the press will read something sinister into it.* ❑ *Those are the facts; read into them what you will.*

read off
You **read off** a number of items *eg* from a list when you say them aloud one after the other: *He read off the numbers on the meter, and I wrote them down.*

read out
You **read** something **out** when you say it aloud as you read it: *They had all been there when Moran read out the telegram.* ❑ *His statement was read out in court.*

read over
1 You **read** a piece of writing **over** when you read it carefully in order to check that you understand it or that it is accurate: *When you've finished writing your essay, read it over, paying particular attention to spelling and punctuation.* **2** You **read** something you have learned **over** when you read it again quickly to check that you know it: *Read the poem over once or twice before class to make sure you know it.*

read through
You **read** a piece of writing **through** when you read it from beginning to end: *Take care to read through the documents carefully before signing them.* ❑ *Stirling handed the hand-written note to the general who read it through twice.*

read up *or* read up on
You **read up on** a subject, or you **read up** for something such as an exam, when you find out as much as you can about it or learn as much as you can by reading: *Ray is reading up on the history of Crete before we go on holiday.* ❑ *We recommend that applicants read up on the company and prepare a list of questions about it for their interviews.*

rear /rɪə(r)/: rears, rearing, reared

rear up
1 A horse or other animal **rears up** when it stands on its back legs and lifts its front legs into the air: *The grizzly bear reared up and bared its fangs.* **2** A feature of the landscape **rears up** in

front of you when it rises steeply and unexpectedly from the surrounding area: *A seemingly impenetrable jungle reared up before the exhausted men.* ❑ *A great pillar of lava reared up above St Pierre like an obelisk.*

reason /'ri:zən/: **reasons, reasoning, reasoned**

reason out

You **reason** something **out** when you use careful thought and logical argument to find an answer to it or come to a conclusion about it: *It would take a cleverer person than I to reason out why this should be the case.* [*same as* **work out**]

reason with

You **reason with** someone when you talk to them and use logical and sensible arguments to try to persuade them to do or not do something, or to convince them about something: *They tried in vain to reason with the gunman.* ❑ *He tried to reason with her but she wouldn't be reasoned with.*

rebound /rɪ'baʊnd/: **rebounds, rebounding, rebounded**

rebound on *or* rebound upon

Something you do to someone else with the intention of harming or damaging them **rebounds on** or **upon** you when it ends up having a harmful or unpleasant effect on you as well as, or instead of, your intended victim or target: *He pointed out that that sort of criticism had a habit of rebounding on the critics.* [*same as* **come back on**]

reckon /'rɛkən/: **reckons, reckoning, reckoned**

reckon in

If you are calculating or estimating the total cost of something and you **reckon** an item **in**, you include it in the total: *Have you reckoned in the cost of car hire for the full fortnight?*

reckon on *or* reckon upon

You **reckon on** or **upon** something happening when you expect it to happen, and base your plans on it: *At the very least he would have to reckon on five of his Cabinet colleagues being against him.*

reckon up

You **reckon up** a total when you calculate it by adding several sums or amounts together: *I'll send you an invoice once I've reckoned up the bill.* [*same as* **add up, tot up** (*informal*)]

reckon with

1 You refer to a person as someone to **reckon with** when you think they are very powerful or influential: *Picasso was a massive, overpowering presence to be reckoned with, much as Michelangelo had been in his old age.* **2** If you have problems or difficulties to **reckon with** you have them to deal with: *Even if we manage to get there, we'll still have the problem of transport into the interior to reckon with.* **3** You **reckon with** someone doing something, or something happening, when it is a factor in your plans or calculations: *The police had hoped to catch them all together but they hadn't reckoned with the break-up of the gang.* [*opposite* **reckon without**]

reckon without

You **reckon without** something happening when you have not included it in your plans or calculations because you did not expect it to happen: *He had, however, reckoned without the Earl Marischal.* [*opposite* **reckon with**]

recoil /rɪ'kɔ:l/: **recoils, recoiling, recoiled**

recoil from

You **recoil from** something unpleasant when you draw back from it quickly because it shocks, frightens or disgusts you: *He looked so frightening and strange she instinctively recoiled from his touch.* [*same as* **withdraw**]

reconcile /ˈrɛkənsaɪl/: **reconciles, reconciling, reconciled**

reconcile to

You **are reconciled to** an unpleasant fact or situation when you have accepted it, especially because you know that you can't do anything to change it: *Old Mrs Brown seems quite reconciled to the move to a nursing home.* ❑ *She just couldn't reconcile herself to the new and reduced circumstances she found herself in.*

reduce /rɪˈdjuːs/: **reduces, reducing, reduced**

reduce to

1 A process **reduces** something **to** pieces, or its component parts, when it breaks it down or causes it to form into separate parts. **2** Something **is reduced to** a smaller figure or amount when it is decreased: *The basic rate of income tax has been reduced to 20%.* **3** Someone or something **is reduced to** a low or bad state or condition when they have fallen into that state or condition: *He was reduced to begging in the streets of Paris.* **4** Someone **is reduced to** tears when something has such an upsetting effect on them that it makes them cry.

reek /riːk/: **reeks, reeking, reeked**

reek of

To **reek of** something is to smell very strongly of it: *He swaggered in, reeking of cheap aftershave.* ❑ *The situation reeks of corruption in high places.*

reel /riːl/: **reels, reeling, reeled**

reel back

You **reel back** when you move back suddenly in an uncontrolled way, usually because someone has hit you hard or you have had a shock: *Bruno landed a punch square on his chin and he reeled back against the ropes.* ❑ *She reeled back gasping as the choking fumes filled her lungs.*

reel in

You **reel in** a fishing line when you gradually pull it towards you by turning it around a reel: *Once you feel the salmon has got too tired to fight, start to reel him in gently.*

reel off

You **reel** things **off** when you say them quickly and without having to think; you also **reel** things **off** when you get through them quickly and easily: *She can reel off the relevant statistics at the drop of a hat.* ❑ *Miss Cross began the match well, reeling off the first four games for the loss of only four points.*

refer /rɪˈfɜː(r)/: **refers, referring, referred**

refer to

1 You **refer to** something when you mention it: *Who exactly were you referring to when you talked about people being marginalized?* ❑ *He referred repeatedly to the 'special relationship' that existed between their two countries.* **2** You **refer to** someone or something as a particular thing when that is the name you give them when you are talking to or about them: *He's in the habit of referring to his wife as his old woman.* ❑ *Don't you think it's rather unjust to refer to him as 'that young thug'?* **3** You **refer to** a book or other source of information when you read it or look at it in order to check facts or find something out: *Check your spelling by referring to your dictionary.* ❑ *For guidance on grammar refer to the appendices at the back of the book.* **4** You **refer** someone **to** a source of information when you tell them to look at it because it may be useful to them: *My tutor referred me to a collection of the author's letters held in the university library.* **5** You **refer** someone or something **to** a specialist or expert when you get the specialist or expert to examine them or give their opinion: *If your GP is unable to make an accurate diagnosis, he should refer you to a* *consultant.* ❑ *He was referred to a lawyer who specialized in that area.*

reflect /rɪ'flɛkt/: **reflects, reflecting, reflected**

reflect on *or* **reflect upon**

1 You **reflect on** or **upon** something when you think carefully about it: *You should take some time to reflect on this.* ❑ *When he reflected on his marriage he had to acknowledge to himself that it was a great mistake.* **2** Something **reflects** well or badly **on** the person or group of people associated with it when it causes them to be regarded in a favourable or unfavourable way by others: *His behaviour reflects well on those who were responsible for bringing him up.*

refrain /rɪ'freɪn/: **refrains, refraining, refrained**

refrain from (*formal*)

You **refrain from** doing something when you stop doing it or do not do it: *Please refrain from smoking within the hospital buildings.* ❑ *He wanted to smash his fists against the wall but sensibly refrained from something that would damage only himself.*

rein /reɪn/: **reins, reining, reined**

rein back

1 A rider **reins back** his or her horse when he or she pulls on the reins to stop it moving forward or to slow it down. **2** You **rein back** on something when you slow it down or cut it back to a lower level: *yet another attempt by the Tories to rein back on public expenditure.*

rein in

1 A rider **reins in** their horse when they pull the reins to make it stop or slow down: *He desperately tried to rein in his panic-stricken horse.* **2** You **rein** someone **in** when you do something to control their irresponsible or reckless behaviour and make them behave in a more reasonable manner: *The old man will have to rein that son of his in before he wrecks the entire family business.*

relate /rɪ'leɪt/: **relates, relating, related**

relate to

1 Something that **relates to** something else is concerned with that other thing or has a direct connection with it: *How does this relate to what we were discussing earlier?* ❑ *all the evidence relating to the crime.* **2** You **relate to** another person or their situation when you understand their feelings because you have had similar experiences or feelings yourself: *'I find big crowds terrifying.' 'Yes, I can relate to that.'* ❑ *She was looking for someone she could relate to.*

relieve /rɪ'liːv/: **relieves, relieving, relieved**

relieve of

1 You **relieve** someone **of** something they are holding or carrying, or a responsibility, when you help them by taking it away from them: *Can I relieve you of that heavy suitcase?* ❑ *A measure that effectively relieves the local authority of responsibility for housing homeless families.* **2** Someone **is relieved of** their post or command when they are dismissed, usually because they are incompetent: *The President relieved the general of his command and ordered him home.*

rely /rɪ'laɪ/: **relies, relying, relied**

rely on *or* **rely upon**

1 You **rely on** or **upon** something when you need it or depend on it to exist or survive: *Smokers ought to give up the habit and stop relying on the NHS as a safety-net.* ❑ *a form of socio-economic domination from outside that does not rely on direct political control.* **2** You **rely on** someone when you trust them to do what they should do or what you ask them to do: *You can always rely on*

Adele to help you out in a crisis. ❑ *I have my doubts about Gerry. Do you think we can rely on him?*

remark /rɪˈmɑːk/: **remarks, remarking, remarked**

remark on *or* **remark upon** (*formal*)
Someone **remarks on** or **upon** something when they say something about it or make a comment about it: *He often remarks on Jessica's likeness to his mother.* ❑ *Masterson remarked upon the curious weather they had been having.*

remember /rɪˈmɛmbə(r)/: **remembers, remembering, remembered**

remember to
You ask to be **remembered to** someone that you have known or met in the past when you ask someone who is going to meet them to mention your name to them so that they don't forget you: *Remember me to Peter when you see him.*

remind /rɪˈmaɪnd/: **reminds, reminding, reminded**

remind of
Someone or something **reminds** you **of** someone or something else when they have some quality or characteristic that is like, and therefore makes you think of, that other person or thing: *Some of Niall's expressions and gestures remind me of my father.* ❑ *The music reminded him of home.*

remit /rɪˈmɪt/: **remits, remitting, remitted**

remit to (*formal*)
1 A matter **is remitted to** a higher or more senior body when it is passed to them so that they can make a decision about it. **2** A sum of money **is remitted to** someone when it is transferred to them from someone else, usually through the banking system.

render /ˈrɛndə(r)/: **renders, rendering, rendered**

render down
A solid substance **is rendered down** when it is turned into a liquid using heat: *The fat is rendered down into lard.*

render into (*formal*)
Something such as a work of literature **is rendered into** another language when it is changed from its original language into that other language: *The next test is to render this passage into French.* [*same as* **translate**]

rent /rɛnt/: **rents, renting, rented**

rent out
You **rent out** property or land that you own when you make it available for others to use in return for a regular payment or rent: *I'm going abroad for a year so I'll be renting out my flat in Edinburgh.*

repair /rɪˈpɛə(r)/: **repairs, repairing, repaired**

repair to (*formal* or *humorous*)
You **repair to** a place when you leave the place you are in and go there: *Shall we repair to the lounge for coffee?*

report /rɪˈpɔːt/: **reports, reporting, reported**

report back
If you have been sent somewhere by someone to find something out and you **report back** to them, you tell them what you have found out: *Reporting back after a two-week visit to Kuwait, the fact-finding team said scores of people had been tortured and killed.*

reside /rɪˈzaɪd/: **resides, residing, resided**

reside in (*formal*)
The authority or power to do or decide something **resides in** an individual, a group or an institution when they have

it: *He has his finger on the nuclear button and that power resides with him alone.*

resort /rɪ'zɔːt/: **resorts**, **resorting**, **resorted**

resort to
You **resort to** a course of action that you would prefer not to use, when you adopt it only because other methods or approaches have failed: *We had to resort to bullying him to make him wash his hair occasionally.*

rest /rɛst/: **rests**, **resting**, **rested**

rest on *or* rest upon
Something such as an argument or theory **rests on** or **upon** a particular thing when that is the thing it is built on or based on: *The whole structure of his argument rests on this one rather spurious contention.* ❑ *Their entire economic policy rests upon their stated objective of low inflation and low taxes.*

rest up
You **rest up** when you rest for a time until you recover your strength: *They found a ledge so that they could rest up before the final assault on the summit.*

rest with
The responsibility for something **rests with** a particular person or organization when they have that responsibility: *A Scottish Office spokesman said responsibility for the repairs rested with the local authority.* [*same as* **lie with**]

result /rɪ'zʌlt/: **results**, **resulting**, **resulted**

result from
One thing **results from** another when the first thing is caused by or is a consequence of the second: *Scurvy results from a lack of vitamin C in the diet.*

result in
An action or circumstance **results in** a particular situation or consequence when it causes it to happen: *I predict that the experiment will result in complete disaster for us all.*

return /rɪ'tɜːn/: **returns**, **returning**, **returned**

return to
1 You **return to** a place when you go back there after being somewhere else: *We returned to Bath to find our house had been burgled.* **2** You **return to** a topic or question that has been raised or discussed at some time in the past when you go back to it after dealing with other things: *Returning to the question of pensions, it would be unrealistic to expect the state to provide for anyone other than those in greatest need.* **3** Something that has changed or has been changed **returns to** its previous state when it changes back to that state: *plants rotting away and returning to the earth.* **4** You **return** something **to** someone when you give it back to them: *Would you be sure to return my umbrella to me once you've finished with it.*

rev /rɛv/: **revs**, **revving**, **revved**

rev up (*informal*)
You **rev up** the engine of a car or other vehicle when you press the accelerator to make the engine run faster, usually when the car itself is not moving: *He was already in the car, revving up and impatient to be off.*

revel /'rɛvəl/: **revels**, **revelling** (*AmE* **reveling**), **revelled** (*AmE* **reveled**)

revel in
You **revel in** something when you enjoy it very much: *To all appearances she seems to revel in her new role as wife and mother.* [*same as* **delight in**]

revert /rɪ'vɜːt/: **reverts**, **reverting**, **reverted**

revert to
Something **reverts to** a previous state or condition when it goes back to that state or condition: *You might find that plants grown from seed tend to revert to the colours of the wild form.*

revolve /rɪ'vɒlv/: **revolves**, **revolving**, **revolved**

revolve around *or* **revolve round**
1 Your life **revolves around** or **round** a particular person, group of people or activity when they are your main concern or interest: *Her life revolves around her horses.* **2** A discussion or debate **revolves around** or **round** a particular topic or subject when that is the thing that it is mainly concerned with: *Their discussions tended to revolve around domestic concerns rather than things beyond the home.*

rid /rɪd/: **rids**, **ridding**, **rid**

rid of (*formal*)
You **rid** yourself **of** something when you get rid of it completely: *They came up with some fairly ingenious ways of ridding themselves of the lice that infested the trenches.*

ride /raɪd/: **rides**, **riding**, **rode** /roud/, **ridden** /'rɪdən/

ride out
You **ride out** a difficult or dangerous period when you manage to get through it without suffering a lot of damage or harm: *If we can just ride out the next six months, we should be okay.*

ride up
Clothes **ride up** when they are pulled up out of position when you move your body: *His short bomber-style jacket had ridden up at the back revealing a large scar.*

riffle /'rɪfəl/: **riffles**, **riffling**, **riffled**

riffle through (*informal*)
You **riffle through** papers or the pages of a book or magazine when you turn them over quickly with your fingers: *He was riffling idly through the memo pad on her desk.*

rifle /'raɪfəl/: **rifles**, **rifling**, **rifled**

rifle through
You **rifle through** things when you search through them quickly, looking for something: *Emmy caught Joss rifling through her father's bureau.*

rig /rɪg/: **rigs**, **rigging**, **rigged**

rig out
You **rig** yourself **out** in special or odd-looking clothes when you get them and wear them: *He'd rigged himself out in this pirate's costume; Captain Hook, I think.* ❑ *He was fully rigged out in his dress uniform.*
• *noun* **rig-out**: **rig-outs**
A **rig-out** a set of special or odd-looking clothes: *Is that another new rig-out you've got there?*

rig up (*informal*)
You **rig** something **up** such as a piece of equipment for a particular purpose, when you put together its various parts or some readily-available substitute, and place them in position: *They were able to rig up a sort of temporary hospital on the outskirts of the camp.* ❑ *Can you rig me up a couple of spotlights?*

ring /rɪŋ/: **rings**, **ringing**, **rang** /raŋ/, **rung** /rʌŋ/

ring around see **ring round**

ring back
You **ring** someone **back** when you telephone them for a second time or when you return a call that they have made to you: *Can you ring me back later?* ❑ *John called and asked if you*

would ring him back before lunch. [*same as* **call back, phone back**]

ring in
You **ring in** when you make contact with your office or base by telephone from somewhere outside such as your home: *Gary rang in sick this morning.* [= he telephoned to say that he was too ill to come to work] [*same as* **call in, phone in**]

ring off
You **ring off** when you end a telephone conversation and put the receiver down: *I'm going to ring off now, Mum; I can hear the baby crying.*

ring out
1 Bells **ring out** when they can be heard a great distance way; someone's voice **rings out** when it can be heard very clearly from a long way off. **2** If you try to contact someone by phone and their phone **rings out**, it rings but no-one answers: *I've tried ringing her a couple of times this morning but the phone just rings out.*

ring round
You **ring round** or **ring around** several people when you contact them by phone one after the other, usually to get information of some kind: *Ring round all the suppliers, will you, Dave, and find out who's offering the biggest discounts.* [*same as* **phone round**]

ring up
1 You **ring** someone **up** when you contact them by phone: *The cheeky young devil rang me up and asked me out.* [*same as* **call up, phone up**] **2** A shopkeeper or till operator in a shop **rings up** a sale when they record it on the cash register by pressing the appropriate keys: *Do you want to put this back, sir? I haven't rung it up yet.*

rinse /rɪns/: rinses, rinsing, rinsed

rinse out
1 You **rinse out** clothing when you put it in fresh water to remove dirt, or to remove soap after washing: *She'd rinsed out her tights and hung them on the radiator.* ❏ *The final cycle rinses the soap powder out completely.* **2** You **rinse out** a cup or glass when you clean it quickly using water: *Leonora rinsed out her coffee cup, then eyed the cupboards wondering where to put it.* **3** You **rinse** your mouth **out** *eg* after brushing your teeth with toothpaste or having dental treatment when you take a small amount of water into your mouth, move it around inside, and then spit it out again.

rip /rɪp/: rips, ripping, ripped

rip off
Someone **rips** you **off** when they cheat you *eg* by charging too much for something: *I can't believe they can get away with ripping customers off with these massive bank charges!* ❏ *He said he didn't mind paying, but really resented being ripped off.* [*same as* **cheat, overcharge**]

• *noun* **rip-off**: **rip-offs**: *Is a small shrub at £2.99 a bargain or a rip-off?*

rip through
Something such as a high wind or a fragment from a bomb **rips through** something when it passes through it very quickly causing a great deal of damage: *The bullet ripped through the sleeve of his jacket missing his arm by millimetres.*

rip up
You **rip** something made of paper **up** when you destroy it by tearing it into pieces: *Harry ripped up the photograph and tossed the pieces in the waste bin.* [*same as* **tear up**]

rise /raɪz/: rises, rising, rose /rouz/, risen /'rɪzən/

rise above
You **rise above** a difficult or degrading situation when your character is strong enough or you are determined enough

not be affected by it: *Jocasta rose above those minor setbacks, and continued undeterred with her arrangements.*

rise up

1 To **rise up** is to move upwards: *Smoke rose up in a great black column, obliterating the sun.* ❑ *Their chanting rose up through the vaulted roof of the Cistercian chapel.* **2** Something tall or steep **rises up** when it appears suddenly in front of you: *A massive iceberg rising out of the mist like a floating cathedral.* **3** People **rise up**, or **rise up** against authority, when they rebel and begin to fight against authority: *The peasants rose up against their oppressors.*

• *noun* **uprising**: **uprisings**

An **uprising** is a rebellion: *He had played a prominent role in the anti-Nazi uprising of 1945.*

roll /roul/: rolls, rolling, rolled

roll about *or* roll around

1 You **roll about** or **around** when you lie down on the ground and move around by turning your body over: *In those days kids seemed to have more fun; they could run and roll around and get dirty.* **2** People **roll about** when they laugh so much that they twist and turn their bodies, often having fallen down on the ground first: *Jane watched with delight as he rolled about on the floor with mirth.*

roll back

1 You **roll back** a covering such as a carpet when you remove it by lifting one edge and turning it over and over into a roll: *The rug was rolled back to reveal a trapdoor.* **2** You **roll back** something that has had the effect of steadily increasing something's importance when you make the changes required to cause it to begin decreasing again: *The power of the state is being rolled back in some areas, but is being greatly increased in others.* ❑ *His skill in spotting new frontiers to roll back earned him the admiration of Mrs Thatcher.*

roll by

Days, weeks, months or years **roll by** when time passes, or it seems to pass, fairly quickly: *These small details are so easy to forget as the years roll by.*

roll down

1 Something **rolls down** a sloping or vertical surface when it moves down it turning over as it goes: *Suddenly he found himself rolling down the slope, head over heels.* ❑ *He was staring straight ahead, the tears rolling down his cheeks.* **2** You **roll down** the window of a vehicle when you turn the handle so that it opens.

roll in *or* roll into

1 (*informal*) You **roll in** somewhere, or you **roll into** a place, when you arrive there in a vehicle; someone **rolls in**, or **rolls in** drunk, when they swagger in casually, or come in moving from side to side unsteadily: *The convoy rolled into Sarajevo just before dusk.* ❑ *Iraqi tanks rolling into Kuwait* ❑ *He rolled in two hours late and seemed surprised at her indignation.* **2** (*informal*) People **are rolling in** somewhere when they are arriving in large numbers; money **is rolling in** when you are receiving large amounts of it: *Visitors to the palace are rolling in at the rate of ten thousand a day.* ❑ *Once we start selling the houses money should start rolling in and we'll be out of the bad patch.*

roll on

1 Time or a process **rolls on** when it continues steadily and smoothly: *And thus the years rolled on, uneventful but nonetheless happy.* **2** You can say '**roll on**' something when you want to let people know you are impatient for it to happen: *'Roll on tomorrow night,' he moaned. 'It can't come quick enough.'*

roll out

1 You **roll** something **out** when you form it into a smooth flat shape by pressing down on it with a roller or rolling-pin: *Roll out the pastry to an* *oblong measuring 8 x 12 inches.* **2** Products **roll out** of a factory when they come off the production line and are available on the market: *By that time, the company's Alpha technology will begin to roll out in volume.* **3** (*informal*) A person or thing **is rolled out** when they are brought into public view, rather like a new make of car or aircraft is: *Ringo Starr was rolled out for the encores and thrashed about enthusiastically enough.*

roll over

1 You **roll over** when you turn your body round so that you are lying on the opposite side: *He rolled over on to his back and stared at the ceiling.* **2** A sum of money from one period **is rolled over** to the next when it is added to it: *Last week's jackpot has been rolled over again to make a total jackpot this week of a massive forty-two million.*

roll up

1 You **roll** something **up** when you turn or fold it over again and again so that it forms a roll; you **roll up** your sleeves when you turn the cuffs back until your sleeves are above your elbows, especially as a way of preparing for a spell of hard work: *He was carrying a rolled-up copy of the Evening Standard.* ❑ *He says we need a lot more heavy rain before he can roll up and put away his prayer mat.* ❑ *He rolled up his sleeves immediately and got to work.* **2** People **roll up** to an event or entertainment such as a circus when they come to it or are attracted to it in large numbers: *'Roll up, roll up! See the amazing monkey woman!'*

romp /rɒmp/: romps, romping, romped

romp through

You **romp through** a task when you do it very quickly, or very quickly and easily: *They romped through the speeches, determined to get to the most important thing, the banquet itself.* ❑ *This time he had real difficulty with a maths paper that he would normally have romped through.* [*same as* **rattle through** (*informal*)]

root /ruːt/: roots, rooting, rooted

root about *or* root around

(*informal*)

A person or animal **roots about** or **around** when they search in the earth, or in every part of a place, or through a collection of things, trying to find something: *Henry fell to his knees and began rooting about in his files of cuttings.* ❑ *Coatis' long mobile noses are used for rooting around in search of small animals.* [*same as* **rummage about**]

root for (*informal*)

You **root for** someone involved in a competition or doing a difficult task when you support them, hoping that they will win or succeed: *Just go out and do the best you can. You know we'll all be rooting for you.*

root out

1 To **root out** something, or to **root** it **out**, is to identify it after a determined search and remove it completely: *His aim is to root out corruption in the police force.* **2** You **root** something **out** when you only succeed in finding it or obtaining it with a great deal of hardship or difficulty: *The descendants of the once magnificent Mayan civilization are rooting out a meagre living in isolated villages.*

root up

To **root up** a plant is to pull it out of the ground, taking it all away, including the roots: *Smaller wine producers have been rooting up their vines and planting cereals in their place.*

• *verb* **uproot: uproots, uprooting, uprooted**

To **uproot** a plant is to pull its roots out of the ground: *The gales had uprooted thousands of trees, some of which were a hundred and fifty years old.*

rope /roup/: **ropes**, **roping**, **roped**

rope in *or* **rope into**
You **rope** something **in** or **into** a small area when you confine it there and put up a rope barrier to prevent it getting out: *The bulls may have been tied up and roped in but he was still wary of going too near them.*

rope off
An area **is roped off** when it is separated from the surrounding areas by a long rope suspended from poles stuck in the ground: *Will we be roping off the area to keep the public at a safe distance?* ❑ *The area of investigation was roped off and marked out with luminous tape.*

rot /rɒt/: **rots**, **rotting**, **rotted**

rot away
Materials such as wood **rot away** when they gradually break down and disappear: *She passed the old chalets, their paintwork peeling and their woodwork rotting away.*

rot down
Plant or other organic material **rots down** when it breaks down into a dark mass resembling earth: *As the compost rots down it gives off heat which further accelerates the process.*

rough /rʌf/: **roughs**, **roughing**, **roughed**

rough out
You **rough** something **out** when you make a rough outline or sketch to demonstrate your ideas or as a guide for a more detailed version: *He had spent the morning roughing out a few ideas for the new garden layout.*

rough up (*informal*)
If someone **roughs** you **up** they hit or beat you, usually in order to intimidate you: *'You roughed up a man from Belfast a few days ago.' 'Yes,' they said, 'but it was a mistake.'* [*same as* **beat up**]

round /raund/: **rounds**, **rounding**, **rounded**

round down
You **round** a figure **down** when you ignore any fraction and include only whole numbers, tens, hundreds, *etc*: *To be strictly accurate, the figure is 4.23, but we've rounded it down to 4.*

round off
You **round off** something when you do something that has the effect of making it complete: *They rounded off their formal education with a cookery or arts course.* ❑ *Charles finds that a glass or two of port is a very pleasant way to round off a good dinner.*

round on
You **round on** someone who has been annoying or attacking you when you suddenly lose patience and attack them in turn: *He taunted the police until one of them rounded on him and threatened him with arrest.* [*same as* **turn on**]

round up
1 To **round up** people or animals is to gather them together in a group so that they can be kept in one place or driven elsewhere: *It looks like one of those dogs that round up sheep; a collie or something.* ❑ *Those that have tried to escape have either been killed or rounded up.* **2** You **round up** a figure that includes a fraction when you make the fraction into a whole number: *His official salary is £23,750 but it's been rounded up to £24,000 to make it easier to divide by 12.*
• *noun* **round-up**: **round-ups**
1 A **round-up** is the gathering together of animals that have been wandering freely in the countryside into a closely-packed group: *The roundup took two weeks and the army found they had to move 232 elephants.* **2** A **round-up** is also a short summary of facts, news or information: *We're now returning to the studio for a quick news round-up.* [*same as* **summary**]

round /raund/

Round is an adverb and a preposition. It is a very common word in English and has many different senses. It occurs in a large number of phrasal verbs in this dictionary, in nine main senses. In most of these senses, **round** can frequently be found forming new phrasal verbs.

In many of the phrasal verbs in which **round** appears, **around** and **about** can replace it in some senses with no change in meaning.

1 MOVING

The literal meaning of **round** relates broadly to movement in different directions, and it is used in a large number of phrasal verbs with this kind of movement as part of their meaning, such as **look round**. **Round** combines freely with verbs to form other, often informal, phrasal verbs with this meaning, such as *chase round*, *trudge round*, *swagger round* and *busk round* in the following examples: *It's nice to be popular, but it's not so nice to be chased round.* ❑ *There are long periods spent ashore, trudging round doing routine customs work.* ❑ *He swaggers round handing roses to all the women.* ❑ *Dan had left college and was busking round trying to see something of the world.*

Many similar phrasal verbs refer to movement or action in different places, such as **phone round**, or to action that results in something being put in or taken to different places, such as **hawk round** and **hand round**.

2 TURNING

The second most common occurrence of **round** is in phrasal verbs that refer to the action of turning, usually of turning once to face the opposite direction, as in **look round**, **swing round** and **wheel round**. **Round** can often be found forming new phrasal verbs with this meaning, such as *pull round* and *switch round* in the following examples: *Elaine pulled his face round and planted a wet sticky mouth on his own.* ❑ *Eliot would switch his chair round to face the guest settled opposite.*

Spin round, **swivel round** and **turn round** can refer to the action of turning repeatedly in a circular motion, and this repeated movement can be emphasized by repeating the particle, as in: *The lights spin round and round in time to the music until everyone's head is in a total whirl.*

Round can occasionally be found forming new phrasal verbs with this meaning, as in *dance round* and *churn round* in the following examples: *The Husayn twins and Khan were dancing round a case stuffed with priceless porcelain.* ❑ *It was a day of noisy traffic churning round the roundabout.*

3 SURROUNDING

Round appears in a small number of phrasal verbs that have the idea of surrounding as part of their meaning. For example, you **wrap** something such as a blanket **round** someone when you surround them with it, to keep them warm; when you ask people to **gather round** you want them to come together in a group that surrounds you or some other central point. Here again, **round** combines readily with verbs to form phrasal verbs with this meaning, as in *seat round*, *fasten round*, *bind round* and *pour round* in the following examples: *The company was seated round card tables.* ❑ *They fastened the garrotte string round her neck.* ❑ *It took all day to bind the cloths round her aching knees.* ❑ *Her hair poured round her, sticky with electricity.*

4 FOCUSING

A few phrasal verbs with **round**, such as **centre round** and **revolve round**, refer to something that all other things relate to or are linked to, or something that everyone concentrates their attention on. Occasionally, **round** can be found forming new phrasal verbs with this meaning, such as *weave round* and *frame round* in the following examples: *A number of Victorian novelists continued to weave romances round great houses.* ❑ *The terms of the settlement are framed round the concept of a trust beneficiary.*

5 AVOIDING

In some phrasal verbs, the idea of moving past something on a circular course is extended to refer to the avoiding of something. In **talk round** and **skirt round** you avoid talking about something or dealing with it; in **go round** and **get round** you avoid a problem or obstacle. New phrasal verbs with **round** in this sense are not very common; *meander round* occurs in the following example: *I have meandered round the issue for too long.*

6 PERSUADING
The idea of turning to face the opposite direction is extended in a small number of phrasal verbs that refer to the act of persuading someone to change their opinion or decision, such as **bring round, talk round** and **win round**. You **come round** when you allow yourself to be persuaded.

7 VISITING
Round features in a small number of phrasal verbs that refer to visiting, such as **call round, drop round** and **go round**. The visit is usually informal and brief. **Round** can occasionally be found forming new phrasal verbs with this meaning, such as *pop round* in the example: *The next day it was fine, so Maureen popped round to see what we were up to.*

8 MAKING OR BECOMING CONSCIOUS AGAIN
When someone has lost consciousness, you try to **bring** them **round** or **pull** them **round**. You **come round** when you become conscious again after fainting.

9 LACK OF ACTIVITY OR PURPOSE
There are a few phrasal verbs with **round** that refer to lack of activity or purpose, such as **stand round** and **hang round**. You can occasionally find new and often informal phrasal verbs with **round** in this sense, such as *cruise round* in the example: *The bikes are cruising round outside, waiting for a call.*

rout /raʊt/: routs, routing, routed

rout out (*informal*)
You **rout** someone or something **out** when you find where they are hidden and force them to come out: *Go and rout that lazy boy out of his bed. It's past ten.* ❑ *The terriers dashed to and fro routing out the rats and mice from the haystacks.*

rub /rʌb/: rubs, rubbing, rubbed

rub along (*informal*)
People **rub along** together when they are able to tolerate each other reasonably well and can live or work together fairly successfully: *They've been rubbing along in that way for years; not exactly close friends but never having any serious disagreements.*

rub down
You **rub** yourself **down**, or you **rub down** an animal such as a horse, when you use a towel or something similar to rub water or sweat off your skin, or off the animal's coat: *He rubbed himself down briskly until his skin tingled.* ❑ *He was rubbing the great Clydesdales down with a handful of straw.*
• *noun* **rubdown**: *Davies, the groom, led the sweating horse away and gave him a thorough rubdown.*

rub in (*informal*)
You can say that someone **is rubbing** it **in** when they go on talking about something embarrassing concerning you or a mistake that you have made, that you are already aware of: *'You seem to have put on a bit of weight!' 'Yes, I know; don't go rubbing it in.'*

rub off *or* rub off on
1 You **rub** marks or dirt **off** a surface when you remove them by rubbing with eg a cloth: *The teacher had rubbed the examples off the board before I had time to take them down.* ❑ *Will these marks rub off or will we have to paint over them?* **2** When one person's way of doing things, or the way they are feeling, **rubs off** or **rubs off on** another person, that other person is influenced by them and begins to behave or feel as they do: *We're hoping that some of the older boys' obvious enthusiasm will rub off on him.*

rub out

You **rub out** something that has been written in pencil or chalk when you remove it using a rubber or cloth: *She wasn't satisfied with what she had written so she rubbed it out and started again.*

ruck /rʌk/: rucks, rucking, rucked

ruck up

Fabric or clothing **rucks up** when it is pushed upwards so that it forms a series of uneven folds: *She was dancing around in the stream with her skirt rucked up and tucked into her knickers at the back.*

rule /ruːl/: rules, ruling, ruled

rule off

You **rule off** a piece of paper when you draw a series of lines on it, *eg* to create columns or a grid: *Rule off the sheets into ten equally-spaced columns.*

rule out

1 You **rule** something **out** when you decide not to consider it or include it: *The French still have interest rates above the German level and they don't rule out a devaluation of the franc.* ❑ *The Labour leader hadn't actually ruled out proposals on electoral reform.* **2** One thing **rules out** another when the first makes the second impossible or impractical: *A hairline fracture of the finger ruled him out of the match.* **3** You **rule out** a certain type of behaviour when you get rid of it because it is not appropriate or acceptable: *This would rule out racial and sexual discrimination.*

rumble /ˈrʌmbəl/: rumbles, rumbling, rumbled

rumble on

An argument, disagreement or conflict **rumbles on** when it continues for a long time without being resolved or settled: *And so it was that the dispute rumbled on for months, then years, with neither side prepared to give an inch.*

rummage /ˈrʌmɪdʒ/: rummages, rummaging, rummaged

rummage about *or* rummage around

You **rummage about** or **around** in a place or container when you search through the things that are in it in a hurried or disorganized way: *He was rummaging about in the office complaining he could never find anything on Dee-Dee's day off.* ❑ *Gary unzipped his schoolbag and rummaged about for a pencil.*

run /rʌn/: runs, running, ran /ran/, run

run about

You **run about** when you move quickly from one place to another: *She prepared the food and I ran about acting as kitchenmaid.* [see also **run around**]

• *noun* **runabout: runabouts**

A **runabout** is a small or inexpensive car used for short journeys: *Her husband promised to buy her a little runabout.*

run across

You **run across** someone or something when you meet them or find them by chance: *Did you happen to run across any of my old acquaintances while you were in Oxford?* [*same as* **come across**]

run after

1 You **run after** someone of the opposite sex when you follow them around and make it too obvious that you want to have a romantic relationship with them: *He's got all those silly little girls running after him. Is it any wonder he's conceited?* **2** (*informal*) You **run after** someone when you do everything for them such as cleaning up the mess they make: *If you think your mother's going to go on running after you when you've grown up, think again!*

run along

You tell someone, especially a child, to **run along** when you want them to go away: *Run along now, Janey. I want to speak to your aunt.*

run around

1 People or animals **run around** or **about** when they move quickly from place to place within an area in an excited or energetic way: *No-one seemed to know what to do. They were all running around in a blind panic.* ❑ *When she got to the park she let the dog off the lead so that it could run around.* **2** You **run around** or **about** doing something when you move quickly from place to place getting the things you need or attending to many different things: *The daily chores fell mainly to the women; shopping, running around to find particular things.* **3** (*informal*) You say that people **are running around** or **about** when they are moving about in public going from one place to another in a purposeless or threatening way: *It terrifies me to think of people running around the streets carrying guns.*

• *noun (informal)* **run-around**

When you say that someone has given you the **run-around** you mean that they have purposely delayed dealing with something that they ought to have done, or they have deceived you intentionally: *I don't think he's got any intention of giving me a direct answer; I've been getting the run-around for weeks now.*

run around with

You **run around with** someone when you have a casual romantic or sexual relationship with them; you **run around with** a gang or similar group of people when you are involved with them and take part in their activities: *Six months ago she was involved with a known criminal; now she's running around with a married man.* ❑ *He runs around with some pretty unsavoury characters.*

run away

1 You **run away** when you get away from someone or something by running: *I ran away as fast as I could.* ❑ *The policeman tried to speak to the young girl but she ran away.* ❑ *The boys would ring the neighbours' doorbells and run away.* **2** Children **run away** from home when they leave without telling anyone they are going because they are unhappy there: *He ran away to the Army when he was 17.* **3** You **run away** from something that you don't want to deal with when you avoid it or refuse to face it: *You can't run away from the fact that you are ten years older than you were then.*

• *noun* **runaway: runaways**

A **runaway** is a child or young person who has run away from their home: *Many of London's homeless are young adults and teenage runaways.*

run away with

1 You **run away with** someone when you leave your home so that you can be with them: *Ursula met Justin, the writer's moody adolescent brother, and ran away with him.* **2** Your tongue **runs away with** you when you talk too much or you accidently say more than you intended to; your emotions **run away with** you when you can't control them: *I'm sorry I upset you. You know how my tongue runs away with me sometimes.* ❑ *This is silly; you're letting your emotions run away with you.* **3** You **run away with** a mistaken idea if you believe that it is true: *People shouldn't run away with the notion that they are more important than other members of the cast.*

run down

1 You **run down** somewhere when you move quickly to a lower level; you **run down** to a place when you go there quickly either on foot or by car: *He ran down the slope to meet Sue.* ❑ *Would you run down to the shops and get a loaf of bread?* **2** You **run** someone **down** when you criticize them unfairly:

It won't do much for his confidence if people are always running him down. **3** A business **is being run down** when it is being reduced in size and in its range of activities, often with the intention of closing it down completely: *The factory is being run down and closure is scheduled for 1997.* **4** A supply **is run down** when it is reduced: *The $25 million reserve fund had been run down to $8 million.* **5** A mechanism or battery **runs down** when it gradually stops working or loses power: *I think the batteries in this radio are running down.* **6** A vehicle or its driver **runs** someone **down** when they hit them and injure them: *He was about to be run down by the motorcycle.* **7** (*informal*) You **run down** someone or something you have been searching for when you eventually find them: *I ran him down in a seedy little hotel on the Left Bank.*

• *adjective* **run-down** *or* **run down**

1 Something that is **run-down** is in a bad state of repair: *a run down shack* ❑ *The whole area looked shabby and run down.* **2** You feel **run down** when you feel very tired and ill: *'She's been a little run down lately. Needs a tonic, I would say.'*

• *noun* **rundown**

A **rundown** is a brief spoken summary of something's main points: *George gave us a rundown of the day's events.*

run in

1 You **run in**, or **run into** a place, when you move quickly inside: *Run in and get an umbrella.* ❑ *He ran into the kitchen, shouting excitedly.* **2** (*informal*) Someone **is run in** by the police when they are arrested: *They ran him in on some trumped-up charge.* **3** In the past, a new car **was run in** for a period just after it was bought when it was carefully driven so as not to put too much strain on the engine: *With modern cars, there's no need to run the engine in as you used to have to do.*

• *noun (informal)* **run-in: run-ins**

You have a **run-in** with someone when you have a fight or argument with them: *She had a bit of a run-in with the headmaster about how her department should be run.*

run into

1 You **run into** someone when you meet them unexpectedly: *'Did you run into anyone interesting on your travels?'* ❑ *I stayed outside in case I ran into Father.* [*same as* **bump into, run across**] **2** You **run into** difficulties when you are suddenly faced with them and have to deal with them: *One of the residents was a chap about my age who had run into problems after his wife died.* **3** A sum of money **runs into** a stated amount if it reaches that amount: *The cost to government, employers and insurance companies could run into millions.* **4** A vehicle **runs into** another, or **into** a stationary object such as a wall, when it hits it: *The Benetton ran straight into the front of the Williams.* ❑ *The Hurricane was badly damaged and ran into a parked aircraft on landing.* **5** One thing **runs into** another when the one merges with the other so that there is no distinct division between them: *It was late one night running into horribly early the next morning.* ❑ *red running into purple, then into a deep blue.*

run off

1 You **run off** when you leave, running: *He shouted at them and they ran off, laughing.* **2** You **run off** somewhere when you go there without telling anyone you are going: *He ran off to London.*

run off with

You **run off with** someone when you unexpectedly leave with that person without intending to return: *Apparently her husband ran off with some girl half his age.*

run on

1 You **run on** when you continue running in the same direction after a brief pause or after you have reached a particular place; you **run on** ahead when you go ahead of others, running: *He reached the garden gate at a trot, hesitated for a moment, and then ran on.* ❑ *The wee boy ran on ahead into the gallery.* **2** Someone **runs on** when they go on talking for an unnecessarily long time: *She runs on a bit, your gran, doesn't she?*

run out

A supply of something **runs out** when there is none of it left: *What're they going to do when North Sea oil runs out?*

run out of

You **run out of** something when you have no more left because you have used it all: *Buy the most powerful PC you can afford, then there's less risk of running out of memory.* ❑ *I thought I'd better tell you you've run out of toilet paper.*

run out on

Someone **runs out** on you when they leave you to deal with a difficult situation alone: *I might have known the little rat would run out on us.*

run over

1 You **run over** to a person or place when you go towards them, running; people also say they **are running over** somewhere when they are going there by car: *She ran over to me to show me her new dolly.* ❑ *I'll be running over to Exeter this afternoon to do some shopping.* **2** Something containing a liquid **runs over** when liquid begins to spill over its upper edge: *They found the bath running over, but there didn't seem to be anyone in the house.* **3** A person or animal **is run over** when a vehicle's wheels pass over them, injuring or killing them: *Hundreds of toads are run over every year on Britain's roads.* ❑ *He tried to run me over with his tractor.* [compare **run down, knock down**] **4** You **run over** something when you practice it or check it to make sure it is correct: *I'd like you to run over these accounts with me sometime.* **5** Something **runs over** its allotted time when it goes on for longer than it should: *We're running over by at least ten minutes.*

• *verb* **overrun: overruns, overrunning, overran, overrun**

Something **overruns** when it takes longer than it should: *The concert overran by half an hour.*

• *adjective* **overrun**

A place is **overrun** with or by people or animals when they occupy it in great numbers: *The town was overrun with rats.*

run through

1 You **run through** a place when you pass through it, running: *They ran through the fields waving their arms and shouting to him to stop.* **2** Something such as a road or river **runs through** a place when its route goes through that place: *a long straight road running through agricultural land dotted with occasional clumps of trees.* **3** Something that **runs through** something else is found all through it: *What makes it interesting are the various sub-plots that run through the entire novel.* **4** You **run through** something when you use it all up: *We seem to be running through a huge amount of paper.* ❑ *I predict that they'll manage to run through all the money before Christmas.* **5** You **run through** something when you check it to make sure it is agreed or understood, or is being done properly: *I just want to run through the times of the flights again so that you all know when you should be where.*

• *noun* **run-through**

A **run-through** is a rehearsal or practice: *Let's have a quick run-through of the soprano part.*

run to

1 You **run to** someone for help or support when you go to them so that they can give it to you: *You won't always be able to run to your parents whenever something goes wrong in* *your life.* ❑ *What if he goes running to the police?* **2** You can **run to** something when you can afford it: *My salary doesn't run to expensive weekends in fancy hotels.* **3** Something **runs to** a stated amount when it reaches that amount: *The report ran to more than two thousand pages, not including the appendices.* **4** You can say that someone's tastes **run to** a particular thing when they like that thing: *Unusually for a teenager, his taste in music runs to more sophisticated things like opera.*

run up

1 You **run up** a debt when you get things without paying for them at the time, or you use other people's money that has to be repaid eventually: *How much debt do you run up on your credit card at this time of year? Too much, that's for sure.* **2** A flag **is run up** when it is raised on a flagpole so that it flies from the top: *They ran up the Jolly Roger.*

• *noun* **run-up**

The **run-up** to an event is the period of time before it and the activities preparing for the event during that period of time: *The warm weather proved to be a disadvantage in the run-up to autumn trading.* ❑ *in the run-up to the next general election.*

run up against

You **run up against** opposition or a problem when you are suddenly faced with it: *You've been lucky so far, but one of these days you'll run up against a problem that you can't solve so easily.*

rush /rʌʃ/: rushes, rushing, rushed

rush in *or* rush into

You **rush in**, or **into** something, when you start doing it immediately without thinking about it or preparing for it: *Andy's always getting into scrapes; he just rushes in without thinking.* ❑ *I wouldn't rush into marriage if I were you.*

rush out

You **rush out** to do something when you go and do it immediately without giving any thought to whether it is the best or most appropriate thing to do: *Don't rush out immediately and buy all the textbooks on the list.*

rush through

Something **is rushed through** when it is made or processed in a great hurry because it is needed urgently: *Everything was rushed through before they had time to think.* ❑ *The report implied that they may have rushed the product through without adequate testing.*

rust /rʌst/: rusts, rusting, rusted

rust away

A metal object **rusts away** when it is broken down and eventually destroyed by the effects of rust: *The iron railings hadn't been painted for years and were slowly rusting away.*

rustle /ˈrʌsəl/: rustles, rustling, rustled

rustle up

You **rustle up** something, especially a meal, when you prepare it quickly using whatever is readily available: *If you can wait ten minutes, I'm sure we can rustle up some hot soup and bread, at least.* ❑ *Can you rustle us up some coffee and sandwiches, Miss Peters?*

S

saddle /'sadəl/: **saddles**, **saddling**, **saddled**

saddle up
To **saddle up** a horse is to put a saddle on it so that it is ready to ride: *His young rider saddled him up and started to trot him round the practice ring.*

saddle with
Someone **is saddled with** a job or responsibility when they are given one that they don't want: *She offered herself in order to saddle him with someone else's child.* ❏ *The company is moving away from a family-dominated group, saddled with an out-of-date share structure.* [*same as* **lumber with** (*informal*)]

sail /seɪl/: **sails**, **sailing**, **sailed**

sail through
You **sail through** a difficult or testing experience when you deal with it easily and successfully: *Oxbridge interviews are supposed to be stiff, but Wilkie sailed through.* [*same as* **romp through**, **walk it** (*informal*)]

sally /'salɪ/: **sallies**, **sallying**, **sallied**

sally forth (*literary or humorous*)
Someone who **sallies forth** begins a journey or a task, usually with energy and determination: *Within just a few weeks, the young cub will sally forth to make his own way in the world.*

salt /sɔːlt/ *or* /sɒlt/: **salts**, **salting**, **salted**

salt away (*informal*)
To **salt** money **away** is to save it for the future, especially secretly: *We listened open-mouthed as we were told of the thousands she had somehow managed to salt away.* [*same as* **put by**, **put away**, **stash away** (*informal*); compare **save up**]

sand /sand/: **sands**, **sanding**, **sanded**

sand down
You **sand down** a surface of wood, or sometimes metal, when you make it smooth by rubbing it with sandpaper or other abrasive material: *I gave the table three coats of varnish and sanded it down between coats.* [compare **rub down**]

save /seɪv/: **saves**, **saving**, **saved**

save up
1 You **save up** when you gradually gather a sum of money, made up of all the smaller amounts you haven't spent, so that you can buy something you want; you can also say that you **save up** money, or an amount of money: *I had saved up and gradually built up my set of golf clubs.* ❏ *She saved up enough money to take a manicuring class.* [compare **put away, put by**] **2** You **save** something **up** when you keep it to be used or dealt with later: *I'd saved up quite a stock of scrap paper for the kids to draw on.* ❏ *Note down any queries and save them up for the next meeting.*

savour (*AmE* **savor**) /'seɪvə(r)/: **savours**, **savouring**, **savoured**

savour of

You can say that a situation or action **savours of** a particular quality, especially a quality that you disapprove of, when it has it or seems to have it: *It wasn't the first time that team selection had savoured of favouritism.* [*same as* **smack of**]

saw /sɔː/: **saws**, **sawing**, **sawed**, **sawn**

saw off

To **saw** something **off** is to cut it off using a saw: *A man was sawing and he sawed his fingers off.* ❑ *We sawed off the point with a neighbour's hacksaw.*

• *adjective* **sawn-off**

Sawn-off is used to describe something that has been made shorter by sawing a piece off: *Punishment was meted out with a sawn-off cricket bat.*

saw up

To **saw** something **up** is to cut it into pieces with a saw: *The smaller branches would be sawed up for firewood.*

say /seɪ/: **says** /sɛz/, **saying**, **said** /sɛd/

say for

When people talk about there being something to **say for** a particular situation they are commenting on the good aspects it has; when they talk about there being not much to **say for** it they are commenting on how bad or unsatisfactory it is: *We have virtually no traces of bacteria in the finished product, which is more than can be said for cheeses from some other Common Market countries.* ❑ *It doesn't say much for their organization if they can't even get the stuff mailed out on time.* ❑ *It says a lot for both clubs that they can produce such an exciting and entertaining game at this level.*

scale /skeɪl/: **scales**, **scaling**, **scaled**

scale down

To **scale** something **down** is to reduce its size, extent or value: *By the end of the '80s, armies were scaled down enormously and we waited for the peace dividend.*

scale up

To **scale** something **up** is to increase its size, extent or value: *Production had to be scaled up to meet the demands of a growing market.*

scare /skɛə(r)/: **scares**, **scaring**, **scared**

scare away *or* scare off

1 To **scare away** a person or animal, or **scare** them **off**, is to frighten them so that they go away or stay away: *The radio had been left on to scare burglars away.* ❑ *All the recent police activity scared him off and he left in quite a hurry.* **2** To **scare** someone **away**, or **scare** them **off**, is to make them unwilling to do what they had wanted or intended to do: *An overprotective father is guaranteed to scare off even the most committed boyfriend.* ❑ *Potential investors had been scared away by rumours of interest-rate rises.* [*same as* **put off**, **deter**, **discourage**]

scatter /'skatə(r)/: **scatters**, **scattering**, **scattered**

scatter about *or* scatter around

Things that **are scattered about** or **scattered around** have been carelessly and untidily left in various places: *There were lots of crisp packets and chocolate papers scattered about the yard.* ❑ *Old bits of iron and wood lay scattered around.*

school /skuːl/: **schools**, **schooling**, **schooled**

school in

People **are schooled in** a particular skill, attitude or type of behaviour when they are taught it, or are encouraged to develop it: *Children from* *that kind of background are schooled in the art of self-promotion.* ❑ *David and Earl were both schooled in the macho preference for raucous art.*

scoop /skuːp/: **scoops**, **scooping**, **scooped**

scoop up
You **scoop** something **up** when you lift it in a quick circular movement with your hand placed underneath: *Alice scooped the little one up from behind and tried to propel her into safer water.* ❑ *One by one, the gerbils were scooped up, inspected, and dropped back.*

score /skɔː(r)/: **scores**, **scoring**, **scored**

score off
Someone **scores off** you when they try to make themselves appear clever or amusing by using you as the object of an insulting or unkind remark: *We were to be treated to an evening of Alan and Fay scoring off each other.*

score out
You **score out** something written or printed when you cancel it by drawing a line through it: *The manuscript reveals that he had chosen a much more prosaic title at first, and later scored it out.* [*same as* **cross out**]

scout /skaʊt/: **scouts**, **scouting**, **scouted**

scout around *or* scout round
You **scout around** for something, or **scout round** for it, when you look for it in several different places: *I was still scouting around, vaguely aware that I had, in fact, actually found it.* ❑ *He was soon scouting round for logs and pieces of wood.* [*same as* **look around**]

scrabble /ˈskrabəl/: **scrabbles**, **scrabbling**, **scrabbled**

scrabble about *or* scrabble around
You **scrabble about** or **scrabble around** when you search with your hands for something in a clumsy or desperate way: *It was a pitiful sight to watch him scrabbling about under the frames.* ❑ *Like many voluntary organizations, they had to scrabble around to put together small pockets of resource.* [compare **scratch about**]

scramble /ˈskrambəl/: **scrambles**, **scrambling**, **scrambled**

scramble for
Several people **scramble for** something when each struggles to get more of it than the others: *The lesser media companies are left to scramble for coverage of the smaller tournaments.*

scrape /skreɪp/: **scrapes**, **scraping**, **scraped**

scrape along
You **scrape along** when you continue to manage to live on very little money: *They scraped along for over a year until a small windfall made life a little easier.* [*same as* **scrape by, get by**]

scrape by
You **scrape by** when you manage to live on very little money: *We will have to depend on dad for money or else scrape by on Social Security.* ❑ *Those who had possessions pawned them; others did what they could to scrape by.* [*same as* **scrape along, get by**]

scrape in *or* scrape into
Someone who **scrapes into** a job or other position only just manages to be accepted for it; you can also say that they **scrape in**: *I expect the Tories'll scrape into office on the slimmest of margins, like they always do.* ❑ *She was a poor scholar and only scraped in because of her sporting prowess.*

scrape through
You **scrape through** when you only just manage to pass an examination or test, or survive a difficult or testing experience: *I gather I scraped through the interview on the cut of my suit more than the cut of my wit.* ❑ *The aim is to*

cut costs enough to scrape through today's recession.

scrape together
You **scrape together** an amount of something, usually money, when you only manage to gather or collect it with great difficulty: *I managed to scrape enough together to feed my children and keep my flat going.* ❑ *Watson had succeeded in scraping together eleven players, although two of them were over fifty.* [*same as* **scrape up**]

scrape up
You **scrape up** an amount of something, usually money, when you only manage to gather or collect it with great difficulty: *Chilton and his wife scraped up £250 and persuaded the manufacturer to produce an unwaxed batch.* [*same as* **scrape together**]

scratch /skratʃ/: **scratches**, **scratching**, **scratched**

scratch about *or* **scratch around**
You **scratch about** or **scratch around** when you struggle to gather or collect all you need: *He was worrying his head off, scratching about for the rent and weathering one disappointment after another.* ❑ *Although they won the game 60-18, the Barbarians too scratched around for fluency.* [compare **scrabble about**]

screen /skriːn/: **screens**, **screening**, **screened**

screen off
You **screen off** part of a room when you separate it from the rest, with something such as a screen or curtain: *He worked in the dining room, at a desk that was screened off.* [compare **cordon off**]

screw /skruː/: **screws**, **screwing**, **screwed**

screw around (*informal*)
1 Someone who **screws around** has brief and casual sexual relationships with different people: *People who screw around nowadays know they are putting themselves at risk.* **2** Someone who **screws around** with something treats or handles it foolishly or too casually, not realising the serious harm or damage they could do: *He should have known better than to screw around with people's livelihoods.*

screw down
You **screw** something **down** when you fasten it down firmly using screws: *The lid had been screwed down.*

screw out of (*informal*)
You **screw** something **out of** someone when you use persuasion or threats to make them give it to you: *Albums, tee-shirts and endless other merchandising gimmicks are designed to screw, on average, another £12 out of each punter.*

screw up
1 You **screw up** your eyes when you close them tightly; you **screw up** your face when you twist it out of its normal shape, usually in an expression of disgust: *Stephen screwed his eyes up; nothing could have prepared him for this sight.* ❑ *You put down a lovingly cooked meal and your child just screws up her face at it.* **2** You **screw up** paper when you squash it into a ball-like shape with your hands: *Jason screwed the letter up nonchalantly and tossed it into a bin.* [*same as* **scrunch up**] **3** You can say that you **screw up** your courage when you make a great effort to deal bravely with something frightening: *Screwing up her courage, Polly turned the handle slowly.* [*same as* **summon up**, **muster up**] **4** (*informal*) You **screw** something **up** when you spoil it or deal with it badly or foolishly; you **screw up** when you make a foolish mistake that spoils something: *The drugs business has screwed up his chances of going to the world championships next summer.* ❑

We can just pretend that the computer has screwed up again. [*same as* **mess up** (*informal*), **cock up** (*vulgar slang*), **foul up** (*informal*)] **5** (*informal*) Something **screws** you **up** when it makes you nervous, uneasy and confused about how you should feel or think: *Outwardly you have to be unemotional and cynical, but inside it can really screw you up.*

• *adjective* **screwed-up**

1 A piece of **screwed-up** paper has been screwed up into a ball: *She must have put the screwed-up five-pound notes on the chest.* **2** (*informal*) A **screwed-up** person feels nervous, uneasy and confused about what to feel and think: *The kids who are pushed too much can turn into really screwed-up adults.*

scrunch /skrʌntʃ/: **scrunches, scrunching, scrunched**

scrunch up

You **scrunch up** paper when you press it into a rough ball-like shape with your hands: *He scrunched up sheets of newspaper and stuffed them between the logs.* [*same as* **screw up**]

seal /siːl/: **seals, sealing, sealed**

seal off

To **seal off** a place or area is to prevent people from getting in by blocking the entrances to it: *Forensic were on the scene and the whole area had been sealed off.* [*same as* **cordon off**; compare **screen off, cut off**]

seal up

You **seal** something **up** when you close or fasten it tightly and securely: *It is unwise to seal the vents up completely with tape, as changes in atmospheric pressure may cause damage.*

search /sɜːtʃ/: **searches, searching, searched**

search out

You **search out** someone or something when you find them after a long search: *With John in the band, we began to search out new songs.* [*same as* **hunt out**]

search through

You **search through** numerous things, or **through** what contains them, when you look at each in an attempt to find the thing you are looking for: *He came to London and systematically searched through the various agencies that might have employed her.* ❑ *We searched through all his bags, but could find no evidence of it.* [*same as* **look through**]

second /sɪˈkɒnd/: **seconds, seconding, seconded**

second to

Someone who **is seconded to** a place or a job from another job or place has been sent there, or sent to do it, temporarily: *Wilkins had been seconded to Special Branch, who thought his knowledge of dog tracks might come in useful.*

secure /sɪˈkjʊə(r)/: **secures, securing, secured**

secure against

You **are secured against** something when you are protected from it: *The clip secures the slate against wind uplift.* ❑ *There is no way you can secure the system against unlicensed access by hackers.*

see /siː/: **sees, seeing, saw** /sɔː/, **seen**

see about

You **see about** something when you take action to have it done, dealt with or provided: *I phoned up to see about having the bed delivered.* ❑ *They'd left us to see about the broken washing machine.* ❑ *'So he wants to get rid of the strike leaders, does he? We'll see about that!'* [compare **see to**]

see as

A person or thing **is seen as** a particular

thing, or having a particular role or function, when that is what they are considered to be: *Charlie Buchan was seen as the man to inspire and lend experience to a faltering Arsenal attack.* ❑ *Some works have been intended by their authors to be seen as art.* ❑ *He seemed to see himself as part of a fashionable play.*

see beyond

1 You are able to **see beyond** or **past** a certain point of time in the future when you can imagine, and perhaps plan for, what will happen after it: *At the moment we can't see beyond paying the car insurance, let alone Christmas.* **2** You can't **see beyond** or **past** someone when you are so emotionally involved with them that you aren't able to accept that they have any faults: *Don't criticize him in front of his Mum. She's never been able to see past him.*

see in

1 You **see** a particular quality or characteristic **in** someone or something when you believe that they have it, or when you recognize it in them: *The extent to which universities opposed her policies can be seen in the Oxford vote not to give her an honorary degree.* ❑ *It's uncanny how much of his father I see in him.* ❑ *We couldn't see what a beautiful girl like Anna could possibly see in Jim.* **2** You **see in** a new time or period when you are present at the beginning of it: *I went round to Bob's flat and we saw the New Year in together.* [compare **usher in**]

see of

People often use **see of** when talking about how often they see or meet someone: *I didn't see all that much of her while she was growing up.* ❑ *I've seen a great deal of my family since I moved back to Scotland.*

see off

1 You **see** someone **off** when you say goodbye to them as they leave: *She comes out on the terrace to see them off to school.* ❑ *We've just come down to see off a friend of my sister's.* **2** You **see off** an opponent when you defeat them: *They defeated Spurs, then saw Chelsea off with ease.* **3** You also **see** someone **off** when you force them to go away: *The dogs are left in the yard to see off intruders.* [*same as* **chase off**]

see out

1 You **see** someone **out** when you go with them as far as the door or other exit they are leaving by: *See the inspector out please, Marilyn.* [*same as* **show out**] **2** You **see** a period of time **out** when you continue or survive until the end of it: *He can expect to see out the remainder of his two-year term as prime minister.* [*same as* **last out**]

see over *or* see round

You **see over** a place, or **see round** it, when you look at or inspect all parts or areas of it: *It took over three hours for us to see over the extensive grounds.* ❑ *I saw round the factory on my last visit.* [*same as* **look round**]

see past see see beyond.

see through

1 You can **see through** something when you can see from one side of it to the other: *The latest radar equipment enables them to see through layers of cloud.* ❑ *She could see the bones through the skin.* **2** You can **see through** a person, or their behaviour, when you understand what their true intentions are, although they try to hide them: *She presents herself as the victim of men she sets out to attract and soon sees through and rejects.* **3** You **see** something **through** when you continue with it until it is finished: *It would be a bold attack requiring determination to see it through.* **4** Something **sees** you **through** a difficult time when it helps you to survive it: *The points secured will see England through to the finals.* **5** Something **sees through** a period of time when it lasts until the end of it: *The despised suburban style looks like* *seeing the century through.* ❑ *He doubted he would see the winter through, and he died the following spring.*

• *adjective* **see-through**

See-through clothes are made of cloth that is so thin you can see the skin or underwear of the person who is wearing them: *I'd prefer something that was a little more see-through.*

see to

You **see to** something when you do it or arrange for it to be done or dealt with: *I would also need to see to the matter of costumes.* ❑ *Who's seeing to the travel arrangements?* ❑ *'Would someone please organize some coffee and sandwiches for our visitors.' ' Yes, I'll see to it.'* [*same as* **attend to, deal with, take care of**]

seek /siːk/: seeks, seeking, sought /sɔːt/

seek out

You **seek out** something or someone when you try to find them: *It is well worth seeking out an unpasteurised Camembert.* ❑ *She did not have the energy to seek them out.* [compare **track down**]

seize /siːz/: seizes, seizing, seized

seize on

You **seize on** something such as an opportunity or an idea, or **seize upon** it, when you take it or accept it eagerly: *The money-conscious Sir Henry seized on the suggestion of a £2000 fee.* ❑ *Such lapses were seized upon by Lewis's jealous academic colleagues.*

seize up

1 Part of your body **seizes up** when it becomes painfully stiff, usually because the muscles in it have been exercised too much: *Lamb's right calf seized up and he had to leave the field.* **2** You can also say that something such as a machine or system **seizes up** when its moving parts fail to move, so that it doesn't work properly: *To the strikers' dismay, Britain did not seize up without trains.* [*same as* **jam**]

sell /sɛl/: sells, selling, sold /sould/

sell off

Someone **sells** something **off** when they get rid of it by selling it: *They were forced to keep the land because of the particular problems associated with selling it off.* ❑ *He was often broke and was gradually forced to sell off his library.*

• *noun* • **sell-off**: **sell-offs**

A **sell-off** is the sale of something, usually part of a business company: *They would have to delay the sell-off by up to six months.*

sell out

1 A shop **sells out** of something when they have none of it left to sell: *Sega is anticipating selling out within a week of the game's release.* **2** A film, play or other performance **is sold out** when all the tickets have been sold: *The concert sold out two hours after the box office opened for business.* **3** (*informal*) Someone who **sells out** betrays their principles or their friends: *Educationalists have sold out to those who have imposed attainment on the education system.* ❑ *He didn't want to be accused of selling out to the arts establishment.*

• *noun* **sell-out**

1 A **sell-out** is a play, film or other performance for which all the tickets have been sold: *Other shows had been a sell-out at around five or six thousand seats.* **2** You can also refer to action or behaviour that betrays friends or principles as a **sell-out**: *Feminist interpreters will consider her video a sell-out.*

sell up

Someone who **sells up** sells everything they have, such as their home or their business: *They didn't sell up completely but granted leases of land wanted for development.* ❑ *It looked as if they might have to sell up and move into* *rented accommodation.*

send /sɛnd/: **sends**, **sending**, **sent** /sɛnt/

send ahead
You **send** something, or someone, **ahead** when you arrange for them to arrive at a place before you get there: *We can arrange for your luggage to be sent on ahead to each of the overnight stops.* ❑ *He sends parties of slaves ahead at intervals.*

send away
1 You **send** someone **away** when you ask or order them to leave: *She was dying to get on with her work but not wanting to send him away in this mood.* **2** You **send away** for something when you send a letter to the supplier asking them to send it to you: *Mum's sent away for their spring catalogue.* ❑ *Morrison's said they would have to send away for the part and it might be two weeks before it arrived.* [*same as* **send off**]

send back
You **send** something **back** when you return it, usually by post: *Send them one of your pieces and ask them to match it and send their sample and yours back.* ❑ *They took the bills away but didn't send back the cheque.*

send down (*informal*)
Someone who **is sent down** is sent to prison: *This time he'll be sent down for life.*

send for
1 You **send for** something when you send a letter to the supplier asking them to send it to you: *Before launching out to buy new materials, send for literature from each company.* [*same as* **send away**] **2** You **send for** someone when you send a message asking or ordering them to come and see you: *I advised him to send for the leaders of the other two parties.*

send forth (*literary*)
People sometimes use **send forth** when referring to something that is produced or created: *Songbirds send forth their music over a troubled land.* ❑ *The plant will grow rapidly and send forth its runners.* ❑ *He's worked selflessly for the party, sending forth a barrage of witty editorials.* [*same as* **send out**]

send in
1 You **send** something **in** when you send it by post to someone who will judge it or deal with it officially: *To win a prize, send in your caption together with any suitable photos.* ❑ *Complete the form opposite and send it in to our Marathon team.* **2** You **send** someone **in** when you invite or order them to enter a room: *Mrs Pygling sent her in to spy on Jane.* **3** People such as police or soldiers **are sent in** when they are ordered to go and deal with a difficult situation: *The banks don't want to send in managers or directors.* ❑ *It's one of these situations where they usually end up sending in a SWAT team.*

send off
1 You **send** something **off** when you post it: *He hasn't forgiven her for sending it off without telling him.* **2** You **send off** for something when you send a letter to the supplier asking them to send it to you: *She cuts out coupons from magazines and sends off for make-up samples.* [*same as* **send away**] **3** You **send** someone **off** when you ask or order them to leave, especially to go somewhere specific: *They sent us off on a wasteful course of negative research.* ❑ *She wouldn't listen to him and sent him off feeling more bitter and frustrated than ever.* **4** A footballer or other sportsperson **is sent off** when they are ordered to leave the field as punishment for breaking the rules: *He's back from a one-match ban after being sent off against Crystal Palace.*

• *noun* **send-off**
A **send-off** is an occasion when people gather to give their good wishes to someone who is leaving: *His colleagues gave him a memorable send-off.*

send on
You **send on** something you have received when you send it to someone else: *Sheen closed the list with a message of thanks, asking that it be sent on.*

send out
1 You **send** something **out** when you post it to someone: *Eleven weeks before departure, we will send out a final invoice showing the balance.* **2** People often use **send out** to refer to something that is produced or created: *The tree sends out shoots from a dry and seemingly lifeless trunk.* [*same as* **send forth**]

send up (*informal*)
You **send** something **up** when you use humour to make it appear ridiculous: *This is a state which Zuckerman experiences and which he sends up.* ❑ *He sends up politicians and TV personalities brilliantly.*
• *noun* **send-up**: *It's obviously a send-up of 'Newsnight' and of Jeremy Paxman in particular.*

separate /ˈsɛpəreɪt/: **separates**, **separating**, **separated**

---

separate out
You **separate** things **out** when you divide them into groups, or separate them from others: *It is not useful to separate any one out from the group.* ❑ *The effect of the rotation is to separate things out from the original mixture.* [compare **sort out**]

serve /sɜːv/: **serves**, **serving**, **served**

---

serve as
You can use **serve as** to say what something is used for, especially if it is used for a purpose that is not its original purpose: *The room for general living often has to serve as a study.* ❑ *His name served as a seal of approval that a deal would go ahead.* [*same as* **do as** (*informal*), **do for** (*informal*)]

serve on
1 People **serve on** something such as a jury or committee when they are a member of it: *Serving on the General Purposes Committee gave him a certain insight into how they did things.* **2** (*technical*) Someone who is presented with a legal document that requires them to do something has that document **served on** them: *Writs were served on the two firms last March.*

serve under
Someone who **serves under** a particular person works for an organization which has that person as its leader: *From 1851 to 1854 he was in Canada, returning in 1854 to serve under Sir Henry James.*

serve up
1 You **serve up** food when you give it to people: *Dot had not seen an egg served up like that before.* [*same as* **dish up**] **2** You can also use **serve up** when talking about something that is offered or presented: *Some served up their erotic fantasies while others explored their inner beings.*

set /sɛt/: **sets**, **setting**, **set**

---

set about
1 You **set about** doing something when you begin to do it, often with energy and enthusiasm: *I took off my jacket and set about clearing the tables.* ❑ *In Africa, the Italian army set about building an empire.* **2** (*informal*) Someone **sets about** you when they attack you; you can also say that you **set about** something when you vigorously or violently tackle it or deal with it: *Then they set about him with sticks.* ❑ *I fetched the iron and set about a pile of shirts.* ❑ *I set about the lump with the woodcarver.*

set against
1 People or groups **are set against** each other when they take or are made to take different sides in opposition to each other: *Both groups were set against each other, each determined not*

to give in to the other. ❑ *The community and the individual are set against each other.* **2** Two or more people or things **are set against** each other when they are compared in order to show how different they are: *You have the intellectual subversive set against the 'clean, ordered British bobby'.* **3** You **set** negative things **against** positive things when you compare them to discover what the average or overall effect is: *They have only two wins and two draws to set against four defeats.* **4** You **are set against** something when you are opposed to it: *I can't see why you're so set against the idea.* **5** You can use **set against** when talking about the circumstances that surround or act as the background to an event or story: *The book is set against the breakdown of the pattern of Savoyard life.*

set apart

You **set** something such as a room or period of time **apart** when you keep or reserve it for a special purpose: *areas of woodland set apart for recreational and educational purposes.*

set apart from

One thing that **is set apart from** others is regarded or treated as different, often better: *Cases involving negligence have been set apart from cases of positive acts.* ❑ *They emphasised the power that sets him apart from other strikers.*

set aside

1 You **set aside** something such as time or money when you save it for a special purpose: *I don't know how they had scraped up the money set aside for the roof repairs.* ❑ *The last day had been set aside for a hunting trip.* [*same as* **set apart**, **put aside**] **2** You **set aside** things such as feelings and beliefs when you disregard them for the sake of something that is more important: *He should set aside his obsession with results and experiment with tactics and players.* [*same as* **put aside**]

set back

1 Something **sets** you **back**, or **sets back** your progress, when it delays or reverses your progress: *A bad training class could have set Toby's development back months.* [compare **hold up**] **2** (*informal*) Something that **sets** you **back** a specified amount of money costs you that much: *The white evening gloves set her back the equivalent of two weeks' wages.* [*same as* **knock back** (*informal*)] **3** A building that **is set back** from a road or other landmark is built some distance back from it: *The house is ideally suited, being slightly set back from the busy and noisy seafront.*

• *noun* **setback**: **setbacks**

A **setback** is any disadvantage or inconvenience, especially something that delays or reverses progress: *Problems in Japan are blamed for the setback.* ❑ *It all caused me severe emotional stress and a career setback.*

set down

1 You **set** something **down** when you write it down: *An author is taking his revenge in setting down these judgements.* [compare **take down, note down, jot down**] **2** You can use **set down** to talk about what is stated in laws or official rules: *Many aspects of our proposals are being implemented, such as the need to set down what is meant by 'an acceptable level'.* [*same as* **lay down**] **3** You **set down** something you've been holding when you put it on to a table or other surface, especially carefully or gently: *Little Jane, set down by Dorothy, staggered out to join the others.* [*same as* **lay down**] **4** You can use **set down** when talking about where a bus or train stops to let people get off: *They asked to be set down in what looked to us to be totally featureless moorland.*

set down as

You can say that you **have set** someone **down as** a certain kind of person when you have decided what kind of person they are, especially when you later discover that they are different: *Her* *family had, of course, set him down from the start as an opportunist, only interested in her money and social status.* [*same as* **have down as, put down as**]

set forth (*formal*)

1 You **set forth** when you begin a journey: *The two armies finally set forth on the third anniversary of the Battle of Hattin.* ❑ *At once, Richard set forth for Cyprus.* [*same as* **set off, go forth**] **2** You **set forth** things such as opinions, ideas and suggestions when you present or explain them: *This recalls the doctrine set forth in the Old Testament.* ❑ *He sets forth an idealistic view of society.* [*same as* **put forth**]

set in

An unpleasant condition **sets in** when it begins and seems likely to continue: *Root crops must be dug up before severe frosts set in.* ❑ *A sort of bunker mentality quickly sets in.*

set off

1 You **set off** when you begin a journey: *He collected his offspring and set off home.* ❑ *He could set off to walk south and try to cross enemy lines.* ❑ *Some 13,000 Scots would set off at first light.* ❑ *She tucked the case under her arm and set off down the alley.* [*same as* **set out**] **2** To **set off** a bomb is to cause it to explode; to **set off** an alarm or other device is to cause it to sound or to function: *Believing that a man is about to set off a bomb won't make our soldier do anything.* ❑ *Exhaust fumes could set off the alarm.* [*same as* **trigger off**; compare **go off**] **3** Something **sets off** a process or a chain of events when it causes it to begin: *It can accidentally set off a very volatile and dangerous sequence of events.* [*same as* **trigger off, spark off**] **4** Something **sets** someone **off** when it makes them begin to do something, such as laugh or cry, that they continue to do for some time: *The stop sets one dog off barking and others join in.* ❑ *We'd just calmed her down when a chance remark from Don set her off again.* **5** One thing **sets off** another it is next to when it provides a contrast in shape or colour that makes the other more noticeable and striking: *His luminous head with its burning eyes is set off against a whirlpool of darkness.* ❑ *Soft surrounding plants set off spiky, yellow-bloomed irises.* [*same as* **bring out, show off**]

set off against

You **set** expenses **off against** tax you are due to pay when you subtract them from the earnings that will be taxed; one thing **is set off against** another when the one reduces the amount, extent or effect of the other: *If you sue for a return of this, I shall set off my larger claim against it.*

set on

1 You **are set on** some course of action when you have firmly decided to do it, or it will definitely or inevitably happen: *Is this a priest who strides towards us, implacably set on some atavistic rite?* ❑ *Within fifteen years, Germany was set on a course of revanche.* ❑ *It was clear that both parties were set on a collision course.* ❑ *He has set the Group on a course for long-term growth.* **2** Someone **sets on** you when they attack you; you can also say that you **are set upon** by them: *Without warning, they set on the ragged marchers with batons.* ❑ *Farrell was set upon by a gang of thugs wielding iron bars.* **3** Someone **sets** dogs or other animals **on** you when they cause them to attack you: *The farmer threatened to set his Alsatian on us if we didn't get off his land.*

set out

1 You **set out** when you begin a journey: *Wycliffe set out along the road which was really a lane.* ❑ *Four horses and riders set out to complete the cross-country course.* ❑ *You are about to set out on an interesting and formative experience.* [*same as* **set off**] **2** What you **set out** to do is the final result you hope to achieve by your actions: *Artists* *and poets set out to explore their own island in search of the picturesque.* ❑ *They did not succeed in doing what they had set out to do.* **3** Something that **is set out** is explained or stated in speech or writing: *In each course, the method of assessment is set out at the beginning of the session.* ❑ *Your attention is drawn to the proviso set out in Clause 3.* ❑ *Its functions and powers are set out in Schedule 1 to the Act of 1986.* [*same as* **set forth** (*formal*)] **4** Something that **is set out** somewhere is placed or arranged there in an ordered way: *Bog plants can be set out in their permanent position.* ❑ *Set the tiles out so that they are centred on the area concerned.* [*same as* **lay out**]

set to

1 You **set to** when you begin an activity with energy and determination: *Mungo set to, enjoying the work.* **2** (*old*) Two people **set to** when they begin fighting or arguing: *After a moment's pause, they set to again, beating each other with their little fists, biting and kicking.*

• *noun (old)* **set-to**

A **set-to** is a fight or argument: *They had a right set-to while I went to look for my knitting.*

set up

1 You **set up** equipment when you install it and make it ready to use: *I bought the computer, brought it home and set it up immediately.* **2** You also **set** something **up** somewhere when you build it there, or fix it into position there: *The best solution would be to set a roadblock up at the exit to the estate.* ❑ *They set up two photo-detectors on either side.* [*same as* **erect** (*formal*)] **3** You **set up** something such as a company, an organization or a system when you create it: *Licences were issued to any company wanting to set up a sawmill.* ❑ *There are still those who would advocate setting up a separate Parliament.* ❑ *I set up a little deception plan.* **4** You **set up** in business when you begin to operate a business: *He decided to set up as a psychotherapist.* ❑ *They would contribute to the cost of setting up in areas of high unemployment.* **5** You **set** something **up** when you cause it, or take action that makes it happen: *The disquiet that he had set up among the brothers would go on echoing for some time.* ❑ *He ended a fine performance by setting up wing Byram for a try.* ❑ *He set up his victory by establishing a new course record in the third round.* ❑ *That victory set the Swede up for a seemingly difficult task against Wheaton in the sixth round.* **6** Something that **sets** you **up** makes you feel healthy and full of energy: *Self-massage sets you up perfectly for the day ahead.* **7** (*informal*) Someone who **sets** you **up** tricks or deceives you, especially by making you appear guilty of a crime or other wrongdoing: *It was then that he realised he'd been set up by Marie.* ❑ *He tried to set us up.*

• *noun* **set-up**: **set-ups**

1 You can refer to a situation or a system as a **set-up**: *Under the old set-up, I ran a course on the problems of language-learning.* **2** (*informal*) A **set-up** is also a trick or deception, especially one that makes you appear guilty of a crime or other wrongdoing: *It was a set-up, designed to flush the big-shots in the drugs cartel into the open.*

settle /ˈsɛtəl/: settles, settling, settled

---

settle back

You **settle back** when you lean or lie back comfortably, *eg* in a chair: *She settled back on the pillow.* ❑ *He'd just settled back to enjoy the film when the baby started crying again.*

settle down

1 You **settle down** to do something when you begin to do it, in a calm or serious way: *With its political base ensured, the government could now settle down to enjoy the fruits of* *recovery.* ❑ *The old hands were less excited and settled down to daydream the time away.* **2** You **settle** yourself **down** somewhere when you make yourself comfortable there and rest or relax: *We settled ourselves down in a first-class compartment.* **3** To **settle down** is to begin to live an ordered life, more or less permanently in the same place or with the same partner: *They're considering building a house and perhaps settling down.* **4** People or situations **settle down** when they become calm or quiet after being noisy, busy or affected by strong feelings: *Things had just settled down again when the air-raid siren sounded for a second time.* ❑ *'Settle down now, children. The programme is just about to begin.'*

settle for

You **settle for** something when you choose or accept it, especially when your preferred choice is not available: *The breakfast on offer looked revolting, so I settled for tea and muesli.* ❑ *He wasn't proposing to settle for just any job.* [compare **plump for**]

settle in

You **settle in** when you become used to, and begin to feel familiar with, a new situation such as a new house or job: *They had stayed to help her settle in.* ❑ *No doubt it'll all seem a bit strange at first, but you'll soon settle in.*

settle into

You **settle into** a certain kind of activity or behaviour when you begin to do it and will do it for some time: *They gave up the game and settled into cosy domesticity.* ❑ *We appear to be settled into a period of relative calm on the political front.*

settle on

You **settle on** something when you finally decide to do or have it: *After some discussion, we settled on lunch together the following day.* [*same as* **decide on**; compare **agree on**]

settle up

You **settle up** with someone when you pay them the money that you owe them: *I don't get paid until next week. Can I settle up with you then?* ❑ *You go ahead and I'll settle up the bill.*

sew /sou/: sews, sewing, sewed, sewn

sew on

You **sew** something **on** when you attach it to something by sewing it with a needle and thread: *The doctor said he could have sewn the fingers back on.* ❑ *There were garlands with bells sewn on.*

sew up

1 You **sew up** fabric that is torn when you repair it by sewing: *Take your jacket off and I'll sew up the tear.* ❑ *The surgeon had sewed up the patient leaving a swab inside.* **2** (*informal*) You can also say that you **have got** something **sewn up** when you are sure you will gain, achieve or win it: *Mount Patrick appeared to have the race sewn up.*

shack /ʃak/: shacks, shacking, shacked

shack up (*informal*)

One person **shacks up** with another, or they **shack up** together, when they start living together as lovers: *Elizabeth said quite firmly that she didn't believe in young men and women shacking up together.*

shackle /ˈʃakəl/: shackles, shackling, shackled

shackle with

You can say that someone **is shackled with** something when it limits or restricts them in some way: *When you give it attributes, you are shackling it with meaning, imprisoning it with adjectives.* [compare **lumber with** (*informal*), **saddle with**]

shade /ʃeɪd/: **shades**, **shading**, **shaded**

shade in
You **shade in** an area on a drawing or painting when you cover it with pencil lines or dark colours: *Once she'd shaded in the shadows the picture was almost complete.*

shade into
One thing **shades into** another when it becomes the other, so gradually that it is impossible to identify where one ends and the other begins: *It was criticism all right, shading into vitriol and downright bitchiness.* [*same as* **blend into**, **merge into**]

shake /ʃeɪk/: **shakes**, **shaking**, **shook** /ʃʊk/, **shaken** /ˈʃeɪkən/

shake down (*informal*)
You **shake down** somewhere when you make a temporary bed and sleep there: *The shearers usually shake down at the back of the sheds, maybe building a camp fire if it's cold.* [*same as* **bed down**, **doss down** (*informal*)]
• *noun (informal)* **shakedown**: **shakedowns**
A **shakedown** is somewhere to sleep as a temporary bed: *Muffled snores were coming from Bluey's shakedown in the kitchen.*

shake off
You **shake off** someone or something when you manage to get rid of them: *It was just an attempt to shake off a pervasive boredom.* ❑ *Many of the island-groups still have to shake off the mastery of foreign powers.* ❑ *The red-brown tentacles of London's suburbs had at last been shaken off.* [compare **throw off**]

shake out
You **shake out** a cloth when you shake it, either in order to get rid of dirt or to spread it out when it has been folded: *She shook her duster out on to the roses.*

shake out of
You **are shaken out of** feelings or behaviour of a particular kind when someone forces you to feel or behave differently: *She will be shaken out of her depression with violence.*

shake up
1 Something that **shakes** you **up** shocks or upsets you: *The news from home had really shaken him up.* **2** To **shake up** something such as an organization or a system is to make great changes to it, usually in order to improve it or make it more efficient: *We need some system for shaking things up.*
• *noun* **shake-up**: **shake-ups**
1 A **shake-up** is a major change to something: *There is speculation among MPs that a limited Cabinet shake-up is still on the cards.* **2** A **shake-up** is also an experience that shocks or upsets you: *Individuals survive the shake-up of midlife change, and often emerge from it stronger.*

shame /ʃeɪm/: **shames**, **shaming**, **shamed**

shame into
You **shame** someone **into** doing something when, by making them feel ashamed, you force them to do something to correct what they are ashamed of: *My teacher said I was a disaster and my father was shamed into paying for extra lessons for me.*

shape /ʃeɪp/: **shapes**, **shaping**, **shaped**

shape up (*informal*)
You can ask how something **is shaping up** when you want to know how well it is developing or progressing; you can say that it **is shaping up**, or **shaping up** nicely, when it is developing or progressing well: *How's the new apprentice shaping up?* ❑ *According to preliminary reports the scheme seems to be shaping up pretty well.*

share /ʃeə(r)/: **shares**, **sharing**, **shared**

share out
You **share** something **out** when you give each of several people a share of it: *She used to count us all and share it all out.* ❑ *Then home we would go and share out the proceeds of our trip.* [compare **give out, dish out**]

sharpen /ˈʃɑːpən/: **sharpens, sharpening, sharpened**

sharpen up
1 You **sharpen** something **up** when you make it sharp or sharper: *Sharpening up the mower blades regularly will ensure a good cut.* ❑ *The helmets were sharpened up with the help of a file.* **2** You also **sharpen** something **up** when you make it better: *The primary function of the plan is to sharpen up the best of good practice.*

shave /ʃeɪv/: **shaves, shaving, shaved**

shave off
You **shave off** hair when you remove it by shaving: *This was attached to the one lock of her hair that had not been shaved off.* ❑ *No-one recognised him when he'd shaved off his beard and moustache.*

shear /ʃɪə(r)/: **shears, shearing, sheared**

shear off
A metal part of a machine or other structure **shears off** when it breaks off because there is too much pressure on it: *One of the bolts fixing the mast had sheared off.*

sheet /ʃiːt/: **sheets, sheeting, sheeted**

sheet down (*informal*)
Rain **sheets down** when it falls very heavily: *They looked out at the monsoon rain sheeting down and turning the roads into muddy rivers.* [*same as* **pour down, lash down**]

shell /ʃɛl/: **shells, shelling, shelled**

shell out (*informal*)
You **shell out** money on something when you spend what you think is a large or unreasonable amount on it: *And then he had to shell out five hundred quid to have the car fixed.* [*same as* **fork out** (*informal*), **splash out** (*informal*); compare **cough up**]

shin /ʃɪn/: **shins, shinning, shinned**

shin down
You **shin down** something such as a tree when you climb down it holding on with your legs as well as your hands: *The burglar made his escape by shinning down a drainpipe.*

shin up
You **shin up** something such as a tree when you climb up it holding on with your legs as well as your hands: *The next moment he was shinning up the rope as if his life depended on it.*

shine /ʃaɪn/: **shines, shining, shone** /ʃɒn/

shine out
1 A light **shines out** when it shines so brightly that it can be seen from far away: *The reassuring flash of the Arnamurchan light shone out across the darkened sea.* **2** You can also say that a quality **shines out** when it is immediately and easily noticeable: *Her kindness and concern shone out like a beacon.*

shine through
A quality **shines through** when it is immediately and easily noticeable: *Hugh McIlvanney's feeling for his fellow-man shines through.*

ship /ʃɪp/: **ships, shipping, shipped**

ship in
Goods that **are shipped in** are brought

to a place by ship: *Emergency aid was being shipped in by the tonne.*

ship off (*informal*)
People or things **are shipped off** when they are sent away somewhere, usually, but not necessarily, by ship: *Many children were shipped off to the relative safety of the US and Canada.*

ship out
Goods that **are shipped out** somewhere are taken there by ship: *The crates were eventually shipped out of Africa.*

shock /ʃɒk/: shocks, shocking, shocked

shock into
You **are shocked into** doing something, or into action of a particular kind, when a shock or surprise you receive causes you to do it: *She'd been shocked into complete silence.*

shoo /ʃuː/: shoos, shooing, shooed

shoo away *or* shoo off
You **shoo** an animal **away**, or **shoo** it **off**, when you wave your hands to make it go away: *Now she flapped her hands as if shooing something away.*

shoot /ʃuːt/: shoots, shooting, shot /ʃɒt/

shoot down
1 An aircraft **is shot down** when bullets or missiles fired at it hit it and cause it to crash to the ground: *They moved the anti-aircraft units to the Isle of Wight, making it possible to shoot the V1s down before they reached the London area.* ❑ *Two of the pilots were eventually shot down in 1986.* [*same as* **bring down**] **2** Someone **is shot down** when a bullet or bullets fired at them wounds or kills them and causes them to fall to the ground: *They organized escape routes for pilots who'd been shot down over France.* [*same as* **bring down**] **3** (*informal*) To **shoot** someone **down** is also to dismiss their ideas or suggestions as ridiculous or impossible: *When I tried to put my side of the story, he shot me down in flames.*

shoot off
1 (*informal*) You **shoot off** when you leave, at speed or in a hurry: *Alistair said he was shooting off to the country for a long weekend.* [*same as* **dash off**; compare **clear off**] **2** Part of something **is shot off** when it is destroyed by bullets or missiles: *You order one of these heads and they send it with the nose shot off.* [compare **blow off**]

shoot out
Something **shoots out** when it comes out, is forced out, or is extended out, at great speed: *The male catches the young as they shoot out of the female.* ❑ *The dragon shoots out foam and spume from her nostrils.* ❑ *As Graham's hand touched the gate she shot her hand out and grabbed him.*

• *noun* **shootout: shootouts**
A **shootout** is a fight between people who shoot at each other with guns: *a shootout between FBI agents and the terrorists.*

shoot up
1 Something **shoots up** when it grows or rises rapidly: *They watched the flames shoot up the chimney.* **2** A child who **is shooting up** is growing very fast or becoming very tall: *Don't worry if his growth seems slow; he'll probably shoot up when he reaches 14 or 15.* **3** Someone who **shoots up** a place causes great damage by repeatedly firing a gun: *They wheeled around the perimeter shooting up buildings.* **4** (*informal*) Someone who **shoots up** injects themselves with drugs for pleasure: *addicts shooting up in a disused warehouse.*

shop /ʃɒp/: shops, shopping, shopped

shop around
1 You **shop around** when, before

buying something, you compare the price or quality of it in each of several shops: *This is a bargain time for buyers prepared to shop around.* **2** You can also say that you **shop around** when you examine what is offered by each of several companies or organizations before deciding what to accept: *They encouraged people to shop around among insurers.* ❑ *In the 'internal market', local doctors could shop around for health care.*

shore /ʃɔː(r)/: **shores**, **shoring**, **shored**

---

shore up
1 To **shore up** a wall or other structure is to support it with something that will prevent it from falling or collapsing: *Mines were built under the walls, shored up with timber.* **2** You **shore up** anything that is failing or weakening when you do something to strengthen or support it: *Investment was intended to shore up the pound against the dollar.* [*same as* **prop up**]

shout /ʃaʊt/: **shouts**, **shouting**, **shouted**

---

shout down
Someone speaking in public **is shouted down** when others force them to stop speaking by shouting: *Each time he tried to make himself heard, he was shouted down by a militant faction.* [*same as* **howl down**]

shout out
You **shout out** when you shout something, so that others will listen or pay attention; you can also say that you **shout** something **out**: *Lilley shouted out that there was trouble ahead.* ❑ *I shouted out to her but she walked past.* ❑ *They heard Angus's name shouted out.* [*same as* **call out**]

shove /ʃʌv/: **shoves**, **shoving**, **shoved**

---

shove about *or* **shove around**
(*informal*)
Someone who **shoves** you **about**, or **shoves** you **around**, rudely or unfairly orders you to do things, in a way that suggests they think they are more important or powerful than you: *Because their character is independent, they don't like being shoved around.* [*same as* **push around**]

shove off (*informal*)
Someone who tells you to **shove off** is telling you rudely to go away: *He told us to shove off; so we shoved off.* [*same as* **push off** (*informal*), **clear off** (*informal*)]

shove up (*informal*)
If someone says '**shove up**' to you they want you to move to make room for them: *Shove up and let Russell sit on the couch.* [*same as* **budge up** (*informal*)]

show /ʃoʊ/: **shows**, **showing**, **showed**

---

show around *or* **show round**
You **show** someone **around**, or **show** them **round**, when you guide them round a place so that they can see all parts of it: *He made apologies as he showed me round.* ❑ *He's promised to show us around the factory.*

show down
• *noun* **showdown**: **showdowns**
A **showdown** is any situation in which two people or groups are finally brought into a contest or conflict with each other, which will decide who is the stronger: *The brothers are heading for another showdown at Cheltenham on Sunday.*

show in
Someone **shows** you **in** when they lead you into a room or building: *Hubert Molland was in the waiting-room when Peter was shown in.* [opposite **show out**]

show off
1 When someone is trying to make

others notice how clever or skilful they are, you can say disapprovingly that they **are showing off**: *They speak in English to each other to show off.* **2** You **show off** something you are proud of when you display it to others, expecting them to admire it: *You can acquire a cloth badge to show off your membership.* ❑ *They vie with each other in generosity, showing off their wealth.* **3** To **show** something **off** is to make it seem as impressive or admirable as possible: *She strode forward with that swing in her hips that showed off her tall, slim figure.* [compare **set off**]

• *noun* **show-off**: **show-offs**
You can call someone a **show-off** if you disapprove of the way they are trying to make others notice and admire something they are proud of: *What a little show-off she is!*

show out
Someone **shows** you **out** in when they lead you into a room or building: *Show Mr McGregor out, would you.* ❑ *She allowed herself to be shown out.* [opposite **show in**]

show through
Something **shows through** when others can see or notice it, although it may be hidden or concealed by something: *It's a rich voice with a touch of his native Somerset showing through.*

show up
1 (*informal*) Someone or something **shows up** when they arrive or appear: *Sooner or later the brothers would show up in London.* ❑ *He was supposed to come yesterday but he didn't show up.* [*same as* **turn up**] **2** Something **shows up** when it can be clearly seen or distinguished: *This was the only medium that showed up against the pattern of the timber.* ❑ *It changes colour so that it doesn't show up against whatever vegetation it happens to be on.* **3** You can use **show up** to talk about what is revealed by a test or investigation: *The analysis shows up imperfections in the processing.* **4** Someone **shows** you **up** when their behaviour makes you feel ashamed or embarrassed that you know them or are associated with them: *Promise you'll behave. I don't want to be shown up in front of my colleagues.*

show up as
You can use **show up as** to talk about what the true identity or nature of something or someone is revealed to be: *When his so-called treatments were scrutinized by proper scientists he was shown up to be a complete fraud.*

shower /ʃaʊə(r)/: showers, showering, showered

shower on *or* shower upon
Things **are showered on** or **upon** someone or something when they are given them in great quantities: *During their trip, they were showered with gifts by local tribesmen.*

shrink /ʃrɪŋk/: shrinks, shrinking, shrank, shrunk

shrink away
1 You **shrink away** when you move away in fear: *The terrified mongrel shrank away from his touch.* **2** Something **shrinks away** when its size or importance gets less and less and finally disappears: *It's funny how ideas shrink away when people are put on the spot.*

shrink back
You **shrink back** when you move back in fear: *He shrank back fearfully as the horns scythed back and forth.* [*same as* **draw back, pull back**]

shrink from
You can say that you **shrink from** something when you feel, or show that you are, unwilling to do it or accept it: *He claimed she was not a fit partner and shrank from his attentions with loathing.* [*same as* **shy away**]

shrivel /ˈʃrɪvəl/: **shrivels, shrivelling** (*AmE* **shriveling**), **shrivelled** (*AmE* **shriveled**)

shrivel up

Something **shrivels up** when it shrinks, or its surface becomes lined or curled, because it has lost the moisture it contained and is no longer fresh: *Ferns tend to shrivel up in a centrally-heated room.* ❑ *All we were offered was a glass of water and a plate of some sort of shrivelled-up meat, that may or may not have been ham.*

shroud /ʃrɑud/: **shrouds, shrouding, shrouded**

shroud in

Things that **are shrouded in** something such as fog are completely hidden or concealed by it: *He reopens the Kennedy assassination debate, which many Americans were all too ready to shroud in convenient official explanations.* ❑ *At the Department of Transport, all is shrouded in secrecy.*

shrug /ʃrʌg/: **shrugs, shrugging, shrugged**

shrug off

You **shrug off** something that is likely to upset you when you say or show that you don't think it is serious or important, or that you're not bothered by it: *For years, that was shrugged off as Unionist propaganda.* ❑ *A detective inspector shrugs this criticism off.* [compare **play down**]

shuffle /ˈʃʌfəl/: **shuffles, shuffling, shuffled**

shuffle off

You **shuffle off** a burden or an unwelcome duty when you get rid of it or ignore it, often by indirect means: *Special Hospitals can shuffle off their responsibilities by claiming that they have no suitable facilities.* ❑ *... what dreams may come, when we have shuffled off this mortal coil, must give us pause.*

shut /ʃʌt/: **shuts, shutting, shut**

shut away

1 You **shut** a person or an animal **away** when you put them in a place that they can't escape from, or in a private or secret place where others can't see them: *You can't just shut her away in some mental hospital and forget all about her.* **2** You **shut** yourself **away** when you go to a private or secret place to be alone: *When she wasn't at the poly, she was shut away in her attic, working on it.*
[*same as* **lock away, shut in**]

shut down

1 A business or factory **shuts down**, or **is shut down**, when it closes completely, either permanently or for a limited period: *Any of our pubs can, at a moment's notice, be shut down or altered by uncaring owners.* ❑ *Many of the East European firms have shut down.* **2** Machines, usually large industrial machines, **shut down**, or **are shut down**, when they stop working completely for a limited time: *The turbines were shut down until the water supply could be restored.* [*same as* **switch off, shut off**]

shut in

1 You **shut** a person or an animal **in** when you put them in a place that they can't escape from: *The policy consisted mainly of shutting them in and letting them be.* ❑ *The dogs were shut in all day.* [*same as* **lock in, imprison**] **2** You **shut** yourself **in** a room when you refuse to come out and meet other people: *He'd shut himself in in a fit of pique.* [*same as* **shut away, lock away**]

shut off

1 To **shut off** an engine or other large machine is to stop it working by stopping its power supply: *In this case, the engines shut off automatically.* [*same as* **switch off, turn off**] **2** To **shut** something **off** is to prevent it from being seen: *The garden was shut off from the street by a tall screen of* *conifers.* [*same as* **block out**] **3** You **shut** yourself **off** when you stay away from others and have no contact with them, or when you refuse to speak to them or listen to them: *She never acquired that emotional immunity, that almost instinctive shutting off.* [*same as* **cut off**; compare **shut away, shut in**]

shut out

1 Something **shuts out** light or sound when it prevents it from being seen or heard: *Heavy brocade curtains were drawn, shutting out all the natural light.* [*same as* **block out**] **2** You **shut out** unpleasant thoughts when you stop yourself thinking them: *She won't admit that it ever happened. She's shut it out completely.* [*same as* **block out, blot out**] **3** You **shut** someone **out** when you prevent them from entering a place, *eg* by locking doors: *The strikers were shut out of the factory.* **4** You **shut** someone **out** when you deliberately exclude them, or prevent them from communicating with or reaching you: *Hopes are high that the Polish attack can be shut out and the points secured that will see the English team safely through.*

shut up

1 (*informal*) Someone who tells you to **shut up** is telling you rudely to stop talking; someone **shuts** you **up** when they do or say something that stops you talking; you **shut up** when you stop talking: *Shut up and listen!* ❑ *The joke got a laugh but didn't shut the lady up.* ❑ *A glance from Skinner shut him up.* ❑ *You find yourself wishing they would shut up.* **2** You **are shut up** somewhere when you are kept there and prevented from escaping: *The dogs had to be shut up in the little room off the kitchen.* [*same as* **shut in, imprison**; compare **coop up**]

shy /ʃaɪ/: shies, shying, shied

shy away

You **shy away** when you avoid something because you are nervous or afraid: *He confronts problems that other men would shy away from.* ❑ *Horses are sensible to shy away at the sound of a hiss.* [*same as* **back away**]

sick /sɪk/: sicks, sicking, sicked

sick up (*informal*)

You **sick up**, or **sick up** food, when you vomit: *Mum! Mark's sicked up all over the back seat!* [*same as* **throw up** (*informal*), **chuck up** (*informal*), **bring up**]

side /saɪd/: sides, siding, sided

side against

People **side against** you when they join with each other to oppose or fight you: *China had sided against the leadership which had prevailed.* [*opposite* **side with**]

side with

You **side with** someone when you support them in an argument or conflict: *Jess didn't know if she should side with the Law or her own interests.* [*opposite* **side against**]

sidle /ˈsaɪdəl/: sidles, sidling, sidled

sidle up

Someone **sidles up** to you when they approach you quietly and secretively, as if not wanting to be noticed by others: *A desperate-looking character sidled up to me and asked me if I wanted to buy a watch. I fled.*

sift /sɪft/: sifts, sifting, sifted

sift through

You **sift through** a number of things when you examine each one carefully, looking for something or trying to make a choice: *The judges have sifted through over 8,000 entries.* ❑ *They were sifting through the untidy muddle like rescue workers scrabbling in rubble for survivors.* [*same as* **look through,** search through]

sign /saɪn/: signs, signing, signed

sign away

You **sign** something **away** when you give away your ownership of it by signing a legal document stating that you have agreed to do so: *Mary, Queen of Scots, signed away her Scottish kingdom.* [compare **hand over**]

sign in *or* sign into

1 You **sign in** when you record your arrival in a place by signing your name in an official register; you also say that you **sign into** a place: *I had no choice but to slink away or sign in. I signed in.* ❑ *He'd signed himself into a detoxification unit without telling his family.* [*same as* **book in, check in**] **2** You **sign** someone **in** when, as member of a club, you enable them to enter it by signing your name next to theirs in an official register: *You can't use the facilities unless a member signs you in.*

sign off

1 You **sign off** when you end a letter by signing your name; a radio presenter **signs off** when they end a radio programme by saying their name. **2** A doctor **signs** you **off** work when they sign an official form stating that you are too ill to work, for a limited period: *The doctor's signed him off for a fortnight.*

sign on

1 An unemployed person **signs on** when they go to a government unemployment office to formally register the fact that they are not working and to claim their unemployment benefit: *I was over-qualified and signing on.* **2** Someone who **signs on**, or **is signed on**, signs an official agreement or contract to join something, such as a course of study, or a company as an employee: *After the war, he signed on as a trainee pilot.* [*same as* **sign up**]

sign out

You **sign out** when you record the fact that you are leaving a place by signing your name in an official register: *Remember to sign out when you leave the office at night.* [*same as* **book out, check out**]

sign over

You **sign** something **over** when you give someone else ownership of it by signing a legal document stating that you are doing so: *They found that he'd already signed his house over to his wife.*

sign up

1 You **sign up** for something, such as a course of study, when you officially join it by signing your name: *Kate signed up for an intensive course at the Berlitz school.* **2** Someone who **is signed up** is acquired as an employee or a team member: *The Springbok stand-off is not about to be signed up in South Wales.*

silt /sɪlt/: silts, silting, silted

silt up

A river or other stretch of water **silts up** when it becomes blocked with mud and sand, preventing water from flowing properly, or at all: *The North Sea inevitably began to silt up.*

simmer /'sɪmə(r)/: simmers, simmering, simmered

simmer down

Someone who has been angry **simmers down** when they become calm again; you can also say that a situation **simmers down** when the people involved become calm: *When I'd simmered down a bit, I phoned him back and apologised.* [*same as* **calm down, cool down**]

sing /sɪŋ/: sings, singing, sang /saŋ/, sung /sʌŋ/

sing up

You **sing up** when you sing more loudly: *You boys at the back'll have to sing up* *if you want to be heard.*

single /'sɪŋgəl/: **singles**, **singling**, **singled**

single out

You **single** someone or something **out** when you choose them from among others and give them special attention or special treatment: *Four main factors are singled out by Chris Green.* ❑ *Vichy's anti-Semitism had singled out Jews for contempt and discrimination.* [compare **set apart**]

sink /sɪŋk/: **sinks**, **sinking**, **sank** /saŋk/, **sunk** /sʌŋk/

sink back

1 You **sink back** when you lie or sit backwards into a more comfortable position: *The convulsion was over and she sank back quite exhausted.* **2** You can say that someone **sinks back** into a former state or condition when they return to it: *Cameron let his temper sink back to normal.* ❑ *Barnfield would sink back into anonymity once more.*

sink down

You **sink down** when you let your body fall or slide into a lower position: *She sank down to the ground.* ❑ *She sank down into a chair.*

sink in

You can say that something **sinks in** when you understand, appreciate or accept it: *I couldn't believe it. It took a while to sink in.*

sink into

1 You **sink into** a chair when you let your body fall into it, *eg* because you are tired: *Sighing, she sank into an armchair.* **2** You can use **sink into** to describe how something sharp goes into a soft surface: *A dog sank its teeth into his face.* **3** You **sink into** an unpleasant or undesirable state or condition when you allow yourself to enter it: *He was just about to sink into a state of total collapse.* ❑ *Kids are in danger of sinking into a subculture of drugs and crime.* [*same as* **lapse into**] **4** Someone who **sinks** money **into** something spends or invests a lot of money on or in it: *He'd sunk most of his inheritance into the ill-fated venture.*

siphon *or* **syphon** /'saɪfən/: **siphons**, **siphoning**, **siphoned**

siphon off

1 You **siphon off** a liquid when you draw it out of a container through a tube: *The sand can be raked and any mud syphoned off at the same time.* **2** You can say that a portion of anything **is siphoned off** when it is taken away or separated.

sit /sɪt/: **sits**, **sitting**, **sat** /sat/

sit about *or* sit around

Someone who **sits about** or **sits around** does nothing except sit and relax or be lazy: *They sit about in stolid idleness.* ❑ *I've more to do than sit about.* ❑ *My plan was to sit around and wait.* ❑ *He didn't sit around. He got out and did the work.*

sit back

1 Someone who **sits back** relaxes into a seated position with their back resting against the back of a chair or other support: *Sit back and relax.* ❑ *Just leave them on the floor and sit back in the chair.* **2** You can also say that someone **sits back** when they take no action, at a time when action is needed or expected: *Steve couldn't sit back while the animals suffered.* [*same as* **sit by**]

sit by

Someone who **sits by** sits on the sidelines and takes no action, at a time when action is needed or expected: *Should society sit by and allow them to get away with it?* ❑ *The females hunt in a pack. One male sits by, watching.* [*same as* **sit back**]

sit down

1 You **sit down**, or **sit** yourself **down**,

when you lower your body into a sitting position: *She makes me sit down while she laces my boots.* ❑ *He sat down at his desk.* **2** You **sit** someone **down** when you tell them or force them to sit down: *She sat Nicandra down on her own chair.* **3** When someone **sits down** to do something they sit so that they can begin to do it, especially with determination: *Representatives of the Cricket Union and the National Sports Congress sat down together in a Johannesburg hotel.* ❑ *Over 130 sat down to a five-course meal.*

sit for

Someone who **sits for** an artist or photographer serves as a model to be painted or photographed: *I have very unpleasant memories of sitting for him, having not to move.*

sit in

Someone who **sits in** on a meeting, an interview or a discussion is present at it: *Would you object if my lawyer sat in on our discussion?*

• *noun* **sit-in**: **sit-ins**

A **sit-in** is a protest by a number of people, in which they continue to sit inside a place, usually their place of work, until they achieve their aim.

sit on

1 Someone who **sits on** something such as a committee is a member of it: *members who'd been appointed to sit on the Commons Select Committee.* **2** You can say that someone **is sitting on** something when they are not dealing with it or allowing it to be used: *It would appear that he'd been sitting on the loan application for three weeks.*

sit out

1 You **sit out** when you sit outdoors, rather than indoors: *They would sit out in their deckchairs in brilliant sunshine.* **2** You **sit** something **out** when you stay until the end of it: *They were desperate to get away but had to sit it out until the speeches were over.* **3** You also **sit** something **out** when you don't take part in it: *Tony sat it out in my tent.* ❑ *If you don't mind, I think I'll sit the next couple of dances out.*

sit through

You **sit through** something such as a performance when you stay until the end of it, even though you find it boring or otherwise unpleasant: *those who sat through last night's results on TV.*

sit up

1 You **sit up** when you move your body into an upright sitting position, after lying down or leaning back: *Sit up a little and touch your right elbow.* ❑ *Sit up straight and pay attention.* **2** You **sit up** when you stay out of bed until after your usual bedtime: *A few staff sit up late at night to prepare lectures.* **3** Something makes someone **sit up** when it suddenly captures all their attention or interest: *This will really get the banks to sit up and take notice.*

• *noun* **sit-up**: **sit-ups**

Sit-ups are exercises in which you raise your body from a lying position to a sitting position without using your hands to support your weight: *Do ten press-ups and twenty sit-ups each day.*

size /saɪz/: sizes, sizing, sized

size up

You **size** someone or something **up** when you form an opinion or a judgement about them: *Three pairs of eyes were about to turn and size him up.* [*same as* **weigh up**]

skate /skeɪt/: skates, skating, skated

skate around *or* skate round *or* skate over

You **skate around** something, or you **skate round** or **skate over** it, when you avoid talking about it or dealing with it directly: *We've been skating around the subject for too long. Now is the time to face facts.* [*same as* **skirt round**]

sketch /sketʃ/: **sketches, sketching, sketched**

sketch in

1 Someone who is drawing **sketches** something **in** when they add it to the drawing, roughly and perhaps temporarily: *She'd already done the background wash and sketched in some of the details.* **2** You also **sketch** something **in** when you give a few brief details about it to give a general impression of what it is like: *It will be necessary first to sketch in a general historical picture.* ❑ *During our journey, I'd sketched in the background to his coming to England.* [*same as* **outline**]

sketch out

You **sketch** something **out** when you give a brief general description of it: *The party president sketched out the contours of a new socialist movement.* [*same as* **outline**]

skim /skɪm/: **skims, skimming, skimmed**

skim off

1 To **skim off** a substance floating on the surface of a liquid is to remove it with shallow scooping movements of a spoon or similar implement: *Boil the ham in plenty of water, skimming off any scum that rises to the surface.* **2** Someone who **skims off** parts or elements of something takes the best parts or elements and leaves the rest: *They'd been skimming the profits off and reinvesting them elsewhere.* [*same as* **cream off**]

skim through

You **skim through** something written or printed when you look briefly at several of the pages, to get a general impression of what it is about but without reading the details: *Skimming through his notes, she'd missed the reference to Auden.* [*same as* **flick through**]

skimp /skɪmp/: **skimps, skimping, skimped**

skimp on

You **skimp on** something when you don't use enough of it, or when you don't spend enough time, money or effort on it, and so produce something that is unsatisfactory: *Buy only the best ingredients; skimping on them will produce an inferior result.*

skirt /skɜːt/: **skirts, skirting, skirted**

skirt around *or* skirt round

1 You **skirt around** something, or **skirt round** it, when you go around the edge of it, rather than going through or across it: *There's a tunnel up ahead but you must skirt round it.* **2** You also **skirt around** something, or **skirt round** it, when you avoid talking about it or dealing with it directly: *We skirted round the vexed question of what was to be done with the children.* [*same as* **skate around**]

skive /skaɪv/: **skives, skiving, skived**

skive off (*informal*)

Someone who **skives off** avoids work or avoids something else they should be doing: *I spent more and more of my time skiving off to extra-mural classes.*

slacken /'slakən/: **slackens, slackening, slackened**

slacken off

Something **slackens off** when it becomes less busy, active or intense: *We waited until the rain and wind had slackened off before setting out.* ❑ *Recently, the volume of work seems to be slackening off.*

slag /slag/: **slags, slagging, slagged**

slag off (*informal*)

Someone **slags** you **off** when they criticize you, especially in a very unkind way: *Most of his resignation speech was taken up with slagging off his former colleagues.*

slam /slam/: **slams**, **slamming**, **slammed**

slam down
You **slam** something **down** when you put or throw it down onto a surface with great force, usually in anger: *He slammed his fist down angrily.* ❑ *He delighted in slamming the rod down on the top of the tousled head below.* [*same as* **slap down**]

slam on
The driver of a moving vehicle **slams on** the brakes when he or she puts the brakes on suddenly, usually in order to avoid a collision: *He had to slam on the brakes when a dog ran out in front of him.* [*same as* **jam on**]

slam to
You **slam** a door **to** when you close it with great force, often in anger; you can also say that a door **slams to** when it closes with great force: *She nearly jumped out of her skin when the door of the barn slammed to behind her.*

slap /slap/: **slaps**, **slapping**, **slapped**

slap around
Someone who **slaps** you **around** hits you repeatedly with their hands or fists: *I was charged, and when I wouldn't grass on my mates, was slapped around.* [*same as* **rough up**]

slap down
1 You **slap** something **down** when you put or throw it down with great force: *He slapped down the book and shouted: 'I don't believe it!'* [*same as* **slam down**] 2 (*informal*) Someone who **is slapped down** is prevented from continuing to speak or act by being spoken to very severely or unkindly, or has their ideas or suggestions dismissed as ridiculous: *Kids who are slapped down repeatedly tend to lose self-confidence.* [compare **put down**]

slap on *or* **slap onto** (*informal*)
1 You **slap on** something such as paint when you put it on a surface roughly, carelessly or in large amounts: *We left him slapping whitewash on, getting more on himself than on the walls.* **2** You can say that things such as extra charges or price increases **are slapped on** when they are added in a way that seems to you to be unfair or excessive: *They'll slap on massive bank charges if you go over your overdraft limit.*

slave /sleɪv/: **slaves**, **slaving**, **slaved**

slave away
Someone who **slaves away** works very hard at something: *Mum was slaving away in the kitchen, as usual.*

sleep /sliːp/: **sleeps**, **sleeping**, **slept** /slɛpt/

sleep around
Someone who **sleeps around** has brief and casual sexual relationships with different people: *He was sleeping around a lot.* ❑ *Despite all the health warnings, drink and drugs and sleeping around were still the favoured recreations of some young people.* [*same as* **screw around** (*informal*)]

sleep in
You **sleep in** when you continue to sleep past your usual or intended time for waking up: *Her excuse for sleeping in was that her alarm clock hadn't gone off.*

sleep off
You **sleep** something **off** when you sleep in order to overcome its unpleasant effects: *He would read the Sunday papers then sleep off the drink.* ❑ *Ronnie spent many mornings sleeping it off.*

sleep on
You can say that you will **sleep on** something when you want to delay making a decision about it until the following day: *I'll sleep on it tonight, and tomorrow we'll do our best to come up with a solution.*

sleep through
You **sleep through** noise or other disturbance when you are not woken up by it: *Both of them slept through 'Today' on the radio.*

sleep together
1 Two people, usually people who are not married to each other, **sleep together** when they have sex with each other: *She and Jonathan stopped sleeping together.* ❑ *Don't you think that sleeping together automatically provides us with a kind of contract?* **2** You can also say that two people **sleep together** when they share the same bed: *All four children slept together in one big bed.*
[compare **sleep with**]

sleep with
1 To **sleep with** someone means to have sex with them: *Angelo offers her a bargain: if she will sleep with him, her brother shall live.* **2** To **sleep with** someone also means to sleep in the same bed as them: *Little Katy always sleeps with four teddies and a fluffy rabbit.*
[compare **sleep together**]

slew /sluː/: slews, slewing, slewed

slew round
Something, especially a heavy vehicle or piece of machinery, **slews round** when it turns, suddenly or out of control, to face in the opposite direction: *The articulated lorry had slewed round blocking both lanes.* ❑ *Then he slews round hard in his chair.*

slice /slaɪs/: slices, slicing, sliced

slice into
You **slice into** something when you insert a knife or other sharp instrument into it: *The knife slipped and sliced into his thigh.*

slice off
You **slice** something **off** when you remove it by cutting: *The executioner sliced off her head with a sweeping blow of the sword.*

slice up
You **slice** something **up** when you divide it into smaller parts or slices by cutting: *Slicing up the Christmas cake, she offered a piece to each of the carol singers.*

slick /slɪk/: slicks, slicking, slicked

slick down
Someone **slicks down** their hair when they make it flat and smooth by rubbing oil or other hair application on it: *With his Armani suit and slicked-down hair he was a different person.*

slip /slɪp/: slips, slipping, slipped

slip away
1 You **slip away** when you leave quietly or secretly, without others noticing: *We edged back and managed to slip away without attracting notice.* [*same as* **slip off**] **2** Something that **slips away** disappears quickly and easily: *She opened the window and felt her exhaustion slip away from her.* **3** Things such as chances and opportunities **slip away** when you lose them: *The keeper let two points slip away.* ❑ *She felt their life together slipping away.*

slip by
1 Time or an event **slips by** when it passes: *The hours slipped by so quickly that she had no time to brood.* **2** You **slip by** when you move past someone or something without being noticed: *I feel as if I can slip by, no-one will notice or comment.*

slip down
1 Something **slips down** when it slides into a lower position: *Ward slipped down into the driving seat.* **2** (*informal*) You can say that a drink **slips down** when you enjoy drinking it: *This cognac is slipping down a treat.*

slip in
1 You **slip** something **in** when you put or place it somewhere quietly, easily or secretly: *I could just slip it in and out of my jeans pocket.* **2** You **slip in** when you enter quietly, easily or secretly: *The raiders slipped in past the patrols.*

slip into
1 You **slip** something **into** a place when you put or place it there quietly, easily or secretly: *This illegal cash is made legal by slipping it into the banking system.* **2** You **slip into** a place when you enter it quietly, easily or secretly: *I cross the road, slip into an alley, and wait.* **3** You **slip into** a piece of clothing when you put it on quickly and easily: *Mary Rose slipped into a mink coat.* [*same as* **slip on**] **4** You **slip into** a habit or a way of behaving when you gradually adopt it, without noticing or perhaps without wanting to: *I have now slipped into the comfortable habit of accepting proffered cigarettes.*

slip off
1 You **slip off** when you leave a place quietly or secretly: *Tens of thousands are slipping off to sanctuaries abroad.* [*same as* **slip away**] **2** Something **slips off** when it falls by sliding: *He wakes up to find he's slipped off the bed.* **3** You **slip off** a garment when you take it off quickly and easily: *She sits down beside me and slips her shoes off.* ❑ *Molly sinks into a chair and slips off one shoe.* [*opposite* **slip on**]

slip on
You **slip** a garment **on** when you put it on quickly and easily: *Slip this protective apron on over your head.* [*opposite* **slip off**]

• *noun (plural)* **slip-ons**

Slip-ons are shoes without laces or fastenings. [compare **lace-ups**]

slip out
1 You **slip out** of a place when you leave it quietly or secretly: *The small motor fishing vessel slipped out of Ness Harbour.* ❑ *I slipped out while the priest was talking.* [*same as* **slip away**] **2** You can say that something **slips out** when you tell it to someone without intending to: *She might have let the plan slip out prematurely to Allan Stewart.* ❑ *I'm sorry, I didn't mean to say that; it just slipped out.* [compare **come out with**]

slip through
1 Something that **slips through** passes through a barrier or procedure that should not have allowed it through: *Matrons were vetted strictly but a few negligent ones slipped through.* **2** You can say that something such as a chance or opportunity **slips through** your grasp or your fingers when you lose it or fail to take advantage of it: *Norman had let the US title slip through his fingers.*

slip up
You **slip up** when you make a mistake: *It seemed that they were all waiting for her to slip up.* [compare **mess up, foul up**]

• *noun* **slip-up**: **slip-ups**

A **slip-up** is a mistake: *We can't afford any slip-ups this time round.*

slob /slɒb/: slobs, slobbing, slobbed

slob about *or* slob around
(*informal*)

You **slob about** or **slob around** when you spend time lazily doing nothing, wearing old clothes and not caring about your appearance: *The great thing about working from home is that, if you want to, you can slob about in an old tracksuit.* [compare **laze about, lounge about**]

slog /slɒg/: slogs, slogging, slogged

slog away
Someone who **slogs away** continues to work hard: *You're not still slogging away at those accounts, are you?* [*same as* **slave away, beaver away**]

slop /slɒp/: **slops**, **slopping**, **slopped**

slop out
In some prisons, prisoners **slop out** when, in the morning, they empty the buckets in their cells which they have used as a lavatory while they have been locked up: *'No in-cell sanitation' is just a euphemism for having to slop out.*

slop over
A liquid **slops over** when it spills over the edge of its container: *The water level had risen so high it was beginning to slop over the edge of the dam.*

slope /sloup/: **slopes**, **sloping**, **sloped**

slope off (*informal*)
You **slope off** when you leave or go away quietly or secretly, especially in order to avoid an unpleasant task or duty: *I just worked that day out and sloped off home.* [compare **slip away, clear off**]

slot /slɒt/: **slots**, **slotting**, **slotted**

slot in
1 You **slot** something **in** when you place or fit it somewhere, especially quickly and easily: *You can open up your PC and slot the card in.* **2** Something **is slotted in** when it is included as part of a schedule or programme of events: *I think we can slot the slide show in at 2 pm.* ❑ *Jackson was easily slotted in with the other unlikely pop stars.*

slot into
1 You **slot** something **into** a place when you place or fit it there, especially quickly and easily: *The drill bits are quickly slotted into place.* **2** Something **is slotted into** a schedule or programme of events when it is included in it: *The Prime Minister's surprise announcement was slotted into the evening schedule at the last moment.*

slouch /slautʃ/: **slouches**, **slouching**, **slouched**

slouch about *or* slouch around
Someone who **slouches about** or **slouches around** doesn't hold their body straight and erect but moves about slowly or leans against something in a relaxed and slovenly way, often because they are lazy or bored: *There was a group of leather-clad youths slouching about in the doorway.* [compare **lounge about, laze about**]

slough /slʌf/: **sloughs**, **sloughing**, **sloughed**

slough off (*literary*)
Someone who **sloughs** something **off** gets rid of it: *They did everything they could to slough off the reputation they had acquired for dubious business practice.*

slow /slou/: **slows**, **slowing**, **slowed**

slow down
1 Something that **slows down**, or **is slowed down**, begins to move or happen more slowly: *A black BMW slowed down and drew abreast of them.* ❑ *It is used when fermentation begins to slow down.* ❑ *It was decided to slow down the growth in the UK.* ❑ *Slow the pace down for two minutes before hiking it up again.* **2** Someone who **slows down** begins to work less hard or become less active or energetic: *I had gone too far and experienced too much, I needed to slow down.*
[*same as* **slow up**; *opposite* **speed up**]

slow up
1 Something that **slows up**, or **is slowed up**, begins to move or happen more slowly: *It slowed things up too much, having to keep putting it away and taking it out.* **2** Someone who **slows up** begins to work less hard or become less active or energetic: *After twenty years of continual hard work, it was inevitable that he should slow up a little once he was financially secure.*

[*same as* **slow down**; *opposite* **speed up**]

sluice /sluːs/: **sluices**, **sluicing**, **sluiced**

sluice down

To **sluice** something **down** is to clean it all over with a powerful flow of water, such as from a hose: *The whole area had to be sluiced down with strong disinfectant.* [compare **wash down**]

smack /smak/: **smacks**, **smacking**, **smacked**

smack of

You can say that something **smacks of** a particular quality, especially one that you disapprove of, when you think it has that quality to some degree: *All this activity smacked of sedition.* [*same as* **savour of, smell of**]

smarten /ˈsmɑːtən/: **smartens**, **smartening**, **smartened**

smarten up

1 To **smarten** someone or something **up** is to make them look cleaner and tidier: *Eddie had an iron to smarten up dog-eared labels.* ❑ *Smartened up, it gleams with whitewash.* [*same as* **spruce up**] **2** (*informal*) When someone tells you to **smarten up,** or **smarten** yourself **up,** they are telling you to improve your performance or do better than you have been doing: *You'd better smarten your ideas up if you don't want to end up being unemployed.*

smash /smaʃ/: **smashes**, **smashing**, **smashed**

smash down

To **smash down** something such as a door is to cause it to break and fall to the ground by hitting it very hard: *The tanks surged forward, smashing down the barricades and scattering the protestors.*

smash in

To **smash** something **in** is to break it by forcing pieces of it inwards: *The windscreen had been smashed in and the radio stolen.*

smash up

To **smash** something **up** is to destroy it by using violence to break it into pieces: *Simon told me that he'd smashed that kiosk up.* ❑ *You smash up your opponent's force before he knows what's hit him.*

• *noun (informal)* **smash-up**: **smash-ups**

A **smash-up** is a road accident, especially one in which much damage and many injuries are caused: *The policeman said it was the worst smash-up he'd ever seen in twenty years on the force.*

smell /smɛl/: **smells**, **smelling**, **smelled** *or* **smelt**

smell of

To **smell of** something is to have its smell, or a smell like it: *The whole place smelled of putty and turpentine.* ❑ *She also had a teething baby, pinched and veined and smelling of milk.*

smell out

1 An animal **smells** something **out** when it finds it using its sharp sense of smell: *Pigs were traditionally used to smell out the rare black truffles.* [*same as* **sniff out**] **2** (*informal*) You can also say that you **smell** something **out** when you find or discover it, especially when it is hidden or secret: *She has this uncanny ability to smell out a traitor to the cause.* [*same as* **sniff out, root out**]

smoke /smouk/: **smokes**, **smoking**, **smoked**

smoke out

1 To **smoke** an animal **out** is to force it to come out by filling its hiding-place with smoke: *They built a fire of damp brushwood to smoke the bear out of the cave.* **2** You can also say that you **smoke** someone **out** when you force them out of their hiding-place or when you force them to identify themselves: *Their task was to smoke out the enemy agents.*

smooth /smuːð/: **smooths, smoothing, smoothed**

smooth down
You **smooth down** clothing or hair when you make it neat by flattening and straightening it with your hands: *Nervously, she smoothed down her hair.* ❑ *They were suddenly self-conscious, smoothing down their tattered skirts.* [compare **slick down**]

smooth out
1 You **smooth out** a surface when you make it flat and smooth by pressing it down: *Gingerly, he unfolded the tattered old map and smoothed it out on the table.* **2** You can also say that you **smooth out** a situation when you make it easier, removing problems or difficulties: *Both he and his accountant tried to smooth out the problems with his bankers, without success.*

smooth over
You **smooth over** a situation when you make it easier by dealing skilfully with problems or difficulties: *Don't you think it would make more sense to smooth things over by allowing him some of the freedom he is demanding?* [compare **gloss over**]

snap /snap/: **snaps, snapping, snapped**

snap at
1 An animal **snaps at** you when it makes a sudden attacking movement towards you with its teeth, intending to bite: *The Alsatian snapped at her and took the top of her finger off.* **2** Someone who **snaps at** you suddenly and unexpectedly speaks very angrily to you: *'Get in here,' he snapped at me.* ❑ *I don't know what's the matter with her. She's been snapping at everyone all morning.*

snap up
You **snap** something **up** when you buy or take it immediately, before others buy or take it and it becomes unavailable: *So many locations that would before have been snapped up by the professionals are now available to the amateur.* ❑ *The best roles have already been snapped up.* [*same as* **seize on, pounce on**]

snarl /snɑːl/: **snarls, snarling, snarled**

snarl up
Something, especially traffic or a road, **is snarled up** when free movement or progress is impossible because of a blockage or because too many things are trying to move in different directions at the same time: *The book soon snarls up in a mess of motives and half-finished characters.* ❑ *He rushed headlong into the fence snarling his clothes up in the barbed wire.* [compare **pile up**]
• *noun* **snarl-up**: **snarl-ups**: *Nothing could break through a six-lane snarl-up.*

snatch /snatʃ/: **snatches, snatching, snatched**

snatch up
You **snatch** something **up** when you pick it up suddenly or with violence: *Smoke billowed up. Jane snatched the cat up.* ❑ *She bent down and snatched up a roll of paper.*

sneeze /sniːz/: **sneezes, sneezing, sneezed**

sneeze at
You can say that something **is** not **to be sneezed at** when you think it is valuable or important, even though it might not seem so: *I was surviving, and that was nothing to be sneezed at.* [*same as* **sniff at**]

sniff /snɪf/: **sniffs, sniffing, sniffed**

sniff at

1 You **sniff at** something when you smell it, especially briefly or by taking short inward breaths through your nose: *Olive took the glass of wine, sniffed at it and downed half in one go.* **2** You can say that something **is** not **to be sniffed at** if you think that it is valuable or important, even though it may not seem so: *A government grant of 25% towards our set-up costs isn't to be sniffed at.* [*same as* **sneeze at**]

sniff out

1 An animal **sniffs** something **out** when it finds it using its sharp sense of smell: *The terriers could sniff out and dispatch a rat quicker than any other dog.* [*same as* **smell out**] **2** (*informal*) You **sniff** something hidden or concealed **out** when you find or discover it: *See if you can sniff out what it is they're up to.* [*same as* **smell out, root out**]

snip /snɪp/: snips, snipping, snipped

snip off

You **snip** something **off** when you remove or detach with a single quick cut of the scissors: *She snipped off one of the best blooms by mistake.*

snoop /snuːp/: snoops, snooping, snooped

snoop about *or* snoop around

Someone who **snoops about** or **snoops around** searches for things, secretly or dishonestly: *A couple of journalists were snooping around in the backyard.* ❑ *There was most definitely someone snooping around outside.*

snow /snoʊ/: snows, snowing, snowed

snow in

You **are snowed in** somewhere when heavy snow prevents you from leaving: *Almost the entire population of the Shetlands were snowed in for three days.* [*same as* **snow up**]

snow under

Someone who **is snowed under** has enormous amounts of work to do: *We're pretty snowed under at work.*

snow up

You **are snowed up** somewhere when heavy snow prevents you from leaving: *They were snowed up for a fortnight in a remote cabin in the Rockies.* [*same as* **snow in**]

snuff /snʌf/: snuffs, snuffing, snuffed

snuff out

1 You **snuff out** a candle or other flame when you stop it burning by covering it or pinching it with your fingers: *She'd snuffed out the candles and was sitting in the dark.* [*same as* **put out, extinguish**; compare **blow out**] **2** To **snuff** something **out** is to destroy it or put an end to it: *High interest rates would have snuffed out any natural upturn.* ❑ *Any independent thought had been snuffed out early on.*

snuggle /ˈsnʌgəl/: snuggles, snuggling, snuggled

snuggle down

You **snuggle down** when you lower your body into a warm, comfortable position, *eg* under bedclothes: *Snuggling down further into the bed and pulling the blankets over her head, she felt cosy and secure.*

snuggle up

You **snuggle up** to someone when you make yourself warm and comfortable by leaning or lying against their body: *The puppies snuggled up to their mother's body for warmth.* [*same as* **cuddle up**]

soak /soʊk/: soaks, soaking, soaked

soak in

1 Something **is soaked in** a liquid when the liquid covers it or is absorbed into it: *He took bread soaked in ale every* *couple of weeks.* **2** You **soak** something **in** when you give your whole mind or body to experiencing it as fully as possible: *She played the record non-stop and soaked it in until it was her heartbeat.* [*same as* **soak up**] **3** You can also use **soak in** to emphasize how much of a quality something has: *The place was literally soaked in history.* [*same as* **steep in**]

soak through

Something that **is soaked through** is thoroughly wet: *My shirt is soaked through.* ❑ *They were soaked right through to the skin.*

soak up

1 Something such as a sponge **soaks up** liquid when it takes the liquid into itself: *It soaks up water and acts as a reservoir for the plants roots.* [*same as* **absorb**] **2** Someone who **soaks up** sunshine enjoys having the sun shine on their body: *thousands of holiday-makers soaking up the sun on the Costa del Sol.* **3** You can say that you **soak** something **up** when give your whole body or mind to experiencing it as fully as possible: *You sit in one of the small roadside restaurants and simply soak up the atmosphere.* ❑ *He spends his time painting and soaking up the culture of the land.* [*same as* **soak in, drink in**] **4** Something that **soaks up** resources such as money or time uses up a lot very quickly: *It'll soak up any contingency fund you may have in no time.* [*same as* **eat up**; compare **eat into**]

sober /'soubə(r)/: sobers, sobering, sobered

sober up

Someone who has been drunk **sobers up** when they become sober again: *We soon sobered up when we saw her hurt expression.* [compare **dry out**]

sod /sɒd/: sods, sodding, sodded

sod off (*vulgar slang*)

Someone who tells you to **sod off** is telling you very rudely to go away: *'I said Sod off!' the youth repeated.* [*same as* **clear off** (*informal*), **bugger off** (*vulgar slang*), **piss off** (*vulgar slang*)]

soften /'sɒfən/: softens, softening, softened

soften up

To **soften** someone **up** is to make them more willing to agree with you or do what you ask, *eg* by paying them a compliment: *They tried softening him up by cooking his favourite meal.* [compare **butter up**]

soldier /'souldʒə(r)/: soldiers, soldiering, soldiered

soldier on

You **soldier on** when you continue doing something, when it is very difficult or unpleasant or when you very badly want to stop: *I admire the way he's soldiered on with the course.* ❑ *Should we abandon the car or soldier on?* [*same as* **press on**]

sort /sɔːt/: sorts, sorting, sorted

sort out

1 People often use **sort out** to refer to action of any kind that solves a problem, corrects a fault, or makes the situation satisfactory again: *Sorting all that out has taken up half the visit.* ❑ *The history department is trying to sort out its timetable.* ❑ *We'll hopefully get the bleeper sorted out by then.* [*same as* **see to, clear up, straighten out**] **2** You also **sort** things **out** when you separate them into different types or groups, or when you identify one type and separate them from the rest: *It takes time to sort out the real issues from the party politics.* [*same as* **separate out**] **3** You **sort out** people who are acting in a confused or disorganized way when you show or tell them what to do: *There were some kids* *trying to push in behind the Germans and he had to go and sort them out.* [*same as* **organize**] **4** (*informal*) You **sort** someone **out** when you punish them or do something to prevent them doing wrong again: *Someone'll have to sort him out, before he gets involved in worse crimes.* [*same as* **deal with**]

sound /saʊnd/: **sounds**, **sounding**, **sounded**

sound off (*informal*)
Someone who **sounds off** speaks in a loud, self-important, or boastful way that annoys or bores others: *Oliver's always sounding off about the injustice of the tax system.* [compare **hold forth**]

sound out
You **sound** someone **out** when you ask them what their opinions are: *He wanted to sound Eleanor out on the subject of Liz.* ❏ *He instructed the Chief Whip to sound out MPs.*

soup /suːp/: **soups**, **souping**, **souped**

soup up
To **soup up** a vehicle, or its engine, is to adjust it to make it more powerful: *Once he's souped it up, he'll be able to use it as a rally car.*
• *adjective* **souped-up**: *He drives a souped-up Chevrolet.*

space /speɪs/: **spaces**, **spacing**, **spaced**

space out
You **space** things **out** when you arrange them in a way that leaves spaces or intervals between each one: *The grouse were driven towards the butts spaced out across the hillside.* ❏ *Spacing the paragraphs out gives the letter a better appearance.*
• *adjective* **spaced out** *or* **spaced-out** (*informal*)
You can describe someone who cannot think clearly because they are under the influence of drugs, or perhaps alcohol, as **spaced out**: *They appeared to be spaced out on some form of hallucinogenic drug.* ❏ *In the Sixties he was one of those spaced-out hippies.* [compare **dope up**]

spark /spɑːk/: **sparks**, **sparking**, **sparked**

spark off
Something **sparks off** an event or a condition when it causes it to happen or exist: *Thorez's accusations sparked off what has become known as the Nizan case.* ❏ *The riots had been sparked off by police mishandling of a case.* [*same as* **set off**, **trigger off**]

speak /spiːk/: **speaks**, **speaking**, **spoke** /spoʊk/, **spoken** /'spoʊkən/

speak about
1 You **speak about** something when you discuss it: *We've just been speaking about the unemployment problem in the village.* **2** People often use **speak about** to refer to what a situation involves or concerns: *We are not speaking about small static parcels of land.*
[*same as* **talk about**]

speak for
1 You **speak for** a person or group when you state their opinions to others and make decisions that affect them: *They pay people like Bobby to speak for them.* ❏ *Her behaviour could prove dangerous to the causes she speaks for.* [*same as* **represent**] **2** You **speak for** yourself when you state your own opinions; people often say they **are speaking for** themselves when they want to suggest that others may not have the same opinion as them: *She does often manage to speak for herself.* ❏ *'I've never seen the point of dieting.' 'Speak for yourself, most women of our age are obsessed by their weight.'* **3** When you say that something **speaks for** itself, you mean that no further proof, information or explanation is needed: *The figures speak for them-*

selves. **4** Something that **is spoken for** already belongs to someone, and is not available to others; you can say that someone **is spoken for** when they are married or they have a partner: *Is this seat spoken for?* ❑ *You can't ask Sheila out; she's already spoken for.*

speak on

You **speak on** something when you talk about it, especially when you give a formal talk or speech on that subject: *Next will be Professor Greenberg who'll be speaking on the latest developments in bioengineering.*

speak out

Someone who **speaks out** states their opinions openly or publicly: *Carrie dared not speak out, for fear they would question her.* ❑ *An anonymous female member of the Saudi royal family has spoken out about the reality of life for women in Saudi Arabia.* ❑ *He did speak out very strongly one evening against it.*

speak up

1 You **speak up** when you speak more loudly than before: *There were cries of 'Speak up! What did he say?'* **2** Someone who **speaks up** states their support for someone or something openly or publicly: *It is a watchdog organization that speaks up for citizens as well as consumers.*

speed /spiːd/: speeds, speeding, speeded

speed up

Something **speeds up** when it moves or progresses faster; you **speed** it **up** when you make it move or progress faster: *Access with database files doesn't speed up noticeably.* ❑ *The driver speeds up by pulling hard on the lines.* ❑ *This should speed proceedings up.* ❑ *The reforms have speeded up the pace of resource management.* [compare **hurry up**]

spell /spɛl/: spells, spelling, spelled *or* spelt

spell out

1 You **spell** a word **out** when you say in sequence each letter that forms that particular word: *That's an odd name. Would you spell it out for me?* **2** You **spell** something **out** when you explain it fully or in great detail: *The Special Report spells out the nature and function of the different sections.* ❑ *It is typical of him to spell things out so literally.* [*same as* **set out**]

spew /spjuː/: spews, spewing, spewed

spew out

Something that **spews out** flows out with great speed or force: *Great screeds of flimsy paper spewed out of the machine.* [*same as* **pour out**]

spew up (*informal*)

You **spew up** when you force the contents of your stomach out through your mouth: *Then he went into the gents and spewed up.* [*same as* **throw up** (*informal*), **sick up** (*informal*), **be sick, vomit**]

spice /spaɪs/: spices, spicing, spiced

spice up

You **spice** something **up** when you make it more interesting or exciting: *He spices up his music with exotic touches drawn from swing and jazz.* [*same as* **jazz up** (*informal*), **liven up**]

spill /spɪl/: spills, spilling, spilled *or* spilt

spill out

1 Things **spill out** of their container when they flow or fall out over the edge; you **spill** them **out** when you remove them by spilling or tipping: *Many of the sacks had burst in transit with corn spilling out onto the floor.* ❑ *They take their washing along and spill it out onto a hopefully clean floor.* **2** Something that **spills out** comes out of a place, or is produced or created, in large amounts or with great force:

Music spilled out from the main hall below. ❑ *The lime-coloured light spills out onto white sheets.* [*same as* **pour out**]

spill over
1 Things, usually liquids, **spill over** when they flow out over the sides of their container because the container isn't large enough to hold them: *It was just at the point where the river spills over the weir.* **2** You can say that one thing **spills over** into another when it becomes the other or develops into it: *Pent-up hurt and frustration had spilled over into violence.* ❑ *Debates about the problems of the British constitution spill over into a case for reconstructing the constitution itself.*

spin /spɪn/: **spins**, **spinning**, **spun** /spʌn/

---

spin off
• *noun* **spin-off**: **spin-offs**
A **spin-off** is a useful additional thing that is unexpectedly created as a result of a process or activity: *I find the teaching and research spin-offs the most exciting part.* ❑ *Much of this business is a spin-off from its base of mainframes.*

spin out
You **spin** something **out** when you make it last as long as possible: *Frankie tried to spin out the discussion as long a possible to allow time for them to arrive.* [*same as* **draw out, drag out, prolong**]

spin round
Something **spins round** when it turns quickly, either repeatedly in a circular motion, or once to face the opposite direction; someone who **spins round** turns quickly to face in the opposite direction: *The birds can hang in the air or spin round at breakneck speed.* ❑ *A voice broke the stillness and made them spin round.*

spirit /'spɪrɪt/: **spirits**, **spiriting**, **spirited**

---

spirit away *or* **spirit off**
You **spirit** someone or something **away**, or **spirit** them **off**, when you take them away quickly, secretly or mysteriously: *The aircraft was unloaded and the crew spirited away by car.* ❑ *Captain Hook spirits Banning's children away.* [compare **whisk away**]

spit: **spits**, **spitting**, **spat** /spat/

---

spit at
Someone **spits at** you when they aim saliva forced out of their mouth at you: *The crowd jeered and spat at him as he was dragged to the scaffold.*

spit out
1 You **spit out** something in your mouth when you force it out of your mouth: *She had the sense to spit it out when she found it wasn't a mint.* **2** You can say that someone **spits** words **out** when they say them angrily: *Bono stiffens in his chair and spits out the list.* **3** You can tell someone to **spit** it **out** as a way of encouraging them to say something they are unwilling to say: *'I'll never know what's the matter with you unless you tell me. Come on, spit it out!'*

splash /splaʃ/: **splashes**, **splashing**, **splashed**

---

splash about
You **splash about** in water when you wave your arms or kick your legs in the water to make it splash: *We were soon splashing about in the surf.*

splash down
A space vehicle **splashes down** when it lands in the sea on its return to Earth: *The astronauts will be splashing down in the Atlantic, where they'll be picked up by an US aircraft carrier.* [compare **touch down**]

splash on
1 You **splash on** something such as paint when you put it on a surface quickly or carelessly: *He took a hand in the redecoration personally,*

splashing on new paint and putting up wallpaper. [*same as* **slap on**] **2** Liquids that **splash on** a surface fall in large drops: *The first heavy drops splashed in coin shapes on the pavement.* ❑ *The yellow liquid floated beside Byrkin's face then splashed on his tunic.*

splash out (*informal*)
You **splash out** when you spend a lot of money, perhaps in a carefree way: *It can be tempting to splash out on the first splendid specimen that catches your eye.* ❑ *Building societies were splashing out on brochures offering fancy loans.* [*same as* **lash out** (*informal*); compare **fork out, cough up**]

split /splɪt/: splits, splitting, split

split off
1 Something **splits off**, or you **split** it **off**, when it breaks off or becomes divided or separated: *My nails are so brittle they split off once they've grown to a certain length.* ❑ *The gales had split large branches off and even toppled some of the smaller trees.* **2** People who **split off** from a group stop being members of it, and perhaps form their own separate, smaller group: *one of the Nationalist groups who'd split off from the IRA for one reason or another.* [*same as* **break away**]

split on (*informal*)
You **split on** someone when you betray them by telling others, especially people in authority, about the bad or criminal things they have done: *A former gang member had split on them and told the cops where the money was stashed.* [*same as* **tell on, grass on** (*informal*), **rat on** (*informal*)]

split up
1 You **split** things **up** when you divide them into types or groups: *It's the way they are split up that promotes the development of greater strength.* ❑ *We'll be split up into smaller groups and led through.* [*same as* **divide up**] **2** People who are together **split up**, or **are split up**, when they separate and go to different places or travel in different directions: *They split up again when Gandalf rides off with Pippin and Merry sets off with Aragorn.* ❑ *We were split up. I was billeted with a family outside Göttingen. Bruno was sent to stay with a farmer near Weimar.* **3** People who are married or in a relationship **split up** when they end their relationship: *Andy and I had already split up before he met her.* ❑ *Mum and Dad are splitting up.* [*same as* **break up, separate**]

spoil /spɔɪl/: spoils, spoiling, spoiled

spoil for
Someone who **is spoiling for** trouble or a fight is eager for it: *Major was spoiling for a fight, and fight he did.*

sponge /ʃpʌndʒ/: sponges, sponging, sponged

sponge down
You **sponge** something **down** when you clean it by wiping it with a wet sponge: *It gets right through your clothes so that you have to stand in the bath and sponge yourself down.* [compare **wipe down**]

sponge off *or* sponge on
Someone who **sponges off** other people, or **sponges on** them, continues selfishly to take help and money from them without intending to pay it back or offer anything in return: *It's very unjust to accuse them of sponging off the state.*

spoon /spuːn/: spoons, spooning, spooned

spoon out
You **spoon** food **out** when you serve it with a spoon: *Spoon the mixture out until it half fills an eight inch cake tin.*

spoon up
You **spoon** food **up** when you eat it with a spoon: *She's just learned how to spoon up her baby food.*

sprawl /sprɔːl/: **sprawls**, **sprawling**, **sprawled**

sprawl out
Someone who **sprawls out**, or **is sprawled out**, sits or lies lazily or relaxedly with their arms and legs extended away from their body: *Tricia was sprawled out on the grass with her sunhat over her face.*

spread /sprɛd/: **spreads**, **spreading**, **spread**

spread out
1 You **spread out** something that is folded or bundled when you open it fully and lay it flat: *I stripped off and spread my garments out to dry.* ❑ *A map of the course was spread out over the console before him.* [*same as* **open out**] **2** Things that **are spread out** have gaps or spaces between them: *The permanent jumps are spread out and not in a ring.* [*same as* **space out**] **3** You **spread** your fingers or toes **out** when you extend them fully so that there are spaces between each of them. **4** People who are grouped together **spread out** when they each go or move in a different direction: *We spread out, some diving down to the school of fish below.* **5** You can use **spread out** to emphasize how wide something is or how large an area it covers: *Beyond, the sea spread out like a ploughed field.* ❑ *The wide sweep of the Bay of Naples spread out far below them.* ❑ *He was standing alone with the world spread out at his feet.*

spread over
You **spread** something **over** a period of time when you do it or make it happen gradually or at intervals during that time, rather than all at once: *You can incur expenses of £200 plus, spread over three, four or five years.* ❑ *The cost was spread over a few months.*

spring /sprɪŋ/: **springs**, **springing**, **sprang** /spraŋ/, **sprung** /sprʌŋ/

spring back
Something **springs back** when it quickly returns to its original position or shape after being pushed or stretched: *No matter what she did her hair always sprang back into those wiry curls she hated so much.*

spring from
1 One thing **springs from** another when it develops from it or when it happens as a result of it: *Ideas are self-generating now, they spring from what I've done before.* **2** (*informal*) When you are surprised by the sudden appearance of someone or something, you can ask where they **have sprung from**: *Who was the boy? Where had he sprung from?*

spring on
You **spring** something **on** someone when you surprise them by presenting or introducing something suddenly and unexpectedly: *They're fond of springing those little surprises on you. It seems to give them some sort of perverted pleasure.*

spring up
1 Something that **springs up** appears or develops suddenly: *Reform circles were springing up all over the country.* [*same as* **sprout up, shoot up**] **2** You **spring up** when you stand up suddenly: *Bertha sprang up with surprising alacrity.* [*same as* **jump up**]

sprout /sprɑut/: **sprouts**, **sprouting**, **sprouted**

sprout up
Something that **sprouts up** appears or develops suddenly: *Aerials sprouted up like weeds on the roof.* [*same as* **spring up, shoot up**]

spruce /spruːs/: **spruces**, **sprucing**, **spruced**

spruce up
You **spruce** something **up** when you make it look clean and neat; you can also **spruce** yourself **up**: *The old caravan had been spruced up and given a lick of paint.* ❑ *He'd even spruced himself up in a clean shirt and a fairly respectable-looking jacket.* [*same as* **smarten up**]

spur /spɜː(r)/: **spurs**, **spurring**, **spurred**

spur on
Something **spurs** you **on** when it encourages you to continue to try to do or achieve something: *They were partially spurred on by the success of Apple's PC drive.* [*same as* **urge on**]

sputter /ˈspʌtə(r)/: **sputters**, **sputtering**, **sputtered**

sputter out
1 A candle or other flame **sputters out** when its flame burns erratically for a time before it finally stops burning: *The flame sputtered out when the door was opened.* **2** You can also says that something **sputters out** when it suddenly stops working or comes to an end abruptly: *Their sudden burst of frenzied activity sputtered out when the heat began to have its effect.* [compare **fizzle out, peter out**]

spy /spaɪ/: **spies**, **spying**, **spied**

spy on
Someone who **spies on** you watches you secretly: *You've been spying on them, have you?* ❑ *She couldn't help glancing back, in case Jasper was spying on her.*

spy out
You **spy** something **out** when you discover it, especially by watching or observing secretly: *Small patrols were dispatched to spy out the enemy positions and report back.*

square /skwɛə(r)/: **squares**, **squaring**, **squared**

square off
You **square** something **off** when you give it a square shape, or make its surface perpendicular to the surface next to it: *Square off the edges of the cardboard and draw a line down the centre.*

square up (*informal*)
You **square up** when you pay a bill, *eg* in a restaurant or hotel: *Have you squared Tom up for the taxi fare?* [*same as* **settle up**]

square up to
1 Two people **square up to** each other when they face each other, ready to fight: *As they squared up to each other, the spouses implored them not to fight.* **2** You **square up to** a problem or difficulty when you deal with it: *We'll need the services of a lawyer to square this one up.*
[compare **face up to**]

square with
Two or more things **square with** each other when they match in some way or give the same results: *How do you square the needs of an ever-increasing population with diminishing world resources?* ❑ *The monthly unemployment statistics don't square with the real facts.* [*same as* **agree with, be consistent with**]

squash /skwɒʃ/: **squashes**, **squashing**, **squashed**

squash in *or* squash into
1 You **squash in**, or **squash into** a place, when you push to get in, because there is little room; you can also say that you **squash** something **in**, or **squash** it **into** a place: *If you move up a little, I'll be able to squash in beside you.* [*same as* **squeeze in**; compare **push in**] **2** You can also use **squash in**

and **squash into** to emphasize how little room there is for something to fit in: *They were all squashed into a couple of small rooms, with no indoor plumbing.* [*same as* **squeeze in**]

squash up
Someone or something that **is squashed up** is pressed hard against others: *There was plenty of room in the front of the bus, but they chose to sit squashed up at the back.*

squat /skwɒt/: **squats**, **squatting**, **squatted**

---

squat down
1 You **squat down** when you lower your body from a standing position by bending your knees and moving your bottom towards your heels: *Squat down with your feet just over shoulder width apart.* [*same as* **hunker down**] **2** You can also say that you **squat down** when you sit down, especially when you sit on the floor with your legs crossed: *He sighed and squatted down by her feet.*

squeal /skwiːl/: **squeals**, **squealing**, **squealed**

---

squeal on (*informal*)
To **squeal on** someone is to betray them by telling others about the wrong things they have done: *'Don't worry, Johnnie ain't gonna squeal on his own brothers.'* [*same as* **split on** (*informal*), **grass on** (*informal*), **rat on** (*informal*), **tell on**]

squeeze /skwiːz/: **squeezes**, **squeezing**, **squeezed**

---

squeeze in *or* squeeze into
1 You **squeeze in**, or **squeeze into** a place, when you push to get in, because there is little room; you can also say that you **squeeze** something **in**, or **squeeze** it **into** a place: *We arrived late and had to squeeze in at the back of the hall.* ❑ *Several large and formidable-looking ladies were squeezed into the tiny car.* **2** You can also use **squeeze in** and **squeeze into** to emphasize how little room there is for something to fit in: *It was difficult to squeeze the new symbol into the box on the ballot paper.* ❑ *There was a tiny cottage squeezed in the corner.* [*same as* **squash in**] **3** You **squeeze** something **in**, or **squeeze** it **into** your schedule, when you manage with difficulty to find time to do it: *The Lions had squeezed in two light training sessions before the match.* [*same as* **fit in**]

squeeze out
1 You **squeeze** liquid or air **out** of its container when you press the container to force the liquid or air out: *You don't have to mix your colours, squeeze your tubes out.* **2** Someone or something that **is squeezed out** is forced out or excluded: *These projects might otherwise get squeezed out.* ❑ *He yawned to squeeze the bad thoughts out of his head.* **3** (*informal*) You **squeeze** something **out** of someone when you force or persuade them to give it to you: *I'm surprised no-one's tried to squeeze more out of me.*

squeeze through
You **squeeze through** when you manage with difficulty to pass through a narrow gap: *He doubted he'd be able to squeeze through that hole again.*

squirrel /ˈskwɪrəl/: **squirrels**, **squirrelling** (*AmE* **squirreling**), **squirrelled** (*AmE* **squirreled**)

---

squirrel away
You **squirrel** something **away** when you put it somewhere safe or secret and keep it there: *The auction has lost its sparkle slightly since the National Gallery squirrelled away the Holbein.* [*same as* **hoard away**, **stash away** (*informal*)]

stack /stak/: **stacks**, **stacking**, **stacked**

---

stack up
1 You **stack** things **up** when you arrange them in a pile or stack: *Stack*

the clean plates up on the sideboard and I'll put them away later. **2** (*informal*) You can say that things don't **stack up** when they don't make sense: *He was seen in the High Street at 2 o'clock, but his employer said he was in a meeting at the time. It doesn't stack up.* [*same as* **add up**]

staff /stɑːf/: **staffs**, **staffing**, **staffed**

staff up

A company **staffs up** when it increases the number of workers it has: *They'd staffed up for a major expansion programme.*

stake /steɪk/: **stakes**, **staking**, **staked**

stake on

People often say they would **stake** money, or their reputation or their life, **on** something to show how firmly they trust or believe that it's true or that it will succeed: *It was amazing to find him staking his life on this principle.* ❑ *He will come back. I'd stake my life on it.* [*same as* **bet on**]

stake out

1 Someone who **stakes out** an area of land marks its boundary with posts, to show either that they own it or would like to claim it: *The whole area had been staked out by gold-hungry prospectors from the east.* [compare **mark out, mark off**] **2** To **stake** anything **out** is to show or state what its limits or boundaries are: *They'd staked out their territory firmly in the middle ground of politics.* **3** (*informal*) Police officers **stake out** a building when they secretly watch it continually, checking who goes in and who comes out: *The FBI had been staking the place out for weeks, hoping for evidence that it was being used as a safe house for Soviet spies.*

stamp /stamp/: **stamps**, **stamping**, **stamped**

stamp on

1 You **stamp on** something when you bring your foot forcefully down on it, in order to break or crush it: *We stamped on the cockroaches as they scuttled out from under the fridge.* [compare **trample on**] **2** You can say that someone **stamps** themselves or their personality **on** something when they have a strong influence, or make a strong impression, on it: *He'd stamped his larger-than-life personality on all his businesses, and dealt with opposition ruthlessly.*

stamp out

To **stamp out** something unwanted or undesirable is to take firm action, or use force, to get rid of it: *The Church had tried, and failed, to stamp out those ancient pagan customs.* [*same as* **crush**]

stand /stand/: **stands**, **standing**, **stood** /stʊd/

stand about *or* stand around

You **stand about** or **stand around** when you stand doing nothing, *eg* because you are lazy, you are waiting for something, or you don't know what to do: *People were standing about on the dried mud of the half-built streets.* ❑ *Hundreds of people are standing around, waiting to be told which platform their train is leaving from.* [compare **hang about, lounge about**]

stand apart

Someone who **stands apart** doesn't involve themselves with others, or with what they are doing: *The speaker stands apart from the political parties, and is directly answerable to the Commons.* ❑ *There is one who stands apart, dissociating himself from his companions.*

stand aside

1 You **stand aside** when you move to let others pass: *She stood aside to motion him in.* [*same as* **step aside, move aside**] **2** You can also say that you **stand aside** when you don't involve yourself in the affairs or arguments of others: *The UN will be standing aside to allow NATO to take over the role of peacekeepers.* [*same as* **stay out of**]

stand back

1 You **stand back** when you move back and away from something or someone: *He stood back to let us pass.* [*same as* **step back**] **2** You can say that you **stand back** from a situation you are involved in when you try to judge it in the way that someone who is not involved would judge it: *He will have little opportunity to stand back and examine the data.* [*same as* **step back**] **3** A building that **stands back** from a road or other feature does not lie next to it, but at some distance from it: *Standing some 50 metres back from the main street, the museum was hidden from view until you were right in front of it.* [*same as* **set back**]

stand between

People often use **stand between** when referring to a person or thing that prevents something from happening or being achieved: *Now there was nothing standing between her and the fulfilment of her lifetime ambition.* [compare **come between**]

stand by

1 Someone who **stands by** fails to take action to prevent something unpleasant from happening: *Governments stand by while the industry collapses.* ❑ *He would not stand by and watch her impulsively throw her life away.* **2** Someone who **is standing by** is ready to take action when asked or when it is needed: *Mr Venables was standing by to offer encouragement.* **3** You **stand by** someone when you remain loyal to them and give them support in a difficult situation: *Think of all the hassle she's had from standing by her father.* [*same as* **stick by**] **4** You can say that you **stand by** something such as a promise or agreement you made earlier to show that you have not changed your mind, even though circumstances may have changed: *I think you have to stand by what you believe.* [*same as* **stick by, abide by, adhere to**]

• *noun* **bystander: bystanders**

A **bystander** is someone who sees something happen but is not involved in it: *His words were received with enthusiasm by the bystanders.* ❑ *Affray consisted of fighting in public to the terror of innocent bystanders.*

• *noun* **standby** *or* **stand-by**

1 A **standby** is something that can be used if needed, perhaps in place of something else that might fail or might not be available; you can also say that such a thing is on **standby**: *I am asked if I can be on standby if transport is needed.* **2** A **standby** is also a ticket, especially for air travel or for a theatre performance, that you buy immediately before the journey or performance, at a reduced price: *We can offer you a stand-by at a third of the normal fare.*

stand down

Someone who **stands down** gives up their job or position: *He's about to stand down on grounds of age and health.* [*same as* **step down**]

stand for

1 An abbreviation **stands for** a word or set of words that it represents or refers to: *Somebody writes TNT on the board and says what does that stand for?* **2** You can say that you won't **stand for** something when you won't tolerate it or allow it to happen: *Put him into Mrs McGill's class. She won't stand for any of his nonsense.* [*same as* **put up with, tolerate**] **3** Someone who **stands for** certain principles or values supports them or is regarded by others as representing them: *Guys like him stand for everything that's rotten.* **4** Someone who **stands for** something such as an election is a candidate in it: *He's standing for the Tories at the by-election.* [compare **put up**]

stand in

You **stand in** for someone when you

do their job, or do something that is normally their responsibility, because they are absent: *Barbara Bonney was standing in for an indisposed Lillian Watson.* ❑ *Would you be able to stand in at short notice if one of the committee doesn't arrive?*
• *noun* **stand-in**: **stand-ins**: *Brierley was the obvious stand-in for Bob Kimmins.*

stand off

• *noun* **stand-off**: **stand-offs**
A **stand-off** is a situation in which two opposing people or groups confront each other as if ready to fight or argue, but without either side taking any action: *Both cats were tense and bristling with aggression, in a stand-off that went on for fifteen minutes.*

stand out

1 Something that **stands out** can be seen clearly: *The caravans are painted white so that they stand out against the green landscape.* ❑ *Mount Kanchenjunga with its bright plume of snow stands out like a triumphal flag.* **2** Something that **stands out** is noticeably much better than others of its kind: *In my opinion, she stands out as being the most confident and self-assured of the four candidates.*
• *adjective* • **outstanding**
1 Something **outstanding** is very good indeed, especially much better than others of its kind: *In this respect, Mrs Mackay's porridge was outstanding.* **2** Something that is **outstanding** has not yet been dealt with: *They're demanding payment of the outstanding £1250.*

stand out against

You **stand out against** something when you publicly state your opposition to it, or when you remain opposed to it even though others disagree with you: *The lyric is not debarred from standing out against the state.* ❑ *He continued, despite overwhelming pressure, to stand out against entry into the ERM.*

stand out for

You **stand out for** something when you continue to insist that you want it, and refuse to accept anything less: *Don't let them bully you. Stand out for what is rightfully yours.* [*same as* **hold out for**]

stand over

Someone **stands over** you when they watch what you're doing closely, especially in order to make sure you do it, or do it properly: *Dad would stand over us and make sure we did our homework.*

stand together

People or groups **stand together** when they remain loyal to each other by together continuing to oppose or fight something or someone that threatens them both: *The Armed Services needed to stand together to mitigate the worst excesses of the reforms.* [*same as* **stick together**]

stand up

1 You **stand up** when you raise your body from a sitting or lying position into a standing position: *Push the hips forward and stand up straight.* ❑ *We were asked who would volunteer to stand up and read their poem.* **2** You can say that things such as arguments, explanations or excuses **stand up** if they prove to be true or seem likely to be true: *The evidence against him is purely circumstantial and would never stand up in court.* **3** (*informal*) You **stand** someone **up**, especially a boyfriend or girlfriend, when you deliberately don't go to meet them as you had agreed you would: *How dare he stand her up and then get that woman to phone and make his excuses?*

stand up for

You **stand up for** someone or something, especially when they are being attacked or criticized, when you defend, support or protect them: *They could not be relied on to stand up for British interests.* [*same as* **stick up for**]

stand up to

1 Something or someone that **stands up to** severe treatment survives it and remains relatively unharmed or undamaged: *This enables them to stand up to heavy wear.* [*same as* **withstand**] **2** You **stand up to** someone who is attacking you when you defend yourself bravely and with determination: *I would never have thought he had the courage to stand up to her.* [compare **face up to**]

stare /steə(r)/: **stares, staring, stared**

---

stare down *or* stare out

To **stare** someone **down**, or **stare** them **out**, is to look aggressively into their eyes and force them to look away, in order to make them feel weak or inferior: *The stupid man thought he could stare the tiger out, and ended up being eaten.*

start /stɑːt/: **starts, starting, started**

---

start back

1 You **start back** somewhere when you begin the journey to return there: *It's six o'clock. We ought to be starting back.* **2** You also **start back** when you make a sudden movement backwards, away from something that gives you an unexpected shock or fright: *Starting back in alarm from the edge of the pavement, she just avoided being hit as the bus careered out of control.*

start for

You **start for** a place when you begin the journey to go there: *Everyone should get packed up this evening. We'll be starting for Etosha first thing in the morning.*

start in

You **start in** when you begin to do or deal with something: *She'd already started in on the pile of ironing.*

start in on (*informal*)

Someone **starts in on** you when they begin to speak angrily to you, blaming or criticizing you for something: *'Oh, don't start in on me, just because he wouldn't give you the car.'* [*same as* **start on** (*informal*), **lay into** (*informal*), **tear into** (*informal*)]

start off

1 You **start off** by doing something, or **start off** doing it, when that is the first thing you do: *Start off by standing upright with our arms by your sides.* ❑ *You start off being coy about drinking brandy.* ❑ *We started off with some introductions.* **2** You **start off** when you begin a journey: *They gave up and started off home.* ❑ *The signal was given and the train started off.* [*same as* **set off, set out, start out**] **3** You can use **start off** when talking about the original position, state or nature of something: *Bullens Creek had started off tiny and tedious and gone downhill from there.* ❑ *The membranes start off positively charged.* [*same as* **start out**] **4** You **start** something **off** when you cause it to begin to happen: *Consider the Big Bang that started off the Universe.* **5** You **start** someone **off**, or **start** them **off** doing something, when you give them the signal to begin something, or when you do or say something that makes them behave in a certain way: *He made this stupid remark about how awful boarding school could be which started her off crying again.*

start on

1 You **start on** something when you begin to deal with it or do it: *You may find that when you first start on your weight control programme.* ❑ *She started on the thick vegetable soup.* **2** (*informal*) Someone **starts on** you when they begin angrily criticizing you or blaming you for something: *Then he started on poor Lucy, shouting and bawling at the top of his voice.* [*same as* **start in on** (*informal*), **lay into** (*informal*)]

start out

1 You **start out** when you begin a journey: *Before you start out, make* *sure the mountain rescue know when you intend to return.* [*same as* **start off, set off, set out**] **2** You can use **start off** when talking about the original position, state or nature of something: *A take that started out as three or four minutes long may eventually be edited to a ten-second shot.* ❑ *He had started out in Cleveland, Ohio playing 3,000 people.* ❑ *It's a fair achievement having started out on a Youth Training Scheme.* [*same as* **start off**] **3** What you **started out** to do is what you began to do, or what you intended to do: *He had started out to make a rough count of the houses.*

start over (*especially AmE*)
You **start over** when you do something again, from the beginning: *The whole thing collapsed and we had to start over.*

start up
1 You **start up** an engine, vehicle or machine when you switch it on so that it begins working: *They heard an ambulance start up and move off.* **2** You **start up** something such as a business when you begin it: *There was a positive decision against starting up a tourism enterprise.* [*same as* **set up, establish**]

starve /stɑːv/: starves, starving, starved

starve for
You **are starved for** something when you have not had it for some time and you want or need it badly: *Starving for some attention, he deliberately set the kitchen on fire.* [compare **starve of**]

starve into
Someone who **starves** a person **into** something forces them to do it by not giving them food until they agree to do it: *His main tactic was to starve them into submission.*

starve of
To **be starved of** something is to suffer from not having it or not having enough of it: *The heating system is starved of water due to losses not being replaced.* ❑ *The regional council is being starved of funds and cannot carry out the necessary refurbishment.* [compare **starve for**]

starve out
To **starve** someone **out** is to force them to come out of their hiding-place by preventing them from getting food: *Laying seige to the city, Alexander hoped to starve the occupants out.*

stash /staʃ/: stashes, stashing, stashed

stash away (*informal*)
You **stash** something **away** when you hide it somewhere or save it in a secret place: *They looked under the floorboards for that fortune he was supposed to have stashed away.* ❑ *He's probably got thousands stashed away.* [compare **salt away**]

stave /steɪv/: staves, staving, staved

stave off
You **stave off** something unpleasant when you prevent it from happening or appearing, perhaps only for a limited period: *There are emergency measures to stave off a winter economic crisis.* ❑ *The longer you stave that off, the less time you will spend building fatigue toxins.* [*same as* **ward off, avert**]

stay /steɪ/: stays, staying, stayed

stay ahead
You **stay ahead** when you remain in a stronger position than your rivals or opponents: *Stay ahead by deploying modest numbers of state-of-the-art aircraft.* ❑ *Peters managed to stay ahead throughout the race.* ❑ *If Scotland can stay ahead of Sweden in their group they have an excellent chance of qualifying.*

stay away
You **stay away** when you don't go

somewhere: *Many voters simply stayed away rather than vote against the proposals.* ❑ *We're asking those without tickets to stay away.*

stay back
You **stay back** when you remain in a place after others have left: *He stayed back at the ranch with the women.* [*same as* **stay behind**]

stay behind
You **stay behind** when you remain in a place after others have left: *Both of them were told to stay behind after school.* [*same as* **stay back**]

stay down
Food you have eaten **stays down** when it remains in your stomach and is not vomited up again: *He said a little of Mamma's chicken broth might stay down.* [compare **keep down**]

stay in
You **stay in** when you stay at home rather than go out to places such as restaurants or theatres: *If I can't afford to go out we stay in and read together.*

stay off
1 You **stay off** something when you don't eat, drink or otherwise consume it: *Maintain good health and stay off drugs.* ❑ *He managed to stay off alcohol for the first time.* [*same as* **lay off** (*informal*), **keep off**] **2** You **stay off** work or **off** school when you don't go, perhaps because you are ill: *You can't stay off school just because you feel like it, you know.*

stay on
You **stay on** when you remain in a place longer than other people or longer than expected: *She had come to Glasgow to nurse her father and stayed on after his death.* ❑ *The men who were there had no choice but to stay on.*

stay out
1 You **stay out** when you remain away from home longer than expected or intended: *He stayed out until after midnight without phoning his wife to tell her where he was.* **2** Striking workers **stay out** when they remain on strike: *The miners stayed out for a number of weeks.*

stay out of
You **stay out of** something such as a fight or argument when you don't get involved: *'Stay out of this,' she yelled, 'it's none of your business!'*

stay over
You **stay over** when you spend the night in a place you have been visiting: *John and Mark are welcome to stay over if they want.*

stay up
You **stay up** when you don't go to bed until after your usual time: *We attempted to miss a night's sleep and stay up all night.*

stay with
1 You **stay with** someone when you live in their home for a time: *Staying with friends can be very disorientating.* ❑ *Bruno was sent to stay with a family near Weimar.* **2** You **stay with** something when you continue to discuss it, deal with it or use it, rather than changing to something else: *Staying with the economy, is it the Labour Party's intention to increase public expenditure on education?* ❑ *He'd looked at a few other cars, but in the end decided to stay with Fords.* [*same as* **stick with**]

steal /stiːl/: **steals**, **stealing**, **stole** /stoul/, **stolen** /'stoulən/

---

steal away
You **steal away** when you leave quietly or secretly: *They stole away from the fort under cover of darkness.* [*same as* **slip away**]

steal up on
You **steal up on** someone when you approach them slowly and quietly or secretly, in order to surprise them; something **steals up on** you when it

happens gradually, and takes you by surprise because you don't notice it: *Middle age steals up on you like a mugger in a dark lane.* [*same as* **creep up on**]

steam /stiːm/: **steams**, **steaming**, **steamed**

steam off
You **steam off** something that is stuck to a surface when you remove it using steam: *She gave him the envelopes so that he could steam off the stamps for his collection.*

steam up
1 A glass surface such as a window **is steamed up** when steam that has condensed on it makes it difficult to see through: *We couldn't see in. The windows had steamed up.* [*same as* **fog up, mist up**] **2** (*informal*) You can say that someone **is steamed up** when they are angry or excited: *He had got all steamed up over nothing.*

steep /stiːp/: **steeps**, **steeping**, **steeped**

steep in
You can use **steep in** to emphasize how much of a quality something has: *Another sporting triumph gave reassurance to the nation, especially those steeped in the amateur spirit.* ❑ *Djogo's work is steeped in folklore.* [*same as* **soak in**]

steer /stɪə(r)/: **steers**, **steering**, **steered**

steer away from
You **steer away from** something when you try to avoid it; you **steer** someone **away from** something when you try to make them avoid it, or keep them from noticing it: *I'll steer away from men like him in future.* ❑ *Steering teenagers away from situations where there's likely to be drugs isn't as easy as you might think.*

stem /stɛm/: **stems**, **stemming**, **stemmed**

stem from
You can use **stem from** when talking about the cause or origin of something: *His love of writing stems from his analytical training at university.* [*same as* **spring from**]

step /stɛp/: **steps**, **stepping**, **stepped**

step aside
1 You **step aside** when you move in order to let others pass: *When he stepped aside we could see into what looked like an Aladdin's cave.* **2** You also **step aside** when you give up your job or position so that someone else can take it or be appointed to it: *He chose to step aside at this juncture, for he felt he'd nothing more to offer.* [*same as* **step down, stand down**]

step back
1 You **step back** when you move back, perhaps in order to let others pass: *The opponent launches a front kick, which you evade by stepping back.* **2** You **step back** from a situation you are involved in when you try to judge it from the position of someone who is not involved: *Instead of struggling with them, I step back and let thoughts and feelings come and go.* ❑ *Once he had stepped back from the day-to-day struggle, he realised how pointless it had all been.*

step down
You **step down** from your job or position when you give it up: *The Prime Minister has confirmed that he will step down shortly.* [*same as* **step aside, stand down**]

step forward
You **step forward** when you offer to do something: *Frankly, we hadn't expected anyone to step forward and take on willingly such a difficult task.* [*same as* **come forward**]

step in
Someone who **steps in** involves themselves in a situation that others have been dealing with: *Some got stranded at the airport but luckily others were on hand to step in.* ❑ *Television and radio stepped in and killed the art of storytelling.*

step up
Something that **is stepped up** is increased in amount, extent or intensity: *Lenin appealed to the Ukraine to step up its aid.* ❑ *The Community's role in this area should be stepped up.* ❑ *My blood tests were stepped up to once a week.*

stick /stɪk/: **sticks**, **sticking**, **stuck** /stʌk/

---

stick around (*informal*)
You **stick around** when you stay in a place, often in order to wait for something: *If you find something better, great; if not, stick around.* ❑ *Just stick around here until we can think of something.* [*same as* **hang around** (*informal*)]

stick at
1 You **stick at** something you are doing when you continue to do it, although you might want to stop: *Grandad told me to stick at my lessons and get into a good university if I could.* [*same as* **keep at**] **2** To **stick at** a particular level, stage or point is not to go beyond it: *After doing so well, her weight stuck at 9 stone 6 pounds.* **3** You can say that you will **stick at** nothing in order to achieve something as a way of emphasizing that you will use every possible means to achieve it: *Some of the more extreme elements in the party will stick at nothing to achieve what they've set out to do.* [*same as* **stop at**]

stick by
1 You **stick by** something you have always believed, supported or used when you continue with it and don't change: *I think you should stick with what I say or get somebody else who can do it better.* **2** You **stick by** someone when you remain loyal to them and give them support in a difficult situation: *Somehow he'd taken it for granted that she would stick by him. She didn't.* [*same as* **stand by**]

stick in
1 You **stick** something sharp **in** an object when you push it into the object firmly, especially so that it stays there: *She turned the fish over and stuck the knife in just beneath the gills.* **2** Something **sticks in** your mind when you have very clear memories of it: *I don't know why his words stuck in my mind.* **3** (*informal*) You get **stuck in** when you begin a task with energy and determination: *You choose your college, find a course, and get stuck in.* [*same as* **wire in** (*informal*)]

stick on (*informal*)
You can say that you **are stuck on** someone or something when you like them very much: *Julie seems pretty stuck on that boy.*

stick out
1 Something that **sticks out** extends beyond the edge of the thing or things that it is next to, and can be easily seen: *His left elbow was sticking out of the window.* ❑ *The helmeted head of some hero would stick out through the roof.* [*same as* **jut out**, **protrude** (*formal*)] **2** You can say that anything obvious or noticeable **sticks out**: *Dressed like that you'll certainly stick out in a crowd!* [*same as* **stand out**] **3** You **stick out** a difficult or unpleasant task or situation when you continue to do it, or stay in it, although you might want to stop or leave: *Fordyce stuck it out for as long as he could.*

stick out for
You **stick out for** something when you continue to insist that you want it and will accept nothing less: *The unions seem determined to stick out for a shorter working week.* [*same as* **hold**

out for, stand out for]

stick to

1 You **stick to** laws or rules when you obey them: *Find the rules to work by and then stick to them.* [*same as* **abide by**] **2** You **stick to** something when you continue to do or use it, rather than changing to something else: *It is sometimes best to stick to the familiar, cling to the known.* ❑ *Knighton is publicly sticking to the line that his offer will proceed.* **3** You **stick to** a subject when it is the only thing you talk about or discuss: *I think writers should stick to the facts.* **4** You **stick to** someone when you remain loyal to them and support them in a difficult situation: *Despite the questions about his loyalty, he's sticking to the President, so far at least.* [*same as* **stick by**, **stand by**]

stick together

People who **stick together** remain loyal to each other, giving each other help and support in a difficult situation: *All we have to do is stick together and tell the truth.*

stick up

1 Something that **sticks up** points upwards, or extends upwards beyond the edge of the thing or things next to it: *Some of them had electrodes on their heads that stuck up like a second pair of ears.* **2** (*informal*, *old*) To **stick up** a place such as a bank is to rob it using a gun or other weapon to threaten violence: *He said jokingly that the only way out of his problems would be to stick up a bank.* [*same as* **hold up**]

• *noun* **stick-up**

A **stick-up** is an act of robbing a bank or similar place using a gun or other weapon to threaten violence: *'Put your hands above your heads. This is a stick-up.'* [*same as* **hold-up**]

• *adjective* **stuck up**

Someone who is **stuck up** doesn't involve themselves with others because they think they are better or more important than they are: *She's too stuck up to talk to the likes of us.* ❑ *What a stuck-up little horror she's turned out to be!* [*same as* **snobbish**]

stick up for

You **stick up for** someone when you defend them against attack or criticism: *All the kids stuck up for him.* [*same as* **stand up for**]

stick with

1 You **stick with** something when you continue to do or use it, and don't change to something else: *Stick with it and you'll get there in the end.* **2** You **stick with** someone when you stay close to them, going where they go: *You stick with me, kid, and I'll show you the ropes.* [*same as* **stay with**] **3** Things **stick with** you when you have very clear memories of them: *Their experiences in Burma had stuck with them for all these years.* [*same as* **stay with**] **4** You can say that you **are stuck with** something when you have been forced to keep it or accept it, although you don't want it: *Experimenters are stuck with observing physical events.* ❑ *The Democrats are stuck with Mr Clinton.* [*same as* **lumber with** (*informal*), **saddle with**]

sting /stɪŋ/: stings, stinging, stung /stʌŋ/

sting for (*informal*)

Someone who **is stung for** an amount of money is forced to pay it: *Then the cab driver stung me for fifty quid!*

stir /stɜː(r)/: stirs, stirring, stirred

stir in *or* **stir into**

You **stir** something **in** when you add it to a substance by stirring with a spoon, to form a mixture; you can also say that you **stir** it **into** a substance: *Wait until the sugar has dissolved then stir in the honey.* ❑ *Last of all, stir the treacle and milk mixture into the flour and fruit.*

stir up

To **stir up** trouble or unpleasant feelings

is to cause them to be produced: *How dare this stranger stir up these doubts in so private an area?* ❑ *This action is commonly attributed to the fear of a working class stirred up by the course of events in France.*

stitch /stɪtʃ/: **stitches**, **stitching**, **stitched**

stitch up

1 A surgeon **stitches up** a wound when they close it by sewing with a surgical needle and thread: *When he'd stitched me up, he asked me how I'd come to get a wound like that.* [*same as* **sew up**] **2** (*informal*) Someone who **is stitched up** is made to appear guilty of committing a crime they didn't really commit: *Becket was stitched up. New evidence has come to light that proves he didn't do it.* [*same as* **frame**] **3** You can say that you have something **stitched up** when you have definitely achieved or obtained it: *He was jubilant, saying he had the deal stitched up.* [*same as* **sew up**]

stock /stɒk/: **stocks**, **stocking**, **stocked**

stock up

You **stock up** with things, or **stock up** on them, when you gather a supply of them to be used later: *Complex campaigns may take days, so stock up on rations.* [*same as* **store up, lay in**]

stoke /stoʊk/: **stokes**, **stoking**, **stoked**

stoke up

1 You **stoke up** a fire when you add more fuel to make it burn more strongly: *Stoking up the boilers was one of the janitor's tasks.* **2** Something **stokes up** feelings such as anger or jealousy when it causes people to have them: *This will only stoke up trouble for the future.* [*same as* **stir up**]

stoop /stuːp/: **stoops**, **stooping**, **stooped**

stoop to

Someone who will **stoop to** something, or **stoop to** doing it, is willing to do it if the situation makes it necessary, however wrong, unpleasant or unworthy it is: *Give me a goddess's work to do and I will do it. I will even stoop to a queen's work if you will share the throne with me.* [*same as* **descend to, resort to**]

stop /stɒp/: **stops**, **stopping**, **stopped**

stop at

You can say that you will **stop at** nothing in order to achieve something as a way of emphasizing that you will use every possible means to achieve it: *Will she stop at nothing to get herself elected?* [*same as* **stick at**]

stop away

You **stop away** when you don't go to a place: *Most of their supporters had stopped away.* [*same as* **stay away**]

stop behind

You **stop behind** when you stay in a place after others have left: *Bert stopped behind to look after the animals.* [*same as* **stay behind**]

stop by

You **stop by** when you visit a place briefly: *At 11.30, a few regulars stopped by to find the door locked.* ❑ *I reminded myself to stop by at Frasers.* [*same as* **drop by, drop in**]

stop in

1 You **stop in** when you stay at home, instead of going out to places such as restaurants or theatres: *'Are you coming?' 'No, I'm stopping in with our kid.'* [*same as* **stay in**] **2** You **stop in** when you visit a place briefly: *She's stopping in at Hamish's on her way south.* [*same as* **drop in, look in**]

stop off

You **stop off** somewhere when you spend a short time there before continuing your journey to another place:

I stopped off at Jim Groeling's place to discuss some architectural drawings. ❑ *They stopped off in Wolverhampton to change trains.*

stop on

You **stop on** somewhere when you stay longer there than you originally intended, or longer than others stay: *Are you lot stopping on here? We're going down the pub.* [*same as* **stay on**]

stop out

1 You **stop out** when you remain away from home: *Will you be stopping out again tonight?* **2** Striking workers **stop out** when they remain on strike: *The railwaymen stopped out for another week.*
[*same as* **stay out**]

stop over

1 You **stop over** somewhere when you sleep there before continuing your journey to another place: *He is merely stopping over en route from the Republic.* [compare **stop off**] **2** You **stop over** when you visit a place briefly: *Jane'll be stopping over in Frankfurt on her way home.* [*same as* **stop by, drop by**]

• *noun* **stopover: stopovers**
A **stopover** is a short stay somewhere during a longer trip or journey, or the place where you stay: *It was one of these tedious stopovers that we often had to endure.* ❑ *Easy access makes this place a favourite stopover with camper-vanners and tenters.*

stop up

1 You **stop up** a hole or passage when you fill or cover it so that nothing can get in or out: *Don't stop up that vent. It keeps damp out of the chimney.* [*same as* **block up**] **2** You **stop up** when you don't go to bed until after your usual time: *Patrick stopped up to watch the American football.* [*same as* **stay up**]

store /stɔː(r)/: **stores, storing, stored**

---

store away

You **store** something **away** when you put it or keep it somewhere safe so that it can be used later: *Fortunately they'd stored away enough tinned and dried food to see them through the winter.* [compare **hoard away, stash away** (*informal*)]

store up

1 You have a supply of something **stored up** when you have gradually gathered it and are keeping it for later use: *The universe grew ever faster, as energy stored up in hitherto unexpected fields of energy was released.* [*same as* **save up**] **2** You **store up** feelings such as anger or bitterness when, instead of expressing them, you keep them inside, allowing them to grow: *Elizabeth stored this slight away until she could think of a good way of getting her revenge.* [*same as* **bottle up**]

storm /stɔːm/: **storms, storming, stormed**

---

storm in *or* storm into

Someone who **storms in** enters a place suddenly and noisily, especially because they are angry; you can also say that they **storm into** a place: *Davis stormed in, his face black with rage, and demanded to know who had been tampering with the generator.*

storm off

Someone who **storms off** rushes away in an angry mood: *He hurled a chair across the set and then stormed off to his dressing-room.*

storm out

Someone who **storms out** leaves a place suddenly and in an angry mood: *She stormed out without further words.* ❑ *Mazzin stormed out, clearly upset.*

stow /stoʊ/: **stows, stowing, stowed**

---

stow away

1 You **stow** something **away** when you put it carefully in a safe place while it is not needed or not being used, often in a place specially designed to contain it: *A six-pack of beer, which someone had forgotten to stow away, slid back and forth.* ❑ *The musical instruments had been stowed away in the glass-fronted cabinets.* [compare **store away**] **2** Someone **stows away** on a ship or aircraft when they hide on it with the intention of travelling in secret or without paying the fare: *In order to escape, they stowed away on a tanker bound for Europe.*

• *noun* **stowaway: stowaways**

A **stowaway** is someone who hides on a ship or aircraft with the intention of travelling in secret or without paying the fare.

straighten /'streɪtən/: **straightens, straightening, straightened**

straighten out

1 You **straighten out** something that is bent, twisted or otherwise forced out of shape when you make it straight again or put it back into its normal shape: *He tried to straighten out the brim, but it had been curled and folded so often it was beyond repair.* **2** You **straighten out** a confused or troublesome situation when you put things right or solve problems: *When is someone going to straighten out this mess?* [*same as* **straighten up, put right, sort out**] **3** You **straighten out** someone who is confused or worried, or who misunderstands something, when you help them to think clearly or calmly, or explain things to them: *Alan had got the wrong end of the stick, so we had to straighten him out and reassure him that we hadn't intended to criticize his work.* [*same as* **put straight, put right**] **4** You **straighten out** someone who is behaving badly or foolishly when you persuade them to behave in a sensible or acceptable way: *It'll take more than a prison sentence to straighten him out.* [*same as* **put right**]

straighten up

1 You **straighten up** when you move your body into an upright position after bending over: *Katherine straightened up in the chair.* ❑ *Straightening up again for a brief rest, he worked out a method of getting through the opening.* ❑ *Forster straightened himself up.* [compare **stand up**] **2** You **straighten up** a confused or troublesome situation when you put things in order or solve problems: *How are we going to straighten up the mess we've got ourselves into?* [*same as* **straighten out, put right, sort out**]

strain /streɪn/: **strains, straining, strained**

strain at

An animal **strains at** a rope that it is tied up or controlled with when it pulls hard in an attempt to get free: *Archie was straining at the lead, eager to move on again.*

strain off

You **strain off** a liquid when you separate it from solid bits contained in it by pouring it through a sieve or similar utensil: *Strain off the liquid for the consommé by passing it through a piece of muslin.*

strap /strap/: **straps, strapping, strapped**

strap in *or* strap into

You **strap** yourself **in** when you fasten yourself firmly and safely to the seat of a vehicle by fastening the seat-belt; you can also say that you **strap** yourself **into** the seat or **into** the vehicle: *The kids were safely strapped in and survived the accident with only minor cuts and bruises.* ❑ *They found the pilot, still strapped into his ejector seat, dead.*

strap on

You **strap** something **on** when you fit or attach it to your body by fastening straps: *Strapping his skis on his back, Karl set off on foot.*

strap up
An injured part of your body **is strapped up** when it has bandages wrapped round it: *He came back onto the field with his injured ankle strapped up.*

stray /streɪ/: **strays**, **straying**, **strayed**

stray from
To **stray from** things such as principles or standards is to behave in a way that departs from or abandons them; to **stray from** the subject being discussed is to discuss other things: *Ollivier and Gramont strayed from the prepared text.* [*opposite* **stick to, keep to**]

stretch /strɛtʃ/: **stetches**, **stretching**, **stretched**

stretch away
Something, usually an area of land, **stretches away** when it extends into the distance: *The autobahn E35 stretched away into the distance.* ❑ *A long formal garden stretched away past ponds and flower beds.*

stretch out
1 You **stretch out**, or **stretch** yourself **out**, when you lie in a comfortable position with your body fully extended, taking as much space as you like: *Two medics were lying stretched out on the floor.* **2** You **stretch** an arm or leg **out** when you extend it fully: *Parents and children stretched out flailing arms towards each other.*

strike /straɪk/: **strikes**, **striking**, **struck** /strʌk/

strike at
To **strike at** someone or something is to attack them with words or actions: *The old man stepped forward and made to strike at him with his stick.*

strike back
You **strike back** when you attack in turn someone who has attacked you: *Karpov struck back in the very next game.* [*same as* **hit back**; compare **get back at**]

strike down
Someone who **is struck down** is killed; you can also say that someone **is struck down** when they suddenly and unexpectedly contract a serious illness that prevents them living a full life: *He lay like something fallen or struck down.* ❑ *Their eldest was struck down by polio at aged 8.*

strike off
A professional person such as a doctor or lawyer **is struck off** when, usually as punishment for behaving unprofessionally, their status is officially taken away so that they can no longer work in the profession: *A member would be struck off the register or have his professional certificate suspended.*

strike out
1 Someone who **strikes out** involves themselves in new activities or new business, especially independently of groups or organizations they belonged to before: *His sisters struck out for themselves.* **2** You **strike out** somewhere when you begin to walk or travel in that direction, perhaps with energy or determination: *Swimming against the current, he struck out as smoothly as a seal.* **3** You **strike out** something written or printed when you cancel it by drawing a line through it; to **strike out** anything is to cancel it: *Strike out any references to the USSR and substitute the Russian Federation.* ❑ *Any foods you suspect are causing problems must be struck out of your diet.* [*same as* **cross out, delete**] **4** (*informal*) You **strike out** when you fail to achieve or obtain something: *Arnie couldn't get anyone to go to the prom with him. He'd struck out again.*

strike up
1 You **strike up** a friendship or a conversation with someone, especially one that is unplanned and develops naturally and pleasantly, when you

begin it: *We met on the cross-Channel ferry and struck up a conversation.* **2** Musicians **strike up** when they begin to play; you can also say that their music **strikes up** when it begins, or that they **strike up** a particular tune when they begin to play it: *A small group of musicians struck up the opening bars of the first hymn.*

string /strɪŋ/: **strings**, **stringing**, **strung** /strʌŋ/

string along (*informal*)

1 Someone **strings** you **along** when they deceive you into doing or believing something: *Try to string her along for a while longer. We've almost got everything we want.* [*same as* **lead on**] **2** You **string along** with someone when, for a short while, you travel with them or spend time with them: *He'd strung along with a group of settlers heading west.* [*same as* **go along, tag along**]

string out

1 You **string** something **out** when you make it last longer or as long as possible: *There's no point in trying to string it out for any longer than a week. By then it'll have lost its impact.* [*same as* **spin out**] **2** Things that **are strung out** are arranged in a line with spaces, distances or intervals between them: *A few poorly-manned look-out posts were strung out along the coast.*

string together

You **string** things **together** when you add them to each other to form a unit or sequence: *The performance strings together every possible Celtic cliché.* ❑ *They string several services together.*

string up

1 You **string** something **up** when you hang it up by a string or other cord: *Gaily-coloured bunting was strung up along the main street of the town.* **2** (*informal*) Someone who **is strung up** is killed by being hanged by the neck: *He was captured and strung up there and then.*

strip /strɪp/: **strips**, **stripping**, **stripped**

strip away

1 You **strip** something **away** when you remove it from a surface that it is covering, or to which it is stuck: *Stripping away the wallpaper they found what looked like the original silk wall-coverings beneath.* **2** You **strip away** something that conceals the real nature or character of something when you remove it: *Strip away the hype and there is some original thought, substance and strength.*

strip down

You **strip down** something that is made up of many connected parts, particularly engines, when you disconnect all its parts: *At the end of the month, begin to strip down hanging baskets and replant them.*

strip of

Someone **is stripped of** something such as a quality, right or privilege when it is taken away from them: *He should be stripped of his powers and reduced to a representative role.* ❑ *the kind of cold criticism that strips itself of every shred of temperament.*

strip off

1 (*informal*) Someone who **strips off** takes off all or some of their clothes; you can also say that they **strip off** their clothes: *This once-respectable female began stripping off and sitting in front of the cameras.* ❑ *He put his cup down and stripped off his apron.* **2** You **strip** something **off** when you remove it from a surface it is covering or attached to: *You have to strip off the paint from the binding edge.*

struggle /'strʌgəl/: **struggles**, **struggling**, **struggled**

struggle on

You **struggle on** when you continue with something that is difficult or unpleasant: *The brave old horse put her head down and struggled on through* *the driving sleet, her flanks glistening with sweat.* [*same as* **soldier on**]

strut /strʌt/: **struts**, **strutting**, **strutted**

strut about *or* strut around

Someone who **struts about** or **struts around** walks about in a proud or self-important way: *Don't you think you look a trifle ridiculous strutting about on stage dressed in tights?*

stub /stʌb/: **stubs**, **stubbing**, **stubbed**

stub out

To **stub out** a cigarette or cigar is to stop it burning by pressing the burning end into an ashtray or against a hard surface: *Mrs Hepton's hands shook as she stubbed out her cigarette and immediately lit another.* [compare **put out**]

stumble /'stʌmbəl/: **stumbles**, **stumbling**, **stumbled**

stumble across *or* stumble on

You **stumble across** someone or something, or **stumble on** them, when you meet someone, or discover something, unexpectedly and by chance: *Exploring the caves, he stumbled across a quantity of guns and ammunition.* ❑ *They found the track and, on the second night, stumbled on the signal light.* [*same as* **come across**, **come upon**, **chance on** (*formal*)]

stump /stʌmp/: **stumps**, **stumping**, **stumped**

stump up (*informal*)

You **stump up** when you pay an amount of money for something, often unwillingly; you can also say that you **stump up** an amount of money: *Gerry made him stump up for a brand-new fishing rod to replace the one he'd broken.* ❑ *British Rail surprisingly stumped up £500,000 for short-term repairs.* [*same as* **cough up** (*informal*)]

subscribe /sʌb'skraɪb/: **subscribes**, **subscribing**, **subscribed**

subscribe to

1 You **subscribe to** a magazine when you pay in advance to receive regular copies of it: *Father subscribed to 'Punch' as well as 'National Geographic'.* **2** (*formal*) You **subscribe to** a view, opinion or theory when you have it or believe it, along with others: *I can't subscribe to the theory that man should always be 'bloody, bold and resolute'.* ❑ *There is not a single one of these platitudes that I don't subscribe to.*

suck /sʌk/: **sucks**, **sucking**, **sucked**

suck up to (*informal*)

To **suck up to** someone in a position of authority is to try to please them, *eg* by flattering them, in order to win their support or favour: *He likes his people to suck up to him, and they do.* [*same as* **fawn on**]

sum /sʌm/: **sums**, **summing**, **summed**

sum up

1 You **sum** something **up** when you state its main features or characteristics: *I would sum it up by saying that cars are for work, not for worship.* ❑ *A happy holiday course in a sublime setting sums up Ufford Park nicely.* [*same as* **summarize**] **2** You **sum up** someone or something when you quickly form an accurate opinion of what they are like: *A good thing is the ability to sum up your close colleagues.* [*same as* **size up**] **3** Something **sums up** a situation when it represents it accurately because it is typical of it: *The word 'disastrous' would pretty accurately sum up the whole sorry escapade.* [*same as* **epitomize**, **typify**, **symbolize**] **4** At the end of something such as a formal discussion, you **sum up** when you state the main points that

were discussed or the agreements that were reached; a court judge **sums up** when he or she reminds the jury what the main evidence and arguments are, before the jury considers its verdict: *When summing up, the trial judge said the counsel's comment was improper.*
• *noun* **summing-up: summings-up**
1 A **summing-up** is a generalized opinion or judgement of someone or something: *The evaluation is a summing-up which places the work in the experience of others.* **2** A court judge's **summing-up** is his or her statement to the jury of the main evidence and arguments of a legal case, made before the jury considers its verdict: *The judge emphasized this point more than once in his summing-up.*

summon /'sʌmən/: summons, summoning, summoned

summon up

1 You **summon up** a quality such as courage or patience when you try to find within yourself as much of it as possible, in order to deal with a situation: *There is still a way out of this economic crisis, if Mr Gorbachev can summon up the courage to take it.* ❑ *Before I can summon up some energy, Gordon is hoisting a huge rucksack onto his back.* [*same as* **muster up**] **2** Something **summons up** a thought or memory when it causes you to think it; you **summon** something **up** when you remember it: *The taste of sun-dried tomatoes summons up images of Tuscan hillsides bathed in sunshine.* ❑ *He concentrated on passages he knew and summoned them up word for word.* [*same as* **conjure up, call up**]

surge /sɜːdʒ/: surges, surging, surged

surge forward

A crowd of people **surges forward** when they all suddenly move towards a place or position in front of them: *The protestors surged forward waving placards and driving the riot police back along the boulevard.*

surge up

Things such as feelings **surge up** when they are suddenly and strongly felt or experienced: *Blind uncontrollable rage surged up inside him.*

suss /sʌs/: susses, sussing, sussed

suss out (*informal*)

You **suss out** someone or something when you discover what they are really like so that you understand their true nature: *Have you sussed out what it is they're trying to achieve in this production? Whatever it is, it's gone right over my head!* [*same as* **figure out**]

swab /swɒb/: swabs, swabbing, swabbed

swab down

You **swab down** a floor or other surface when you clean it thoroughly with a mop and water: *Most of their time was spent swabbing down the decks or helping in the galley.* [compare **sluice down**]

swab out

You **swab out** something when you clean it thoroughly using some sort of cloth and water: *She was trying to swab out the filthy cooking pot with a lace hankie.*

swallow /'swɒlou/: swallows, swallowing, swallowed

swallow down

When you swallow something you can also say that you **swallow** it **down**: *He turned his head with a little toss and swallowed down his wine.*

swallow up

1 Something that **is swallowed up** becomes part of something larger and loses its separate identity: *Brown Mills was eventually swallowed up by the* *expanding city.* ❑ *Tory ideology was about to be swallowed up by the centrist Christian Democrats.* [*same as* **absorb**] **2** To **swallow** something **up** is to use large amounts of it, or all of it, very quickly: *The National Curriculum swallowed up most teaching time.* ❑ *France's nuclear weapons swallow up almost a third of defence spending.* **3** One thing **is swallowed up** by another when the other hides it so that it seems to disappear: *When the sun finally appeared, the reds and golds were swallowed up in daylight.*

swamp /swɒmp/: **swamps**, **swamping**, **swamped**

swamp with

You can say that you **are swamped with** things when you have a lot of them to deal with: *After the broadcast, their office was swamped with inquiries from concerned women.* [*same as* **flood with**, **inundate with**]

swap *or* **swop** /swɒp/: **swaps**, **swapping**, **swapped**

swap over

You **swap** two things **over** when you put each in the place the other was in before: *He hadn't noticed that she'd swapped the cups over so that he had the one with the chip.* [*same as* **change over**]

swap round

You **swap** two or more things **round** when you put each in the place the other, or one of the others, was in before: *One day the settee is opposite the door, the next it is where the telly was before it was swapped round with the nest of tables.* [*same as* **switch round**, **change round**]

swear /swɛə(r)/: **swears**, **swearing**, **swore** /swɔː(r)/, **sworn** /swɔːn/

swear at

Someone who **swears at** you attacks you with rude and insulting words: *He leapt onto the back of the chair and swore at me.* ❑ *He swore at the door and at the siren still wailing.*

swear by

You can say that you **swear by** something when you always use it for a particular purpose, because you find that it always works well: *Bill always swore by what is now considered to be an old-fashioned remedy for colic.*

swear in

Someone who **is sworn in** makes a formal promise to do what is asked, especially in a court of law or when accepting an official position: *I was sworn in as a constable.* ❑ *The girl could not be sworn in to give evidence.*

swear off (*informal*)

You **swear off** something such as alcoholic drink when you decide or promise to end your habit of taking it: *A reformed character is he these days, since he swore off the demon drink.* [*same as* **give up**]

sweat /swɛt/: **sweats**, **sweating**, **sweated**

sweat off

1 You **sweat off** body weight when you lose it by causing yourself to sweat a lot, especially by taking strenuous exercise: *Piggott had to sweat off the extra pounds in the sauna to make the weight.* **2** You **sweat off** an illness when you make yourself sweat in order to get rid of the illness and recover: *Keep him warm and he'll have sweated it off by tomorrow.*

sweat out (*informal*)

Someone who **sweats out** a difficult or unpleasant experience or period of time suffers or endures it until the very end, waiting for it to finish: *They left us to sweat it out for the next three days.*

sweat over

You **sweat over** something when you work very hard to get it done: *Kitty left him sweating over the final few pages* *of his novel.*

sweep /swiːp/: **sweeps**, **sweeping**, **swept** /swɛpt/

sweep aside

To **sweep** something **aside** is to remove it or dismiss it: *A sudden revolution from below swept aside the old leaders.* [compare **brush aside**]

sweep away

1 To **sweep** something **away** is to destroy it or remove it completely: *He joined the Kennedy administration and began sweeping away waste wherever he could find it.* ❑ *We would expect a Labour government to sweep away all these laws.* **2** Natural forces such as winds and waves **sweep** objects **away** when they destroy them or carry them away: *The storm raged on, sweeping away huts and trees.* ❑ *They believe the volcano will erupt and sweep away the new Christian retreat being built on its slopes.* **3** You **are swept away** by emotions or feelings when they control your behaviour, especially causing you to behave foolishly: *A flow of desire swept her away at the thought of being together with Lucy.* [*same as* **carry away**]

sweep out

You **sweep out** a room when you sweep its floor thoroughly: *The attic'll have to be swept out and everything rearranged.*

sweep up

1 You **sweep up** dirt or litter when you gather it with a brush and lift it off the floor or the ground with the aid of a shovel of some kind: *He was using the broom to sweep up a broken wine glass.* **2** You **are swept up** in something when you quickly or suddenly become deeply involved in it, perhaps without wanting or expecting to: *Even people who might never have expected to own their own home were swept up in this new enthusiasm for property-ownership.* [*same as* **catch up**]

sweeten /ˈswiːtən/: **sweetens**, **sweetening**, **sweetened**

sweeten up

You **sweeten** someone **up** when you make them willing to agree or co-operate with you by doing something nice for them: *He tried to sweeten me up by telling me I was still beautiful.* [*same as* **soften up**; compare **butter up**, **win over**]

swell /swɛl/: **swells**, **swelling**, **swelled**, **swollen** /ˈswoulən/

swell up

1 Part of your body **swells up** when it becomes unnaturally large and round as a result of an injury or illness: *The horse's head was swollen up with stings.* [*same as* **puff up**] **2** You can say that feelings **swell up** when they become very strong: *Pride swelled up in the bosoms of the children's parents.* [compare **well up**]

swing /swɪŋ/: **swings**, **swinging**, **swung** /swʌŋ/

swing round

Someone **swings round** when they turn their body quickly round to face in the opposite direction; something **swings round** when it turns quickly to face in the opposite direction: *They watched Donald half turn to the crowd, then swing back round and raise his gun.* ❑ *The Audi followed, spinning slightly on the wet road, the back end swinging round as the driver revved too hard.* ❑ *His arm swung round and pointed north.* [*same as* **swivel round**]

switch /swɪtʃ/: **switches**, **switching**, **switched**

switch off

1 You **switch off** televisions and other electrical appliances when you stop them working by pressing the switch that cuts the supply of electricity: *Don't forget to switch it off after leaving the office.* ❑ *Switching the recorder on and*

off without being seen proved more difficult than he'd expected. ❑ *They were watching television and didn't even switch off when he came in.* **2** You can say that you **switch off** when you stop listening or giving attention to someone or something: *As soon as you mention politics, they just switch off.* **3** You can say that someone **switches off** behaviour of a certain kind when they suddenly stop behaving that way, perhaps so suddenly that it makes you think their behaviour wasn't genuine: *She can switch the charm off and on like a light.*
[*same as* **turn off**]

switch on
1 You **switch on** televisions and other electrical appliances when you make them begin working by pressing the switch that lets electricity flow to them: *She filled the kettle and switched it on.* ❑ *He climbed into the car and switched on the radio and the heater.* **2** You can say that someone **switches on** behaviour of a certain kind when they suddenly begin behaving that way, perhaps so suddenly that it makes you think their behaviour is not genuine: *You can tell she's bored rigid. She's never been able to switch on an expression of interest or enthusiasm like some can.*
[*same as* **turn on**]

switch over
1 When you are watching television, you **switch over** when you press a switch that allows you to watch a programme on a different channel: *Switch over to BBC1; 'One Foot in the Grave' is just coming on.* **2** You **switch over** from one thing to another when you begin to use or do the second thing instead of the first: *London switched over to the new system.* [*same as* **change over**]

switch round
You **switch** things **round** when you put each in a position that one of the others was in before: *Someone must have switched the bottles round.* [*same as* **swap round**]

swivel /ˈswɪvəl/: **swivels**, **swivelling** (*AmE* **swiveling**), **swivelled** (*AmE* **swiveled**)

swivel round
You **swivel round** when you quickly turn to face in the opposite direction: *She swivelled round to face me.* ❑ *She'd swivelled round in her chair.* [*same as* **swing round**]

swoop /swuːp/: **swoops**, **swooping**, **swooped**

swoop down
1 A bird **swoops down** when it flies suddenly down towards the ground: *One of our local bluetits swooped down upon a friend's Mercedes.* ❑ *We watched the hungry birds swooping down.* **2** You can say that a group of people **swoop down** when they suddenly approach and attack someone or something: *Police and customs men had swooped down on them as they tried to bring the drugs ashore.* [compare **pounce on**]

swop see **swap**

swot /swɒt/: **swots**, **swotting**, **swotted**

swot up *or* **swot up on** (*informal*)
You **swot up** a subject of study, or **swot up** on it, when you study it intensively, or intensively review what you have learned in preparation for an examination: *Paul spent the next few weeks swotting up on the relevant EC legislation.* [*same as* **mug up** (*informal*)]

syphon see **siphon**

t

tack /tak/: **tacks**, **tacking**, **tacked**

tack down
You **tack** something **down** when you fix it firmly to the floor or other surface using tacks or nails: *The carpet hadn't been tacked down properly.*

tack on
Something that **is tacked on** is added, perhaps as an afterthought, or to something that is already complete: *He tacked on tendentious continuations to things Raskolnikov said.* [*same as* **tag on**, **add on**]

tag /tag/: **tags**, **tagging**, **tagged**

tag along
Someone who **tags along** with you joins you or goes with you, especially when you have not asked them: *His little brother always tagged along when we went anywhere.*

tag on
Something that **is tagged on** is added, perhaps as an afterthought, or to something that is already complete: *The comment about costs was tagged on at the end of his letter.* [*same as* **tack on**, **add on**]

tail /teɪl/: **tails**, **tailing**, **tailed**

tail away see **tail off**

tail back
Traffic that **is tailing back** has formed a long queue that is moving slowly or waiting to move: *A huge queue of cars and lorries tailed back from the scene of the accident.* [compare **snarl up**]

• *noun* **tailback**: **tailbacks**: *a five-mile tailback on the M5.*

tail off *or* **tail away**
Something **tails off** when it gradually decreases in strength, intensity or value, especially before disappearing completely: *Acceleration only begins to tail off above 120mph.* ❑ *His voice tailed off and he sat down heavily.* ❑ *Initial enthusiasm tails off as the new aid becomes a routine element of lessons.* [*same as* **drop off**, **fade away**, **peter out**]

take /teɪk/: **takes**, **taking**, **took** /tʊk/, **taken**

take aback
Something that **takes** you **aback** surprises you greatly or shocks you: *She was clearly taken aback at this suggestion.* ❑ *They were taken aback as the huge hangar doors blew open.*

take after
You **take after** an older member of your family when you are similar to them in the way you look or behave: *My family say I take after my mother in that she could make do and be happy.* ❑ *She had a trace of dark hair on her pate, just to show she took after her parents.*

take against
You **take against** someone or something when you begin to dislike them, or decide you dislike them: *For some unknown reason, the dog seems to have taken against the new gardener.* [*opposite* **take to**]

take along

You **take** someone or something **along** when you take them with you: *She always takes at least one doll along with her wherever she goes.* [compare **go along, come along**]

take apart

1 You **take** something **apart** when you separate it into the different parts that it is made up of: *They had to take the engine apart to find the fault.* **2** (*informal*) To **take** someone or something **apart** is to defeat them convincingly or criticize them severely in an argument or fight: *Don't get into an argument with him because he'll take you apart.* [compare **tear apart**]

take aside

You **take** someone **aside** when you separate them from others they are with, in order to speak to them privately: *Try to take him aside and warn him not to say too much.* [compare **put aside, set aside**]

take away

1 You **take** something **away** when you remove it from where it was and take or put it somewhere else: *She took her hand away from Anna's mouth.* ❑ *The contractors take it away and dilute it before spreading it thinly on the soil.* ❑ *When the roof was taken away, ruin took over and spread throughout.* **2** To **take** something **away** is also permanently to remove it or make it disappear: *Work has taken away the identity we had before.* ❑ *They kill; they take away another's life.* ❑ *The guards at the airport took it away and ate it.* ❑ *Removal men came to take away the sets.* **3** Someone who **is taken away** is forced to leave with others, especially police officers: *'What is the charge? You have taken away innocent men.'* ❑ *They were taken away for questioning.* ❑ *The police would come and take me away.* ❑ *His father came and took him away to Hambury.* **4** You **take** something **away** when you ignore it or disregard it: *When you take away all the sociological claptrap, policing is all about dealing with folk.* **5** What you **take away** from an experience is what you learn from it, or what memories or impressions of it stay in your mind when it is over: *The abiding impression I'll take away from Namibia is the vastness and emptiness of the country.* **6** You **take** one number or amount from another when you find the difference between them by subtracting one from the other: *Taking 55 away from 102 leaves 47.* **7** To **take away** from something is to make it less important, impressive or valuable: *His dirty trainers rather took away from what was otherwise a smart and businesslike appearance.*

• *noun* **takeaway**: **takeaways**

1 A **takeaway** is a shop or restaurant that sells cooked food that you take home to eat: *an Indian takeaway.* **2** A **takeaway** is also a meal bought at such a shop or restaurant: *Do you fancy a takeaway?*

• *adjective* **takeaway**: *a takeaway pizza.*

take back

1 You **take** something **back** when you take it to where it was earlier: *You'll have to take that chair back into the house if it starts to rain.* **2** You **take back** something you have borrowed when you return it to the person who lent it to you: *'Oh no! I've forgotten to take my library books back!'* **3** You **take back** something you have bought when you return it to the shop and ask for a replacement, or for your money to be returned, because it is faulty or no longer suitable; the shop **takes** it **back** when they agree to give you a replacement or return your money: *If it isn't working properly you should take it back.* ❑ *You've obviously used it, so we can't take it back.* **4** You **take back** something you used to own or possess when you take possession of it again, perhaps using force: *Our mission* *was to take back from the Boche those few miles of battered ground.* [*same as* **regain** (*formal*)] **5** You **take** someone or something **back** when you take them with you when you leave: *She could not take him back to America with her.* ❑ *They took the duck back to the cabin.* **6** Something **takes** you **back** when it causes what happened or existed earlier to happen or exist again: *This week's rise takes many pensioners back to where they were 18 months ago.* ❑ *This took gold prices back to where they were the day before Iraqi tanks rolled into Kuwait.* **7** After ending your friendship or relationship with someone, you **take** them **back** when you agree to start up your friendship or relationship again: *Aunt Lucy would not have taken her back.* [*same as* **have back**] **8** You **take back** something you have said when you admit that you should not have said it and that it is not right or true: *'If you don't take that back, I'll smash your face!'* [*same as* **retract** (*formal*)] **9** You can say that something **takes** you **back** when it makes you remember or think about a past time or period: *Hearing that old recording again really takes me back.*

take down

1 You **take** something **down** when you move it from a higher position to a lower one: *He reached up and took it down.* **2** You **take down** something that is fixed to a wall or other vertical surface when you remove it: *The vines were taken down from their wires and their ends tied.* ❑ *Alan had decided to take down all the posters in his bedroom.* **3** You **take down** something that has been built when you separate it into the parts it has been built from: *The exhibition's being taken down today.* ❑ *It's time we took down the Christmas decorations.* [*same as* **dismantle** (*formal*); *opposite* **put up**] **4** You **take** something **down** when you make a written note of it: *The vehicle's details were taken down and reported back to Holbaek.* ❑ *She took down his words in her swift hand.* [*same as* **note down, jot down**] **5** You can use **take down** when talking about taking something or someone to any place at some distance from where you are: *He's setting up a golf course in Cornwall and he's taken Margaret and Suzie down there with him.* ❑ *Take this down to desk number twenty-three.* ❑ *We'll take you down to the town centre in the minibus.*

take for

1 You **take** one person or thing **for** another when you mistakenly identify one for the other: *He made a small, indefinite sound that could well have been taken for agreement.* **2** People often say 'what do you **take** me **for**?' in angry response to someone who has suggested they might behave foolishly or inappropriately: *'I would never hit a woman. What do you take me for?'*

take in

1 You **take** something or someone **in** when you take them with you when you enter a place: *He went into the study taking the case in with him.* **2** An establishment or organization **takes** someone **in** when it accepts or admits them as a guest or a member: *It's one of the few organizations that will take in homeless families and help them get back on their feet.* ❑ *She supplements her pension by taking in lodgers.* **3** You **take** something **in** when you understand, notice, observe or judge it: *I haven't had time to take everything in.* ❑ *You need to be highly intelligent to take in the situation instantaneously.* ❑ *They strolled around the gardens taking in the various delights on offer.* [compare **pick up**] **4** To **take in** something is to include it as a part of something larger: *This enlarged area now takes in much land amenable for agricultural purposes.* ❑ *Their area of responsibility takes in some of the city's most deprived estates.* **5** You **are taken in** by someone when you are fooled or deceived by them: *We were completely* *taken in by his appearance of friendly concern.* **6** You **take** something **in** when you visit it or go to see it, while staying in or touring a place: *Not surprisingly, they'll be taking in all the usual touristy sites, like the Parthenon.* **7** You **take** something **in** when you take it into your house from outside: *They make ideal houseplants if you take them in for the winter.* **8** Someone who **takes in** work such as washing earns money by doing other people's washing in their own home: *The inhabitants made a precarious living by taking in each other's washing.* **9** You use **take in** when talking about substances such as food, water and air that enter your body: *Plants take in carbon dioxide and give out oxygen.* **10** To **take in** a piece of clothing is to make it narrower by repositioning the joins at the edges: *The dress'll have to be shortened and taken in at the waist.* [*opposite* **let out**]

• *noun* **intake**

1 The **intake** in an establishment, especially a school or college, is the group or number of people who join it at a particular time: *The training course has just begun the autumn term with a new intake.* **2** A person's **intake** of food or drink is the amount they eat or drink: *An adequate intake of vitamins and minerals is essential.* **3** An **intake** of breath is the act of breathing in suddenly and so sharply that others hear it, especially as a result of surprise or shock: *His arm slackened with a painful intake of breath.*

take into

1 You **take** someone or something **into** a place when you take them with you when you enter: *The woman persuaded the kidnapper to let her take the child into a shop to get some baby food.* ❑ *Father would take us into Newcastle to buy Mama's perfume.* **2** To **take** something or someone **into** a particular state or condition is to cause them to be in that state or condition: *The story took her into an exotic, adult world.* **3** Substances such as food, drink and air **are taken into** your body when they enter it: *Worms are deposit feeders, taking mud into their guts and extracting nutrients from it.* **4** To **take** someone **into** an establishment or organization is to accept or admit them as a guest or member: *Some of those with the strongest objections were taken into the Catholic Church.*

take off

1 You **take off** a piece of clothing you are wearing when you remove it from your body: *The man had taken his shoes off and hung his feet over a chair.* ❑ *He knelt to take off the laced boots.* [*opposite* **put on**] **2** You can use **take off** in any of numerous ways which have the idea of removing something or making something disappear as part of their meaning: *Put the cloth on for the winter and take it off in summer.* ❑ *We can take the top off and feel the wind in our hair.* ❑ *That should take the strain off your back.* ❑ *That takes a load of pressure off me.* ❑ *Just take these other duties off my shoulders.* ❑ *Take off eye make-up gently with a cotton bud.* ❑ *The Captain had been either dismissed or taken off the case.* ❑ *They're taking Test cricket off TV in order to boost the radio audience.* [*opposite* **put on**] **3** An aeroplane or a bird **takes off** when it leaves the ground and begins flying: *It's not unusual to see pilots take off towards a heavy rain shower.* ❑ *We were supposed to take off for Malta twelve hours ago.* **4** Something that **takes off** suddenly or immediately becomes very successful or very popular: *The enterprise which had begun to take off in Napoleonic Paris had made enormous progress.* **5** You can also say that something **takes off** when it suddenly rises sharply to a very high level: *This is the unemployment rate which stops inflation taking off.* **6** You **take** your mind, eyes or attention **off** something when you think, look, or give your attention to, something else: *He just couldn't take his eyes off her.* ❑ *The accounts may take my mind off* *being cross with you.* ❑ *The Holbein case had taken the focus off the Canaletto and Zoffany.* **7** You **take** time **off** when you have a period not doing what you normally do, especially not working: *These jobs enable women to take time off to have children.* ❑ *He has elected to take 24 hours off.* [compare **take out**] **8** You **take off** when you begin a journey, or begin an activity of any kind: *They plan to take off in a camper van.* ❑ *Before you take off on your campaign, make sure you know you can meet voters' needs.* **9** (*informal*) You also **take off** when you leave: *He took off as soon as he saw the policeman heading towards him.* [compare **shoot off**] **10** You **take** someone **off** somewhere when you take them with you when you go there, perhaps suddenly or unexpectedly: *She had taken Maggie off to the sunshine.* **11** You **take** something **off** someone who owns or possesses it when you use force to take possession of it: *Peter came running to his Mum saying the bigger boys had taken his ball off him.* [*same as* **get off**] **12** (*informal*) You **take** someone **off** when you imitate the way they look or behave, especially in order to amuse others: *She's brilliant at taking off the boss; has us all in fits of laughter.* [*same as* **mimic**; compare **send up**] **13** You **take off** an amount when you reduce a total by that amount: *It's slightly damaged so we'll take 10% off the price.* [*same as* **subtract, deduct**; *opposite* **put on, add on**]

• *noun* **takeoff: takeoffs**

1 Takeoff is an aeroplane's rising into the sky and beginning to fly. **2** A **takeoff** of someone is an amusing imitation of the way they look or behave: *Will you do your takeoff of the bumbling old judge?*

take on

1 You **take** something **on** when you accept it as a job or responsibility: *He will perhaps set up home with someone else and take on a new job.* ❑ *There is the reluctance of central government to take on new expenditure.* ❑ *They will find it harder to take on large loans.* **2** Someone who **is taken on** is accepted as an employee or member: *The university was willing to take on an inspector.* ❑ *Clubs tended to take on large numbers of hopefuls at low rates.* **3** (*informal*) To **take** someone **on** is to challenge or fight them: *He had the courage to stand up to Dublin and take Dublin on.* ❑ *They voted to take on the powers of the Yugoslav assembly.* **4** Something that **takes on** a new or different quality begins to have that quality: *Any liberal democracy will eventually take on an expansionist line.* ❑ *The search for beauty seems to take on a different aspect.* ❑ *Faces took on a different expression.* ❑ *Free-market economics took on a different meaning last week.* **5** A vehicle **takes on** passengers or cargo when passengers join it or cargo is loaded on: *They stopped at Tarbert to take on water and fuel.*

take out

1 You **take** something **out** when you remove it from the place it was in, or from its container: *I take a handful out every day.* ❑ *Don't take everything out of the freezer yet.* ❑ *It will look better if we take out those awful shoulder pads.* ❑ *At this request, passengers would take small change out of pocket or handbag.* ❑ *He had taken out a little yellow fiddle and was warming up.* ❑ *Goldberg took out his polka-dotted handkerchief.* **2** You can use **take out** in any of numerous ways in which the idea of removing something or making it disappear is part of the meaning: *These gases have to be taken out before bottling.* ❑ *Prune when you see long growths taking the goodness out of the tree.* ❑ *Money would be taken out of the economy.* [*opposite* **put in**] **3** You **take** someone **out,** *eg* to a restaurant or cinema, when you take them there with you and pay for their entertainment, often as a way of forming a romantic relationship with them: *She had been willing to take her and her friends out for meals.* ❑ *He took her out; they fell in love and started to live together.* ❑ *Perhaps he would take the nurse out after he was home from hospital.* [compare **go out with**] **4** You often use **take out** when talking about formal or legal agreements in which money is paid: *Four million people are estimated to have taken out the new savings scheme.* ❑ *We will take out insurance against the repatriation of profits.* ❑ *Take out a subscription today and we'll enter you in our fabulous prize draw.* ❑ *Do you take out a new loan before the old one is paid off?* **5** You **take** time **out** when you spend time doing something different from what you normally do: *Ned was able to take a year out from his university course.* [compare **take off**] **6 a** (*slang*) To **take** someone **out** is to kill them: *There are rogue cops out there taking out IRA terrorists.* [*same as* **knock off** (*informal*), **bump off** (*informal*); compare **do in**] **b** Soldiers **take out** an enemy's vehicle, building or other location when they destroy it: *It'll be a night mission so we can take out the enemy positions under cover of darkness.*

take out of

1 (*informal*) You can say that something **takes** it **out of** you, or **takes** a lot **out of** you, when it makes you feel very tired: *I've only been out of prison three months. It takes it out of you.* ❑ *A long session of step aerobics can really take it out of you. Be careful you don't overdo it.* **2** Something **takes** you **out of** yourself when it makes you forget your problems or the difficult situation you are in: *You should go to the party. It'll take you out of yourself.*

take out on

You **take** your bad feelings **out** on someone when you release those feelings by unfairly behaving angrily towards someone who is not responsible for the way you feel: *Don't over-react; don't take it out on your children.*

take over

1 You **take over**, or **take** something **over**, when you gain control of something, or responsibility for something, in place of someone else, either by using force or authority, or when invited after someone else has finished: *The management committee will take over and run the whole operation.* ❑ *These are the contenders to take over leadership of the mainstream computer industry from IBM.* ❑ *I think Mary and Janice had better take over junior Biology.* ❑ *They called on Nu to take over as Prime Minister.* ❑ *They would take over some of the tasks now carried out by management.* ❑ *Whitehall has the power to take over the duties of local authorities.* ❑ *I gather you're taking over this case as well.* ❑ *They allowed the military to take over the railways to get supplies.* **2** You **take** someone **over** to a place when you take them with you when you go there: *We'll take him over to the embassy for a J-1 visa.* **3** Something that **takes over** becomes more important, powerful, influential or popular: *What happens to the diet when stress and temptation take over?* ❑ *She told herself not to let negative thoughts take over.* ❑ *This is the time for jazz to take over from calypso.* **4** You **take over** a place when you begin living or working there after someone else has left: *His son'll take over the farm when he retires.* **5** Something that **takes** you **over** occupies all your attention, energy or thoughts, perhaps making you behave strangely or unreasonably: *It started as a hobby, but now it's an obsession that's taken him over completely.* **6** You **take** time or trouble **over** something when you are careful to do it properly or well: *Look at all the trouble she's taken over dinner.*

• *noun* **takeover**: **takeovers**

1 A **takeover** occurs when one business company takes control of another by buying it: *The Hong Kong and Shanghai Bank will go ahead with its takeover of Midland Bank.* ❑ *A Swiss-based consultancy was about to launch a takeover bid.* **2** A **takeover** is the act of using force to gain control of a country or other territory: *the Communist takeover of the region.*

take round

Someone **takes** you **round** a place when they give you a tour of it, showing you all its interesting parts or features: *After lunch we were taken round the grounds.* [*same as* **show round**; compare **look round**]

take through

1 You **take** someone or something **through** when you take them with you when you go to a different room: *He took Sarah through to the parlour.* ❑ *Yanto took the empty glasses back through to the main bar.* **2** You **take** someone **through** a procedure when you show or explain it, or perform it with them, from beginning to end: *The film takes us through a day at WRAC headquarters.* **3** To **take** something **through** to a later or further stage is to cause it to progress to that stage: *This takes the patient through to the next potency level.* ❑ *A 4-3 victory takes the A's through to their second World Series in a row.* [compare **go through**]

take to

1 You **take to** someone or something when you begin to like them or decide you like them: *My mother never really took to her.* ❑ *I wondered how they would take to steak and kidney pud.* ❑ *No-one could have been better suited for the role, nor taken to it with more enthusiasm.* [*opposite* **take against**] **2** You **take to** something, or **take to** doing it, when you begin to do it as a regular habit or activity: *Henry had taken to aeronautics recently.* ❑ *A number of competitors have taken to slinging innuendos around.* **3 Take to** is sometimes used to refer to the action of someone who, suddenly or and with a definite purpose, goes to a particular place, often in order to escape from something or someone: *Her own son had taken to the hills.* ❑ *Severe flooding had forced the villagers to take to higher ground, salvaging what they could as they fled.*

take up

1 You **take** something or someone **up** when you take them with you when you go or move to a place or position that is, or is thought to be, higher than where you start from: *A new rail service was introduced that would take them up twice a week to Irvine.* ❑ *A van stood by to take the bottles up to the municipal bottle bank.* ❑ *The therapist supports the leg and takes it up gently.* ❑ *She took him up the front steps.* ❑ *The administrator took us up in a lift.* **2** (*formal*) You **take** something **up** when you lift it and begin to hold or carry it: *He had paused before taking up his pen.* ❑ *Disgust filled me whenever I took up a brush and shovel.* ❑ *He took the poker up and turned a log over.* [*same as* **pick up**] **3** You **take** something **up** when you start doing it as a regular activity, hobby or job: *You decided to take up floristry because you saw an advertisement.* ❑ *None of them had taken up smoking.* **4** You can also use **take up** when talking about states or conditions that are beginning to exist: *They have to complete such courses before taking up employment.* ❑ *It would be necessary for her to take up more permanent residence at the Lodge.* **5** Something **takes up** time, space or effort when it uses it or occupies it: *Sorting out the clothes took up literally half the visit.* ❑ *A great deal of time is taken up with swopping spies.* ❑ *Routine maintenance will continue to take up time.* ❑ *In a public place it will not take up any space.* ❑ *The greater part of the first volume is taken up with a narrative of past events.* **6** You **take up** a particular position or attitude when you adopt or assume it: *The group would dismount and take up their* *preliminary positions.* ❑ *Your opponent takes up a left fighting stance.* **7** You **take** something **up** when you discuss it or deal with it: *The honourable member for Stafford will take that up with his Conservative colleagues.* ❑ *I should indeed take the matter up with the Senate.* ❑ *The number of cases taken up by Amnesty now stands at over 42,000.* [see also **take up with**] **8** You **take up** something that is offered or is available when you accept it: *Theological colleges were eager to take up the new opportunities.* ❑ *'Do let's take up the offer'.* ❑ *Not every woman takes up that challenge.* ❑ *Twenty per cent of pensioners do not take up benefits they are entitled to.* **9** You **take up** something that has stopped, or that someone else has finished, when you continue it: *Peter Dew takes up the story.* **10** You **take up** something that is fixed to the floor or the ground when you detach it and lift it: *All the floorboards will have to be taken up, and the timbers treated.* ❑ *Leave the onions to dry off before taking them up and storing them.* **11** To **take up** a substance is to absorb it, especially from the ground or from a lower place: *With this system the tomato plants will take up essential minerals more readily.* [compare **take in**] **12** To **take up** something such as a dress or coat is to make it shorter by folding the bottom edge up and stitching it: *We'll have to take the curtains up about six inches.* [*opposite* **let down**; compare **take in**]

take up on
You **take** someone **up on** an offer they have made when you accept it: *'I am sorry, I won't be able to take you up on your offer.'*

take up with
You **take up with** someone when you begin to spend time with them and be their friend: *He's dropped out of college and taken up with some animal liberation group.* [see also **take up**]

talk /tɔːk/: talks, talking, talked

talk about
1 You **talk about** something when you discuss it: *She was unwilling to talk about her background and past.* ❑ *She explained why she couldn't talk about the Mills case at home.* ❑ *We have things to talk about.* **2** You **talk about** something, or **talk about** doing it, when you consider doing it: *We talked about it and decided we weren't ready.* ❑ *A weekend away was still talked about though not realized.* **3** People **talk about** you when they say unpleasant things about you or discuss your private affairs in an unpleasant way: *She remembered thinking how mean his mother was to talk about him.* ❑ *He was more talked about than if he'd been open.* [compare **talk of**]

talk around see talk round

talk at
Someone **talks at** you when they talk to you without ever pausing or letting you reply, perhaps because they think their own opinions are more important than anyone else's: *She has this habit of talking at you, not to you.*

talk away
Someone who **talks away** talks continuously for a long time: *There she was in the corner talking away as usual, ten to the dozen.*

talk back
Someone **talks back** to a person in authority when they answer them in a rude or disrespectful way: *Many of them now stand up and talk back to the managing director.* [*same as* **answer back**]

talk down
1 You **talk** something **down** when you criticize it or say that it's not very good: *They're fed up with the Labour Party's attempts to talk down and undermine the Health Service.* [*same as* **do down** (*informal*)] **2** You **talk down** someone who is speaking when you interrupt

them loudly or forcefully and force them to stop talking: *Mary made more than one attempt to object but each time was talked down by the overly-officious chairman.* [*same as* **shout down**]

talk down to

Someone **talks down to** you when they speak to you in a way that shows they think they are more important, experienced or intelligent than you: *They are fed up of being talked down to and dictated to.* [*same as* **patronize**]

talk into

You **talk** someone **into** something, or **talk** them **into** doing something, when you persuade them to do it: *They had to be talked into even showing up at all.* ❑ *I'm definitely not going, so don't try to talk me into it.* [*opposite* **talk out of**]

talk of

You **talk of** something when you speak about it or discuss it: *Would such a man talk about fairies like that?* ❑ *The new Tories talk about 'being on the side of the people'.* [*same as* **talk about**]

talk out

You **talk** something **out** when you discuss it in detail, and perhaps decide how to deal with it: *We've talked it out and come to the following conclusion.*

talk out of

You **talk** someone **out of** something, or **talk** them **out of** doing it, when you persuade them not to do it: *He threatened to stop eating but I talked him out of it.* [*opposite* **talk into**]

talk over

Two or more people **talk** something **over** when they discuss it: *I'll talk it all over with Alan.* ❑ *They'll be talking over old times in Santander this week.*

talk through

1 You **talk** something **through** when you discuss it in detail, and perhaps decide how to deal with it: *Theological issues like redemption and salvation have to be talked through carefully.* ❑ *I'm glad I talked that through with you.* **2** Someone **talks** you **through** something, either something that has happened or will happen, when they explain or describe it: *Don't worry, I'll talk you through it first before you actually have to do anything.*

talk to

1 You **talk to** someone when you have a conversation with them or address spoken words to them: *John is the only person I could talk to about it.* ❑ *She's better to talk to than write to.* ❑ *Cats like to be talked to.* ❑ *'How dare you talk to me like that!'* **2** You **talk to** someone who has done something wrong when you speak angrily to them: *The headmaster will have to talk to you if your behaviour doesn't show a marked improvement.*

• *noun* **talking-to**: *Dad gave us a real talking-to.*

talk with (*usually AmE*)

You **talk with** someone when you have a conversation with them: *The field-worker was talking with two plain-clothes men.* ❑ *Daggy comes over and talks with me and Marie a bit.*

tamp /tamp/: tamps, tamping, tamped

tamp down

To **tamp** something **down** is to press or flatten it with repeated downward blows: *The hardcore is tamped down with a special machine before the tarmac is laid.*

tamper /'tampə(r)/: tampers, tampering, tampered

tamper with

Someone who **tampers with** something touches or handles it without pemission, causing disturbance or damage: *There's been a strong temptation to tamper with it.* ❑ *You must not remove or tamper with the* *labels.* [*same as* **mess with** (*informal*), **meddle with**]

tangle /'taŋgəl/: **tangles**, **tangling**, **tangled**

tangle up
1 Something such as a rope **is tangled up** when it is twisted or knotted untidily and is difficult to untie or straighten; something that **is tangled up** is twisted or knotted in a rope and is difficult to get free: *Each released dog shows a marked enthusiasm for getting tangled up again.* ❑ *The fairy lights were tangled up with old pieces of tinsel and ribbon.* **2** You can also say that something **is tangled up** when there are problems or difficulties involved in it: *The discussions had got tangled up with arguments over land ownership.*

tangle with (*informal*)
You **tangle with** someone when you involve yourself in a fight or other conflict with them: *You had to be able to tangle with fairly tough and earthy people.* ❑ *I strongly advise you not to tangle with Jake.* [*same as* **mess with** (*informal*)]

tank /taŋk/: **tanks**, **tanking**, **tanked**

tank up (*informal*)
Someone who **is tanked up** has drunk a lot of alcohol and is very drunk: *He'd sometimes get tanked up before a performance. Then I just couldn't work with him.*

tap /tap/: **taps**, **tapping**, **tapped**

tap for (*informal*)
You **tap** someone **for** something when you obtain it from them by asking or persuading them: *He's always tapping me for money.* [compare **sponge off**, **do out of**]

tap in
1 You **tap in** something such as a nail when you cause it to go into a surface by hitting it with repeated soft blows: *Tap in the dowels and then screw the two pieces together.* **2** You **tap in** information when you enter it into a computer by typing: *She tapped in the password and waited.* [*same as* **key in**]

tap into
To **tap into** a store or supply of something is to gain access to it: *The smaller machines tap into the central database.* ❑ *They seemed designed to tap into an audience's desire to atone.* ❑ *You're tapping into a person's past.*

tap out
You **tap out** sounds when you make them with repeated light blows: *They tapped out messages on the hot water pipes.*

tape /teɪp/: **tapes**, **taping**, **taped**

tape up
You **tape** something **up** when you close or seal it by sticking tape over it: *The police taped up the door to prevent anyone getting in.*

taper /'teɪpə(r)/: **tapers**, **tapering**, **tapered**

taper off
Something **tapers off** when the level or amount of it gradually lowers or decreases, perhaps until it disappears completely: *The rise in the unemployment rate has tapered off in the last couple of months.* [*same as* **fall off**, **die out**, **fade away**]

tart /tɑːt/: **tarts**, **tarting**, **tarted**

tart up (*informal*)
1 Someone who **tarts** themselves **up** makes themselves smart and attractive, perhaps in a rather obvious or vulgar way: *She'd tarted herself up in a ghastly pink dress and high heels.* [*same as* **doll up** (*informal*)] **2** To **tart** a place **up** is to make it look smart and attractive, perhaps in rather an obvious or vulgar way: *They've tarted the place up a bit since we were here last.* [*same as* **do up**]

taste /teɪst/: **tastes**, **tasting**, **tasted**

taste of
To **taste of** something is to have the flavour of it: *This tea tastes of soap!* [compare **savour of**]

team /tiːm/: **teams**, **teaming**, **teamed**

team up
Two or more people **team up** when they form a team or partnership, ready to work together: *Peter Reid is about to become a vital part of the new Manchester City regime by teaming up again with Howard Kendall.*

tear /tɛə(r)/: **tears**, **tearing**, **tore** /tɔː(r)/, **torn** /tɔːn/

tear apart
1 To **tear** something **apart** is to destroy it by violently pulling pieces off it: *Once they'd brought the animal down, the dogs tore it apart within seconds.* **2** To **tear** a place **apart** is to violently disarrange or break the furniture and other things in it: *Even though they tore the place apart, they found nothing incriminating.* **3** Someone who **is torn apart** suffers severe mental or emotional pain: *You had to have suffered tremendously, been torn apart, come close to death.* **4** An event or situation **tears** people **apart** when it causes violent disagreements or conflicts between them: *British athletics will be torn apart by a £7 million four-year contract which the sport is about to sign with ITV.*

tear at
To **tear at** something is to violently attack it with the intention of pulling pieces off it: *She is set upon by hunting dogs who tear at her blood-red head gear.*

tear away
1 You **tear** someone **away** from a place or an activity when you force them to leave it and come away with you: *She tore herself away to hang the Do Not Disturb sign on the door.* **2** To **tear** something **away** is violently to pull it away from what it is attached to: *The falling door tore the frame away.*
• *noun* **tearaway**: **tearaways**
(informal, old)
A **tearaway** is a young person who behaves in a wild, perhaps violent way: *Past attempts to stop the tearaways have failed.*

tear between
You **are torn between** two or more choices or possibilities when you find it difficult or impossible to make a decision: *The horse will be in a state of confusion, torn between two or more courses of action.*

tear down
1 To **tear down** buildings or other structures is to destroy or demolish them: *We can turn our backs on the divisions of the past, tear down the barriers that divide us.* **2** To **tear down** something that is fixed to a wall, or fixed to something above you, is to remove it by violently pulling it: *They tore down pictures of President Ceausescu.* [*same as* **pull down**]

tear into (*informal*)
Someone **tears into** you when they attack you with angry words of blame or criticism: *I called him into my office and really tore into him.*

tear off
1 You **tear off** clothes you are wearing when you remove them quickly and roughly or violently: *One of the Americans tore off his fur hat and screamed.* **2** To **tear** something **off** is to remove it from the thing it is attached to by violent pulling: *Try to pull it apart, tear bits off it.* ❑ *They were tearing off sections of print-out as it came tumbling forth.* **3** (*informal*) You **tear off** when you leave in a hurry: *Gordon always seems to be tearing off to some high-powered meeting or other.* [*same as* **dash off**; compare **clear off**]

tear out
To **tear** something **out**, especially a page from a book, is to detach or separate it by violent pulling: *After learning the poem by heart, he would tear out the page.*

tear up
1 To **tear up** paper or cloth is to reduce it to small pieces by tearing it with your hands: *The card came the next morning. My immediate reaction was to tear it up.* ❑ *Have a sheet of paper that you can tear up to make the scene start with a dramatic focus.* [*same as* **rip up**] **2** A place or area **is torn up** when it is badly damaged: *They are completely tearing up the whole site.*

tease /tiːz/: teases, teasing, teased

tease out
You **tease** something **out** when, gradually or with great care or effort, you discover, reveal or separate it: *She listened to the story and teased out the relevant details.* ❑ *The fringes of the carpet had been teased out so that the individual strands could be seen.*

tee /tiː/: tees, teeing, teed

tee off
Golfers **tee off** when they play the first shot in a game of golf: *He watched the first few matches tee off.*

tee up
A golfer **tees up** when he or she places the ball on a tiny wooden or plastic stand stuck in the ground, ready to hit it at the beginning of each hole in a game of golf: *Now Woosnam's teeing up for the vital eighteenth hole.*

teem /tiːm/: teems, teeming, teemed

teem down
Rain **teems down** when it falls very heavily: *They struggled to put up the tents as the rain teemed down.* [*same as* **pour down, bucket down** (*informal*)]

tell /tɛl/: tells, telling, told /tould/

tell about
To **tell** someone **about** something is to give or reveal information about it to them: *I'll just ring my mother and tell her about it.* ❑ *I wish you'd tell me more about this Zbigniew Nowak.* ❑ *Libet's experiments tell us something interesting about the brain.*

tell against
Facts or circumstances **tell against** someone when they make that person less likely to succeed: *His lack of experience told against him at this more demanding level.* [*same as* **go against, count against, weigh against**]

tell apart
You can **tell** similar people or things **apart** when you can identify which is which, not mistaking one for the other: *The different works are not always easy to tell apart.* [compare **tell from**]

tell from
You can **tell** one person or thing **from** another when you can identify which is which, not mistaking one for the other: *I'm no expert. I can't tell one red wine from another.* [compare **tell apart**]

tell off
Someone who **tells** you **off** speaks to you angrily because you have done something wrong: *His mum told him off for being such a cheat.* ❑ *He is, in effect, told off by Maeve Binchy.*
• *noun* **telling-off**: **tellings-off**: *She'd had a telling-off for leaving the gate open.*

tell on
You **tell on** someone who has done something wrong when you tell someone in authority about it: *Please don't tell on me; I'll do anything you say.* [*same as* **grass on** (*informal*), **split on** (*informal*)]

tempt /tɛmpt/: tempts, tempting, tempted

tempt into
You **are tempted into** something, or **tempted into** doing it, when you are persuaded to have or do it by the benefit or advantage it would bring you: *Tyson and Bruno will be tempted into profitable confrontation.*

tend /tɛnd/: **tends**, **tending**, **tended**

tend towards
1 You **tend towards** something when you favour or support it in preference to other things: *Young voters tended towards the tabloid press and Radios 1 and 2.* **2** You can also use **tend towards** to say that someone or something has qualities of one particular kind rather than another: *She has a conversational style that tends towards the monologue.* [*same as* **lean towards**]

tense /tɛns/: **tenses**, **tensing**, **tensed**

tense up
1 You **tense up** when the muscles in your body become uncomfortably stiff, *eg* because you have been doing too much exercise: *His neck was stiff and his back had tensed up.* **2** You also **tense up** when you become nervous or tense: *She tensed up as the dentist approached with the drill.*

thaw /θɔː/: **thaws**, **thawing**, **thawed**

thaw out
1 Something that is frozen **thaws out** when warmth or heat causes it to come out of its frozen state: *Stand the gateau in a warm place until it's thawed out.* [*same as* **defrost**] **2** You can also say that you **thaw out** when you become warm again, after being uncomfortably cold: *As my fingers thawed out and the blood began to flow, they tingled.*

thin /θɪn/: **thins**, **thinning**, **thinned**

thin down
You **thin down** a liquid when you make it less thick or dense, *eg* by adding water: *If necessary, acrylics can be thinned down with water.*

thin out
You **thin out** things that are grouped together when you remove some, or move them all further apart, so that there is more space between each: *Thin the young plants out to about 3 inches apart.*

think /θɪŋk/: **thinks**, **thinking**, **thought** /θɔːt/

think about
1 You **are thinking about** something when it is in your mind or occupying your thoughts: *I think about the years that passed.* ❑ *We encourage them to think about their future.* **2** You can also say that you **are thinking about** something, or **thinking about** doing it, when you are trying to decide whether or not to have or do it: *We can think about rescheduling another programme.* ❑ *To think about reform is to think about its consequences.*

think ahead
You **think ahead** when you consider what will happen in the future and usually make plans for dealing successfully with it: *This is caused by poor basic training and not thinking ahead.* ❑ *You should try to think ahead to your financial future.*

think back
You **think back** when you make an effort to remember something in the past: *I look at the glass and think back to the work and the mistakes I've made.* ❑ *She thought for a few seconds, thinking back to the Thursday of the fire.* [compare **look back, hark back to**]

think of
1 You can say that you **are thinking of** something, or **thinking of** doing it, when you are trying to decide whether or not to have or do it: *Don't worry; I wasn't thinking of messing around with*

him. ❑ *He's seriously thinking of accepting the offer.* **2** You can **think of** things that you know, or once knew, when you can remember them or bring them into your mind: *I think of what it was like after the War.* ❑ *I can only think of two times he has watched me doing that.* **3** People often use **think of** when talking about opinions, and say they **think** a lot **of** things they like, and don't **think** much **of** things they don't like: *It would be unwise even to think of him as a gentleman.* ❑ *What do we all think of yesterday's historic decision?* ❑ *I didn't think much of his speech.* **4** You **think of** other people when your thoughts are occupied by concern for their health, happiness or needs: *You know Gran always thinks of others before herself.* **5** You **think of** something when you discover or invent it in your mind: *The solution was so easy I wished I had thought of it myself.* ❑ *I thought of the following stratagem to bring him within range.* **6** You can say that you would not **think of** something, or would never **think of** it, as a way of stating firmly that you would not allow it or do it: *I would never think of asking him to lend me the money.*

think out

You **think** something **out** when you plan each stage of it before you do it: *He has to think out what to do next.*

think over

You **think** something **over** when you consider it carefully in order to reach an opinion or decision: *Can you give me a couple of days to think it over?* ❑ *Once he'd thought it over, he decided it wasn't such a good idea after all.*

think through

You **think** something **through** when you consider all its aspects, or all its possible effects or consequences: *You owe it to yourself to think all the implications through.* ❑ *He tried to think it through properly.* ❑ *Smokey thinks through the problems of modern love.*

think up

You **think** something **up** when you invent or create it in your mind: *It's time to start thinking up new ideas.* ❑ *Thinking up suitable costumes kept the ladies occupied for weeks beforehand.*

thirst /θɜːst/: thirsts, thirsting, thirsted

thirst for

You can say that you **thirst for** something when you want or desire it very much: *Children all around him were thirsting for education.* [*same as* **hunger for**]

thrash /θraʃ/: thrashes, thrashing, thrashed

thrash about

Someone who **thrashes about** violently moves their arms or legs around in different directions: *I threw myself in the middle of the room, screaming and roaring and thrashing about.*

thrash out

People **thrash out** a difficulty or problem when they discuss it thoroughly in order to reach a solution or decision: *This is where Shankly and his managerial descendants thrashed out every set piece.* [compare **work out**]

throttle /ˈθrɒtəl/: throttles, throttling, throttled

throttle back *or* throttle down

The driver of a vehicle or, more usually, the pilot of an aircraft, **throttles back** or **throttles down** when he or she uses the controls to make the vehicle or aircraft go slower: *When you throttle back it doesn't half make the old adrenalin start flowing.*

through see panel on next page

through-put /ˈθruːput/ see **put through**

throw /θrou/: **throws**, **throwing**, **threw** /θruː/: **thrown**

throw about *or* throw around

1 You **throw** things **about**, or **throw** them **around**, when you throw them violently in all directions, or playfully throw them to one person who throws them to another in turn: *The political divisions of the 60s can be sorted out by Kevin Costner throwing a baseball around with his ghost dad.* **2** Someone who **throws** money **about**, or **throws** it **around**, spends large amounts of it foolishly: *The way he throws cash around, you'd think he'd won the lottery.*

through /θruː/

Through is an adverb and a preposition. **Through** has various meanings when it is used in combination with verbs. The basic meaning refers to movement that goes in at one side of something and out at the other side, so that when you **walk through** the park you make your way from one side of it to the other.

1 MOVEMENT OR PROGRESS FROM ONE SIDE TO THE OTHER
There are many phrasal verbs using **through** in its basic sense of movement or progress from one side of something to the other. These include **pass through, amble through, whizz through, dart through** and **mosey through.**

2 PASSING FROM ONE SIDE TO THE OTHER OF A SOLID OBJECT OR BARRIER
This sense also refers to movement from one side to the other but is used more specifically to refer to movement from one side to the other of a barrier or solid object. For example, you **cut through** something when you use a knife or other sharp implement to make a cut that separates it into two or more parts; the sun **breaks through** the clouds when it suddenly appears from behind the clouds that have hidden it until then; and a liquid **soaks through** something when it goes in one side and comes out at the other. Some phrasal verbs with this sense have a metaphorical meaning. For example, you **see through** someone else's attempts to hide their real intentions when you aren't deceived by them.

3 DOING SOMETHING THROUGHLY OR PROPERLY
Through is also used in many combinations to show that something is done thoroughly. For example, you **think** something **through** when you think about it very carefully and logically; you **heat** cold food **through** when you heat it so that it becomes throughly warm or hot; and, you **sift through** a large number of things when you examine each one individually, removing the ones that you want and discarding the ones that you don't.

4 ACCOMPLISHING OR COMPLETING
Through used in this sense suggests that something, usually something that involves a struggle or some degree of difficulty, is completed or ends successfully. For example, you **see** something **through** when you continue with it until it is completed, even though it may be difficult and unpleasant; you **carry through** a plan when you manage to put it into practice; and, someone who has been very ill **pulls through** when they recover. Something **sees** you **through,** or **carries** you **through** a time of difficulty or shortage when it enables you to survive or endure during that period. You **wade through** a large amount of work when you work until you manage to finish it; and, you **work through** a problem when you manage to solve it in stages. You **follow through** a series of actions or movements when you perform the action or movement that makes the series complete.

5 LOOKING AT OR READING
Through as a preposition is often combined with verbs to indicate that something is looked at, examined or read from the beginning to the end. For example you **leaf through** or **glance through** a book or magazine when you turn the pages quickly, looking briefly at each one.
Through is also used in the idiomatic phrasal verb **fall through** meaning to fail or fail to happen.

throw aside

You **throw** something **aside** when you dismiss or reject it: *Throwing aside her inhibitions, she stood up and sang.*

throw away

1 You **throw away** something you no longer want or need when you get rid of it, *eg* by putting it in a bin: *The American family was throwing away an average of 750 cans a year.* ❑ *Throw that old anorak away immediately.* **2** You **throw away** something such as a chance you are given, or an ability you have, when you fail to make proper use of it and waste it: *They didn't expect their rivals to throw their lead away in such a foolish manner.*

• *adjective* **throwaway**

1 A **throwaway** product is designed to be thrown away after it has been used once or a few times: *It's one of these throwaway cameras that you only use once.* **2** A **throwaway** remark is one made casually, without being considered or planned beforehand: *She'd found out about it from a throwaway remark made by one of his colleagues.*

throw back

1 You **throw** something **back** when you return it to someone, or to where it was before, by throwing it or roughly passing it: *I swish the weed in a bucketful of pondwater then throw the water back.* **2** You **throw back** a cover when you remove it by pulling sharply or violently, revealing what is underneath: *Throw back the quilt and move onto your side.* ❑ *Julie threw back the cellar hatch and came hurtling forth.* **3** You **throw back** your head or your arms when you move them backwards sharply or violently, *eg* when laughing or expressing surprise: *His head is thrown back as he yells the words aloud.* **4** To **throw back** light, heat, sound or other energy or force is to reflect it: *Light from the object is thrown back onto the camera lens.* **5** You **throw back** a drink when you drink it quickly, especially in one gulp: *Having first thrown back a large whisky, he began to talk in an urgent undertone.* [*same as* **knock back** (*informal*)]

• *noun* **throwback**: **throwbacks**

You can refer to a person or animal as a **throwback** when they are like the people or animals that were their early ancestors, rather than being like their parents: *It seems to be a sort of throwback to prehistoric times.*

throw back at

You **throw back at** someone something they did wrong in the past when you remind them of it, as a way of attacking them or hurting them: *He'll always find some way of throwing back at you anything that he perceives as an insult.*

throw down

1 You **throw down** something you are holding when you throw it to or towards the ground, or let it fall heavily: *Daddy was up on the roof of the Landrover throwing bikes down.* ❑ *The wind lifted us up and threw us back down again.* **2** You **throw** something **down** when you eat or drink it hurriedly: *Throwing down the whisky with a shudder, she switches off the bedside lamp.* **3** You **throw** yourself **down** when, with a single movement, you move your body onto the ground or another lower surface: *He throws himself down on the bed.* **4** You can say that soldiers **throw down** their arms when they surrender: *When they saw the size of the force ranged against them they threw down their arms and surrendered.*

throw in

1 Something that **is thrown in** is included or added as an extra or bonus: *We're selling some of the horses and cows and we're quite willing to throw in the sheep.* **2** You **throw in** a comment when you add it, especially casually: *She was babbling on, with her husband throwing in the occasional remark whenever she paused for breath.* **3** When someone is arrested and put in a prison cell, you can say that they **are thrown in** prison: *I would throw them all into jail and get them off the streets.*

throw into

1 You **throw** yourself **into** a task or activity when you do it with great energy or enthusiasm: *Since the divorce, I've thrown myself into my job.* **2** You **throw** money or other resource **into** a project when you spend it in large amounts on that project: *They'd thrown all their energies, and their cash, into the venture.* **3** To **throw** something **into** a state or condition is suddenly or unexpectedly to cause it to be in that state or condition: *Three middle-aged couples are thrown into a frenzy.* **4** When someone is arrested and put into a prison cell, you can say that they **are thrown into** prison: *It has been suggested that he was thrown into debtor's prison.*

throw off

1 You **throw off** clothes when you remove them hurriedly or with sudden rough movements: *He wanted to throw off his T-shirt and jeans, crawl under the covers and go to sleep.* ❑ *She threw off the covers and swung her feet to the floor.* **2** You **throw off** something that is preventing movement or progress when you free yourself of it: *Will the honourable gentleman throw off the veto of his Minister of State and have the courage to meet with us?* **3** Something that **throws off** heat, light or other energy produces or releases it, especially in large quantities: *Tremendous heat was being thrown off by burning timbers.* [compare **throw out, give off**] **4** Something that **throws** you **off** disturbs or upsets you and interferes with your ability to do something properly or accurately, and causes you to make a mistake: *Her body spun in the opposite direction, throwing her aim off completely.*

throw on

1 You **throw on** clothes when you dress yourself hurriedly or with sudden rough movements: *I threw my coat on over my nightdress.* **2** You **throw** yourself **on** something when you move your body onto it with a sudden rushing movement: *He threw himself on the bed with his head on my stomach.* ❑ *Without thinking, she had thrown herself on the screaming child to smother the flames with her body.* **3** To **throw** light **on** something is to reveal something about it, making it easier to understand; to **throw** doubt or suspicion **on** something is to cause people to have doubts or suspicions about it: *Such devices throw light on the character being played.* ❑ *Doubt was thrown on his claims when no-one managed to duplicate the experiment.*

throw out

1 You **throw out** something you no longer want or need when you get rid of it, *eg* by putting it in a bin: *If an attractive chair gets damaged, don't throw it out.* **2** Someone who **is thrown out** of a place or job is forced to leave it: *He was thrown out of hospital only two days after a gall bladder operation.* ❑ *He was thrown out of the choir for setting off a firework during rehearsals.* **3** You **throw out** something such as a proposal or suggestion when you dismiss or reject it: *A deal struck by the leaders was thrown out by the Reform Alliance's members.* **4** Something **throws out** light, heat or other energy when it produces or releases it: *The heat thrown out by such an explosion can be felt up to five miles away.* [compare **throw off, give off**] **5** You **throw out** an arm or a leg when you push it out away from your body with a sudden or violent movement: *Throwing her arms out to the side, she succeeded in wedging herself between the rocks.* **6** People **throw out** things such as ideas or proposals when they express them casually, as they enter their minds: *Chandler threw out the suggestion that there may have been some dirty dealings.*

throw over

Someone who **throws over** their boyfriend or girlfriend ends their relationship with them: *She became suicidal when her boyfriend threw her over for another girl.*

throw overboard

1 Someone on a ship **throws** something **overboard** when they throw it into the water: *A corked bottle, attached to a line, was thrown overboard and allowed to drift.* **2** You can also say that something **is thrown overboard** when it is dismissed or rejected completely: *The old system of division of labour is thrown overboard.* ❑ *They have already thrown the first proposition overboard.*

throw together

1 You **throw** something **together** when you prepare or create it hurriedly and roughly: *There was a twenty-six-day break in which he threw together a small book.* ❑ *Her outfit looked as if it had been thrown together, but was this intentional?* [compare **cobble together**] **2** People who **are thrown together** by events or circumstances are forced to meet each other as a result of them and often go on to develop a friendship or relationship with each other: *Noreen was more and more thrown together with him.* ❑ *families are thrown together by marriage or accident.*

throw up

1 To **throw up** something such as dust or dirt is to cause it to rise into the air: *Blood mingled with the dust thrown up by the battle.* **2** (*informal*) Someone **throws up** when they force the contents of their stomach out through their mouth: *Not unless they think a client's about to throw up over the upholstery.* [*same as* **be sick, vomit**] **3** You **throw** something **up**, especially your job, when you stop doing it or you give it up: *You can't just throw up your job and go off without telling anyone where you're going.* **4** To **throw up** things such as problems or ideas is to create them or produce them: *No amount of lonely pacing could throw up any alternative in his mind.* ❑ *They deal as effectively as possible with whatever problems these casual encounters throw up.*

thrust /θrʌst/: thrusts, thrusting, thrust

thrust upon (*formal*)

You have something such as a task or responsibility **thrust upon** you, when you are forced to do it or deal with it: *After my father died, heavy responsibility was thrust upon us older children.* ❑ *People need to know what their colleagues are doing, without having it distractedly thrust upon their attention.*

thumb /θʌm/: thumbs, thumbing, thumbed

thumb through

You **thumb through** something such as a book when you turn the pages quickly, briefly glancing at the contents: *Thumbing through an old copy of 'Cosmopolitan', I found this article on women in the church.* [*same as* **flick through, skim through**]

thump /θʌmp/: thumps, thumping, thumped

thump out

1 Someone **thumps out** a tune when they play it loudly by pressing hard on the keys or strings of their instrument: *He puts so much into thumping out a rhythm that the sweat drips from the end of his guitar.* **2** Things such as opinions **are thumped out** when they are stated firmly or aggressively: *She thumped out what her policy objectives were at every opportunity, whether people were prepared to listen or not.*

tick /tɪk/: ticks, ticking, ticked

tick away

1 You can use **tick away** to describe the continuous ticking sound made by a clock or watch: *A collection of the most curious-looking clocks ticked away merrily on the mantelpiece.* **2** Time **ticks away** when it passes, especially when it seems to pass too quickly: *The minutes ticked away and she felt her palms grow damp and her heart begin to thump.* [*same as* **tick by**]

tick by

Time **ticks by** when it passes, especially when it seems to pass too quickly: *As the seconds ticked by, the fear of being grabbed started to well up.* ❑ *Even in the capital, life ticked by with the rhythm of the rice-growing cycle.*

tick off

1 You **tick off** an item on a list when you write a mark next to it, to show that it has been dealt with: *She should have ticked off Miss Vine's name on her list.* **2** (*informal*) Someone **ticks** you **off** when they speak angrily to you because you have done something wrong: *His aunt ticked him off for being rude to Sophia.*

• *adjective (informal)* **ticked off**
Someone who is **ticked off** is angry or irritated: *Gerry was pretty ticked off when you didn't turn up.*

• *noun* **ticking-off: tickings-off**
Someone who gives you a **ticking-off** speaks angrily to you because you have done something wrong: *The policeman gave me a ticking-off for not indicating that I was going to turn left.*

tick over

1 A vehicle's engine **ticks over** when it runs at its steady minimum rate while the vehicle is not moving: *Sleep is not a period when the body is marking time and just ticking over.* **2** You can say that work, or a business, **is ticking over** when progress is slow but steady or regular: *The Christmas period kept stores ticking over.*

tide /taɪd/: tides, tiding, tided

tide over

Something that **tides** someone **over** allows them to survive a brief or temporary period of difficulty: *She gave us enough money to tide us over until I got paid.* [*same as* **see through, get through**]

tidy /ˈtaɪdɪ/: tidies, tidying, tidied

tidy away

You **tidy** things **away** when you store them away somewhere, leaving the place they were in before in a tidy state: *Remember to tidy away all those toys before you go to bed.*

tidy out

You **tidy out** something such as a room or a cupboard when you put the things in it into a neat and tidy order, and throw away the things you no longer want or need: *I found his letters when I was tidying out the desk.*

tidy up

1 You **tidy** something **up** when you arrange the things in it in a neat and tidy order; you can also say that you **tidy up**: *We tidied up and I gave her a hug.* **2** You **tidy** yourself **up** when you make yourself look neat and smart: *They tidied him up to his satisfaction.* ❑ *I had my hair cut, to tidy it up.* **3** You also **tidy** something **up** when you satisfactorily complete what was left unfinished or undone: *The budget plan will tidy up your current financial position.* ❑ *We used the editing features to tidy it up.*

tie /taɪ/: ties, tying, tied

tie back

You **tie** something **back** when you draw it away from the front or middle of something and fasten it so that it stays away: *She had beautiful long fair hair tied back from the brow.*

tie down

1 You can use **tie down** to talk about limits or restrictions: *It's not easy to get away for a holiday. I feel more tied down than ever before.* ❑ *They* *originate from a broadly defined area but cannot be tied down to a specific village or town.* **2** You **tie** something **down** when you fasten it to the floor or a surface with ropes or straps: *The patient was tied down so that he couldn't struggle during the treatment.* [*same as* **lash down**] **3** Soldiers are **tied down** when their enemy prevents them from making progress and forces them to stay in one place: *Their brigade was tied down by Serb artillery.*

tie in with

One thing **is tied in with** another when it is suitably or properly similar to it or connected with it: *It ties in with her comments on child abuse.* [*same as* **fit in with**]

tie up

1 You **tie** something **up** when you wrap string round it to fasten it or make it secure: *Tie it up as close to the fingers as you can.* **2** An animal that **is tied up** is fastened by rope to a post or other fixture to prevent it from moving or escaping; a person who **is tied up** has had their arms or legs, or both, tied together to prevent them from moving or escaping: *The four youths had tied up a fourteen-year-old boy.* **3** (*informal*) Something that **is tied up** is being used or occupied, and is therefore not available for any other purpose or for anyone else to use: *Parent companies have their capital tied up in idle stocks.* ❑ *You have to be prepared to tie up £1000 for at least two years.* **4** (*informal*) You can say that you **are tied up** when you are busy with something and not available to do something else: *Mr Saunders is tied up until late afternoon, but he could probably fit you in tomorrow sometime.* **5** (*informal*) To **tie** something **up** is to settle or finish it, *eg* by making decisions or completing what was previously left undone: *We still have to tie up a few minor details, but the contract will almost certainly go ahead.* [compare **wind up, wrap up** (*informal*)] **6** You **tie up** your shoelaces when you tie them in a bow in order to fasten your shoes. **7** A boat that **is tied up** is tied to a post or other fixture, *eg* in a harbour. **8** One thing **is tied up** with another when it is closely connected or related to it: *The crisis in Asia would become tied up with the course of events in Europe.*

tighten /'taɪtən/: tightens, tightening, tightened

tighten up

1 You **tighten up** something such as a nut on a bolt when you make it tighter: *You pull the line above the hook to tighten it up.* **2** To **tighten up** things such as rules or laws is to make them stricter: *This has caused many local authorities to tighten up their procedures.* **3** Muscles **tighten up** when they become stiff or tense: *His chest tightened up making breathing difficult.* **4** To **tighten** something **up** is also to make it operate more efficiently or effectively: *The Welsh team has worked hard to tighten up their pack.*

tinker /'tɪŋkə(r)/: tinkers, tinkering, tinkered

tinker about *or* tinker around

You **tinker about** or **tinker around** when you occupy yourself with small, unimportant tasks: *Will's happiest when he's tinkering about in the garage.*

tinker with

You **tinker with** something when you make slight changes intended to improve it, but which perhaps result in harm or damage: *The temptation to tinker with the existing legislation proved to be overwhelming.* [compare **tamper with**]

tip /tɪp/: tips, tipping, tipped

tip off (*informal*)

You **tip** someone **off** when you warn them that something secret is going to happen, or tell them that it has

happened: *The press had been tipped off that the Health Secretary was going to make an announcement.*
• *noun* **tip-off**: **tip-offs**: *The letter purported to be a public-spirited tip-off from a concerned MP.*

tip over
You **tip** something **over** when you cause it to fall onto its side or turn upside down: *The big man stood up, tipping his chair over.*

tip up
You **tip up** a container when you turn it upside down so that its contents pour or spill out: *Tipping the jar up, he poured the last of the honey into his mouth.*

tire /taɪə(r)/: **tires**, **tiring**, **tired**

tire of
You **tire of** something when you lose interest in it and become bored by it: *Mr Gorbachev never tires of reminding us of that fact.* ❑ *We met Europeans who were tiring of conventional holidays.*

tire out
Something that **tires** you **out** exhausts you or makes you very tired: *Now that she's getting on in years, a couple of hours with the grandchildren tires her out.* [*same as* **wear out**]

to see panel on next page

toddle /'tɒdəl/: **toddles**, **toddling**, **toddled**

toddle along (*informal*)
1 You can say that you **toddle along** when you leave or go away: *We'd better be toddling along soon or we'll be late for the train.* **2** You can also say that a person, especially an elderly person, **toddles along** when they make their way on foot to a place, especially when they walk slowly or with some difficulty: *Each morning, she toddles along to the village shop to make her modest purchases.*

tog /tɒg/: **togs**, **togging**, **togged**

tog out (*informal*)
The clothes you **are togged out** in are the clothes you are wearing: *Richard was togged out in his dress uniform.*

tog up (*informal*)
You can say that you **are togged up** in certain clothes when you are wearing them: *Do I really have to get togged up in a formal suit and bow tie? Isn't it just a family party?*

together see panel on next page

toil /tɔɪl/: **toils**, **toiling**, **toiled**

toil over
You **toil over** a difficult task when you work hard to do or achieve it: *Don was toiling over the annual accounts, trying to reconcile the figures.* [*same as* **slave over**, **labour over**]

tone /toun/: **tones**, **toning**, **toned**

tone down
To **tone** something **down** is to make it less intense, severe or extreme: *Attempts to tone down Dixons' garish image have yet to bear fruit.*

tone in
One thing **tones in** with another, or they both **tone in**, when together they make a suitable or pleasing combination: *The browns and yellows of their plumage tone in perfectly with vegetation, making them difficult birds to spot.* ❑ *Caroline felt herself to be ostracized because her views didn't quite tone in with those of the rest of the group.* [*same as* **blend in**, **go with**]

tone up
Someone **tones up** their body or their muscles when they make their muscles stronger with physical exercise: *A sensible diet with regular exercise to tone up the muscles should be enough to keep you fit and healthy.*

to /tuː/ *or* /tə/

To is a preposition and an adverb.

It is a very common word in English, often having very little meaning other than its function as a linking word showing the relationship between things. It is used as a preposition with many verbs to show that the movement or action is directed towards a particular place, person or end. For example, you **go to** Paris when you travel there; you **propose to** someone when you ask them to marry you; you **admit to** something when you confess that you have done it or are guilty of it; you **adhere to** a rule or vow when you abide by it; you **allude to** something when you mention it indirectly; you **look to** someone to give you something when you expect them or rely on them to give it to you; and, a responsibility or duty **falls to** you when you are the person that has that duty or responsibility.

To is used as an adverb in a small number of phrasal verbs. Most of these combinations have to do with moving something such as a door or window so that it closes. For example, you **push** or **slide** a door **to** when you push against it or slide it so that it closes. The other verb + adverb combinations are **set to** and **come to** meaning to begin doing something, and to recover consciousness, respectively.

To often forms the third element of phrasal verbs, as in **get down to, get up to, get through to, put up to** and **stand up to**.

together /tə'gɛðə(r)/

Together is an adverb.

Its basic meaning has to do with joining or combining two or more people or things, or bringing them close to each other.

1 CLOSENESS OR IN CLOSE CONTACT

Together is combined with verbs to indicate that two or more people or things are in a position close to each other, or they share some sort of relationship with each other. For example, you **gather** things **together** when you collect them from various places and bring them all to one place; you **glue** two things **together** when you attach one to the other using glue. Two people **sleep together** when they sleep in the same bed, or have a sexual relationship; and, if you say that two people of the opposite sex **are going together** you mean that they are having a romantic or sexual relationship. People **live together** when they share the same home; and, two or more people **room together** when they share the same room, as in the following example: *Courier and Agassi roomed together at Nick Bolletieri's tennis academy.*

2 FORMING A WHOLE OR UNIT

Some verbs with **together** show how people or things fit with each other to form a whole or unit. For example, things **go together** or **belong together** when they match or fit well with each other. You **piece** something **together** when you use a number of separate parts to create the whole; and you **lump** several people or things **together** when you consider them as a whole or as being of the same type, even though they may be quite different. Some combinations with this sense are more idiomatic: for example, when you say that ideas **gel together** you mean that they combine to form a whole in a satisfactory way; and, when things don't **hang together** they can't be combined satisfactorily.

3 CO-OPERATING

Together is also used to indicate that a number of people form a group to do or achieve something that they wouldn't be able to do alone. For example, groups of people **band together** when they join together to form a larger group; a number of people **club together** to buy or pay for something when they each make a contribution to the cost; and, people **get together** to do something when they meet or join with each other in order to share ideas or do something in each others' company.

tool /tuːl/: **tools**, **tooling**, **tooled**

tool up
1 To **tool up** is to prepare for a job or task by acquiring the proper tools or equipment: *The factory is tooling up to cope with a massive order from the Middle East.* **2** (*informal*) People, especially soldiers or gangsters, **tool** themselves **up** when they arm themselves with guns: *Police intelligence has discovered that the paramilitaries are tooling themselves up for a renewed outbreak of violence.*

top /tɒp/: **tops**, **topping**, **topped**

top off
To **top** something **off** is to end it with something even more impressive, or something that makes it even worse: *It was a terrible week, and to top it all off there were dispiriting revelations about Liverpool's manager, Graeme Souness.* [*same as* **round off**, **crown**]

top up
You **top up** a container of liquid when you add more liquid to make it full or make a complete measure; you can also say that you **top up** the liquid, especially when it is an alcoholic drink: *Keeping the pots topped up with water raises humidity.*
• *noun* **top-up**: **top-ups**
A **top-up** is another serving of a drink in the same glass or cup as the first: *Let me give you a top-up.*

topple /ˈtɒpəl/: **topples**, **toppling**, **toppled**

topple over
Something **topples over** when it becomes unsteady and falls to the ground: *The calf toppled over and went into a convulsion.* ❑ *The steeple was leaning precariously and in imminent danger of toppling over.* [compare **keel over**]

toss /tɒs/: **tosses**, **tossing**, **tossed**

toss about *or* **toss around**
1 Something that **is tossed about** or **tossed around** is lifted and dropped, or shaken, with rough or violent movements: *It was a stormy sea in which he was tossed about in a little boat.* **2** People who **toss** something **about** or **toss** it **around** mention it often or casually: *The superlatives were still being tossed around for Arazi, who won impressively at Saint Cloud.*

toss for
Two or more people **toss for** something when they decide who will have or do it according to which of them correctly guesses which side a spinning coin will land on: *If you can't decide who's going to do the driving, you'll have to toss for it.* [compare **toss up**]

toss up
Two or more people **toss up** when they spin a coin and decide who will do or have something according to who correctly guesses which side the coin will land on: *They tossed up and the home team won, choosing to play into the wind for the first half.*
• *noun* **toss-up**
You can call a situation a **toss-up** when both of the possible results seem equally likely, or both of two choices equally attractive: *It was a toss-up whether to try for acceptance in the front row or work towards qualifying for the back row.*

tot /tɒt/: **tots**, **totting**, **totted**

tot up (*informal*)
You **tot up** several amounts when you add them together to find their total: *You need not tot the calories up for everything you eat.*

touch /tʌtʃ/: **touches**, **touching**, **touched**

touch down
An aircraft **touches down** when it lands: *A lone plane touched down and took him off.* [*opposite* **take off**]

• *noun* **touchdown**: *There were also the hazards of having higher touch-down speeds.*

touch for (*informal*)
Someone **touches you** for money when they ask to borrow it from you: *He shuffled up to me and tried to touch me for a fiver.* [compare **sponge off**]

touch off
An action or circumstance **touches off** something, especially violent behaviour, when it causes it to happen: *This thoughtless comment touched off a heated argument between my parents.* [*same as* **spark off**]

touch on *or* **touch upon**
You **touch on** something, or **touch upon** it, when you mention it or refer to it: *This is a problem which I will touch on in the next chapter.* ❑ *These are the themes touched upon by some of the films being screened.*

touch up
1 To **touch** something **up** is to make slight changes to alter or improve it: *Someone suggested she touch up her lipstick.* **2** (*informal*) To **touch** someone **up** is to get sexual pleasure from touching their body, usually without being invited to: *He's one of those creeps who thinks it's amusing to touch up the waitresses.* [*same as* **feel up** (*informal*)]

touch upon see **touch on**

toughen /ˈtʌfən/: **toughens, toughening, toughened**

---

toughen up
To **toughen** someone **up** is to make them stronger physically or mentally: *His parents thought the sometimes harsh discipline of a military academy would toughen him up a bit.*

tow /tou/: **tows, towing, towed**

---

tow away
A vehicle that has been parked or has broken down **is towed away** when it is attached to another vehicle and pulled by it to another place: *I discovered that my car had been towed away.*

towards see panel on next page

---

tower /ˈtɑuə(r)/: **towers, towering, towered**

---

tower above *or* **tower over**
1 One person or thing **towers above** another, or **towers over** them, when they are, or it is, much taller than they are: *The tall bulky building towered above him.* ❑ *The dog jumped on me, towering over me with his paws on my shoulder.* **2** You can also say that one person or thing **towers above** another, or **towers over** them, when they are far better than them or far more impressive: *He towered above all the other poets of his generation.*

toy /tɔɪ/: **toys, toying, toyed**

---

toy with
1 You **toy with** a possible course of action when you try to decide whether or not to take it: *We toyed with the idea of bringing her down from the gallery onto the stage.* **2** Someone **toys with** you when they enjoy keeping you in a state of uncertainty, *eg* by not giving you a direct answer or by delaying a decision: *Roy was only toying with me, eventually agreeing to participate in good spirit.* **3** You **toy with** an object when you handle it with small movements, casually or while concentrating on something else: *He looked abstractedly into the distance, toying with his silver cufflink.* [*same as* **play with**]

track /trak/: **tracks, tracking, tracked**

---

track down
You **track** someone or something **down** when you find them after a long search: *The prisoner will be tracked down and*

caught. ❑ *He would track her down mercilessly.* ❑ *Have you managed to track down that missing file yet?*

trade /treɪd/: **trades**, **trading**, **traded**

trade in
You **trade in** something you own when you give it as part payment for a newer, more expensive replacement: *Some retailers will allow you to trade in your old PC for a more up-to-date model.*
• *noun* **trade-in**: *My car is ten years old. How much will you give me in a trade-in?*

trade on
Someone who **trades on** something makes unfair use of it in order to obtain or achieve something: *He's been trading on his privileged position as advisor to the government to further his career in the media.* [*same as* **exploit**]

trail /treɪl/: **trails**, **trailing**, **trailed**

trail away *or* **trail off**
A speaker's voice **trails away** or **trails off** when it gradually becomes softer before they stop speaking altogether, without finishing what they were saying: *Her bewildered voice trailed*

towards /təˈwɔːdz/

Towards is a preposition. In *AmE* the form **toward** is often used.
Its two basic meanings are of movement in the direction of someone or something, or being in a position facing someone or something. For example, if someone **walks towards** you they walk in your direction gradually coming closer and closer to you; and, a window **faces towards** the sea when you can look in the direction of the sea from it.

1 MOVEMENT IN THE DIRECTION OF
Phrasal verbs with the literal meaning of movement in the direction of someone or something include **advance towards, blow towards, glance towards, head towards, march towards, move towards, point towards, progress towards** and **run towards. Towards** can be used to form new phrasal verbs with this sense, especially when referring to the way in which something moves in a particular direction. For example, something **careers towards** you when its movement in your direction is so rapid that it seems unable to slow down or stop; and, you **are impelled towards** something when you are pushed or forced to move in that direction. This basic meaning is used in certain combinations to show that there is movement in a particular direction in a figurative rather than a literal sense. For example, someone **leans** or **inclines towards** a particular view or opinion if they have a tendency or inclination to favour that view or opinion; and, when you **gear** your activities **towards** a particular objective you organize things in a way that is designed to achieve that objective.

2 IN OR TO A FACING POSITION
The second literal meaning of **towards** when used in phrasal verbs refers to being in a position facing someone or something. Phrasal verbs with this sense include **face towards, turn towards** and **look towards.**

3 ATTITUDE OR FEELINGS
The third sense of **towards** occurs in a small group of phrasal verbs with more idiomatic meanings. It is used to indicate how the action relates to the person or thing concerned, so that what you **feel towards** someone are the feelings you have for them or the attitude you have to them.

4 PURPOSE
Another sense of **towards** when combined with verbs refers to doing or using something for a particular purpose. For example, you **put** money **towards** something when you contribute some money to meet part of the cost of that thing; you **work towards** something when you work over a period of time with a particular goal in mind; and, something **counts towards** a score or total when it can be taken into account or included in the total.

away. ❑ *He let his words trail off.*

train /treɪn/: **trains**, **training**, **trained**

train on

You can use **train on** to refer to the action of aiming something, such as a gun, at a target: *German machine guns were permanently trained on the lip of the British trench.*

train up

To **train** someone **up** is to teach or train them in order to improve their skills: *You train them up for the extra work ahead.*

trample /'trampəl/: **tramples**, **trampling**, **trampled**

trample down

People or animals **trample** something **down** when they cause damage by repeatedly walking on or over it, flattening it: *Herds of elephants were constantly breaking through the fences and trampling down the new crops.*

trample on

1 People or animals **trample on** something when they damage it by repeatedly walking on or over it: *Visitors must keep to the paths so that they don't trample on the rare species of orchid and other protected plants growing in the reserve.* **2** Someone who **is trampled on** is treated very unfairly or cruelly: *You have to stand up for yourself or else they'll trample on you.*

trap /trap/: **traps**, **trapping**, **trapped**

trap into

Someone **traps** you **into** something, or **traps** you **into** doing it, when they make you do it by tricking or deceiving you: *They tried to trap him into admitting he had been there.*

treat /triːt/: **treats**, **treating**, **treated**

treat of (*formal*)

Something such as a written essay or article **treats of** something when it has it as its subject: *a blasphemous manuscript that treats of witchcraft.* [*same as* **deal with**]

trespass /'trɛspəs/ *or* /'trɛspas/: **trespasses**, **trespassing**, **trespassed**

trespass on *or* trespass upon

(*formal*)

You **trespass on** something, or **trespass upon** it, when you involve yourself in it, and especially make changes to it, without having the right or permission to do so: *Macmillan trespassed on the modern constitutional convention.* ❑ *He was accused of trespassing upon the rights of an already disadvantaged group.*

trick /trɪk/: **tricks**, **tricking**, **tricked**

trick into

Someone **tricks** you **into** something, or **tricks** you **into** doing it, when they make you do it by deceiving you: *He reckons he can trick the doctor into giving him an alibi.*

trick out

Some people use **trick out** when referring to what someone is wearing, or how something is decorated: *Her hair was tricked out with bows and jewelled combs.* [*same as* **deck out**]

trifle /'traɪfəl/: **trifles**, **trifling**, **trifled**

trifle with

To **trifle with** someone or something is to treat them too casually, failing to show them proper respect: *She wanted her revenge on this man who had trifled so blatantly with her affections.* ❑ *Don't trifle with me; I want the truth.*

trigger /'trɪgə(r)/: **triggers**, **triggering**, **triggered**

trigger off

Something **triggers off** an action, or series of actions, when it causes it to happen or makes it operate: *It triggered off a chain of events that no-one could have anticipated.* ❑ *Genetic material lies dormant for years until something triggers it off.* [compare **spark off, touch off**]

trim /trɪm/: **trims, trimming, trimmed**

trim away *or* **trim off**
You **trim** an unwanted part of something **away**, or **trim** it **off**, when you remove it: *Trim away any surplus mortar with the trowel.* ❑ *The knot is tightened and a length eventually trimmed off.*

trim down
You **trim** something **down** when you reduce its size or amount by removing non-essential parts: *Trim down the end of the stick until you have a fairly sharp point.* ❑ *He gave them a trimmed-down version of events.*

trip /trɪp/: **trips, tripping, tripped**

trip on *or* **trip over**
You **trip on** something, or **trip over** it, when you catch your foot or leg against it, causing you to stumble or fall over: *He'd tripped on the dog's lead and fallen headlong into the hedge.* ❑ *Be careful to avoid walking on, or tripping over, electric cables.*

trip up
1 You **trip up** when you catch your foot or leg against something, causing you to stumble or fall over; someone **trips** you **up** when they deliberately create an obstacle, often their own foot or leg, for you to catch your foot or leg against in this way: *He tripped up as he approached the queen and fell in an undignified heap at her feet.* ❑ *Every time I ran past he hit me again or tripped me up.* **2** You **trip** someone **up** when, with clever arguments, you cause them to say something wrong, make a mistake or reveal a secret: *You had better have your story straight because their lawyer will do everything he can to trip you up and rubbish your evidence.*

trot /trɒt/: **trots, trotting, trotted**

trot off (*informal*)
You can say that someone **trots off** somewhere when they leave to go there: *She trotted off with her shopping basket bursting to tell everyone in the High Street the news.*

trot out (*informal*)
You can use **trot out** to emphasize how boringly familiar, or casually expressed, are the ideas, excuses or explanations that someone offers: *These easy phrases are trotted out in the course of gossip.*

truckle /'trʌkəl/: **truckles, truckling, truckled**

truckle to (*formal*)
To **truckle to** someone in a position of power or authority is to behave towards them in a very respectful way, perhaps too respectful, and perhaps out of weakness: *All her friends were in on it, truckling to this ghastly woman.* ❑ *She must truckle too, to the whole lot of them.* [compare **crawl to, suck up to**] (*informal*)]

trump /trʌmp/: **trumps, trumping, trumped**

trump up
To **trump up** something such as evidence or proof is to invent it, often in order to make an innocent person appear guilty: *They'd trumped up a charge of treason as a convenient method of getting rid of her once and for all.* [compare **dream up**]

truss /trʌs/: **trusses, trussing, trussed**

truss up (*informal*)
Someone who **is trussed up** has their freedom of movement restricted, either by having their limbs tied together with

rope, or by having to wear very tight clothes: *I've got a man trussed up here on the floor like a Christmas turkey.*

try /traɪ/: **tries**, **trying**, **tried**

try for

You **try for** something when you attempt to achieve or obtain it: *I don't know whether to try for a place in the front row or work towards qualifying for the back row.* ❑ *This encouraged him to try for promotion.*

try on

1 You **try on** a piece of clothing when you put it on to find out if it fits or if you like it: *Take your coat and things off and try it on.* ❑ *She had gone into a shop and tried on dress after dress.* **2** (*informal*) To **try** it **on** with someone is to behave towards them in a mischievous, rude or attacking way, in order to test what their reaction will be: *I was irritable because of David trying it on with Sara.* ❑ *We all know his reputation for violence, but if he tries it on here, he'll be sorry.*

try out

1 You **try** something **out** when you do or use it for the first time in order to find out if you like it or if it is useful or effective: *It was too wet and windy to try it out.* ❑ *I took these two guitars into the studio to try them out.* **2** You **try** someone **out** when you give them a short task as a test of their ability: *He's trying out new skating partners.*

tuck /tʌk/: **tucks**, **tucking**, **tucked**

tuck away

1 Something that **is tucked away** is stored or hidden in a safe or secret place: *He looked in the mirror he kept tucked away among his things.* **2** You can also say that something **is tucked away** when it is in a quiet or private place, away from where most people go: *The development is tucked away behind shops.* ❑ *It was a little shop tucked away down an alley.* **3** (*informal*) To **tuck away** food is to eat large amounts of it: *You know her; she can tuck away a whole box of chocs in less than half an hour.* [*same as* **pack away, put away**]

tuck in

1 You **tuck in** a garment such as a shirt or vest when you push its lower end under the top edge of a skirt or pair of trousers, to keep it in place; the garment **is tucked into** *eg* a shirt or pair of trousers when it is pushed under its top edge: *He's alleged to wear his shirt tucked into his underpants.* ❑ *Tuck your T-shirt in.* **2** You **tuck in** covers on a bed when you push the edges of them under the mattress, to keep them in place; you can also say that you **tuck** someone **in**, especially a child, when you tuck in the covers on their bed: *Off to bed now and I'll come up in a moment to tuck you in.* **3** You **tuck in** a part of your body that is sticking out when you draw it in so that it is in line with the rest of your body: *Stand straight and tuck in your bottom.* [*same as* **pull in**] **4** (*informal*) You **tuck in,** or **tuck into** something, when you eat, or begin to eat, hungrily and with great enjoyment: *The taste panel tucked into ready-made Christmas cakes.* ❑ *The food's ready. Tuck in, everyone.*

tuck up

To **tuck** someone **up** in bed is to make them warm and comfortable there, perhaps by tucking in the covers on their bed: *She found herself tucked up under the covers again.*

tug /tʌg/: **tugs**, **tugging**, **tugged**

tug at

To **tug at** something is to pull it with repeated short violent movements, in order to move or detach it: *The man had gripped his arm and had started to tug at him.*

tumble /'tʌmbəl/: **tumbles**, **tumbling**, **tumbled**

tumble down
When something falls down you can say that it **tumbles down**, especially when it falls heavily: *Jack and Jill did not tumble down the hill without someone giving a push.*
• *adjective* **tumbledown**
A **tumbledown** building is in very poor condition, perhaps with some of its pieces having fallen off: *He could see the tumbledown shed across an expanse of garden.*

tumble to (*informal*)
You **tumble to** something when you suddenly understand that it is happening, or understand its true nature: *He'd been embezzling Scout funds, and we didn't tumble to it until he suddenly disappeared.*

tune /tjuːn/: tunes, tuning, tuned

tune in *or* **tune into**
You **tune in** when you listen to a particular radio programme or watch a particular television programme; you can also say that you **tune into** a programme: *Listeners who tune in next week will hear the result of our competition.* ❑ *You should have tuned into '40 Minutes' (BBC2) on the subject of geriatric romance.*

tune up
Musicians **tune up** when they test the sound their instrument makes and adjust it so that it produces the right notes: *People were already taking their seats and the orchestra was tuning up when the announcement was made.* ❑ *I tune up just before Bryan goes on.*

turf /tɜːf/: turfs, turfing, turfed

turf out (*informal*)
1 Someone who **is turfed out** is forced to leave a place: *It was the officer who had turfed me out of the church yesterday.* **2** You **turf out** unwanted things when you get rid of them, *eg* by putting them in a bin: *'Do you want any of these old clothes?' 'No, just turf them all out.'* [*same as* **throw out**]

turn /tɜːn/: turns, turning, turned

turn about
• *noun* **turnabout**
A **turnabout** is a sudden and complete change in a person's attitude or judgement: *It represented a complete turnabout in traditional Labour policy.*

turn against
Someone, especially someone you usually rely on for support, **turns against** you when they change their alliance and begin to oppose you; someone who **turns** them **against** you persuades them to do this: *The Maronites and other Christian groups turned against the French.* ❑ *Muslims have missed a great opportunity to turn public opinion against Salman Rushdie.*

turn around *or* **turn round**
1 Someone or something **turns around**, or **turns round**, when they turn to face the opposite direction: *He told us not to turn around and to give him our money.* ❑ *We turned round for a look.* **2** To **turn around** something that is failing, or **turn** it **round**, is to reverse its poor progress so that it begins to become successful: *The Herald hopes that her financial aplomb will turn around its ailing circulation.*
• *noun* **turnaround** *or* **turnround**
A **turnaround** or **turnround** is a sudden and unexpected change from failure to success: *a turnaround in Labour's electoral fortunes* ❑ *There was an unprecedented turnround in its financial performance.*

turn away
1 You **turn away** from someone or something when you turn your body into a position of no longer facing them: *I turned away so that Jeff wouldn't be able to see my tears.* **2** You **turn** something **away** from someone or something when you turn it into a position of no longer facing them: *Marie turned her face away.* ❑ *Do not*

turn your hips away from your opponent. **3** Someone who **is turned away** is dismissed or rejected, or not allowed to enter: *It has refused to turn refugees away from its embassy.*

turn back

1 You **turn back** when you start travelling in the opposite direction, going back towards where you came from: *We got onto the summit crest but were forced to turn back.* **2** You **turn back** when you change your mind and decide not to do something: *In the fluid world of Thai politics, he may have gone too far to turn back.*

turn down

1 To **turn** someone **down** is to refuse what they are asking or offering; to **turn** something **down** is to refuse to accept it: *He turned down the role.* [*same as* **decline, reject**] **2** You **turn down** an appliance when you adjust its controls to reduce the flow of power to it, which reduces the sound, heat, *etc* that it produces; you can also say that you **turn down** the sound, heat, *etc*: *Turn the heating down; it's far too hot in here.* ❑ *Turn that TV down. I can hear it at the other end of the house.* **3** When you leave a main road you are driving on and enter a minor one that it connects with, you can say that you **turn down** that minor road: *From there, turn down Follyhouse Lane.*

• *noun* **downturn**: **downturns**
There is a **downturn** in something when the level of it begins to fall or decrease: *The seasonal downturn may have flattened out a bit.* ❑ *There is evidence of an advertising downturn.* [*opposite* **upturn**]

turn in

1 You **turn in** something you have borrowed, or something in your possession, when you give it to someone in authority: *They could turn their guns and knives in without fear of prosecution.* [*same as* **hand in**] **2** You **turn in** written work you have finished when you give it to the person or authority who has asked for it or who will judge it: *Those who haven't turned in their essays by the end of the week won't have them marked.* [*same as* **submit**] **3** (*informal*) You **turn in** when you go to bed: *After you've gorged yourself on all the fun and nightlife that Benitses has to offer, you can turn in for the night and leave it all behind.* **4** To **turn** someone **in** is to tell the police or other authority that they have committed a crime or other wrong-doing, or perhaps take them to the police: *It would be better for everyone if he turned himself in.*

turn into

1 You use **turn into** to talk about what someone or something becomes, or changes to become; you **turn** someone or something **into** someone or something different when you cause them to become that different person or thing: *He was the entrepreneur who turned Bass into a great Victorian company.* ❑ *A witch turned his two daughters into swans.* ❑ *A low estimate can easily turn into a high bill.* **2** You **turn into** a road or street when you enter it from another connected to it: *Turning into the lane, they could see the house up ahead.*

turn off

1 You **turn off** an appliance when you adjust its controls to stop power flowing to it, so that it stops working; you can also say that you **turn** the power **off**: *Drain the tank and turn the electricity off.* ❑ *The last one out turns off the lights.* **2** You **turn off** a road you are travelling on when you leave it: *I turned off by the stop sign.* ❑ *I turned off the road when I drew alongside the Brigadier.* **3** Something that **turns** you **off** causes you to lose interest or enthusiasm: *Her rather high-pitched speaking voice was thought by her image-makers to turn voters off.* [*same as* **put off**; *opposite* **turn on**] **4** You can also say that something **turns**

you **off** if it causes you to lose sexual interest, or prevents you from developing any: *All his attempts to arouse her seemed only to turn her off.* [*opposite* **turn on**]

• *noun* **turn-off**: **turn-offs**

1 A **turn-off** is something that causes you to lose sexual excitement, or prevents you from developing any: *Those woolly tights are a total turn-off.* **2** A **turn-off** is also something that causes you to lose interest or enthusiasm: *He loved medicine, but found the administrative side of things a complete turn-off.* **3** A **turn-off** is also a junction at which you leave the road you are travelling on: *Could it have driven up the turn-off?*

turn on

1 You **turn on** an appliance when you adjust its controls to allow power to flow into it, causing it to start working: *I turn off the light above my seat.* **2** You can say that someone **turns on** a particular kind of behaviour when they suddenly begin to display it, suggesting it is not genuine or sincere: *When he feels like it, he can turn on the charm like turning on a tap.* **3** An angry person or animal **turns on** you when they suddenly or unexpectedly attack you, violently or with angry words: *You will upset them and they may turn on each other.* **4** To **turn** something such as a gun or light **on** someone or something is to move it into a position of aiming or pointing at them: *She doesn't like it when the spotlight is turned on her.* **5** When one thing **turns on** another it depends on that other thing happening: *Liability was seen to turn on the question of whether the victim was likely to respond.* ❑ *The outcome turns on the block votes of union delegates.* [*same as* **hang on**, **hinge on**] **6** Something that **turns** you **on** makes you sexually excited: *The sight of all that naked flesh doesn't turn me on in the slightest.* [*same as* **arouse**] **7** You can also say that something **turns** you **on** when it causes you to become interested or excited: *He says that he gets turned on by the danger.*

turn out

1 People often use **turn out** when talking about what finally or eventually happens or what is finally or eventually discovered to be true: *Two of the men turned out to have family problems.* ❑ *It might simply turn out to be a consequence of bad taste.* ❑ *The photos didn't turn out too well.* ❑ *It turns out Lewis had checked with the college.* ❑ *Thankfully it has turned all right for baby and mother.* ❑ *It turned out that East German security wanted to take their identity away.* **2** You **turn out** an appliance, especially a light, when you adjust the controls to stop the flow of power to it, causing it to stop working: *Be sure to turn out the lights when you leave.* **3** Someone who **is turned out** of a place is forced to leave it: *She turned everyone else out of her room.* ❑ *They were turned out of their cottages and forced off the land.* [*same as* **put out**, **throw out**, **evict**] **4** You **turn out** a container when you empty it of its contents, especially by lifting it up and pouring the contents out: *Her small son had opened the biscuit box and turned out the contents on the kitchen floor.* **5** To **turn** things **out** is to produce them, especially in large quantities: *Some of the stuff they turn out is absolute rubbish.* ❑ *The purpose of 'English' was to turn out critics.* **6** People who **turn out** for an event go there to take part or watch: *Large crowds would turn out to support the Fair.* **7** You can say that someone **is** well **turned out** when they have a neat or smart appearance: *She's always neatly turned out in a smart skirt and jacket.*

• *noun* **turnout**

The **turnout** for an event is the number of people who go there to take part or watch: *Turnout for the poll was 62.5 %.* ❑ *He describes the turnout for the race as a disaster.*

turn over

1 You **turn** something **over** when you turn it in such a way that the top or upper side becomes the bottom or lower side: *He turned her hands over and examined the backs.* ❑ *He takes up the poker and turns over another log.* **2** You **turn** something **over** to someone when you formally give them possession of it or responsibility for it: *They turned their country over to Syria.* **3** You **turn** something **over** to a different use when you change its use: *Millend had left the cloth trade and been turned over to corn and saw milling.* **4** You **turn over** someone who has committed a crime or other wrongdoing when you take them to the police or other authority: *They'll be turned over to the French police once the extradition formalities are completed.* **5** When you are watching television or listening to the radio, you **turn over** when you begin to watch or listen to a different programme; you can also say that you **turn** the television or radio **over**: *Boy had turned it over to a boxing match.* **6** (*informal*) To **turn** a room or other place **over** is to cause great damage by carrying out a thorough search: *They returned to find the office had been turned over by the police.* **7** An engine **turns over** when it works steadily at its minimum rate of power: *Keep the engine turning over, engage first gear, and draw away slowly.* [*same as* **tick over**] **8** You **turn** something **over** in your mind when you think about it carefully: *When he'd had a quiet moment to turn it all over in his mind, he realized that he had probably made a grave mistake.*

• *noun* **turnover**

1 A business company's **turnover** is the value of the goods or services it sells in a given period: *Trading in sterling amounts to almost half the daily turnover.* ❑ *Turnover edged ahead to £127 million.* **2** A **turnover** is a rounded pastry case with a sweet filling: *an apple turnover.*

turn round see **turn around**

turn to

1 You **turn to** someone when you ask them to give you help or advice: *There is a wealth of support to turn to when you need help.* ❑ *The couple must now turn to the Investors' Compensation Scheme.* ❑ *There are voices you turn to as a friend.* **2** To **turn to** a subject is to begin to discuss or deal with it, after discussing or dealing with something else: *Turning to English, we review Jonson, Herbert and Rossetti.*

turn up

1 To **turn up** is to arrive or appear: *The classroom teacher may be concerned with the parents that don't turn up.* ❑ *Surely Dennis wouldn't turn up late?* ❑ *Everton supporters turn up in their thousands week after week.* ❑ *He had turned up for work as usual.* **2** Something that is **turned up** is discovered by chance: *They'd been nosing about and had turned up some pretty unsavoury details about his private life.* **3** You **turn up** an appliance, especially one that produces sound or heat, when you adjust its controls to increase the power supplied to it, causing it to work more intensively; you can also say that you **turn up** the power, or **turn up** the energy the appliance produces: *The pop music had been turned up quite loud now.* ❑ *We turn up the volume.* ❑ *It was like the mantle of a gas lamp turned up very slowly.* **4** To **turn up** a piece of clothing such as a dress or pair of trousers is to shorten it by folding the bottom edge or edges and sewing the fold: *These jeans will have to be turned up by at least two inches.* [*same as* **take up**]

• *noun* **upturn**: **upturns**

An **upturn** in something occurs when it starts to improve or increase: *It has been helped by the recent upturn in the gold price.* ❑ *There was an upturn of the fortunes of thousands of prisoners of conscience.* [*opposite* **downturn**]

• *adjective* **upturned**

Something that is **upturned** has been turned or thrown upside down: *They attached themselves to the upturned hull.*

type /taɪp/: types, typing, typed

type in *or* type into

You **type in** information when you enter it into a computer by typing; you can also say that you **type** it **into** a computer: *Type in your name; then the password.* ❑ *I sit at home, typing this book into a word processor.* [*same as* **key in**]

type out

You **type out** something written when you produce a copy of it on a typewriter: *He asked her if she was prepared to type out his thesis for him.*

type up

You **type up** something written, especially something written roughly or in the form of notes, when you produce a neat or complete copy of it on a typewriter: *We'll send you the report as soon as it is typed up.*

u

under see panel below

under /ˈʌndə(r)/

Under is a preposition and an adverb. It is a fairly common word in English, but it occurs in only a small number of phrasal verbs in this dictionary.
Its main sense relates to the position of something that has something else above it or on top of it. It appears in phrasal verbs in two main senses.

1 MOVEMENT AND POSITION
Under occurs in phrasal verbs whose meaning relates to the movement of one thing to a position below another, or below a surface, as in **pull under**.

2 AUTHORITY
The sense of being below something in position is extended in a few phrasal verbs that refer to the position of someone who is given orders by a person in authority, such as **come under, work under** and **buckle under**.

3 DEFEAT OR DESTRUCTION
Under also features in a few phrasal verbs that have defeat or destruction as part of their meaning, such as **go under**.

up see panel on page 409

upkeep /ˈʌpkiːp/ see **keep up**

upon see panel on following page

uprising /ˈʌprising/ see **rise up**

uproot /ʌpˈruːt/ see **root up**

upturn /ˈʌptɜːn/ see **turn up**

upturned /ʌpˈtɜːnd/ see **turn up**

urge /ɜːdʒ/: **urges**, **urging**, **urged**

urge on *or* **urge upon**

1 You **urge** a person or animal **on** when you do or say something to encourage them to continue with something or go faster: *The horse was faced with a frightening object that he didn't want to go past, and yet was being urged on by his rider.* ❑ *The Prime Minister, urged on by her newest economic advisor, forced through the most anti-Keynesian budget of modern times.* **2** You **urge** something **on** or **upon** someone when you try to persuade them to accept it: *Klein was urging equipment that we couldn't afford on us, all the time insisting that we couldn't do without it.* ❑ *We were afraid to refuse the food that they urged upon us.*

use /juːz/: **uses**, **using**, **used**

use up

1 You **use** a supply of something **up** when you consume it bit by bit, and leave none: *We've used up all the spare light bulbs.* ❑ *The rockets flew in a straight line until their fuel was used up.* ❑ *Sprinters often collapse when they cross the line because they've used up the reserves of oxygen in their blood.* **2** You **use** something **up** when you make sure that none of it is wasted or has been thrown away: *Karen made a stir-fry to use up the remains of the turkey.*

up /ʌp/

Up is an adverb and a preposition.
It is one of the commonest words in English and is the particle that occurs most frequently in phrasal verbs.
The basic sense of **up** relates to the movement of something from a lower to a higher level or place. It features in phrasal verbs in this dictionary with twelve main meanings.

1 MOVEMENT AND POSITION
In its literal sense, **up** is used in phrasal verbs that refer to the action of moving to a higher place or position, such as **look up**, **move up**, **push up**, **reach up** and **shin up**. New and often informal phrasal verbs with **up** in this sense are fairly common, such as *crane up*, *jerk up*, *suck up* and *ghost up* in the following examples: *He cranes hopefully up at the windows.* ❑ *The impact was so strong that she jerked up in bed.* ❑ *Camels can suck up literally gallons of water in a matter of seconds.* ❑ *Archie, moving fast and silently, ghosted up the stairs.*
Very often, these phrasal verbs refer to the movement of a person's body into an upright or standing position, as in **draw up**, **get up**, **jump up**, **sit up** and **stand up**.
Up is also used in a handful of phrasal verbs of movement that refer specifically to a person's moving to make room for others, such as **budge up**, **move up** and **squeeze up**.
Another related sense is that of lifting something to a higher place or position, as in **jack up**, **lift up**, **pick up**, **scoop up** and **spoon up**.
Sometimes, this movement up is from below the surface of something, as in **bob up**, **bubble up**, **dig up**, **grub up** and **poke up**.

2 INCREASING
A very common use of **up** is in phrasal verbs that have the idea of increasing as part of their meaning, such as **brighten up**, **cheer up**, **firm up**, **grow up**, **hike up**, **hurry up**, **pile up**, **save up**, **speed up** and **turn up**.

3 IMPROVING
Related to the notion of increasing is the idea of improving, and there are numerous examples of phrasal verbs with **up** in this meaning, such as **brush up**, **do up**, **perk up**, **smarten up**, **spice up** and **tone up**.

4 FINISHING AND COMPLETING
One of the most common occurrences of **up** in phrasal verbs is where the meaning relates to something finishing or being finished, as in **drink up**, **eat up**, **gobble up**, **swallow up** and **wind up**.
Up can occasionally be found forming new phrasal verbs with this meaning, such as *sup up* in the example: *He talked to Aunt Tossie while she supped up her soup delightedly.*
Linked to the notion of finishing is the idea of something coming, or being brought, into a final state or condition, as in **dry up**, **heal up**, **fill up**, **lock up**, **soak up**, **tidy up**, **wash up** and **wrap up**.
New phrasal verbs are sometimes created with this meaning of completeness, as in *button up* meaning to work something out successfully, and *noise up* meaning to succeed in annoying someone so that they lose their temper, as in the following examples: *I'm afraid I don't have this thing buttoned up yet.* ❑ *His purpose seemed to be to noise them up and create chaos.*
The idea of completeness is extended in a number of phrasal verbs with **up** to refer to the complete destruction of something, or the breaking of it into pieces, as in **break up**, **burn up**, **grind up**, **mash up**, **rip up** and **tear up**.

5 FASTENING, AND FORMING A BARRIER
Up also occurs frequently in phrasal verbs whose meaning relates in some way to the idea of fastening, such as **button up**, **hook up**, **lace up**, **screw up**, **stitch up**, **tie up** and **zip up**.
Related to these phrasal verbs of fastening is a group of combinations that suggest the idea of a gap or space being filled to form a barrier, such as **board up**, **brick up**, **cork up**, **dam up**, **plug up**, **shore up** and **stop up**.
The notion of a barrier is extended in a number of phrasal verbs in which some sort of blockage is created that prevents proper movement or use, such as **bung up**, **clog up**, **freeze up**, **jam up**, **mist up** and **steam up**.

continued over page

6 SPOILING AND DAMAGING
In a large number of phrasal verbs, **up** is used to convey the idea of something being spoiled or damaged, as in **churn up, break up, hold up, mess up** and **mix up**. Many of these are informal, such as **foul up, louse up** and **muck up**; several are vulgar, such as **bugger up, cock up** and **screw up**.

7 PREPARING
Many phrasal verbs with **up** have the idea of preparing something, such as a meal, as part of their meaning. These include **brew up, cook up, fry up, heat up, rig up, saddle up, start up, tune up** and **warm up**.

8 GATHERING
Numerous phrasal verbs with **up** contain the idea of gathering things, such as **bunch up, heap up, pile up, round up, stack up** and **sweep up**. Many of these refer to the idea of people coming together as a group, or as a pair, such as **gang up, join up, meet up, pair up** and **team up**.

9 APPROACHING, REACHING AND TOUCHING
There are many phrasal verbs with **up** that have the idea of approaching as part of their meaning, such as **close up, creep up, draw up, loom up, pull up** and **steal up. Up** can sometimes be found forming new and often informal phrasal verbs with this meaning, such as *schmooz up* and *cosy up* in the following examples: *Bud schmoozed up the local press.* ❑ *The Greeks embarked on an argument during the course of which they cosied up to Serbia.*
Often, the meaning is extended a little, so that what is approached is also reached, as in **catch up** and **come up to**, sometimes with the suggestion that the two are now equal in some way, as in **balance up, even up, level up, line up, measure up** and **square up**.
In other combinations, there is the idea of two people or things coming so close to each other that they touch or stay in contact, as in **cuddle up, nestle up** and **snuggle up**.

10 GIVING
A small number of phrasal verbs with **up** have the idea of giving as part of their meaning, such as **cough up, deliver up, pay up, settle up** and **stump up**. Related to these is a group of informal phrasal verbs that refer to the action of vomiting: these include **bring up, sick up, spew up** and **throw up**.

11 INVENTING AND PRODUCING
A few phrasal verbs with **up** have the idea of inventing or producing as part of their meaning, such as **come up with, conjure up, cook up, dream up, make up** and **think up**. Sometimes, the meaning is more of something being produced, as in **spring up** and **sprout up**, and this is extended in a few phrasal verbs that refer to things happening or appearing, such as **come up, crop up, pop up, show up** and **turn up**.

12 DIVIDING
A small number of phrasal verbs with **up** relate to the action of dividing things, or cutting them into portions, such as **carve up, cut up, divide up, saw up** and **slice up**. In some combinations, the sense is of things, or more especially people, being separated. For example, the phrasal verbs **break up, bust up** and **split up** can all refer to the ending of a relationship or partnership between people.

13 CRUSHING OR SQUEEZING
Up is used in phrasal verbs, such as **screw up** and **scrunch up**, that have to do with the actions of pushing, crushing or squeezing something so that it becomes compressed. New and often informal phrasal verbs sometimes appear with this sense, as in *ball up*, *scrumple up* and *squinch up* in the following examples: *Pieces of torn-up newspaper balled up and used as padding.* ❑ *Issey Miyake has always made clothes that can be scrumpled up and still look great when they're unpacked.* ❑ *He slams his eyes shut and squinches up his face to figure it out.*

usher /ˈʌʃə(r)/: ushers, ushering, ushered

usher in *or* usher into

1 You **usher** someone **in** when you

politely but firmly show them the way in; you **are ushered into** a place when someone politely but firmly shows you the way: *A tall officer was making a small ceremony of ushering in a man with long grey hair and a black coat.* ❑ *At the restaurant they were ushered into a small, extremely hot cocktail lounge.* **2** Something **is ushered in** by something else when it is brought in by that thing: *Winter was ushered in by a week of especially hard frosts.*

usher out

You **are ushered out** of a place when you are shown out, often rather quickly: *We were ushered out by a grim black-coated butler.*

---

upon /ʌ'pɒn/

Upon is a preposition.
It is not a very common word in English. However, because it is a more formal variant of **on**, **upon** can occur in a large number of phrasal verbs, although **on** is far more common. People don't usually use **upon** instead of **on** in phrasal verbs which are informal, slang or vulgar.
The different meanings of **upon** in phrasal verbs are mostly the same as the meanings of **on**, although a small number of phrasal verbs only occur with **upon**, such as **loose upon** and **put upon**.

vamp /vamp/: **vamps**, **vamping**, **vamped**

vamp up
Something **is vamped up** when it is made more interesting or attractive by decorating it or adding things to it: *She'd vamped up the plain court shoes by adding diamanté clip-on bows.*

varnish /'vɑːnɪʃ/: **varnishes**, **varnishing**, **varnished**

varnish over
You **varnish over** something's unpleasant or distasteful aspects when you hide them and pretend that they are not there: *Their attempts to varnish over the rift in the party hadn't been wholly successful.* [*same as* **paper over**, **draw a veil over**]

veer /vɪə(r)/: **veers**, **veering**, **veered**

veer off
Something that has been moving along in a straight line **veers off** when it suddenly turns to one side and stops, or begins to follow a different course: *An oil tanker had veered off and steamed right through Heaven Sound.* ❑ *Initially we talked about work and exams, but soon the conversation veered off into more personal matters.*

venture /'vɛntʃə(r)/: **ventures**, **venturing**, **ventured**

venture forth (*formal or literary*)
You **venture forth** when you go outside or go somewhere, especially somewhere that might turn out to be unpleasant or dangerous: *It's much too cold to think of venturing forth unless your journey is absolutely necessary.*

verge /vɜːdʒ/: **verges**, **verging**, **verged**

verge on *or* **verge upon**
One thing **verges on** or **upon** another when it is very close to being or becoming that thing: *Then they would break into convulsions of laughter, verging on hysteria.* [*same as* **border on**]

vest /vɛst/: **vests**, **vesting**, **vested**

vest in
Power or authority **is vested in** an individual or institution when they have it or are given it: *Martha Simmonds and her companions vested in Mayler their apocalyptic hopes.*

vest with
Power or authority **vests with** an individual or institution when they have it or are given it: *All the bankrupt's property shall thenceforth vest with the trustee.*

vie /vaɪ/: **vies**, **vying**, **vied**

vie with
You **vie with** someone for something when you compete with them to get it: *Local MPs vied with each other to be in the vanguard of the 'war against drugs'.* ❑ *Thoughts raced about her head, vying with each other for verbal expression.*

visit /ˈvɪzɪt/: **visits**, **visiting**, **visited**

visit on *or* **visit upon** (*old or literary*)

To **visit** a punishment **on** or **upon** someone is to inflict it on them: *He felt as if the wrath of the entire community was being visited upon him.*

visit with (*AmE*)

Someone **visits with** you when they pay you a visit, especially at your home: *You can take it with you when you're visiting with your aunt in the fall.*

vote /voʊt/: **votes**, **voting**, **voted**

vote down

A proposal **is voted down** when a majority votes against it: *A Liberal MP tabled an amendment that was subsequently voted down in the Commons.*

vote in

An individual **is voted in** when they win an election and take their place on a council, committee or in parliament; a political party **is voted in** when they win an election and form a government: *He was voted in again with an increased majority.*

vote on

You **vote on** something when you take a vote to decide whether it will be done: *When they come to vote on it, it's likely to be very close-run thing.*

vote out

An individual **is voted out** when he or she loses their seat on the council or in parliament at an election; a political party **is voted out** when it loses an election and can therefore no longer govern the country: *Quite unexpectedly, Winston Churchill and the Conservatives were voted out in the post-war election.*

vote through

Something **is voted through** when a majority of people vote for it and it can be put into effect: *These changes were voted through at the last council meeting.*

vouch /vaʊtʃ/: **vouches**, **vouching**, **vouched**

vouch for

1 You **vouch for** someone when you are able to guarantee that they will behave properly, and will make yourself responsible for their behaviour: *He's a good lad and I'd certainly be prepared to vouch for him.* [*same as* **answer for**]
2 You **vouch for** something if you know and can give a guarantee that it exists or is reliable: *You'll have to find someone who will vouch for the existence of another will.*

wade /weɪd/: **wades**, **wading**, **waded**

wade in (*informal*)
1 You **wade in** when you attack someone vigorously either physically or with words: *He always the first to wade in at the least sign of trouble.* **2** You **wade in** when you begin to work at a difficult or daunting task with great energy and determination: *There were hundreds of parcels to sort through so we all had to wade in.*
[*same as* **pitch in**, **get stuck in** (*informal*)]

wade into (*informal*)
1 You **wade into** someone when you attack or criticize them in a very forceful and determined way: *The Labour Deputy waded into the Tories in a rousing speech yesterday.* [*same as* **launch into**, **tear into** (*informal*)] **2** You **wade into** a difficult or daunting task when you start dealing with it with great energy and determination: *All his friends waded into the tidying-up and soon the house was back to normal.* [*same as* **get stuck into** (*informal*)]

wade through (*informal*)
You **wade through** things such as a great many boring or difficult books or other written material when you read or deal with them slowly and with a great deal of effort: *Then he's got to wade through the red boxes before going to bed.* [*same as* **plough through**]

wager /ˈweɪdʒə(r)/: **wagers**, **wagering**, **wagered**

wager on
1 (*old*) People **wager** money **on** the result of *eg* a horse race when they make a bet that a particular horse will win: *He'd wagered on the king's champion.* [*same as* **bet on**] **2** (*rather formal*) When you **wager on** something happening or being the case you are confident that it will happen or turn out to be the case, though there is a risk that it will not: *I wouldn't wager on his being there if I were you.* [*same as* **gamble on**]

wait /weɪt/: **waits**, **waiting**, **waited**

wait about *or* **wait around**
You **wait about** or **wait around** somewhere when you remain there doing nothing till the person or thing you are expecting arrives, or the thing you are expecting to happen, happens: *Film-making involves acting for ten minutes and then waiting about for two hours.* ❑ *I waited around in the car park until I saw him come out.* ❑ *'I didn't feel like spending my life waiting around for the parts that David Niven turned down,' was how he expressed it.* [*same as* **hang about** (*informal*)]

wait behind
When others have left a place and you **wait behind**, you stay there *eg* because you want to talk to someone in private: *She asked her to wait behind after the meeting finished.* [*same as* **remain behind**, **stay behind**]

wait in
You **wait in** when you stay at home

instead of going out because you are expecting someone to visit or telephone you, or in order to be there when something is delivered to your home: *I waited in all morning but the workmen didn't turn up.* [*same as* **stay in**]

wait on *or* **wait upon**

1 The people who **wait on** you in a restaurant are the people employed to serve you with the food and drink that you have ordered. **2** You **wait on** or **upon** someone else when you do everything for them and get them everything they need or want: *You got fed regularly and women waited on you and asked you how you felt.* ❑ *'You do not think or care, lying here day after day, waited upon and given in to, without worries or anxiety.'* **3** (*informal*) You **wait on** someone when you wait for them, staying where you are for a time until they arrive: *Kevin was waiting on me at the bus-stop.* **4** (*informal*) If someone says **'wait on'** to you they are asking you to wait for them until they are ready to come with you, or they are asking you to stop what you are doing: *'Wait on, I think I may have found what we were looking for.'* [*same as* **hang on** (*informal*)] **5** You **wait on** somewhere when you stay there for longer than you had originally planned, to allow more time for someone to arrive or something to happen: *Jack waited on in her dressing-room until after eleven.* [*same as* **stay on**] **6** (*formal*) You **wait on** or **upon** an event when you wait until it happens before acting or making a decision: *'What are you waiting on?'* ❑ *Parliament had to wait upon the king's response.*

wait out

You **wait out** a period of time, especially one that is difficult or unpleasant, or you **wait** it **out**, when you wait patiently, doing nothing or remaining where you are until it ends: *There's nothing more we can do until the police get in touch again. We'll just have to wait it out.* ❑ *Impatiently, Maria waited out the month until his return.* [*same as* **sit out**]

wait up

1 You **wait up** when you don't go to bed at night at your usual time because you are waiting for someone's arrival or return, or some other event: *My mother always waits up for me, even when I come in after midnight.* ❑ *I'll be back late; don't wait up for me.* [*same as* **stay up**] **2** (*informal*) If you are about to leave or are ahead of someone and they say **'wait up'** they are asking or telling you to wait for them: *'Wait up, Ken, I'll just be a minute.'* [*same as* **hang on** (*informal*)]

wait upon see **wait on**

wake /weɪk/: **wakes**, **waking**, **woke** /wouk/, **woken** /'woukən/

Note that in American English **waked** is often used as the past tense and past participle of **wake**.

wake up

1 You **wake up**, or you **waken up**, when you stop sleeping and become conscious; someone or something **wakes** you **up** when they do something to make you stop sleeping, such as shaking you or making a loud noise: *He woke up in the middle of the night and couldn't get back to sleep.* ❑ *Margaret woke up cold. What had woken her up? A noise? A bad dream?* ❑ *a thin, piercing sound, like the wail of a child that has just wakened up and found himself alone.* **2** Something **wakes** you **up** from an inactive state resulting from laziness or boredom, or it **wakens** you **up**, when it causes you to be more active or feel more energetic: *A word from you might wake him up a bit and make him start working.* ❑ *The by-election defeat had the effect of wakening up the Conservatives who'd been pretty complacent about winning until then.* **3** If someone tells you to **wake up** or **waken up** they are telling you rather rudely to be pay more attention to what is going on around you: *Wake up, you lot. That was a dismal performance.* ❑ *You'd better waken up if you don't want to end up at the bottom of the league.*

wake up to
You **wake up to**, or **waken up to**, an unpleasant fact, problem or situation which you had not identified or recognized beforehand, when you suddenly become aware of it or realize that it exists: *By the time he woke up to the fact it was too late to do anything about it.* ❑ *Here every delegate vote counts equally and they are increasingly waking up to the power of the voting card.* ❑ *The brewers have at last woken up to the fact that their high-street shops are dinosaurs slouching towards extinction.*

waken /'weɪkən/: **wakens**, **wakening**, **wakened** see **wake**.

---

walk /wɔːk/: **walks**, **walking**, **walked**

---

walk away see walk off

walk away from
Someone who **walks away from** a situation leaves or abandons it because they no longer want to be involved in it or it is too difficult or complicated for them to deal with: *Do what Jackson wants and get out. You've walked away from worse situations than this before.* ❑ *But she found she couldn't just walk away and leave them in a jam.*

walk away with (*informal*)
You **walk away with** a prize when you win it easily: *There doesn't seem to be anyone who can stop him walking away with the World Driver's Championship.* [*same as* **walk off with** (*informal*)]

walk in
1 If someone **walks in** they come into the room where you are: *They were talking about Edith and the money when Henry walked in.* ❑ *He has this annoying habit of walking in without knocking.* **2** If people are able to **walk in** somewhere they can get in very easily because the doors are not kept locked or there is no proper security system: *There's no security guard and just about anyone could walk in.*

• *adjective* **walk-in**
A **walk-in** cupboard is a cupboard with a large enough entrance and enough floor space inside for you to walk into and stand upright in.

walk in on
You **walk in on** someone or something when you disturb people unintentionally by entering a room while they are doing something that they want to keep private: *Jilly found she'd walked in on a full-blown argument between the so-called lovers.*

walk into
1 You **walk into** trouble or a dangerous situation when you get into it unintentionally, or through lack of good judgement: *He turned the corner and walked straight into a rioting mob of football hooligans.* ❑ *You can't just walk into a war zone and expect to be protected from the carnage.* **2** You can say that someone **walks into** a job when they get the job without much apparent effort: *It seems to me that people from his sort of background can just walk into any job they like.*

walk off
1 Someone **walks off** or **walks away** when they leave or move away from you on foot: *Zen waggled his finger at me and walked off up the street.* **2** You **walk off** a large meal or a mood such as anger when you go for a walk outdoors to get rid of its unpleasant effects: *Tim went down to the beach to walk off his rage and frustration.*

walk off with
1 You **walk off with** the honours or the prize in a competition when you win them easily: *It seems as if the top ten*

firms are walking off with all the prizes these days. [*same as* **walk away with**] **2** (*informal*) Someone who **walks off with** something steals it or takes it without the owner's permission: *It seems that he calmly walked off with about ten thousand pounds worth of jewels.*

walk on
1 You **walk on** when you go on walking or you reach a place and then continue beyond it on foot: *They walked on in silence.* ❑ *Walk on round the cliffs and you come to what seems like utterly derelict sheds hanging on the side of the precipice.* **2** In the theatre, an actor **walks on** when they have a very small part in a play with few or no lines and often with only a brief appearance on stage.
• *adjective* **walk-on**
A **walk-on** part in a play is a minor one in which the actor has very few or no lines to say, or makes only a brief appearance on stage.

walk out
1 Employees **walk out** when they stop working and leave their workplace in a group as a protest against their employer: *The lads in the machine shop are threatening to walk out if they don't get a pay rise this year.* **2** You **walk out** of a meeting or a performance in the theatre when you leave it abruptly before it has ended to show your anger or disapproval: *He walked out of the Cabinet, and resigned.* ❑ *There were boos and cat-calls, and some of the audience walked out.*
• *noun* **walkout**: **walkouts**
A **walkout** is a form of strike in which employees stop working and leave their workplace in a group.

walk out on (*informal*)
You **walk out on** someone you have been living with, or someone who is dependent on you, such as your family or partner, when you leave them and don't intend to return: *Her husband had walked out on her a couple of years before.* [*same as* **leave**, **abandon**]

walk over (*informal*)
If you let someone **walk over** you, you allow them to treat you very badly, because you are too timid or weak to stop them: *She lets those kids walk all over her.* ❑ *They were fed up with being walked over and treated like dirt.*
• *noun* **walkover**
People sometimes refer to a success or victory as a **walkover** when it has been very easily won or achieved: *'Thanks for your congratulations. It was quite a walkover,' she said smugly.*

walk through
A theatre or film director **walks** the actors **through** their parts when he or she shows them where they are to stand or how they are to move in the final performance: *'There's nothing very complicated for you to do. In any case, you'll be walked through it before we start filming.'*
• *noun* **walk-through**: *It wasn't so much a rehearsal; more a quick walk-through.*

wall /wɔːl/: walls, walling, walled

wall in
1 An area **is walled in** when it is completely surrounded or enclosed by a wall or walls: *The kitchen garden was walled in and couldn't be seen from the big house.* **2** Someone or something **is walled in** when they are completely surrounded by a solid barrier which prevents them from moving or escaping: *Rhoda felt trapped, walled in on every side by people who wanted to get something from her.* [*same as* **fence in**, **hem in**, **pen in**]

wall off
You **wall off** part of an area when you build a wall round it to separate it from the rest of the area: *She worked in the squalid rat-infested refugee camp, walled off from the rest of the city and patrolled inside and out by armed gunmen.* [compare **partition off**]

wall up
1 To **wall up** something such as a room or door is to build a wall to cover the opening or entrance to close or seal it permanently: *The sarcophagus was walled up in a hidden inner chamber.* **2** Someone **is walled up** inside a small space when a wall is put up to prevent them getting out: *He got rid of her by walling her up in a courtyard specially built for the purpose.*

wallow /ˈwɒloʊ/: **wallows**, **wallowing**, **wallowed**

---

wallow in
You **wallow in** an emotion or sensation, whether pleasant or unpleasant, when you allow yourself to enjoy it for a long time in a way that is thought by others to be self-indulgent: *What hope can they have if they see you slumping about wallowing in self-pity?*

waltz /wɔːlts/ *or* /wɔːls/: **waltzes**, **waltzing**, **waltzed**

---

waltz in (*informal*)
Someone **waltzes in** or comes **waltzing in** when they walk into a place in a casual, confident way: *Nurse Bodkin winked in delight as he waltzed in.* [*same as* **breeze in**]

waltz off with (*informal*)
1 You **waltz off with** a prize when you win it easily: *Keep this standard up and you'll waltz off with all the prizes.* **2** Someone **waltzes off with** something when they steal it: *Someone had broken into their van and waltzed off with three guitars, including a Stratocaster.* [*same as* **walk away with**, **walk off with**]

waltz out (*informal*)
Someone **waltzes out**, or goes **waltzing out**, when they walk out of a place in a casual, confident way: *Then he waltzes out without even so much as a goodbye.* [*same as* **breeze out**]

wander /ˈwɒndə(r)/: **wanders**, **wandering**, **wandered**

---

wander about *or* **wander around**
You **wander about** or **around** when you move from place to place without any particular purpose or without knowing where you are going next: *Endhill left the library and wandered about in a daze.* ❑ *He wandered around for a bit and then came back to the hotel.* ❑ *I wandered around with no idea where I was or where I was going.*

wander off
Someone **wanders off** when they leave without knowing or telling others where they are going: *Once we reached Liverpool Station, he just wandered off aimlessly.* ❑ *My brain wandered off surveying the absurdity of it all.*

want /wɒnt/: **wants**, **wanting**, **wanted**

---

want for
You can say that someone doesn't **want for** a particular thing, or they **want for** nothing, when they have or are given as much of that thing as they need, or they have or are given everything they need to make their life comfortable and pleasant: *She certainly won't want for anything money can buy.* ❑ *They were sublimely happy and wanted for nothing.*

want in (*informal*)
When others are involved in a business deal or other arrangement that you find attractive, and you say you **want in,** you mean that you want to become involved or have a share in it so that you can profit or benefit too: *Jackson has let it be known that he wants in on the deal.* [*opposite* **want out**]

want out (*informal*)
When you are involved in a situation and you **want out**, or **want out** of it, you want to escape or free yourself from it because it is bringing you no benefit or is becoming too difficult for you to deal with: *It's my feeling that he doesn't want a reconciliation. he just wants out of the marriage.* [*opposite* **want in**]

ward /wɔːd/: **wards, warding, warded**

ward off

1 If someone or something is trying to hit you, you **ward off** their blows by using something to shield or protect yourself against them: *He used his umbrella to ward off her blows.* ❑ *She was holding up her arm, as if he was striking her, and she warding off the blow.* [*same as* **fend off**] **2** You **ward off** something unpleasant such as danger, evil or illness when you do something that prevents you from being affected or harmed by it: *He always has a big bowl of porridge in the morning to ward off, as he says, those winter chills.* [*same as* **fend off**]

warm /wɔːm/: **warms, warming, warmed**

warm over (*especially AmE; informal, derogatory*)

To **warm over** something that has been used before, or to **warm** it **over**, is to use it again, often because you cannot think of anything new or original: *It's just the same old policy, warmed over.* ❑ *You're not going to give a warmed-over version of that old chestnut again, are you?* [*same as* **rehash**]

warm through

You **warm** cold food **through** when you heat it gently until it is warm but not hot: *Serve the sauce cold; or warm it through before serving.*

warm to *or* warm towards

1 You **warm to** a task or an idea when you become more enthusiastic about it or interested in it: *After initial nervousness, he found himself warming to the task.* **2** You **warm to** or **towards** a person when you begin to like or approve of them more: *I think Mother's warming to you at last.* ❑ *Almost despite herself, Candice found herself warming towards this strange little man.*

warm up

1 You **warm up** cold food when you heat it gently until it is warm enough to eat: *She served us some warmed-up left-overs.* **2** The weather **warms up** when the temperature rises; a place that has been cool or cold **warms up** when it gradually gets warmer: *The high pressure will be forced northwards and it will warm up considerably in the next few days.* ❑ *The kitchen had warmed up enough for them to shed their outdoor clothes.* [*opposite* **cool down**] **3** You **warm up** when your body gradually gets warmer after having been cool or cold; something **warms** you **up** when it makes you feel less cold or gives you a feeling of warmth: *He put his hands inside his jacket to warm them up.* ❑ *A nice bowl of hot soup will warm you up.* [*opposite* **cool down**] **4** An event or activity **warms up**, or the pace of something **warms up**, when it gets more lively or more intense: *Now the competition is really warming up, with three throwers battling for the lead.* [*same as* **hot up**] **5** An engine or other machine **warms up** when it reaches a condition where its parts are warm and it is running smoothly a short time after you have switched it on or started it: *Let the engine warm up before you disengage the choke.* **6** A performer or comedian **warms up** an audience when they make them relax and begin to enjoy themselves by telling them jokes or amusing them before the main show: *He used to warm up the 'Have I Got News For You' audience before stardom beckoned.* **7** An athlete or sportsman **warms up** when he or she does a series of relatively gentle exercises or practices shots to prepare for an event: *The substitute goal-keeper's warming up on the sidelines. It looks as if Mark Bosnich is coming off.* [*same as* **limber up**]

• *noun* **warm-up**: **warm-ups**

A **warm-up** is a series of relatively gentle exercises or a short spell of practice that you do before a race or sporting event: *He'd pulled a muscle during yesterday's warm-up.* ❑ *He described the bout as a warm-up for* *the World title.*

warn /wɔːn/: **warns**, **warning**, **warned**

warn against
You **warn against** something, or you **warn** people **against** it, when you tell people it is likely to be dangerous or harmful: *Young people are being continually warned against the dangers of smoking.*

warn away *or* warn off
You **warn** people **away** from something, or you **warn** them **off**, when you try to force them to go away, or you persuade them to stop their investigations into something, by threatening them with danger or punishments: *Her father had warned me off repeatedly saying that if I tried to contact her I'd be sorry.*

wash /wɒʃ/: **washes**, **washing**, **washed**

wash away
Something **is washed away** when it is removed or carried away by water or a flood: *The Legionnaires camp had been washed away by a flash flood.* ❑ *The thin layer of topsoil had been washed away exposing the bare rock.*

wash down
1 You **wash** a surface **down** when you clean the dirt off it using water: *Wash down the walls with a fungicide solution.* **2** You **wash down** a pill when you take a drink to help you swallow it; you **wash down** solid food when you drink something while you are eating it or just after you have eaten: *I'll need something to wash the aspirins down with.* ❑ *They had roast beef and Yorkshire pudding washed down with an excellent claret.*

wash off
1 You **wash** dirt **off** something when you remove it from its surface using water: *Go and wash off all that make-up; you look like a clown!* **2** You **wash** yourself **off** when you use water to remove dirt or other unwanted material from your body: *His body and clothing were covered in blood. He washed himself off in a nearby stream.*

wash out
1 You **wash out** a container, or you **wash** it **out**, when you use water to remove any dirt from inside it: *He'd washed out an old jam jar and filled it with honey.* [*same as* **rinse out**] **2** You **wash out** a dirty mark or stain on fabric when you remove it by washing the fabric with soap and water; a stain or mark **washes out** when you are able to remove it by washing: *Washing the stains out of the loose covers, she then hung them out to dry.* ❑ *I don't know if that blackcurrant stain will wash out.* **3** A sporting event **is washed out** when it is prevented from starting or it is stopped before the end by heavy rain. [compare **rain off**] **4** Something **washes** you **out** when it makes you feel very tired and lacking in energy.

• *adjective* **washed-out**

1 Washed-out colours are pale or faded-looking: *a pair of washed-out denims.* **2** You can say that someone is or looks **washed-out** when they are very pale or tired: *'This is the wife,' he said, indicating a thin washed-out-looking little mouse of a woman.*

• *noun* **washout**: **washouts**

You can refer to an event as a **washout** when it is a total failure or disaster: *The rally turned out to be a complete washout.*

wash over
1 A feeling **washes over** you when it seems to flow suddenly through your whole body: *Relief washed over her.* **2** If something that others are or would be affected by **washes over** you, you don't notice it or are unaffected by it: *Heidi let the whole thing wash over her as if she had no personal involvement in it at all.*

wash up

1 You **wash up** when you wash the dirty dishes and cutlery that have been used to prepare and serve a meal: *I'll wash up if you dry.* **2** (*AmE*) You **wash up** when you wash yourself with soap and water to remove any dirt from your body, especially from your face and hands: *You boys go and wash up before dinner.* **3** Something **is washed up** by the sea or a river when it is carried to and left on the shore by the force of the waves or current: *He collected pieces of driftwood washed up along the shore.* ❑ *After a couple of days the bodies are usually washed up further downstream.*

• *adjective* **washed up** (*informal*)
You can say that someone is **washed up** when they have failed and have nothing of value to offer; you can also say that something such as a relationship is **washed up** when it has deteriorated so much that it cannot go on: *He'll never go on stage again; as an actor, he's all washed-up.*

• *noun* **washing-up**
You do the **washing-up** when you wash the dishes and cutlery that have been used for a meal: *Christmas dinner was great; except for the mountains of washing-up afterwards.*

waste /weɪst/: **wastes**, **wasting**, **wasted**

---

waste away

Someone **wastes away** when they gradually become thinner and weaker, usually because of illness or disease: *We had to watch helplessly as he wasted away before our eyes.*

watch /wɒtʃ/: **watches**, **watching**, **watched**

---

watch for

You **watch for** something when you pay careful attention to make sure you notice it when or if it happens: *Parents should watch for the tell-tale signs, such as abnormal sensitivity to light and a skin rash.*

watch out

If someone tells you to **watch out** they are telling you to be careful so that you avoid danger or trouble: *Watch out! There's a lorry pulling out of that side street.* [*same as* **look out**]

watch out for

1 You **watch out for** something when you pay careful attention or stay alert so that you will notice it when it appears or happens: *Even after snow ploughs have cleared the snow from the roads, you have to watch out for patches of black ice.* **2** You **watch out for** someone when you look after them and prevent them from getting into any trouble or danger: *We asked our friends' son to watch out for Jason when he went to Gordonstoun.* [*same as* **look out for**]

watch over

You **watch over** someone or something when you guard them or look after them: *shepherds watching over their flocks.*

water /'wɔːtə(r)/: **waters**, **watering**, **watered**

---

water down

1 You **water down** a liquid such as wine or beer when you make it thinner or weaker by adding water to it: *Sometimes the children were given wine; watered down, of course.* [*same as* **dilute**] **2** You **water down** things such as comments, criticisms or proposals when you alter them to make them less controversial or extreme, so that they are easier to accept: *After sustained pressure from wealthy landowners, the legislation was heavily watered down.* [*same as* **tone down**]

wave /weɪv/: **waves**, **waving**, **waved**

---

wave aside

You **wave aside** an idea, objection or criticism, or you **wave** it **aside**, when you show that you are not willing to consider it because you think it is unimportant or irrelevant: *Our protests were waved aside; they carried on regardless.*

wave away

You **wave** someone **away** when you make a signal to them with your hand to show that you want them to move away or that you don't want them to approach you: *I went to speak to Josh, but he waved me away and hobbled back into the shack.* [*same as* **wave off**]

wave down

You **wave down** a moving vehicle when you get it to stop by making a signal to the driver with your hand: *He went down into the street to try to wave down a taxi.* [*same as* **flag down**]

wave off

1 You **wave** someone **off** when you wave goodbye to them as they leave: *Our entire class came to wave us off at the airport.* **2** You **wave** someone **off** when you make a signal with your hand to show that you want them to move away or you don't want them to approach you: *A figure in the distance appeared to be waving us off with frantic gestures.* [*same as* **wave away**]

wave on

You **wave** someone **on**, especially the driver of a vehicle, when you signal to them with your hand to show that you want them to continue going forwards: *We slowed down to see what had happened but an angry-looking policeman waved us on impatiently.*

wave through

1 Someone **waves** you **through** a barrier or checkpoint when they signal to you that you can pass through it, often without checking what you are carrying with you or whether your documents are in order: *I was waved through the frontier barrier by a spotty boy-soldier.* **2** You **wave** something **through** when you give permission for it to happen or be used without investigating or checking it properly or thoroughly: *They hope to convince the regulators in the US that the drug is safe (most other countries having already waved it through).*

wean /wiːn/: weans, weaning, weaned

wean off

You **wean** someone **off** something that they find very difficult to give up when you help them by gradually removing it or reducing it until they have stopped using it or wanting it: *He had to be weaned off the tranquillizers gradually.*

wean on

If someone says they **were weaned on** a particular thing they mean that they were given it or were made familiar with it from a very early age: *They'd been weaned on stories of the Wild West.* [*same as* **brought up on**]

wear /wɛə(r)/: wears, wearing, wore /wɔː(r)/, worn /wɔːn/

wear away

1 A material **wears away,** or it **is worn away**, when it gradually becomes thinner or disappears completely because of repeated pressure or rubbing: *The stone was gradually worn away by the drip drip of water over the centuries.* ❑ *The leather was wearing away at the top of the boots near the ankle.* **2** A period of time **wears away** when it passes slowly: *The afternoon wore away and still the sun beat down.* [*same as* **wear on**]

wear down

1 Something **wears down,** or **is worn down,** when it gradually gets shorter or thinner because of repeated pressure or rubbing: *Eventually, the action of the sea will wear down the rocks until sand is formed.* ❑ *His clothes were clean but shabby, and the heels of his boots were worn down.* **2** Something **wears** you **down** when it is repeated so often or goes on for so long that it weakens you or makes you less and less able to resist it: *Charlie was trying to wear her down; writing, phoning, calling unexpectedly in the middle of the afternoon.*

• *adjective* **worn-down**: *a worn-down tyre* ❑ *He had a worn-down expression.*

wear off

A feeling or the effect of a drug **wears off** when it becomes less and less and finally disappears: *Hopefully, by that time the effects will have worn off.* ❑ *After the first awkwardness wore off, the party went with a swing.*

wear on

Time **wears on** when it passes slowly: *The years wore on and there was still no word of her missing girl.*

wear out

1 If something that has been used a lot **wears out**, or **is worn out**, it gets so weakened or rubbed through that it can no longer be used: *We disturb wildlife, pollute air, drop litter and literally wear out the footpaths.* **2** Someone or something **wears** you **out**, or you **wear** yourself **out** doing something, when they make you, or you become, physically or mentally exhausted: *Their longer than usual visit had obviously worn her out.* ❑ *Chris wore herself out trying to get the harvest in single-handed.* [*same as* **tire out**]

• *adjective* **worn-out**: *When you die you simply leave your worn-out body behind.*

wear through

Something **wears through**, or **is worn through**, when a hole or gap is made in it by repeated pressure or rubbing: *The cheapest beds have a non-woven fabric which wears through very quickly.*

weary /ˈwɪərɪ/: weariest, wearying, wearied

weary of (*formal or literary*)

You **weary of** something when you get tired of it or lose interest in it: *It wasn't long before he wearied of the constant media attention.* [*same as* **tire of**]

weed /wiːd/: weeds, weeding, weeded

weed out

You **weed out** the people or things that you don't want from a group or collection when you identify them and get rid of them: *This test is designed to weed out the candidates that don't have the kind of attitude we're looking for.*

weigh /weɪ/: weighs, weighing, weighed

weigh against

1 A factor or circumstance **weighs against** you when it is likely to prevent you being successful: *The fact that he's unmarried is likely to weigh against him in the selection process.* [*same as* **go against, tell against**] **2** You **weigh** one factor **against** another when you consider how important the one is in relation to the other: *The advantages of trying to do so as fully as possible have to be weighed against the disadvantages of imposing fetters on business.*

weigh down

1 You **are weighed down** by a load or burden when it is so heavy that it stops you moving or progressing easily: *We passed a line of donkeys weighed down by great bundles of firewood.* **2** You **are weighed down** by problems or worries when they make you depressed and anxious: *Paul is so weighed down by the stresses of his job that he has become silent and introverted.*

weigh in

1 A wrestler or boxer **weighs in** before a fight, and a jockey **weighs in** before and after a race, when they are weighed officially to check their weight: *The American contender weighed in at nearly 18 stones.* **2** (*informal*) You **weigh in** when you join in an argument or fight in a forceful or determined way;

if there is a lot of work to be done and you **weigh in** you begin the work with determination and energy: *Predictably, Gerry weighed in with his opinion.* ❑ *The whole village weighed in and cleared the debris up before it got dark.* **3** (*informal*) You **weigh in** with support or help for someone when you contribute what you can to help or support them: *Unless some white knight weighs in with a substantial amount of cash, takeover seems inevitable.*

• *noun* **weigh-in**

A **weigh-in** is the official weighing of boxers before a match or jockeys before and after a horse race: *We'll try to interview Bob Champion after the weigh-in.* ❑ *the pre-fight weigh-in.*

weigh into (*informal*)

You **weigh into** someone when you start to attack them violently, either physically or with words: *Dennis Healey weighed into him in his characteristic style.*

weigh on

A problem **weighs on** or **upon** you when you worry about it so much that it makes you depressed: *They don't tell us their procedures to prevent gossip and simplistic interpretations of raw statistics weighing on our minds.*

weigh out

You **weigh** something **out** when you measure the quantity you need by weight, using scales: *Weigh out six ounces of plain flour, and six ounces of caster sugar.*

weigh up

1 You **weigh** a situation **up** when you study it carefully so that you know all about it and are therefore able to make a judgement about it: *I was sorry I hadn't weighed it up more thoroughly beforehand.* **2** You **weigh up** two or more alternatives when you consider each carefully before deciding on one of them: *We have to weigh up the benefits of medical assistance and of letting Nature take its course.* **3** You **weigh** someone **up** when you make a careful study of their behaviour or reactions so that you know what they are like: *He thought he'd got me weighed up and eating out of his hand.* [*same as* **size up**]

weigh upon see weigh on

weigh with

Something **weighs with** people if they are impressed or influenced by it: *What weighed more heavily with some Tories was the thought that the positive values of the Thatcher years had been gradually eroded.* [*same as* **carry weight with**]

weight /weɪt/: weights, weighting, weighted

weight down

Something **is weighted down** when something heavy is attached to it to prevent it moving or floating away: *The body had been weighted down with stones.*

weld /wɛld/: welds, welding, welded

weld together

1 To **weld together** two pieces of metal is to join them to one another using heat or pressure to create a solid bond: *Two strips of metal are welded together lengthways.* **2** People or things **are welded together** when they are combined or made into a single unit by creating a strong unbreakable bond between them: *He confined his remarks to generalities about free trade welding nations together for mutual benefit.*

well /wɛl/: wells, welling, welled

well up

1 Tears **well up** in someone's eyes when they start to fill their eyes: *Nancy could feel the hot tears welling up in her eyes.* **2** A feeling or emotion **wells up** inside you when it seems to rise through your body without you having any control over it: *Compassion for him welled up* *inside her, and she put her arms around him.*

welsh *or* **welch** /wɛlʃ/: **welshes**, **welshing**, **welshed**

welsh on (*derogatory*)
People sometimes say that someone who has purposely failed to repay a debt **has welshed on** the debt; you can also say that someone **has welshed on** an agreement or promise when they have failed to keep it: *I don't think there's any risk they will welsh on the agreement at this late stage.*

wheel /wiːl/: **wheels**, **wheeling**, **wheeled**

wheel round *or* **wheel around**
A person or animal that has been facing in one direction **wheels round** or **around** when they suddenly turn to face in the opposite direction: *He wheeled round and looked to see where the noise had come from.* ❑ *Lieutenant Erickson wheeled around to scream at Miles.*

wheel in (*informal*)
When someone asks you to **wheel** someone or something **in** they are asking you, in a way that is intended to be humorous or off-hand, to bring that person or thing in so that they can see them: *'Mr Peters is here for his interview.' 'Okay, wheel him in.'*

wheel out (*informal*)
You **wheel** something **out** when you take it out of the place where it has been kept or stored so that people can inspect it or look at it: *The Household Cavalry are wheeled out in full fig for state occasions.*

while /waɪl/: **whiles**, **whiling**, **whiled**

while away
You **while away** the time doing something if you spend it in that way: *Meg and Harry while away the hours until dinner doing jigsaws.*

whip /wɪp/: **whips**, **whipping**, **whipped**

whip away
You **whip** something **away** when you remove it with a snatching movement: *He'd whipped it away before I had a chance to look at it.*

whip up
1 You **whip up** cooking ingredients such as cream or eggs when you use a fork or whisk to beat them until they are stiff or thoroughly mixed. **2** You **whip up** excitement or anger in people when you do or say things that encourage it: *It took only a few well-organized agitators to whip up political unrest that was difficult to contain.* **3** The wind **whips up** the surface of the sea when it makes the water rise upwards into waves and frothy spray. **4** You **whip up** a horse or ox when you use a whip to make it go faster: *The coachman whipped up the horses and they disappeared into the night.* **5** (*informal*) You **whip up** something such as a meal when you prepare it in a hurry: *His wife usually whips them up a snack of hot soup or cheese and toast when they come in from the hill.*

whisk /wɪsk/: **whisks**, **whisking**, **whisked**

whisk away
Someone or something **is whisked away** when they are taken away very quickly, as if by magic: *He was whisked away in an official car to nearby Cape Town.* ❑ *Lucy was bundled on a trolley and whisked away through swing doors.*

whisk up
You **whisk up** egg whites or cream when you stir them rapidly with a whisk until they are stiff, thick and light.

whistle /ˈwɪsəl/: **whistles**, **whistling**, **whistled**

whistle for (*informal*)
When you say that someone can

whistle for something that they want, you mean that they aren't going to get it or you aren't going to give it to them: *'He wants to borrow a thousand pounds apparently.' 'Well, as far as I'm concerned he can whistle for it.'*

whistle up (*informal*)
You **whistle up** something that is needed urgently when you obtain it or create it in a hurry: *We can usually whistle up enough people to help us with the harvest.*

whittle /'wɪtəl/: **whittles**, **whittling**, **whittled**

---

whittle away *or* **whittle away at**
You **whittle** something **away** when you reduce it bit by bit until there is very little or none of it left; you **whittle away at** something when you take small parts off or from it until there is very little or none left: *He sat on a stump, whittling away at a hazel branch with a penknife.* ❑ *Taxes had been whittling away at the family fortune until there was nothing left to pass on to the next generation.*

whittle down
Something **is whittled down** when it is reduced in size or extent by removing parts or pieces of it bit by bit: *During his ministry, the Social Security budget had been whittled down by 30% in real terms.*

whoop /wuːp/: **whooops**, **whooping**, **whooped**

---

whoop up
People **whoop** it **up** when they spend time enjoying themselves in a noisy or boisterous way: *A group of young people were whooping it up down on the seafront.*

wimp /wɪmp/: **wimps**, **wimping**, **wimped**

---

wimp out (*informal, derogatory*)
You **wimp out**, or you **wimp out** of something dangerous or difficult, when you don't do it because you are too cowardly or afraid: *I might have known he would wimp out of it.* [*same as* **chicken out** (*informal*)]

win /wɪn/: **wins**, **winning**, **won** /wʌn/

---

win back
You **win back** something that you have lost when you get it back again, especially after a great deal of effort: *British companies are going all out to win back the markets they lost during the recession.*

win out
When several people or organizations have been competing for something and one **wins out**, that person or organization eventually succeeds in getting it: *He said that he had been quite sure that I would win out in the end.*

win over *or* **win round**
You **win** someone **over**, or you **win** them **round**, when you succeed in persuading them to agree with you or give you their support: *an attempt by Labour to win over Middle England* ❑ *It took some persuasion, but we won him round in the end.*

win through
You **win through** when you survive or get through a difficult situation after an effort or struggle: *The selection process for a parliamentary candidate is not unlike that for a giant multinational corporation, and those that win through have some similarities to corporate executives.*

wind /waɪnd/: **winds**, **winding**, **wound** /waʊnd/

---

wind back
You **wind back** the tape in a film or music cassette when you make it move backwards to a position at or nearer the beginning. [*same as* **rewind**]

wind down
1 You **wind down** the window of a

vehicle when you lower it by turning a handle inside: *He wound down the passenger window and asked if I wanted a lift.* **2** A clock, clockwork device, or machine **winds down** when it is about to stop and works more and more slowly: *The toy wound down and came to a halt under the kitchen table.* **3** You **wind down** some activity when you gradually bring it to an end: *You've arrived a bit late; the conference is winding down.*

wind on *or* wind forward

You **wind on** a video or music cassette or a film in a camera, or you **wind** it **forward**, when you move it forward to a position at or nearer the end. [*opposite* **wind back**]

wind up

1 You **wind up** a mechanical clock or watch when you turn a key to tighten the spring mechanism that makes it work. **2** A business **is wound up** when it is closed or ceases trading: *He's thinking of winding up the company unless he can find a suitable buyer soon.* **3** You **wind up** an activity when you bring it to a conclusion or end: *They wound up the conference by singing 'The Red Flag'.* **4** You **wind up** the window of a vehicle when you close it by turning a handle inside. **5** (*informal*) You **wind** somebody **up** when you amuse yourself by pretending that something is true or has happened so that you can enjoy their reaction: *'That's not true; you're winding me up, aren't you?'* [*same as* **kid on** (*informal*)] **6** (*informal*) You also **wind** somebody **up** when you do or say something to them that makes them very annoyed or upset: *She sometimes winds him up so much, it takes all his self-control not to strangle her.* **7** (*informal*) You **wind up** somewhere when you find yourself in that place or position, often when you didn't set out to get there: *He's one of those kids that generally winds up in young offenders' institutions* [*same as* **end up, land up** (*informal*)]

• *noun* **wind-up**

A **wind-up** is something that someone does or says to you that is deliberately intended to mislead you or annoy you: *Pay no attention; it's just a wind-up.*

• *noun* **winding-up**

The **winding-up** of a business is the process of closing it down.

wink /wɪŋk/: winks, winking, winked

wink at

You can say that someone, especially someone in a position of authority, **winks at** something improper or illegal when they pretend not to notice that it is going on, usually because they secretly approve of it: *It's to be hoped that his successor won't wink at Mafia activity in the same way.*

winkle /ˈwɪnkəl/: winkles, winkling, winkled

winkle out

To **winkle** something **out** is to get it or discover it with great difficulty: *She'd managed to winkle the truth out of his younger brother.*

wipe /waɪp/: wipes, wiping, wiped

wipe away

You **wipe away** liquid or dirt when you remove it using your hand or a cloth: *He took her in his arms and wiped away her tears.*

wipe down

You **wipe down** a surface, or you **wipe** it **down**, when you clean it throughly using a damp cloth or sponge: *These easy-clean surfaces need only be wiped down with a damp cloth.*

wipe off

1 You **wipe** something **off** a surface when you remove it by rubbing it with your hand or a cloth: *Apply the adhesive to both surfaces, wiping off any excess.* **2** A large proportion of the value of something **is wiped off** when it is lost: *Millions will be wiped off our share value.*

wipe out
1 You **wipe out** a container when you clean its inside surfaces with a cloth: *Wipe the wok out with a damp cloth.* **2** Things **are wiped out** when they are destroyed or got rid of completely: *The snow has virtually wiped out today's racing programme.* [*same as* **eradicate**] **3** A debt **is wiped out** when it is repaid in full.
• *noun* **wipe-out**
A **wipe-out** is a total and humiliating defeat: *The Fifth Test was a wipe-out.*

wipe up
You **wipe up** spilled liquid when you remove it from a surface with a cloth.

wire /waɪə(r)/: **wires**, **wiring**, **wired**

---

wire in (*informal*)
You **wire in**, or get **wired into** a task, when you begin it with great determination and energy: *He was shown what to do and got wired into it right away.*

wire up
You **wire up** an electrical or electronic apparatus when you fit it with electrical wires so that it can be connected to the power supply: *The bomb had been wired up to the heating system.*

wise up /waɪz/: **wises**, **wising**, **wised**

---

wise up (*informal*)
You **wise up** when you discover or realise the real facts of a situation: *You'd better wise up if you don't want to end up dead.*

wish /wɪʃ/: **wishes**, **wishing**, **wished**

---

wish away
You **wish** something **away** when you try to get rid of it by wishing that it wasn't there: *You'll just have to accept it. There's no point in trying to wish it away.*

wish on *or* **wish upon**
You **wish** something **on** or **upon** someone when you hope very much that it will happen to them: *It's been an experience that I wouldn't wish on my worst enemy.*

with see panel on next page

---

wither /ˈwɪðə(r)/: **withers**, **withering**, **withered**

---

wither away
Something **withers away** when it fades, dries up and eventually disappears: *The cord withers away after a few days, and drops off.*

without see panel below

---

without /wɪˈðaut/

Without is a preposition.
It is a fairly common word in English, but it only occurs in three phrasal verbs in this dictionary; **do without**, **go without** and **reckon without**; all of which have the idea of a lack or absence of something as part of their meaning.

wolf /wulf/: **wolfs**, **wolfing**, **wolfed**

---

wolf down
A person or animal **wolfs down** food when they eat it very quickly without chewing it properly: *We watched as he wolfed down a whole plate of jam doughnuts.*

wonder /ˈwʌndə(r)/: **wonders**, **wondering**, **wondered**

---

wonder at
You **wonder at** something when you are surprised or puzzled by it: *Quentin could only wonder at her extraordinary cheek.*

work /wɜːk/: **works**, **working**, **worked**

---

with /wɪð/ *or* /wɪθ/

With is a preposition.

It is one of the most common words in English and it occurs in a fairly large number of phrasal verbs in this dictionary.

Its basic sense relates to connections or links between people and things. It occurs in phrasal verbs in five main senses.

1 CONNECTIONS RELATING TO PEOPLE

With is used in many phrasal verbs that have the idea of a connection between people as part of their meaning. This group includes the combinations **acquaint with**, **live with**, **meet with**, **sleep with** and **visit with.** The idea of people coming together in some way is also found in the phrasal verbs *link with*, *correspond with*, *collude with* and *mingle with* in the following examples: *This is why we are asking your church to link with us in a Christian response to AIDS.* ❑ *He sent some of the cards on to colleagues who wanted to correspond with people in the UK.* ❑ *There is the suspicion that police were colluding with the attackers.* ❑ *They turned nomadic and mingled with the nomads of the Sudan.*

Phrasal verbs such as **mess with**, **tangle with** and **trifle with** all suggest arguments or confrontations between people. Sometimes, the meaning relates to the breaking or ending of relationships between people, as in **break with** and **finish with**.

2 CONNECTIONS RELATING TO THINGS

In a second group of phrasal verbs, **with** relates to connections between things. Included in this group are the frequently used phrasal verbs **deal with**, **do with** and **lie with**, used to refer to the subject, nature or cause of something. You can occasionally find **with** forming new phrasal verbs with this meaning, such as *die with* in the example: *We are now caring for one in four of those dying with AIDS in this country.*

3 TAKING ACTION

With occurs in a number of phrasal verbs that have the idea of taking action as part of their meaning, such as **grapple with**, **juggle with** and **wrestle with**, in which a problem of some kind is being tackled. Often, the action is unwanted or unwelcome, as in **interfere with**, **meddle with**, **mess with** and **tamper with**.

4 GIVING AND PROVIDING

In a few phrasal verbs containing **with**, the idea of giving or providing is present. These verbs are most commonly found in the passive. For example, you can say that someone **is endowed with** qualities or talents when they have them or have been given them. Sometimes, what is given is unwanted or unwelcome, as in **land with**, **lumber with** and **saddle with**.

5 GIVING SUPPORT

The idea of giving your support to someone is found in a few phrasal verbs containing **with**, such as **agree with** and **side with**. The idea of continuing support, for a person or for something such as a belief or decision, is found in **hold with**, **stay with** and **stick with**.

You can occasionally find **with** forming new phrasal verbs with this meaning, such as *ride with* in the example: *We remember the writer Isaac Babel, who rode with Budyonny's Red Cavalry.*

With often occurs as the third element in phrasal verbs, as in **come up with**, **get away with**, **keep in with** and **take up with**.

work at

You **work at** a difficult task or problem when you put at lot of thought or energy into solving it or completing it successfully: *Writing doesn't come naturally to him. He has to work at it.*

work away *or* work away at

You **work away**, or **work away at** something, when you devote effort or thought to it continuously over a period of time: *Rescue workers worked away through the night, trying to free the people trapped in the rubble.* ❑ *He was working away at the loose tooth with his fingers.*

work in *or* work into

1 To **work** something **in** is to incorporate it in a mixture gradually and thoroughly; something **is worked into** a mixture when it is incorporated in the mixture: *Work the oil into the mixture until it forms a soft dough.* **2** You **work** something **into** something such as a conversation when you manage to introduce it or include it: *How are we going to work the subject of Bet into the conversation without being too obvious about it?* ❑ *The puppy had worked his way into all our affections by that time.*

• *noun* **work-in**: **work-ins**

A **work-in** is a form of protest by workers whose factory is to be closed in which they take over the factory and keep it running.

work off

1 You **work off** a feeling such as anger or frustration when you do some energetic activity to get rid of it; you **work off** excess weight when you take exercise to get rid of it; you **work off** the effects of a large meal when you take exercise to make yourself feel better: *Going to the gym is a great way of working off stress.* **2** If you owe someone money and you **work off** the debt, you do work for them as a way of repaying them. **3** A machine **works off** electricity or some other source of power when it uses that power source in order to operate: *Will this machine work off the mains?* [compare **work on**]

work on

1 You **are working on** something when you putting effort or thought into finishing it or improving it: *'Have you finished that report yet?' 'I'm working on it.'* **2** When you **work on** someone you use various means of persuasion to try to make them agree to something: *June said she was working on the boss to give her an extra week's holiday.* **3** Something **works on** batteries when it takes the power it needs to operate from them: *She bought me a radio, the kind that worked on batteries.*

work out

1 You **work out** a mathematical problem when you find the answer by calculation; you **work out** a problem when you solve it by thinking about it carefully and logically: *Let me show you how to work out percentages on your calculator.* ❑ *This is the figure that will be used to work out their roof tax.* [*same as* **figure out**] **2** You **work out** the details of a plan when you finalize them by thinking about them, discussing them with others or making calculations: *We are working out ways of using new course structures, perhaps with part-time study.* ❑ *If you'd given me more notice, I'd have worked out a much more interesting alibi for you.* **3** You **work** problems or difficulties **out** when you manage to solve them successfully: *They'll have to work out a solution that suits both partners.* **4** You say you can't **work** someone **out** when their behaviour is too strange or difficult for you to understand: *He's not like anyone I've ever met before. I can't work him out.* [*same as* **figure out**, **make out**] **5** You can say that things **have worked out** when they have come to a satisfactory or successful conclusion. **6** Something **works out** well or badly when it has a good or bad result or ending: *We had a few minor panics, but it all worked out okay in the end.* [*same as* **turn out**] **7** You **work out** when you do a series of exercises regularly in order to keep fit and healthy: *'He works out, you know, and plays a lot of handball and tennis.'* **8** You **work out** your contract or your notice when you continue to work at your job until the end of your contract or period of notice.

• *noun* **work-out**

A **work-out** is a period spent doing a series of exercises in order to keep your body fit and healthy: *You need someone to devise a work-out for someone of your level of fitness.*

work out at

Something **works out at** a certain amount if it is calculated to be that amount: *The bill worked out at more than twenty pounds a head.* [*same as* **come out at**]

work over (*informal*)

To **work** someone **over** is to beat or hit them repeatedly and violently, often as a punishment: *Once his so-called mates have worked him over he isn't likely to want to talk to us.*

work through

You **work through** a problem or difficulty when you deal with it by a series of gradual and logical steps or stages in order to find a solution: *These problems have to be worked through, and fortunately they can often be resolved successfully.*

work towards

You **work towards** a particular aim or objective when you work steadily over a period of time in order to achieve it: *He's only a bit-part player but he's working towards bigger roles.*

work under

You **work under** someone when you do a job under their direction or with them as your boss: *You'll be working under Miss Hopeton in Accounts.*

work up

1 You **work** yourself or others **up** into a state of *eg* anger or excitement, when you make yourself or them get into that state: *By then, he'd worked himself up into a frenzy.* **2** You **work up** an appetite when you do some sort of activity that makes you hungry; you **work up** the courage or enthusiasm to do something when you gradually develop it: *By the time I'd worked up the courage to ask him, he'd left for the evening.*

work up to

1 You **work up to** the most important point in something when you approach it gradually in a series of careful steps: *The opera works up to a glorious climax in the final aria.* **2** You **work up to** a more senior position when you start in a junior post and are gradually promoted to that higher post: *Starting as a cub reporter and working up to editor had been his schoolboy dream.*

worm /wɜːm/: worms, worming, wormed

worm out

You **worm** information **out of** someone when you get them to tell you it by questioning them cleverly: *We managed to worm his little secret out of him.* [*same as* **screw out of, coax**]

worry /ˈwʌrɪ/: worries, worrying, worried

worry at

A dog **worries at** something when it grips it in its teeth and shakes it from side to side: *The fox terrier worried at the fluffy slipper, obviously a little unsure quite what it was.*

wrap /rap/: wraps, wrapping, wrapped

wrap round

1 You **wrap** something such as paper or cloth **round** something when you put it round it so that it covers it or protects it: *young pines trees with cloth wrapped round the top shoots to stop deer eating them.* **2** You **wrap** your arms or fingers **round** something when you put them round it tightly: *I picked her up and she wrapped her little arms around my neck.* **3** The text on a computer screen **wraps round** if it starts a new line as soon as the last character space on the previous line is filled.

wrap up

1 You **wrap up** something, or you **wrap** it **up**, when you enclose it in paper or cloth to form a package or parcel: *You'd better wrap up those Christmas presents before anyone sees them.* ❑ *The sleeping child was wrapped up in* *his coat.* **2** People **wrap up** when they put on warm clothes to protect them from the cold: *The skaters on the frozen loch were all wrapped up warmly.* **3** (*informal*) You **wrap up** a deal or task when you bring it to a satisfactory or successful conclusion: *I'm pretty confident we can wrap this up before the close of business tonight.*

wrap up in
You say that someone **is wrapped up in** something such as their work when they think about it all the time:

wrench /rɛntʃ/: wrenches, wrenching, wrenched

wrench off
To **wrench** something **off** is to pull it away from the place where it was attached with a violent tearing or pulling movement: *The door had been wrenched off its hinges and was lying on the ground.*

wrestle /ˈrɛsəl/: wrestles, wrestling, wrestled

wrestle with
You **wrestle with** a problem that you are finding difficult to solve when you try very hard to find a solution: *Aaron spent a sleepless night wrestling with his conscience, and in the morning had resolved to tell her the truth.* [*same as* **grapple with**]

wriggle /ˈrɪgəl/: wriggles, wriggling, wriggled

wriggle out of (*informal*)
You **wriggle out of** a duty, responsibility or trouble when you cleverly manage to avoid it or avoid being punished for it: *He's always getting into trouble but somehow he always manages to wriggle out of it.*

wring /rɪŋ/: wrings, wringing, wrung /rʌŋ/

wring out
You **wring out** a wet cloth or wet clothing when you squeeze it and turn it in both hands to get the water out of it: *The window cleaner wrung out his cloth and waited for her to get his money.* [*same as* **squeeze out**]

wring out of
You **wring** information **out of** someone when you force them to tell you it even though they don't want to: *I'll get him to tell me the truth, even if I have to wring it out of him.* [*same as* **squeeze out of**]

write /raɪt/: writes, writing, wrote /rout/

write away
You **write away** for something when you send a letter to the organization that can supply it asking them to send it to you: *I'm interested in VSO and I'm going to write away for details.*

write back
If you write a letter to someone and they **write back**, they reply to your letter by writing you a letter: *The company wrote to me asking me if I could do some work for them. I wrote back to tell them I wouldn't be available until March.*

write down
You **write** something **down** when you record it by writing it on paper with a pen or pencil: *I know I wrote his telephone number down somewhere, but I can't remember where.* [*same as* **note down**]

write in
1 You **write in** to a radio or television station or a magazine when you send them a letter: *Listeners should write in with suggestions for new word games.* ❑ *I think that programme was a disgrace; I'm going to write in and complain.* **2** If you are filling in a form and you **write** details **in** you write them in pen or pencil in the appropriate places: *Write your name and address in at the bottom of the form.*

write into
Something such as a condition or arrangement **is written into** a contract or agreement when it is included in it: *We'll have what we've just been discussing written into your contract.*

write off
1 You **write off** to a company or organization when you send a letter to them asking for something: *He wrote off for their winter seed catalogue.* **2** You **write off** money that someone owes you, or that you have lost, when you accept that you will not get it back: *The high-street banks have had to write off millions of pounds in bad debts.* **3** You **write** someone **off** when you lose all hope that they will return, recover from a serious illness, or begin to behave reasonably: *You shouldn't write him off just because he made one mistake.* ❑ *I must admit we'd written him off, but then he seemed to make a miraculous recovery.* **4** You **write** something **off** when you decide that it is not going to succeed and that you will not spend any more time, effort or money on it: *He said he wasn't going to waste any more time on it; he'd written it off as a bad experience.* **5** You **write** your car **off** when you crash it and damage it so badly that it is not worth the cost of repairs.
• *noun* **write-off**: **write-offs**
A vehicle is a **write-off** if it is so badly damaged, usually in an accident, that it is not worth repairing.

write out
1 You **write** something **out** when you write it on paper in full: *I wrote out my name and address on the back of the cheque.* **2** You **write out** something such as a cheque when you fill in all the necessary details and sign it: *He said he would write me out a cheque but I insisted on cash.* ❑ *The doctor said he would write out a prescription and I could collect it the next morning.*

write up
1 You **write up** something such as a report or notes when you write or rewrite them in a complete, neatly laid out form: *'Have you written up this patient's notes yet?'* **2** You **write up** a journal or your diary when you record your activities in it up to the present time: *The plane journey gave her the opportunity to write up her journal.*
• *noun* **write-up**: **write-ups**
A **write-up** is an article about something such as a new product, new activity or a holiday destination written for a newspaper or magazine: *Did you see the write-up on him in yesterday's 'Independent'?*

y

yearn /jɜːn/: **yearns**, **yearning**, **yearned**

yearn for (*formal or literary*)
You **yearn for** something when you have a strong desire or longing for it: *It was so chaotic it made one almost yearn for the tedious but reassuring routine of one's schooldays.* [*same as* **long for**]

yell /jɛl/: **yells**, **yelling**, **yelled**

yell out
Someone **yells out**, or they **yell out** for something, when they shout, or make their needs known in a loud or forceful voice so that people will pay attention to them: *'Party, party,' she yelled out.* ❑ *The policeman yelled out to him to stop.* [*same as* **shout out**]

yield /jiːld/: **yields**, **yielding**, **yielded**

yield to
1 You **yield to** pressure or someone's demands when you give way and do what they want you to do, after you have resisted for a time: *She yielded to temptation and had another slice of chocolate cake.* ❑ *He was trying his best not to yield to pressure from big business.* [*same as* **give in to, give way**] **2** (*formal*) One thing **yields to** another when the first thing is replaced by the second: *Harsh winter had yielded to gentle spring.* **3** (*especially AmE*) When you are driving a vehicle on the road and you **yield to** traffic coming from the right, or from the left, you let it go first. [*same as* **give way to**]

yield up (*formal*)
1 You **yield up** something that you have control of, or you **yield** it **up**, when you hand control of it over to someone else, especially to an enemy who has defeated or conquered you: *He refused to yield up his find to the authorities.* ❑ *They were forced to yield up land that had been Serbian for generations.* [*same as* **surrender**] **2** Someone or something **yields up** a secret when they reveal it or disclose it: *Moon rock yielding up its chemical secrets.* [*same as* **give up**] **3** Something such as rock, soil, the earth or the sea **yields up** something interesting or useful when it produces or supplies it: *The North Sea continues to yield up vast quantities of oil and gas.*